...ers of the
Black Museum

By the same author

Neither the Sea Nor the Sand
Dragon Under the Hill
Adam's Tale
Red Watch
Nagasaki 1945
The Edge of Heaven
Royal Wedding
The Year of the Princess
Selfridges
TV-am Celebration of the Royal Wedding
Siren Song
More Murders of the Black Museum
The Complete Murders of the Black Museum
Beach

Murders of the Black Museum

1875–1975

THE DARK SECRETS BEHIND MORE THAN A HUNDRED YEARS OF THE MOST NOTORIOUS CRIMES IN ENGLAND

Gordon Honeycombe

JOHN BLAKE

Published by John Blake Publishing Ltd,
3 Bramber Court, 2 Bramber Road,
London W14 9PB, England

www.johnblakepublishing.co.uk

First published in hardback in 2009

ISBN: 978-1-84454-715-9

British Library Cataloguing-in-Publication Data:

A catalogue record for this book is available from the British Library.

Design by www.envydesign.co.uk

Printed in the UK by CPI William Clowes, Beccles NR34 7TL

1 3 5 7 9 10 8 6 4 2

© Text copyright Gordon Honeycombe

Papers used by John Blake Publishing are natural, recyclable products made from wood
grown in sustainable forests. The manufacturing processes conform to the environmental
regulations of the country of origin.

Every attempt has been made to contact the relevant copyright-holders, but some were
unobtainable. We would be grateful if the appropriate people could contact us.

ACKNOWLEDGEMENTS

The author and publishers wish to thank the following: Her Majesty's Stationery Office for permission to reproduce the 1980 criminal statistics (pp *xii, xiii)*; George Walpole & Company, Official Shorthand Writers to the Central Criminal Court, London EC4, for permission to quote from trial transcripts; Times Newspapers for permission to quote from trial reports; Michael Joseph Limited for permission to quote from *No Answer to Foxtrot Eleven* by Tom Tullett (pp 246–55); and Harrap Limited for permission to quote from *Executioner: Pierrepoint* by Albert Pierrepoint (pp 283–87); *Pierrepoint, A Family of Executioners* by Steve Fielding, published by John Blake Publishing.

CONTENTS

Foreword ix

Introduction xiii

1   Charles Peace: The Murder of Arthur Dyson, 1876   1
2   Jack the Ripper: The Whitechapel Murders, 1888   11
3   Florence Maybrick: The Murder of Mr Maybrick, 1889   25
4   Mrs Pearcey: The Murder of Mrs Hogg, 1890   33
5   Dr Cream: The Murder of Matilda Clover, 1891   41
6   Frederick Deeming: The Murder of Miss Mather, 1891   46
7   William Seaman: The Murder of John Levy, 1896   52
8   Milsom and Fowler: The Murder of Henry Smith 1896   60
9   Mrs Dyer: The Murder of Doris Marmon, 1896   64
10   Richard A Prince: The Murder of William Terriss, 1897   68
11   Samuel Dougal: The Murder of Miss Holland, 1899   76
12   Alfred and Albert Stratton: The Murders of Mr and Mrs Farrow, 1905   87
13   Dr Crippen: The Murder of Cora Crippen, 1910   90
14   Steinie Morrison: The Murder of Leon Beron, 1911   99
15   Mr and Mrs Seddon: The Murder of Eliza Barrow, 1911   104
16   George Smith: The Murder of Bessie Mundy, 1912   118
17   Alfred Bowes: The Attempted Assassination of Sir Edward Henry, 1912   128
18   David Greenwood: The Murder of Nellie Trew, 1918   134
19   Major Armstrong: The Murder of Mrs Armstrong, 1921   136
20   Ronald True: The Murder of Gertrude Yates, 1922   144
21   Freddy Bywaters and Edith Thompson: The Murder of Percy Thompson, 1922   149
22   Patrick Mahon: The Murder of Emily Kaye, 1924   167
23   Norman Thorne: The Murder of Elsie Cameron, 1924   180
24   John Robinson: The Murder of Minnie Bonati, 1927   188
25   Browne and Kennedy: The Murder of PC Gutteridge, 1927   193
26   Samuel Furnace: The Murder of Walter Spatchett, 1933   203

27   Parker and Probert: The Murder of Joseph Bedford, 1933   206
28   Charlotte Bryant: The Murder of Frederick Bryant, 1935   210
29   Leslie Stone: The Murder of Ruby Keen, 1937   215
30   Edward Chaplin: The Manslaughter of Percy Casserley, 1938   219
31   William Butler: The Murder of Ernest Key, 1938   226
32   Udham Singh: The Murder of Sir Michael O'Dwyer, 1940   228
33   Harold Trevor: The Murder of Mrs Greenhill, 1941   231
34   Gordon Cummins: The Murder of Evelyn Oatley, 1942   234
35   Jones and Hulten: The Murder of George Heath, 1944   249
36   Jack Tratsart: The Murders of John and Claire Tratsart, 1945   245
37   Neville Heath: The Murder of Margery Gardner, 1946   249
38   Jenkins, Geraghty and Rolt: The Murder of Alec de Antiquis, 1947   259
39   Donald Thomas: The Murder of PC Edgar, 1948   264
40   Harry Lewis: The Murder of Harry Michaelson, 1948   267
41   John Haigh: The Murder of Mrs Durand-Deacon, 1949   269
42   Daniel Raven: The Murder of Mr Goodman, 1949   280
43   Craig and Bentley: The Murder of PC Miles, 1952   283
44   John Reginald Christie: The Murder of Mrs Christie, 1953   295
45   John Donald Merrett: The Murders of Vera Chesney and Lady Menzies, 1954 317
46   Ginter Wiora: The Murder of Shirley Allen, 1957   320
47   Michael Dowdall: The Murder of Veronica Murray, 1958   323
48   Guenther Podola: The Murder of DS Purdy, 1959   327
49   Roberts, Witney and Duddy: The Murders of DS Head, DC Wombwell   333
     and PC Fox, 1966
50   Reggie and Ronnie Kray: The Murders of George Cornell   347
     and Jack McVitie, 1966-7
51   Stanley Wrenn: The Murder of Colin Saunders, 1969   358
52   Mustapha Bassaine: The Murder of Julian Sessé, 1970   361
53   Arthur and Nizamodeen Hosein: The Murder of Mrs McKay, 1970   365

Appendix A   382
Appendix B   385
Appendix C   388
Appendix D   390
Afterword   392
Select Bibliography   393

Note

The years given above refer to the year of the crime in which the named victim was killed, not the year in which the ensuing trial took place. In cases of multiple killing the victim listed is the one for whose death the accused was tried. Neither Tratsart nor Merrett ever came to trial.

FOREWORD

The Black Museum is now called the Crime Museum. The original Black Museum came into being in 1875, when exhibits that had been acquired as evidence and produced in court in connection with various crimes were collected together and privately displayed in a cellar in 1 Palace Place, Old Scotland Yard, Whitehall. Ten years later, the augmented collection was moved to a small back room on the second floor of the offices of the Convict Supervision Department. By then the objects on display, consisting mainly of weapons, and all carefully labelled, numbered about 150.

In 1890, when the Metropolitan Police began moving into their impressive new headquarters at New Scotland Yard on the Victoria Embankment (designed by Norman Shaw, RA), the museum went too. It was then called the Police Museum, its primary object being to provide some lessons in criminology for young policemen and its secondary one to act as a repository for artefacts associated with celebrated crimes and criminals. Privileged visitors, criminologists, lawyers, policemen and people working with the police were guided around the museum by the curator, who over the previous century has always been a former policeman, with a special responsibility for the cataloguing, maintenance and display of the exhibits, and for dealing with correspondence from criminologists all over the world.

In 1968, when the Metropolitan Police moved into their modern high-rise premises at 10 The Broadway, London SW1, the museum – by now officially called the Crime Museum – occupied a large room on the second floor. Eleven years later, on the 150th anniversary of the founding of the Metropolitan Police force, it was decided to reassess, reorganise and modernise every aspect of the museum – as well as the three other Metropolitan Police museums: the Historical Museum on the top floor of Bow Street police station; the Thames Museum at Wapping; and the Training Museum in Hendon Training School. The last had taken over the instructional role previously shared with the Crime Museum, which was now able to fulfil its entire function as a museum. Its original title was restored, and on 12 October 1981 the Black Museum, on the first floor of New Scotland Yard, was officially reopened by the Commissioner, Sir David McNee.

The Black Museum's historical collection of articles and exhibits was and is unique. It covers more than murder. Other sections deal with Forgeries, Espionage, Drugs, Offensive Weapons, Abortions, Gaming, Housebreaking, Bombs and Sieges, and Crime pre-1900. The museum also houses displays concentrating on particular crimes, such as the Great Train Robbery and the attempted kidnapping of Princess Anne, and possesses such peculiar exhibits as Mata Hari's visiting card, a fake Cullinan diamond, a loving-cup skull with silver handles, two death masks of Heinrich Himmler, and thirty-two plaster casts of the heads of hanged criminals, men and women, executed in the first half of the nineteenth century at Newgate in London, at Derby and York. The heads, still bearing the mark of the rope, are said to have been made to record the features of those who were executed. Many criminals then used aliases, and the only way of identifying them after death (before the use of photographs and fingerprints) was to keep these plaster likenesses. In addition, some if not all of the heads were probably made for doctors or phrenologists bent on proving theories about the physiognomy of criminal types by examining the bumps and shape of a criminal's head after its owner was dead and gone.

Visitors' books, also maintained in the museum, contain records of a different sort: the signatures of such notable persons as King George V, Edward, Prince of Wales, Stanley Baldwin, Sir Arthur Sullivan, WS Gilbert, Captain Shaw of the London Fire Brigade, and William Marwood, executioner.

There is an undisplayed mass of other material (newspapers, cuttings, photographs, documents, letters and miscellaneous objects) relating to the exhibits on show and to other crimes. This material is kept under lock and key, generally in cabinets or cupboards below the showcases and mainly because space is restricted, but also because some of the items – for instance, the police photographs of Gordon Cummins's victims – are too obscene to be shown. The museum was rearranged and refurbished early in 2008.

I first visited the Black Museum in 1979. It was a most interesting and very disturbing experience. There was a certain grim fascination in seeing the actual instruments and implements used by criminals, infamous or otherwise, and in seeing other more innocuous items given a sinister cast in the context of their use. But the effect of the exhibits on display was cumulatively shocking. They presented a dreadful picture of ruthlessness, greed, cruelty, lust, envy and hate, of man's inhumanity to man – and especially to women. There was nothing of kindness or consideration. There was no nobility, save that of the policemen murdered on duty. There was very little mercy. But the museum made me realise what a policeman must endure in the course of his duty: what sights he sees, what dangers he faces, what depraved and evil people he has to deal with so that others may live secure. The museum also made me curious to know more about the people whose stories were shadowed by the exhibits on display.

This book deals with a very few of the murders investigated by the officers of the Metropolitan Police between 1875 and 1975. This hundred-year period embraces many of the major murder cases in the history of Scotland Yard as well as the major advances in crime detection. The museum has some exhibits relating to murders before 1875 (notably a letter written by the poisoner William Palmer) and several associated with murders after 1975 (notably the murder of Lesley Whittle by Donald Neilson in 1975 and the murders of Dennis Nilsen a few years later). But, writing in 1982, I felt that the grief suffered by families whose relatives had been murdered after 1975 was too recent to be revived by a detailed account. The murder that ends this book, that of Mrs Muriel McKay, seemed a fitting conclusion to the whole sequence, having been more publicised than most and being in many ways extraordinary.

The accounts of these particular murders of the Black Museum have been dealt with as case histories, with an emphasis on factual, social and historical detail, and on the characters and backgrounds of both the victim and the killer. Principal sources are listed at the back of the book, but in the main, statements and court proceedings have formed the basis for each story. No dialogue has been invented; it has been reproduced from statements and evidence given by the murderer as well as by witnesses and the police. What was said or alleged at the time by those most closely involved in a murder case may not always be true, but it is, I feel, of paramount importance in understanding the events that lead up to an act of murder and the complex motives and personalities of those most closely concerned. Like the superintendent or inspector in charge of a case I have tried to find out exactly what happened and why. It is my impression that the police officers investigating a murder ultimately have a clearer understanding of character, method and motive than some of the lawyers who take part in the ensuing trial. A court of law is seldom a place where the whole truth is told or revealed. It is in some respects a theatre of deception, with witnesses, defendants and barristers seeking to deceive the jury and each other. Even the judge, the arbitrator of truth, can mislead and be misled through ignorance or bias. But in a police station, although a suspect may lie as much as he likes, a truer picture of events and character is more likely to be attained in the end. Police reports concerning a murder and sent to a chief constable or commissioner are most sensible, lucid presentations of comment and fact. It is a pity they are not also available to the members of a jury in a court of law.

In researching and writing this book in the early 1980s, since revised for this edition, I was afforded the constant and generous cooperation of New Scotland Yard. I would particularly like to thank the following for their individual assistance at the time: Peter Neivens; Patricia Plank and the staff of the Commissioner's Reference Library; the Museums' Coordinator, Paul Williams; and the then Curator of the Black Museum, Bill Waddell. More recently, various Home Office and Ministry of Justice departments have also been helpful in updating information about the subsequent lives and deaths of those in this book who were given a prison sentence or detained in Broadmoor, and in this instance I would like to thank Les Blacklaw, Miss L Douglas, Kathryn Coleman, Emma Reed, David Keysell and Dave Norris, as well as Syd Norris and Sandy

Macfarlane. The two Curators of the Museum who succeeded Bill Waddell have also been unfailingly helpful. My special thanks to John Ross, and to Alan McCormick, the present Curator of the Crime Museum.

INTRODUCTION

M urder is a very rare event in Britain. Its exceptional nature is, in fact, part of its fascination. More than ten times as many people are killed on the roads each year as are victims of a murderer.

In 1980, 564 cases of murder, manslaughter and infanticide, all now classed as homicide, were currently recorded in England and Wales. On the roads of Britain in 1979-80, 6,352 people were killed and 81,000 injured. It must be said, however, that these figures for death on the roads were the lowest for thirty years and that the homicide figure was unnaturally high. Indeed, the car-death figure, when compared with that of other decades and with the number of cars on the roads, shows an astonishing decrease in fatalities. In 1931, for instance, when 1,104,000 cars and vans were on the roads, 6,691 people were killed and over 200,000 injured. Yet in 1979-80, with over 15 million cars on the road, the death toll was much lower, as was the number of those injured. The worst year for road fatalities was, significantly, 1941, the second full year of the Second World War, when the blackout was in full force: 9,169 people were killed that year. It is worth noting that deaths caused by reckless driving are not classified as homicide by the police, who recorded 235 such deaths on the roads in Britain in 1980.

The year 1980 was unusual in terms of homicide in that, of 564 homicides, seventy occurred in fires – thirty-seven in a Soho club and ten in a hostel in Kilburn. In addition, twenty-three deaths that had occurred in fires in the Hull area between 1973 and 1978, when they were regarded as accidental, were recorded as homicides in 1980. This meant that the homicide figure for 1980, without the unusually high figure of deaths in fires, would have been under 500 – a great reduction on the 551 homicides recorded in 1979. Instead, with the figure of seventy deaths in fires included, the overall number of recorded homicides in 1980 (564) was the highest on record.

Although this figure was very small when compared with road fatalities and when seen against the total population of this country, it nonetheless showed a small increase in deaths by murder, manslaughter and infanticide. The figure, seen as a percentage per million of the population of England and Wales, was 11.5. In 1970, when 339 homicides were ultimately recorded, the figure was seven per cent.

There is no doubt that we live in an increasingly violent society, in which more violence is being committed by the young and in which even more is directed against women and the elderly. In London in 1980, there were 13,984 incidents involving robbery, mugging and violent theft – an increase of 20 per cent on the previous year. Of the victims involved in these incidents, nearly 2,000 were over the age of sixty, and 3,387 were over fifty. And in the 584,137 serious offences recorded in London in 1980, 25 per cent of those arrested were aged between ten and sixteen.

Nonetheless, although there has been a vast increase in all types of crime since 1900, the comparative rise in murder is very slight, and there is little variation in the kinds and causes of murder. The commonest murders are still domestic ones – of a wife by her husband, of a woman by a lover, of a child by a parent. Of 456 murders examined in the period 1957–60 (70 per cent of those victims over the age of sixteen were women) the victim and the murderer were related in 53 per cent of all cases. In 27.9 per cent they were known to each other and 19.1 per cent were strangers. This is very similar to the Home Office statistical interpretation of the figures for homicide between 1970 and 1980: when about 50 per cent of the victims and killers were related, when over 30 per cent knew each other and about 19 per cent were strangers. A notable feature of the Home Office statistics is that infants less than one year old, viewed as a percentage of that age group in the population, were most at risk.

The survey of the 1957–60 murders, carried out by Terence Morris and Louis Blom-Cooper, also found that a very high percentage of the murderers had previous criminal records, usually for property offences, and that 70 per cent of the men convicted of capital murder in 1960 had previous convictions. It was also found that murderers were predominantly of the lower classes; that many of these had been in the services or were merchant seamen; that not a few were coloured; and that many murders were associated with heavy drinking.

Sir John MacDonnell wrote in 1905 that murder was 'an incident in miserable lives in which disputes, quarrels, angry words and blows are common'. This still applied 75 years later – as the 1980 Home Office Criminal Statistics for England and Wales show when listing the apparent circumstances of homicides in 1970 and in 1980.

	1970	1980
Quarrel, revenge or loss of temper	173	239
In furtherance of theft or gain	34	56
Attributed to acts of terrorism	0	4
While resisting or avoiding arrest	0	2
Attributed to gang warfare or feud	4	5
The result of offences of arson	0	84

Homicide of women undergoing illegal abortion	4	0
Other circumstances, including sex attack	51	66
Not known, because:		
The suspect committed suicide	19	20
The suspect was mentally disturbed	34	39
Other reasons	20	49
Totals	339	564

Compared with the 1950s, there was less shooting or gas poisoning in the 1970s, and a much-reduced use of the blunt instrument – a reflection of changing social conditions. One constant was, however, murder by strangulation or asphyxiation.

The Home Office list of figures for offences recorded as homicide in the decade 1970-1980 by apparent method of killing was as follows.

	1970	1980
Sharp instrument	107	160
Strangulation or asphyxiation	70	89
Hitting, kicking, etc.	57	94
Blunt instrument	43	61
Shooting	23	19
Drowning	12	14
Poison or other drugs	9	14
Burning	1	94
Explosion	0	0
Other	15	19
Not known	2	0
Totals	339	564

The increasing use of sharp instruments in violent crimes from 1998 to 2007 has become a cause for some alarm. National Health Service statistics published in 2008 showed that in the previous ten years there had been a 32 per cent rise in the number of patients being treated for stab wounds or similar injuries. Home Office statistics also revealed that police in England and Wales had recorded 22,151 offences involving knives in 2007. Of these, 7,409 offences had occurred in London, where twenty teenagers had died. In one week in July 2008, twelve people were stabbed to death in the UK. Despite these knife-crime figures, the Home Office said that overall crime in 2008, as recorded by the police, was down by 9 per cent.

The term 'homicide' covers the offences of murder, manslaughter and infanticide. Murder and manslaughter are common law offences that have never been defined by statute. In the Home Office statistics for 2005-2006, covering the period up to 9

October 2006, it should be noted that 'homicide offences are shown according to the year in which the police initially recorded the offence as homicide' and do not necessarily mark the year in which the homicide occurred.

A summary of these statistics reveals that 766 deaths in England and Wales in 2005-2006 were recorded by the police – a decrease of 9 per cent since 2004-2005. Of that number, 67 per cent were male deaths. The most common method of killing, at 28 per cent, involved a sharp instrument. Compared to the seventy-five victims who were shot and killed in 2004-2005, only fifty were shot in 2005-2006. In general, female victims were more likely to be killed by someone they knew. For instance, 54 per cent of female victims knew the main suspect, compared with 38 per cent of male victims. But the main suspect was known by 67 per cent of victims under the age of sixteen, 44 per cent of whom had been killed by their parents. At 38 per million of the population, children aged one year old and less were the age group most at risk, baby boys being the most vulnerable.

Several multiple deaths this century have bumped up the annual homicide statistics. The London bombings of 7 July 2006, in which fifty-two people died, accounted for 7 per cent of the homicides in 2005-2006. In 2003-2004, in Morecambe Bay, twenty cockle-pickers were drowned; 172 victims were attributed to Dr Harold Shipman in the 2002-2003 statistics – although well over 200 deaths were later accredited to him; and in the period 2000-2001, fifty-eight people in a group of Chinese nationals being smuggled into the UK in a lorry suffocated en route.

Of some interest is the fact that suicide (there were 4,200 in Britain in 1979), homicide and mental illness are connected and complementary. Between 1900 and 1949, 29 per cent of the persons suspected of murder committed suicide, a proportion that rose to 33 per cent in the next decade. Again, between 1900 and 1949, 21.4 per cent of the persons found guilty of murder were also adjudged to be insane or unfit to plead. This figure rose in the next decade to 26.5 per cent. It seems that a person suffering from morbid depression, frustration or anxiety, whose mental balance is disturbed, may, as that mental stress or illness increases, commit either suicide or murder. If it is murder, that person may recover as a result of such an act, or become insane. There also seems to be a case for viewing murder as an act of displaced self-destruction, when the disturbed person, unable to kill himself or herself, kills someone near as a substitute. Some women, unable to kill themselves or a husband or a lover, direct their act of destruction against someone more vulnerable – a child – almost as a token sacrifice.

Another factor connected with the causes of murder is the actual or subconscious yearning of a nonentity for notoriety, a desire inflamed these days by the ease with which other nonentities achieve a spurious fame through appearing on television or from the inflated attentions of the press. People desire to be noticed, to be distinguished in some way by what they are or do. In some cases, where a person is totally undistinguished and untalented, desperate measures are taken to remedy the defect.

Bruce Lee, aged twenty – his real name was Peter Dinsdale – killed people by setting fire to the houses in which they lived in and around Hull. Said to be suffering from a psychopathic personality disorder, he admitted in court to twenty-six cases of manslaughter on the grounds of diminished responsibility and to ten charges of arson. He was committed on 20 January 1981 to a psychiatric institution in Liverpool for an indefinite period. His counsel, Mr Harry Ognall, QC, said at Dinsdale's trial: 'No words of mine could assist this crippled, solitary and profoundly disordered young man. This pathetic nobody has, by his deeds, achieved a notorious immortality.' Perhaps this was one of Dinsdale's unacknowledged desires.

It was certainly the aim of seventeen-year-old Marcus Serjeant, from Capel le Ferne in Kent, who on 13 June 1981 fired five blank shots at the Queen as she rode down the Mall to the ceremony of Trooping the Colour in Horse Guards Parade. Tried under Section 2 of the Treason Act, he was sentenced to five years in jail. He claimed he had been influenced by the shooting of John Lennon and by the assassination attempt on President Reagan. To a friend he wrote: 'I am going to stun and mystify the whole world with nothing more than a gun … I may in a dramatic moment become the most famous teenager in the whole world. I will remain famous for the rest of my life.'

Such a desire was probably not shared by Crippen, Christie or Haigh. But the last two certainly relished their notoriety, and they may have been subconsciously influenced by a desire to be different, to do something alien, at least to become notable by doing something notorious, like taking another person's life.

One interesting trait shared by many murderers is their use of pseudonyms. It appears that they assume false names not only to evade detection, but chiefly to invent for themselves new personas – as though they cannot bear to be what they are.

In most if not all premeditated murders, the act of murder is not the only solution to a particular emotional or mental problem. Yet it is the one way out that a potential murderer chooses. There are many and complex reasons for this, apart from the minor factors outlined above. There is supposedly an X factor, a chemical reason – strictly speaking, an extra Y chromosome in the genetic structure of a few people – that turns them into psychopaths, if not into killers. There is undoubtedly a rage in the blood and in the mind that leads to murder, whatever its cause. But what the murderers in this book have in common – and most are to some degree amoral, vain, cunning, cruel, avaricious, selfish, stupid and bad – is that without exception they are, and behave, like fools.

What is also interesting is the fact that not a few, earlier in their lives, suffered blows to their heads or were involved in accidents that might have resulted in such damage. Could it be that damage to their frontal lobes impairs those areas of the brain controlling common sense, compassion, pity and remorse, and that physical or chemical factors should be added to genetic factors of omission and excess?

There is one other factor that the case histories in this book reveal – the apparent significance of *place* in the perpetration of a murder. This may only be an oddity. But in this connection it should be noted that of the thirty-seven women poisoners executed for murder between 1843 and 1955 (sixty-eight women in all were hanged in this period), twenty lived in towns and seventeen in the country. Of the latter, five lived in or near Boston in Lincolnshire and six in and around Ipswich in Suffolk. The Ipswich murders may have been imitative – they all occurred within a period of eight years – but the Boston murders were many years apart.

In considering the murders described in this book, one wonders how great a part chance and coincidence played in the following facts: that Miss Holland and Mrs McKay were murdered within a few miles of each other, and near Bishop's Stortford, near where the poisoner George Chapman ran a pub and where Harry Roberts went to ground; that Mrs Deeming and Mr Maybrick died within a few miles of each other in Liverpool; that Frederick Deeming, Mrs Maybrick, Mahon, Armstrong, Kennedy and Wrenn at some time all lived in Liverpool; that Parker and Probert, Haigh, Thorne and Mahon killed within a twenty-mile radius of Lewes in Sussex (at Portslade, Crawley, Crowborough and Langney); that Mrs Pearcey and Samuel Furnace killed within a few hundred yards of each other in Camden – a mile away from Crippen's house and 2 miles from where the Seddons lived; and that of forty-one murders in the London area, only eight were committed south of the River Thames.

And why is it that so many victims and murderers in this book have visited and stayed at Bournemouth? The town has had some sensational murders, such as that of Irene Wilkins in 1921 by Thomas Allaway, that of Mr Rattenbury by George Stoner in 1935, that of Walter Dinivan by Joseph Williams in 1939, and that of Doreen Marshall by Neville Heath in 1946. But Samuel Dougal, George Smith, Major Armstrong, the Thompsons, Ronald True, Emily Kaye, Frederick Browne, Neville Heath – and Montague Druitt – all stayed there within a few months of a murder. They did not choose other resorts nearer London for their visits, like Brighton or Eastbourne, or any further away to the north. Why Bournemouth?

What is most remarkable, however, is the number of murderers – indeed, mass murderers – who were born and brought up west and south of Leeds. The Wartime Ripper, Gordon Cummins, was born in New Earswick, to the north of York. Although Haigh was not born in Yorkshire, he was brought up from an early age in Outwood, south of Leeds. Christie was born and lived in a suburb of Halifax. The Black Panther, Donald Neilson, was born in Morley south of Leeds and lived in Bradford to the west; and the Yorkshire Ripper, Peter Sutcliffe, was born in Shipley and brought up in Bingley. To them can be added Peter Dinsdale, the killer-arsonist who came from Hull – to the east of Leeds, but on the same latitude – and Dr Harold Shipman. Although Shipman was born in Nottingham, he graduated from the Leeds School of Medicine in 1970, and spent his first few years as a doctor in the West Riding of Yorkshire, where it is thought he first began to kill.

Finally, besides these mass murderers, there are ten Yorkshiremen who between them caused the deaths of over 1,200 men and women. James Berry, chief executioner, was born in Heckmondwike, south-west of Leeds (between Christie and Haigh), and lived in Bradford. The three Pierrepoints – Tom, Harry and Albert, all chief executioners, who between them hanged 834 people – came from Clayton, a western suburb of Bradford. The last two also lived in Huddersfield, as did another executioner, Thomas Scott. Executioner Steve Wade was yet another Yorkshireman, from Doncaster. The four executioner Billingtons – father James and his three sons, Thomas, William and John – all came from Bolton in Yorkshire. Whoever said that God was a Yorkshireman was worshipping some strange gods indeed.

CHARLES PEACE

THE MURDER OF ARTHUR DYSON, 1876

Murder is often compounded with theft and sex – which is to say that it frequently results from a compulsive desire to deprive, or a compulsion not to be deprived of, one's desire. Fortunately, much thieving seems to be related to a low or inadequate sexual capability. But not always. A randy thief or robber has therefore more problems than his undersexed counterpart – problems that can lead to murder. As they did in the case of Charles Frederick Peace.

He was born in Sheffield on 14 May 1832, the son of a respected shoemaker. He was not a good scholar, but was very dexterous, making artistic shapes and objects out of bits of twisted paper. Apprenticed at a rolling mill, he was badly injured when a piece of red-hot steel rammed his leg, leaving him with a limp. He learned to play the violin with sufficient flair and skill to be billed at local concerts as 'The Modern Paganini'. He also took part in amateur theatricals. When he was about twenty, in search of other excitements and reluctant to earn a living, he began to thieve. He was unsuccessful at first, and was jailed four times, with sentences of one month, four, six and seven years. During this period he wandered from town to town, and in 1859 met and married Mrs Hannah Ward – a widow with a son, Willie. He returned to Sheffield in 1872. Three years later, he set up shop in Darnall as a picture-framer and gilder. He was also a collector and seller of musical instruments and bric-a-brac.

In 1875, Peace was forty-three. He was, according to a police description: 'Thin and slightly built, 5 ft 4 ins or 5 ins, grey hair … He looks ten years older. He lacks one or more fingers of his left hand, walks with his legs rather wide apart, speaks somewhat peculiarly, as though his tongue was too large for his mouth, and is a great boaster.' He was also shrewd, cunning, selfish, salacious, ugly, agile as a monkey and very strong.

Peace became involved with his neighbours in Britannia Road, the Dysons. Very tall (6 ft 5 in) and genteel, Arthur Dyson was a civil engineer, working with railway companies. He was in America when he met his future wife, a young Irish girl called Katherine. She was tall, buxom and blooming, and fond of a drink. They married in Cleveland, Ohio. The couple often had rows. Peace – 'If I make up my mind to a thing I am bound to have it' – became familiar with the Dysons and enamoured of young Mrs Dyson, who unwisely responded to his attentions. It seems they visited pubs and music halls together and that their place of assignation was a garret in an empty house between their two homes. Peace took to calling on the Dysons at any time, including mealtimes. Mr Dyson put his foot down. But Mrs Dyson continued, accidentally or intentionally, to associate with Peace. In June 1876, he was forbidden to call on them any more. Arthur Dyson wrote on a visiting card, 'Charles Peace is requested not to interfere with my family,' and threw it into Peace's yard.

This was something Peace could not endure. He pestered and threatened the Dysons. 'We couldn't get rid of him,' said Mrs Dyson, talking later to the *Sheffield Independent's* reporter. 'I can hardly describe all that he did to annoy us after he was informed that he was not wanted at our house. He would come and stand outside the window at night and look in, leering all the while ... He had a way of creeping and crawling about, and of coming upon you suddenly unawares ... He wanted me to leave my husband.'

One Saturday in July 1876, Peace tripped up Mr Dyson in the street, and that evening pulled a gun on Mrs Dyson as she stood outside her house complaining to neighbours about the assault. He said: 'I will blow your bloody brains out and your husband's too!' A magistrate's warrant was obtained for his arrest and he fled with his family to Hull, where Mrs Peace ran an eating-house.

For a time the Dysons were, it appears, undisturbed. But on 26 October, they moved house, to Banner Cross Terrace in Ecclesall Road, and when they arrived (their furniture had gone ahead), Peace walked out of their front door. He said: 'I am here to annoy you, and I will annoy you wherever you go.'

A month later, on Wednesday, 29 November 1876, Peace was seen hanging about Banner Cross Terrace between 7 and 8 pm. It was later suggested in court that Mrs Dyson and Peace had had a rendezvous in the Stag Hotel the evening before.

At eight o'clock on the 29th, Mrs Dyson put her little boy, aged five, to bed. She came downstairs, to the back parlour where her husband was reading, and about ten past eight she put on her clogs, took a lantern and, leaving the rear door open, went to the outside closet, which stood in a passage at the end of the terrace. It was a moonlit night. Peace later claimed that she left the house when he whistled for her. Her closet visit was brief. When she opened the door to emerge, Peace stood before her. 'Speak, or I'll fire,' he said, presumably meaning the opposite. She shrieked, slammed the door and locked it. Mr Dyson rushed out of the rear door of the house and around the corner of the building. As he did so his wife fled from the closet. He pushed past her, pursuing Peace down the passage and on to the pavement. According to Peace, there was a struggle. He fired one shot, he said, to frighten Dyson. It missed. 'My blood was up,' said Peace. 'I knew if I was captured, it would mean transportation for life. That made me determined to get off.' A second shot was fired, striking Dyson in the head. The shots were fired in quick succession. Mr Dyson fell on to his back, and his wife screamed: 'Murder! You villain, you have shot my husband!' Within minutes Arthur Dyson was dead.

Peace ran off, but in doing so dropped a small packet, containing more than twenty notes and letters and Dyson's card requesting Peace not to interfere. The notes, clearly written by a woman, included lines such as: 'You can give me something as a keepsake if you like' – 'Will see you as soon as I possibly can' – 'You must not venture for he is watching' – 'Not today anyhow, he is not very well' – 'I will give you the wink when the coast is clear – 'He is gone out, come now for I must have a drink' – 'Send me a drink. I am nearly dead' – 'Meet me in the Wicker, hope nothing will turn up to prevent it' – 'He is out now so be quick.'

From then on Charlie Peace was on the run, wanted for murder, with a reward on his head of £100. Burgling as he went from town to town and narrowly evading capture, he came in time to London, where he eventually settled in 5 East Terrace, Evelina Road, Peckham. His wife, Hannah, was installed in the basement with her son, Willie. Peace occupied the other rooms with a widowed girlfriend, Susan Grey (or Bailey), aged about thirty – 'A dreadful woman for drink and snuff,' said Peace. They passed themselves off as Mr and Mrs Thompson and before long she bore him a son. The house was richly furnished, adorned with a quick turnover of other people's possessions, and alive with dogs, cats and rabbits, canaries, parrots and cockatoos. As the women were always quarrelling it must have been a very clamorous household. In the evenings, Peace sometimes entertained friends and neighbours with musical soirées, at which he played a fiddle he had made himself, recited monologues and sang.

Meanwhile, he continued his trade, driving around south London by day in his pony and trap to look for likely 'cribs' to crack, returning to them at night with his tools concealed in a violin case. He dressed well – 'The police never think of suspecting anyone who wears good clothes' – and looked quite different from his Sheffield self, having shaved off his beard, dyed his hair black and stained his face; he also wore spectacles. He became more successful, more daring than ever, and although his burglaries attracted much attention in the papers, no one knew who the culprit could be. Every Sunday he went to church with Susan Thompson.

It seems in the end that someone grassed on him, perhaps one or other of his women. Certainly the police were out in unusually large numbers in the early hours of Thursday, 10 October 1878 in the south-eastern London suburb of Blackheath.

About 2 am PC Edward Robinson noticed a flickering light in the rear rooms of 2 St John's Park. He summoned the assistance of PC William Girling and Sergeant Charles Brown, and the latter went round to the front and rang the doorbell, while the other two hovered by the garden wall at the rear. They saw the roving light inside the house go out and a figure make a quick exit from the dining-room window on to the lawn. PC Robinson chased him across the moonlit garden, and was 6 yards away when Peace turned and shouted: 'Keep back, keep off, or by God, I'll shoot you!' PC Robinson said: 'You had better not!'

Peace fired three times, according to Robinson, narrowly missing the constable's head. He rushed at Peace. A fourth shot missed, but as they struggled – 'You bugger, I'll settle you this time!' cried Peace – a fifth shot entered Robinson's right arm above the elbow. Undaunted, but no doubt now enraged, Robinson flung Peace on the ground, seized the revolver and hit Peace with it several times. 'You bugger!' said Peace, 'I'll give you something else!' And he allegedly reached for some weapon in one of his pockets. But by then Girling, followed by Brown, had come to Robinson's assistance and Peace was overpowered.

While he was being searched, Peace made another attempt to escape and was incapacitated by a blow from Girling's truncheon. A spirit flask, a cheque book and a letter-case, stolen from the house, were found on the captive burglar, as well as a small crowbar, an auger, a jemmy, a gimlet, a centre-bit, a hand-vice and two chisels.

As Robinson was now feeling faint from loss of blood, the other two policemen took charge of Peace. He was escorted to Park Row police station near the Royal Naval College at Greenwich and not far from the River Thames. There he was charged with burglary and with the wounding of PC Robinson with intent to murder. He gave his name as 'John Ward', and when asked where he lived he replied: 'Find out!' Inspector John Bonney of Blackheath Road police station was put in charge of the case, and later that morning Peace was brought before Detective Inspector Henry Phillips, local head of the newly formed Criminal Investigation Department of Scotland Yard, the CID.

DI Phillips later wrote a full, vivid and as yet unpublished memoir of his involvement with Peace. Writing in 1899, he said that Peace's 'repulsive' appearance could be verified by the wax image of him in Madame Tussauds – where it is to this day.

On the morning of 10 October 1878, Phillips and Bonney tried to elicit information from the bloody-minded burglar, who exclaimed: 'If you want to know where I live, find out! It's your business!' Bonney threatened to thrash him – 'All to no purpose,' Phillips wrote.

Peace was then lodged in Newgate Prison, where he was visited by DI Phillips more than once. Phillips wrote later: 'He was very talkative and boasted of his misdeeds as if they were something to be proud of.' Phillips concluded that although Peace could seem 'religious-minded' and a 'nice quiet old man', he was really 'a canting hypocrite'.

The following month, on 19 November 18978, Peace was tried under the name of John Ward at the Central Criminal Court in the Old Bailey, charged with the attempted murder of PC Edward Robinson. The judge was Mr Justice Hawkins; Mr Pollard was the prosecutor and Mr Montague Williams spoke on the prisoner's behalf.

After a four-minute consultation, the jury found Peace guilty. Asked by Mr Reed, the clerk of the court, if he had anything to say before judgement was pronounced, the prisoner made a lengthy, whining, almost grovelling speech that apparently impressed most of his listeners except the judge. Peace said:

I swear before God I never had the intention to kill the policeman. All I meant was to frighten him in order that I might get away. If I had the intention to kill him I could easily have done it ... I declare I did not fire five shots. I only fired four shots ... I really did not know the pistol was loaded, and I hope, my lord, you will have mercy upon me. I feel that I have disgraced myself and am not fit to live or die ... Give me a chance, my lord, to regain my freedom, and you shall not, with the help of God, have any cause to regret passing a merciful sentence upon me. Oh my lord, you yourself do expect mercy from the hands of your great and merciful God. Oh my lord, do have mercy upon me, a most wretched, miserable man – a man that am not fit to die. I am not fit to live; but with the help of my God, I will try to become a good man ...

Peace was sentenced to penal servitude for life.

The judge then called PC Robinson forward, commended his courageous conduct, recommended him for promotion and for a reward of £25. Robinson was duly promoted to sergeant, and for many years a waxwork of him stood in Madame Tussauds beside that of Charles Peace.

The prisoner was incarcerated in Pentonville Prison, which in 1878, wrote Phillips, was 'a preparatory prison for all convicts sentenced to Penal Servitude. It was here they performed the first nine months of their sentence, under what was known as the solitary system.'

Meanwhile, under pressure from the police, Susan Thompson had revealed the true identity of Mr Thompson, alias John Ward. She told DI Phillips: 'He is the greatest criminal that ever lived and so you will find out. He used to live at Darnall near Sheffield and is wanted for murder and there is a reward for his arrest.' Susan Thompson eventually claimed and received that reward – £100.

Phillips was sent north by the Director of the CID, Mr Howard Vincent, to pursue his inquiries and to find Hannah Peace (or Ward), who had returned with her son to Sheffield. It seems that Phillips had never been north of Finchley, and his experiences over the next few weeks left a lasting impression. Over twenty years later he wrote: 'We went by the Midland Railway, all the way in the dark. The Country looked very dismal, but was lighted up by various bonfires, it being the 5th November.' He was also very impressed by the Yorkshire police – 'I had never got in contact with such men before. They seemed to have the Knack of making you feel you had known them for years.'

Hannah Peace (or Ward), by now aged fifty, was traced to a cottage in Darnall – 'a wild barren-looking country, the more so in November,' wrote Phillips. In the cottage he found a number of items which he deemed to be stolen property and arrested Hannah Peace. She appeared before the Sheffield magistrates, was remanded for a week, and some time before Christmas was taken by Phillips back to London on an overnight train. She then appeared at the Old Bailey on 14 January 1879, charged with receiving stolen goods. She was acquitted, however, on the grounds that she was Peace's wife – although this was never actually proved – and therefore acted under his authority.

Early on the morning of Wednesday, 22 January 1879, Peace was taken, manacled and in his convict's garb, from Pentonville Prison to Sheffield for the magistrate's hearing into the Dyson murder. Attended by two warders, he was put on the 5.15 am express from London to Sheffield. It was very cold; up north there was snow on the ground. Peace was very troublesome during the journey, but all went well until the train neared Sheffield. It passed through Worksop and going full speed reached the Yorkshire border, where the railway line ran parallel with a canal. Phillips wrote:

> Peace was well acquainted with the locality. He expressed a wish to pass water, and for that purpose the window was lowered and he faced it. He was wearing handcuffs and with a chain six inches long, so that he had some use of his hands – and he immediately sprang through the window. One of the warders caught him by the left foot. There he held him suspended, of course with the head downwards. He kicked the warder with the right foot and struggled with all his might to get free. The Chief Warder was unable to render his colleague any assistance because the Warder's body occupied the whole of the space of the open window. He hastened to the opposite side of the Carriage and pulled the Cord to alarm the Guard, but the Cord would not act. But some gentlemen in the next compartment, seeing the state of affairs, assisted the efforts of the Chief Warder to stop the train. All this time the struggle was going on between the Warder and the Convict, and eventually Peace succeeded in kicking off his shoe and, his head striking the footboard of the Carriage, he fell on the line.

When the train eventually came to a halt, the two warders ran for over a mile back along the railway line and found their prisoner prostrate in the snow and apparently dead. To their relief he soon recovered consciousness, professing to be in great pain from a bloody wound in his head and dying of cold. A slow train heading for Sheffield chanced to appear and was stopped by the two warders. Peace was lifted up and dumped in the guard's van at the rear. The train then proceeded on its way, arriving at Sheffield at 9.20 am.   Phillips later described the scene:

> An immense crowd had assembled to get sight of this great Criminal and the excitement became intense when the 8.54 Express arrived without him. The Guard reported that Peace had escaped. The crowd were unbelieving and they suggested that the statement was a ruse to get the crowd away. But when they saw a sword and a rug and a bag belonging to the Warders brought from an empty carriage and handed to Inspector Bird, it was then generally believed that the statement was true and that Peace had escaped from Custody and that the Warders were on his track. At the Sheffield Police Court great preparations had been made for the reception of Charles Peace and the Court was crowded. All the persons required to be in attendance were present, except one, and that was the Prisoner ... Mr Jackson, Chief Constable of Sheffield, entered the Court in a state of some excitement and made the startling statement to the Bench that Peace had escaped from the Warders. The ordinary

business of the Court proceeded, when it suddenly became known that Peace had been captured and was actually in Sheffield.

In a police station cell, Peace was examined by two surgeons. He had a severe scalp wound and concussion and vomited periodically. He complained of being cold. His wounds were dressed and he was laid on a bed in the cell and covered with rugs. 'There the little old man lay,' wrote Phillips, 'with his head peeping out of the rugs, guarded by two Officers. During the first hour he was frequently roused and he partook of some brandy. At first, force had to be used to get him to take it, but subsequently he drank without any trouble. At the same time he said he should prefer whisky.'

Two days later, the surgeons certified that Peace was fit enough to attend court. In fact the court went to him, and the magistrate's hearing was held on Friday, 24 January, by candlelight in the corridor outside his cell.

Still swathed in rugs and bandages and hunched on a chair, Peace cursed, groaned, complained and endlessly interrupted the proceedings. 'What are we here for? What is this?' he protested. The magistrate replied: 'This is the preliminary enquiry which is being proceeded with after being adjourned.' Said Peace: 'I wish to God there was something across my shoulders! I'm very cold! It isn't justice. Oh, dear. If I killed myself it'd be no matter. I ought to have a remand. I feel I want it, and I must have one!'

The hearing was attended by Mrs Dyson, who had been brought back to England from America, whither she had gone after her husband's death. As the prosecution's principal witness she seemed to enjoy the drama of her situation and was evidently not put out by Peace's appearance and aspersions. When she took the oath without lifting her veil, Peace remarked: 'Will you be kind enough to take your veil off? You haven't kissed the book.'

Committed for trial at Leeds Assizes, he was taken by train to Wakefield Prison. A large crowd again assembled at Sheffield's railway station, this time to witness his departure. Professing to be helpless, he was carried from the police van by prison warders. He looked pale and haggard, despite his brown complexion, and had a white bandage around his head. 'He wore his Convict suit,' wrote Phillips, 'and very comical he looked in the cap surmounting the bandage and appeared as feeble as a Child.'

In Wakefield Prison, Peace spent the next few days writing penitential and moralising letters. One, on 26 January, was to Susan Thompson:

My dear Sue – This is a fearful affair that has befallen me, but I hope you will not foreșake [sic] me, as you have been my bosom friend, and you have oftimes said you loved me, and would die for me. What I hope and trust you will do is sell the goods I left you to raise money to engage a Barrister to save me from the perjury of that villainous woman Kate Dyson … I hope you will not forget the love we have had for each other … I am very ill from the effects of the jump from the train. I tried to kill myself to save all further trouble and distress, and to be buried at Darnall. I remain your ever true lover till death.

Sue Thompson replied:

Dear Jack, I received your letter and am truly sorry to receive one from you from a Prison ... I sold some of the goods before Hannah and I went away and I shared with her the money that was in the house ... I had nothing to depend upon, and have not a friend of my own, but what have turned their backs upon me, my life indeed is most miserable. I am sorry you made such a rash attempt upon your life ... You are doing me a great injury by saying I have been out to work with you. Do not die with such a base falsehood upon your conscience, for you know I am young and have my home and character to redeem. I pity you and myself to think we should have met ... Yours, etc – Sue.

On Tuesday, 4 February 1879, Charles Peace was put on trial at Leeds Assizes before Mr Justice Lopes; the prosecutor was Mr Campbell Foster, QC, and the accused was defended by Mr Frank Lockwood. The court was packed, many of the women being armed with opera glasses. Peace, wizened and unshaven, his scarred head and hollow features bristling with thin grey hairs, sat in an armchair within a spiked enclosure.

The prosecution's chief witness, Mrs Dyson, although evidently embarrassed by the implications of some of the prosecution's more personal questions, behaved with a degree of indecorum, even levity. When asked by Campbell Foster how wide the passage was outside the closet she replied: 'I don't know, I am not an architect.' To the question: 'Did anything touch your husband before he fell on his back?' she replied: 'The bullet touched him.' 'I didn't ask that,' scolded Campbell Foster. 'Did Peace touch him with his foot?' She retorted: 'No, but the *bullet* touched him.' There was laughter in court. Campbell Foster was more successful in implying that Mrs Dyson had had an association with Peace, that he gave her a ring, that she continued to meet him after her husband had expressed his dislike of Peace, and had been photographed with him at the Sheffield Summer Fair in 1876. She denied that letters and notes referring to assignations were in her handwriting. But she was forced to admit when confronted by witnesses, that she had gone with Peace to some pubs and music halls. However, she denied that she had ever been evicted from a pub for being drunk, and that she was with Peace in the Stag Hotel the night before her husband was killed.

Various witnesses corroborated the circumstances surrounding the shooting of Arthur Dyson. Mr Lockwood, defending, proposed that the shooting was accidental, that Peace's threats were meaningless, and that the prosecution's principal witness was unreliable and her evidence tainted and uncorroborated. The judge told the jury that the plea of provocation failed altogether 'where preconceived ill-will against the deceased was proved'.

The jury took fifteen minutes to reach a verdict of 'guilty of wilful murder', and Peace was sentenced to death. On being asked if he had anything to say, he murmured: 'Will it be any use for me to say anything?'

Peace was removed to Armley Jail in Leeds where, in penitential mood, he made a full confession of all his crimes to the Reverend JH Littlewood, vicar of Darnall. In it, he revealed that he had shot another policeman – and killed him – in Manchester on 1 August 1876, four months *before* the death of Arthur Dyson.

Peace's story was that PC Nicholas Cock and another constable had disturbed him when he was about to burgle a group of prosperous houses called Whalley Range. PC Cock surprised Peace as he climbed over a wall and shouted at him to stand where he was. 'This policeman was as determined a man as myself,' said Peace, 'and after I had fired wide at him, I observed him seize his staff, which was in his pocket, and he was rushing at me and about to strike me. I then fired the second time. "Ah, you bugger," he said, and fell. I could not take as careful an aim as I would have done, and the ball, missing the arm, struck him in the breast. I got away, which was all I wanted.'

Two young Irish brothers called Habron, farm labourers, were accused of the crime at Manchester Assizes and one of them, William Habron, aged nineteen, was sentenced to death on 28 November 1876 – the day before the murder of Arthur Dyson. William's brother, John was found not guilty, and the jury added a recommendation for mercy to William Habron 'on the grounds of his youth'. For three weeks he was confined in a condemned cell. But on 19 December the Home Secretary granted a reprieve and William's sentence was commuted to one of penal servitude for life. He was sent to Portland Prison, where he remained for over two years.

Peace had watched the Habron trial from the public gallery and kept silent. He said later: 'What man would have done otherwise in my position?' But now that he was to be executed himself, he told the Reverend Littlewood that he thought it right 'in the sight of God and man to clear the young man'. He ended his confession by saying: 'What I have said is nothing but the truth and this is my dying words. I have done my duty and leave the rest to you.'

Charles Peace was hanged by William Marwood at Armley Jail in Leeds at 8 am on 25 February 1879.

His last days were spent in interminable letter-writing and prayer and the Christian exhortation of others. But his reprobate real self prevailed. Of his last breakfast he said: 'This is bloody rotten bacon!' And when a warder began banging on the door as Peace lingered overlong in the lavatory on the morning of his execution, he shouted: 'You're in a hell of a hurry! Are you going to be hanged or am I?' On the scaffold he refused to wear the white hood – 'Don't! I want to look' – and insisted on making a speech of forgiveness, repentance and trust in the Lord. Four journalists who were present wrote down his last words, spoken as his resolution left him: 'I should like a drink. Have you a drink to give me?' As he spoke, Marwood, the executioner, released the trap door.

Peace fell; the vertebrae at the base of his head fractured and dislocated, and his spinal cord was severed.

He wrote his own epitaph for the memorial card which he himself had printed in jail: 'In memory of Charles Peace who was executed in Armley Prison, Tuesday, February 25th 1879. For that I done but never intended.'

On 19 March, William Habron was moved from Portland to Millbank Prison in London and then set free with a full pardon. He was told that his father had died six months earlier 'of a broken heart'. He was given £1,000 in compensation 'to ease his pain and anguish'.

In due course, DI Henry Phillips donated some items that had been used by Peace in his burglaries to the Black Museum at Scotland Yard. A hundred years later, Phillips's very informative, hand-written memoir was in turn donated to the museum by lorry driver Peter Coyle, on behalf of Phillips's great-niece, Mrs Bell.

JACK THE RIPPER

THE WHITECHAPEL MURDERS, 1888

Fiction far outweighs fact in the volume of words used to describe the crimes, motives and character of Jack the Ripper. The facts are few, almost as few as the five murders he is believed to have committed. The fictions stem from the fact — despite mountains of theory and speculation — that no one knows for certain who he was. No single writer, in the last seventy years, has been able to establish the identity of the 'Whitechapel Murderer', as he was originally called. Significantly, the first full-length work on the subject, The Mystery of Jack the Ripper, *was not published until more than a generation, forty-one years, after the murders. It was written by an Australian journalist, Leonard Matters. Since then, and despite confident claims by various writers that they have found* The Answer, *or* The Final Solution, *they have not. They fail to convince, to provide conclusive proof, their causes and case histories being spoiled by misconception, misreporting, error, and the perpetuation of earlier journalistic imaginings, assumptions and fancy unsupported by fact. The identity of the Whitechapel murderer is and will remain an enigma. He is not even definitely named in the so-called secret files of Scotland Yard.*

Five murders are known to have been committed by the Ripper, but two others were once thought to have been his work as well. The first was of Emma Smith, an ageing prostitute, who lived at 18 George Street, Spitalfields. She was attacked in Osborn Street in the early hours of 3 April 1888. Her face and ear were cut, and some instrument, not a knife, had been thrust violently up her vagina. She said she had been assaulted by four men, but could or would not identify them. She died the next day in the London Hospital of peritonitis. Four months later, at 3 am on 7 August, the body of Martha Tabram, aged thirty-five, was found on a staircase landing in George Yard Buildings in Commercial Street. Her throat and stomach had been stabbed or pierced thirty-nine times with something sharp like a bayonet. Earlier that night, she and another prostitute had been seen in the company of two soldiers, who were arrested and paraded with others in front of the second prostitute. But she failed or refused to identify either her own or the other woman's partner.

It should be remembered that in 1888 the East End of London, a few square miles, was inhabited by about 900,000 people, virtual outcasts living in conditions of extreme depravity, poverty and filth. Fifty-five per cent of East End children died before they were five. Each squalid room in each rotting lodging house was occupied by between five and seven persons – men, women and children. In Whitechapel, about 8,500 people crammed into 233 lodging houses every night, paying as much as 4d for a bed. The parish of Whitechapel was infested with about 80,000 artisans, labourers and derelicts, of whom the better-off – the poor, as opposed to the very poor – earned about £1 a week. The more menial tasks yielded a shilling a day, women being paid less than men. People lived from day to day, earning or stealing what they could to eat and stay alive. Drunkenness and prostitution were rampant. The Metropolitan Police estimated that in October 1888 about 1,200 of the lowest sort of prostitute plied their trade in the dingy Whitechapel streets. Consequently, women were assaulted and injured every night. Some were killed.

Twenty-four days after the death of Martha Tabram there occurred the first of the accepted Ripper killings. At about 3.30 am on Friday, 31 August, Mary Ann Nichols, a forty-two-year-old prostitute, was murdered. She was found in Buck's Row, lying on her back, her skirt pushed up above her knees; her eyes were open. Her throat had been slashed twice, from left to right, the second eight-inch-long cut almost severing the head. Blood from the cut had been absorbed by her stained and shabby clothes: a brown ulster, a brown linsey frock, two petticoats, stays and black wool stockings. She also wore a black straw bonnet. Her face was bruised. She was 5 ft 2 in tall and had lost five of her front teeth. It was not until her body was removed to the mortuary by the old Montague Street workhouse that other injuries were revealed. Her stomach had been hacked open and slashed several times. Mary Ann Nichols, also known as Polly, had lodged at 18 Thrawl Street, Spitalfields, as well as at 56 Flower and Dean Street. She was last seen alive at 2.30 am on the corner of Osborn Street, staggering drunkenly down Whitechapel Road towards Buck's Row (now Durward Street).

Because she, Tabram and Smith were all murdered within 300 yards of each other and were prostitutes, a connection was made between them that now seems insubstantial. A man known to have ill-treated prostitutes and to have been seen with Nichols became a prime suspect. Known as Leather Apron, he was a Jewish bootmaker, John Pizer – also called Jack.

The next murder was eight days later. The body of Annie Chapman, aged forty-five, also known as Dark Annie, Annie Siffey or Sievey (she had lived with a man who made sieves), was found in the back yard of 29 Hanbury Street at 6 am on Saturday, 8 September. She lay on her back beside steps leading from a passage into the yard. Her knees were wide apart and her dirty black skirt pushed up over them. Her face was swollen and her chin and jaw were bruised; her tongue protruded from her mouth. Two deep and savage cuts had practically separated her head from her body. Her stomach had been torn open and pulled apart; sections of skin from the stomach lay on her shoulder – on the right was another piece of skin and a mess of small intestines. It was later established that she had been disembowelled – her uterus, part of the vagina and the bladder had been carved out and taken away.

Slight bloodstains were discovered on the palings of a fence beside the body and specks of blood spattered the rear wall of the house above the prostrate corpse. Her rings were missing – they had been torn from her fingers. At her feet lay some pennies and two new farthings; a comb also lay by the body. Presumably this and the coins had been in the pocket under her skirt that had been ripped open. Other adjacent items, which probably had nothing to do with the murder, included part of an envelope stamped 28 August 1888 and bearing the crest of the Sussex Regiment on the back, as well as a piece of paper containing two pills – and a leather apron soaked with water and about two feet from a communal tap.

Annie Chapman was a small (5 ft), stout woman with dark hair, blue eyes, a thick nose and two teeth missing from her lower jaw. She had lodged at 35 Dorset Street, from where she had been evicted at 2 am because she lacked the few pennies for a bed. Drunk and ill, she had wandered off towards Brushfield Street. She was last seen alive at 5.30 am (a clock was striking the half-hour) by a park-keeper's wife who was on her way to market. She saw Chapman standing outside 29 Hanbury Street, haggling with a foreign-looking man, aged about forty, who was shabbily but respectably dressed and wearing a deerstalker, probably brown. Number 29 was a lodging house, occupied by seventeen people, none of whom heard anything untoward. But the street was not quiet: carts and workers were already moving up and down on their way to work.

Several suspects were taken to Commercial Street police station for questioning on Sunday, 9 September, and in the early hours of Monday the 10th, John Pizer, Leather Apron, was found at 22 Mulberry Street and arrested. Witnesses said that two months earlier he had been ejected from 35 Dorset Street and that he wore a deerstalker hat. The police found five long-bladed knives in his lodgings, of a sort thought to have been used by the murderer. Pizer said that he used them in his boot-making trade. He protested his innocence, and his story that he had been in hiding in the Mulberry Street house for four days, since Thursday, was backed up by his stepmother and brother who lived there. He also had an alibi for the night Mary Ann Nichols was murdered – he was in a lodging house in Holloway Road.

At the inquest on Annie Chapman, the leather apron found in the back yard not far from her body was identified as the property of John Richardson, whose widowed mother lived in 29 Hanbury Street. She had washed the apron on Thursday, leaving it by the fence, where it was found on Saturday by the police. Richardson had actually visited the house about 4.45 am on his way to work, to check that his mother's padlocked cellar, which had recently been robbed, was intact. In the dawn light, he saw that it was and that the yard was empty.

Another yard was the scene of the murder of Elizabeth Stride, a forty-four-year-old Swedish prostitute, also known as Long Liz. She was killed about 1 am on Sunday, 30 September, a wet and windy night. Her body was discovered by a hawker, Louis Diemschutz, who worked as a steward in a Jewish Socialist Club that backed onto the yard in Berner Street. As he drove into the yard in a pony and trap, the pony shied to the left, doing so twice and drawing the hawker's attention to a heap of clothes on the ground. He poked at it with his whip and lit a match, which was snuffed out by the wind. But he had seen enough. He fetched help from the club, where the rowdy members were singing and dancing.

Long Liz lay on her muddy left side, her legs drawn up, right arm over her stomach, her left arm extended behind her back, the hand clutching a packet of cashew nuts. Her right hand was bloody, and her mouth was slightly open. The bow of a check silk scarf around her throat had pulled tight and had turned to the left of her neck. The scarf's lower edge was frayed, as if by a very sharp knife, which had also slit her throat from left to right, severing the windpipe. Bruises on her shoulders and chest indicated that she had been seized and forced down onto the ground when her throat had been cut. Her body was still warm. Evidently the murderer had been frightened off by the returning pony and trap. There were no other injuries or mutilations. It was noted at the mortuary that the dead woman had no teeth in her left lower jaw.

Like Nichols and Chapman, Stride was married but separated from her husband. Like them, she was something of an alcoholic. She had lived in Fashion Street with a labourer called Michael Kidney, who had then moved to 35 Dorset Street. But on the Tuesday before her death she had walked out, lodging instead at 32 Flower and Dean Street. On the Saturday night she had been seen by a labourer, William Marshall, at about 11.45 pm in Berner Street, talking to a mild-voiced, middle-aged, stout and decently dressed man, wearing a cutaway coat. He had looked like a clerk to Marshall: he wore no gloves, carried no stick or anything else in his hands, and on his head was 'a round cap with a small peak to it' like a sailor's hat. He kissed Long Liz and he said: 'You would say anything but your prayers.' Then they walked down the street.

She was seen again in Berner Street at about 12.30 am by a policeman, PC Smith. He described Stride's companion as they stood and talked together as 'of respectable appearance ... He had a newspaper parcel in his hand.' The man was about 5 ft 7 in tall, wore an overcoat and dark trousers and had a dark, hard felt deerstalker on his head. Smith gave the man's age as 'about twenty-eight'. The *Police Gazette* later expanded this description to 'complexion dark, small dark moustache; dress, black diagonal coat, hard felt hat, collar and tie'.

A third witness, a box-maker, James Brown, crossed Berner Street at about 12.45 am and noticed a couple standing by a wall. He heard the woman say: 'Not tonight. Some other night' A glance revealed to him that the man was wearing a long dark coat. The *Gazette* elaborated Brown's description as follows: 'Age about thirty, height 5 ft 5 ins; complexion fair, hair dark, small brown moustache, full face, broad shoulders; dress, dark jacket and trousers, black cap with peak.'

Are Smith and Brown describing the same man? And was he the man who killed Elizabeth Stride at about 1 am and on being disturbed by the pony and trap fled westwards towards Aldgate?

Just after 1.30 am and half a mile to the west in Duke Street, three Jews, one of whom was a Mr Lawende, saw a man talking to a woman in Church Passage, which led into Mitre Square. She was wearing a black jacket and bonnet and was about three or four inches shorter than the man. He was later described in the *Police Gazette* as: 'Aged thirty, height 5 ft 7 ins, or 8 ins; complexion fair, moustache fair, medium build; dress: pepper and salt colour loose jacket, grey cloth cap with peak of some material, reddish neckerchief tied in knots; appearance of a sailor.' The woman was Catherine Eddowes, aged forty-three. Less than ten minutes later she was dead.

She had been married to a man called Conway, but for seven years she had lived at 6 Fashion Street with another man, John Kelly, and accordingly called herself Kate Kelly. That Saturday night she had been arrested in Aldgate about 8.30 pm: she was drunk and disorderly. Taken to Bishopsgate police station, she had been left to sober up in a cell and was discharged at 1 am – at the same time as Elizabeth Stride's throat was cut in the yard off Berner Street. Eddowes walked off southwards, down Houndsditch towards Aldgate High Street and Mitre Square, as Stride's murderer hurried westwards towards her.

At 1.45 am, her body was discovered by the bull's-eye lamp of PC Watkins as he walked on his beat through the square. It lay on its back in a corner. 'I have been in the force a long while,' said Watkins, 'but I never saw such a sight.' The body had been ripped open, said Watkins, like a pig in the market. The left leg was extended and the right leg bent. The throat had been deeply slit and the face had been slashed and cut. There were also abrasions on both cheeks. Both sets of eyelids had been nicked and part of the nose and the right ear had been sliced off. The trunk had been torn apart from the sternum to the groin by a series of disjointed thrusts, the pointed knife that was employed being angled from right to left. The woman had been disembowelled – entrails had been thrown across her right shoulder. The uterus and the left kidney had been cut away and removed.

Police sketches and photographs of Catherine Eddowes's body greatly minimise the view that the murderer had some anatomical knowledge, or took 'at least five minutes' over his work. He clearly worked in a frenzy – cutting the throats of his victims, *ripping* their bodies and pulling out organs with neither care nor skill, and all in a couple of minutes at the most. He would have worked with speed, frantic with bloodlust and also fearful of being caught. He may have had a very rough knowledge of anatomy, sufficient for him to knowingly silence each victim by severing her windpipe, and he might have known what a womb looked like (he removed two) and have been able to distinguish such a comparatively small and obscure item among the mass of organs in the gut. But this does not mean that he had had any actual medical experience or had been a butcher, slaughterman, farmer or hunter of any sort.

The idea propounded at the time by some doctors, that the throats of the victims had been cut (the cause of death) as they lay on the ground, is in reality not very likely – unless the women were already unconscious, or dead. For despite their dirty clothes and drunken state, they are unlikely to have stretched out on the much dirtier, muddy ground to have sex. This service would most likely have been provided standing up against a wall, with their backs to it – or facing it. And it is unlikely that the women were suffocated or strangled *before* their throats were cut. If they *had* been strangled, they would surely have fought for their lives. But in no case was there any sign of a struggle, nor were any bruises found on the women's necks where pressure in strangulation would have been applied. Despite the cut throats, some such marks, if they had been there, must have remained. There were, however, bruises and abrasions on the *faces* of the women, about the chin and jaw. Stride's shoulders were also bruised.

It seems likely that the murderer seized the women from behind, with his left arm or hand gripping face or chin and forcing it upwards, thereby stifling any cry and exposing the throat to the long-bladed knife in his right hand. He would then cut from left to right. In every case, the drunken women were taken by surprise. Despite the fact that people were awake and within a few yards of the murders, there was evidently never any resistance or any sound.

Catherine Eddowes wore a black cloth jacket with an imitation fur collar; her black straw bonnet was trimmed with beads and velvet; her dark green dress was patterned with michaelmas daisies and lilies. In her pockets were a handkerchief, a comb, two clay pipes, a cigarette case, a matchbox containing some cotton, a ball of worsted, a mitten, a small tin box containing tea and sugar, five pieces of soap and a blunt table-knife. Around her neck was a ribbon and 'a piece of old white coarse apron', presumably in place of a scarf. The three previous victims had also worn scarves. Part of this bloodstained apron had been cut off, and was found at the bottom of some common stairs leading to 108–119 Wentworth Dwellings, Goulston Street (north-east of Mitre Square and on the way to Spitalfields) at 2.55 am.

PC Long, who noticed the bloody rag during his night patrol, stated that at 2.20 am it had not been there. Nor, he said, had a five-lined message written in chalk on a black-bricked wall in the passage: 'The Juwes are / The men that / Will not / be Blamed for nothing.' When the Commissioner of the Metropolitan Police, Sir Charles Warren, arrived in Goulston Street about 5 am, he ordered the words to be rubbed out, even before a daylight photograph could be taken of this possible clue. The words, however, were copied. Warren's action was explained by his concern to avoid the exacerbation of prevailing anti-semitic prejudice. For apart from the fact that some main suspects had been Jews, the last four women had been murdered in Jewish areas and near buildings occupied by Jews.

The 'double event' of the murders of Eddowes and Stride provided the press with even more sensational and lurid headlines and reports, and added further fuel to the clamour for the resignation of Sir Charles Warren and the Home Secretary. It was felt that not enough was being done to identify and apprehend the murderer, and the police were strongly criticised. Vigilance committees were formed, petitions signed and demonstrations made. Thousands of letters about the murders and the murderer's identity were sent to the police and to the press, exhibiting every sort of social, sexual and racial prejudices.

Meanwhile, in the East End, where large morbid crowds had gathered in the streets to view the scenes of the murders and indulge in rabid speculation, a 'terrible quiet' descended.

Then a letter and a postcard, received by the Central News Agency, were published with the permission of the police on 3 October. From now on the murderer had a name – Jack the Ripper.

The letter, addressed to *The Boss, Central News Office, London City*, was dated 25 September 1888 and posted in the East End on 27 September, the Thursday *before* the double murder in the early hours of Sunday, 30 September. It read:

Dear Boss

I keep on hearing the police have caught me but they wont fix me just yet. I have laughed when they look so clever and talk about being on the right track. That joke about Leather Apron gave me real fits. I am down on whores and I shant quit ripping them till I do get buckled. Grand work the last job was. I gave the lady (Annie Chapman) no time to squeal . . . I love my work and want to start again. You will soon hear of me with my funny little games. I saved some of the proper red stuff in a ginger beer bottle over the last job to write with but it went thick like glue and I cant use it. Red ink is fit enough I hope ha ha. The next job I do I shall clip the ladys ears off and send to the police officers just for jolly wouldnt you. Keep this letter back till I do a bit more work, then give it out straight. My knife's nice and sharp I want to get to work right away if I get a chance. Good luck.
yours truly
Jack the Ripper

Dont mind me giving the trade name
wasnt good enough to post this before I got all
the red ink off my hands curse it. No luck yet.
They say I'm a doctor now ha ha.

The letter was followed a few days later by a postcard. It was postmarked 1 October – the Monday after the double murder and *not,* as many writers have said, on the same day – even 'a few hours after' the murders of Stride and Eddowes. The postcard was probably written at least 24 hours after the murders, and after details of them had been sensationally splashed in the Monday morning papers. It was addressed to: *Central News Office, London City, EC*:

I wasnt codding dear old Boss when I gave you the tip. youll hear about saucy Jackys work tomorrow double event this time number one squealed a bit couldnt finish straight off. had no time to get ears for police thanks for keeping last letter back till I got to work again.
Jack the Ripper

The postcard might have been written on Sunday the 30th, anything from twelve to twenty hours after the murders, which were within the few hours after midnight. It might have been written by someone in the locality who had heard of the 'double event', or indeed by a journalist, or by anyone connected with the police or medical investigations. In no way does the postcard betoken any foreknowledge of the murders.

Misconception and myth also cloud the next alleged communication from the murderer. Seventeen days after the murders of Stride and Eddowes, on Tuesday, 16 October, at either 5 pm or 8 pm (there were two postal deliveries in the evening in those days), a builder, Mr George Lusk, who was chairman of the Whitechapel Vigilance Committee and lived in Alderney Street, Mile End, received a small brown paper parcel, 3 ½ inches square. Within was a cardboard box that contained half a kidney. The postmark was indecipherable, although post-office workers thought the parcel could have been posted in the Eastern or East Central areas. A brief letter came with the stinking kidney, with an address at the top – 'From hell'.

Sor I send you half the kidne I took from one women prasarved it for you tother piece I fried and ate it was very nise I may send you the bloody knif that took it out if you only wate a whil longer.
signed Catch me when you can Mishter Lusk

The writer of this note is probably not the same man who penned the 'Jack the Ripper' epistles. Apart from the fact that the handwriting is different, the spelling of the Ripper letter and card are superior and written in quite a neat copper-plate. A curious feature of the note to Mr Lusk is the oddly illiterate spelling – it seems deliberate. Words like 'half', 'piece', 'fried' and 'bloody' are properly spelt, yet 'kidne', 'prasarved', 'nise', 'knif', 'wate' and 'whit' are not, being given a sort of phonetic spelling which in three cases is merely attained by the omission of the last letters – 'kidne', 'knif' and 'whit'. Yet in the last two words, the silent letters 'k' and 'h' are included. There is also an obvious Irishness to the spelling of 'Sor' and 'Mishter'.

Mr Lusk had already been bothered by a prowler and other letters, and was at first inclined to dismiss the kidney as a disagreeable hoax. But friends advised him to submit the half kidney to the inspection of the police and doctors, and on 18 October Dr Openshaw, at the Pathological Museum, after examining the offensive organ, concluded that the kidney had come from a woman who drank, had Bright's Disease, and that it was part of a *left* kidney. He thought it had been removed within the last three weeks. It had also been preserved in spirits after its removal.

It has since been assumed that the kidney was the one missing from the body of drunken Catherine Eddowes. There is no proof of this. Eddowes was buried in the City of London Cemetery at Ilford on 8 October, so there was no chance of direct verification or of comparing the alleged length of renal artery attached to the postal kidney and that still in the murdered woman. It is also virtually impossible – it would have been completely so in 1888 – to tell whether a kidney comes from a woman or a man. Moreover, Bright's Disease, which infected the kidney, is not necessarily caused by alcoholism, and the postal kidney had been put in spirits within a few hours of its removal – something the murderer of Eddowes would surely not have thought of or had time to do.

Assumptions and error have gilded the half-kidney since it was sent to Mr Lusk. The sender was most probably a morbid hoaxer, possibly a medical student or hospital worker, who must have been much gratified by the success of his little device. On 29 October, another illiterate letter was sent, this time to Dr Openshaw:

Old boss you was rite it was the left kidny i was goin to hopperate agin clos to your ospitle just as i was goin to dror my nife along of er bloomin throte them cusses of coppers spoilt the game but i guess i wil be on the job soon and will send you another bit innerds Jack the ripper.

An interesting feature of the letters quoted above, one or two of which are thought by some to have possibly been written by the actual Whitechapel murderer, is that the addresses were correct (and correctly *spelt*) and that none of them was addressed to the police – who, in fact, received thousands of letters. This is odd, for murderers with a literary leaning invariably feel bound to communicate with the police, and with no one else – with the exception of Dr Cream, who wrote to everyone.

Sir Robert Anderson, who became head of the CID at the Yard in September 1888, said later: 'The "Jack the Ripper" letter which is preserved in the Police Museum at New Scotland Yard is the creation of an enterprising journalist.' And Sir Melville Macnaghten, who became Assistant Chief Constable at the Yard in 1889 and head of the CID in 1903, wrote: 'In this ghastly production I have always thought I could discern the stained finger of the journalist – indeed, a year later I had shrewd suspicions as to the actual author! But whoever did pen the gruesome stuff, it is certain to my mind that it was not the mad miscreant who had committed the murders.'

The fifth and final murder generally attributed to the Ripper happened forty days after the 'double event'. It was different in that the victim, a prostitute, was young and attractive, was killed indoors and more horribly and extensively mutilated than any female murder victim before, or perhaps since.

Mary Jane Kelly – also known as Dark Mary, Mary Ann and Marie – aged twenty-four, was murdered in the early hours of Friday, 9 November, in a back room of 26 Dorset Street. Two women in nearby but separate rooms said they heard a woman cry 'Murder' about 3.45 am. Mary Kell's lodging, rented for four shillings a week, was Room 13 in the house and had its own entrance, a side-door opening into a passage called Miller's Court. Until 30 October she had shared the room with her common-law husband, Joseph Barnett. After a stormy row he left her, since when another prostitute had stayed with her occasionally.

Kelly's body was discovered about 10.45 am by her landlord's assistant, Thomas Bowyer, who had been sent to ask her for the thirty-five shillings she owed in rent. Getting no answer to his knocking – the door was locked – he peered through a broken window, removing rags that filled the gap and pulling aside a curtain to do so. The police were sent for, but as the Commissioner, Sir Charles Warren, had chosen to resign the day before, the police force were in some confusion. Kelly's room was not entered (at first by the window) until 1.30 pm.

The bloodstained room was sparsely furnished. Mary Kelly, wearing the remains of a chemise or slip, was lying on her back on a bed, where she had been placed after the murderer cut her throat. By the light of a fire, fuelled by clothes and other items he found in the room (although Kelly's clothes, folded on a chair, were not so used), he set to work mutilating the body, which was stabbed, slashed, skinned, gutted and ripped apart. Her nose and breasts were cut off and dumped on a table; entrails were extracted; some were removed; other parts lay on the bed. Mary Kelly was nearly three months pregnant.

The last person believed to have seen her alive was George Hutchinson, an unemployed labourer. He had known Kelly for three years. He met her in Thrawl Street as he walked towards Flower and Dean Street about 2 am. She said: 'Hutchinson, will you lend me sixpence?' 'I can't,' he replied. 'I've spent all my money going down to Romford.' She shrugged. 'Good morning,' she said. 'I must go and find some money.' She walked off, and a man coming in the opposite direction accosted her – they both laughed. Hutchinson watched. He heard Kelly say: 'All right.' 'You'll be all right for what I've told you,' said the man. They walked towards Hutchinson and passed him – he was standing under a lamp outside a pub, the Queen's Head. The man lowered his head and his hat as he passed. But Hutchinson was later able to describe him as being about thirty-four, 5 ft 6 in tall, dark-haired, with a small moustache curled up at the ends. He was dressed in a long dark coat, with a dark jacket and trousers; his waistcoat was as pale as his face, and across it was a gold chain. He wore a white shirt, button boots with gaiters and his black tie had a horseshoe-shaped pin in it. He seemed quite respectable, and Jewish.

Hutchinson's description is very exact: it seems too good to be true. He goes on to say that he followed Kelly and her pick-up into Dorset Street, where they stood talking by Miller's Court for a couple of minutes. He heard Kelly say: 'All right, my dear. Come along – you'll be comfortable.' The man kissed her, and they went into Miller's Court. Hutchinson waited, but they failed to reappear.

Nothing is known about Hutchinson that might lend credence or otherwise to his statement. The man he saw need not have been Kelly's murderer – she was not killed until at least an hour and a half later. Unlike the dark gentleman who chatted quite carelessly outside Miller's Court, the murderer would have been very careful, one imagines, about *not* being seen with Mary Kelly and certainly not so near her room.

The rest is silence, apart from the clamour of speculation at the time, as well as generations later, about the identity of the Whitechapel murderer.

Another heavy-drinking prostitute, Alice McKenzie, was murdered in Whitechapel, in Castle Alley, on 17 July 1889. She was found in the street with her throat cut (or rather, stabbed twice); her dress had been pushed above her knees, and there were cuts and scratches on her stomach. However, the death of 'Clay-pipe Alice' is not thought to have been the work of the Ripper, who is generally believed to have died or to have been imprisoned for other crimes soon after the murder of Mary Kelly.

Who was he? What happened to him? No one can say for certain. Sir Charles Warren is reported by his grandson to have believed the murderer 'to be a sex maniac who committed suicide after the Miller's Court murder – possibly the young doctor whose body was found in the Thames on December 31st 1888.' Sir Robert Anderson, who became head of the CID in September 1888, wrote in his memoirs: 'I am almost tempted to disclose the identity of the murderer … In saying that he was a Polish Jew, I am merely stating a definitely ascertained fact.' A note scribbled in a copy of his memoirs given years later to the Crime Museum indicates that he believed the Ripper to be in fact a Polish barber, Aaron Kosminski.

Sir Henry Smith, Acting Commissioner of the City Police at the time of the murders, thought the murderer must be the man described by Joseph Lawende. Chief Detective Inspector Abberline, who was the senior Yard detective investigating the murders, thought George Chapman (his real name was Severin Klosowski) was the killer. Chapman, a hairdresser's assistant in Whitechapel in 1888, when he was twenty-three, was ultimately hanged in 1903 for poisoning his three wives – another kind of murder altogether. Other police officers involved at the time, such as Leeson and Dew, disagreed, writing in their autobiographies: 'Nobody will ever know' – 'I am as mystified now as I was then.'

In February 1894, one man, Sir Melville Macnaghten, wrote what must be the most sensible account of the murders. It was a hand-written seven-page memorandum deposited in the Ripper file to discredit and disprove a newspaper story that a deranged fetishist, Thomas Cutbush, was the Ripper. Cutbush was arrested in 1891 for maliciously wounding two women by stabbing them in the rear. He was found guilty but insane, and incarcerated in an asylum. Macnaghten states: 'The Whitechapel murderer had 5 victims – & 5 victims only.' They were: Nichols, Chapman, Stride, Eddowes and Kelly. Macnaghten continued:

> It will be noticed that the fury of the mutilations increased in each case, and, seemingly, the appetite only became sharpened by indulgence. It seems, then, highly improbable that the murderer would have suddenly stopped in November 88, and been content to recommence operations by merely prodding a girl behind some 2 years and 4 months afterwards. A much more rational theory is that the murderer's brain gave way altogether after his awful glut in

Miller's Court, and that he immediately committed suicide, or, as a possible alternative, was found to be so hopelessly mad by his relations, that he was by them confined in some asylum. No one ever saw the Whitechapel Murderer, many homicidal maniacs were suspected, but no shadow of proof could be thrown on any one. I may mention the cases of 3 men, any one of whom would have been more likely than Cutbush to have committed this series of murders:

(1) A Mr MJ Druitt, said to be a doctor and of good family, who disappeared at the time of the Miller's Court murder, and whose body (which was said to have been upwards of a month in the water) was found in the Thames on 31st Dec – or about 7 weeks after that murder. He was sexually insane and from private info I have little doubt but that his own family believed him to have been the murderer.

(2) Kosminski, a Polish Jew and resident in Whitechapel. This man became insane owing to many years indulgence in solitary vices. He had a great hatred of women, especially of the prostitute class, and had strong homicidal tendencies. He was removed to a lunatic asylum about March 1889. There were many crimes connected with this man which made him a strong 'suspect'.

(3) Michael Ostrog, a Russian doctor, and a convict, who was frequently detained in a lunatic asylum as a homicidal maniac. This man's antecedents were of the worst possible type, and his whereabouts at the time of the murders could never be ascertained.

Next to nothing is known about Kosminski and Ostrog. Much more has since been revealed about Montague Druitt.

Born on 15 August 1857 at Wimborne in Dorset, he was educated at Winchester College, where he was a prefect, played cricket for the First Eleven, was the best at playing Five's, and won a scholarship to New College, Oxford. There he studied Classics and obtained a Third Class Honours degree in 1880. He may then have studied medicine for a year (he had a cousin who was a doctor) before switching to law, enrolling at the Inner Temple in May 1882. While he studied law, he taught at a crammer's school in Blackheath, where forty-two boys were boarders. He was called to the Bar in April 1885. His father died in September, after which Druitt rented chambers at 9 King's Bench Walk in the Temple. His career as a barrister was undistinguished and unrewarding; he continued to teach at the Blackheath school until he was sacked around 1 December 1888. The reason for the dismissal is not known: he may have shown homosexual tendencies or behaved unreasonably or oddly – the latter being not unlikely, as his mother had been certified as insane in July that year and put in a mental home in Chiswick. He apparently feared for his own sanity. Last seen alive on Monday, 3 December 1888, he penned a note – 'Since Friday I felt I was going to be like Mother and the best thing was for me to die' – weighted the pockets of his overcoat with stones and jumped or waded into the Thames. His body was found floating in the river near Chiswick on Monday, 31 December, four weeks after his disappearance. He was thirty-one.

Was he the Ripper? We know that he was a keen cricketer. A member of the MCC, for several years he played for Blackheath and also for teams in Dorset. The day after Mary Ann Nichols was murdered (about 3.30 am on Friday, 31 August), MJ Druitt played cricket for Canford against Wimborne in Dorset (on Saturday, 1 September). Some *five hours* after the murder of Annie Chapman (about 5.45 am on Saturday, 8 September) Druitt was playing cricket for Blackheath in south London. Where was he, one wonders, on the night of 29–30 September and at dawn on Friday, 9 November? To the question 'Could he have committed such atrocious crimes and then played cricket?' the answer must be 'Yes.'

Of all the suspects, Druitt and Kosminski seem the ones most likely, from what we know now, to have been the Whitechapel murderer. But as in every other case there is no definite, conclusive proof. Other theories, about doctors, butchers, Jews, freemasons, lodgers, other murderers and a member of the monarchy (the Duke of Clarence), may reasonably, if regretfully, be dismissed. Of all the books written about the Whitechapel murders, the most useful are those by Donald Rumbelow, a police sergeant in the City, and Richard Whittington-Egan (see the Bibliography).

One area of interest remains – the actual scenes of the murders and the addresses of the victims: Nichols, Chapman, Stride, Eddowes and Kelly. Why Whitechapel – rather than other areas of prostitution? And why, when about 1,200 prostitutes are said to have worked in Whitechapel, did the five murdered women, although murdered some distance apart, all live within a few hundred yards of each other? It is conceivable that they not only visited the same pubs and touted for custom in the same streets, but actually knew each other, at least by sight. Annie Chapman lived in 35 Dorset Street – so did Jack Pizer and Michael Kidney, with whom Elizabeth Stride used to live. Mary Kelly lived in and was killed at the back of 26 Dorset Street. Nichols, Stride and Eddowes all lodged at one time or another in Flower and Dean Street – as the last two also did in Fashion Street. Is it coincidence that these five possible acquaintances were killed?

It's also possible that all five women were neighbours of the Ripper and were known to him, at least by sight, and that he also lived in or near Flower and Dean Street or Fashion Street or Thrawl Street, which were all parallel to each other and led off the main north-south artery in Whitechapel, Commercial Street. It seems highly probable that the Ripper was a local man, well acquainted with all the streets, alleys, yards, pubs and lodging houses in the area, as well as the beats paraded nightly by the police. With bloody clothes he can't have ventured far from the scenes of the murders, and a local man would have known the darkest, most poorly lit and less-populated routes back to where he lived. The cut-off piece of Eddowes's bloodstained apron was found in Goulston Street, north-east of Mitre Square where Eddowes died. North-east of Goulston Street itself were the parallel streets of Flower and Dean, Fashion and Thrawl. It's likely that the Ripper, hurrying away from Mitre Square, was on his way home when he dropped or discarded the piece of apron.

He took great risks, killing where he did and displaying the bodies as he did. But that must have been part of his murderous urge, the thrill of the kill. And he killed in order to cut, not strangle his victims, swiftly and savagely using his knife. And if his victims knew him, at least by sight, they would not have felt unduly alarmed, especially if his manner and appearance were unexceptional, and not evidently those of a maniac or murderous psychopath, as fiction pictures him, but pleasant and persuasive, as actual murderers often are.

From the many statements made by witnesses who might have seen him before or after the murders, some generalisations might be made – he was about thirty, about 5 ft 6 in and wore a hat or cap and had a moustache. And he probably lived in or near Flower and Dean Street, selecting his victims from among the many prostitutes he lived among.

FLORENCE MAYBRICK

THE MURDER OF MR MAYBRICK, 1889

Judges cannot ever be truly impartial, being inevitably led by their own opinions, background, education, sex and social position to exhibit an occasionally less than objective attitude to the accused, especially if the accused is a woman. Such bias was shown by the learned gentlemen who judged Edith Thompson, Alma Rattenbury, Ruth Ellis – and Florence Maybrick.

Miss Florence Elizabeth Chandler was an American, a Southern belle from Alabama, who at the age of eighteen married Mr James Maybrick in London on 27 July 1881. She was the daughter of a banker from Mobile, and she and her future husband met on the White Star liner *Baltic* when she was on a tour of Europe with her mother. He was a forty-two-year-old English cotton-broker, a frequent visitor to America. His two brothers disapproved of the match, believing that Florence was as flighty, as suspect, as her thrice-married mother, Baroness von Roques.

The Maybricks settled in Liverpool in 1884, eventually purchasing an imposing mansion, Battlecrease House (complete with modern flush toilets), in a southern suburb of the city called Aigburth. Living beyond their means, they were attended by four servants: a cook, two maids, and a nanny called Alice Yapp, who looked after the two young Maybrick children, a boy and a girl. Mrs Maybrick was given £7 a week by her husband to pay not only for the food and domestic requirements but also all the servants' wages. Naturally, she was soon in debt.

James Maybrick was a boorish, irascible man, and a lifelong hypochondriac. Ever complaining of being out of sorts, of pains and numbness and problems with his liver and his nerves, he was a believer in homoeopathic medicines, and was forever swallowing pills and pick-me-ups to improve his health and sexual potency; the mixtures included strychnine and arsenic. 'I think I know a good deal of medicine,' he once told a doctor.

He maintained a mistress on the side, as Florence discovered by chance in 1887. The unhappy young woman found some consolation in the arms of one of her husband's Liverpool friends, a tall and handsome young bachelor, Alfred Brierley, whom she met at a dance at Battlecrease House. In March 1889, the couple spent a weekend together in a London hotel. Mrs Maybrick made the arrangements. They planned to be there a week, but for some reason they left the hotel – Flatman's in Henrietta Street – on the

Monday, when Brierley paid the bill; Mrs Maybrick spent the rest of the week with friends. She said later: 'Before we parted, he gave me to understand that he cared for somebody else and could not marry me, and that rather than face the disgrace of discovery he would blow his brains out. I then had such a revulsion of feeling I said we must end our intimacy at once.' She returned to Liverpool on Friday, 28 March.

The next day, she went to Aintree with her husband for the Grand National. There she happened to meet Brierley, and despite her revulsion and her husband's wishes, she left his carriage and walked up the course with the young man. Maybrick was furious. She returned home on her own. He arrived ten minutes later. There was a row and at one point he punched her. Alice Yapp said later: 'I heard Mr Maybrick say to Mrs Maybrick: "This scandal will be all over the town tomorrow!" They then went down into the hall, and I heard Mr Maybrick say: "Florrie, I never thought you would come to this." They then went into the vestibule, and I heard Mr Maybrick say: "If you once cross this threshold you shall never enter these doors again!"' Mrs Maybrick had in fact ordered a cab and threatened to walk out of the house, but Nanny Yapp intervened, reminding her of her children – 'I put my arm around her waist and took her upstairs. I made the bed for her that night and she slept in the dressing-room.'

On Sunday, Mr Maybrick made a new will, excluding his wife. She went to see the family doctor, Dr Hopper, who said later:

She complained that she was very unwell, that she had been up all night ... and she asked my advice. I saw that she had a black eye. She said that her husband had been very unkind to her ... and he had beaten her ... She said that she had a very strong feeling against him, and could not bear him to come near her.

She wanted a divorce. But the doctor was able to effect a reconciliation. She asked her husband's forgiveness for considerable debts she had incurred (£1,200) and he paid them off – presumably with difficulty, as he was in debt himself.

On 13 April, Mr Maybrick journeyed to London on business connected with his wife's debts and stayed with his bachelor brother, Michael Maybrick, a singer and composer, in his flat in Wellington Mansions, Regents Park. Using the pseudonym Stephen Adams, Michael composed such hymns as 'The Holy City' and 'Star of Bethlehem'. James Maybrick consulted Michael's doctor, complaining of pains in his head and numbness in his right leg. After an hour-long examination the doctor concluded there was very little wrong with him, apart from indigestion, and he prescribed an aperient, a tonic, and liver pills. Mr Maybrick returned to Liverpool on 22 April.

Soon after this, he met a friend of his – Sir James Poole, a former mayor of Liverpool, in the Palatine Club – who said later: 'Someone made the remark that it was becoming the common custom to take poisonous medicines. [Maybrick] had an impetuous way and he blurted out: "I take poisonous medicines." I said: "How horrid! Don't you know, my dear friend, that the more you take of these things the more you require, and you will go on till they carry you off?"' The previous year, in June, Mrs Maybrick had visited Dr Hopper. He said later: 'She told me that Mr Maybrick was in the habit of taking some very strong medicine which had a bad influence on him; for he always seemed worse after each dose. She wished me to see him about it, as he was very reticent in the matter.'

There seems no doubt that he was an eater of arsenic, among other poisons, and three American witnesses at the trial vouched that he often took arsenic in a cup of beef tea, saying it was 'meat and liquor to him' and 'I take it when I can get it.' A chemist from Norfolk in Virginia attested to the fact that Mr Maybrick's consumption of '*liquor arsenicalis*' given in a tonic, increased over eighteen months by 75 per cent.

On or about Monday, 23 April, Mrs Maybrick bought one dozen flypapers from a chemist in Aigburth. She told him that the flies were troublesome in her kitchen. Each paper contained about one grain of arsenic, although the experts at her trial disagreed about the actual amount, saying it depended on whether the arsenic was extracted by boiling the papers or by soaking them in cold water.

On or about that Monday, flypapers were seen by the nanny and a maid soaking in a basin on the Maybricks' bedroom wash-stand. Mrs Maybrick later explained that the arsenic which she extracted from those flypapers was for a cosmetic preparation, a face-wash, something she had used for years; she wanted to clear up some skin trouble before going to a ball. A hairdresser, Mr Bioletti, later agreed that there was 'an impression among ladies that it is good for the complexion'. It was also used, he said, as a depilatory.

The following Saturday, the 27th, Mr Maybrick felt funny and was sick. He went to the Wirrall Races in the afternoon, got wet in the rain, and later dined with friends; his hands were so unsteady that he upset some wine.

On Sunday morning the children's doctor, Dr Humphreys, was sent for. Mr Maybrick was in bed, complaining about pains in his chest and his heart, caused, he said, by a strong cup of tea. He was afraid of becoming paralyzed. The doctor prescribed some diluted prussic acid, and forbade him to drink anything other than soda water and milk. Mrs Maybrick told the doctor that her husband had taken an overdose of strychnine. Two months earlier she had spoken to him about her husband's habit of dosing himself with strychnine and had written in some concern to his brother, Michael, saying she had found a certain white powder which her husband habitually took. When Michael obliquely asked his brother about this, James Maybrick expostulated: 'Whoever told you that? It's a damned lie!'

Dr Humphreys saw his patient again on 29 and 30 April. He concluded that Maybrick was a chronic dyspeptic and put him on a diet. On the night of 30 April, Florence Maybrick went to a fancy-dress ball with her brother-in-law, Edwin, a bachelor cotton merchant, who was staying in Battlecrease House after a recent visit to America.

James Maybrick was back in his office on Wednesday, 1 May. Said brother Edwin: 'Mrs

Maybrick gave me a parcel to take to his office … It contained a brown jug in which there was some farinaceous food in liquid form [Barry's Revalenta]. My brother poured the liquid into a saucepan and heated it over the fire, and he then poured it into a basin and partook of it. He remarked: "The cook has put some of that damned sherry in it, and she *knows* I don't like it!'"

By Friday, Maybrick was ill again and Dr Humphreys was summoned about 10 am. He later stated: 'I found Mr Maybrick in the morning-room on the ground floor. He said he had not been so well since the day before, and he added that he did not think my medicine agreed with him. Mrs Maybrick was present and said: "You always say the same thing about anybody's medicine after two or three days."' Dr Humphreys's advice was 'to go on the same for two or three weeks'. He went away and was called back at midnight. In the interim Mr Maybrick had gone out and had a Turkish bath. He was now in bed; he had been sick twice and complained of gnawing pains in his legs.

On Saturday, his hands felt numb, and he was constantly sick. The doctor told Maybrick he should 'abate his thirst by washing out with water or by sucking ice or a damp cloth'. On Sunday, his sore throat and foul tongue troubled him; Valentine's meat juice was prescribed as well as the prussic acid solution. Mrs Maybrick then thought that a second opinion was unnecessary. She said: 'He has seen so many [doctors] and they have done him so little good.' She was in constant attendance on him day and night, sleeping in the dressing-room adjacent to the Maybricks' bedroom.

At 8.30 am on Monday, 6 May, Dr Humphreys was back. 'I told [him] to stop the Valentine's beef juice … I was not surprised at it making Mr Maybrick sick, as it made many people sick.' Humphreys now prescribed some arsenic, Fowler's solution, which contained in all 1/25th of a grain, and that evening the patient was fed with Brand's beef tea, some chicken broth, Neave's food, and some milk and water. He continued to vomit, and a blister was applied to his stomach. On Tuesday morning he seemed better and told Dr Humphreys: 'I am quite a different man today.' Nonetheless, a second opinion was now sought by Edwin Maybrick. His choice, Dr Carter, arrived about 5 pm. Carter's conclusion was that the patient was suffering from acute dyspepsia, resulting from 'indiscretion of food, or drink, or both'. He prescribed a careful diet and small doses of sedatives. Both Carter and Humphreys thought Maybrick would be well in a few days.

But on Wednesday, 8 May, there was a general turn for the worse. Two of the invalid's friends, Mrs Matilda Briggs and Mrs Martha Hughes (they were sisters), called at the house in the morning and were told by Nanny Yapp about the soaking flypapers and other suspicious matters. Mrs Briggs took immediate action. She told the exhausted wife to send for a trained nurse. She spoke to Edwin. She also telegraphed Michael Maybrick in London – 'Come at once. Strange things going on here.'

The nurse arrived at 2.15 pm. About three o'clock, Mrs Maybrick came to the garden gate and gave Alice Yapp a letter to post. The young nanny was minding the Maybricks' three-year-old daughter and walked to the post office with the child. On the way there the letter, according to Alice, was dropped in the dirt, and needed a new envelope. At any rate, she read the letter, failed to post it and handed it over to Edwin about half-past five. The letter was addressed to A. Brierley and had been written in reply to a somewhat frosty missive from him suggesting that he and Florence did not meet again until the autumn. Mrs Maybrick had written:

Dearest – Since my return I have been nursing M day and night – he is sick unto death*!*
... And now all depends upon how his strength will hold out ... We are terribly anxious
... But relieve your mind of all fear of discovery now and in the future. M has been
delirious since Sunday and I know now he is perfectly ignorant of everything ... and
also that he has not been making any enquiries whatever*!*

This was reported to Michael when he arrived from London that night. Edwin instructed the nurses to let no one else attend his sick brother, while Michael discussed the family's suspicions with Dr Humphreys.

The following day the patient was weaker, complaining of much pain in his rectum: he now had diarrhoea. His faeces and urine, a bottle of brandy and a bottle of Neave's food were all examined for arsenic. None was found.

That evening the cook (also called Humphreys) was followed downstairs by Mrs Maybrick, who said: 'I am blamed for all this.' 'In what way?' asked the cook. 'In not getting other nurses and doctors,' Mrs Maybrick replied. She went into the servants' hall and began to cry. She said her position in the house was not worth anything, that Michael Maybrick, who had always had a spite against her, had turned her out of the master's bedroom. The cook, who thought her mistress had been 'very kind' to Mr Maybrick and 'was doing her best under the circumstances', was much moved and said: 'I would rather be in my own shoes than yours.'

Nurse Gore came on duty at 11 pm and gave her charge some Valentine's meat juice, and noticed how Mrs Maybrick removed the bottle (which had been provided by Edwin) and took it into the dressing room. She closed the door; a few minutes later she returned, placed the bottle in a 'surreptitious manner' on a bedside table, and sent the nurse to fetch some ice. Mrs Maybrick later explained:

After Nurse Gore had given my husband beef tea, I went and sat on the bed beside him.
He complained to me of being very sick and very depressed and he implored me then to give
him this powder, which he had referred to early in the evening, and which I had declined to
give him. I was overwrought, terribly anxious, miserably unhappy, and his evident distress
utterly unnerved me. He had told me that the powder would not harm him, and that I could
put it in his food. I then consented.' But, she said, he didn't take any of the powder, as he
was asleep when she returned to the bedroom; later he was sick. The bottle was later found
to contain half a grain of arsenic.

On Friday, 10 May, James Maybrick was much weaker, with a very faint but rapid pulse; he was very restless and his tongue was foul. He was given sulphonal, nitro-glycerine, cocaine (for his throat) and some phosphoric acid (for his mouth). In the afternoon, Michael Maybrick caught Mrs Maybrick changing medicine from one bottle to another. 'Florrie! How dare you tamper with the medicine!' he cried. No arsenic was later found in the bottle that he removed.

Later on that day, the duty nurse, Nurse Gallery, was administering some medicine, assisted by Florrie, when the patient said: 'Don't give me the wrong medicine again!' That evening, according to Nurse Wilson, Mr Maybrick, who was now delirious, said to his wife: 'Oh, Bunny, Bunny, how could you do it? I did not think it of you.' 'You silly old darling,' said Mrs Maybrick. 'Don't trouble your head about things.' Later, Mrs Maybrick said her husband had been referring to a whispered conversation she had had with him, confessing to her affair with Brierley, assuring him it was over, and asking for his forgiveness.

On Saturday, 11 May, the doctors had a consultation after midday and concluded that their patient would never recover: his case was hopeless. His children were brought to him at 5 pm. James Maybrick died some three hours later. Florence Maybrick swooned and then retired to her bed in the dressing room. She was more or less confined there by the dead man's brothers while a hasty search was made of the bedroom and the house by the servants, the nurses, the doctors, the brothers and Mrs Briggs.

A sealed packet with a red label that read *Arsenic, Poison* ('for cats' had been added) was found in a trunk. Arsenic was later detected in an imperfectly cleaned jug of Barry's Revalenta and in two ordinary medicine bottles. Several small bottles and a scrap of handkerchief were discovered in a chocolate box: the scrap had traces of arsenic. Three bottles found in a man's hat-box contained varying solutions of arsenic. In another hat-box were a glass and another handkerchief: both bore traces of milk and arsenic. More traces were found in the pocket of Mrs Maybrick's dressing gown. There was enough arsenic in the house to poison fifty people.

On Monday, 13 May, a post mortem was carried out by Doctors Carter, Humphreys and Barron. They concluded that death had been caused by some irritant poison acting on the stomach and bowels. But when the body was exhumed on 30 May, less than half a grain of arsenic (two grains would have been a fatal amount) was the total found in his liver, kidneys and intestines. There was none in his stomach, spleen, heart or lungs. There were, however, traces of strychnine, hyoscine, prussic acid and morphia.

In the meantime, Mrs Maybrick had been detained on suspicion of causing her husband's death. She had been removed to the hospital in Walton jail, after a magistrate formally opened the investigation in her bedroom, but not before a letter she wrote to Brierley – 'Appearances may be against me, but before God I swear I am innocent' – was intercepted by Mrs Briggs and given to the police.

When Mrs Maybrick appeared at the brief magisterial hearing on 13 June, she was hissed at by a large number of women as she left the court. She hoped her trial would take place in London. 'I shall receive an impartial verdict there,' she wrote to her mother, 'which I cannot expect from a jury in Liverpool, whose minds have come to a "moral conviction" ... The tittle-tattle of servants, the public, friends and enemies, besides their personal feelings for Jim, must leave their traces and prejudice their minds, no matter what the defence is.' She was advised otherwise, and the trial began at Liverpool Summer Assizes on Wednesday, 31 July 1889.

There was an all-male Lancashire jury, including three plumbers and two farmers. Mrs Maybrick was defended by Sir Charles Russell, QC, MP, later the Lord Chief Justice. The medical experts agreed that Mr Maybrick had died of gastro-enteritis, but disputed whether this had been caused by arsenic, impure food or a chill. The defence claimed that there was an absence of most symptoms usually associated with arsenical poisoning, that the deceased had overdosed himself and died of natural causes, that Mrs Maybrick had no need to adopt the clumsy and uncertain contrivance of soaking flypapers (so openly) to get arsenic, when so much was available elsewhere in the house. She gave no evidence, but made an ill-advised statement, explaining her reasons for soaking the flypapers and what she was doing with the meat juice.

The summing-up of the judge, Mr Justice Stephen, who was himself a very sick man, lasted two days. It was a rambling peroration, not without some errors of fact, laying emphasis on the accused's admitted adultery with Brierley. The judge said:

> For a person to go on deliberately administering poison to a poor, helpless, sick man, upon whom she has already inflicted a dreadful injury – an injury fatal to married life – the person who could do such a thing must indeed be destitute of the least trace of feeling ... Then you have to consider ... the question of motives which might act upon this woman's mind. When you come to consider that, you must remember the intrigue which she carried on with this man Brierley, and the feelings – it seems horrible to comparatively ordinary innocent people – a horrible and incredible thought, that a woman should be plotting the death of her husband in order that she might be left at liberty to follow her own degrading vices ... There is no doubt that the propensities which lead persons to vices of that kind do kill all the more tender, all the more manly, or all the more womanly, feelings of the human mind.

The jury, after an absence of three-quarters of an hour, found Florence Maybrick guilty of murder. Before sentence of death was passed she said: 'With the exception of my intimacy with Mr Brierley, I am not guilty of this crime.'

The judge was booed as he left the court. Meetings were held, letters were sent, petitions organised, and articles written (by doctors and lawyers) decrying the verdict – there was no appeal court then. Leading Americans, including the President, brought pressure to bear on the English authorities. The Home Secretary and the Lord Chancellor reviewed the case and interviewed the judge. Meanwhile, in Liverpool, Mrs Maybrick heard the gallows being erected in Walton jail.

Then, on 22 August, the Home Office announced that the sentence had been commuted to penal servitude for life, without 'the slightest reflection on the tribunal by which the prisoner was tried' and with 'the concurrence of the learned judge'. A message announcing the reprieve reached Walton jail at 1.30 am on 23 August, three days before the date set for Florence's execution.

Despite further efforts to obtain her release, Florence Maybrick remained in jail for fifteen years. The first nine months of her sentence were spent in solitary confinement; she was fed on bread and gruel, wore a brown dress marked with arrows and had to make at least five men's shirts a week. Her imprisonment began in Woking jail and ended in Aylesbury. She was freed on 25 January 1904, when she went to France and visited her aged mother before returning to America, where she had not been for more than twenty years. For a time she was something of a celebrity and wrote a book called *My Fifteen Lost Years*. Soon after it was published, the Court of Criminal Appeal was established in 1907.

She died in squalor, surrounded by cats in a Connecticut cottage, on 23 October 1941. She was seventy-eight. It was fifty-two years since her husband's death and many years since the death of the judge, Mr Justice Stephen. He retired soon after the trial and died in a lunatic asylum.

4
MRS PEARCEY

The Murder of Mrs Hogg, 1890

Women rarely commit murder. Those who have done so have generally been poor, illiterate, aggressive if not volatile, mentally unstable, and poison is their usual method of bringing death. More than half (thirty-seven) of the women hanged for murder (sixty-eight) between 1843 and 1956 were poisoners. The murders women commit are mostly domestic ones – of a child, husband or lover, and occur when the murderess can no longer endure the anguish of a relationship or a situation. Children have often been murdered by women in a kind of misdirection of their anguish – as a substitute for the husband or lover, or for the suicide of the murderess herself. A very few women have murdered for gain, to improve their economic or social conditions. Some murder out of spite. Associated causes of murder where women have been concerned are sexual frustration, nymphomania, lesbianism, post-natal depression, the menopause, alcoholism and feeble-mindedness. In the case of Mrs Pearcey, sexual jealousy has been mooted as the mainspring of the murders she committed. They are more likely to have arisen from circumstances similar to those described in Congreve's famous sentence: 'Heaven has no rage like love to hatred turned, nor hell a fury like a woman scorned.'

Mrs Pearcey was not, in fact, married. Her real and maiden name was Mary Eleanor Wheeler. But when she went to live with a man called Pearcey, she assumed the name and title of his wife, retaining both when, for reasons unknown, he left her. Male reporters later portrayed her as being tall and powerful, with striking almost masculine features, a full figure and fine eyes.

A woman correspondent of the *Pall Mall Budget* described her as being 'a woman of about five feet six, neither slight nor stout. There is nothing of the murderess in her appearance; in fact, she is a mild, harmless-looking woman. Her colouring is delicate and her hands are small and shapely. But she has not a single good feature in her face. Her eyes are dark and bright … Her mouth is large and badly formed, and her chin is weak and retreating.'

Eleanor Pearcey's emotional instability and depressing loneliness – her nearest relatives were an aged mother and an older sister – seem to have led her into a series of affairs, further solaced by drink. In 1890, at the age of twenty-four, she was on her way to being a full-time courtesan. The three rooms she occupied on the ground floor of 2 Priory Street, Kentish Town, were paid for by an admirer, Mr Crichton of Gravesend in

Kent, who called on her once a week. The rooms were small but attractively furnished. On the left of the entrance hall of the house was her front parlour, in which there was an upright piano; folding doors opened on to a bedroom overlooking the yard at the rear. There was a tiny kitchen.

Another admirer was a furniture remover, Frank Samuel Hogg. Him she apparently loved; she used to put a light in her window to let him know when she was free. A feckless, sentimental and selfish man, who had known Eleanor Pearcey for some time, he was vain enough, it appears, to imagine that all women who looked on him loved him, and was pleased to be proved right. One conquest, however, turned out to be a careless triumph in more ways than one. She became pregnant, and such was the weight of her family's opinion, backed up by several large brothers, that Frank Hogg was persuaded to marry her. The marriage was not happy, and when his wife, Phoebe, a large, plain woman, duly produced a baby girl, also called Phoebe, this apparently so lowered her bearded husband's self-esteem and increased his self-pity that he used to speak of suicide to his young bosom-friend, Eleanor Pearcey. He would weep in her arms and bemoan his wretched state, adding his frustrations to hers. As an alternative to suicide he talked of emigration. Both were anathema to Mrs Pearcey.

Although she had known Phoebe Hogg before her marriage to Frank Hogg and had been friends with his sister Clara – the actual relationship between the three women appears to have been quite complex – Mrs Pearcey seems to have become increasingly jealous of Mrs Hogg and full of hate. Apparently Eleanor Pearcey felt that Frank was essential to her happiness and that the realisation of his happiness must be her prime aim. She wished to be his wife, to have him all to herself.

In her letters she besought him not to kill himself, to go on living for her sake if not for his. In one, she wrote:

You ask me if I was cross with you for coming only such a little while. If you knew how lonely I am you wouldn't ask. I would be more than happy if I could see you for the same time each day, dear. You know I have a lot of time to spare and I cannot help thinking. I think and think until I get so dizzy that I don't know what to do with myself. If it wasn't for our love, dear, I don't know what I should really do, and I am always afraid you will take that away, and then I should quite give up in despair, for that is the only thing I care for on earth. I cannot live without it now. I have no right to it, but you gave it to me, and I can't give it up.

It must have seemed that her emotional dilemma could only be resolved by the destruction of Phoebe Hogg, and all Mrs Pearcey's passionate envy and frustration focused on the other, older woman, who had the benefit of Frank's company every night and every day.

Frank and Phoebe Hogg lived with his sister Clara and his mother in rooms at 141

Prince of Wales Road, Kentish Town. On Thursday, 23 October 1890 Mrs Hogg (now aged thirty-one) received a note from Mrs Pearcey inviting her to 2 Priory Street for tea. She showed the note to her sister. It said: 'Dearest, come round this afternoon and bring our little darling. Don't fail.' But Mrs Hogg was for some reason unable to go there that day. Her sister later told the police that Mrs Pearcey had once invited Phoebe to go with her to Southend and look over an empty house.

The next day, Friday the 24th, Eleanor Pearcey gave a small boy a penny to deliver a second note, and this time, without telling anyone where she was going, Phoebe Hogg left her house about 3.30 pm and set out, pushing her daughter in a bassinette or pram down Kentish Town Road and into Royal College Street towards the drab little road (now Ivor Street) where Mrs Pearcey lived. Mrs Hogg pulled the pram up the steps and parked it in the narrow entrance hall. Carrying the child, she then followed the younger, smaller woman either into the front parlour or into the pokey kitchen at the end of the hall.

It was in the kitchen that Phoebe Hogg was slaughtered, despatched with a poker and more than one knife. Her skull was fractured and her throat so severely cut that her head was almost severed from her body. It seems that Mrs Hogg was not easy to kill, that she struggled and fought for her life: the arms of both women were bruised. Two window panes were broken and the kitchen's walls and ceiling were spattered with blood. Mrs Pearcey's neighbours heard what they called 'banging and hammering' at about four o'clock. Another neighbour said she heard a child screaming – or what sounded like a child. But like most good neighbours they hesitated to intrude, readily assuming in a noisy neighbourhood, where cries and fights were not unknown, that the rumpus was in some way connected with workmen repairing a pub on the corner.

Afterwards, Mrs Pearcey probably washed her hands and the weapons, took off and washed her top-skirt, tried to scrub out the bloodstains on a rug, on the curtains and on an apron. At some point she heaved the body of the murdered woman into the pram, in which the little girl, whether alive or dead, also lay. She covered them both with an antimacassar. About six o'clock Mr and Mrs Butler, who lived in the second floor flat at the top of the stairs, returned separately to 2 Priory Street. Both knocked against the bassinette parked in the darkened hallway: Mrs Pearcey heard them and called out to each of them to take care.

Some time after this, when it was quite dark, she put on her bonnet and went out, bumping the pram down the few steps at the front door on to the pavement and, turning right, wheeled her dreadful load away from the house into Chalk Farm Road, then up Adelaide Road and into Eton Avenue. Pushing the weighty pram before her, she sought some deserted place in the gas-lit streets where she might unburden herself, unobserved, of the pram and what it contained. The body of Mrs Hogg was deposited by a partly built house in Crossfield Road, near Swiss Cottage. The child was dumped on some waste land in Finchley Road.

By now the child was dead, having suffocated, it is said, in the pram – no signs of violence were found on her. On the other hand, the little girl may have been suffocated in the house, perhaps by a cushion. The child is unlikely to have remained silent while her mother was murdered, or when both were put in the pram.

As if in a daze, as if tied to the now empty pram, Eleanor Pearcey walked on for over a mile through the quieter, richer streets around Abbey Road, finally abandoning the pram in Hamilton Terrace, between Maida Vale and St John's Wood. She then began the long walk home through the shadowed streets. In all, she walked about 6 miles that night.

Evidently the horror of her deeds was too much for her. She was seen about 8 pm by a friend – possibly before she started out on her terrible errand – standing on a pavement near her home, staring vacantly about her, her face drawn and pale, her clothes much disordered and her hat askew. The friend, who had at first failed to recognise her, assumed that Mrs Pearcey was drunk and passed on without a word.

Eleanor Pearcey seems not to have returned to her home until late at night. For at about 10 pm, Frank Hogg called on her. He had a latch-key and let himself in. No one answered his calls. Apart from a lamp in the bedroom, Mrs Pearcey's rooms were in darkness, he said later. He peered, he said, into the front parlour, saw nothing untoward and withdrew. But he left a note saying 'Twenty-past ten. Cannot stay.'

Frank Hogg later alleged that he was unaware that his wife and Mrs Pearcey were on friendly terms. It seems that after calling at the house in Priory Street on his way home from work about ten o'clock, he walked on to Prince of Wales Road, where his wife's absence had apparently caused no alarm. It was assumed in the Hogg household that Phoebe had gone to visit her sick father in Rickmansworth. Nonetheless, Frank Hogg sat up until 2 am awaiting her return.

On Saturday morning he left home soon after six o'clock and went to work – he was employed in the furniture-moving business by his brother. He came home for breakfast about 8 am. About the same time the Hoggs' landlady, Mrs Styles, who had heard rumours of a murder in Hampstead, said to Clara Hogg: 'Have you heard of this dreadful murder?' 'What do you mean?' asked Clara, adding 'Tell me all about it. My sister-in-law has not been home all night. You gave me quite a turn. We have been enquiring in all directions and can't find a trace of her.' Clara went out to buy a morning paper and read that the body of a woman, brutally murdered, had been found by a police constable in Hampstead on Friday night. She talked to her brother and he set off for Rickmansworth to see if his wife was there. She decided to visit Mrs Pearcey.

Eleanor Pearcey was at home, and the two women conversed in the front parlour. Clara Hogg asked Mrs Pearcey if she had seen or heard of Phoebe. Mrs Pearcey said 'No.' Clara rephrased the question and Mrs Pearcey then replied: 'Well, as you press me, I will tell you. Phoebe wished me particularly not to say anything, and that is why I said "No." She did come round at five o'clock. She asked me to mind the baby for a little while, and I refused. She also asked me to lend her some money. I could not lend her any, as I only had 1s 1 ½d in my purse.' Phoebe, said Mrs Pearcey, then left the house. Clara Hogg was puzzled: she thought it most unlikely that her sister-in-law, who had a horror of being in debt, would ask for a loan, even a small one. However, she made no comment, only remarking that she intended to visit the Hampstead police and to ask to see the body of the woman who had been murdered the night before, in case it was Phoebe. She asked Mrs Pearcey to accompany her, for moral support.

For some reason, Mrs Pearcey agreed – she could, after all, have invented some excuse. But her part in the murder of Mrs Hogg had probably been blotted out of her mind. DI Thomas Bannister took the two women from the police station to the Hampstead mortuary, where they were both shown the body of Mrs Hogg. The baby's body was not found until the morning of the following day.

Eleanor Pearcey said she was unable to recognise the unwashed, bloody mask of the woman on the mortuary table. 'That's not her,' she said. 'It's not her. It's not her! Let's go away!' She became hysterical. Clara said: 'That's her clothing.' But she could not identify the features.

DI Bannister took the two women out of the room and said to Clara: 'Surely if she is a relative and you have been living together, you can form a reliable opinion as to whether it is the person or not.' Both women were brought back to look at the body. Clara was still doubtful, and when she attempted to touch the corpse's clothing, Mrs Pearcey cried out: 'Oh, don't touch her!' and tried to pull Clara away. 'Don't drag me!' scolded Clara. A doctor in attendance at the mortuary was then asked by Bannister to wash the face of the corpse. When this was done, Clara said: 'Oh, that's her. Don't *drag* me!' she added again.

Detective Murray then took both women to see the bassinette, which Clara Hogg identified. Sergeant Beard was sent to accompany the women back to 141 Prince of Wales Road, where Frank Hogg and Mrs Styles were questioned. He was searched and in a pocket his key to 2 Priory Street was found. All three women and the unhappy husband were then asked to come to Hampstead police station for further questioning, and Mrs Pearcey was detained there. DI Bannister, mystified and made suspicious by her excessive and odd reaction in the mortuary, asked if one or two of his men could inspect her apartments. She agreed and said: 'I would like to go with them.'

About 3 pm she returned to Priory Street with Sergeants Nursey and Parsons. They examined her rooms. One of the sergeants then went out to send a telegram to DI Bannister. The other sergeant stayed and engaged Mrs Pearcey in conversation in the front parlour, where she played the piano and sang. She also talked about her 'poor dear dead Phoebe', whom she loved so much, and about the 'dear baby, who was just beginning to prattle, oh, so prettily'.

On receiving the telegram, DI Bannister went straight to 2 Priory Street. He spoke to Mrs Pearcey, questioned her as well as her neighbours and searched her rooms with one of his sergeants; she appeared to him to be distraught and her speech was somewhat incoherent. In the bloodstained kitchen he found two carving-knives, their handles similarly stained. A recently washed apron and skirt were also discovered, as well as a stained rug, smelling strongly of paraffin as if an attempt had been made to clean it. The curtains were missing – they and a bloody tablecloth were found in an outhouse. In the fender of the kitchen grate was a long, heavy poker with a ring handle: it was smeared with matted hair and blood.

Bannister took the knives and the poker into the parlour, where Mrs Pearcey was now whistling and affecting indifference. Asked what she had been doing with the poker, she responded: 'Killing mice, killing mice!'

She could offer no sensible explanation for the bloodstained rooms. Bannister said to her: 'Mrs Pearcey, I am going to arrest you for the murder of Mrs Hogg last night, also on suspicion of murdering the child, Phoebe Hogg.' Mrs Pearcey jumped up and said: 'You can arrest me if you like. I'm quite willing to go with you. But I think you have made a mistake.' He took her to Kentish Town police station. On the way she commented: 'I wouldn't do such a thing. I wouldn't hurt anyone.'

In the police station, she was charged and searched. When she removed her gloves, her hands were seen to have cuts on them. She wore two rings: one of brass, the other a broad gold wedding ring, which was later proved to have been removed from Phoebe Hogg's fingers. The search also revealed that Eleanor Pearcey's underclothes, unchanged for twenty-four hours, were saturated with blood. They were removed and she was supplied with workhouse garments.

Mrs Pearcey appeared at the Marylebone police court on 27 October charged with the murder of Mrs Hogg. She was sent for trial at the Central Criminal Court in the Old Bailey and appeared there, before Mr Justice Denman, on 1 December 1890. Mr Forrest Fulton and Mr CF Gill led for the Crown and the accused was defended by Mr Arthur Hutton. Still wearing her workhouse clothes, Mrs Pearcey gave no evidence and remained stonily impassive throughout the trial, seemingly indifferent to everything. The trial ended on its fourth day, when she was found guilty and sentenced to death.

Eleanor Pearcey was hanged at Newgate Prison on Tuesday 23 December 1890, on a bitterly cold and foggy morning. A crowd of about 300 people gathered outside the prison gates. A reporter in the *Pall Mall Budget* wrote:

The bell of St Sepulchre's church commenced tolling at a quarter to eight, the tones ringing out sharply on the morning air. It had no effect upon the crowd, many of whom were women, and obscene and ribald jokes could be heard among every group, the females especially being fiercely denunciatory of the convict's conduct … At one minute before eight o'clock a yell from the crowd proclaimed the fact that the black flag was hoisted, and directly after the crowd gave vent to their feelings in a loud cheer.

The day before her execution, Mrs Pearcey was visited by her solicitor, Mr Palmer. She asked him to distribute certain trinkets as keepsakes to relatives and friends. She also asked him to put an advertisement in the Madrid papers, addressed to certain initials. Mr Palmer inquired if this had anything to do with the case. 'Never mind,' said Mrs Pearcey. He asked her: 'Do you admit the justice of the sentence?' 'No,' she replied. 'I do not. I know nothing about the crime.' 'Are you satisfied with what we have done for your defence and the efforts we have since made on your behalf?' 'I am perfectly satisfied,' she said. He continued: 'If you have any facts to reveal and will let me know them, even at this late hour, I will lay them before the Home Secretary in the hope of obtaining mercy.' 'I have nothing more to say,' she replied. 'Don't forget about those things. Goodbye.' She walked away across the yard to her cell.

She had repeatedly asked to see Frank Hogg, and permission had at last been given for him to visit her between two and four o'clock that Monday afternoon. Her expectation of seeing him again was great. But as time passed and he did not appear, she became 'nervous and impatient'. When she realised that he would never appear she was overcome, and lay on her prison bed, her hands over her face, sobbing. After a while she controlled herself and got to her feet, her face now quite calm and composed. She sat down at a table in the cell and began to read.

Her executioner was James Berry, a Yorkshireman and a former policeman and boot salesman, aged forty-two, who had been hangman since 1884. During this more recent occupation he hanged 131 people, including five women. In his autobiography he described Eleanor Pearcey's last hours:

> The night before her execution was spent in the condemned cell, watched by three female warders, who stated that her fortitude was remarkable. When introduced to her, I said: 'Good morning, madam,' and she shook my proffered hand without any trace of emotion. She was certainly the most composed person in the whole party. Sir James Whitehead, the Sheriff of the County of London, asked her if she wished to make any statement, as her last opportunity for doing so was fast approaching, and after a moment's pause she said: 'My sentence is a just one, but a good deal of the evidence against me was false.' As the procession was formed and one of the female warders stepped to each side of the prisoner, she turned to them with a considerate desire to save them the pain of the death scene and said: 'You have no need to assist me, I can walk by myself.' One of the women said that she did not mind, but was ready and willing to accompany Mrs Pearcey, who answered: 'Oh, well, if you don't mind going with me, I am pleased.' She then kissed them all and quietly proceeded to her painless death.

She weighed 9 stone and was given a 6 ft drop. Reporters, who had been excluded from the execution by special order of the sheriff, were also refused permission to see the body, which was, however, viewed by the coroner's jury.

Her final message duly appeared in the papers. It was: 'Have not betrayed – Eleanor.' After her death, Frank Hogg sold several items and furnishings connected with the murder, including the poker and the pram, to Madame Tussauds for a large fee, and for many years these items and a tableau containing a waxwork of Mrs Pearcey was a popular attraction there.

5

DR CREAM

THE MURDER OF MATILDA CLOVER, 1891

There is a kind of crazy vanity in murderers that prompts some of them to put their heads in the lion's mouth. They go out of their way to meet and talk to the investigating police, and often pose as conscientious citizens eager to assist police enquiries. In addition, such murderers sometimes cannot resist writing taunting letters to the police or notes containing useless information. One man who pushed this literary bent to extremes was Neill Cream.

At about 7.30 pm on 13 October 1891, a young prostitute, Ellen Donworth, aged nineteen, was plying her trade along Waterloo Road when she staggered and collapsed on the pavement. A man called James Styles ran to her and half-carried her to her nearby lodgings in Duke Street, off Westminster Bridge Road. She was in agony, but she was able to gasp that a tall gentleman with cross-eyes and a silk hat had given her some 'white stuff' to drink from a bottle when she met him earlier that evening in the York Hotel in Waterloo Road. She died on the way to hospital. A post mortem revealed strychnine in her stomach. A jeweller's traveller was later arrested in connection with her death but soon released.

The coroner officiating at her inquest, Mr GP Wyatt, received a letter on 19 October from 'G O'Brian, Detective'. It said: 'I am writing to say that if you and your satellites fail to bring the murderer of Ellen Donworth, alias Linell … to justice, I am willing to give you such assistance as will bring the murderer to justice, provided your government is willing to pay me £300,000 for my services. No pay if not successful.' Another letter, from 'H Bayne, Barrister' was sent to Mr WFD Smith, MP, a member of the newsagent family, WH Smith and Son Limited. The letter said that two incriminating letters from Ellen Donworth had been found in her possession and the writer offered his services as 'counsellor and legal adviser'.

A week after her death, on 20 October, the cries of another prostitute, twenty-six-year-old Matilda Clover, aroused the house of ill-fame in Lambeth Road run by Mother Phillips, in which she had a room. Matilda was also mother of a two-year-old boy. Writhing and screaming in agony she managed, before she died, to say that a man called Fred had given her some white pills. A servant-girl, Lucy Rose, recalled seeing this Fred, who was tall and moustached, aged about forty, and wore a tall silk hat and a cape.

Matilda's death was attributed to DTs caused by alcoholic poisoning – not unreasonably, as she drank heavily, morning, noon and night. She was buried in a pauper's grave in Tooting in southwest London.

A month later, a distinguished doctor in Portman Square, Dr William Broadbent, was astonished to get a letter on 28 November 1891 from 'M Malone' accusing him of the murder of Matilda Clover, who had been 'poisoned with strychnine', and threatening him with exposure unless he paid £2,500. In December, Countess Russell, a guest at the Savoy Hotel, received a blackmail note naming her husband as Matilda's murderer. Then the poisoner's epistles and murderous activities suddenly ceased. He had fallen in love and had become engaged.

But several months later, on 12 April 1892, two more young prostitutes died in agony. They were Emma Shrivell and Alice Marsh, who both lived in second-floor rooms in 118 Stamford Street, a brothel run by a woman called Vogt. Before they died, the girls told a policeman that a doctor called Fred had visited them that night and after a meal of bottled beer and tinned salmon he had given each of them three long thin pills. He was stoutish, dark, bald on top of his head, wore glasses, and was about 5 ft 8 in or 9 in. The policeman, PC Cumley, recalled seeing such a man leave the building at 1.45 am. It was established later that both prostitutes had been poisoned with strychnine, and the newspapers speculated wildly about the identity of the Lambeth Poisoner. Could he be Jack the Ripper, whose activities had suddenly ceased in 1888?

'What a cold-blooded murder!' exclaimed Dr Neill (as Thomas Neill Cream called himself) when he read about the inquest on the two girls in a newspaper on Easter Sunday, 17 April. He told his landlady's daughter, Miss Sleaper, that he was determined to bring the miscreant to justice. A tall, bald, cross-eyed, broad-shouldered man, who wore tall hats and glasses specially made for him in Fleet Street, Dr Cream had rented a second-floor room in 103 Lambeth Palace Road since 9 April, after returning to London from Canada. He had stayed there before, between 7 October the previous year and January, when he took a trip to America. In December, he had become engaged to a girl called Laura Sabbatini, who lived with her mother in Berkhamsted. He made out a will in her favour. On Christmas day he dined with the Sleapers in his lodgings, joining in their family entertainments, singing hymns in the evening and playing the zither. He was no trouble, going out at night alone to places of entertainment and debauchery.

In those days, that area south of the River Thames between Westminster and Waterloo bridges was thronged with bars, theatres, prostitutes and other amusements. There was Astley's circus and playhouse; the Surrey, with its rowdy melodramas (gallery, 6d; pit, 1s); the Canterbury music-hall, with its picture gallery; and the Old Vic – which had, however, become respectable, with blameless programmes and temperance bars, since Emma Cons became director in 1880.

Cream was ready, it seems, to converse with any man about plays or music, but his favourite topic was women, about whom he spoke quite crudely. He would describe his tastes and pleasures and exhibit a collection of indecent pictures that he carried about with him.

An article published later in the *St James's Gazette* said he dressed with taste and care and was well informed. It continued: 'His very strong and protruding under jaw was always at work chewing gum, tobacco or cigars ... He never laughed or even smiled ... He occasionally said "Ha-ha!" in a hard, stage-villain-like fashion, but no amount of good nature could construe it into an expression of gentility.' The article also referred to his 'never-ending talk about women' and referred to the fact that he swallowed pills that he said had aphrodisiac properties.

In the same lodging house as Dr Cream was Walter Harper, a young medical student from St Thomas's Hospital. Cream told Miss Sleaper most forcibly that it was Harper who had killed the girls. The police had proof, he said, and the girls had been warned by letter. Miss Sleaper, a girl of spirit, replied that he must be mad. Unabashed, Cream wrote to young Harper's father, a doctor in Barnstaple, accusing his son of the murders and offering to exchange such evidence as he had for £1,500. He wrote: 'The publication of the evidence will ruin you and your family for ever, so that when you read it you will need no one to tell you that it will convict your son ... If you do not answer at once, I am going to give evidence to the coroner at once.'

Cream was just as outspoken with a drinking acquaintance, an engineer named Haynes, who also happened to be a private enquiry agent. Haynes showed great interest in what Cream had to say, and in due course disclosed all he had discovered to Police Sergeant McIntyre of the CID. Sergeant McIntyre arranged a meeting with Cream and Cream confidentially showed him a letter that had allegedly been received by the Stamford Street victims of the Lambeth Poisoner, warning them about a Dr Harper, who would serve them, it was alleged, as he had served Matilda Clover and a woman called Louise Harvey.

It was a fatal error. Dr Cream had indeed given Louise Harvey some pills to take the previous October. But she had only pretended to swallow them. She was very much alive, and was able to be interviewed by the police.

She told the police how, on 25 or 26 October, she had met Cream in Regent Street about 12.30 at night, having seen him earlier that evening in the Alhambra Theatre at the back of the dress circle. She spent the night with him in a Soho hotel and met him again the following night on the Embankment, opposite Charing Cross underground station. 'Good evening. I'm late!' he said, giving her some roses and inviting her to take a glass of wine with him in a nearby pub, the Northumberland. The night before he had commented on some spots on her forehead and promised to provide her with a remedy for them. After they left the Northumberland, they walked along the Embankment and then he produced some pills that he said would effect a cure. Something in his manner put Harvey on her guard, though. He insisted she took the pills and she pretended to swallow them, putting her hand to her mouth. But when he happened to look away, she threw them over the Embankment wall into the River Thames. The solicitous doctor then bade her farewell. But before he left he gave her five shillings to go to a music hall.

Oddly enough, she saw him again about three weeks later, in Piccadilly Circus. He failed to recognise her, and when she approached him he invited her to a bar in Air Street, to join him for a glass of wine. 'Don't you know me? Don't you remember?' she asked. 'You promised to meet me one night outside the Oxford.' 'I don't remember you. Who are you?' 'Have you forgotten Lou Harvey?' she asked. He hurried away.

As described by Lou Harvey, Dr Cream was a 'bald and very hairy man; he had a dark ginger moustache, wore gold-rimmed glasses, was well-dressed, cross-eyed, and spoke with an odd accent.' It was what would now be called a transatlantic accent. In fact, Thomas Neill Cream was Scottish, having been born in Glasgow on 27 May 1850, although he and his parents emigrated to Canada when he was thirteen. His father was the prosperous manager of a shipbuilding and lumber firm. Young Cream graduated as a doctor at McGill University, Montreal, in 1876. But thereafter he led an obsessional life of crime that included arson, abortion, blackmail, fraud, extortion, theft and attempted murder – each crime being often followed up by a demand for some kind of payment. Three women died under his care as a doctor. A fourth, whom he had tried to abort, he was forced by her father to marry. She died of consumption when he was completing his medical studies in Edinburgh, where he qualified as a physician and surgeon. While practising as a doctor of the 'quack' variety in Chicago – he performed illegal abortions for prostitutes, at least one of whom died – he had an affair with a young woman, Mrs Julia Stott, and poisoned her elderly and epileptic husband. Daniel Stott had been taking Dr Cream's medicinal cures, and Cream had thoughtfully tried to insure his life. Mr Stott died on 14 July 1881 after imbibing one of Cream's remedies, given to him by his wife. Before absconding with Mrs Stott, Cream wrote to the coroner and the District Attorney accusing a chemist of malpractice and implying that Mr Stott had not died of natural causes and should be exhumed. He was, and was found to have been poisoned with strychnine.

The couple were apprehended and Mrs Stott turned state's evidence. Cream was sentenced to life imprisonment in Joliet prison, Illinois. He was released, unexpectedly early, in July 1891. In the meantime, his father had died, leaving him $116,000.

Cream left America, arriving in England on 1 October 1891, the month in which Ellen Donworth and Matilda Clover died and Louise Harvey escaped death. In December, he became engaged to Miss Sabbatini. In January, he returned to America and also visited Canada, where, in Quebec, he had 500 hand-outs printed (but never distributed) notifying the guests of the Metropole Hotel in London that one of the employees there had poisoned Ellen Donworth. Then, on 9 April, he returned to London. Emma Shrivell and Alice Marsh died three days later.

After Cream's conversation with Sergeant McIntyre, the police began a cautious investigation. Louise Harvey was found and interviewed. Cream's lodgings were watched, and he himself shadowed. He told an acquaintance who pointed this out to him that the police were keeping an eye on young Harper. On 17 May, another woman escaped poisoning when, in her room off Kennington Road, she wisely refused 'an American drink' that Cream prepared for her.

On 26 May, Inspector Tunbridge of the CID called on Cream in his rooms in Lambeth Palace Road. Cream complained about being followed by the police and showed Tunbridge a leather case containing, among other drugs, a bottle of strychnine pills, which he said could only be sold to chemists or doctors. The police toiled on. Next, on 27 May, Inspector Tunbridge went to Barnstaple and saw Dr Harper, who showed him the threatening letter that was clearly in Cream's handwriting. But it was not until 3 June that Cream was arrested at his lodgings, having already booked a passage on a ship to America. 'You have got the wrong man!' he exclaimed. 'Fire away!'

He was first charged at Bow Street with attempting to extort money from Dr Joseph Harper. The inquest on Matilda Clover (exhumed on 5 May) began on 22 June. Its conclusion was that Thomas Neill, as he was still being called, had administered poison to her with intent to destroy life. Now charged with her murder, he was put on trial at the Old Bailey before Mr Justice Hawkins on 17 October 1892. The Attorney-General, Sir Charles Russell, led for the Crown, and Mr Gerald Geoghegan appeared for the accused. Insolent and overbearing in court, Cream was convinced he would be acquitted. But the evidence was conclusive. After sentence of death was pronounced, he muttered: 'They will never hang me.'

He never slept the night before his execution, pacing up and down his cell or lying awake on his bed. White as a sheet and shaking, he was hanged at Newgate Prison on 15 November 1892 at the age of forty-two. Madame Tussauds bought his clothes and belongings for £200.

Although he made no confession, it is alleged that on the scaffold he said: 'I am Jack the – ' moments before he fell; that claim is clearly an impossibility, as at the time of the Whitechapel murders Cream was very definitely under lock and key in Joliet prison, Illinois. The executioner, James Billington, who had taken over from James Berry as chief hangman in August 1891, was, it seems, a bit of a joker, and may have invented Cream's last words. Another version of them is that Cream exclaimed: 'I am ejaculating!' before plummeting to his death.

FREDERICK DEEMING

THE MURDER OF MISS MATHER, 1891

Barristers defending persons accused of murder quite often claim that the defendant is insane. How else can the accused's apparently normal behaviour before and after the horrible event be explained? Sometimes, indeed, more time is spent on discussing medical theories about mental states than on the actual circumstances of the murder. In these instances, the defence usually suffers from the difficulty that the defendant looks and sounds far from mad, and is on the contrary the very picture of an agreeable, sometimes good-looking person, wrongfully accused and naturally aggrieved at being so. Seventy years ago and more, juries appear not to have been too bothered with technicalities and took a simpler, black-and-white view of right and wrong. They were not too worried, it seems, whether the accused was mad or not, since oddness, eccentricity and even abnormal behaviour were perhaps more usual – and more tolerated – than they are now. The question then was whether or not the accused had been satisfactorily proved to have done the murderous deed – and if he had, then he deserved to hang.

Frederick Bailey Deeming was certainly an unusual man, an adventurer in every way, engaging, larger than life, dedicated to enjoying himself and avoiding work whenever possible. Other members of his family also seem to have been rather odd. According to Fred's older brother Edward, their father, a tinsmith, 'died an imbecile in Tranmere Workhouse, Birkenhead' and before this had tried four times to commit suicide by cutting his throat. Fred himself, born on 30 July 1853 in Birkenhead, Cheshire, on the River Mersey opposite Liverpool, was the youngest of seven children and spoiled by his puritanical, Sunday School teacher mother. As a boy he was, according to Edward, 'hysterical and peculiar in his habits' and known as 'Mad Fred'. It seems he was supported by his parents for many years, only doing enough in the way of work to pay for his pleasures in Liverpool. It is said that when he was eighteen he became a steward on a liner and disappeared for several years. On his return he was, it seems, transformed, full of tales of adventure in the South African gold fields, and flamboyantly attired. From then on he kept disappearing overseas and reappearing, bejewelled anew, with a new suit and a new lady-friend by his side. Women, it seems, were fascinated by him. But he never exploited them financially, acquiring his money instead through theft, extortion and fraud. He was a plumber by trade.

When his mother died in 1875, her youngest son (according to brother Edward):

... was greatly distressed and very ill, and subsequently went on several voyages, visiting, amongst other places, Calcutta, where he had a severe attack of brain-fever ... Afterwards his mind appeared to be affected [and] he did the most extraordinary things ... He represented himself as being a person of distinction and would dress in peculiar ways. Sometimes he insisted on going out of doors in the morning wearing an evening dress coat [and] on other occasions he would go out as if dressed for a funeral, wearing deep mourning. [He was] subject to delusions, and frequently, after his mother's death, declared that he had seen her vision, and that she had directed him to do certain things.

His travels took him not only into Europe but to America, Australia, New Zealand and South Africa. At some point he married an English girl, of whom little is known except that she bore him four children, was abandoned in Australia (where she sang in the streets of Sydney to earn money) and again at Cape Town in South Africa when she managed to follow him there. He was imprisoned for bankruptcy in Australia in 1887 and was apparently also in prison in Johannesburg in 1888.

In 1890, Frederick Deeming was forty-seven, a large, muscular, hard-faced, handsome man with fair hair, a ginger moustache and light-blue eyes. Early in 1890, he was in Antwerp, posing as Lord Dunn, and was accepted as such by the town's smart society. But some piece of embezzlement or other misdemeanour soon occasioned his departure and he returned to his home territory on Merseyside.

He took up residence at the Railway Hotel, Rainhill, a few miles south of St Helens and east of Liverpool. He informed people that he worked for the government and was an Inspector of Regiments. Such was his ostentatious style of living that the hotel proprietor ventured to suggest that his hotel was too humble, even inadequate to cater for such a guest. Deeming was gracious. He said he was in Rainhill to look for a modest but comfortable little house within convenient distance of Liverpool on behalf of a friend, Baron Brook. The proprietor was pleased to recommend a charming villa near Rainhill, which an acquaintance, Mrs Mather, wished to let furnished to a good tenant.

Supplied with a letter of introduction, Deeming visited Mrs Mather that afternoon and viewed the property, Dinham Villa, which he pronounced to be entirely suitable and satisfactory. He was shown over the house by Mrs Mather's twenty-six-year-old daughter, Emily, a small brown-haired woman, five feet tall and slightly built.

Captivated by Deeming's personality, persiflage and protestations, Mrs Mather let him move into the villa without paying any rent in advance. Believing her handsome tenant to be a single man, she was intrigued to hear that Baron Brook had insisted on being Deeming's best man when he married. To everyone's satisfaction, the courtship of Emily Mather proceeded apace.

Before long, however, Deeming's wooing of Miss Mather was interrupted by the unexpected arrival – by cab and with little luggage – of his incorrigible wife and her four children. She had found her way back to England, to his brothers' families in Liverpool, and thence to Rainhill. She was determined to live with him as his wife.

Miss Mather heard about the new arrivals and wondered who they were. Deeming teased her, mocking her casual curiosity and revealing at last that the woman was not his wife but his sister. Her husband, he said, had recently obtained a lucrative position abroad, and she had come to holiday briefly with her brother to discuss some private financial matters that had to be settled before she left England.

From Deeming's point of view, the sooner she went the better. Her presence and that of the children was inconvenient. When he quarrelled with her, the children cried – it was intolerable. People would soon find out who she really was and then his flourishing romance with Miss Mather would be ruined. As Mrs Deeming refused to leave him – and he was reluctant this time to abandon her yet again (he was planning to marry Miss Mather) something had to be done.

After some thought, he went to Mrs Mather and said that, with her permission, he proposed to make one or two alterations to the villa, which would render the house more desirable to Baron Brook, who possessed a number of valuable carpets acquired in his travels. The floorboards at the villa were poorly laid, uneven, and let in the damp, and Deeming proposed at his own expense to cement the ground beneath the floorboards and then to re-lay them, so that they were flat and formed suitable surfaces for the Baron's carpets. Mrs Mather agreed.

Deeming then called on a local builder, buying a pickaxe and a large quantity of cement. He said his sister and her family had just left, and so, with the house to himself, he proposed to begin the alterations at once.

Over the next few days he cemented the ground-floor rooms himself, with a local carpenter re-laying the floorboards. As soon as this was done he celebrated by giving a little party in the villa. There was dancing in the kitchen, light refreshments being served in other rooms. The culmination of the party was the announcement of the engagement of Miss Mather and Mr Deeming – he had proposed that night and she had accepted. The healths of the happy couple were drunk and the merry guests danced happily over the now even floors – under which, encased in cement, lay the bodies of Mrs Deeming and all four children.

The Inspector of Regiments then suddenly announced that his duties required him to visit Australia. The wedding must therefore take place before he left. At the same time he revealed that Baron Brook had abandoned the idea of acquiring a house near Liverpool, and Mrs Mather was obliged to agree that it would be convenient if Deeming vacated the villa and stayed with her until he married her daughter. For some reason the marriage took place, on 22 September 1891, at Beverley in East Yorkshire.

Weeks later the couple, now known as Mr and Mrs Williams, set sail on the *Kaiser Wilhelm II*. They arrived in Australia, at Melbourne, in December 1891, and rented a small furnished house in Andrew Street, Windsor. Within a few days, on or about 20 December, Emily Mather was cemented in under the dining-room hearth and Mr Williams had disappeared.

The carelessness of a hurried repeat performance meant that, without the benefit of professional assistance, the floorboards were badly re-laid. The owner of the house was compelled to put right the poor workmanship, and in doing so uncovered part of a trussed and naked body. The police were sent for. They eventually dug out the remains of Miss Mather, who had been hit on the head six times before her throat was cut.

Deeming was not traced until March 1892, by which time his real identity had been established. He was found in Western Australia, in Perth, where he had been making plans to marry yet again, in this case a certain Miss Rounsevell. Arrested by Detective Cawsey, Deeming was brought in the last week of March by train to Albany, a sea port on the state's south coast. On the way to Albany the train stopped at York and a large, hostile crowd demonstrated at the railway station. When the train pulled out Deeming had a fit – whether real or faked is not clear – writhing and kicking for about an hour. At Albany, where Deeming and his captors embarked on a steamer for the 1,500-mile voyage to Melbourne, the prisoner shaved off his moustache. He subsequently denied that he had ever had one. Nonetheless, he was identified by several people when he was paraded before them in the yard of Melbourne jail.

He appeared at Melbourne's criminal court in the last week of April 1892, charged with the murder of Emily Mather. The judge was Mr Justice Hodges; the prosecutor was Mr Walsh; and the accused was defended by Mr Deakin. Meanwhile in England, Mrs Mather, informed of the method of her daughter's burial, had been horribly reminded of the cementing of the floors of Dinham Villa. When they were dug up, the remains of Deeming's wife and four children were found where he had laid them. Their throats too had been cut.

In Melbourne, Deeming's trial aroused a great deal of local interest, and crowds mobbed the court house every day. His defence was that he was insane. It was suggested that he suffered from epileptic fits. He was certainly infected with VD, and this may have impaired his mind, for he was moody and loquacious and fantasised about his past. He claimed that his dead mother had told him to kill Miss Mather, and that he had sometimes been overwhelmed by an irresistible impulse to slaughter the current lady in his life. He was thoroughly examined by at least six doctors, who were interested in the criminal mentality, and was even examined by an eye specialist, Dr Ruddal – who said the prisoner's eyes were perfectly normal.

Dr Shields, a prison doctor, said of the accused: 'I have frequently conversed with him, but I cannot believe anything he says.' Asked by Dr Shields whether he had any standards of right and wrong, Deeming had replied that stealing, for example, was a matter of conscience. If a person in needy circumstances stole money from one who could well afford it, that was quite justifiable and proper. Murder, he said, was also permissible in certain circumstances – he had several times gone out with a revolver searching for the woman who had given him VD, intending to kill her. He believed in the extermination of such women. Mr Dick, Inspector-General of Lunatic Asylums in Victoria, examined the prisoner five times, testing his memory and inspecting his eyes, head and general appearance. He was unable to detect any signs of insanity and he concluded that Deeming was 'an instinctive criminal'. During the trial no doctor, not even those who spoke for the defence, would unequivocally say or concede that Deeming was insane.

Towards the end of the trial, on Monday, 2 May, Deeming, with the judge's permission, made a speech – 'I wish to say a few words in my defence.' He spoke for nearly an hour, rambling on without hesitation or nervousness, denying the accusations against him and making some of his own. He began: 'I have not had a fair trial. It is not the law that is trying me, but the press. The case was prejudiced even before my arrival by the exhibition of photographs in shop-windows, and it was by means of these that I was identified … If I could believe that I committed the murder, I would plead guilty rather than submit to the gaze of the people in this court – the ugliest race of people I have ever seen …' He ended: 'I am as innocent as a man can be. That is my comfort.' The Reuter's correspondent in the court wrote: 'While this extraordinary scene was being enacted, daylight faded into darkness. Gas and candles were lighted, and the whole scene was weird in the extreme. The judge then summed up.'

The all-male jury were out for just over an hour. To their verdict that Deeming was guilty they added a rider that he was *not* insane.

After sentence of death had been passed, Fred Deeming thanked the judge, smiled at the jury, waved at friends and with his hands in his pockets disappeared from view.

In the three weeks before his execution, Deeming wrote his autobiography, which was destroyed with all his papers after his death. His writings were said by the authorities to have been 'a compound of ribaldry and folly'. In prison, Deeming, who was alternately angry and depressed and at times incoherent, upbraided his solicitor, Mr Lyle, bewailed his fate, declared his innocence and said he would kill himself if he could. He also made a will leaving the little he had to Mr Lyle and Miss Rounsevell, whom his mother's spirit, he said, was nonetheless still urging him to kill.

A long and closely argued petition was prepared by Mr Lyle and sent to the Melbourne Executive, asking for further enquiries and medical examinations to be made as well as for a stay of execution. The petition was dismissed on 9 May. Another petition was then sent to the Privy Council in England in a last attempt to have the case reconsidered. It included evidence from Edward Deeming and his wife concerning the prisoner's insanity. This petition was lodged at the Privy Council's office in Downing Street on 18 May, and the matter was discussed the following day with the Lord Chancellor in the chair. On the morning of Friday, 20 May, the Lords of the Judicial Committee of the Privy Council reported to Her Majesty that the petition for special leave to appeal should be dismissed.

On Monday, 23 May 1892, just before ten o'clock, Frederick Deeming walked to his execution smoking a cigar. A very large crowd of ticket-holding officials and pressmen were present, and in an attempt to remain incognito the hangman wore a false white beard while his assistant wore a false black one. Asked by the sheriff if he had anything to say, Deeming replied faintly: 'May the Lord receive my spirit.' The cap was put over his head and the entire burial service was read remorselessly by a chaplain before the lever was pulled.

While he was in prison Deeming claimed to be Jack the Ripper – an impossibility, as he had been in jail in South Africa at the time of the Whitechapel murders. Nonetheless, after his execution a plaster death mask was made of his head in case his claim was verified, and his brain and skull were studied by doctors interested in phrenology and the criminal mind. His body had also been examined to determine whether there was any evidence of degeneration, which would assist in identifying the 'criminal type'.

The head, sent to Scotland Yard, soon found a home in the Black Museum, where it was actually displayed for some time as the death mask of Jack the Ripper – thus perpetuating yet another myth.

WILLIAM SEAMAN

THE MURDER OF JOHN LEVY, 1896

Murder is often the outcome and fatal climax of a life of squalor, deprivation and crime. It as if the criminal involved becomes in time so indifferent to his fate, to other people and to life itself, so desperate and despairing, that he takes another person's life to bring his own miserable, meaningless existence to an end. Seaman's execution made history of a sort as he was one of three men hanged in the last triple execution carried out at Newgate Prison in 1896.

William Seaman was moved to commit a double murder by bitter feelings of hatred and revenge. He was said on his arrest to be a 'stoutly built man of middle height', with dark-brown whiskers, moustache and beard, and the appearance of 'a Russian Pole'. Said also to be a lighterman and 'diver', he was a convicted felon, aged forty-six, calloused by years of base and brutal living, in prison and out. He allegedly told another convict during his latest incarceration: 'There's a bloody fence and his whore at Whitechapel that owe me £70 on a deal. I'm going to their place for the money when I get out, and if the old bugger squeals at paying, I'll put his light out sure enough.'

That fence was a Jew, John Goodman Levy, aged seventy-five, who lived in a house on the corner of Turner Street and Varden Street, halfway between the sites of Jack the Ripper's first and third murders, committed in 1888. The area, less than eight years after the Ripper murders and in the year before Queen Victoria's Diamond Jubilee, was still a centre of seething criminal activity, of prostitution, pawn-broking, thievery and insalubrious pubs. Jews thrived locally with second-hand clothes and money-lending businesses, and as pawnbrokers and fences (receivers of stolen goods), though they conducted their lives and occupations, including crime, with more acumen than their neighbours, and with more profit and success. Such a one was old Levy, a retired umbrella-maker with crippled hands. 'Especially the right,' according to his stepson, Jacob Myers. 'Owing to the use of shears in his business.' Mr Myers, another umbrella-maker, who lived in Bow, also attested to the fact that Levy was 'very deaf' and 'too good and kind' for anyone to bear him any ill will. Myers and Levy had been in business together until December 1895, when the partnership was dissolved.

The last time Mr Myers saw his stepfather alive was in Levy's home at 31 Turner Street on the afternoon of Thursday, 2 April 1896. The following night, Levy had a supper party in his house, which was attended by three women: Mrs Annie Gale, aged thirty-seven, who had been Levy's housekeeper for about eleven years and lived on the premises; her sister, Mrs Alice Weiderman, the wife of a walking-stick carver, who lived in Battersea; and an elderly cousin of Mr Levy, Miss Martha Laughton, who was somewhat deaf and lived nearby, at 35 Turner Street. She and Mrs Weiderman both left the house about 9.45 pm that Friday night, after Miss Laughton had accepted Levy's invitation to lunch with him the following day. It was the Easter Bank Holiday weekend and a time for visits by family and friends.

On the morning of Saturday, 4 April, Mrs Annie Gale was seen opening the shutters of the ground-floor windows, and she talked to a dairyman, telling him not to forget about leaving some milk on the doorstep on the Bank Holiday Monday. Although it seems that Jacob Myers had until recently rented two rooms in the house, Mr Levy and his housekeeper were now the only occupants. And although Saturday was the Jewish Sabbath, it seems that Levy was not in the habit of attending the local synagogue and stayed at home that morning.

At 1 pm, Miss Laughton, following up Levy's invitation to lunch that day, called at Number 31 and knocked at the door. There was no response. A small boy from nearby Sydney Street was hovering outside the house and when he approached her she spoke to him. He later told the coroner's court what he presumably told Miss Laughton, that he had gone to the house earlier that morning (on an errand, it seems) received no reply to his knocking, noticed that there was no fire in the basement kitchen, and returned home to his mother, who had then sent him back to Levy's house. After more knocking at the front door, Miss Laughton must have expressed some concern, even alarm, to the small boy at the lack of response within. Both of them continued to hover outside the house, unaware that an intruder had stood for a while on the other side of the front door, debating with himself whether or not to open the door and let the visitors in. 'If I had,' as he later said, 'I would soon have floored them, so as they would not have walked out of that house again alive.'

Some other people would later say that odd sounds from within the house could be heard above the rattle and rumpus of horse-drawn vehicles, carts and people passing up and down, and the clatter of trams in Commercial Road. No doubt some of these sounds were reported to the deaf and elderly spinster by the little boy who, possibly encouraged by her, went off to have a look at the back of the house from Varden Street. While there he saw a man wearing a cap peer at him over a garden wall.

By 1.30 pm Miss Laughton was much perturbed and, going next door, communicated her worries to the couple who lived therein, Mr and Mrs Schafer. William Schafer, who was a tailor, determined to check the back of Number 31. He went into his back yard or garden and placed a ladder against the wall that separated Levy's yard from his. He climbed up and saw a man inside Levy's outhouse. Glimpsed by Schafer through a little outhouse window, the man, wearing a cap, was looking or bending down and, said Schafer later, 'appeared to be doing something with his hands'. Schafer shouted: 'What are you doing there?' The man looked up, then ducked down out of sight. Schafer called out again, whereupon the man straightened up, left the outhouse and disappeared into the basement of Levy's house.

The alarm was raised. Schafer instructed his wife to keep an eye on the back of the house while he went outside, to the front of Number 31. There he told Miss Laughton to fetch the police. By this time a small crowd had begun to gather and the intruder was again spotted out in the yard. When PC Walter Atkinson and another constable, both in plain clothes, arrived, they were taken through the Schafers' house to their yard, from where the constables gamely climbed over the dividing wall and entered the yard of Number 31.

There was a scullery and a lavatory in the outhouse and there was blood on the scullery floor. Within the lavatory lay Mr Levy in a bloody, crumpled heap, face upwards, his clothing disarranged, his throat cut from ear to ear.

PC Atkinson hurried through the house to the front door, where Miss Laughton was now dispatched to fetch a doctor and Mr Schafer admitted to identify the body. The two constables then began checking all the rooms in the house. Atkinson said later: 'In the top-floor front bedroom I saw the body of Mrs Gale, who was lying on her back on the floor. The body was lying nearest the door, and I could see that her throat had been cut. There was a quantity of blood at the foot of the bed and some on the bed. The room was in great disorder and boxes had been pulled out.'

Such was his agitation at finding the bodies, he apparently failed to register a ragged hole in the lathe and plaster ceiling, an old brown overcoat on the bed, both covered with fallen plaster, and an iron chisel and a long-bladed, bloodstained butcher's knife, also on the bed. He rushed downstairs.

Meanwhile, out in the street, someone in the swelling crowd spotted a man on the roof and shouted. At that moment PC Edward Richardson arrived at the scene with PC Wensley and seeing the man on the roof entered the house, leaving Wensley to observe the intruder from below. Pounding up the stairs, he came to the ransacked bedroom, in which Mrs Gale lay dead, saw the hole in the ceiling, got onto the bed, and intent on making an arrest pulled himself up through the hole in the ceiling, into the attic space below the roof. Once up there he stumbled about and slipped and one of his feet broke through the ceiling, making another hole.

Daylight was flooding into the attic from a man-sized hole in the roof. Cautiously clambering out through the hole and on to the tiles, clutching his truncheon, PC Richardson saw a man about 15 yards away, edging along a gutter towards the outer parapet. As Richardson called out to Wensley down below in the street, shouting a warning, the man stepped onto the parapet and jumped. He fell about 40 ft.

Below, the crowd shrieked and scattered as he fell. His fall was partly broken by a little girl, whom he struck and was said later to have slightly injured. Seriously injured himself and unconscious, he was seized by the police. PC Wensley said later: 'With considerable difficulty the man was got inside the house, and not before his coat had been torn from his back by the excited crowd, who would have lynched the prisoner if it had not been for the police.' After being examined inside Levy's home by a doctor, who merely diagnosed a fractured arm, the man was taken in a horse-drawn ambulance to the London Hospital in Whitechapel Road, along with the little girl.

A gold chain, a two shilling piece, a pair of eyeglasses and a gold seal had fallen from the man's pockets as he was manhandled in the street. These items and some money, amounting to 1s 3d, were gathered up by helpful citizens and the police. Other items found in the man's bloodstained clothing included brooches, earrings, a gold watch, a jewelled pin and 10s 9d in silver. The jewellery was Mrs Gale's. A stolen wedding ring and a diamond ring had been worn by Mr Levy. It seems that the murderer was disturbed by Mr Schafer's shout while he was in the outhouse rifling Mr Levy's pockets, for a purse containing 9d in stamps, a silver snuff box and a diamond-and-sapphire necktie pin were found on Levy's body.

Some money and a purse were also found on the roof, as well as a broken hammer and a woman's cap. The hammer's shaft had snapped off near the head. The cap, with a hat-pin in it, was Mrs Gale's. Jacob Myers would later say that she had worn it when she did her housework. Presumably the killer stole it because of the hatpin and then dropped or discarded it on the roof.

The hammer had been used to stun both Mrs Gale and Mr Levy before their throats were cut. It had also been used to make the holes in the bedroom ceiling and the roof. The police discovered that another hole had been made in the roof, from the outside, and there was hole in the chimney breast in the attic. It seems that the killer had tried to effect his escape by breaking through the chimney wall into the Schafers' house next door. About a dozen bricks had been removed. When this proved to be too difficult and when he was out on the roof, he then tried to break back into the house. But this attempt was foiled when the hammer broke. Weaponless, without chisel or knife and with the police at his heels, he jumped off the roof into the street. Why he never ventured to scale the garden wall and flee into the street or escape through another property is a mystery. Perhaps the agitation and activities of Mr Schafer, Miss Laughton and the little boy had attracted a crowd so quickly and so aroused the neighbourhood that he felt himself to be caught in a trap.

Thousands of people visited the scene of the Whitechapel Murders, as they became known, over the Bank Holiday weekend, and on an overcast Easter Monday 31 Turner Street was added to other popular holiday attractions like the British Museum (6,000 visitors), the National Gallery (11,550), the South Kensington Museums (17,900), Hampstead Heath, Hampton Court Palace, and the Royal Gardens at Kew (50,000 went there that day).

For several days after he regained consciousness, the prisoner refused to reveal who he was, and at the coroner's inquest, on Tuesday, 7 April, the possibility that the injured man was Mrs Gale's husband was investigated but dismissed. George Gale, a grocer's assistant and currently a carman (a van driver or carrier), had separated from his wife about ten years earlier; all their children were dead. So said Mary Clark, a baker's widow living in Sidney Street and Annie Gale's mother by adoption. She had viewed the accused man in hospital and was sure he was not George Gale.

At the inquest, PCs Atkinson, Richardson and Wensley gave evidence, as did Jacob Myers, Alice Weiderman, Miss Laughton, Mr Schafer, the dairyman and the little boy (William Whittaker, aged seven). Doctors described the injuries of the two dead persons. Mr Levy's body, when examined at the house, was still warm. He had died about half an hour before being discovered. Six of his ribs and his skull had been fractured and there were cuts on his head. The wound in his throat was eight inches in length, the 'windpipe and gullet having been cut right through.' Mrs Gale had been dead for about two hours. Her skull was fractured in several places and 'the force used in inflicting the wound in the throat had been so great that the knife had actually cut into the vertebrae.'

In the London Hospital, William Seaman's identity was eventually revealed, and it was established that he lodged in Claude Street, Millwall, on the Isle of Dogs. He had lived there for some time, and claimed to be engaged in perfecting an invention that he was trying to sell. Two policemen guarded him daily in the hospital ward, occasionally making notes of what he said. These 'voluntary' statements were later read out in court. It is not known whether Seaman signed them. But perhaps the Millwall inventor and ex-convict, worn down by pain and weary of his guards' questions, of his own wretched existence, became careless about what he said.

On the day after the double murders, Constable Hacchus, who had helped carry Seaman into Number 31 after he dived off the roof, was endeavouring to give the patient some milk when Seaman allegedly said: 'I know what's in front of me, and I can face it. If a man takes a life he must suffer for it. I don't value my life a bit. I have made my bed and I must lie on it.' On 17 April, PC Hacchus was helping a nurse to wash the patient, when Seaman said: 'Never mind washing anything else, as I shan't be here long … I don't want to hide anything, and I shan't try to. I did it. I've been prompted to do it thousands of times. I knew the old man had been the cause of all my trouble, and I would like to kill myself now. I'm sick of life.'

Earlier, on 11 April, PC Bryan was present when Seaman remarked: 'I suppose old Levy is dead and buried by this time.' 'I don't know,' PC Bryan replied. 'I'm glad I've done for him,' Seaman is said to have continued. 'I've been a good many times for the money, amounting to £70, and the old man always made some excuse. I made up my mind to do for him. I'm not afraid of being hanged.' The next day, Seaman allegedly said, on waking up: 'If the old Jew had only paid me the £70, the job would not have happened. You don't know what I've had to put up from him. But this finishes the lot …' On another day he said: 'I've been crushed since I was nineteen years old. I've done fourteen years and two sevens.'

On Friday, 1 May, Seaman appeared at the Thames Police Court to be charged. *The Times* noted: 'The prisoner was lifted into the Court seated on an armchair and was evidently suffering considerable pain. Seaman, who was undefended, was on Thursday night interviewed by Mr Bedford, solicitor, but declined that gentleman's service.'

Seaman was charged with larceny, as well as with the two murders. He chose to question none of the witnesses, only asking both PCs Richardson and Wensley, as if to prove their lack of observation: 'You saw only one hole?' He complained strongly, however, when the various voluntary statements attributed to him were read out in court. Referring to PC Bryan he said: 'The whole lot of his statement is a complete fabrication. I never had anything to say to him. Or the other one. They are the last two officers I should speak to. He and his companion were always questioning me. The rest of the evidence by the other witnesses is correct, but there is no truth in this.' He was then committed for trial.

This took place at the Central Criminal Court by Newgate Prison on Monday, 18 May 1896, a year after the second trial there of Oscar Wilde, convicted of gross indecency (which implied 'homosexual acts not amounting to buggery') and sentenced to two years' hard labour in prison, a sentence that he was currently serving in Reading Jail.

Seaman's trial was the first of the May sessions in 1896, which were formally opened by the Lord Mayor of the City of London attended by various aldermen, sheriffs and officials. Ninety-one persons were to be tried during the sessions: five for murder, one for manslaughter, two for attempted murder, two for rapes and assaults on girls, one for arson, seven for bigamy, eleven for burglary, eleven for larceny, and seventeen for unspecified misdemeanours. Other charges in fact included forgery, libel, letter stealing, perjury, receiving stolen goods and one robbery with violence.

The judge at William Seaman's trial was Mr Justice Hawkins. Mr CF Gill and Mr Horace Avery appeared for the prosecution. There was no counsel for the defence, and Seaman turned down the judge's offer of a barrister to act as a watching brief. He was indicted for the wilful murders of John Goodman Levy and Annie Sarah Gale, but only tried on the first charge.

Mr Gill detailed the prosecution's case and called witnesses in support. All Seaman did was to refute some of the statements he allegedly made in hospital. These included his own (alleged) account of the murders. Mr Gill said that the accused, on the morning of 4 April and after breakfast at his Millwall lodgings, went out between 8 and 9 am, having a hammer, chisel and knife in his possession. Reading from a statement allegedly made by Seaman and written down by PC Bryan, Mr Gill told the jury: 'The prisoner said that on that morning he went to the house and knocked at the door. Mr Levy opened it and he walked in. Mr Levy said the girl was upstairs. The prisoner, continuing, said: "I then went upstairs and found her in her bedroom. She then had her dress on and was leaning over the bed. When she saw me she shouted and began to struggle. But I soon stopped her kicking. I then got downstairs and soon put the old Jew's lights out."'

Why was Mrs Gale the first to die? And why did Levy apparently do nothing about escaping from the house while Seaman ran up the stairs and killed the housekeeper?

PC Bryan's statement, which had also been read earlier, at the Thames Police Court, reported that Seaman also said: 'After the job was finished, I heard someone knocking at the door.' Whether this was done by the little boy or Miss Laughton was not revealed. As Mrs Gale was surmised to have died some two hours before her body was found (i.e., at about 11.30 am), what was Seaman doing in the intervening time, and where was Mr Levy? It was thought that he had died about 1 pm. Why did he not flee from the house?

If what Seaman is alleged to have said is true, Levy opened the door to him about 11.30. Did an argument then take place, during which Mr Levy was struck with the hammer and left for dead? Did Mrs Gale then appear, see what had happened and run screaming up the stairs to her bedroom, pursued by Seaman? Did she try to put her bed between them, whereupon he hit her with the hammer more than once? Having silenced her, did Seaman, thinking that Levy was dead below, spend some time ransacking the bedroom, and possibly other upstairs rooms, before finding that Levy had disappeared, having crawled away and hidden himself in the outhouse lavatory? Although Levy was 'very deaf', it seems inconceivable that he would potter about downstairs, not trying to escape, knowing that Seaman was in the house.

It seems likely that the old man was attacked in the hall of Number 31 and hit by several blows of the hammer. Left for dead, he revived, and despite his fractured ribs and fractured skull was able to drag himself out of the house and hide in the outhouse. Perhaps in his condition he was unable to reach the front-door handle or latch and accordingly headed for the back door of the house, which may have been open, it being a warm spring day. Unable to attract any neighbour's attention, he then may have locked himself in the lavatory in the outhouse. When Seaman came downstairs, to find that Mr Levy's body was not in the hall, a trail of blood and the open back door may well have led him to the outhouse, where he cut the old man's throat.

At the conclusion of the prosecution's evidence, the accused man, when asked what he had to say to the jury in his defence, instead complained about prejudicial remarks about him in a weekly newspaper. The judge then asked Seaman if he had anything to say with regard to the charge against him. Seaman replied that he had nothing to say and no witnesses to call.

Mr Justice Hawkins, during his summing-up, said that there was no evidence to support the accused's statement that Mr Levy owed the prisoner £70. The jury found Seaman guilty and he was sentenced to death.

A few days later, on 21 May, Albert Milsom and Henry Fowler were also sentenced to death by Mr Justice Hawkins, and it was decided, probably to save time, trouble and cost, to hang them along with Seaman. These two, in the course of a burglary in Muswell Hill, north London, in February, had battered and killed another wealthy old man in his home. During their three-day trial, Fowler, a heavily built man, had tried to strangle his partner,

Milsom, in the dock. So, on the scaffold, Seaman was placed between them. 'It's the first time I've been a bloody peacemaker,' he said to the chief executioner, James Billington.

The triple execution within Newgate Prison was carried out on 9 June 1876. Seaman's weight, reduced by his hospitalisation and physical suffering, had fallen to 138 lb. Indifferent to the exhortations and prayers of the chaplain, Seaman was hanged with Milsom and Fowler at 9 am.

MILSOM AND FOWLER

The Murder of Henry Smith, 1896

The phrase 'partners in crime' has a special meaning when that crime is murder. For there seems little doubt that the intense association of two persons, often criminally inclined, acts as a catalyst, so that one of them, becoming grossly exhibitionistic, kills a third person as a result. In the following case as in several others of a similar sort, the victim was old and feeble, and the attack both needlessly brutal as well as cowardly.

Henry Smith, aged seventy-nine and a widower, was a retired engineer who lived alone, although attended by servants, in Muswell Lodge, a decaying mansion at Tetherdown, off Fortis Green in north London. Wealthy Mr Smith was apprehensive about being robbed, and his gardener had obligingly set up man-traps and alarms in the grounds of the house, trip-wires that were supposed to trigger guns into firing a warning shot.

On the night of 13-14 February 1896, no gun-shot was heard, but on the morning of Friday the 14th, the gardener, Charles Webber, discovered the body of Mr Smith in his nightshirt, lying on the kitchen floor. There had been something of a struggle before the old man died from repeated blows on his head – twelve in all, probably delivered by two people. His arms had been tied to his body by strips of a tablecloth, part of which, with a towel, had been wrapped around his head. Pieces of rag had also been used as a gag. Two penknives, employed to rip the cloth, lay one on each side of the body.

Two penknives suggested two men, and from the start a pair of burglars was sought. It was evident they had tried to force the sitting-room and scullery windows with a jemmy before entering the house through a kitchen window. The noise of their entry had clearly awakened Mr Smith, who on coming downstairs to investigate had been bludgeoned to death in the kitchen. The safe in his bedroom had been opened and ransacked. But apart from the pair of penknives, the only clue was a toy lantern found near the body of Mr Smith.

Police investigations revealed that two men had been seen lurking in the neighbourhood of Muswell Lodge two days before the murder, and a detective who had been keeping a watchful eye on an ex-convict out on parole noticed that the man had vanished from his usual haunts. This was a large brute of a man, Henry Fowler, aged thirty-one, whose known partner in petty crime was a small, mean crook called Albert Milsom, aged thirty-three, who lived in Southern Street, King's Cross. Both were labourers by trade.

Their families were questioned, and the brother of Milsom's wife, a fifteen-year-old youth called Henry Miller – who used to call Fowler 'Bunny' – added certainty to suspicion when he positively identified the toy lantern as his own.

A warrant was obtained for the arrest of Milsom and Fowler, who in the meantime had disappeared. A postmark on a letter eventually led to their apprehension on Sunday, 12 April 1896, in a shop in Monmouth Street, Bath. Fowler resisted arrest and was incapacitated by several blows to his head from a police revolver. In the intervening weeks he and Milsom had been to Liverpool, Manchester, Cardiff, London and Swindon as well as Bath, part of the time with a travelling show, in which they had purchased a partnership, calling themselves Taylor and Scott.

Milsom made a statement admitting the robbery but denying any involvement in the murder, which he said had been committed by Fowler while he, Milsom, was outside. He told his brother, Fred – 'Fowler killed the old man. I begged and prayed of Fowler to save the old man's life, and I ran away and Fowler ran after me. Fowler fetched me back, and Fowler went and done the robbery.' He also told the police where in the grounds of Muswell Lodge the pair had buried their tools.

Fowler claimed that his partner, Milsom, 'a dirty dog', had killed the old man. He said: 'He first put his foot on the old man's neck and made sure he was dead.'

Their three-day trial at the Old Bailey began on 19 May 1896, before Mr Justice Hawkins. Mr CF Gill and Horace Avory appeared for the Crown. Milsom was defended by Mr Hutton and Mr Rooth, and Fowler by Mr Woodfall and Mr Abinger. The evidence was overwhelming – a £10 note stolen from the Smith residence had also been found in Fowler's possession.

While the jury were out considering their verdict the two accused remained in the dock, and Fowler, determined that Milsom should die – if not hang – fell upon the other man. He almost succeeded in strangling Milsom before he was forcibly subdued by attendant warders and policemen. A correspondent from *The Times* wrote:

> *The constables climbed into the dock from the body of the Court to aid the warders. In the course of the struggle part of the glass partition which is on one side of the dock was smashed. Meanwhile there was great excitement in the body of the Court and in the gallery, both of which were crowded to excess. The members of the bar present and the rest of the spectators rose in their places in order to obtain a better view of what was going on, many of them standing on the seats.*

Sentenced to death on 21 May, they were hanged together in Newgate Prison on 9 June 1896, sharing a triple execution with the Whitechapel murderer, William

Seaman. The executions, timed for 9 am, were attended by about two dozen officials and warders, but not by any newspaper reporters, who were not admitted on the orders of the High Sheriff. Nonetheless, reporters were able to piece together an account of events from what they were told. The correspondent from *The Times* correspondent noted:

> *The condemned men, it is said, passed a restless and disturbed night, but Fowler ate a hearty breakfast. The bell of the prison began to toll at a quarter to 9 o'clock, by which time a large crowd had assembled outside the gaol … The men wore the clothes in which they were tried. A procession was formed and made its way to the scaffold, which is situated under a shed in a yard of the prison, the chaplain reciting the first portion of the Burial Office … Seaman was placed between the Muswell Hill murderers. As 9 o'clock struck the executioner withdrew the bolt, and the drop fell. The execution was over less than four minutes after the first man was pinioned. Prior to his death, Milsom said he was innocent, Seaman said he had nothing to say, and Fowler made no statement at all. As the black flag denoting the sentence had been carried out was hoisted on the roof of the gaol, the crowd in the precincts cheered.*

What *The Times* correspondent apparently did not know was that a horrid accident had occurred at the hanging. To prevent any strife between Milsom and Fowler, or any resistance from all three, James Billington, the chief executioner, had been given three assistants – one of whom was William Warbrick. Four warders also stood in close attendance. One of the warders happened to obscure Warbrick from Billington's view as he knelt down on the trap-door to pinion the feet of one of the doomed men. Warbrick was still thus employed when Billington, acting hastily on the stroke of nine, withdrew the bolt that released the trap-door below the three condemned men, catapulting his assistant into the pit. Warbrick instinctively managed to grab the legs of the man in front of him. He ended up swinging below the bodies of the three dead or dying men.

This scaffold, described by Billington's successor, Harry Pierrepoint, as 'the finest scaffold in the whole country, being fitted to hang three persons side by side' was moved to Pentonville Prison in 1902, when Newgate Prison was demolished. The first hanging at Pentonville took place on this scaffold on 30 September 1902, an event that was also marked by the discontinuance of the practice of flying a black flag when an execution occurred. Instead, a bell was tolled.

In 1903 the number of people executed for murder in Britain rose to its highest level for over seventy years – twenty-seven people being hanged. This, however, was below the average for the years between 1811 and 1832, when about eighty people were hanged every year – and far less than the average rate of executions which, in the brief reign of Edward VI (1547-53), reached record heights, about 560 people being executed each year at Tyburn alone.

It was in 1903 that building on the site of the demolished Newgate Prison began, concluding three years later. The new edifice, topped by a large bronze figure of Justice, was the imposing Central Criminal Court, soon to be known by the name of the street in which it stood: the Old Bailey.

MRS DYER

THE MURDER OF DORIS MARMON, 1896

Some sorts of murder in the nineteenth century arose out of the economic and social conditions peculiar to that age. They could never happen now, having been eliminated by social progress and improvements in housing, wages, hygiene and the status of women. Baby-farming was a peculiarity of late Victorian England, when unwanted or inconvenient babies and children, whether illegitimate or merely burdensome, were farmed out to women acting as foster mothers who were paid to 'adopt' the infants or to look after them for months or years. Such a surrogate mother was Mrs Dyer, who killed at least seven children, and in her twenty years as a baby farmer may have killed many more. Mrs Dyer also has the distinction of being the oldest woman to have been hanged in Britain between 1843 and 1955.

A native of Bristol where she was born (in about 1839), brought up and married, Mrs Amelia Elizabeth Dyer was a member of the Salvation Army. She began acting as a midwife and foster mother about 1875 if not before. In 1880, she was jailed for six weeks for running a baby farm in Long Ashton, a village south-west of Bristol. Between 1891 and 1894, she was thrice admitted to lunatic asylums for a month or so – twice, it is said, because she had tried to commit suicide while in prison. In June 1895, she left Barton Regis workhouse with an old woman called Granny Smith and went to Cardiff, where the pair lodged with Mrs Dyer's married daughter, Mrs Mary Ann (Polly) Palmer, for a few months. During this period, Polly Palmer had a baby that died of 'convulsions and diarrhoea' and probably neglect. Her husband, Arthur, was twenty-five and unemployed. Mrs Dyer's husband, William, whom she had left many years earlier, worked in a vinegar factory in Bristol.

In September 1895, evading creditors and the police, the Palmers, Mrs Dyer and Granny Smith absconded from Cardiff and travelled east to Caversham, a village outside Reading. Here Mrs Dyer, using an assumed name, advertised her trade, and children for adoption or boarding began to arrive. She was assisted in this business by her daughter and presumably by Granny Smith; Arthur Palmer remained out of work.

The ten-month-old baby daughter of a barmaid probably arrived first: the mother, Elizabeth Goulding, paid Mrs Dyer £10. A nine-year-old boy, Willie Thornton, was next, followed by another baby and a girl aged four.

In January 1896, the Palmers moved to London, renting two rooms in Willesden for seven shillings a week and taking with them an infant called Harold, another of Mrs Dyer's charges. She herself moved from Piggott's Road to her third address in Caversham, Kensington Road, and using yet another alias, Mrs Thomas, carried on as before. The children she now acquired were Ellen Oliver, aged ten; Helena Fry, who was fifteen months old; and two illegitimate babies of servant girls.

On 30 March 1896, bargemen on the River Thames at Reading fished the body of a baby girl out of the water. She had been wrapped in a brown paper parcel and weighted with a brick. The infant (who was Helena Fry) had been strangled with a tape. On the brown paper was inscribed 'Mrs Thomas, Piggott's Road, Lower Caversham.' The next day, in Cheltenham, Mrs Dyer was paid £10 by Evelina Marmon to take care of her illegitimate four-month-old daughter, Doris.

Miss Marmon, aged 25, a farmer's daughter and now a barmaid, who had given birth to a baby girl in her lodgings in January 1986, had seen a newspaper advertisement that said: 'Married couple with no family would adopt healthy child, nice country home. Terms £10.' Evelina wrote to the woman whose name appeared at the foot of the ad, Mrs Harding, who replied: 'I should be glad to have a dear little baby girl. We are plain homely people … I don't want a child for money's sake, but for company at home and comfort … I have no child of my own. A child with me will have a good home and a mother's love.' Evelina Marmon wanted to make the payment in weekly instalments, but Mrs Harding insisted on the £10 being paid in full.

The day after Doris Marmon was handed over to Mrs Dyer in Cheltenham, she and her daughter Polly were at Paddington Station in London, where they collected a baby boy, Harry Simmons, from a Mrs Sargeant, whose maid had given birth to him a year before and then disappeared. Mrs Sargeant was relieved no doubt to dispose of the baby to the kindly elderly woman whose advertisement in the *Weekly Dispatch* had caught her eye: 'Couple having no child would like the care of one or would adopt one. Terms £10.'

The following day, 2 April, the two babies, Doris and Harry, who had both been strangled with tape, were dumped in the Thames in a weighted carpet bag.

Two days later, the police at last identified Mrs Thomas of Piggott's Road as Mrs Dyer of Kensington Road. She was arrested on 4 April. At Reading police station she tried unsuccessfully to kill herself with a pair of scissors and then by choking herself with a bootlace. Her daughter Polly and her son-in-law, Arthur Palmer, were also arrested. 'What's Arthur here for?' asked Mrs Dyer. 'He's done nothing.' The two babies found in her house in Kensington Road were returned to their mothers and Willie Thornton and Ellen Oliver were eventually found other homes. A four-year-old boy who arrived after the arrests was sent away by Granny Smith.

The River Thames was dragged for other bodies, and the decomposed corpse of a baby boy was recovered from the river on 8 April, as was that of another boy two days later. Neither was ever identified. Also on 10 April, the carpet bag containing Doris

Marmon and Harry Simmons was retrieved from the river bed. Miss Goulding's baby was dredged up on 23 April and another unidentified baby boy was discovered a week later. The total had now reached seven.

Meanwhile in Reading Prison Mrs Dyer tried to ease her mind and save her daughter and son-in-law by writing a letter to the Superintendent of Police. 'I feel my days are numbered,' she wrote. 'But I do feel it is an awful thing, drawing innocent people into trouble. I do know I shall have to answer before my Maker in Heaven for the awful crimes I have committed, but as God Almighty is my Judge in Heaven as on Earth, neither my daughter, Mary Ann Palmer, nor her husband, Arthur Ernest Palmer, I do most solemnly swear that neither of them had anything at all to do with it. They never knew I contemplated doing such a wicked thing until too late.'

The matron at Reading Prison, Ellen Gibbs, said to Mrs Dyer: 'By a letter like this, you plead guilty to everything.' 'I wish to,' remarked the prisoner. 'They cannot charge me with anything worse than I have done ... Let it go.' She never revealed how many children she had killed, merely saying later: 'You'll know all mine by the tape round their necks.'

The charges against Palmer and his wife were never proved, and Polly Palmer became the chief witness for the prosecution, giving evidence against her mother at the magistrate's hearing on 2 May and later at the Old Bailey trial. Mrs Palmer's story was that on 31 March her mother turned up in Willesden carrying a ham and a carpet bag and holding a baby, Doris Marmon, temporarily 'for a neighbour'. The baby must have been strangled, said Mrs Palmer, while she was out fetching some coal, for when she returned the baby had disappeared and Mrs Dyer was shoving the carpet bag under the sofa. Harry Simmons, she said, must have been killed (again in Willesden) the following night, before she, her mother and her husband went out to a music hall. At any rate, he had disappeared by the following morning – Mrs Dyer had slept on a sofa in the living room – although there was an odd parcel under the sofa beside the carpet bag. 'What will the neighbours think if they saw you come in with a baby and go away without it?' Polly asked, allegedly. To which her mother replied, allegedly: 'You can very well think of some excuse.' Later that day the Palmers accompanied Mrs Dyer to Paddington Station. While Mrs Dyer went to buy some cakes to eat on the Reading train, Palmer held the now bulging carpet bag.

Mrs Amelia Dyer was charged with the murder of baby Doris Marmon and tried at the Old Bailey on 21 and 22 March 1896 before Mr Justice Hawkins. The trial began on the afternoon of the day on which Mr Justice Hawkins had sentenced to death Albert Milsom and Henry Fowler.

The Crown's case at Mrs Dyer's trial was put by Mr AT Lawrence and Mr Horace Avory. Mr Kapadia, who defended her, accepted that she was guilty but tried to prove that she was insane. Dr Logan of Gloucester Asylum said that in 1894 she had been violent and had suffered from delusions: she heard voices and said birds talked to her. Dr Forbes Winslow, who saw her twice in Holloway Prison, said she was suffering from delusional insanity, depression and melancholia. He did not believe she was shamming insanity. Two other doctors appearing for the prosecution said that her insanity was feigned. One of them, Dr Scott, the medical officer of Holloway, who had seen her daily, said he had discovered nothing in her that was inconsistent with her being a sane person, beyond her own statements. The jury agreed, taking a mere five minutes to find her guilty, and not insane.

Mrs Dyer, aged fifty-seven, a short, squat woman with thin white hair scraped into a bun behind her head, was hanged by James Billington at Newgate Prison on 10 June 1896. Before she died she made a long statement or confession, written in five exercise books, explaining some of her actions and thoroughly exonerating her daughter and son-in-law. When urged by the chaplain to confess, she indicated the exercise books and asked: 'Isn't this enough?' Her statement ended: 'What was done I did do myself. My only wonder is I did not murder all in the house when I have had these awful temptations on me. Poor girl [Polly], it seems such a dreadful thing to think she should suffer all this through me. I hope and trust you will believe what I say, for it is perfectly correct, and I know she herself will speak the truth, and what she says I feel sure you can believe.'

The Reading baby farmer evidently had some feelings for her own and only surviving child.

10
RICHARD A PRINCE

THE MURDER OF WILLIAM TERRISS, 1897

Murderers often tend to play a part, to assume other names, achievements and emotions, to invent autobiographical details, to pose, pretend and lie. They would make, one imagines, good actors. On the other hand, only one actor in the UK is believed to have committed a murder. He was Richard Prince, whose ambitions were scorned, his affections spurned, and his whole existence mocked. He was more than neurotic and just a little mad, and his victim was an actor like, but much better than, himself.

His real name was Richard Millar Archer, though he also called himself William Archer and William Archer Flint. Short, dark, with a thin black moustache waxed at both ends, he was Scottish, having been born in 1858 on a farm on the Baldoran Estate just outside Dundee. His father was a ploughman. His mother, Margaret Archer, later attributed the fact that Richard was 'soft in the head' to the summer day when she left him as a baby out in a harvest field in the sun. He was educated in Dundee, and as a lad was employed in a minor capacity at the Dundee Theatre for two years. In 1875, when Richard was seventeen, the Archers came temporarily to London, and the fantasies of the stage-struck youth must have been set alight by the glamorous world of the gas-lit West End theatres, in which the idols of the stage – before films and television eclipsed their glory – declaimed and emoted to much effect and immense adulation. But before long, the Archers were back in bleak Dundee.

Little is known of Prince's movements over the next twelve years. Presumably, like many young aspiring actors, he was more out of work than in, finding employment where and however he could. His native accent may have limited his chances on the London stage, although he probably modified and disguised it as best he could. What he was unable to alter was an increasingly theatrical manner, a slight squint and a villainous appearance that meant he was invariably cast as a 'heavy'. However, in 1887 he was in London, employed as a 'super' or extra at the Adelphi Theatre in the Strand, appearing in *The Union Jack*. He stayed with the play on its provincial tour, and is also said to have toured in *Alone in London* and *The Harbour Lights* (in 1889). This was a revival of the play written by George R Sims and Henry Pettit that in December 1885 had established the Adelphi as the home of popular melodrama. It had also established the romantic association of its two stars, Jessie Millward and William Terriss, which was also played out in private: she was his mistress.

William Terriss (real name William Charles James Lewin) was one of the most popular actors at that time on the English stage. Popularly known as Breezy Bill, he was born in London on 20 February 1847, educated privately and also at Christ's Hospital, and took up various occupations before he became a full-time actor. As a youth he joined the merchant navy for a few weeks (he liked the uniform), embarking as a cadet on a sailing ship at Gravesend and disembarking at Plymouth, having discovered a sailor's life was not for him. He also tried his hand at silver-mining and horse-breeding in America and at sheep-farming in Australia and the Falkland Islands, where his daughter, Ellaline Terriss, a future Gaiety Girl and wife of Seymour Hicks, was born. Her mother was Isabel Lewis, who on holiday in Margate had been captivated by the athletic figure of young William Lewin sporting in the sea. They were married in 1868 when he was twenty-one. Before long the family left the Falklands and returned to England, and Terriss, who had dabbled in amateur theatricals, obtained his first notable professional engagement. In 1871, he was cast as Robin Hood in a Drury Lane extravaganza and appeared in *Rebecca,* which was based on Sir Walter Scott's *Ivanhoe.* The *Observer* critic, Clement Scott, noted of his performance: 'It is really pleasant to find anyone determined to speak as ordinary people speak on the boards of the theatre, whereon strange tones and emphases prevail.'

Terriss's face, figure and voice being his fortune, he soon became successful, establishing his reputation as an actor with Henry Irving's company at the Lyceum Theatre. Aged thirty-one when he joined the company, Terriss gave several acclaimed performances: as a brother in *The Corsican Brothers;* as Squire Thornhill in *Olivia,* with Ellen Terry as Olivia and Irving as Dr Primrose; as Nemours in *Louis XI;* as the King in *Henry VIII;* and as Henry II, with Irving in the title role of Tennyson's play, *Becket,* which was given a royal command performance in Windsor Castle in 1893 before Queen Victoria. In 1895, Irving was knighted, the first actor to be so honoured.

Several years before this, in October 1882, Jessie Millward, then aged twenty-one, had appeared as Hero in the Lyceum's production of *Much Ado about Nothing;* Terriss was Claudio. It was three years after this, in December 1885, that they made a name for themselves as a romantic team in *The Harbour Lights,* in which Terriss played Lieutenant David Kingsley and Jessie Millward the lovely Lina. One critic said of Terriss's performance: 'He does not act, he *is* the frank, handsome sailor whose joyous laugh, bright eye and sturdy ringing voice bring life and hope to the darkest hour. The fine presence, boyish, handsome face and free, fearless gestures suit the role to perfection.'

From then on, Terriss and Jessie Millward often appeared in the same productions, touring Britain and America. In London in the 1890s he used to dally with her in her flat off Oxford Circus, while his wife (they were both Catholics) kept up appearances and the family home in Bedford Park, West London.

It was in September 1894 that Terriss and Jessie Millward – he called her 'Sis' and she referred to him as 'my comrade' – embarked on the series of popular successes at the Adelphi that affirmed their national reputation, appearing in plays such as *The Fatal Card*, *The Girl I Left Behind Me*, *One of the Best*, *Boys Together*, and *Black-eyed Susan*. He invariably played gallant sailors or soldiers. In *One of the Best* (1895) he was court-martialled and falsely convicted of espionage. As the drums rolled, the marks of his rank, his collar and cuffs, were torn from his uniform, his face the while depicting the agony he suffered. But when his medals were seized he cried out: 'Stay! You may take my name, my honour, my life! But you cannot take my Victoria Cross!'

Capitalising on his manly mien and personality, Breezy Bill, now approaching fifty and wearing pince-nez in private, strode nightly about the stage, declaring his love for Queen, country and innocent womanhood, foiling the foe at every turn. The audience loved him. Admired and acclaimed, living up to his motto *Carpe Diem*, blessed with a wife, three children and a loving mistress, with good business sense and membership of the better London clubs, he seemed unassailably successful, without a care or enemy in the world.

The year 1897 marked Queen Victoria's Diamond Jubilee. Terriss had turned fifty, though was said to be younger, and Jessie Millward was thirty-six. Richard Prince, who gave his age as thirty-two, was now thirty-nine and in a dangerous, desperate plight. Nothing is known about how Prince became acquainted with Terriss. It may have been during the run of *The Union Jack* in 1888. Perhaps Terriss gave the younger actor a walk-on job; it was not unusual for struggling actors to be encouraged or patronised by an established star. Perhaps there was some ground for the uncharitable rumours that were later circulated about some sexual association. What is known is that during the run of *The Harbour Lights,* Terriss caused Prince to be sacked after the swarthy Scot had made an offensive remark about him. Later on Terriss, out of generosity it is said, sent, or caused to be sent, small sums of money to Prince when he was out of work via the Actors' Benevolent Fund, and he apparently used his influence to get the younger man on the provincial tours in which Prince occasionally appeared.

But the managers of these touring companies found him increasingly unemployable. One of them, Ralph Croydon, a theatre manager in Newcastle, hired Prince towards the end of October 1897, at 25s a week, but soon sacked him, because in rehearsal he was 'absolutely incapable . . . absurdly dramatic' and unable to remember the lines of quite a small part. 'Ah!' exclaimed Prince on hearing of his dismissal, 'I have *two* enemies now!' He informed the manager that the other was Terriss – 'the dirty dog'. 'You're mad!' said Mr Croydon. 'Yes!' said Prince. 'And the world will ring with my madness!' Another manager received a letter from Prince that said: 'You hell-hound! You Judas! You have got me out of my engagement by blackmailing me to get on yourself! You cur! I am not a woman, you hound! How dare you blackmail a Highlander!'

Abject but useless apologies would follow such outbursts, which were also heard in theatre dressing rooms, where Prince was known as Mad Archer. He wearied company members with diatribes about the management and other actors, who he claimed had impeded or prevented his advancement. Prince was just as rabid with his pen, sending effusive messages of congratulation and condolence to politicians and royal persons whenever the occasion, birthday or bereavement, arose. He also wrote poems and plays, one of which, *Countess Otto,* he sent to an up-and-coming young actor, Fred Terry. It was written in longhand in exercise books. Terry made no immediate acknowledgement or return of the script and soon received the following postcard – 'Sir, please return play *Countess Otto* at once. If you are hard up for money will send it. Terriss, the Pope, and Scotland Yard. I will answer in a week – Richard A Prince.'

Despite the consolation of Sunday services in Westminster Abbey, which he often attended, Prince's professional and private life must have been miserable. When 'resting', he was employed in an ironworks in Dundee, where the workmen 'used to torment him because he was soft'. He was 'very strange in his ways', according to a foreman, 'and very jealous'. Once in 1895, when his wretchedness or sense of drama got the better of him, Prince jumped in the Regent's Canal. His vanity probably kept him from killing himself. 'I am a member of the handsomest family in Scotland!' he is said to have exclaimed.

But in November 1897, after being sacked by the Newcastle manager, his poverty was extreme. Existing on handouts from the Actors' Benevolent Fund, which had been prompted by a letter from Terriss, Prince lived in a bed-sit near Victoria Station, in Buckingham Palace Road. The rent was 4s a week, which a sympathetic landlady, Mrs Darby, reduced to 3s. He had no luggage or possessions; his clothes, apart from those he wore, had been pawned. He fed on bread and milk. On 9 December he received what was to be his last payment (10s) from the Benevolent Fund.

On Monday, 13 December, he tried to get a complimentary seat for a show at the Vaudeville Theatre by showing his card at the box office. It read: 'Richard Archer Prince, Adelphi Theatre'. Asked if he was employed there, he replied: 'No, I'm not. But I was. I suppose I should have written "Late Adelphi Theatre". But other people don't, so why should I?' No ticket was given him, and he became so abusive that he had to be removed from the theatre foyer. He said he would go to the Adelphi a few yards away and tell Mr Gatti how he had been treated. Mr Gatti owned both the Vaudeville and the Adelphi. Prince failed to see him, but at the stage door of the Adelphi he inquired as to when Mr Terriss arrived at the theatre and when he left.

That night or the next, Miss Millward heard raised voices in Terriss's dressing room; Prince was there. She asked Terriss later if anything was the matter; he was dismissive and said: 'This man's becoming a nuisance.' On Wednesday, she again visited his dressing room, haunted by a feeling of impending ill – she had had a dreadful dream in which Terriss, dying, fell into her arms in some barren room. She asked for some remembrance of him. Amused, he gave her his watch and chain, with her picture in the lid. Another member of the Adelphi company who had a prophetic dream of death was Terriss's understudy, Mr Lane. Meanwhile the show went on. It was called *Secret Service*. Written by William Gillette, it was a four-act drama set during the American Civil War.

In another part of London, Mrs Darby asked her poor Scottish lodger when he would be able to pay his overdue rent. He told her she would be paid when he received a certain letter; he would then be 'one way or the other'. Mrs Darby asked him what he meant. Prince replied: 'That is best known to God and man.'

That certain letter arrived on the morning of Thursday, 16 December. It informed him that the Benevolent Fund had terminated his grant. Penniless, starving and poorly clad under his slouch hat and cloak, he set off on foot towards the West End for the last time. In the Strand he happened to meet his step-sister and asked her for some money. She said she would rather see him dead in the gutter than give him anything. If she had, he said later, he would never have bent his steps towards the Adelphi Theatre. He waited outside its warmth and glamour with a crazy resolve to kill.

Will Terriss spent the early part of that Thursday afternoon playing poker with Fred Terry in the Green Room Club. At four o'clock, he and a friend, Harry Greaves, a surveyor, dined in Jessie Millward's flat in Princes Street, Hanover Square. The two men settled down to play chess after their meal, and at about seven o'clock Jessie Millward left them to finish their game while she went on ahead. 'I must get down to the theatre,' she said. 'I hate being rushed.' They followed soon afterwards, riding in a hansom cab to Maiden Lane, the narrow street that runs behind the Adelphi and the Vaudeville. They got out at the street-corner and walked the short distance towards the rear of the Adelphi. Its stage door was then in Bull Inn Court.

There was another entrance, a pass door, which also served as the royal box entrance. This was in Maiden Lane. It now serves as an exit door of the present theatre, being marked, then and now, by the royal crest above the door; the present stage door is right beside it. Terriss used this pass door to avoid his fans, and Greaves accompanied him to the theatre, probably in case a particular person should prove again to be a nuisance. The door was kept locked. In the dank, gas-lit street Terriss fumbled in a pocket for his key.

As he inserted it in the lock and opened the door, a dark figure that had been lurking near Rule's Restaurant rushed across the street and with great force stuck a kitchen knife in Terriss's back. Another blow slashed Terriss's side as he turned. A third thrust penetrated his chest.

The attack was carried out in silence. Jessie Millward, in her dressing room above the door, heard Terriss arrive and the door open – and then nothing. Suddenly apprehensive, she ran down the stairs with her maid, Lottie, and saw Terriss leaning against the wall by the open door. 'Here are my keys, Lottie,' he said, quite calmly. 'Catch that man.' The maid ran outside. 'Sis,' he whispered, gazing at Jessie. 'Sis, I am stabbed.' Although she tried to support him he collapsed, and they both fell on the bare boards of the hall at the foot of the stairs. 'Mr Terriss has met with an accident!' she cried. 'Send for a doctor!' She held him in her arms as shocked company members crowded around. Doctors from the nearby Charing Cross Hospital soon arrived, as well as the police.

Out in Maiden Lane, Prince, who made no resistance, had been seized by Greaves and Lottie and was now handcuffed and in the charge of a uniformed constable. The knife was found in his pocket. He was reported to have said after the murder: 'I did it for revenge. He had kept me out of employment for ten years, and I had either to die in the street or kill him.' He was taken past Covent Garden to Bow Street police station, where five pawn tickets were found on him but no money. Meanwhile, Terriss still lay on the floor of the little hall, supported by Jessie Millward, whose control was such she did not, or could not cry. Nothing could be done for him; he was dying and barely conscious. Once or twice he murmured: 'Sis ... Sis ...' Five or six minutes before the curtain was due to rise, he died.

The audience were already aware that something was amiss, as no orchestra had appeared, the footlights were not lit, and the sound of agitated voices could be heard behind the curtain. A minute or so before 8 pm the curtains parted and the shadowy figure of the assistant stage manager, Mr Budd, appeared. Lifting a hand for silence, he announced: 'Ladies and gentlemen, I am deeply grieved and pained to announce to you that our beloved friend, Mr Terriss, has met with a serious, nay terrible, accident, which will make the performance of *Secret Service* this evening quite impossible. I will ask you to be good enough to pass into the street as quietly as possible, and it is hardly necessary for me to add that your money will be returned on application at the pay boxes.' Those who went to the stage door to inquire what had happened soon learned that William Terriss had been stabbed to death. Word quickly spread; crowds gathered, and within an hour special editions of the evening papers were on the streets with the news.

At Bow Street police station Prince was charged with murder, and having admitted the charge said: 'Can you give me something to eat?'

The following morning Bow Street court, opposite the Royal Opera House, Covent Garden, was crammed with theatre-goers, actors and actresses, who greeted Prince's appearance in the dock with loud sounds of disapprobation. But the villain of the piece was suitably unmoved and smiled disdainfully. Indeed, he clearly relished his leading role in front of a full house, nodding, grimacing, smiling, stroking his moustache, twirling the ends, as he listened to the witnesses. Reporters described him as 'Mephistophelian'. The audience's loathing increased as the hearing proceeded, and when he was committed for trial – when he bowed and smiled – a torrent of shouts and yells accompanied his exit.

The funeral of William Terriss took place at 1 pm on 21 December, a bitterly cold and windy day. The funeral procession was half a mile long and took an hour to make the journey from the Terriss family home in Bedford Park to Brompton Cemetery; many thousands of people lined the route. Sir Henry Irving was the most celebrated of the mourners; he had been asked by the Queen to convey her condolences to Terriss's family. He also personally conveyed Jessie Millward to the funeral service; she had hardly slept or eaten since Terriss's death. Mrs Terriss did not attend the service, the family being represented by Terriss's two sons – his daughter, Ellaline, had just lost her first baby and was very ill in Eastbourne. It is said that ten thousand people gathered at the cemetery.

The Adelphi Theatre remained closed for over a week, reopening on Monday, 27 December, with Mr Herbert Waring in place of Terriss and May Whitty taking over Jessie Millward's role. For many months the stage door in Bull Inn Court became a place of pilgrimage for morbid and mistaken sensation-seekers and fans.

Richard Prince was tried at the Old Bailey on 13 January 1898 before Mr Justice Channell. The prosecutor was Mr CF Gill, assisted by Mr Horace Avory; Mr WH Sands represented the accused, who was swathed in an Inverness cape. The gas-lit courtroom was packed.

At the start Prince pleaded 'Guilty with provocation' and was advised to change this plea. He said: 'I am guilty, but I have to ask a favour. I believe the law of England allows me a Queen's counsel. I have a counsel, but I should like a Queen's counsel to watch the case on my behalf. I have no friend, and my mother cannot help me with a penny for my defence.' His request was refused, and he eventually accepted Mr Sands's advice and changed his plea to 'Not guilty'.

Prince again behaved with much theatricality, but the audience was this time more subdued. The defence was insanity, and his family and several Scottish neighbours and associates were produced to vouch for his strangeness. Two doctors spoke of his 'insane delusions' and said he was 'of unsound mind'. When his mother gave evidence, Prince was much amused and often laughed, loudly translating her Dundonian accent for the benefit of judge and jury. She said: 'He was born mad, and he grew up wi' passions that pit him wrang in his mind.'

The trial lasted one day. The jury retired at 6.35 pm and after a thirty-minute deliberation found the accused 'Guilty, but according to the medical evidence not responsible for his actions.' The judge consigned Prince to the criminal lunatic asylum at Broadmoor, to the prisoner's evident relief. He embarked on an oration of thanks, which was interrupted by the judge. Prince was removed from the court.

In Broadmoor he was apparently happy, a leading light in the entertainments of the inmates. He conducted the prison orchestra, and declaimed Shakespeare in a garden courtyard, hanging his cloak on a tree. But was he really insane? Irving thought otherwise, and is reported to have said: 'They will find some excuse to get him off – mad, or something. Terriss was an actor.'

Secret Service ended its run at the Adelphi on 20 January, a week after the trial. The enterprising Gatti management transferred another play from Islington to the Adelphi. Preceded by a farce, *BB,* it opened at 8.30 pm on 21 January. The play was a drama about the assassination, by knife, of Jean Marat, and was called *Charlotte Corday.*

Some months before this, Terriss's wife, it is said, had happened to be reading the reviews of *Charlotte Corday* and had told her husband that she thought the part of Marat would suit him very well. 'Ah, no,' he replied. 'Horrible! I couldn't bear that scene with the knife!'

11

SAMUEL DOUGAL

THE MURDER OF MISS HOLLAND, 1899

The character of some murders is determined in part by the nature of society. As social conventions and inhibitions alter, so do kinds of murder, some vanishing, others developing. Murder in the course of a terrorist hijack or kidnapping has become a feature of recent times. A feature of the late-Victorian and Edwardian eras was the number of single and susceptible women with money who were courted by unscrupulous but charming rogues, whose sole aim was to deprive the ladies of their savings and sometimes of their lives. The circumstances surrounding the murder of Miss Holland and the social situation of those involved belong to a different age, when manners made a man and might unmake a maid.

Miss Camille Cecile Holland was a little spinster lady of fifty-five in 1898 when she met Samuel Herbert Dougal, then aged fifty-two, either at the Earl's Court Exhibition or through an advertisement in some journal dealing with persons seeking friendship and/or matrimony. Miss Holland, born in India, where her French mother had married a Liverpudlian merchant, was brought up largely in England by an aunt who ran a girls' school. When Aunt Sarah retired, Miss Holland became her companion and finally her heiress in 1893. She inherited about £6,000 in investments – a great deal of money then – as well as all her aunt's furniture and jewellery. Thus enriched and freed from family considerations – her only living relatives were two nephews and a niece – Miss Holland, then aged fifty, flowered, disguising the ravages of middle age by powdering her face, dying her hair red-gold and being most particular about her dress. She was not unattractive to gentlemen, who appreciated her very Victorian accomplishments: she played the piano, composed sentimental songs (both words and music), painted sentimental watercolours and, as a good Catholic, regularly went to church. But it seems she retained her virtue, left intact for many years after an early object of her affections, a young naval officer and the brother of a schoolfriend, drowned. In fond memory of him she always wore his cornelian ring.

Yet something was missing from her life, something she needed so desperately that at the age of fifty-five she sacrificed her virtue and her Victorian propriety by going away with a most unsuitable middle-aged married man and living with him as his wife. It was not as if she were mindlessly besotted with him, although she romanticised their association to start with, referring to him as her 'sweetheart'. Before long, she had realised just what a mercenary rogue he was – and yet she still went to live with him.

Samuel Herbert Dougal was a ruthless, amoral and utterly engaging beast. He possessed an animal vitality and magnetism that helped him to deprive women of their virtue and both men and women of their money. With few scruples he used his attractions and abilities to exploit others. His aim, it seems, was always enjoyment, whether as Jekyll or Hyde, and he had humours to match. Born at Bow in the East End of London in May 1846, he was given a basic education and acquired a job as an apprentice in a civil engineering office. But this was far too humdrum for his extrovert, adventurous nature, and when his debts and dissipations and the strictures of his father became intolerable he joined the army, enlisting at Chatham in the Royal Engineers on 6 March 1866. He remained with the RE for twenty-one years, serving in Ireland, Wales, and Nova Scotia, where he lived for ten years. He worked as a surveyor and a clerk, ending his service on 22 March 1887 as the chief clerk for the RE at Aldershot, with the rank of quartermaster-sergeant. His conduct and character were described as 'very good' and he was commended as being 'a very good clerk'.

His domestic life was not so good. In 1869, when he was twenty-three, he married a Miss Griffiths. She had four children by him and much unhappiness; apparently he drank and ill-treated her. They put up with each other for sixteen years until, towards the end of his ten years in Halifax, Nova Scotia, she suddenly fell ill, dying in agony within twelve hours. This was in June 1885. Two months later, after a brief leave in England, he returned to Halifax with a second wife, who in October was also suddenly taken ill. Vomiting excessively, she died. Both wives were buried in Halifax within twenty-four hours of their deaths which, having occurred in military quarters, were not required to be entered in a civil register. When his regiment returned to England early in 1887, the year of Queen Victoria's Golden Jubilee, he brought with him a young girl from Halifax, passing her off as his wife; he was now forty. Evidently she believed that his intentions were honourable and included marriage. She had a baby, but was so abused and beaten by him that she returned with her child to Halifax, posing as a widow.

After leaving the army Dougal became in turn a salesman, storekeeper, the steward of two Conservative clubs, publican, surveyor and clerk, along the way acquiring as many women as jobs (if not more) to keep him company and in a manner to which he had not hitherto been accustomed – most notably a widow who bore him two children and absconded when his brutality became unbearable. For a time he ran a pub at Ware in Hertfordshire with the help of an elderly woman and her money. But not for long: both the pub and a house insured by Dougal caught fire. He applied for the insurance but was arrested instead and tried at St Albans in December 1889. On being acquitted through lack of evidence he moved to Ireland, to Dublin, where he met Sarah White, eventually marrying her on 7 August 1892. She was his third wife and bore him two children.

Two years later he was back in London, wifeless but not a widower, seeking some other lady to support him. The unlucky woman this time was Miss Emily Booty, who met him as she emerged from a Camberwell bank. With her money they leased and furnished a house in Watlington, Oxfordshire, and at his invitation the third Mrs Dougal, more enduring than his other wives or women, brought her children to England and moved into Miss Booty's house. She suffered this and Dougal's behaviour for a few months, during which the youngest Dougal died of convulsions. But when she began packing her boxes Dougal became so threatening that she fled and went to the police. They searched *his* boxes and found within them some of Miss Booty's minor possessions: a linen-duster, two tea cloths and 4 yards of dimity. Arrested and charged with larceny, Dougal appeared at Oxford Quarter Sessions in April 1895, where he defended himself so impressively that the jury, also impressed it seems by his fine army record, found him not guilty.

The jury at the Central Criminal Court in January 1896 were not so impressionable when he was charged with forging the signature of Lord Frankfort on a cheque in Dublin, and he was sentenced to twelve months' hard labour. This he served in the Cane Hill Lunatic Asylum, where he was taken from Pentonville Prison suffering from acute melancholia after half-heartedly trying to hang himself in his cell.

He was pronounced sane and discharged in December 1896. By then he was fifty, and having served a prison sentence and lost his army pension as a result he found it difficult to get work. He was saved by his brother, Henry, who provided him with some clerical work at Biggin Hill for over a year, during which time Mrs Dougal returned to him and then left again, retreating to Dublin with her surviving child, Olive, when her husband's immoral and immoderate behaviour became too much for her. It also became too much for Henry, who sacked his brother and in so doing sent him back to London and into the arms of Miss Holland.

They met in September 1898 when she was staying at 37 Elgin Crescent, Bayswater, in a boarding house run by Mrs Florence Pollock, a widow. He visited Miss Holland there twice, posing as Captain Dougal, and once the middle-aged couple spent a weekend together at the Royal Hotel, Southend. Sometime in November, Miss Holland's dressmaker, Annie Whiting, calling on her one morning before (as she thought) Miss Holland was due to go off to Brighton with her sweetheart, was told: 'We've parted. I've found out he doesn't want me, only my money. What do you think – he wants me to withdraw all my money and let him invest it in his name. But I won't do it – so we've entirely parted.' Common sense had prevailed.

Yet so plausible and persuasive was her burly, bearded wooer, and his rude virility so bewitching, that on 2 December Dougal rented a furnished house, Parkmoor, at Hassocks near Brighton, at £6 a month. The money was Miss Holland's. Three days later she left Elgin Crescent and travelled to Brighton, ostensibly on her honeymoon. 'We were under the impression that Miss Holland was going away to be married,' remarked Mrs Pollock later. 'But some of my gentlemen thought not.'

The couple spent Christmas and New Year at Parkmoor, during which Dougal devised the scheme that would lead to Miss Holland's death. It is unlikely that he derived any satisfaction from the association, for his preference was for buxom girls. But he had to humour her, and possibly grimly amused himself in doing so.

It was doubtless on his persuasion that Miss Holland bought a farm for £1,550. A contract was drawn up in January 1899 by Dougal and an estate agent. It was in his name and he signed it. Then Miss Holland, showing unexpected wariness and independence, caused it to be destroyed and a new one to be made out in *her* name. This was signed on 19 January. A week later the couple moved to lodgings in Saffron Walden in Essex to be near their property – Coldhams Farm, Quendon near Clavering, soon to be renamed by Dougal as Moat House Farm, a name that would one day become notorious.

They remained at Saffron Walden for three months while the deeds and furnishing of the farm were finalised, occupying a bedroom and a sitting room in 4 Market Row. Dougal used to frequent local hostelries, including those at Bishop's Stortford. It is more than likely that he met and socialised with the landlord of The Grapes there, one George Chapman, who was later to be hanged for the murder by poison of his three wives.

Miss Holland, posing as Mrs Dougal, became quite friendly with her landlady, Mrs Henrietta Wisken, who later described her as follows: 'The lady I knew as Mrs Dougal, when dressed, looked about fifty years of age, but when in bed ten or fifteen years older. She had golden hair, grey or blue eyes, powdered face. She was about 5 feet 2 or 3 inches in height, and had a good figure for an aged person. She had very small feet, also very small hands. She had a very nice set of teeth.'

Although Mrs Wisken believed that Mrs Dougal was well educated and a lady, she was not fooled by her guest's pretences; she knew that the other woman dyed her hair, and without comment pushed letters under the Dougals' bedroom door that were marked 'Miss CC Holland'. She liked Mrs Dougal and her little brown-and-white dog called Jacko, and was doubtless intrigued by the middle-aged lovers, who seemed devoted to each other. Although Mr Dougal would sometimes be detained overnight in London 'by business', he would dutifully send telegraph messages to this effect, and on his return would greet his spouse most warmly, assuaging her evident suspicions. 'I don't believe he need stay up at all,' Miss Holland once said to Mrs Wisken. 'He could have come back if he'd wanted.' But on his return from Moat House Farm (where he was supervising the takeover of the property) he would ring the bell of his bicycle as he entered Market Row, and Miss Holland would leave her little sitting room and go to the front door to let him in, when he would greet her with a kiss.

On 27 April, she and Dougal left Saffron Walden in a pony and trap and were driven by an ancient farm-worker, Henry Pilgrim, to Moat House Farm. In three weeks' time, Miss Holland was dead.

The small, neat farmhouse was surrounded by a wide moat and reached by a little bridge. Fir trees and apple trees screened it from view – unnecessarily, as it was isolated in some bleak countryside, at that time but sparsely peopled. The nearest house, Rickling Vicarage, was about half a mile away.

Two days after the couple moved in, a twenty-year-old girl, Lydia Faithful, previously engaged by Miss Holland as a domestic servant, arrived. She moved out a week later, perhaps driven away by the attentions of Dougal – as was the next maidservant, Florence Havies, aged nineteen, who was hired by Miss Holland at Bishop's Stortford on 9 May. She arrived on Saturday 13 May, and departed a week later – the day after her new mistress disappeared.

Florrie's story, as told to the court, of her own and Miss Holland's last days at Moat House Farm, was as follows: 'The first night I slept in a little bedroom at the back of the house … The next morning I got up about six o'clock and commenced my duties. I was the only one up. About half an hour afterwards the prisoner came down alone and into the scullery where I was. He came up unawares and kissed me. I objected very much, and as soon as I saw Miss Holland I made a complaint to her.' Miss Holland was even more upset and cried bitterly. She also begged the girl not to leave, probably anxious on her own account, even apprehensive, wondering how she could extricate herself from her uncomfortable situation. However, she was not too timid to upbraid Dougal for his objectionable conduct.

A few days later, on the evening of Tuesday 16 May, Florrie retired to bed about nine o'clock. She said: 'Miss Holland went to bed at the same time. The prisoner remained downstairs in the dining room. Soon after, about ten minutes after, someone came to my door, I knew the voice … He called "Florrie" three times in an undertone, and pulled at the door with all his might.' The door had a bolt and he nearly pulled it off. 'I screamed for Mrs Dougal. Miss Holland came to my door and I had hysterics. After I came to, I made a complaint to Miss Holland. She took me into the prisoner's bedroom. He was in bed and pretending to be asleep. Mrs Dougal said: "It's no use pretending to be asleep." In consequence of what happened Miss Holland and I slept together in the same bed that night. I had made up my mind to go home, but yielding to pressure from Miss Holland I agreed to stay on.' Again, Miss Holland burst into tears and begged the girl not to leave her. Florrie felt oddly sorry for her. As she said later: 'She was so kind to me … I did not like to leave her alone.'

Reassured by each other's presence, the two women slept together in the spare bedroom on Wednesday and Thursday nights. During the day Florrie observed that no tradesmen or postmen called at the house, supplies being fetched by Dougal in the trap, and letters being taken by him off the postman at the outer gate.

On the early evening of Friday, 19 May, about half-past six, Miss Holland entered the kitchen where Florrie was at work: 'Do you mind if I go into the town to do a little shopping?' she asked. Replied Florrie: 'No. Not so long as Mr Dougal goes with you.' He would be doing so, said Miss Holland – he was driving the trap. She was wearing a dark dress with a bustle and a fall of lace at her throat; on her head was a white sailor hat with a veil. Before they left, Miss Holland called: 'Goodbye, Florrie. I shan't be long.' Florrie watched her go down the path, across the little bridge and get into the trap with Dougal. She never saw her again.

It grew dark; night fell and there was still no sign of either Dougal or Miss Holland. Florrie must have become very worried. Then at last the trap returned. It was now about half-past eight. Dougal entered the kitchen, alone. 'Where's the mistress?' Florrie exclaimed. He replied: 'Gone to London.' 'What!' cried Florrie, aghast. 'Gone to London and left me here all alone?' 'Yes,' said Dougal. 'But never mind, she's coming back, and I'm going to meet her.' He then went out to feed the pony, returning to the kitchen at about nine o'clock, remaining in the house for ten minutes or so. Then he went out again, saying he was going to meet Mrs Dougal at the station. He disappeared, but Florrie did not hear the trap depart. He was back half an hour later, saying: 'She hasn't come back. I suppose she'll come by that train something after ten o'clock.' A few minutes later he again left the house, saying he was going to meet the train. In half an hour he again returned. 'No, she hasn't come,' he said. 'I suppose she will come by the twelve o'clock train.' He disappeared yet again, not returning this time until a quarter to one. 'The mistress has not come,' he said. 'You had better go to bed.'

Florrie said later: 'I went up to the spare bedroom and stayed there, without undressing, for the rest of the night. I was awake and sat by the window all night' – ready to leap out should Dougal try to force the door. At 6.30 am he knocked at her door to wake her up. But she did not come downstairs until some farm labourers had arrived. He had made the breakfast: tea, bacon and eggs. He told her he had received a letter from Mrs Dougal, saying she had gone on holiday and that a woman friend would be coming to stay. Florrie paid little attention – she only wanted to leave. She was, in fact, waiting for her mother to arrive. The previous day she had sent her mother a note, which so alarmed Mrs Havies that as soon as she received it she hired a trap to get her from Newport to Moat House Farm.

On her arrival, she told Dougal what she thought of him and that she had come to take her daughter away. Dougal retorted that he had not harmed her, and relieved, no doubt, to get rid of the pair, put a month's wages for Florrie on the kitchen table and enough money for their return train fares to Waltham. They departed that morning and Dougal immediately telegraphed his real wife, telling her to come to Moat House Farm. That evening he and Pilgrim picked her up at Newport station.

Dougal had written to her some time before this, suggesting that she take up residence in a cottage in the vicinity. Instead, as Miss Holland was no longer there, she moved with her little daughter, Olive, into Moat House Farm, and was presented to the vicar of Clavering and his wife as Dougal's widowed daughter – as she was to the next maidservant to arrive at the farm, Emma Burgess. Not as fearful as Florrie, Emma remained for just under a year, when an 'indisposition' caused her temporary absence. In the meantime, all pretence at Mrs Dougal's kinship was dropped and she became generally known as what she was: Dougal's wife. For a time, despite frequent quarrels, she made the most of her situation as mistress of Moat House Farm. She wore some of Miss Holland's clothes, altered by Emma, and told the vicar's wife that Miss Holland was away yachting.

At one point the little dog, Jacko, ran away, turning up 6 1/2 miles away at Saffron Walden outside Mrs Wisken's house. She was delighted to see the dog and presumed she would soon be seeing his mistress, from whom she had heard nothing for over six months. No mistress appeared, and Mrs Wisken duly wrote to Moat House Farm, requesting some instructions concerning the dog. Dougal replied, and it was he who reappeared one night in Market Row to take the dog away. All Mrs Wisken's enquiries about Miss Holland were ignored.

Soon after Miss Holland's disappearance, Dougal had begun to forge her signature on cheques and letters, and by stages over the next two years he acquired the rest of her capital, which he banked in his own name. By September 1901 he had accumulated £2,912 15s. He also transferred the ownership of Moat House Farm to himself. Thus enriched and unthreatened, he dropped the pretence of being a farmer, although he still kept some cows, chickens and pigs. He bought a car, the first ever seen in that part of the country, and pursued the convivial pleasures of a country gentleman – hunting, shooting, smoking, drinking and generally enjoying himself. On one occasion he gave naked girls bicycle lessons in a field behind the farmhouse. Along the way he also sired several children on servant girls and other women, and at one time was pleasuring three sisters as well as their mother.

Naturally, rumours abounded in the neighbourhood about the goings-on at Moat House Farm, and in due course (January 1902) Mrs Dougal upped and left – in company with an engine driver, George Killick. Divorce proceedings were instituted by Dougal in May and, the suit being undefended, he was given a decree nisi on 1 August 1902. In September another servant girl, Kate Cranwell, aged eighteen, went home to have a child. This time, however, there was a paternity suit, which Dougal foolishly chose to contest, thus inviting the ire of the women in the case and the attention of the local law.

'You have had twelve months for forging cheques,' said Eliza Cranwell, who had gone with Dougal to Tenby to serve notice of divorce on his wife. 'You'll be hung next for the killing of that woman.' Eliza, a dressmaker, was Kate's older sister. Another sister, Millie, aged sixteen, who for some months had been a servant at Moat House Farm at the same time as Kate, was taken away from the farm by Mrs Dougal when she left. A fourth sister, Georgina Cranwell, became Dougal's last female servitor, staying at the farm in the winter of 1902-3.

In January 1903, a month after the birth of Kate Cranwell's child, the matter of Miss Holland's disappearance began to arouse more concern than ever. Where was she? That was the question that now concerned the King's Proctor, whose representative was investigating whether or not the decree nisi should be made absolute. Miss Holland was missing, allegedly abroad. But many if not all of her personal possessions remained at Moat House Farm. Was the local rumour true that Dougal had killed and buried her true? Fired by these enquries and by his own suspicions, PC Drew wrote to his Chief Constable at the end of January 1903. His letter began: 'Sir, I have the honour to report, for your information that it is a talk in this Village Clavering about Mr Herbert Samuel Dougal.'

Official police enquiries were set in motion and Miss Holland's nephews, her bankers and solicitors were contacted. Superintendent Pryke visited Moat House Farm five days before the decree nisi was actually rescinded on 9 March. He and Dougal had a friendly talk concerning 'a scandal in the village' and the whereabouts of Miss Holland. Said Pryke: 'I thought he had told me the truth, and I shook hands with him on leaving.' But the financial investigations of DI Bower of the CID at Scotland Yard, and DI Marden of the Essex Constabulary, gave them grounds for much unease. Of particular concern was a cheque dated 28 August 1902, made out to 'Mr J Heath' and signed 'Camille C Holland'. Her nephew, Ernest Holland, said the signature was definitely not his aunt's.

Meanwhile, Dougal had determined on flight. The day after Pryke's visit he withdrew £605 from his accounts and went up to London, where he stayed at the Central Hotel, Long Lane, returning to Moat House Farm a week later. He was only there for one night, his last in the place that had been his home for nearly four years.

On Friday, 13 March, he moved out with a pile of luggage, staying that night once again in the Central Hotel. Here he was joined on the Saturday by Georgina Cranwell, pregnant and also bearing a quantity of luggage, which she left in the cloakroom of Liverpool Street Station. She and Dougal then travelled on to Bournemouth for a weekend of pleasure, which included a steamer trip to Swanage. They stayed at the Coburg Hotel. On Tuesday they returned to London, where Dougal remained while Georgina went back to Essex and Moat House Farm.

On Wednesday, 18 March at about 1.30 pm, he entered the Bank of England in the City and presented fourteen £10 notes, which he wanted changed into smaller currency. The cashier, William Lawrence, on glancing at the notes, realised that some bore numbers of notes that had been stopped. He told Dougal: 'I am sorry, but I shall have to ask you to accompany me to the secretary's office.' Dougal demanded: 'Why? Are the notes stopped?' 'Some of them are,' said Lawrence, adding that the other man would not be detained long. He asked Dougal to endorse one of the notes, and Dougal wrote: 'Sydney Domwille, Upper Terrace, Bournemouth'.

As Dougal sat in the secretary's office, DI Henry Cox, on duty at the bank, was sent for. After a brief discussion with the secretary, Mr Dale, DI Cox approached Dougal and questioned him, concluding with a request that he should come to the detective's office in Old Jewry. 'Your name is Dougal,' said DI Cox casually. 'Yes,' admitted Dougal, and accompanied the inspector into the street, where he unexpectedly bolted, running towards Cheapside and then into Frederick's Place. It was a cul-de-sac. There Cox collared the hapless felon. They both fell to the ground in the ensuing struggle, but with the assistance of a constable, Cox soon overpowered the older, overweight man.

When Dougal was searched there were found on him eighty-three £5 notes, eight £10 notes, £63 in gold, a £5 gold coin, seven rings (five of them made for a woman and one being Miss Holland's cornelian ring), five watches, several items of feminine jewellery, six moonstones, a walking stick, a pipe and a cloakroom ticket. He was charged with the forgery of the cheque made out to Mr J Heath and taken the following day to the police station at Saffron Walden. That day, a search for the remains of Miss Holland at Moat House Farm began.

The police moved in, led by DS Scott, who took up residence in the farmhouse. He and his helpers, having examined every inch of the house, began to dig, concentrating mainly on the moat, which was drained. For five weeks they dug, until the farm looked like a battlefield. Little Jacko roamed about, deaf now and almost blind. Then Inspector Bower heard locally that Dougal had caused a drainage ditch to be filled in soon after his arrival at the farm; it had run from the horse pond to the moat and was full of sewage and manure – 'black liquid filth', according to DS Scott. His men opened it up.

On the afternoon of Monday, 27 April, four years to the day since Miss Holland's arrival at Moat House Farm, a small boot was unearthed by a pitchfork. Inside was a skeletal foot.

Slowly, all that remained of Miss Holland's fully clothed corpse was revealed, partly preserved by blackthorn branches that had been laid on top of her. The remains were dug out in a slab, which was then placed on two chairs in a conservatory. Mrs Wisken managed to identify the body, chiefly through its many garments, some of which she had stitched and altered herself. On the day she died Miss Holland had been wearing, apart from a dress, two pairs of combinations, steel-framed corsets, two underbodices, stockings, bloomers and two petticoats. She had been shot at close range. The bullet from a revolver that was proved to have belonged to Dougal was found inside the skull. It had entered a few inches above and behind the right ear and had been fired, according to the pathologist, Dr Pepper, 'by a person in a higher position than the deceased'. Evidently Dougal, from his seat in the trap, had leaned over and shot Miss Holland as she stood on the ground with her back to him.

On Monday, 27 April 1903, the *Essex County Chronicle* noted: 'Throughout the week people have flocked to Moat Farm in crowds, the majority of visitors being ladies. Oranges and nuts were sold as at a village fair … Souvenir postcards of the Moat House and of the grounds, showing many of the holes made by the police and the tent-like awning which conceals the grave, commanded an enormous sale. A number of sightseers brought Kodaks with them in search of effective snapshots.'

Samuel Dougal was charged on Thursday, 30 April 1903 by DI Alfred Martin with 'wilfully, maliciously, feloniously, with malice aforethought' killing and slaying Miss Holland. He was charged in the dining room of Moat House Farm on a dismal, rainy day, the day on which the inquest was opened in the old barn.

Dougal was remanded several times, finally being committed for trial, protesting his innocence, on 29 May. In the interim he wrote several cheerfully chatty letters to the women in his life, including Mrs Dougal, who became a Roman Catholic and began calling herself Mary Magdalene.

The trial began in the Shire Hall at Chelmsford, Essex, on Monday, 22 June before Mr Justice Wright. Leading counsel for the Crown was Mr CF Gill, KC, while the accused, who gave no evidence, was defended by Mr George Elliott. At 4.50 pm on the following day, after an absence of seventy-five minutes, the jury found Dougal guilty and he was sentenced to death. To this he made no reply.

An appeal was later dismissed. Dougal himself wrote to the Home Secretary, confessing now that he had indeed shot Miss Holland – by accident. His explanation was that on their return from Stansted, where they had done some shopping, 'stopping on the way at the Chequers public-house and had a glass of whisky each', Miss Holland had seated herself on a box at the coach-house door while he stabled the horse. As she gazed at the starlit sky he picked up a loaded revolver lying on a shelf and began unloading it – earlier that day he had done some shooting with it. The gun, he said, was in his left hand when she said: 'Come and look at the beautiful silvery moon.' He moved towards her and 'the revolver accidentally exploded'. Her head fell forward. He said: 'I hope you are not hurt, dear.' Thinking she had fainted he supported her, saying tenderly: 'Speak, Cecily dear.' Then, he said, he ran to the house for some brandy and was confronted by the maid, who asked him where her mistress was. He replied that she had gone to London. He then returned with the brandy, he said, and found that her pulse was still beating:

> I took off her hat and veil and could see no blood, and afterwards removed her cloak, and still saw no blood. At this time I became demented, not knowing what I did. I took her in my arms and carried her up into the fields where there was a breeze, thinking it would revive her ... I went back indoors, and shortly after returned to her and found her dead. I did not know what to do then. I carried her back towards the coach-house, and seeing the open ditch ... I laid her on some straw in the ditch, and returned to the house again. I could not rest, so returned to where she was. I knelt down and kissed her, and placed a piece of lace over her face, and put some straw over her ... Afterwards I placed a branch of a thorn-bush on the straw, so that the fowls could not scratch the straw off her body. After that I walked about the yard.'

He could not sleep that night, he said, and the following morning Alfred Shaw, who had already begun filling in the ditch, continued doing so 'until the trench was level, taking about a fortnight'.

Dougal was hanged at Chelmsford Prison on 8 July 1903 on a bright, sunny morning. He was fifty-seven. The executioner was William Billington, aged twenty-eight, second son of James Billington, who had died in 1901. All three of James's sons became executioners. William, known as Billie Billington, had carried out the last hanging in Newgate Prison in May 1902, that of George Woolfe, executed for the stabbing death of his girlfriend.

At Dougal's execution, a zealous chaplain, determined to save the condemned man's soul on the scaffold, demanded of Dougal, by then hooded and haltered, 'Are you guilty or not guilty?' There was no response. Again the chaplain repeated the question. Dougal's hooded head half-turned and his voice said 'Guilty' as the lever was pulled.

The chaplain's explanation for his conduct, which was criticised by the papers and in parliament, was that Dougal had promised to confess before his execution but had failed to do so. 'My spiritual anxiety became intense,' said the chaplain. 'I prayed earnestly with him during the last quarter of an hour, during which he sobbed … I knew not what to do more, so under strong impulse, and quite on the inspiration of the moment, I made the strong appeal at the scaffold.'

Dougal's body was buried in Chelmsford Prison. On Miss Holland's grave in Saffron Walden churchyard a cross was raised on which was carved the figure of an angel receiving a sweet young girl. The inscription said that she died, aged fifty-six, 'under distressing circumstances'. Little Jacko, who had finally found a home with Mrs Wisken, died a year later; he was stuffed and mounted in a glass case in her parlour.

12

ALFRED AND ALBERT STRATTON

THE MURDERS OF MR AND MRS FARROW, 1905

Petty crime was the background to murder in the case of the Stratton brothers, as it has been so often. But their trial is unique in that for the first time in a British court fingerprint evidence was used to obtain a conviction for murder.

Alfred Stratton, aged twenty-three, and Albert, twenty, both labourers, lived in south-east London, at Deptford. Both had previous convictions for housebreaking and burglary. They came to believe that an elderly local tradesman, seventy-one-year-old Thomas Farrow, kept a cache of money in his chandler's store, which dealt in oil, paint, candles and soap, at 34 High Street, Deptford. He and his wife, Ann, aged sixty-five, lived above the shop, which was owned not by them but by an absentee landlord, Mr Chapman.

At about 7.30 am on Monday, 27 March 1905, their young assistant, William Jones, arrived for work and found the shop door open. This was not unusual, for Mr Farrow often rose early to supply painters and decorators with materials on their way to work. Jones went in and called out. No one responded. He could see that some chairs had been overturned. On going into the back parlour, he found Mr Farrow in his nightshirt dead on the floor and drenched in blood; his head had been badly battered. Mrs Farrow was later discovered in a similar state in her bed upstairs, unconscious; she died in hospital four days later.

Jones ran off to summon help. The police, headed by Chief Inspector Frederick Fox, surmised that the old man had come downstairs at about 7 am in response to someone knocking at the shop door. Attacked by the man or men he let into the shop, he had managed to reach the parlour before being bludgeoned to death with a kind of cosh, a lead ball attached to a piece of rope. His wife, awakened by the rumpus below and calling out anxiously, probably then had also to be silenced by the cosh. The cash box, in which there were only a few pounds, had been broken open and was empty. Two masks made from black stockings that were found in the shop seemed to indicate that two assailants were involved. Fox noticed what looked like a fingerprint on the cash box's metal tray – the print of a bloody right thumb.

The Assistant Commissioner (Crime), Melville Macnaghten, then head of the CID, took a particular interest in the case, especially when he saw the smudged fingerprint on the underside of the cash box's inner tray. He took the tray to the new Fingerprint Bureau at the Yard, which had been established in July 1901.

The Bureau's chief, DI Charles Collins, had had some success with identifying villains through their fingerprints, but this was still a doubtful and doubted science. However, all those who were known to have touched the tray, including the victims, the shop-boy and a policeman, were now carefully fingerprinted. The thumb print belonged to none of them. Chief Inspector Fox thought the murderers must be local men – why had they worn masks unless they feared recognition? So all the minor villains in the Deptford area were sought out and their alibis checked.

The Stratton brothers, already known to the police, were not to be found. But Alfred Stratton's girlfriend, Annie Cromarty, was questioned. Disgruntled and afraid (she had a black eye), she eventually admitted that the brothers had been out all night the previous Sunday, that Alfred had later destroyed the coat he had been wearing, and that he had dyed his brown shoes black. A milkman and his boy assistant revealed that they had seen two men leave the chandler's shop in a hurry about 7.15 am on Monday, leaving the door open. One was wearing a dark brown suit and a cap (Alfred), the other (Albert) a dark blue serge suit and a bowler hat.

The following Sunday, Alfred was picked up in a public house and Albert, the younger brother, in lodgings in Stepney. They were brought to Tower Bridge police station. Both had their fingerprints taken, and Alfred's thumb print was found to match the bloody print on the cash box. There were eleven points of resemblance, it was later said in court.

The Stratton brothers' trial took place at the Central Criminal Court in the Old Bailey in May 1905, before Mr Justice Channell. DI Collins said that the Fingerprint Bureau now had about 85,000 sets of prints. Knowledgeably questioned by the prosecutor, Mr Richard Muir, who had studied the matter, Collins described how the system of fingerprint identification worked. As an example, the fingerprints of one of the jurymen were taken and examined by the rest of the jury. Mr HG Rooth, defending Alfred Stratton, said that the fingerprint system was 'unreliable' – it 'savoured more of the French courts than of English justice' – and this new-fangled evidence was contested by some so-called experts for the defence. The judge himself was dubious about the irrefutable nature of such evidence. But the jury had no doubts and found both brothers guilty. Each blamed the other for the murders. While awaiting trial, Albert, the younger brother, had told a man who worked in the jail: 'I reckon he [Alfred] will get strung up and I shall get ten years.'

In the event they were both hanged together, on 23 May 1905.

The chief executioner was John Billington, James Billington's youngest son. Aged twenty-five, John was assisted by Harry Pierrepoint, a handsome, moustached man, aged twenty-seven, who had first assisted James Billington at an execution in November 1901.

Their wages, unchanged since Berry's time, were still ten guineas for the head hangman and two for his assistant.

Harry Pierrepoint had previously been employed in a worsted mill in Clayton, Yorkshire, before toiling in a butcher's shop and then with a firm of cabinetmakers. He had read avidly about the exploits of the Bradford hangman, James Berry, and more recently about those of James Billington, who had hanged Dr Cream and Mrs Dyer. When he was not yet twenty-three, Pierrepoint wrote in February 1901 (three weeks after the death of Queen Victoria) to the Home Secretary, offering his services as an executioner. His first hanging as chief executioner was in March 1902, when he was twenty-four. His son, Albert, who would hang more men and women than anyone else, before and since, was born on 30 March 1905.

The Strattons were hanged in Wandsworth Prison two months after that event by James Billington, assisted by Harry Pierrepoint. The brothers occupied cells on separate floors, one above the other. The two hangmen peered at the brothers through spy-holes and did their calculations. The elder brother, Alfred, who weighed about 147 lb, would be given a drop of 6 ft 6 in; Albert's drop – he was heavier – would be 7 ft 6 in. A practice drop on the scaffold in the execution shed was carried out with sandbags, and Harry Pierrepoint wrote the names 'Alfred' and 'Albert' in chalk on the wooden trap doors below the appropriate nooses. The following morning the two brothers were brought, arms pinioned behind their backs, in silent procession to the scaffold, the only voice being that of a priest reading the burial service. Their legs were bound and their faces hidden in white bags or caps before the nooses were placed around their heads and drawn tight, with the knot behind the left lower jaw. During this process Albert called out: 'Alfred – have you given your heart to God?' Alfred's muffled reply, after a pause, was 'Yes.' They fell together.

Three years later, in 1908, the hanging of persons under the age of sixteen was abolished. Between 1908 and 1921 inclusively, a period of fourteen years, no woman was hanged, although fifty-one women were convicted of murder, sentenced to death and then reprieved.

DR CRIPPEN

THE MURDER OF CORA CRIPPEN, 1910

Very few doctors have been murderers, but not a few may have committed murder without any suspicion being aroused. They have both the know-how and the wherewithal to bring about illness and death: the instruments, the dangerous drugs and poisons. They can pronounce with authority on the cause of death and sign certificates to this effect. They have also the necessary facility of viewing people as objects. The doctors who have killed (and have been detected) have largely been poisoners, as one would expect. Such a one was Dr Crippen, whose extraordinary story also illustrates the frequent connection between murder and dressing-up, playing a part and the use of pseudonyms.

Hawley Harvey Crippen was born in Coldwater, Michigan, on 11 September 1862, and acquired his medical training through the winning of diplomas in Cleveland, London and New York. His father was a dry-goods merchant called Myron Crippen. In 1887, young Crippen married Charlotte Bell, his first wife; they had a son, Otto. She died in about 1890 and two or three years later in Jersey City, he married Cora Turner, whom he first met when she was seventeen and living with another man, a stove manufacturer. Her real name was Kunigunde Mackamotzki, her father being a Russian Pole and her mother German. Crippen paid for Cora to train as an opera singer, though to no avail, and when they settled in 1900 in London, where he become the manager of a patent medicine firm, she tried to succeed as a music-hall artiste, calling herself Belle Elmore. She sang in various halls in London and elsewhere, going away for about two weeks at a time. Her singing voice, however, was as small as her talents, though her speaking voice was loud and clear with a sharp American twang. She herself was short and stout, and with her dark eyes and hair, bright jewels and colourful clothes, seemed like a plump bird of paradise. Her flamboyant appearance was at odds with her meanness, both of which were mildly tolerated by her husband.

Considerate and courteous, Crippen was a short (5 ft 3 in) slightly feminine man, with thinning hair, a long and straggly sandy moustache, and prominent grey eyes behind gold-rimmed glasses. 'Somewhat slovenly in appearance,' said a later police description. 'Wears his hat at back of head. Very plausible and quiet spoken, remarkably cool and collected demeanour … Throws his feet outward when walking.' He was known as 'Peter'. He worked for a patent medicine company, Munyon's, who paid him £3 a week, and was a partner with Dr Rylance in Yale Tooth Specialists, situated in Albion House, New Oxford Street.

In September 1905, the Crippens moved to 39 Hilldrop Crescent, a semi-detached house that they rented at £52 10s a year. The crescent connected with Camden Road and was less than half a mile from Holloway Prison. They occupied separate bedrooms, and had frequent rows. 'She went in and out just as she liked,' said Crippen, 'and did what she liked. It was of no interest to me … I was rather a lonely man and rather miserable.' By this time Mrs Crippen had acquired many music-hall friends – although on her last appearance on stage, during an artistes' strike at the Bedford and Euston Palace, she was hissed at for being a blackleg. Thenceforth she enthusiastically embraced the office of honorary treasurer of the Music-Hall Ladies Guild. She also persuaded her husband to become a Roman Catholic. They frequently entertained at home but their private lives were quite squalid, mainly spent in the dingy and disorderly basement kitchen. The grimy windows were never opened – she disliked fresh air – and her two cats were never let out. Her gentleman friends were let in, however, when Dr Crippen was at work. They gave her gifts and also, it seems, money.

By this time her husband had also found consolation, having fallen in love with the typist who had worked for him for more than seven years, Ethel le Neve, a shy, soft-spoken, boyishly attractive girl, born in 1883, who was slightly taller than he. By 1910 she had been his mistress for three years. She was twenty-seven; he forty-eight; Mrs Crippen was thirty-five.

Perhaps Ethel le Neve had by then become rather discontented, wishing to be more than a mistress. Certainly Mrs Crippen, aware of her husband's association with his typist, was threatening to leave, to go and live with one of her gentlemen and take all 'her' money with her. Most of their money, £600, was in fact banked in a joint deposit account, to which she had somehow contributed £330. Significantly, on 15 December 1909, she gave twelve months' notice of withdrawal of the whole amount, which would have been paid to her without question in December 1910. Dr Crippen, on the other hand, was in some financial trouble. Entertaining Ethel must have been costly – they made love in hotels – and in November 1909 Munyon's stopped employing him as a manager and only paid him a commission on his sales. Even these payments came to an end on 31 January 1910.

That night, the Crippens gave a small dinner party for two retired music-hall artistes, Mr and Mrs Paul Martinetti. Dinner was served in the breakfast room, next to the kitchen. Later they went upstairs to the parlour, where they played whist. The Martinettis – 'It was quite a nice evening and Belle was very jolly' – left at 1.30 am, saying goodbye on the gas-lit front-door steps that led down to the dark, cold street. 'Don't come down, Belle,' said Clara Martinetti. 'You'll catch a cold.'

When the guests had departed there was a marital row, Mrs Crippen accusing her husband of not having escorted old and ill Mr Martinetti upstairs to the lavatory, when he went there earlier that evening. 'She abused me,' said Crippen in his first statement to the police. 'She said: "This is the finish of it – I won't stand it any longer – I shall leave you tomorrow, and you will never hear of me again!"' She had said this so often, he continued, that 'I did not take much notice of it. But she did say one thing which she had never said before, viz, that I was to arrange to cover up any scandal with our mutual friends and the Guild, the best way I could.'

A fortnight before this, on 17 January, Crippen had ordered five grains of a narcotic poison called hyoscine (for homoeopathic purposes) from a New Oxford Street chemist's, Lewis and Burrows. They had had none in stock, but had been able to deliver the crystals on 19 January. He had signed the poisons register.

The morning after the dinner, on Tuesday, 1 February, Crippen called at the Martinettis' flat in Shaftesbury Avenue to enquire about Mr Martinetti's health. 'How is Belle?' enquired Mrs Martinetti. 'Oh, she's all right,' came the reply. On 2 February and 9 February, Crippen pawned some of his wife's jewellery in Oxford Street for £195, more than he used to earn from Munyon's in a year.

On the afternoon of 2 February Mrs Crippen failed to appear for the usual meeting of the Music-Hall Ladies Guild, held every Wednesday at Albion House in a room loaned by Dr Crippen. Miss le Neve, however, appeared with two letters signed by Belle Elmore, but not in her handwriting, which said that she had been obliged to go to America because of a relative's illness and would have to resign from the Guild.

Crippen said later that Miss le Neve spent the night with him in 39 Hilldrop Crescent. She stayed other nights and he began giving her his wife's jewellery and some of her clothes.

Belle's friends thought it odd when they did not hear from her – not a single letter or a postcard. They were amazed when on 20 February, at the dinner and ball organised by the Guild for their Benevolent Fund at the Criterion (each ticket cost half a guinea), they saw Dr Crippen with Miss le Neve, who was wearing a brooch that had belonged to Belle. Later they saw the typist wearing Belle's furs. Their anxious requests for news about Belle and her address were disposed of by Crippen, who said she was 'right up in the wilds of the mountains of California'. Later they were told that she was seriously ill with double pneumonia. Meanwhile, on 12 March, Miss le Neve moved permanently into 39 Hilldrop Crescent, sometimes posing as the housekeeper, although she had now acquired a French maid.

Since the beginning of February she had in fact spent few nights in her own lodgings, and before she left them on 12 March she gave her landlady, Mrs Jackson, articles of clothing, including six coats, six skirts, five blouses, three nightgowns, stockings and hats, telling her that Mrs Crippen had gone to America. According to Mrs Jackson, Ethel le Neve had been much depressed and in tears in January. 'Very tired and strange,' said Mrs

Jackson. She enquired why. 'It's Miss Elmore,' Ethel had confessed. 'When I see them go away together it makes me realise what my position is … She's been threatening to go away … and when she does that the doctor's going to divorce her and marry me.' She was much more cheerful at the beginning of February, 'Really happy'. When Mrs Jackson jokingly asked her if someone had died and left her money, Ethel answered that 'someone' had gone to America.

On Wednesday, 16 March, Dr Crippen gave his landlord three months' notice of leaving the house. On Thursday, 24 March, he and Ethel, calling themselves Mr and Mrs Crippen, went to Dieppe for five days over Easter. The same morning, Mrs Martinetti received a telegram sent from Victoria Station: 'Belle died yesterday at six o'clock … Shall be away a week. Peter.' It is thought that during the crossing to France, Belle's head, in a weighted handbag, was dropped overboard.

During their absence a notice of her death appeared in *The Era* on 26 March. When the couple returned, Peter set about dealing with mourning friends, calls and letters of condolence. He said his wife had been cremated in America, and in May told people that he had her ashes at home.

Crippen must have felt, after three months had passed, that he and Ethel were secure, for on 18 June he arranged with his landlord to stay on at Hilldrop Crescent until 29 September. But ten days later Mr and Mrs Nash, who were friends of Belle and had recently returned from America where Mrs Nash had been touring the music halls as Lil Hawthorne, called and questioned Crippen about his wife's demise. Dissatisfied with the little doctor's answers, Mr Nash communicated his unease on 30 June to a friend of his, Detective Superintendent Froest at Scotland Yard, who was in charge of the newly formed Serious Crimes squad. Chief Inspector Walter Dew was asked to investigate further, and on Friday, 8 July visited Hilldrop Crescent with DS Mitchell.

There they encountered a French maid and Ethel le Neve, who was wearing one of Mrs Crippen's brooches. Ethel said she was the housekeeper; she agreed to accompany the policemen to Albion House, where Crippen worked. The three of them went by omnibus, and when they reached the building Ethel ran up the stairs to the third-floor office to let the doctor know who had come to see him. Having heard the reason for Dew's visit, Crippen said: 'I suppose I had better tell the truth.' 'Yes, that would be better,' Dew remarked. Crippen continued: 'The stories I have told about her death are untrue. As far as I know, she is still alive.' In between teeth-pulling and making up prescriptions, assisted by Miss le Neve, the doctor dictated a lengthy statement. It took five hours, with a break for lunch with Dew in an Italian restaurant. The doctor said that Mrs Crippen had left him for another man and that she had disappeared by the time he came back from work on 1 February. He said: 'I sat down to think it over as to how to cover up her absence without any scandal.'

At the conclusion of the statement and of the afternoon, Crippen and his assistant-housekeeper accompanied the two police officers back to Hilldrop Crescent, and obligingly allowed the house to be searched. Both Crippen and Ethel watched from a doorway as Dew cast his eye over the coal-cellar. The only thing that seemed odd to him was the fact that Mrs Crippen had left a large quantity of her flashy gowns behind. He left the house, however, fairly satisfied that nothing was amiss, although he wondered why Crippen had gone to such lengths to hide the alleged reason for his wife's disappearance, especially as he seemed to be making the most of her absence with Ethel le Neve.

Over the weekend the inspector pondered, remained unperturbed, and then returned to Albion House on Monday, 11 July for a few more routine enquiries. He was astonished to hear from Crippen's partner, Dr Rylance, that on the previous Saturday Rylance had received a letter from Crippen instructing him to wind up his business affairs and household accounts. Wrote Crippen: 'In order to escape trouble I shall be obliged to absent myself for a time.' Dew learned that Crippen had also sent the office boy out to buy some clothing suitable for a boy.

Dew returned to Hilldrop Crescent. It was occupied by the French maid, whom the police later sent back to France. Of Crippen and Ethel there was no sign. In fact, at that moment they were in Belgium, staying at the Hotel des Ardennes in Brussels, where they remained for eight days. Travel between countries was easier back then – no passports were required.

In London, Crippen's house and garden were searched again and again, on 12 and 13 July, and at last Dew's persistence produced a result beyond anything he expected. Prodding the coal-cellar floor with a poker, he discovered that some of the bricks were loose. He and DS Mitchell prized them out. Underneath was a stinking heap of human flesh: viscera, skin, and hair, but no bones. Dew and Mitchell revived themselves with Crippen's brandy. They had found all that remained of Belle Elmore.

The medical experts who examined the remains were Dr Pepper and Dr Bernard Spilsbury, the latter then aged thirty-three. His consequent appearance in court marked the first occasion he would give evidence for the prosecution in a major murder trial. He and Pepper concluded that the remains had been part of a stout female, who bleached her hair and had had an abdominal operation, apparently when her ovaries were removed: there was a scar. Traces of hyoscine, enough to kill her, were found in various organs. Taken orally in sweet tea or coffee, the hyoscine would have caused delirium, then drowsiness, leading to unconsciousness within an hour, and ending within twelve hours in paralysis and death.

On 16 July, a warrant was issued for the arrest of Crippen and Ethel le Neve, who were wanted for 'murder and mutilation'. The police bill, written by Dew, described Ethel as being 5 ft 5 in, pale-faced, with light brown hair, large grey-blue eyes. 'Nice-looking, pleasant lady-like appearance. Quiet, subdued manner, talks quietly, looks intently when in conversation.'

On Wednesday, 20 July the SS *Montrose* sailed from Antwerp bound for Quebec. Two hours later, the ship's commander, Captain Kendall, became suspicious about two of his saloon passengers – Mr John Philo Robinson and his sixteen-year-old son John – who both came on board in brown suits, soft grey hats, and white canvas shoes – Crippen had shaved off his moustache. The couple were unusually affectionate. Two days later, Captain Kendall sent a lengthy wireless message to the ship's owners in Liverpool, just before the ship steamed out or range of transmitters on land, outlining his certainty that the Robinsons were the wanted couple:

She seems thoroughly under his thumb, and he will not leave her for a moment. Her suit is anything but a good fit. Her trousers, very tight about the hips, are split a bit down the back and secured with large safety pins ... He continually shaves his upper lip and his beard is growing nicely ... The mark on his nose caused through wearing spectacles has not worn off ... He sits about on the deck reading [Pickwick Papers, Metropolis, A Name to Conjure With, *and* The Four Just Men] *... When my suspicions were aroused I quietly collected all the English papers that mentioned the murder ... All the 'boy's' manners at table were most lady-like ... Crippen kept cracking nuts for her and giving her half his salad ... On two or three occasions when walking on the deck I called after him by his assumed name, and he took no notice. I repeated it, and it was only owing to the presence of mind of Miss le Neve that he turned round ... He would often sit on deck and look up aloft at the wireless aerial and listen to the crackling electric spark messages being sent by the Marconi operator. He said: 'What a wonderful invention it is!'*

If Crippen had elected to travel third class, Captain Kendall might have never have noticed him. Had Crippen sailed to New York instead of to Canada, which was a British dominion and thus subject to British law, he might as an American, have avoided immediate arrest and had to be extradited.

The voyage lasted eleven days, during which 'The Chase of Crippen' featured every morning in the *Daily Mail*. The Robinsons, in blissful but anxious ignorance, strolled arm–in–arm along the decks.

As the ship steamed slowly up the St Lawrence River towards Quebec on Sunday, 31 July, a pilot boat came alongside about 9 am. On board was Dew, dressed as a pilot. He had sailed from Liverpool on 23 July on a faster ship, the SS *Laurentic*. Mr Robinson was on deck, relishing the sight of land; in a few hours he would be safe. Master Robinson was in Cabin 5, reading a novel. 'Who are all these people?' Crippen asked the ship's surgeon. 'It's the pilot boat,' came the reply. 'There seem to be a good many pilots,' murmured Crippen. Once on board, Dew went to the bridge and met Captain Kendall. Looking down on the deck below he saw a man he thought he knew. He descended the companion way, his heart pounding. He approached the little man, who looked oddly naked without his moustache. 'Good morning, Dr Crippen' he said. 'I am Chief Inspector Dew.' It was the finest moment of his life. Crippen's arms went up, as if to parry a blow. He replied: 'Good morning, Mr Dew.'

Crippen was formally arrested and charged. Inspector Dew then saw Miss le Neve in her cabin. She was dressed in an ill-fitting boy's suit. 'Miss le Neve?' he enquired. 'I am Chief Inspector Dew.' She looked at him, screamed and fainted.

Later Crippen said: 'I am not sorry – the anxiety has been too much … It is only fair to say that she knows nothing about it. I never told her anything.' Dew sent a triumphant message back to Scotland Yard – *Handcuffs, London. Crippen and le Neve arrested. Dew.*

Detained in Quebec for nearly three weeks, Crippen and Ethel were brought back to England on the SS *Megantic*, boarding the ship from a tug as she sailed towards Quebec from Montreal en route for Liverpool. On board the *Megantic*, Crippen travelled as Mr Nield and Dew as Mr Doyle. Crippen read a lot, mostly love stories, and had many agreeable conversations with his captor. He was kept separate from Ethel le Neve, however, who was guarded by wardresses, and prevented from seeing her.

One evening, Dr Crippen was taking his exercise on the boat deck, walking up and down while handcuffed to Dew, when he suddenly announced: 'I don't know how things may go. They may go right or they may go all wrong with me … I want to ask you if you will let me see her. I won't speak to her. She's been my only comfort for the past three years.'

Dew complied with his request. Crippen was brought to the door of his cabin that night and Ethel to the door of hers. Some distance apart they gazed at each other. Not a word was spoken. Dew felt embarrassed and averted his eyes. The couple next saw each other in court.

Huge crowds booed and jeered the arrival of Crippen and his mistress in England. They were besieged at Liverpool and at Euston station. Both were committed for trial.

A month or so later, Mrs Crippen's remains were interred at Finchley Cemetery on 10 October. Some bits of skin were retained to be put in evidence, and at the trial were passed around the court in a soup plate.

The trial of Dr Crippen began at the new Old Bailey – which had been recently rebuilt and reopened by Edward VII in 1907 – on Tuesday, 18 October 1910, before the Lord Chief Justice, Lord Alverstone. Mr Richard Muir appeared for the Crown and Mr Aspinall Tobin for the defence. Miss le Neve was to be tried separately, and only with being an accessory after the fact. Crippen's moustache once more adorned his face.

His defence was that there was no proof that the remains in the cellar were those of a woman, let alone of Belle Elmore. They had been buried, it was suggested, without the accused's knowledge, even before he came to the house. The prosecution's medical evidence to the contrary was reinforced by the fact that three suits of pyjamas – a piece of one had been found with the remains – had been sent to 39 Hilldrop Crescent by Jones Brothers of Holloway in January 1909, and not in 1905 as Crippen claimed. The pathologist, Bernard Spilsbury, was unable to say whether what remained of the flesh was male of female. But he identified a piece of skin bearing an abdominal scar as being consistent with Mrs Crippen's medical history. The trial ended on its fifth day when Crippen, having been found guilty – the jury were out for twenty-seven minutes – was sentenced to death. 'I still protest my innocence,' he said.

The trial of Ethel le Neve began on 25 October before the same judge and with the same prosecutor. She was defended by Mr FE Smith, KC, afterwards Lord Birkenhead. The trial lasted one day. She did not give any evidence, and was acquitted and freed.

Crippen's appeal was heard and dismissed on 5 November. He was hanged in Pentonville Prison by John Ellis, assisted by William Willis, on 23 November 1910. Harry Pierrepoint was not involved; he had been removed from the Home Office list of executioners after an execution in July when, drunk and 'using the most disgusting language' he had assaulted Ellis.

Three days before his execution, Crippen made a public statement, saying that Ethel le Neve was entirely innocent. He extolled their love:

This love was not of a debased or degraded character. It was ... a good love ... Her mind was beautiful to me ... Whatever sin there was – and we broke the law – it was my sin, not hers ... As I face eternity, I say that Ethel le Neve has loved me as few women love men, and that her innocence of any crime ... is absolute ... Surely such love as hers for me will be rewarded.

Shortly before his execution he wrote a letter to her:

There are less than two days left to us. Only one more letter after this can I write to you, and only two more visits ... Your letter, written early Saturday, came to me last Saturday evening and soon after the Governor brought me the dreadful news about ten o'clock. When he had gone I kissed your face in the photo ... It was some consolation, although in spite of all my greatest efforts it was impossible to keep down a great sob and my heart's agonised cry.

His last request was that a photograph of her, as well as her letters, should be buried with him. They were.

Walter Dew retired from active duty, aged 47, three weeks before Crippen was hanged. His memoirs were published in 1938 and he died at Worthing in 1947.

It has been alleged that Ethel le Neve emigrated to Australia; also that for many years she ran a Tea Room at Jumper's Corner, Iford Bridge, near Bournemouth. But it seems that after Crippen died, she left England for Canada, where she settled in Toronto and worked as a secretary, using the surname Nelson. In 1916 she returned to England and married an accountancy clerk, Stanley Smith, in Croydon, who is said to have looked like Crippen. They had two children. He died some years later of a heart attack. At some point she called herself Ethel Harvey. A grandmother, suffering from cataracts, she died in 1967, aged 84.

14

STEINIE MORRISON

THE MURDER OF LEON BERON, 1911

Leon Beron was a Russian Jew and a forty-eight-year-old widower. His English was poor: he spoke mainly Yiddish and French. He had come to England in 1894 from Paris with his aged father, two brothers and a sister. To all appearances, with his waxed moustache, imperial beard, natty clothes and cosmopolitan affectations, Leon Beron was a man of some substance and even importance. He was indeed a man of property, although the only merit of the nine mean little houses he owned in the East End of London in Russell Court, Stepney, was that they provided him with most of his income. The rents totalled about ten shillings a week. Two shillings of this went towards the payment of his accommodation, a room above a fruit shop in 133 Jubilee Street, Stepney, and one and sixpence a day was spent at the Warsaw restaurant at 32 Osborn Street, Whitechapel, a kosher eating place. There, for an all-inclusive price, he could buy lunch, dinner and countless glasses of tea, and spend the whole day gossiping and arguing with other Jews, mainly emigrés with no leaning towards or need for work.

As a landlord, Beron was more affluent than most and exhibited this status in his dress. He wore a large gold watch and chain, from which also hung a five-guinea piece. In a purse attached to his waistcoat by a safety pin were, it was said, about twenty golden sovereigns.

In December 1910, Steinie Morrison began to be seen in the Warsaw restaurant at Leon Beron's side. Morrison, aged about thirty, was also a Russian Jew, although he claimed to have been born in Australia. His real name may have been Alexander Petropavloff, although at other times he called himself Moses Tagger and Morris Stein. He came to England about 1898. A fine figure of a man (6 ft 3 in tall) and darkly handsome, he was a charmer. His mien and good manners belied the fact that he was a professional burglar who had served five prison sentences, amounting to twelve years, and had in fact been released from jail about six weeks before he and Beron met.

At 8.10 am on Sunday, 1 January 1911, Leon Beron's body was discovered by PC Mumford on Clapham Common. Concealed in some furze bushes near a footpath, it lay on its back with its legs neatly crossed. It had apparently been dragged a short distance, as there was mud on its front, on the backs of the hands and the toes of the boots. Beron, who was wearing a melton overcoat, muffler and patent leather boots, had been struck on the head by a blunt instrument and stabbed three times in the chest as he lay dead on the ground. He had been robbed. No coins or money were found in his possession. There were seven superficial cuts or scratches on his face. Two, one on each cheek, were thought by a police surgeon to be S-shaped and not made accidentally. The surgeon later described them in court 'as being rather like the "f" holes of the violin, on each side of the strings'.

The police discovered that Morrison had worked from late September 1910 for seven weeks for a baker in Lavender Hill and accordingly knew the area, including Clapham Common. They also discovered that on the morning of 1 January, Morrison, calling himself Banman, had deposited a paper-wrapped package in the cloakroom at St Mary's Station, Whitechapel. It contained a revolver and forty-four cartridges. The relevant cloakroom ticket was found in the lining of a billycock hat discovered in his lodging, in the rooms of a prostitute, Florrie Dellow, who resided south of the river at 116 York Road, Lambeth. Morrison had moved in with her on 1 January, after telling his East End landlady at 91 Newark Street – Mrs Zimmerman – that he was off to Paris. He met Florrie at midday – she lived in the house of a watchmaker acquaintance of his – and allegedly asked her if he could live with her. 'Yes,' she replied. 'If you will look after me.' He stayed with Florrie for a week, having, he later said, deposited the revolver in the cloakroom so as not to frighten her. (In fact, he did this *before* he met her.)

Morrison was apprehended at about 9.30 am on Sunday, 8 January, at Cohen's restaurant, Fieldgate Street, just as he finished his breakfast. He was taken to Leman Street police station, ostensibly because, as a convict on parole ('a ticket-of-leave man'), he had neglected to tell the police about his move to Lambeth. Two days later, he was charged with the murder of Leon Beron.

The nine-day trial of Steinie Morrison began at the Old Bailey on 6 March 1911. Mr Justice Darling was the judge. Mr Richard Muir led for the Crown and Mr Edward Abinger for the defence. The trial was characterised by several colourful East Enders, mainly aliens, who gave evidence. They tended to be disputative and unawed by the majesty of the court. On the eighth day, during Abinger's final speech for the defence, Solomon Beron – the dead man's bachelor brother, who lodged for seven pence a night in Rowton House – was so provoked by the suggestion that *he* might have killed his brother that he attacked Abinger and had to be removed, raving, from the court. He was taken to a lunatic asylum.

Throughout the trial, the accused stood – he refused to sit – observing the court with disdain and with one hand on his hip. According to Morrison, he had spent New Year's Eve 1910 selling imitation jewellery. He had supped at the Warsaw restaurant, he said, at about 8 pm. Then he visited the Shoreditch Empire of Varieties, whose artistes that night included Gertie Gitana, Harry Champion and Harry Lauder. He was there from about 8.45 to 11.10 pm. After the show he returned to the restaurant to pick up a flute, wrapped in a paper, which he had left with one of the waiters, Joe Mintz. Morrison had in truth bought a flute for four shillings in the Aldgate that morning. He observed that Beron was in the Warsaw, but did not sit with him, and, having downed a cup of tea, he proceeded, he said, about 11.45 pm to his old lodging in Newark Street, where he went straight to bed, sleeping on a sofa in the Zimmermans' downstairs front room. On his way to Newark Street, he said, he saw Beron and a very tall man on the corner of Sidney Street, soon to be the scene of a famous siege a few days later. 'Bonsoir, monsieur!' Beron had called.

In support of Morrison's account of his movements, Janie Brodski, aged sixteen, and her sister, Esther, told the court that he had indeed been at the Shoreditch Empire on New Year's Eve – somewhat inconsequential evidence, as Beron was murdered at about 2.45 am – although she had neglected to tell the police so when they originally interviewed her. She and her sister, she said, had obtained seats in the orchestra stalls for one shilling each. Morrison was in the same row. Janie's evidence – 'I swear that I saw Morrison there on the night of 31 December. Nobody can deny my own eyes!' – was largely discredited when the acting manager of the Shoreditch Empire said that no seats for the stalls could have been bought at the door as they were all sold, and anyway the price had been raised that night to 1s 6d. It seems that Janie was much enamoured of Steinie Morrison. She had only met him in the last week of December, and within days, she said, he had talked to her of marriage.

The Zimmermans – Maurice and Annie – assured the court that Morrison could not have left their house without rousing them, as the front door had such a noisy bolt that it regularly woke the household. The prosecution pointed out that he could have left by a window.

According to the prosecution Morrison spent most of the evening of 31 December with Beron in the Warsaw – from about 8.30 to 11.45 pm, as alleged by the proprietor, Alexander Snelwar, as well as the waiter, Joe Mintz. Somehow, alleged the prosecution, Morrison had inveigled Beron to go with him to Clapham Common. There, so the prosecution said, in the early hours of the New Year, Morrison murdered the other man by striking him with an iron bar or a jemmy (the skull was fractured) and by stabbing him three times.

The evidence was largely circumstantial, confused, and the prosecution witnesses easily impugned. Beron's belligerent brother, Solomon, had sworn he had seen Leon in Fieldgate Street at 10.45 pm on New Year's Eve. A gasfitter's wife, Mrs Deitch, who also ran a brothel, said she had seen Morrison and Beron in Commercial Road, Stepney about 2.15 am on 1 January. Joe Mintz was not so sure that the package Morrison had left with him about 6 pm on 31 December was indeed a flute – it seemed too long (about 2 ft) and too heavy to be a flute.

Two hansom-cab drivers, Hayman and Stephens, and a taxi-cab driver, Castlin, said respectively (a) that Morrison and Beron had been picked up at about 2 am on 1 January at the corner of Sidney Street and Mile End Road, and had been driven a distance of 6 miles to Lavender Gardens, Clapham, where Morrison had paid the five shilling fare; (b) that Morrison, on his own, had been driven from Clapham Cross to the Hanover Arms near Kennington Church about 3.10 am; and (c) that Morrison and another man had been picked up at 3.30 am at Kennington and taken to Finsbury Gate in north London. Stephens described his 'Morrison' as being about 5 ft 10 in tall and looking like an actor or professional man.

It is odd how the cabmen's accounts detailing Morrison's journeys give him just enough time to dispose of Beron about 2.45 am and then walk across the Common. Moreover, that night there was no moon, and it was so dark that identification cannot have been easy. Two of the cabmen, Hayman and Stephens, had come forward some days *after* 6 January, when the police issued a notice asking cabmen for information about any man or men they had taken to and from Clapham Common between 2 am and 6 am on 1 January. A reward was offered. And by the 6th, Morrison's picture had appeared several times in the newspapers.

In his summing-up, the judge asked the jury about the evidence of the cabmen: 'With what certainty can you, do you think, swear to a man whom you saw on a night like that, by the kind of light there was at these places? Can you feel certain that a man would not be mistaken?'

Mr Abinger sought to imply that Beron was a police spy who had betrayed the anarchists responsible for the Houndsditch Murders (on 10 December 1910), as well as those who died in the Siege of Sidney Street (on 3 January 1911). Accordingly, he had to be killed. The alleged 'S' cuts on the cheeks of Leon Beron signified, he suggested, the Russian or Polish words for 'spy' – 'spic' or 'spiccan'. But DI Wensley, in charge of the case, refuted this last idea, denying that Beron had ever been an informer or was involved with Peter the Painter (allegedly a prominent member of the Latvian criminal gang who were targeted in the Siege of Sidney Street) or any other anarchist. No one put forward the idea that 'S' might signify the *English* word 'spy' – or even 'sodomite'. The prosecution suggested, however, that the supposed double 'S' had been cut by Morrison to confuse the police.

The judge remarked that anyone who could see the letter 'S' in the scratches must have better eyes or a more vivid imagination than he himself possessed. Indeed, police photographs of Beron's corpse show little more than some scratches on his face. Dr Freyberger, who carried out the post mortem, accounted for this by explaining: 'They do not come out well in photographs.' They had also, he said, been distorted by rigor mortis.

It is conceivable, although the point was never raised, that the slight cuts were caused by the furze bushes into which Beron's body was flung. The so-called 'S' cuts, magnified by Morrison's defending counsel and by the press, have since become part of the myths and legends that accumulate around famous trials.

The jury were out for thirty-five minutes. They found Steinie Morrison guilty of murder. As the judge passed sentence of death on him, saying, 'May the Lord have mercy on your soul,' Morrison shouted: 'I decline such mercy! I do not believe there is a God in heaven either!'

Although the verdict was upheld by the Court of Criminal Appeal, the Home Secretary, Mr Winston Churchill, intervened. Morrison was reprieved on 12 April and his sentence commuted to penal servitude for life. He was sent to Dartmoor, and on his way there created a disturbance at Waterloo Station.

He found prison conditions and his existence in jail intolerable, and continually protested his innocence. It is said that he petitioned four times for the death sentence to be carried out. In despair, he staged a series of hunger strikes, and ultimately became so feeble that he died in Parkhurst Prison on 24 January 1921.

Several authorities have thought that Morrison was wrongly convicted, and that although he may have known more about the circumstances of Beron's death than he admitted he was not the murderer. Some have suggested that a third man, looking not unlike Morrison, was involved, that this man drove with Beron to Clapham, and having murdered him joined up with Morrison at Kennington. It certainly seems odd that Morrison should take Beron 6 miles to Clapham Common to rob him and let himself be seen by three cabmen, on the way there and back. Moreover, although Morrison moved to Lambeth, he kept in touch with his friends and did not run away. However, it may be worth noting that the cabman, Alfred Stephens, who said he had driven Morrison from Clapham to Kennington about 3.10 am, was assaulted by four men on 20 January – allegedly because he had kissed the wife of one of his assailants. Stephens said at the time that five days earlier he had been threatened because he was assisting police enquiries.

There seems little doubt that at the Morrison trial more witnesses than usual lied in court about events and people, and that Steinie Morrison, although loved by some, was more loathed than liked – and was a great liar himself. Although the police working on the case were convinced before and after the trial that Steinie Morrison was the guilty man, it is possible that Morrison only acted as a decoy, taking Beron to Clapham Common on some pretext – perhaps to do with some sexual activity or the introduction of Beron to a receiver of stolen goods or 'fence'. Morrison may then have left, whereupon Beron was murdered by some representative of the Houndsditch gang, using a hammer or chisel. The dent on Beron's head doesn't look like a blow from a jemmy – or a flute.

MR AND MRS SEDDON

The Murder of Eliza Barrow, 1911

Money is the mainspring of not a few murders – sheer greed, the acquisition without too much trouble or work of what others have acquired or earned. Some murderers are also very mean about money themselves, never eager to spend but ever eager to get a bargain or something for nothing.

Frederick Henry Seddon was an insurance agent, the district superintendent for Islington of the London and Manchester Industrial Assurance Company, for whom he had worked for over twenty years. In 1911, he was forty, a short, bald-headed, narrow-eyed, wax-moustached, Lancashire businessman, conceited, unfeeling, exact and exacting, who was so obsessed with thrift, money-making and the possession of property that these things had become his religion, with gold as God. He was forever counting his gold sovereigns and notes, totting up sums, zealously plotting and calculating how to save a bit here, make a bit there, and he was never loath to deal in anything that might show a profit, however small. He was not a pleasant man. He exacted 6s a week from his two teenage sons as payment for living at home. He studied the details of wills published in the papers and would say, seeing someone who had died intestate: 'All that money thrown into the gutter. It's criminal!' At a music hall, he once created a scene when he was given change for a florin (2s) instead of half-a-crown (2s 6d). A freemason and formerly a chapel-goer and preacher, his pleasures appear to have included smoking, drinking, music halls and married women.

His wife was three years his junior. A sharp-nosed, weak but capable woman, Margaret Ann Seddon was ruled by her tyrannical husband, whose servants (maid and charwoman) and children (there were five), seemed nervous of him, if not frightened. On the other hand, she ruled their home. As she said: 'I did not tell my husband everything I done, and he never told me everything.' She also commented: 'He never used to take any notice when I said anything to him – he always had other things to think of.' Despite 'a little difference on family matters' (as he put it) at the end of 1909, when there was a brief separation, the marriage seemed quite equable.

The story begins in January 1910, when they moved into 63 Tollington Park, London N4. Seddon, having persuaded the owners to reduce the asking price to £320, bought the house on a mortgage of £220 with a down payment of £100. He intended to turn it into flats, but instead decided to use it himself, sub-letting the top floor. The other two floors and the basement were occupied by the Seddon household, consisting of husband and wife, his old father, William (aged seventy-three), his four children – a fifth child was conceived soon after the separation – and an eccentric servant, Mary Chater, whose brother and cousin were in lunatic asylums. She herself was a former mental nurse and was something of a case herself, shouting and breaking crockery and telling all manner of lying tales.

'This house I live in,' said Seddon in 1912, 'fourteen rooms, is my own, and I have seventeen other properties.' Four of these rooms formed the top-floor flat. Of the other ten, one was his bow-windowed front basement office, another a conservatory, and only three were bedrooms. Mr and Mrs Seddon had a double room on the first floor above the ground-floor drawing room. The first-floor rear room was divided by a partition: the two Seddon daughters and Mary Chater slept on one side, Grandfather William and the two Seddon sons on the other. Apart from the six shillings each of his sons paid for their weekly board, Seddon got five shillings a week from the insurance company as rent for the room used as his office, and twelve shillings and sixpence from the tenant of the four unfurnished top floor rooms. They were occupied for six months, and then were vacated in June.

In July 1910, Miss Eliza Mary Barrow took over the top-floor tenancy. At the time of her death, Miss Barrow was forty-nine; a plump, unprepossessing woman, about 5 ft 4 in tall, who dressed poorly, she was parsimonious, squalid, ignorant, asthmatic, self-indulgent, deaf and drank gin. Her failings were more acceptable to Seddon because she had money, apparently inherited from her mother. According to an engine driver, Robert Hook, she had £420 4s 3d, nearly all in gold coin, kept in fifteen bags in a cash-box, in which were also some banknotes. Mr Hook said he helped her count it out in 1906, when Miss Barrow was living in his sister's house, It was later established that the cash box could hold as much as £1,500 in gold.

She had known Hook since 1896, when she lodged with his mother in Edmonton. When old Mrs Hook died in 1902, Miss Barrow moved in with Robert's sister, Mrs Grant. The Grants were heavy drinkers, it seems, and always feuding, throwing bottles and fire irons about. Mr Grant died in 1906. When Mrs Grant died in 1908, Eliza Barrow took charge of the youngest Grant, six-year-old Ernie, leaving his sister Hilda in an orphanage.

When Robert Hook married in 1909, aged thirty-seven – although he was nine years younger than Miss Barrow, he said they had once been sweethearts – Miss Barrow went to live with a cousin, Frank Vonderahe and his wife, taking Ernie with her. She paid 35s a week for board and lodging for them both. The Vonderahes thought she was excitable, irritable and had peculiar ways; she once spat at Mrs Vonderahe. After a year there was some quarrel and Miss Barrow, 'dissatisfied' according to Frank Vonderahe, moved out, soliciting the help of Robert Hook, who had continued to visit her and now sold her some of his sister's (Mrs Grant's) furniture for her new lodging in Tollington Park. Further, Hook and his wife also moved in, as did Ernie. They lodged with Miss Barrow rent free, in return for Mrs Hook's domestic services.

So, by 1 August 1910, twelve people were crammed into 63 Tollington Park. But before long Miss Barrow, according to Seddon, found fault with the Hooks. She said she was frightened of them, could not trust them, and enquired whether she could leave her cash box, in which she said there was about £35, in Mr Seddon's safe. There was a row, fired by drink, on a Saturday night in the top flat, and on Sunday morning the Hooks took little Ernie with them to Barnet, leaving Miss Barrow in sickness and tears and unattended all day. All this displeased Mr Seddon – 'They were creating a disturbance in the house which I was not used to. They proved undesirable tenants' – so he gave all four notice to quit.

But Miss Barrow was loath to leave. Hook, she said, was the cause of the trouble, and having no friends or advisors at hand she sought the help and advice of the Seddons. Mr Seddon suggested that she give Hook written notice to quit. She did, beginning her note: 'As you and your wife have treated me so badly ...' Hook replied by scrawling on the back of the notice, which had been delivered by Maggie Seddon, then aged fifteen – 'As you are so impudent to send the letter to hand, I wish to inform you that I shall require the return of my late mother's and sister's furniture, and the expense of my moving here and away – Yours RD Hook.'

This brought a summons from Seddon. In Hook's own words:

I went down to see him. He said to me: 'So I see you don't mean to take any notice of Miss Barrow's notice ordering you to leave?' And I said: 'No, not this time of night.' He then gave me an order to clear out within twenty-four hours, and I said I would if I could, and if I could not, I would take forty-eight hours. He said: 'I do not know whether you know it or not – Miss Barrow has put all her affairs in my hands.' And I said: 'Has she?' I asked him if she had put her money in his hands and he said: 'No.' I said: 'I will defy you and a regiment like you to get her money in your hands.'

Seddon took him at his word and pinned his own type-written notice to quit on the Hooks' bedroom door. On Tuesday, 11 August, the Hooks moved out, taking all the furniture in their room. Miss Barrow paid for the removal. As she was now on her own, apart from little Ernie, Seddon suggested that his daughter Maggie might cook and clean for her for 1s a day. Comparative calm returned.

But then the top-floor lodger began to worry and fret about her properties and income. She consulted Mr Seddon. He later stated: 'She came down one Sunday in the month of September into the dining room, and had a chat with me about her property ... She said she had a public-house at Camden Town called the Buck's Head, and it was the principal source of her income. She had had a lot of trouble with the ground landlord, and she said that Lloyd George's budget had upset licensed premises by increased taxation; that her tenants, Truman, Hanbury, Buxton and Co had a lot of licensed houses, and she was afraid they might have to close some of them.' She also owned the adjacent barber's and had invested £1,600 in India stock, which had gone down in value – it had cost her £1,780. What with the gold and notes hoarded in her cash box – she mistrusted banks – and the money in her savings bank, she was worth about £4,000, a small fortune in those days.

Seddon must have been most interested in the extraordinary wealth of his dowdy, dumpy lodger. Further discussions took place, he said later, in which she expressed an interest in purchasing an annuity, as a friend of hers had done. He advised her to consult a solicitor or the post office, but she mistrusted them as well. She chose to put her trust in him. A year later, her fortune had disappeared and Miss Barrow was dead.

On 14 October 1910, Miss Barrow transferred the £1,600 India 3 1/2 per cent stock to Seddon in return for an annuity of £103 4s a year. About this time Mrs Seddon began to change £5 notes for gold at various stores, endorsing them with a false name and address. Twenty-seven £5 notes were eventually traced to Mrs Seddon and six went into her husband's bank account, five on 13 January 1911. The leasehold of the Buck's Head and the barber shop were likewise made over to him on 9 January 1911, for a further annuity of £52 a year. Although the transfers were legally made, there was no written agreement concerning an annuity – at least, none could be found later. But Seddon began paying Miss Barrow £10 a month in advance (for which she gave him a receipt), and allowed her to live in Tollington Park rent-free.

Mrs Seddon's explanation of the £5 notes (the proceeds of cheques paid to Miss Barrow by Truman, Hanbury, Buxton and Co) was that Miss Barrow had asked her to cash them for her. She said: 'I think she had been out herself to get one cashed, and someone would not cash it for her, so she asked me if I would get it cashed. I took it to the post office, and they asked me for my name and address. I thought it was rather funny, as I never cashed a note in my life before, so I gave the first name that came into my head ... M Scott, 18 Evershot Road ... I gave the cash to Miss Barrow when I came back, five sovereigns. After that day Miss Barrow from time to time asked me to change notes for her ... At the shops I went to where I was known I gave my right name and address, because they already knew it ... I always gave the money to Miss Barrow.'

Mrs Seddon gave birth to a baby girl, Lily, on 3 January 1911, and when the annuity transactions were completed, she said, the happy lodger gave Mr Seddon a diamond ring. She herself, she said, was given a gold watch and chain on her birthday and her daughter Maggie was given a gold necklet and locket.

Seddon's explanation of the ring was that it was given to him to defray part of the legal costs in arranging the property transfers – 'She said she had no money to spare ... I wore that diamond ring on my little finger until Miss Barrow's death, and then I had it made to fit this other finger. I have a diamond ring of my own, which is four times the value of that ring.' The prosecution's explanation of these 'gifts' was that they were acquired *after* the lodger's demise.

On 25 January 1911, Seddon instructed Arthur Astle, a stockbroker, to sell the £1,600 India stock. It realised £1,519 16s and was paid by cheque to FH Seddon, who put the money into a deposit account. On 1 February, £119 16s of this was withdrawn and transferred to another bank, his own, where it was split roughly between his current and deposit accounts. Then, on 6 March the remaining £1,400, plus interest, was withdrawn and the account closed. With all this money Seddon bought the leasehold on fourteen houses in Coutts Road, Stepney, and added another £30 to his own deposit account to bring it up to £100.

That month, Miss Barrow went to a funeral. Said Seddon: 'She came in talking about funerals and death and one thing and another and she said, how would it be if anything happened to her now regarding the furniture and the jewellery she had got which had belonged to Ernest and Hilda Grant's parents? I told her that she ought to make a will.' Apparently she was afraid of the Hooks and Vonderahes getting possession of all she had left. He advised her to see a solicitor. But that night he received a letter from Miss Barrow through his wife, in which Miss Barrow named three first cousins, all called Vonderahe, as her nearest relatives and said: 'It is not my will or wish that they, or any other relation of mine, should receive anything belonging to me at my death ... They have not been kind to me, or considered me.' 'I took it that she meant the letter to be a kind of will,' said Seddon, 'and I put it away in my secretaire.'

His salary had just been increased and he was now earning £5 15s 10d a week. About this time the Charing Cross and Birkbeck banks crashed, making Miss Barrow afraid for money she had in a savings bank in Clerkenwell. After closing an investment account she had at the bank in April (£10 7s 9d), she and Mrs Seddon went to the bank on 19 June and drew out £216 9s 7d. It was put into two £100 bags of gold coin, with the rest in loose gold and silver. The account had been opened in 1887 – the last payment was made in 1908 and the last withdrawal in 1907. When the women returned to Tollington Park, Seddon apparently rebuked Miss Barrow for keeping all that gold in a trunk in her room – 'I do not like the idea' – and she said she knew what to do with it. Neither of the Seddons saw the money again, they said.

On 1 August Miss Barrow went to see Dr John Paul in Isledon Road, accompanied by Mrs Seddon. Miss Barrow was suffering from 'congestion of the liver', and constipation. She paid further visits on the 3rd, 17th and 22nd. On the last visit, she complained of asthma. Meanwhile, all the Seddons, Miss Barrow and little Ernie went to Southend-on-Sea for the weekend of 5–8 August. Ernie, now aged ten, delicate and adenoidal, slept with his ageing foster mother. He called her Chickie. Mr Seddon disapproved – 'I advised her to buy a small bed and to let him occupy the room.' But Ernie continued to keep Miss Barrow company in bed.

The last week in August and the first week in September were very hot: London sweltered in a heat wave. On the morning of Friday, 1 September, Miss Barrow felt ill. She sat in the kitchen and complained of feeling sick and bilious. Mrs Seddon took her upstairs, where she lay down on her bed; a cup of tea made her sick. 'I had seen her like this before,' said Mrs Seddon, 'off and on, with these sick bilious attacks every month.' The next day she was still sick and had diarrhoea. Dr Paul was sent for but was too busy to attend. The Seddons' family doctor, Henry Sworn, arrived instead about ten o'clock that night. He prescribed bismuth and morphia, the latter for her stomach pains. He thought she was very ill, and that her mental state was as poor as her health.

Returning on Sunday and Monday, Dr Sworn noticed no improvement. Mrs Seddon told him his patient would not take the thick, chalky bismuth. Instead, Dr Sworn prescribed an effervescing mixture of citrate of potash and bicarbonate of soda and gave her nothing for her diarrhoea, which was not too severe. But he suggested, raising his voice to counteract her deafness, that she should go to hospital. Miss Barrow refused. She also refused to have a nurse. She said Mrs Seddon 'could attend to her very well indeed and she was very attentive'. Indeed, Mrs Seddon, who prepared the patient's food – no solids, just soda water and milk, gruel, milk puddings and Valentine's meat juice – must have been up and down stairs all day, seeing to her various needs. Already the top-floor bedroom stank with the smell of faeces. Because of the heat the windows were open; flies swarmed in. Mrs Seddon and her daughter fanned the patient to keep the flies away.

On Monday, 4 September, Miss Barrow (according to Mrs Seddon) instructed her to get some flypapers, not the sticky ones, but 'those that you wet … I got these flypapers at Meacher's, the chemists', in Stroud Green Road, just around the corner from our house. An old gentleman served me. I think I ordered at the same time a 9s 6d bottle of the baby's food, Horlicks malted milk … I also bought a pennyworth of white precipitate powder, with which Miss Barrow used to wash her head. I have also seen her cleaning her teeth with it.' Mrs Seddon bought four flypapers for threepence, and back in the top-floor bedroom put each one in a saucer of water, wetting them thoroughly. Two saucers were put on the mantelpiece and two on a chest of drawers.

On Tuesday, Miss Barrow was slightly better. She summoned little Ernie to sleep with her, as she did every night. For the next three days, Dr Sworn continued to prescribe the effervescing medicine. But on the 9th he added 'a blue pill which contained mercury' as 'her motion was so very offensive' – so much so, that the stench pervaded the house and carbolic sheets were hung in the rooms. Ernie seemed not to notice the aroma around Miss Barrow, possibly because of his adenoids.

Dr Sworn took a day off on Sunday the 10th, returning on the Monday before midday. His patient was weaker. He advised Mrs Seddon to give her some brandy. It was still very warm and close, and what with the heat and Miss Barrow's weakness he was prepared for a sudden relapse and heart failure. He thought she was in some danger but not in a critical condition: her pulse was rapid and feeble, but her temperature had only once reached 101°F.

That afternoon, Mr Seddon went upstairs to see his ailing lodger, who was worrying again about her possessions. She allegedly told Seddon: 'I don't feel well, and I would like to see, if anything happened to me, that Ernest and Hilda get what belonged to their father and mother.' He advised her, he said, to call in a solicitor, but she asked him to draft a will for her. He agreed.

Mr Seddon's married sister, Mrs Emily Longley, and her daughter, had just arrived on a visit from Wolverhampton, and it was not until about half-past six, after dinner, that he returned to the sick room with his father and his wife as witnesses to Miss Barrow's will. Mrs Seddon later said: 'We propped her up in bed with pillows in a sitting position to get her to sign it ... My husband read the will to Miss Barrow, and then she asked for her glasses to read it herself, which she did, and then she signed it ... I signed it on a little table, and my father-in-law signed it.' The will, revoking all others, made Frederick Henry Seddon sole executor – 'to hold all my personal belongings, furniture, clothing and jewellery in trust' until Hilda and Ernest Grant came of age, when Seddon was to hand them over (or the cash he made from selling them). But no article of jewellery was to be sold to the young Grants. 'Thank you. Thank God, that will do,' said Miss Barrow, according to Seddon. He said later that he fully intended to take the will to a solicitor and get it properly made out. The fact that no mention was made in the will of all the hoarded gold in Miss Barrow's cash box seemed to have escaped his money-conscious attention. He said later: 'I never gave it a thought.'

That evening, as Miss Barrow lay ill in bed with Ernie, Frederick Seddon took his wife, his father and his sister for a night out to the Finsbury Park Empire, leaving his daughter Maggie to look after the lodger.

They returned about midnight and revised the sleeping arrangements. The Seddons moved out of their bed, which was now occupied by Mrs Longley and her daughter, and they took over the bed where the two boys had slept with their grandfather, who in turn were moved into a large extra bed set up in a top-floor room, once occupied by the Hooks and next door to Miss Barrow's bedroom.

Nothing untoward happened on Tuesday the 12th, except that Mrs Seddon knocked one of the flypaper saucers off the mantelpiece. She then put all four papers into a soup plate on a table between the windows. Dr Sworn made no visit that day. But when he called before noon on Wednesday the 13th, he thought his patient was rather worse: she seemed weaker. Her diarrhoea was bad again, but she did not seem to be in much pain. He prescribed a bismuth-and-chalk mixture to be taken after every motion. Mr Seddon himself was not very well that morning. While the rest of the family, apart from his wife and Maggie, went to the White City, he stayed in bed. But at about half-past seven in the evening he went to the Marlborough Theatre, where occurred the row about the wrong change for his half-crown.

About midnight, Mrs Seddon and Mrs Longley were chatting at the gate, waiting for

Frederick's return, when they heard Miss Barrow cry from the open top-floor window: 'I'm dying!'

Mrs Seddon rushed upstairs; her sister-in-law followed. Miss Barrow complained of severe pains in her stomach and that her feet were cold. A flannel petticoat was wrapped around them and hot flannels were laid on her stomach. Seddon, returning about twelve-thirty, was told by his wife about the lodger's 'dying' cry. He looked at his wife and said: 'Is she?' Mrs Seddon said: 'No,' and smiled. Mrs Seddon later explained to the court: 'I have a usual way of smiling at almost everything, I think. I cannot help it. It is my way. No matter how serious anything was I think I would smile.'

Seddon was still complaining about being done out of sixpence at the theatre when Ernie called down the stairs: 'Mrs Seddon, Chickie wants you!' Mrs Seddon was resting on a couch. 'Never mind,' said her husband. 'I'll go and see what she wants.' But both the Seddons went upstairs with Mrs Longley, who was so overcome by the smell and by Ernie's presence on the patient's bed that she soon retreated. Mr Seddon also found the smell nauseating – 'I have a delicate stomach' – and after rebuking the patient for making so many demands on his wife he gave her a drop of brandy.

The Seddons went to bed about two-thirty, and within minutes Ernie called Mrs Seddon again, and again half an hour later. 'She had the diarrhoea bad,' said Mrs Seddon later, adding: 'She did not seem sick – she was only once or twice sick during the night. She seemed to be retching, not proper vomiting, but a nasty froth came up.'

A third time Ernie called, crying: 'Chickie is out of bed!' It was now nearly four o'clock. Seddon told his wife to stay in bed – he would go. 'It's no good you going up,' she said, as on all the other occasions Miss Barrow had to be assisted on and off the commode and given hot flannels. But this time Seddon went with her.

Miss Barrow was sitting on the floor, moaning and in pain; Ernie was holding her up. 'Whatever are you doing out of bed?' asked Seddon. He waited outside while the commode was used and when he was able to enter the room he remonstrated with the exhausted patient. 'You must remember Mrs Seddon has got a young baby and she wants a rest. If Mrs Seddon sits up with you all night she'll be knocked up ... Really we shall have to get a nurse, or you shall have to go to hospital.' Miss Barrow said she couldn't help it. She asked for Ernie, who had been ordered back to his own bed (not for the first time) and was very weary himself. Mrs Seddon thought she had better stay in the bedroom. She said: 'What's the good of going to bed, getting undressed, and being called and having to get up again?' Her husband agreed. 'I'll put a pipe on and keep you company,' he said, and while Mrs Seddon sat in a basket-chair near the end of the bed, he stood at the door smoking his pipe and reading a newspaper. Sometimes he went downstairs to see how the baby was. Miss Barrow seemed to sleep; Mrs Seddon dozed in the chair. For over an hour Miss Barrow snored as dawn began to light the top-floor room at 63 Tollington Park.

Suddenly the snoring softened and stopped. Seddon came forward. 'She's stopped breathing!' he said, rousing his wife. He felt Miss Barrow's pulse, lifted an eyelid and exclaimed: 'Good God, she's dead!' It was just after a quarter-past six, on Thursday, 14 September 1911.

About seven o'clock, Seddon went to Dr Sworn's house and told him his patient had died. Then and there the doctor made out a death certificate, giving the cause of death as 'epidemic diarrhoea'. 'I did not expect it then,' said Seddon.

He returned home, to find that all the blinds had now been drawn down in respect for Miss Barrow's death. His wife and the charwoman, Mrs Rutt, were laying out the body. In the presence of both women he unlocked Miss Barrow's trunk with her keys. Inside was the cash box. He put it on the bed beside the corpse. But no fortune lay within it. In the cash box was only £4 10s. Three sovereigns were later found in a drawer, according to the Seddons, and £2 10s in a handbag. The trunk was ransacked, and apart from clothes, two watches, some brooches and a bracelet were unearthed.

About half-past nine the youngest children, including Ernie, who knew nothing of his foster mother's death, were packed off to Southend. Later in the morning, Seddon visited Mr Nodes, an undertaker, and a cheap and instant funeral was arranged as a favour for £4, which was further reduced to £3 17s 6d when Seddon complained that all the cash he had for the funeral costs and the doctor's fees was the £4 10s found in the cash box. The saving of 2s 6d was regarded by Seddon and Nodes as the former's commission. The cost of the funeral included 'a coffin, polished and ornamented with handles and inside lining, a composite carriage (for the mourners and the coffin), the necessary bearers, and the fees at Islington cemetery'. Miss Barrow was to be buried in a public grave, despite the fact that there was room for her – later denied by Seddon – in a family vault.

Nodes came and measured the body, removing it that night to a mortuary after Seddon had decided the funeral should be the following afternoon – 'It being a slack business day for me.' He later claimed he had typed a letter on black-edged paper to Frank Vonderahe, informing him succinctly of his cousin's death, of the funeral times and of the terms of the will. The letter was addressed to 31 Evershot Road and, he said, it was posted before 5 pm. As it happened, the Vonderahes had moved two months before this to an address in Corbyn Street. Nonetheless, although other letters addressed to Evershot Road eventually reached them at Corbyn Street, they never received Seddon's letter – probably because it was never sent. Nor were any mourning cards, although he had some printed. They were inscribed: 'In ever loving memory of Eliza Mary Barrow' and contained this verse:

A dear one is missing and with us no more;
That voice so much loved we hear not again;
Yet we think of you now the same as of yore,
And know you are free of trouble and pain.

Most of Thursday afternoon was spent by Seddon in his basement office with his two assistant managers, Taylor and Smith, apart from an hour or so when he went to bed complaining of feeling very tired. Meanwhile, the insurance collectors called with their weekly takings, which amounted that day to £63 14s 3d. Smith and Taylor worked from noon to midnight on the accounts. At about 9 pm they observed a large amount of loose gold on Seddon's desk. He was counting it and putting it in four cloth bags, which the assistants later surmised must have held about £400 worth of gold.

In a very good humour, Seddon picked up one of the bags and plonked in on Smith's desk. 'Here's your wages,' he joked. 'I wish you meant it, Mr Seddon,' replied Smith. Seddon then locked all four bags away in a safe. He later denied all this and said he was merely counting the gold and silver brought in by the collectors.

On Friday, 15 September, he was very busy. He made two payments into his bank account that amounted to £96 0s 8d, paid mainly in gold. A sum of £30 was also put into his post-office savings bank, again mainly in gold coin. Mrs Seddon went with him to a jeweller in Holloway Road, where they left a diamond ring and a gold watch for alterations – the ring's band was to be widened; 'EJ Barrow 1860' was to be erased from the back of the watch, and the enamel dial was to be replaced with a gold one. When Mrs Seddon returned home, she was vexed to find that the blinds had been raised by Mrs Longley. 'Let us show a little respect!' exclaimed Mrs Seddon and lowered the blinds once more.

She had already been out with her sister-in-law and father-in-law and had ordered a cross of flowers for the deceased. After lunch, about two o'clock, the same trio took the cross to the undertaker's mortuary in Stroud Green Road, where it was placed on the coffin – but not before the lid had been removed and Mrs Seddon had kissed the corpse.

Later that day, Mrs Longley and her daughter returned to Wolverhampton, and the Seddons to their own beds. The top floor was empty once more.

On Saturday afternoon, Miss Barrow was buried, the two Seddons and Grandfather William travelling with the coffin in the composite carriage from the undertaker's to Islington Cemetery. Less than a year before this, the few remains of Mrs Crippen had also been buried there.

Sunday was a day of rest for all concerned. But on Monday, 18 September, Seddon was active again, buying three shares totalling £90 3s in a building society; he paid in gold coin. The following day he wrote to the society asking about the exact amount required to pay off the mortgage on 63 Tollington Park.

Meanwhile, the Vonderahes happened to hear that their cousin, whom they had not seen in the district for six weeks or so, was ill. Mr Vonderahe called at Number 63 on Wednesday, 20 September and was amazed to be told by the eccentric servant, Mary Chater: 'Don't you know she's dead and buried?' 'No,' he replied, 'when did she die?' 'Last Saturday,' replied the maid. 'But if you call about nine o'clock you will be able to see Mr Seddon and he'll tell you all about it.' When Vonderahe returned with his wife that night, he was told by Maggie that both her parents were out.

The following morning, at about 10 am, Mrs Frank Vonderahe called with her sister-in-law, Mrs Albert Vonderahe, and the two were shown by Maggie into the sitting room. After a long wait, both the Seddons appeared. 'Why didn't you answer my letter and come to the funeral?' demanded Mr Seddon. Mrs Frank Vonderahe replied, 'We never got no letter', whereupon he produced a carbon copy of the letter allegedly sent on the day Miss Barrow died. He also gave Mrs Frank Vonderahe a statement about the terms of the will and the annuity, which died with her, as well as a copy of the will and three mourning cards. Mrs Seddon remarked that they had had a very nice funeral. 'Everything was done very nicely,' she said. Seddon told Mrs Frank Vonderahe that their cousin had been buried in a public grave. 'Fancy!' came the reply. 'And she had a family vault.' 'It's full up,' said Seddon. 'No, it isn't,' she retorted. 'Oh well,' replied Seddon, 'it will be an easy matter for the relatives to remove the body.' Mrs Frank Vonderahe said a public grave was good enough for Eliza Barrow, who had been a wicked woman all her life; she also spoke about unseemly scenes and quarrels that Miss Barrow had caused. 'Really,' she concluded, 'it's a good job for the boy that she passed away ... She even spat at us before we left.' 'She was a woman that wanted humouring,' Seddon opined. 'You ought to take into consideration her infirmities. She was to be pitied.' The Vonderahes then asked about Ernie. Seddon said he was quite prepared to look after the boy, unless any of his relatives could give him a better home. They enquired about the Buck's Head and the India stock. Seddon told them Miss Barrow had been anxious to buy an annuity and had parted with all her investments to this end. 'Well,' said Mrs Albert Vonderahe, 'Whoever persuaded Miss Barrow to do that was a very clever person.'

Neither wife was surprised that nothing had been left to their husbands, the actual cousins of the deceased. They asked if Seddon would see their husbands that evening, but he said it was out of the question – enough time had been wasted and he was going away the next day and he could not possibly see them until his return.

All the Seddons went to Southend on 22 September, where Ernie was informed about his benefactress's death. They returned on 2 October, and several days later Ernie was sent to call on Frank Vonderahe with the message that Seddon was back.

On 9 October, Frank Vonderahe called with a friend, Mr Walker. His brother, he said, was not well. 'What did you want to bring a stranger for?' demanded Seddon, 'This only concerns the next-of-kin.' He said all the information Mr Vonderahe need have or know had already been given to his wife. 'Can I see the will, the original will?' asked Vonderahe. 'No,' said Seddon. 'You already have a copy ... I don't know why I should give you any information. You're not the eldest of the family. You have another brother, Percy.' This brother had, in fact, disappeared some time ago. 'He might be dead for aught I know,' retorted Vonderahe. 'I don't think so,' Seddon returned. 'You've been making enquiries and talked about consulting a solicitor.' (He had been told this by Nodes, the undertaker.) Vonderahe persisted: 'Who is the owner of the Buck's Head now?' 'I am,' came the reply, 'likewise the shop next door ... I am always open to buy property at a price.' 'How did you come by it?' 'I've already told you that.' 'Who bought the India stock?' Seddon answered: 'You'll have to write to the Governor of the Bank of England and ask him. Everything has been done in a perfectly legal manner.'

According to Seddon, the interview ended amicably, with enquiries about the well-being of Ernie and Hilda Grant. But the Vonderahes were very dissatisfied and deeply suspicious about the circumstances of their cousin's death – and the total disappearance of her fortune. They communicated their anxieties to the police.

On 15 November, Miss Barrow's body was exhumed and examined by Dr Bernard Spilsbury and Dr Willcox. The body was remarkedly well preserved, a fact attributed to some preserving agent – such as arsenic. And sufficient traces of arsenic (2.01 grains) were found in the body to suggest that the cause of death was not epidemic diarrhoea and heart failure caused by gastroenteritis, but 'acute arsenical poisoning', although the symptoms were the same. It was thought that a large dose of arsenic had been administered about three days before death, most of it having been purged by the body. It was calculated that one flypaper, if boiled, could produce as much as 5 grains of arsenic (2 grains were said to be fatal) and one flypaper soaked in cold water would produce nearly 1 grain.

While the body was being dissected in St Mary's Hospital, Paddington, Seddon was coincidentally being shown around the hospital in connection with a business deal.

An inquest began on 23 November and was adjourned until the 29th.

At 7 pm on 4 December, Seddon was arrested outside his home. On hearing the charge he said: 'Absurd. What a terrible charge – wilful murder! It is the first of our family that has ever been accused of such a crime … Poisoning by arsenic? What a charge! … Murder … Murder.' Mrs Seddon was arrested on 15 January 1912. On 2 February, both the Seddons were committed for trial.

The arrests had attracted little attention, but the trial was avidly followed and the court was crowded every day. The trial began on Monday, 4 March 1912, at the Old Bailey and occupied ten days. The Attorney-General, Sir Rufus Isaacs, KC, was the prosecutor, assisted by Mr Richard Muir and Mr Travers Humphreys. Mr Edward Marshall Hall, KC, led Seddon's defence and Gervais Rentoul his wife's. The judge was Mr Justice Bucknill.

Both the Seddons gave evidence, Frederick Seddon over a record three days. He was fully in command of himself and his defence, and was never at a loss for an answer. His self-confidence was overweening. His responses were meticulous, his manner sometimes jaunty, but more often cold and arrogant. His whole demeanour, too clever by half, seemed to confirm every prejudice already felt against him and antagonised everyone in the court, even the Attorney-General who, as if from deep personal dislike, concentrated almost entirely on the case against the male accused – as did the judge in his summing-up. If Seddon had not given evidence, revealing himself as a man who certainly seemed capable of the crime as charged, the Crown would have had a harder task and the all-male jury might have given him the benefit of the doubt. For the evidence was entirely circumstantial, concerned mainly with motive and opportunity. There was no evidence that Seddon had ever bought or used any arsenic or knew anything about it. There were also serious doubts about the way the police had conducted the investigation, and the Marsh test, which was applied to the arsenic in the body, was improperly applied to the *quantity* of arsenic therein, not just to the quality. As Seddon himself wrote after the trial: 'There was no motive for me to commit such a crime. I would have to be a greedy inhuman monster, or be suffering from a degenerate or deranged mind, as I was in good financial circumstances. 21 years in one employ, a good position, a good home with every comfort, a wife, five children and aged father depending on me, my income just on £15 per week.'

Despite the fact that the evidence offered against Seddon was the same as that offered against his wife – and, if anything, there was more to incriminate *her* – it was he alone who was found guilty by the jury after an absence of exactly an hour. Mrs Seddon was acquitted.

When she was pronounced 'Not guilty' Seddon leaned across and gave her a resounding kiss. She became hysterical and was taken below in tears. When asked if he had anything to say for himself before sentence of death was passed, he stepped forward in the dock, and made a very long, lucid speech, quoting facts and figures from his notes, explaining this, justifying that, leading to a powerful protestation of his innocence.

The judge, like Seddon, was a freemason. The condemned man concluded his speech by raising a hand as if taking a freemason's oath. He said: 'The prosecution has not traced anything to me in the shape of money, which is the great motive suggested by the prosecution in this case for my committing the diabolical crime, of which I declare before the Great Architect of the Universe I am not guilty, my lord. Anything more I might have to say I do not suppose will be of any account. But still, if it is the last words that I speak, I am not guilty of the crime for which I stand committed!'

The judge's secretary arranged the black cap on his wig; a chaplain appeared; the usher, crying 'Oyez, oyez, oyez!' called on all to be silent as sentence of death was passed. The doors of the court were locked.

The judge replied in a low, faltering voice to the points raised in Seddon's final speech. Seddon nodded twice in grave agreement when the judge said he believed the jury's verdict on Mrs Seddon was the right one and that the trial had been a fair one. Seddon spoke three times, quietly interrupting the judge's words, saying: 'I have a clear conscience … I am at peace … She done nothing wrong, sir.' Towards the end the judge said: 'You and I know we belong to one brotherhood … But our brotherhood does not encourage crime. On the contrary, it condemns it. I pray you again to make your peace with the Great Architect of the Universe. Mercy – pray for it, ask for it.' He was in tears as he said: 'The sentence of the court is that you be taken from hence to a lawful prison, and from thence to a place of execution, and that you be there hanged by the neck until you are dead … And may the Lord have mercy on your soul.'

An appeal was heard on 1 April and dismissed the following day. Meetings were held and a petition organised. It was signed by more than 250,000 people, but to no avail. Seddon was hanged at Pentonville Prison on 18 April 1912, not long after hearing the news that his house had been sold for next to nothing. 'That's finished it!' he exclaimed.

A large crowd of 7,000 people gathered outside the prison as the hour of execution approached. The newspapers were still full of the sinking of the *Titanic*, which had struck an iceberg and sunk with a huge loss of life two days beforehand. The hangmen were John Ellis and Tom Pierrepoint, a quarryman, who had first assisted his younger brother, Harry, at an execution in April 1906. Seddon approached the noose reluctantly and, with his eyes closed, had to be directed towards it by Tom Pierrepoint. The execution was carried out in a record time of 25 seconds.

Frederick Seddon made no confession. But Mrs Seddon did. A few months after the execution, she remarried and moved to Liverpool, eventually emigrating to America. On 17 November the *Weekly Dispatch* published a signed confession in which she said that she had seen her former husband give poison to Miss Barrow on the night she died and that he had compelled her to say nothing by threatening her with a gun. But a fortnight later, *John Bull* published another statement. Mrs Seddon swore on oath that the confession was a lie, that she had made it to stop people saying she was a murderess – and to gain the large sum of money she was offered by the *Dispatch*.

16
GEORGE SMITH

The Murder of Bessie Mundy, 1912

Men who murder women generally do so under the stress of extreme provocation. What varies in each case is the cause of this stress. Some men have found their wives' lack of respect unbearable; others have been incensed by submissiveness. An excess of compliance often encourages a man already vain, unfeeling and bent on gain to believe that he can get away with murder.

Like other lady-killers in this book George Joseph Smith was a charmer, but the most cold-blooded and callous of them all. He was vile. Like many other murderers, he was a petty criminal before he began to kill.

A cockney, born at 92 Roman Road, Bethnal Green, in the East End of London on 11 January 1872, he was only nine years old when he was sentenced to eight years in a Gravesend reformatory: an upbringing and a background that may have developed his criminal tendencies and contempt for the law. When he came out he stayed with his mother. According to his first wife: 'He said he had a stepfather whose name was Smith. He said he had a good mother, but he had broken her heart.'

More thieving and brief spells in jail were followed by three years with the Northampton Regiment. Next, after persuading a woman to steal for him, he was jailed for a year in 1896 for larceny and receiving stolen goods. Released in 1897, he went to Leicester, where he opened a baker's shop at 28 Russell Square, using £115 (the equivalent of two years' wages) from a cash box which the same woman had stolen for him from her employers.

In Leicester, on 17 January 1898, now calling himself George Love, he married Caroline Beatrice Thornhill, aged eighteen (he was twenty-six at the time), despite her bootmaker father's disapproval. She later remarked of her then husband, 'During the time I knew him I never knew him do any work' and described him thus: 'Complexion fair, hair brown, ginger moustache, peak chin, on left arm a very large scar, military walk, stands 5 ft 9 ins.' What this fails to indicate is Smith's evident sexual attraction. He had a masterful way with certain women. There was something hypnotic in the small dark eyes set in a bony face. His first bigamous wife, whom he married in London in 1899, said of him: 'He had an extraordinary power … This power lay in his eyes … When he looked at you, you had the feeling that you were being magnetised. They were little eyes that seemed to rob you of your will.'

He and Mrs Caroline Love moved to London soon after their marriage in 1898. Posing as her employer and providing references for her, he began his peregrinations, finding jobs for her in London, Brighton, Hove and Hastings. Taught by Smith, she stole from the families who employed her as a maid. But in the autumn of 1899 at Hastings, she was arrested in a pawnbroker's shop where she was trying to sell some silver spoons. Sent to prison for twelve months she was able on her release to find, identify and incriminate Smith, who was, on 9 January 1901, jailed at Hastings for two years for receiving stolen goods. One waggish local reporter wrote: 'For his spooning at Hastings, Love has gone to prison.'

Released in 1903, Smith went in pursuit of Mrs Love. To escape him, she emigrated to Canada; though separated from him she remained, despite the pseudonym, his only legal wife. He returned to the middle-aged boarding-house keeper whom he had bigamously married in London before his incarceration. Having milked her of what money he could, he left, and having found what an easy way this was of acquiring bed, board and money without doing a stroke of work, he travelled about the south of England wooing, wedding, and walking out on an unknown assortment of lonely or love-lorn women, whose humiliation led them to say little or nothing of the disappearance of their erstwhile spouse.

Next to nothing is known about his activities for three years. But in June 1908, he met a widow from Worthing, Mrs Florence Wilson. After a three-week courtship they were married in London, where, after pocketing the £30 she withdrew from a post-office savings account, he took her to the Franco-British Exhibition at the White City, went to get a paper and walked out of her life – but not before removing and selling all her belongings, which were left in their Camden digs. That was on 3 July.

On 30 July he married Miss Edith Mabel Pegler in Bristol, using his real name. A dark-haired, round-faced, twenty-eight-year-old, she had replied to his advertisement in a local paper for a house-keeper: he now had a shop in Gloucester Road, Bristol.

From then on, using their various homes as a base for his operations, which necessitated frequent and lengthy absences in pursuit of his trade as an antique-dealer, they moved to Bedford, Luton, Croydon, London and Southend. It was not a regular life, but Edith Pegler accepted it without question. Her husband would disappear for weeks and months at a time, sometimes saying he was off on business or off to help 'a young fellow' with some business deals. During his absences he sent her occasional letters and postcards as well as the odd pound note. When she ran out of money she returned to her mother in Bristol, where he would pick her up or send her a note telling her to come to him. His added wealth after his absences he attributed to the selling of rare antiques, pictures or jewellery. Sometimes he said he had been abroad, to Canada or Spain.

In October 1909, he married a spinster clerk from Southampton, Miss Sarah Freeman. He called himself George Rose, claiming to be a man of means with a mythical monied aunt. He always dressed up for his wooings in a frock coat and top hat. The couple took lodgings in London and he had to wait a few days before she could withdraw all her post-office savings. He had told her he was short of the wherewithal to set up an antique business. She also sold some government stock. He pocketed the lot and took her on 5 November to the National Gallery. She sat and waited while he went to the lavatory. He never returned. While she waited for him he journeyed to Clapham, where he removed and sold her belongings, leaving her totally destitute. In all, he made about £400 out of Miss Freeman, the equivalent of the average wages of a working man over a four year period.

With that money, Miss Pegler and a second-hand furniture shop were for a time established at 22 Glenmore Street, Southend, bought for £270 with £30 remaining on the mortgage. Then the Smiths returned to Bristol, where he bought 86 Ashley Down Road, largely on a loan. Although he ultimately acquired eight properties and was worth a small fortune, he made a loss on the sale of all of them. He was too mean to be a good businessman, ever suspicious, arrogant and demanding in his many ill-spelt, ill-composed letters to solicitors, insurers, banks and building societies. He was also mean with his brides, travelling third class, lodging them cheaply and taking them by bicycle or on foot to places of free public entertainment.

In August 1910, a tall and winsome girl, Miss Beatrice (Bessie) Constance Annie Mundy, aged thirty-one, was living in a boarding house in Clifton. Her father, who had died in 1904, had been a bank manager at Warminster in Wiltshire and had left her well provided for, with over £2,500 in gilt-edged securities, managed for her by a family trust headed by her uncle, who thought her a fool where money was concerned and from whom she received £8 a month.

One day she happened to meet a picture restorer, Henry Williams (a.k.a. George Smith) when out for a walk, and in a matter of days they were on their way to Weymouth, she with no luggage but a hat box. They lodged at 14 Rodwell Avenue and were wed at the registry office on 26 August. 'Dear Uncle,' she wrote. 'I got married today, my husband is writing tonight. Yours truly, B Williams.' Smith wrote: 'Bessie hopes you will forward as much money as possible at your earliest by registered letter. Am pleased to say Bessie is in perfect health, and we are both looking forward to a bright and happy future. Believe me, yours faithfully, Henry Williams.'

But Smith had to wait until 13 December before he could lay his hands on £135, which was the interest that had accrued on her securities. He then absconded, leaving a lengthy letter of instruction for Bessie, repeating everything as if she were a child and cruelly explaining his departure thus:

Dearest, I fear you have blighted all my bright hopes of a happy future. I have caught from you a disease which is called the bad disorder. For you to be in such a state proves you could not have kept yourself morally clean ... For the sake of my health and honour, and yours too, I must go to London ... to get properly cured of this disease. It will cost me a great deal of money, because it might take years ... Tell the landlady and everyone else that I have gone to France. But tell your uncle the truth ... If he happens to ask you about money, tell him that you kept all the money which was sent to you in a leather bag, and two days after I had gone you happened to go on the beach and fall asleep and when you woke the bag of money was gone ... Whatever you do, stick to everything you say. Never alter it or else you will get mixed up and make a fool of yourself ... Mark what I say. Now tear this letter up at once and throw the pieces in the road.

Smith went straight from Weymouth to Bristol, back to Edith Pegler. They moved once more to Southend, where he bought another house. From there they went to London and then back to another address in Bristol, which may have been financed by another 'marriage', for nothing is known about Smith's activities in 1911.

Then, in March 1912, there was a fatal meeting in Weston-super-Mare. Bessie Mundy, who had been lodging with a Mrs Sarah Tuckett since February, went out at 11 am to buy some daffodils. By some extraordinary chance she happened to meet her vanished husband, Mr Williams. She returned at one o'clock. Mrs Tuckett later recalled:

She was very excited. She said as soon as she went out she found her husband looking over the sea.' At 3 pm he arrived at the house. Some women, like Mrs Tuckett, took an instinctive dislike to Smith. 'I asked him,' she said later, 'how it was he had left her eighteen months before at Weymouth. He replied that he had been looking for his wife for more than twelve months ... He knew her relatives and knew where they lived ... Miss Mundy said she wished to go back to her husband. She had forgiven the past. They had been to a solicitor, and she had promised to return to him. I told Mr Williams it was my duty to wire to her aunt to come at once ... She left with him without taking away any of her belongings. She promised to come back that same night, but I never saw her again ...

Smith took Bessie from town to town while he made official enquiries about how he might legally get possession of her fortune. In May, they were in Herne Bay, renting a small house at 80 High Street, which had neither bathroom or bath. On 2 July, Smith heard from his lawyer that if he and Bessie both made wills and she died, he would inherit everything. The information signed her death warrant. This time he had to kill his bride in order to get hold of her money and he had to act quickly, in case her relatives altered the terms of the settlement on her. Wills were drawn up and attested on 8 July. The next day, Smith bought a zinc bath (without taps) from an ironmonger, beating down the asking price of £2 to £1 17s 6d. In fact, he never paid for it, returning the bath six days later, its purpose served.

On Wednesday, 10 July, he took his wife to a young and newly qualified doctor called French, alleging she had had a fit – although all Bessie Mundy had complained of was a headache. At 1.30 am on Friday, Dr French was summoned to 80 High Street – Bessie had apparently had another fit and was in bed. The doctor found nothing amiss. She looked as if she had just woken up, was flushed and heavy-headed: it was a very warm night. The doctor prescribed a sedative. That afternoon he chanced to see the Williamses out of doors; she seemed in perfect health. That night, evidently on Smith's instructions, she penned a letter to her uncle:

> Last Tuesday night I had a bad fit, and one again on Thursday night … My husband has been extremely kind and done all he could for me. He has provided me with the attention of the best medical men here, who are … visiting me day and night … My husband has strictly advised me to let all my relatives know of my breakdown. I have made out my will and left all to my husband. That is only natural, as I love my husband.'

Poor Bessie. The following morning, about 7.30, she prepared to have a bath in a spare room, making about twenty journeys up and down the stairs with a bucket to and from the kitchen, while Smith went out to buy some fish. She got in the bath, her hair in curling-pins. Smith returned.

About 8 am a note reached Dr French as he was dressing – 'Can you come at once? I am afraid my wife is dead.' Delaying to snatch a quick breakfast, the doctor hurried to the house. Mrs Williams was lying submerged in the bath on her back, naked and dead. A bar of Castile soap was clutched in her right hand. When French left the house he informed the police of the fatality, and about ten o'clock PC Kitchingham arrived to take a statement from the bereaved husband. Bessie Mundy's body still lay, bare and uncovered, on the floor by the bath, and it was still there when at 4 pm a woman came to lay the body out.

Smith wired Miss Mundy's uncle: 'Bessie died in fit this morning. Letter following.' The subsequent letter began: 'Dear Sir, words cannot describe the great shock I suffered in the loss of my wife. The doctor said she had a fit in the bath …' There was no post mortem. The inquest, on Monday, 15 July – Smith wept throughout – found that she had died from misadventure. She was buried in a common grave at 2.30 pm on the Tuesday, before any of her relatives could get to Herne Bay. They tried to contest the will, but within six months over £2,500 was paid to Bessie's sole executor and legatee, Henry Williams. He opened several bank accounts, bought seven houses in Bristol and an annuity for himself.

Edith Pegler was instructed in August to join Smith in Margate. She said later: 'I told him I had tried to find him at Woolwich and Ramsgate, and he was very angry about it … He said I should not … interfere with his business, because he did not believe in women knowing his business … He remarked that if I interfered … I should never have another happy day.'

It seems she was not unhappy, although he used to beat her from time to time. From

Margate, they moved to Tunbridge Wells, Bristol, Weston-super-Mare and back to Bristol. Then, in the summer of 1913, Smith disappeared again.

In October he was in Southsea, where he met and married short and plump, twenty-five-year-old Alice Burnham, private nurse to an elderly invalid man and daughter of a Buckinghamshire fruit-grower. Her father, Mr Charles Burnham, met George Smith before the marriage took place and was thoroughly repelled by him. However, there was nothing he could do to stop the marriage, which took place in a Portsmouth registry office on 4 November, Smith using his real name and describing himself as 'bachelor, independent means'. But afterwards, when Smith wrote to Mr Burnham demanding the £104 that Mr Burnham was keeping for his daughter, the suspicious father-in-law got a solicitor to enquire about his son-in-law's antecedents. Soon, Mr Burnham received a postcard from Smith, which read: 'Sir — In answer to your application concerning my parentage, etc. My mother was a bus-horse, my father a cab-driver, my sister a rough-rider over the arctic regions. My brothers were all gallant sailors on a steam-roller.'

The day before the marriage, Alice's life was insured for £500. Smith then set to work, and having got the £27 9s 5d that was in her savings bank, having extracted the £104 which her father owed her and having paid the premium on Alice's insurance, he persuaded her to make a will. They then set off on an out-of-season seaside holiday.

This time Smith chose the main northerly English resort, Blackpool, where they arrived on Wednesday, 10 December 1913, a bleak and breezy day. The first lodging house they visited on spec, in Adelaide Street, had no bath. From here they were directed to 16 Regent Road, which had a bath. The rent was 10s a week. Again, a doctor — Dr Billing — was consulted about the buxom bride's health: she had a headache, not surprisingly after the long and tiring train journey across England from Portsmouth. Mrs Smith was then persuaded to write to her parents – 'My husband does all he can for me, in fact I have the best husband in the world' – and on Friday evening, 12 December, the couple went out for a walk after asking the daughter of their landlady, Mrs Crossley, to prepare a bath. They returned just after eight o'clock.

The bathroom was partly over the kitchen in which, at about 8.15 pm, the Crossleys were having tea. They heard nothing untoward, but then observed that stains were spreading over the ceiling and down a wall – the bath had overflowed. Just about then Smith appeared in the kitchen door, seeming out of breath and rumpled. He had two eggs in his hand. He said: 'I've brought these for our breakfast.' He then went upstairs, and a few minutes later shouted from the landing: 'Fetch the doctor! My wife cannot speak to me!'

The shocked Crossleys waited below as Dr Billing examined the unfortunate Mrs Smith, her body still in the bath. 'Oh, she is drowned – she is dead,' Dr Billing told Mrs Crossley. She could not believe what she must have suspected, but the death in her house

– and Smith's evident callous indifference to it – were too much for her. She could not bear to have him stay there that night; she told him so and he slept next door.

But in the morning, Saturday the 13th, he was back, seeing to the burial and matters to do with his wife's death. In the afternoon he played Mrs Crossley's piano in the front room and drank a bottle of whisky. As a result he was able to be emotional – he wept copiously – at the inquest on Mrs Alice Smith, née Burnham, which was held at 6.30 pm. The verdict was accidental death.

Alice Burnham was buried in a common grave on Monday, 15 December, at noon. Smith refused to have a deal coffin, saying dismissively: 'When they are dead, they are done with.' Immediately after the funeral he took a train back to Southsea. Before he left he gave Mrs Crossley an address card. She wrote on the back – 'Wife died in bath. We shall see him again.' She thought him 'a very hard-hearted man … I did not like his manner.' And as he left the house, she shouted: 'Crippen!'

After selling all Alice Burnham's belongings that had been left in her Southsea digs, Smith rejoined Edith Pegler in Bristol and was soon £500 richer. He increased his annuity. Once more he and Miss Pegler set off on their travels, going to London, Cheltenham and Torquay. By August they were in Bournemouth, and were staying in Ashley Road when the First World War began. 'While there,' said Edith later, 'my husband was out in the evenings. About the middle of September 1914, my husband said he was going to London for a few days.' In fact, he remained in Bournemouth, and wooed and won another bride – a maidservant named Alice Reavil. Dressed in white flannels, white boots and a boater he encountered her as she sat listening to a band in the sea-front gardens. They were married in Woolwich by special licence on 17 September – he called himself Charles Oliver James – and they lodged in Battersea Rise. She was lucky – she wasn't worth killing – and having made £90 out of her by stealing her savings and selling her belongings, Smith left Alice Reavil in some public gardens after a tram-ride. Some of her clothes he generously gave to Edith, saying he had 'been to a sale in London and had bought some ladies' clothing'. The Smiths then returned to Bristol, and he returned to his next victim, whom he had first met in June in Bath.

Miss Margaret Lofty was thirty-eight, the daughter of a clergyman long deceased. Occasionally a lady's companion, her last employment had ended in July and now she lived with her sister and aged mother. Disappointed in love earlier that year (ironically, her fiancé had turned out to be already married) she went out for tea on 15 December – and never returned. Two days later, on 17 December, without telling any of her family, she married 'John Lloyd, estate agent' in Bath. That same day, the Lloyds went to London and took rooms at 14 Bismarck Road (now Waterlow Road), Highgate. The house had a bath. That night 'John Lloyd' took his new bride to see one Dr Bates, and the following morning she went to a solicitor and made her will – her life had already been insured for £700. She wrote to her mother about her marriage, describing her husband as 'a thorough Christian man ... I have every proof of his love for me ... He has been *honourable* and kept his word to me in everything. He is such a nice man.'

About 8 pm on that Friday night, 18 December, she had a bath. At the time, the landlady, Miss Louisa Blatch, was ironing in the kitchen below the bathroom. She said: 'I heard a sound from the bathroom. It was a sound of splashing. Then there was a noise as of someone putting wet hands or arms on the side of the bath, and then a sigh ... a sort of sound like a child might make ...' (At Smith's trial, the medical experts, Dr Spilsbury and Dr Willcox, agreed that Smith probably drowned his brides by raising their legs, his left forearm under their knees, as he thrust their heads under the water with his right hand and held them down.) Next, she heard the harmonium being played in the front room. It was a familiar hymn: 'Nearer my God to Thee'. At about ten minutes later, the doorbell rang. It was Mr Lloyd. 'I forgot I had a key,' he said. 'I have been for some tomatoes for Mrs Lloyd's supper. Is she down yet?'

Margaret Lofty was buried on 21 December, and Smith was back with Edith in Bristol in time for Christmas. One day she told him she was going to have a bath. He replied: 'I would advise you to be careful of those things, as it is known that women have often lost their lives through weak hearts and fainting in the bath.'

The inquest on Margaret Lofty was held on 1 January 1915, and the resulting story in the *News of the World* – 'Bride's Tragic Fate on Day after Wedding' – was read by Alice Burnham's father and by Mrs Crossley. Both were powerfully struck by the similarities between the deaths of Mrs Lloyd and Mrs Alice Smith, and communicated their anxieties to the local police and to Scotland Yard.

On 4 January, Smith called on a solicitor, Mr Davies, at 60 Uxbridge Road, and instructed him to have Mrs Lloyd's will proved and the insurance policy made good. As Smith waited for the money to be paid, the police were pursuing exhaustive enquiries that took them to towns all over England during the next four weeks. At last they had enough information to make a holding charge. When Smith returned to his solicitor on 1 February, he was detained as he left the building by Detective Inspector Neil and two police sergeants. He admitted he was George Smith, who had married Alice Burnham, and was then charged with bigamy.

That same day, Margaret Lofty's body was exhumed and examined by Dr Spilsbury, who later travelled to Blackpool and then to Herne Bay to supervise the exhumations of Alice Burnham and Bessie Mundy and carry out the respective post mortems. Spilsbury had by now become the Home Office's honorary pathologist.

After further police investigations, Smith was charged on 23 March with the wilful murder of Bessie Mundy, Alice Burnham and Margaret Lofty. Remanded at Bow Street several times, he frequently shouted abuse at the witnesses and lawyers, denouncing and reviling them.

The trial of George Smith, aged forty-three, began at the Old Bailey on Tuesday, 22 June 1915, when he was indicted with the murder of Bessie Mundy. It was very hot in

London that month, with temperatures over 80°F, but the court was packed, mainly with women eager to see the accused, whose denunciatory outbursts from the dock – he gave no evidence – became more frequent as the trial proceeded. He called Mrs Crossley a lunatic and Inspector Neil a scoundrel. 'I don't care twopence what they say,' he told the judge. 'You cannot sentence me to death! I have done no murder. I have nothing to fear.' He vilified his lawyers and repeatedly shouted at the judge during the summing-up, complaining 'You'll have me hung the way you are going on!' – 'Sentence me and have done with it!' – 'It's a disgrace to a Christian country, this is! I'm not a murderer, though I may be a bit peculiar.' The prosecutor referred to him as 'a systematic bigamist'.

The trial was long, concluding on Thursday, 1 July. There were 264 exhibits and 112 witnesses. At one point, the jury were taken into an anteroom, where Inspector Neil demonstrated with a nurse (in a bathing costume) and one of the baths how the brides could have been drowned. So convincing was his demonstration that artificial respiration had to be used to revive the nurse.

Smith was defended by Mr Edward Marshall Hall, KC, assisted by Mr Montague Shearman. The prosecutor was the senior Treasury Counsel, Mr Archibald Bodkin, assisted by Mr Travers Humphreys, and the judge was Mr Justice Scrutton. *The Times*, reporting on the trial on 23 June 1915, was full of war news: the Roll of Honour in the paper that day contained the names of over 3,000 soldiers and 80 officers who had been killed; 3,772 servicemen were listed as being Mentioned in Despatches. Justice Scrutton made reference to this larger world picture during his summing-up:

> *Since last August all over Europe … thousands of lives of combatants, sometimes of noncombatants, have been taken daily, with no warning, and in many cases with no justification … And yet, while this wholesale destruction of human life is going on, for some days all the apparatus of justice in England has been considering whether the prosecution are right in saying that one man should die.*

The jury retired at 2.52 pm and took twenty-two minutes to find George Smith guilty. After he was sentenced – and he took this quite calmly – he leaned over the dock and said to Marshall Hall: 'I thank you, Mr Marshall Hall, for everything you have done. I still have great confidence in you. I shall bear up.' The judge commended the police who had carried out the investigation, in particular Inspector Neil, for their care and assiduity. The jury said: 'Hear, hear!' Outside the court, Edith Pegler wept.

Smith's appeal was dismissed. He was removed from Pentonville to Maidstone Prison on 4 August 1915. Unrepentant, though often in tears and prostrated, it is said, by fear, he was taken at 8 am across the sunny prison yard on Friday, 13 August and hanged in a high shed. John Ellis was the executioner.

Inspector Neil formally identified the body, and the errant bridegroom, naked and exposed to strangers as his wretched brides had been, was buried in a pit of quicklime within the jail.

The following day in Leicester, Caroline Thornhill – formerly Mrs Love, Smith's first wife and now a widow – married a Canadian soldier serving with the RE, Sapper Tom Davies, by special licence.

17

ALFRED BOWES

THE ATTEMPTED ASSASSINATION OF SIR EDWARD HENRY, 1912

There is a kind of premeditated murder in which the victim, a person of political, social or religious significance, happens to epitomise all the deep-seated grievances that the assailant has grown to feel and can only exorcise by destroying the imagined symbol or cause of his suffering. Murders where a political motive appears to be paramount are called assassinations. But most of the public figures who are shot at are also the victims of misguided, malignant obsession as well as of a perverted and morbid desire for fame.

E dward Henry was appointed Chief Commissioner of the Metropolitan Police in 1903. Until Sir Joseph Simpson was appointed in 1958, no Commissioner had ever been a policeman himself: they were elderly gentlemen, reputable civil servants, colonial administrators or senior army officers, appointed by the government after years of public service to supervise the Metropolitan Police.

Born in 1850 – his father was a London doctor – Edward Henry was educated at a Roman Catholic school, St Edmund's College in Hertfordshire, and began work at the age of sixteen in the offices of Lloyd's, the celebrated insurance company. Dissatisfied with his position as a lowly clerk, Edward Henry studied for and successfully sat the Indian Civil Service exams and was sent to work for the Bengal taxation service in Calcutta when he was twenty-four. He learned Bengali, played polo and hunted jackals in his spare time, and an unexceptional civil service career might have followed had not his curiosity been aroused one day on a visit to a Calcutta cashier's office, where he first came across the system of identifying illiterate Indian workers that Sir William Herschel, a senior ICS official, had initiated. Each Indian workman made a thumb print by sticking his left thumb in an inkwell, wiping off the excess with a rag and then pressing his thumb on a wages sheet. Edward Henry realised, as others had done, that the resulting prints – no two of which were the same – might be used to identify and track down criminals. But how? Using duplicates of the thumb-print payment sheets of Bengali workmen, he began to study the differences and similarities in the prints and tried to work out some system of classification.

In 1888, the year of the 'Jack the Ripper' murders in London, Edward Henry became a magistrate-collector, presiding over civil courts in which tax claims and disputes were settled. Two years later, aged forty, he married the young daughter of an Irish vicar while he was on leave in Britain. She was called Louisa Moore, and sailed with him back to Calcutta, where he had now lived and worked for sixteen years. The following year the ICS appointed him Inspector-General of Police in Bengal.

He was now able to study the fingerprints of thousands of Indian malefactors, and gradually evolved a numerical system that classified the prints of each finger on a man's hand according to its loops, whorls, arches, composites and lines.

Dr Francis Galton, a cousin of Charles Darwin, published a book called *Fingerprints* in 1892. His conclusions, however, were not favourable towards using them as a positive means of identification: there was still no proof that the line-patterns on people's fingers did not alter between the cradle and the grave; their variety seemed to be endless, and there seemed no simple way of classifying them. In the meantime, Scotland Yard detectives, using a French system, continued to measure and photograph criminals for their records – although some fingerprints were taken in case they might prove useful in identifying villains, many of whom used aliases in those days.

Then, in 1894, Edward Henry at last felt sufficiently confident about his findings and his system to write an official report, describing and advocating his system of identification by fingerprints. He sent it to the Government of India; the system was adopted throughout the country, and Henry published a textbook, *Classification and Use of Fingerprints,* which eventually became the accepted textbook on the subject all over the world. Nonetheless, magistrates in India continued to be reluctant to convict anyone on fingerprint evidence alone.

In 1899, at Galton's suggestion, Henry was invited to address a meeting of the British Association in London about his fingerprint researches and conclusions, and also to liaise with a government body, the Belper Committee, which had been set up to consider the various methods of identifying criminals and determine which might be best. Melville Macnaghten, Assistant Chief Constable in 1899, was a member. And so, after twenty-five years in India, Edward Henry resigned from the ICS and returned with his family to England, hoping to find some senior police post that would enable him to put his theories into practice.

Nothing transpired, and he went to South Africa to take up a police job there, which involved the reorganisation of the Transvaal police force. In so doing, he instituted new labour passes for coloured workers that bore the fingerprints of the holders. But the Boer War put an end to any further experiments and improvements. Then, in 1901, he heard that Sir Robert Anderson, Assistant Commissioner and head of the CID at Scotland Yard, was about to resign. Edward Henry applied for the post and got it. He took up his duties at the Yard on 31 May 1901.

Two months later, the Central Fingerprint Branch of the Metropolitan Police was established at the Yard under Detective Sergeant Charles Stockley Collins. It operated under many difficulties, much doubt and some opposition. Indicative of the scornful mistrust of many was this letter from 'A Disgusted Magistrate' to a national paper:

> *Scotland Yard, once known as the world's finest police organisation, will be the laughing-stock of Europe if it insists on trying to trace criminals by odd ridges on their skins. I, for one, am firmly convinced that no British jury will ever convict a man on 'evidence' produced by the half-baked theories some official happened to pick up in India.*

Another correspondent, writing in 1902, denounced Henry's system as 'hopelessly inaccurate, dangerous, and completely un-British'. But on Derby Day that year, the fingerprints of fifty-four people who had been arrested on Epsom Downs were taken and checked by Henry, DS Collins and a constable against the 2,000 or so that had by that time been filed away by the Fingerprints Branch. Twenty-nine of the fifty-four were found to have had previous convictions, and the next day as a result received heavier sentences from the magistrates who heard the charges against them.

The first trial at the Old Bailey in which fingerprint evidence formed the main part of the prosecution's case involved a burglar called Jackson, newly out of prison, who had left a neat impression of his prints on some new paint in a house he had robbed in Denmark Hill. He was found guilty, chiefly on account of the adept evidence of DS Collins, who had given the young barrister prosecuting Jackson (Richard Muir) a crash course on fingerprint deduction before the trial. However, these successes met with little public attention and even in the Yard Henry's oddball enthusiasm for fingerprints was dismissively regarded by most of his colleagues. But when, in 1903, his book on fingerprints was published for the first time in Britain, police forces in other cities – and other nations – slowly began to put the Henry system into practice; Bradford, in Yorkshire, was the first English town to start its own fingerprint collection.

On the retirement of the Commissioner, Edward Bradford, after thirteen years of service, Edward Henry was asked to be the next Chief Commissioner of the Metropolitan Police; he was fifty-three.

The fingerprint section at the Yard now flourished under Assistant Commissioner Melville Macnaghten and the newly promoted DI Collins. But it wasn't until the murder of the Farrows in Deptford in March 1905 that the value of fingerprinting as evidence of identification became firmly established. At the ensuing trial of the Stratton brothers at the Old Bailey, Richard Muir was again the prosecutor, and the most damning evidence, despite the reservations of the judge, was Alfred Stratton's thumb print on the cash box. A further advance in the science of fingerprinting was made when it was discovered that prints not immediately visible could be made so by dusting them with a very fine yellow powder called licopodium.

Yet it took a candle and a burglary in Huddersfield in 1909 to fix fingerprinting as evidence that was legally beyond all doubt. The burglar, Herbert Castleton, had been convicted of breaking and entering – no defence was put forward and he subsequently appealed. A candle he had gripped and used to light his search for valuables had served to convict him – it bore a fine set of fingerprints. He claimed that various thieving acquaintances had also handled the candle. In the appeal court Justice Darling asked the prisoner's counsel if he could produce anyone else whose fingerprints exactly matched those on the candle. This he could not do and the appeal was dismissed. Thenceforth 'The Castleton Judgement' became a point of law. Three years later, the Commissioner himself appeared in the Old Bailey as a witness for the prosecution in the case of his own attempted murder.

Edward Henry's responsibilities as Commissioner included the protection of foreign potentates and politicians and of the royal family, and as a result he had become acquainted with King Edward VII and Queen Alexandra. When the King died in 1910, Henry supervised the full-scale security operation surrounding the coronation of George V in June 1911. After this, he was knighted. But his biggest security headache was the state visit of the new King and Queen to India later that year. The former Lloyd's clerk and junior ICS official travelled with them, overseeing security arrangements throughout the royal tour, which culminated in the imperial splendours of the grand Durbar at Delhi.

By 1912, Sir Edward had stopped riding a horse to work, as had been his wont, and generally walked the five or six miles between his Kensington home and Scotland Yard. Sometimes, however, he made use of the car and chauffeur officially placed at his disposal, as he did on 27 November that year.

About 7 pm that evening, the car taking him home, driven by Albert English, drew up outside Campden House Court. Sir Edward's wife and his two young daughters were awaiting his arrival – he also had a four-year-old son, who was then in bed. His second daughter, Hermione, aged eleven, watched from the window of her bedroom above the front door porch as her father got out of the car. Sir Edward told English that he would not be needed again that night and turned towards the house. As he did so a young man approached him and said there was something he wanted to talk about. 'Can't speak to you now,' said Sir Edward. 'I'm busy. Call my office.' Whereupon the man pulled out a pistol and fired three times. Two shots missed their target. Wounded by the third, Sir Edward staggered to the front door of his house, opened it, and was helped to a chair by his eldest daughter, Helen, who happened to be in the hall. The gunman had in the meantime been seized by the chauffeur, who was assisted in the resulting struggle by a porter and a decorator working in a house across the road. 'Let me go!' cried the gunman. 'This man has done me a great wrong! Let me go!'

Sir Edward's injury was found not to be serious, but he suffered severely from shock. His assailant was taken to Kensington police station and identified as Alfred George

Bowes, from Acton in west London. It later transpired that, having failed to pass his driving test and having been refused a licence as a taxi driver, Bowes had developed distorted feelings of injustice and humiliation, which focused for some reason on the Commissioner. Bowes imagined that the Commissioner was personally responsible for his failure to get a licence.

He was tried at the Old Bailey. No fingerprint evidence or any other was required, as the accused pleaded guilty. The weapon used was a Remington Colt self-loading pistol. Sir Edward, supporting himself on a stick and still unwell, was the chief witness. He asked the judge to be merciful towards Bowes. 'He was ambitious to become a taxi driver,' explained Sir Edward. 'All ambition is a good thing, and I would not wish him to suffer unduly because of that ambition.'

The judge sentenced Bowes to fifteen years' penal servitude. This distressed Sir Edward, who as Commissioner was in a position to know much more about his assailant's background and character than the usual victim of such an attack. He knew that Bowes, an only son, had been anxious to better himself and earn a good and regular income as a taxi driver so that he could improve his widowed mother's lot: she kept herself from abject poverty by washing and sewing for others.

After Alfred Bowes was imprisoned, Sir Edward periodically drove to Acton, where he dismissed his chauffeur-driven car before calling on Mrs Bowes. He gave her enough money to satisfy her needs and keep herself comfortable and warm. After each visit – and they continued for several years – he returned to Kensington by public transport. For a long time no one, not even his wife, knew about these visits. When Alfred Bowes was released from prison in 1922, Sir Edward paid for his passage to Canada, giving him enough money for him to make a new start in life.

Sir Edward, meanwhile, remained as Commissioner throughout the First World War, although he could have retired in 1915 when he was sixty-five. When in 1918, after years of governmental procrastination, the police went on strike at midnight on 29 August, demanding various improvements in pay, pensions and conditions, Sir Edward, who had supported their cause and had been sadly disillusioned by the whole experience, resigned soon after the government capitulated. The strike lasted two days.

Laden with honours and distinctions bestowed on him for his invention, classification and promulgation of a fingerprint system that was now in successful worldwide use, Sir Edward lived out the rest of his life in a house called Cissbury at Ascot. He became a magistrate. He was chairman of the Athenaeum Club in London and on the central committee of the NSPCC. Then in 1930 his only son, John, who had just completed a three-year course at Trinity College, Cambridge, suddenly became ill and died, aged twenty-two.

Six months later, on 19 February 1931. Sir Edward Henry himself died at the age of eighty.

Meanwhile, further improvements had been made at Scotland Yard. In August 1914, when the First World War began, a PC was earning thirty shillings a week; in 1918 the basic pay was put up to forty-three shillings; and by 1931 it had risen to seventy shillings. By the time of the First World War, the first detective training school had been started and the Criminal Record Office set up. By then, the Metropolitan Police were equipped with a few official bicycles and cars, and in 1921 – twenty years after the first telephone was installed at the Yard – the first police telephone box was erected.

DAVID GREENWOOD

THE MURDER OF NELLIE TREW, 1918

Seldom have more trivial items helped to trap a murderer than the button and badge that were lost from an overcoat and left behind at the scene of this crime. Seldom has a murderer been so hopeless or pathetic, or he and his victim so young.

Nellie Grace Trew was sixteen. A junior clerk, she worked in the offices of Woolwich Arsenal and lived with her parents at Juno Terrace, Eltham Well Hall. She was known as Peg. On the evening of Saturday, 9 February 1918 she left her home to go to Plumstead Library to change a library book. When she failed to return home by midnight, her father went to the police.

Her body was found the following morning on Eltham Common, near the Eltham-Woolwich Road, and about a quarter of a mile from her home. She lay on her back, and although still wearing her knickers, she had been raped. Covered in mud, she had been struck on the head, dragged about 30 yards and strangled manually. Beside her lay her handbag and a library book called *The Adventures of Herr Baby*.

Nearby, trodden into the grass and mud was a replica of the badge of the Leicestershire Regiment, the Tigers, and an overcoat button. The latter had been threaded through two holes – not with cotton or wool but with a piece of wire, one end of which was sharp, the other end being broken. The police acted promptly, and by Monday morning photographs of the badge and button appeared in every popular newspaper.

Ted Farrell, who worked for the Hewson Manufacturing Company in Newman Street between Oxford Street and Tottenham Court Road – the firm made aeroplane parts – drew the attention of the pictured badge to a twenty-one-year-old workmate, a turner called David Greenwood. Farrell thought the badge was just like one that Greenwood wore in the lapel of his overcoat – and he had been wearing it, Farrell felt sure, the previous Saturday. Now it was missing. He pointed at the newspaper and remarked: 'That looks uncommonly like the badge you were wearing.' Greenwood had to agree, and when asked what had happened to *his* badge, replied that he had sold it on Saturday afternoon for two shillings to a man he had met on a tram between Well Hall and Eltham. His colleagues then suggested that for his own good that he should 'clear the matter up' with the police.

Accordingly, at lunchtime, Greenwood went to Tottenham Court Road police station and told his story about the badge and the man in the tram – 'His accent appeared to me as though he came from Belfast,' he stated. 'I should say he was a man that had had an outdoor life.'

The police discovered that Greenwood had been a neighbour of Nellie Trew and lived at Jupiter Terrace, Well Hall. They visited the Hewson works the following day, showed Greenwood the badge, and asked him if it was in fact his. He said it was. He was then asked to accompany Inspector Carlin back to Scotland Yard. En route, the inspector casually enquired: 'What buttons have you on your coat?' adding as he saw for himself – 'Why, I see they are all off.' Indeed they were, and Greenwood said they had been 'off for a long time'. The inspector, taking a close look at the coat worn by the young man beside him, now noticed that there was a little tear where one button had been. 'That is where it was pulled out, I suppose,' Greenwood explained. The button found by Nellie Trew's body was later proved to have come from his overcoat and the wire attachment to have been part of a spring of a type used at Hewson's. Greenwood was arrested and charged.

His trial began at the Old Bailey on 24 April 1918 before Mr Justice Atkin; Sir Travers Humphreys was the prosecutor and Mr Slesser defended. Greenwood, who pleaded not guilty, said he had never liked his overcoat, which had been issued to him on his discharge from the RAMC in 1917. The buttons were poorly sewn on and had come off easily. He was not, he claimed, wearing the coat on the day of the murder.

Mr Slesser revealed the record of Greenwood's valiant war service and tried to get Bernard Spilsbury to admit that Greenwood would not have been able to overpower a healthy young girl. He had enlisted at the beginning of the war when he was seventeen and had fought at Ypres, where he had been buried alive by the earth thrown up by an exploding shell. He was now suffering from neurasthenia, shell-shock and a weak heart. Spilsbury refused to commit himself either way.

The jury took three hours to find Greenwood guilty, adding a recommendation for mercy because of his youth, his services to his country and his good character. Curiously, when asked if he had anything to say before sentence was passed, Greenwood repeated that he was innocent but urged that the recommendation for mercy be disregarded. It was – he was sentenced to death.

He appealed, and was reprieved on the eve of his execution, set for 31 May, being sentenced instead to penal servitude for life. For some years people continued to agitate for his release – petitions were organised and signed by thousands. But he spent fifteen years in jail, being released in 1933 at the age of thirty-six.

MAJOR ARMSTRONG

THE MURDER OF MRS ARMSTRONG, 1921

Very few murderers seem to have been of any great height or, for that matter, of any great weight, and they have had a correspondingly exaggerated idea of their own importance and an excess of personal vanity. Indeed, vanity is a trait to be found in most murderers, who lavish much care on their dress and appearance, especially when appearing in court. One such was Major Armstrong, believed to be the only solicitor in the UK ever to be hanged.

Herbert Rowse Armstrong, a neat little man with ice-blue eyes, was fifty-one at the time of his wife's death. He wore spectacles, spats, a flower in his button hole and a walrus moustache, spikily waxed at each end. Apart from being small (5 ft 3 in), he was also extraordinarily slight, weighing only about 7 stone. He lived with his wife and three young children in the charming Welsh border town of Hay-on-Wye, in the then country of Brecknockshire, where he was clerk to the local JPs, the Worshipful Master of the Hay Lodge of freemasons, and had a reputable solicitor's practice in Broad Street.

He was born in Devon, in Plymouth, on 13 May 1869; his father was a merchant. The family moved to Liverpool and young Armstrong, after studying at St Catherine's College, Cambridge, and then in Liverpool for a law degree, became an articled clerk in that city in 1895. He was commissioned during the Boer War in 1900, serving with the First Lancashire Royal Fusiliers. In 1901, pursuing his profession as a solicitor, he went to Newton Abbott in Devon, lived there for six years, and eventually, after a three-year engagement, married a printer's daughter, Miss Katherine Mary Friend, in Teignmouth in 1907, when she was thirty-four. They moved to Hay-on-Wye, where, at 9 Broad Street, Armstrong became the junior partner of Mr Cheese in a solicitor's firm that was then renamed Cheese and Armstrong. The couple settled in a valley south-east of Hay called Cusop Dingle, where they acquired a large house, Mayfield, as well as three children in as many years: two girls and a boy. The house, situated on the English side of the border (which was marked by a wooded stream running down the valley), had a large garden, a tennis court, and a plethora of plantains and dandelions that required large quantities of weed-killer to keep them under control.

On 26 April 1914, Mr Cheese died (of cancer) and his wife collapsed and died the following day (of a heart attack). The solicitor's practice now became Armstrong's alone, the brass plate at the door changed to read: *Mr H Rowse Armstrong, Solicitor and Notary Public, Clerk to the Justices.* But he had little chance to enjoy his professional elevation– which some people would later see in a very sinister light – for in August war was declared. In November 1914, Armstrong enlisted in the Royal Engineers and served throughout the Great War (although never abroad), becoming a major in 1916, a rank he also held as a part-time soldier after the war in the local Territorial Army. In 1917, Mrs Armstrong, nervous about her children's future, made a will leaving them everything she had, aside from bequests to friends and just £50 a year to her husband.

Major Armstrong was demobbed in May 1920. Two months later, he was entertaining a middle-aged widow in London: they had dinner together and went to a theatre. This was Mrs Marion Gale, who lived with her mother in Ford Cottage, Christchurch. She had first met Armstrong in August 1915 when he was stationed in the Bournemouth area.

It is worth noting here that in April 1920, the body of Mrs Mabel Greenwood was exhumed at Kidwelly in south Wales and found to contain about half a grain of arsenic. Her husband, Harold Greenwood, was a forty-five-year-old solicitor practising in Llanelly, and four months after his wife's sudden death, in June 1919, he had taken a younger woman, Gladys Jones, as his second wife. In June 1920 the jury at the inquest on Mrs Greenwood concluded that she had been poisoned by Mr Greenwood. He was sent for trial. Weed-killer containing arsenic was alleged to have been given to her in a bottle of burgundy at lunch. The case excited much interest, not only in Britain but also in America. It must have caused much comment in that other somnolent town in south Wales, Hay-on-Wye.

A month before the major met Mrs Gale in London, and just about the time that Greenwood was sent for trial, Mrs Armstrong made a new will, leaving everything to her husband and making no special provisions for her three children. The will was in his handwriting and counter-signed by the housekeeper and a maid – although not at the same time, and in the case of the maid not in Mrs Armstrong's presence. Her signature and the will were almost certainly forged.

About this time, her mental state began to deteriorate. She had never been in the best of health, suffering from chronic indigestion, rheumatism and neuritis, and was something of a hypochondriac. She believed in homoeopathic medicines, of which over fifty bottles were found in her bedroom after her death. A tall and gawky, intelligent, cultured woman, who wore spectacles and played the piano with skill, she was also a cranky, teetotal autocrat who allowed no wine, spirits or smoking in the house and who ruled her home, husband and children with some severity. The Armstrongs were nonetheless thought locally to be an affectionate couple – they were impolitely known as Mutt and Jeff – and her public rebukes were borne by the major with mild and good-humoured forbearance.

According to him, he first noticed signs in her of a mental breakdown on 9 August

1920 when (five days after he had bought three tins of powdered weed-killer) he returned home from his office and learned that Mrs Armstrong had told the children they would never see their father again: she believed he had been arrested for something she had done. Her melancholia and delusions arose, it seems, from a deep sense of failure. Acutely introspective, she felt she was unworthy, that she was not looking after the children properly, was defrauding tradesmen and underpaying the servants. She heard voices and footsteps, and was anxious about imaginary intruders. 'She imagined things were happening in the house,' said the elderly housekeeper, Miss Pearce.

These delusions rapidly worsened, and then Mrs Armstrong became really ill. Doctors and family friends were consulted and on 22 August after Sunday lunch, which was attended by Major and Mrs Armstrong, by her sister, her niece and by the major's lifelong friend, a solicitor named Arthur Chevalier, the necessary forms were signed and Mrs Armstrong was driven to Gloucester, to Barnwood House Hospital for Mental Disorders, a private asylum. She was there for five months.

Free of her strictures, the major indulged in his little vices, such as drinking and smoking and going up to London at the weekend, when he pursued the pleasures of a middle-aged philanderer. Before long, he was paying for these pleasures. In November he contracted syphilis, and was not fully cured until the following spring. And in November he must, like everyone else, have read with extraordinary interest that the jury at the Harold Greenwood trial in Carmarthen had brought in a verdict of 'Not guilty'. Indeed, it was not long after this that he began to agitate for Mrs Armstrong's return home, writing letters on the subject to the asylum's superintendent.

On 11 January 1921, he bought a quarter of a pound of arsenic from Mr John Davies, the principal chemist in Hay – in very early anticipation of using it as a weed-killer in his garden. Three days later, he again wrote to the superintendent of Barnwood about his wife's illness, saying: 'The original delusions have absolutely ceased, and I feel sure that a return to her home and light household duties will be beneficial.' Although her general health *had* improved, the superintendent, Dr Townsend, knew that her delusions had persisted – she believed she was being poisoned by the asylum. But as she herself was eager to go home, to redeem herself as a dutiful wife and mother, and as her husband's request could not reasonably be denied, Mrs Armstrong returned to Mayfield on 22 January.

She was still quite feeble and a nurse, Muriel Kinsey, was hired from the 23rd to assist Mrs Armstrong when she washed and dressed. But Nurse Kinsey felt unable to cope with her charge's mental condition after Mrs Armstrong 'asked if it would be sufficient to kill anyone if they threw themselves through the attic window'. A full-time nurse, Eva Allen, took over on the 27th. Meanwhile, the Armstrongs' family doctor, Dr Tom Hincks, a large man with a dark moustache and a fondness for hunting and riding, was puzzled by his patient's reference in an examination to the fact that she felt she was walking on springs. Although an invalid she left her sick-bed every day, anxiously venturing downstairs to check on the running of house and home. On 8 February she was forty-eight.

On Sunday, 13 February Mrs Armstrong was stricken with vomiting, pains and muscular spasms. It was thought she had caught a chill from sitting out on the porch, although she had been wrapped in an eiderdown and had had hot-water bottles at her feet and in her lap. She recovered, but after lunch (boiled leg of mutton, junket and preserved gooseberries), on the 16th she was dreadfully sick again. Dr Hincks noted that her sallow skin had darkened, becoming almost coppery; there were sores about her mouth. That evening she retired to her bed and never left it, being fed on soft foods such as tapioca, sago and Benger's foods, intermittently vomiting and suffering from diarrhoea, with a pulse rate of 120 and terrible pains in her stomach.

Dr Hincks now attended her daily, and raised no objection when the major asked if his wife could take some of her homoeopathic brews – which the major prepared for her himself.

Two days later, Mrs Armstrong's arms and legs became paralysed, and on Monday, 21 February, Dr Hincks told the major that his wife would not recover. Very early the next morning Nurse Allen heard Mrs Armstrong say: 'Nurse, I'm not going to die, am I? Because I have everything to live for – my children and my husband.' At 8 am, Nurse Allen summoned the major from the bedroom he had used since his wife's return; she was all but unconscious. Dr Hincks arrived, and having done what he could for the dying woman he drove the major into town and dropped him off at his office in Broad Street at about nine o'clock. Some fifteen minutes later, Nurse Allen telephoned the major to say that Mrs Armstrong was dead.

Her demise was succinctly noted in Major Armstrong's pocket diary (Full Moon 9.32 am) – 'K died.'

Two nights later, he asked one of the maids, Inez Rosser, to bring a candle to the main bedroom, where Mrs Armstrong's body now reposed in a coffin, her hair twined into two long plaits. The maid watched as, by candlelight, the major soaped his dead wife's fingers and removed her rings.

Dr Hincks continued to be perplexed by the conflicting symptoms of Mrs Armstrong's last illness. Eventually, he wrote on her death certificate that she had died of heart disease, arising from nephritis and gastritis.

She was buried on 25 February. The major coldly noted in his diary – 'K's funeral 3 pm Cusop.'

Within three weeks, Major Armstrong rewarded himself with a month-long holiday in Italy and Malta, where he picked up a skin infection that produced a rash over most of his body. On his return to England he visited Bournemouth and asked Mrs Gale to marry him. She demurred. But the marriage of a solicitor did take place in Hay that summer, on 21 June – that of Mr Oswald Martin and Miss Constance Davies.

Mr Martin, aged thirty-two, was the senior partner in the firm of Griffiths and

Martin, and had become so when old Mr Griffiths died in November 1920. Mr Martin had come to Hay the year before. Wounded in the last months of the Great War, in which he had served throughout as a private, he had sustained an injury that half-paralysed one side of his face. This made him seem to wear a permanent half-smile, which some people found rather disconcerting. Something other than this, however, must have irritated the major during the three months that followed his professional rival's wedding, for on 20 September, a 1 lb box of Fuller's chocolates was posted to Mr Martin by an anonymous well-wisher.

Fortunately neither Martin nor his wife were partial to chocolates, although they sampled one or two. These had no ill-effects and the rest were put aside, to be brought out and placed in a silver sweet-dish on 8 October, when the Martins gave a dinner-party for his two brothers and their wives, who were in Hay on a visit. Of the six Martins only Gilbert Martin's wife, Dorothy, ate any of the chocolates. Later that night she was violently ill – much to the embarrassment of her hosts and the vexation, no doubt, of Major Armstrong.

Oddly enough, a local inspector of taxes was also taken ill at about this time after dining at Mayfield, and an estate agent from Hereford, Mr Willi Davies, at odds with the major over some deal, actually died on 4 October. Local gossip was later to put a poisonous cast on both of these other mishaps.

A month after the chocolate-box incident, the major had definite cause for aggravation apropos Mr Martin. They were both involved in the sale of the Velinnewydd estate: Armstrong was acting for the vendor, Martin for the purchaser. Completion was more than a year overdue. On 20 October 1921, Mr Martin gave written notice of his client's desire to rescind the contract, at the same time demanding repayment of deposits totalling £500, with costs and expenses. This apparently much agitated the major, who wished to defer the matter as his client had, without his previous knowledge, taken out two mortgages on the estate.

However, in an apparent attempt at conciliation, he asked Mr Martin to tea at Mayfield on Wednesday, 26 October. Mr Martin went there by car. He stated later:

> When I arrived at Major Armstrong's house (about 5.10 pm), I met him in the drive. We went round the garden, and went into the house ... into the drawing room on the left as you go into the hall. There was a small table by the window laid for tea, and by it there was a three-tier cake-stand ... The teapot and hot water were brought in by the maid. I sat with my back to the window facing him. It was getting dusk at the time. Major Armstrong poured out a cup of tea and handed it to me, and then he handed me a scone in his fingers.

It was a buttered scone and the gesture was uncharacteristically uncouth. 'Excuse my fingers,' said the major in mitigation. Mr Martin also ate some currant bread.

Within a few hours, Mr Martin began to feel ill. After dinner with his wife (jugged

ANOTHER WHITECHAPEL HORROR.
MORE REVOLTING MUTILATION THAN
EVER.

[WITH FULL PAGE ILLUSTRATIONS.]

On Friday another addition was made to the series of horrible crimes that has created a panic in the East End of London for many weeks past, and has sent a thrill of horror through the country at large. As in the previous cases, the scene of the tragedy lies in the district of Whitechapel, within almost a stone's throw of Hanbury-street, where the unfortunate woman Nicholls was so brutally put to death. The victim was another of the unfortunate class, who occupied a miserably-furnished room in a court off Dorset-street, a narrow thoroughfare out of Commercial-street, not far removed from the police-station. She had lived in the court for some little time, and was known as Mary Jane Kelly, alias "Ginger." She was a Welsh woman, and it is believed was married, but separated from her husband. Recently she had lived with a man who was known in the neighbourhood as Dan, but the couple parted a few days ago. Since that time the murdered woman had been seen several times walking about the locality, and on more than one occasion has been in the company of men. It is supposed that she met the man who was to be her murderer at a late hour on Thursday night, and that he induced her to allow him to accompany her home. Though there is good reason to believe that the murderer was in the house the whole of the night, he did not carry out his terrible purpose until a period later than half-past eight o'clock on Friday morning. At that time the deceased was seen walking along Dorset-street, and it is supposed that she had left the house for the purpose of purchasing provisions for breakfast. She is then said to have appeared cheerful and looking bright and well. Some two hours from this time the unfortunate woman was found lying dead and frightfully mutilated. At half-past eleven o'clock a man went to the room to collect the rent, and failing to gain any answer to his knocking at the door, he looked through the window. It was then seen that the woman was lying naked and bleeding on the bed, and an alarm was at once given.

Above: Mrs Dyson giving evidence against Charles Peace in Sheffield Prison. ©*Topfoto*

Below left: Charles Peace, who shot dead his neighbour, Arthur Dyson. © *Topfoto*

Below right: A newspaper report on one of the Jack the Ripper murders.

© *John Frost Collection*

Above: Police News illustrations relating to the Jack the Ripper murders.

© *John Frost Collection*

Below left: Sketch of the body of Ripper victim, Catherine Eddowes.

Below right top and bottom: James and Florence Maybrick. Florence was found guilty of poisoning her husband in 1889.

© *The Metropolitan Police*

Above: Mrs Deeming and Frederick Deeming   © *The Metropolitan Police*

Below left: A plaster cast of Deeming's head, taken after his execution.

© *The Metropolitan Police*

Below right: Dr Cream, who murdered Matilda Clover.   © *Getty Images*

THE ARREST OF FOWLER.

The Private Stage Door. Adelphi Theatre

Above left: A drawing showing the arrest of Henry Fowler who, along with his partner in crime, Albert Milsom, brutally murdered Henry Smith. © *The Metropolitan Police*

Above right: The theatre doorway in Maiden Lane where William Terriss was stabbed.

© *Mander and Mitchenson*

Below: The Adelphi Theatre in the Strand. © *Mander and Mitchenson*

Above left: Alfred and Albert Stratton   *© The Metropolitan Police*

Above right: Camille Cecile Holland: Samuel Dougal bewitched her before
killing her.   *© Chelmsford Museums*

Below: Searching for Miss Holland's body in the moat at Moat House Farm.

          © Chelmsford Museums

Above left: Dr Crippen

© *Getty Images*

Above right: The cellar where police found Belle Elmore's remains.

© *The Metropolitan Police*

Below left: Eliza Barrow, who became Frederick Henry Seddon's tenant.   © *Mirrorpix*

Below right: Mr Seddon at the time of his trial. He was found guilty of murdering Eliza but his wife was acquitted.

© *Mirrorpix*

Above: Ronald True at the inquest on Gertrude Yates: True was a fantasist and a liar.

©*Mirrorpix*

Below: Norman Thorne posed for press photographers on the spot where he had buried the body of Elsie Cameron.

© *Getty Images*

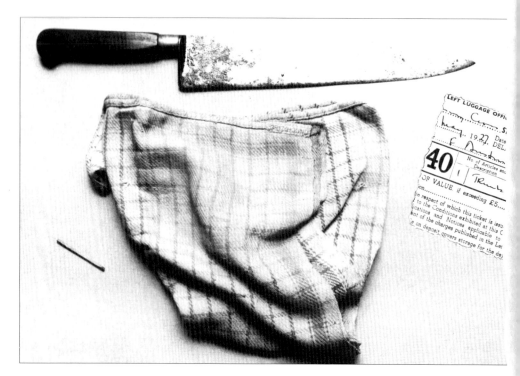

Above: The bloody matchstick, knife, duster and cloakroom ticket that provided the evidence against John Robinson, who hid the dismembered body of Minnie Bonati in a trunk at the left luggage office at Charing Cross station.

© The Metropolitan Police

Below left: Charlotte Bryant, who poisoned her husband, Frederick John Bryant.

© Topfoto

Below right: The Bryants' cottage at Coombe Farm near Sherborne.

© Topfoto

hare and coffee custard), he dashed upstairs and was horribly sick. He continued to retch and vomit throughout the night and was ill for five days in total. Dr Hincks, who attended him, was more than puzzled by this patient's symptoms and rendered most uneasy when Mr Martin's father-in-law, Mr Davies, the town's chief chemist, informed the doctor that the major regularly purchased large quantities of arsenic from his shop. It was Mr Davies who then remembered the sudden sickness of Mrs Dorothy Martin. The two men agreed it might be advisable to have a sample of the invalid's urine analysed – as well as the remaining chocolates, which were still in the Martins' house – and on 31 October, a parcel containing the urine sample and the chocolates was sent to the Clinical Research Association in London. At the same time, Dr Hincks wrote to the Home Office, outlining his suspicions.

The Association's laboratory found that two of the chocolates had been tampered with and that one was stuffed with 2.12 grains of white arsenic. The urine sample contained 1/33 of a grain of arsenic; the Association informed the DPP about this. But Dr Hincks, Mr Davies and the Martins were kept in suspense until 9 December, when a representative of the DPP met Dr Hincks in Hereford. Dr Hincks made a statement and a secret police investigation was instituted straight away.

It lasted for a month, during which the persistently friendly major assailed Mr Martin with further invitations to tea, as he had done throughout November. 'I think I had about twenty invitations to tea,' said Mr Martin, desperately trying to postpone the event with a series of increasingly lame excuses.

To avoid having to pass Mayfield on his way home, he began to take tea in his office. The major began to do likewise, however, and as the two offices were on opposites sides of Broad Street it was most difficult for the intended victim to find plausible reasons for not accepting an invitation whenever the major telephoned and suggested that Mr Martin nip across the road for a genial business chat over a cup of tea – especially after the police instructed him to give the major no cause for alarm.

Matters came to a head when, just before Christmas, Major Armstrong issued a formal invitation to both Mr and Mrs Martin. It was for 28 December. In truth, Martin had by now run out of plausible excuses, though he did manage to scrape up a weak reason for his wife's and his own absence from this festive treat. Then at last, on 31 December, Inspector Crutchett of Scotland Yard came to the rescue.

Accompanied by Sergeant Sharp and Superintendent Weaver, the Deputy Chief Constable of Herefordshire, the inspector called on Major Armstrong in his antiquated office in a converted shop at ten o'clock that morning. They entered his office without knocking and stayed until four.

The major, who was wearing a snappy Norfolk jacket, riding-breeches and trench boots, was asked if he had anything to say about the suspicious circumstances of Mr Martin's recent illness. 'This is a very serious matter,' he replied. 'I will help you all I can.' He then made a detailed statement, after which he was arrested on a charge of attempting to murder Mr Martin, and his clothes and the office were searched. A small packet of arsenic was discovered in one of his pockets. It was the twentieth part, he said, of 1 oz of arsenic purchased to eradicate twenty dandelion roots in his garden. Another 2 oz of arsenic were found in his office desk. Major Armstrong was taken to the local police station, where he was temporarily lodged, to the stunned disbelief of the local worthies, before being remanded in custody in Worcester Jail.

On 2 January 1922, Mrs Armstrong's body was exhumed from the snowy graveyard of Cusop church and examined the following day by Dr Bernard Spilsbury. Her remains, when analysed, were found to contain 3 1/2 grains of arsenic, a remnant of the massive dose that had killed her. As the gravediggers worked in the churchyard on the 2nd, Major Armstrong made his first sensational appearance at Hay in the magistrate's court in which he had often assisted in the processes of justice. Throughout the hearing he was transported by car between Worcester and Hay. He was charged on 19 January with the murder of his wife.

Unseasonal snow was falling when the trial of Major Armstrong began at Hereford Assizes on Monday, 3 April 1922, the day after Cambridge won the Boat Race – a good omen, as it seemed to him. The trial lasted ten days.

The presiding judge was Mr Justice Darling, aged seventy-three. The Attorney-General, Sir Ernest Pollock, led for the Crown. Sir Henry Curtis Bennett, for the defence, suggested that Mrs Armstrong had committed suicide when of unsound mind and had taken the arsenic herself. It was also pointed out that hardly any of the money left to the major by his wife (£2,278) had been touched.

The major, himself a lawyer, was a confident witness and an acquittal was expected. But Mr Justice Darling's questions – he asked over a hundred – were incisive, and Major Armstrong, five hours in the witness box, could give no satisfactory explanation for the presence of arsenic in his office and in his pocket.

'If you were simply dosing dandelions,' inquired the judge, 'why did you make up that one ounce of arsenic into twenty little packets such as that found in your pocket wrapped up in paper?' 'Because of the convenience of putting it in the ground,' replied the major.

The judge: 'Why go to the trouble of making up twenty little packets, one for each dandelion, instead of taking out the ounce you had got and making a hole and giving the dandelions something from the one ounce?' Replied the major: 'I do not really know.'

'Why make up twenty little packets, each a fatal dose for a human being, and put them in your pocket?'

'At the time it seemed to me the most convenient way of doing it.'

Major Armstrong was found guilty of the murder of his wife on Thursday, 13 April. An appeal was dismissed and, having put his affairs in order and given small gifts to his lawyers and his warders, he was taken from his cell in Gloucester Prison on 31 May 1922 and hanged.

The Armstrong children were taken care of by an aunt. Mayfield was sold and its name was changed. Hay-on-Wye returned more or less to normal, and Mr Martin became the leading solicitor in the town. But the attempts on his life, the notoriety and the trial had deeply affected his health. He suffered from depression and became afraid of the dark. In 1924, he and his wife moved to East Anglia, where he died within a few years. Dr Hincks died in 1932 from a heart attack that struck him one day as he rode on the hillside above Mayfield. The judge, the Attorney-General and Sir Henry Curtis Bennett all died in 1936. The twice unhappy widow, Mrs Gale, known at the trial as Madame X and thereafter in reports of the case as Mrs G, outlived them all. She died in a Bournemouth nursing-home in 1960 at the age of ninety-one.

Nothing much – apart from the growth of a plethora of bookshops – has really changed since the murder of Mrs Armstrong in charming Hay-on-Wye.

20
RONALD TRUE

THE MURDER OF GERTRUDE YATES, 1922

More prostitutes have been murdered than persons of any other profession, including policemen, and several men have murdered women for resisting their sexual advances. Sexual problems are indeed at the root of many murders that are not committed for gain. But Gertrude Yates was murdered mainly because Ronald True was mad. An extreme example of the totally amoral murderer who fantasizes and lies, Ronald True had, like so many other convicted murderers, learnt to kill during a war. In fact, a wave of serious crimes followed the First World War, and the Flying Squad was formed to deal with it.

Ronald True was born in Manchester on 17 June 1891, the son of an unmarried sixteen-year-old girl. She married a wealthy man when Ronald was eleven, and he was sent to Bedford Grammar School. Even as a boy he habitually lied, played truant and was cruel to his pony and rabbits. When he left school at seventeen, he did no work and his step-father followed the usual line with family incompetents and misfits by sending him abroad to learn a job, such as farming. For brief periods, True lived and worked in New Zealand, Argentina, Canada and Mexico, leaving each country after being dismissed from his latest job or merely walking out. He kept coming home, as dissolute and as feckless as ever. And then he started taking morphia.

In 1915, he joined the Royal Flying Corps and crashed the following February on his first solo flight at Farnborough, suffering severe concussion. The head injuries he sustained may have affected his mind: his behaviour became odder and he developed an aversion to wearing hats. A month later he crashed again, and then had a nervous breakdown. Pilot Officer Guy Dent said of him: 'He had a feverish air about him. He was always given to rushing about and laughing with a loud voice, and he seemed deficient in common sense … He was unstable, boastful … He was a very bad pilot … He gave me the impression of a man always on a strain – tense.'

Invalided out of the RFC in October, True acquired and soon lost a job as a test pilot at Yeovil. He went to New York, where he regaled ladies at parties with stirring tales of air battles with German planes. As an indirect result, he obtained a brief job as a flying instructor and married an impressionable young actress, Frances Roberts. He was an attractive man, tall (6 ft 1 in), dark and handsome, with large eyes and a moustache.

He wandered with his wife from America to Mexico, to Cuba, and then back to England, whence he was despatched to a Gold Coast mining company in February 1919. His lies and odd conduct again caused his dismissal within six months. In a statement that says much about the social mores of the time, one of his colleagues – John Thompson, an engineer – recalled that True was not only bombastic, irresponsible and erratic but was 'in the habit of laughing and joking and generally playing about with the native black men, which was considered very infra dig [beneath one's dignity] … which no white man does or would do … One must not hob-nob with the blacks.' On True's return to Bedford, his stepfather washed his hands of the young man, giving him an allowance but no further help.

His fantasies by this time had increased, as had his morphia addiction. For eighteen months he was treated for both, in and out of nursing homes. While hospitalised in Southsea, he was wheeled about in a bath chair, which was decked with flags and toys: a monkey, a cat, a hooter and a dog that barked. He giggled a lot; he shouted and swore; at other times he just sat and stared, at a tree, at the sea or the sky. In September 1921, he was convicted and fined in Portsmouth for obtaining morphia from a chemist using forged prescriptions.

Two months later, back home once more, he began displaying hostility towards his wife, who had taken up her acting career again. Anything disagreeable that happened to him was now blamed on another Ronald True, who became his bogeyman and the symbol of his split personality. He believed this man was impersonating him and forging his cheques – the ones that bounced. Sometimes he was violent, sometimes morose and brooding. His wife did what she could to humour and care for him. But when he became hostile towards their two-year-old son, whom he had once adored, she gave up, accepting his mother's decision that he should be certified as insane; he used to wet and comb the child's hair several times a day. He told his aunt, who rebuked him for staying out late: 'I may as well enjoy life when I can. I am going to be killed through a woman soon', adding that three palmists, in Buenos Aires, Shanghai and San Francisco, had told him so.

Early in January 1922, he disappeared in London, where he haunted West End bars and clubs. Now aged thirty, he lived richly, signing dud cheques, walking out of hotels without paying his bill, stealing from coats, purses and people's homes. He was out having a good time every night, dining, drinking, dancing, picking up women and telling fantastic tales about his own achievements, wealth and plans. He formed instant friendships and liaisons, but was always on guard against his enemies – including the imaginary Ronald True.

One friend he acquired in the first week of February was an out-of-work motor tradesman named James Armstrong. They were introduced in the Corner House, Leicester Square. For some reason they took to each other and for the next few weeks were together nearly every day, travelling about, amusing themselves, with True the eccentric but congenial host. Interestingly, it was the *women* he met who thought him insane. During this time, True bought a pistol off Armstrong for £2, to protect himself against the other Ronald True. There was, in fact, a Ronald Trew around at the time, a singer whom True may have seen and heard sing in a club.

His wife, much concerned about his state of mind, traced his whereabouts in London and managed to see him twice over a period of two months. She was so alarmed by his conversation and appearance that on 3 March she sought the help of Scotland Yard – True had vanished again – and employed an enquiry agent to seek him out.

Some weeks before this, on Saturday, 18 February, True met Olive Young – 'a member of the unfortunate class', according to the prosecution at his later trial. Aged twenty-five, her real name was Mrs Gertrude Yates. She had given up working in a shop to become a call girl and was doing rather well, with money in the bank and some rather expensive jewellery. True stayed the night in her basement flat at 13a Finborough Road, Fulham, and on leaving removed a £5 note from her handbag. She resolved not to see him again, and succeeded for a while, although True kept on calling at the flat at night and pestering her with telephone calls.

On 2 March, posing as Major True and while he was staying at the Grand Hotel, Northumberland Avenue, without paying any bills, he acquired a chauffeur-driven car from a hire firm – the driver was Luigi Mazzola – and in unpaid-for luxury drove about with James Armstrong to Richmond, Reading, to tea-rooms, dance halls, hotels and clubs – after which True was penniless. At one tea dance he pointed out a man to an acquaintance, Robert Scales. Mr Scales later told the court: 'He said this man was not treating a girlfriend of his right … He said the man had been at Bedford Grammar School when he first met him. He said the girl lived at Bedford, and that her name was Olive.'

Every night before midnight on the 2nd, 3rd, and 4th of March, Mazzola drove True to Finborough Road and then drove him away. Each time Miss Young was out. But just before midnight on Sunday, 5 March, she was at home, and let him in – Mazzola was dismissed. True spent the night with her.

The following morning, a newspaper boy delivered the *Daily Mirror* at about 7.10 am. The milkman arrived about 7.30 am. Some time after this Ronald True made tea for himself and Miss Young. He took her cup into the bedroom. As she sat up to drink it, he struck her five times on the head with a rolling-pin before strangling her. It appears that he then downed his cup of tea and ate some biscuits. What he did for the next hour or so is not known, though he remained in the flat.

About 9.15 am, Miss Young's daily, Miss Emily Steel, arrived, letting herself into the basement flat with her own key. She went to the kitchen, observing in passing that a man's coat and scarf were in the sitting room and that the glass panel of the bedroom door was newly cracked. She began cooking some sausages for her own breakfast and did some tidying in the sitting room. She was there when True, whom she had seen there before, breezily entered the room from the bedroom.

'Good morning, Major True,' she said. He told her: 'Don't wake Miss Young. We were late last night … She's in a deep sleep. I'll send the car round for her at twelve o'clock.' Miss Steel helped him on with his coat and he gave her half-a-crown before leaving to get a taxi. It was about 9.50 am.

She continued with what she was doing before knocking on the bedroom door to see if Miss Young was awake yet. There was no reply, so she opened the door and went into the room.

Blood was everywhere. There seemed to be a body in the bed, but on pulling back the bedclothes she discovered only two bloodstained pillows. A rolling-pin lay under the eiderdown; the dressing-table had been ransacked; some jewellery had disappeared. She eventually found Miss Young's naked body in the bathroom. A towel had been rammed down her throat and a dressing-gown cord tied around her neck. She had died of asphyxia. Miss Steel ran out of the flat to get some help and in due course, not long after 10.15 am, an inspector from Chelsea police station arrived on his bicycle at the flat.

Meanwhile, True had taken a taxi to a post office, where he phoned Mazzola and then drove on to a menswear shop, Horne's in Coventry Street, where he bought a bowler hat (18s 6d) and a ready-made brown suit (five guineas) which he put on, after showing the salesman some blood on his trousers. The salesman said later: 'He said he had had a smash that morning in an aeroplane and hurt himself in the groin. He said he had come over from France and in landing he had had a smash.' True was very jocular. He then took the same taxi, which had waited, on to 21 Wardour Street. There he had a shave at a barber's shop and then a few doors along (Number 27) he pawned two rings for £25 and redeemed a silver cigarette case and a watch, which he had pledged the previous Saturday. He then met James Armstrong at the Strand Corner House at about eleven o'clock, and with Mazzola at the wheel they drove to Hounslow, to look at engines, then on to Feltham, and to Croydon for tea. There, True bought the *Star*, which featured Olive Young's murder on the front page. They then drove on to Richmond, where he bought a shirt, which he put on. They eventually reached the Hammersmith Palace of Varieties about 8.40 pm, and Mazzola was then dismissed.

He returned to his garage, where the police were waiting. Having heard Mazzola's story, four senior police officers returned with him to the Palace of Varieties, arriving about 9.45 am. Detective Inspector Burton later told the court: 'I saw the accused and the witness Armstrong in a box in the theatre … I entered the box and got hold of the accused by both hands and said to him: "I am a police officer. Come out with me." I took him outside the box, still holding his hands, and Superintendent Hawkins took from his hip pocket a revolver … It was loaded.'

True made a brief statement in which he said that a tall man, aged thirty-one, was in Mrs Yates's flat the previous night when he arrived there, and that he left when a stormy scene ensued.

On 7 March, he was charged with the wilful murder of Gertrude Yates. While being held for observation in Brixton Prison's hospital, he attacked a prisoner whom he thought was stealing his food, and was jolly with Henry Jacoby, an eighteen-year-old pantry boy who had murdered an elderly hotel guest, Lady White. 'Another one to join our Murder Club!' cried True. 'We are only accepting members who kill them right out!'

His trial began at the Old Bailey on Monday, 1 May 1922. The judge was Mr Justice McCardie, who had just sentenced Henry Jacoby to death after a two-day trial. True's defence was that of insanity, two psychiatrists agreeing with the prison doctor that the accused was suffering from a congenital mental disorder, aggravated by his drug addiction. There was a lengthy legal debate about the meaning of homicidal insanity and the McNaughten case was much discussed. (In 1843, this case had helped to establish the test of irresponsibility for a criminal offence on the ground of insanity.) The prosecutor, Sir Richard Muir, called no experts, relying on his cross-examination of witnesses to prove the defendant was not altogether mad. Victor Trew, twin brother of Ronald Trew, was produced at one point – his brother was in hospital with pneumonia – to show that his brother was quite unlike True in appearance, and to say that he never carried a gun and did not know Olive Young.

The jury concurred with the prosecution: the doctors might say True was mad, but they could not believe that he was truly a lunatic. On 5 May 1922, they found Ronald True guilty of the murder of Gertrude Yates. He was sentenced to death.

An appeal was dismissed by the Lord Chief Justice. But while True was in Pentonville Prison he was re-examined by three other medical experts on the orders of the Home Secretary, after which he was indeed declared to be insane. Thereupon he was reprieved and sent to Broadmoor Criminal Lunatic Asylum (later renamed Broadmoor Institution). This caused an outcry in the Commons and the press, especially as Henry Jacoby had just been hanged. It was felt that social position had damned the one and saved the other.

True spent the rest of his life in Broadmoor, where he proved to be a popular and cheerful chap. He died there in 1951, aged sixty.

In the summer of 1922, Reynolds News featured a series of articles entitled 'Ten Years as a Hangman' written by Harry Pierrepoint. He had been suffering a terminal illness for several years and died on 14 December 1922, aged forty-eight. Harry Pierrepoint had officiated at 105 executions, including six double hangings. The greatest number of condemned persons he hanged in one year as chief executioner was nineteen. His account of the execution of Abel Atherton in December 1909 appears in Appendix B.

His son, Albert, was now seventeen. He took possession of all his father's papers and diary and studied them over the next few years. Even at school in Huddersfield he had written an essay when he was eleven that began: 'When I leave school I should like to be the Official Executioner.'

FREDDY BYWATERS AND EDITH THOMPSON

THE MURDER OF PERCY THOMPSON, 1922

Nothing seems to incite one man to kill another as strongly as the urge to be the sole possessor of the other man's woman or wife. Desire for a woman can become so obsessive that nothing but the most drastic action will resolve the situation. Rational thought is seldom employed. In this case, as in that of Mrs Casserley, the wife could have left her husband; she could have deserted him and gone to live with her lover. But she chose not to do so. Love seldom conquers all. Apart from the fact that women are more responsive to social expectations and the sanctity of the status quo than men, some primitive instinct seems to demand that the possessor be aggressively dispossessed and the woman carried away. Moreover, so complex are the interactive feelings of those involved, that two people who become part of an unhappy triangle can only be realigned as a happy pair when the triangular involvement is torn apart.

Frederick Edward Francis Bywaters was a good-looking, virile young man, self-willed and well travelled. Although susceptible to emotion, he was not a man of imagination or a thinker. He was more a creature of instinct and of action, and, although impressionable, not the innocent lad his counsel would later describe. Nor was Edith Jessie Thompson the dominating seductress subsequently portrayed at the trial. A sensual, attractive lady, she was a dreamer, in love with love and anything that lifted her out of the shallows of her pedestrian life in suburban Ilford with Percy Thompson.

They had married on 15 January 1915, when she was twenty-two and he was twenty-six. There were no children. At the time he was a shipping clerk with a firm in the City of London and she was the book-keeper and ultimately the manageress of a wholesale milliner, Carlton & Prior, at 168 Aldersgate Street, EC1, a quarter of a mile north-east of the Old Bailey. Both the Thompsons continued with their jobs for seven years until the night of the murder, she earning as much as he: £6 a week.

In 1916, during the Great War, Percy enlisted in the London Scottish Regiment, but was soon discharged as unfit because he was suffering from heart trouble. At about this time, Freddy's father, a ship's clerk who had also enlisted in the army at the start of the Great War, was killed, and his mother moved from Manor Park to Norwood, south of the river. Two years later, Freddy Bywaters, then aged sixteen, joined the Merchant Navy as a ship's writer or clerk.

In July 1920, the Thompsons took up residence in 41 Kensington Gardens, Ilford – a north-eastern suburb of London, where both had been born and brought up. They bought the terraced house from a crabbed old lady, Mrs Lester, who with her ailing husband remained in the house as the Thompsons' lodgers. Every weekday morning the Thompsons set off about quarter-past eight to work in the City, returning about quarter to seven at night. They dined with friends or went to shows, but seem to have had few interests – except that Edith Thompson was an avid reader of popular fiction and magazines.

On 4 June 1921, Freddy Bywaters, then aged eighteen, returned from a four-month voyage to Australia on the steamship *Orvieto*. He had been friendly with Edith's younger brothers and sister since his schooldays – her maiden name was Graydon – and at Percy's invitation he joined the Thompsons and Edith's sister, Avis Graydon, for a week's holiday at Shanklin on the Isle of Wight. Edith was able to escape from her husband and to have fun with the younger people, going swimming and having tennis lessons. She and Freddy exchanged their first kiss. A year later, on 14 June 1922, she was to write: 'One year ago today we went for that memorable ride round the island in the charabanc, do you remember? – that was the first time you kissed me.'

At the end of the holiday, on 18 June, Freddy was invited by Percy, who liked the young man, to lodge with them – presumably so that Freddy could be nearer the Graydon boys and his presumed girlfriend, Avis. The Graydons lived a mile and a half south of the Thompsons in Shakespeare Crescent, Manor Park. But Freddy's romantic interest in Avis, if it ever existed, had already been diverted. Although both denied in court that they made any declaration of love until that September, Edith wrote in a letter dated 20 June 1922: 'It's Friday now darlint ... I am wondering if you remember what your answer was to me in reply to my question "What's the matter?" tonight of last year. I remember quite well – "You know what's the matter, I love you" ... but you didn't then darlint, because you do now and it's different now isn't it?'

On 20 June 1921, Freddy Bywaters had been lodging with the Thompsons for just two days. Friday, 27 June, was his nineteenth birthday, a date and a day Edith looked back on several times in her letters as being of some significance. They met for lunch in the Holborn Restaurant. Bywaters later told the court: 'Mrs Thompson told me she was unhappy, and I said: "Let me be a pal to you – let me help you if I can" ... Mrs Thompson and I had been having an argument, and she suddenly burst into tears, and I advised her to wait, not to give up hope, and not commit suicide ... I extracted a promise from her to wait five years, so that she should not commit suicide.' In the interim she was to try to obtain a divorce or separation, and if this was not possible they would go away together or both kill themselves in a suicide pact.

A month passed, with Freddy still lodging in Kensington Gardens. By now, the Thompsons had been married for more than six years. She said later: 'I think I was never really happy with my husband,' and added that the question of a separation had been discussed between them long before Bywaters came to stay.

On Monday, 1 August it was aired again. She told the court: 'I had some trouble with my husband that day. I think it originated over a pin.' She was sewing and Freddy went to fetch a pin for her. 'But eventually it was brought to a head by my sister not appearing at tea when she said she would. I wanted to wait for her, but my husband objected, and said a lot of things to me about my family that I resented. He then struck me several times, and eventually threw me across the room.' Her arm was badly bruised. 'Bywaters was in the garden ... He came into the room and stopped my husband. Later on that day there was a discussion about a separation ... I wanted a separation and Bywaters entreated my husband to separate from me. But he said what he usually said, that he would not. At first he said he would, and then I said to him: "You always tell me that ... and later, you refuse to grant it to me."'

Not surprisingly, Freddy was asked by Percy Thompson to leave, and did so four days later. 'We were friends,' Freddy said later of his relationship with Mrs Thompson at that time – 'I was fond of her.' But it seems the affair had already been consummated. In one of the only two surviving letters he wrote to her, found at Carlton & Prior's and written two days before the murder, he wrote: 'I do remember you coming to me in the little room and I think I understand what it cost you – a lot more darlint than it could ever now. When I think about that I think how nearly we came to be parted for ever. If you had not forfeited your pride darlint I don't think there would ever have been yesterday or tomorrow.' The little room was most probably where Bywaters lodged in Kensington Gardens.

After 5 August, he stayed in his widowed mother's small house in Westow Road, Upper Norwood, a long way from Ilford. But he continued to meet Edith – or Edie, as her family called her.

The first extant letter she wrote to him is dated 11 August 1921. It reads: 'Darlingest – Will you please take these letters back now. I have nowhere to keep them, except a small cash box I have just bought and I want that for *my own letters only* and I feel scared to death in case anybody else should read them ...' Apparently, she was referring in the first instance to 'personal' letters written to him by a girlfriend he had acquired in Australia.

Her next letter was a note dated 20 August – 'Come and see me Monday lunchtime, please darlint. He suspects. Peidi.' She explained in court: 'I meant that my husband suspected I had seen Bywaters. I think it was on the Friday previous to that date. I usually saw him on Fridays and I continued to see him until he sailed on the 9th of September.' On Fridays the Thompsons invariably visited her family, the Graydons, in Manor Park. So did Bywaters, calling on Avis and her brothers. Their parents also liked him and made him welcome.

It was before he sailed on the SS *Morea* to the Mediterranean, working as a mess-room steward, that Bywaters and 'Peidi' ('Child') affirmed their love for each other. Their letters – with hers breathing an 'insensate, silly affection' according to the trial judge – now began their lengthy travels across the world.

Forty-nine letters, notes and telegrams were produced as exhibits at the trial – thirty-four were not. This gave undue prominence to Mrs Thompson's apparently incriminating remarks about 'removing' her husband which, if taken in their full context, would have seemed more fantastical and less calculating. The defence never insisted, however, on *all* the letters being put in evidence – for the very good reason that some referred damagingly to Mrs Thompson's abortions.

She wrote more than sixty letters to Bywaters over the period of a year, during which he was at sea five times: from 9 September to 29 October 1921; 11 November 1921 to 6 January 1922; 20 January to 16 March; 31 March to 25 May; and finally from 9 June to 23 September 1922. He kept all her letters in a sea chest. These five voyages were all in the SS *Morea,* where he was employed as a mess-room steward, a writer and then as a laundry steward.

She wrote to him nearly every day, often at her desk in Carlton & Prior's, with a brass monkey – a present from Bywaters – sitting on the desk before her. Some of the letters were very long, running on like a diary from day to day, full of gossip and chat about the weather, relatives, shows, books, her thoughts and feelings. Very often she included newspaper cuttings, advertisements, invitations or other items that she thought might interest him – in fact, fifty enclosures were found with the letters. She also sent him books, chocolates and other gifts, probably using Carlton & Prior's postage. He addressed some of his replies to her office, although later she used a poste-restante address at the Aldersgate post office under the name of 'Miss P Fisher'. He reciprocated as best he could with letters and gifts, and sometimes, it seems, he humoured her fantasies, though on his fifth and longest voyage his enthusiasm was tangibly beginning to flag. Nonetheless, both at the beginning and at the end of their association they were undoubtedly very much in love – obsessively so.

Bywaters's two surviving letters to Edith, written just before the murder, could have been composed by her. The style is very much the same: rambling, effusive, loosely constructed and punctuated, with the occasional French or coded phrase. He signs himself 'Freddy'. He calls her 'Peidi Mia – Ma Chere – Darlint little girl – The darlingest little sweetheart girl in the whole world ... and big pal.'

Always signing herself 'Peidi', she invariably calls him 'Darlingest boy', and ubiquitously 'darlint'. She describes their relationship as 'the Palship of two halves'. 'We're not ordinary human beings,' she wrote. 'We're apart – different – we've never known pleasure ... until we knew each other.'

No letters survive from his first voyage on the *Morea.* Later, she wrote of their reunion on 31 October 1921: 'I'll never forget it, I felt – oh I dont know how, just that I didnt really know what I was doing, it seemed so grand to see you again, so grand to just feel you hold my shoulders, while you kissed me, so grand to hear you say just 3 ordinary commonplace words "How are you?" Yes I did feel happy then.'

They saw each other nearly every day. Then, soon after Freddy's return, he visited Kensington Gardens on the afternoon of Saturday 5 November, specifically to see Percy

Thompson – 'We shook hands when we met' – and asked the other man to agree to a separation from his wife. According to Freddy Bywaters, there was a reason for this confrontation. He said later:

I had taken Mrs Thompson out previously. Apparently he [Mr Thompson] had been waiting at the station for her and he had seen the two of us together. He made a statement to Mrs Thompson – 'He is not a man or else he would ask my permission to take you out' – and she reported that statement to me the following day. In consequence of that I went and saw Mr Thompson ... I said: 'Why don't you come to an amicable agreement? Either have a separation or you can get a divorce.' And he hummed and hawed about it. He ... said: 'Yes – No – I don't see it concerns you.' I said: 'You are making Edie's life a hell. You know she isn't happy with you.' He replied: 'Well, I've got her, and I will keep her.'

On 11 November 1921, Freddy sailed for India on the *Morea,* bound for Bombay via Marseilles, Port Said and Aden. From dreary Ilford, about a week after Freddy left her, Edith Thompson wrote:

At night in bed the subject – or the object the usual one came up and I resisted, because I didnt want him to touch me for a month from Nov. 3rd ... He asked me why I wasnt happy now – what caused the unhappiness and I said I didnt feel unhappy – just indifferent, and he said I used to feel happy once. Well, I suppose I did ... but that was before I knew what real happiness could be like, before I loved you darlint. Of course I did not tell him that but I did tell him I didnt love him and he seemed astounded. He wants me to forgive and forget anything he has said or done ... I told him I didnt love him but that I would do my share to try and make him happy ... I was feeling awful.

In her next letter, undated but written on the 21st or 28th of November, she wrote:

I gave way this week (to him I mean) its the first time since you have been gone. Why do I tell you this? ... We had – was it a row – anyway a very heated argument again last night (Sunday). It started through the usual source, I resisted – and he wanted to know why since you went in August I was different – 'Had I transferred my affections from him to you.' Darlint its a great temptation to say 'Yes' but I did not. He said we were cunning, the pair of us ... He said 'Has he written to you since he has been away,' and when I said 'No' he said 'That's another lie.'

There was more of the same on 6 December.

I am feeling very blue today darlint, you havn't talked to me for a fortnight ... I fear that we, you & I, will never reap our reward, in fact, I just feel today darlint, that our love will be in vain. He talked to me again last night a lot, darlint … He said he began to think that both of us would be happier if we had a baby, I said 'No, a thousand times No' & he began … to plead with me, oh darlint, its all so hard to bear … He hasn't worried me any more, except that once I told you about …You know I always sleep to the wall, darlint, well I still do but he puts his arm round me & oh its horrid …What do you think, he is going to learn dancing – to take me out to some nice ones, wont it be fun … About myself darlint, its still the same & I've not done anything yet – I dont think I shall until next month …

Her birthday was on Christmas Day – she was twenty-eight. On 3 January 1922 she wrote again to Freddy:

Darlint, I've surrendered to him unconditionally now – do you understand me? I think it the best way to disarm any suspicion, in fact he has several times asked me if I am happy now and I've said 'Yes, quite …' Darlint, you are a bad bad correspondent really darlint I absolutely refuse to talk to you at all next trip, if you dont mend your ways. Darlint, are you frightened at this – just laugh at me.

The *Morea* returned to England on 6 January 1923 and Edith saw Freddy the following day. His shore-leave was short, for the *Morea* sailed again on 20 January, bound again for Bombay.

The prosecution was to imply later that the previous letter contained an expression of intent to remove Percy Thompson by poison or some other means. But what it was she had to do becomes clear in a letter written on 24 January, just after he went to sea again:

About 10.30 or 11 am I felt awfully ill – I had terrible pains come all over me – the sort of pains that I usually have – but have not had just lately – do you understand

She fainted in her office three times and at 3.30 pm was taken home in a car with a hot-water bottle in her lap. She went straight to bed.

About 7 something awful happened, darlint I don't know for certain what it was, but I can guess, can you, write & tell me.

This letter was not one of the exhibits read out in court, as the revelation that she had had a miscarriage or abortion would in those days have damaged her defence and damned her in the eyes of the jury. The prosecution and the defence probably made some deal about which letters were to be put in evidence. But the suppression of the foregoing piece of information, which helped the defence, also assisted the prosecution, allowing them to add a murderous intent (as in the letter of 3 January) to anything ambiguous Mrs Thompson wrote. These ambiguities were undoubtedly also assisted by Edith Thompson herself.

10 February 1922 – You must do something this time ... opportunities come and go by – they have to – because I'm helpless and I think and think and think ... It would be so easy darlint – if I had things – I do hope I shall ... Have enclosed cuttings of Dr Wallis's case. It might prove interesting.

The cuttings, from the *Daily Sketch* of 9 February, referred to a story headlined 'Mystery of curate's death'. Dr Wallis had been poisoned by hyoscine – and his wife seemed to be involved. The same letter contained a cutting featuring the lines: *Poisoned chocolates for university chief. Deadly powder posted to Oxford Chancellor. Ground glass in box.* Clearly Edith wished Freddy to provide her with some poison and tell her what to do. On 22 February, she wrote:

I do hate this life I lead – hate the lies hate everything and I tell so many that it hurts ... if only I could make an absolutely clean – fresh start ... Darlingest boy, this thing that I am going to do for both of us, will it ever make any difference between us, darlint; do you understand what I mean. Will you ever think any the less of me ... because of this thing that I shall do. Darlint – if I thought you would I'd not do it ...

A letter dated 14 March 1922 continued this theme:

Will you do all the thinking and planning for me darlint – for this thing – be ready with every little detail when I see you – because you know more about this thing than I, and I am relying on you for all plans and instructions – only just the act I'm not. What about Wallis's case? You said it was interesting but you didn't discuss it with me.

In this letter, a very long one, she also said she had been looking for an unfurnished flat.

Freddy Bywaters returned to England on 16 March. In court, he admitted to having given Edith some quinine – to humour her ideas of suicide, he said, knowing it wouldn't kill her or anyone else. *His* interpretation of the letters in court (as well as hers) was that she was referring in the ambiguous sentences to suicide or to her freedom, which was to be gained by divorce, separation, or by running away – not by murder.

She saw him just before he sailed away again on 31 March, when she gave him a watch as a present. The day before she had written:

After tonight I am going to die ... not really ... but put on the mask again until the 26th May ... This time really will be the last you will go away ... like things are, won't it? We said it before darlint I know and we failed ... But there will be no failure this next time darlint, there mustn't be ... if things are the same again then I'm going with you.

In her next lengthy letter, dated 1 April, she mentions hearing of an unfurnished three-room flat in Kensington for thirty-five shillings a week – 'Darlint it is just the thing we wanted.' She reverts to their farewell a few days earlier and then to more sinister matters:

> *Darlint you're not and never will be satisfied with half and I don't ever want to give you half ... You said to me 'Say no Peidi, say No' on Thursday didn't you – but at that very moment you didn't wish me to say 'No' did you? ... I knew this – felt this – and wouldn't say 'No' for that very reason. Don't keep this piece. About the Marconigram – do you mean one saying Yes or No, because I shant send it darlint I'm not going to try any more until you come back ... He puts great stress on the fact of the tea tasting bitter, 'as if something had been put in it' he says. Now I think whatever else I try it in again will still taste bitter – he will recognise it and be more suspicious still ... I wish we had not got electric light – it would be easy. I'm going to try the glass again occasionally – when it is safe. Ive got an electric light globe this time.'*

Three days later she wrote:

> *He knows or guesses something ... As I was getting into bed a car drew up outside & he came in looking, well you know how with that injured air of mystery on his face attempted to kiss me and then moved away with the expression 'Phew – drink.' ... If he has any sense he could easily put 2 & 2 together. Your last night last time & your last night this time – I went to a theatre on both occasions ... I'm afraid I let go & said several things in haste ... I was told I was the vilest tempered girl living.*

After the Easter holiday, during which she amused herself by going to a tea dance at the Waldorf and by attending a Sunday League Concert at the Ilford Hippodrome, Edith wrote on 24 April: 'I used the "light bulb" three times but the third time – he found a piece – so I've given up – until you come home. I had a doctor's bill in yesterday ... You want me to pay it, don't you darlint – I shall do so.'

She was writing more often now, posting letters to Aden and Bombay which were packed with her thoughts on all manner of things. But the theme of most of these letters was *When?* and *How?*

On 1 May 1922 she wrote:

> *About those fainting fits darlint ... I'm beginning to think its the same as before ... What shall I do about it darlint, if it is the same this month ... I still have the herbs ... We must learn to be patient ... Such a love was not meant to be in vain. We'll wait eh darlint, and you'll try and get some money and then we can go away ... You said it was enough for an elephant. Perhaps it was. But you don't allow for the taste making only a small quantity to be taken ... Darlint I tried hard.*

She was apparently referring to the quinine he had given her.

The mail was in this morning and I read your letter darlint and I cried ... it sounded so sad ... I was buoyed up with the hope of the 'light bulb' and I used a lot − big pieces too − not powdered − and it has no effect − I quite expected to be able to send that cable ... Oh darlint, I do feel so down and unhappy. Wouldnt the stuff make small pills coated together with soap and dipped in liquorice powder ... You tell me not to leave finger marks on the box − do you know I did not think of the box but I did think of the glass or cup ... Do experiment with the pills while you are away − please darlint.

During the trial, Bywaters was asked if he ever believed she had attempted to poison her husband. 'No,' he said. 'It never entered my mind at all. She had been reading books.' Dr Bernard Spilsbury told the court that he had found no trace of any poison and no trace of any large piece of glass or any powdered glass in Percy Thompson's remains, nor any trace of any of these things having ever been administered. Spilsbury's post-mortem examination was carried out on 3 November, a month after the murder.

Earlier that year, Bywaters' fourth long voyage was coming to an end − he was due home on 25 May. Ten days before this, Edith Thompson wrote to him about the money she had lost betting on horse-racing, about the weather − 'It has been a beautiful weekend' − and about her boss, Miss Prior, who had asked Edith to go to the West End and buy some mourning clothes for her newly widowed sister.

There were widows hats with some veils at the back and nobody had the pluck to try them on − they all say it is unlucky − so because of it being unlucky to them I thought it might be lucky to me and tried them all on. I think they all think terrible things are going to happen to me now − but darlint I am laughing I wonder who will be right, they or I?

On 18 May she wrote lengthily about the weather, clothes, cooking, and family news and quoted a passage from a book about the deadly effects of digitalin if taken to excess − 'Is it any use?' She discussed at great length two other books, romantic novels, and then wrote: 'Old Mr Lester died last night. All their side of the house the blinds are drawn. I havent drawn mine and Im not going to. I think they think Im a heathen.'

Two days before his return, she wrote (on 23 May) about an adventure she had had with an admirer − 'The usual type of man darlint ... that expects some return for a lunch.' He had bought her a pound box of marrons glacés. But she was depressed. 'Your news about Bombay − and waiting till next trip, made me feel very sad and downhearted ... You talk about the cage you are in ... that's how I feel ... Mine is a real live cage with a keeper as well.'

He saw her constantly in London during the fortnight he was ashore, before sailing on 9 June on his longest voyage, to Australia via Colombo. As well as lengthy lunches, they had indulged themselves by using her alleged theatre visits to spend a few hours together in hotels such as the Regent Palace. They became increasingly careless, and people began to talk.

Four days after he sailed she wrote, on 13 June:

> *On Thursday – he was on the ottoman at the foot of the bed and said he was dying and wanted to – he had another heart attack – thro me. Darlint I had to laugh at this because I knew it couldn't be a heart attack. When he saw this had no effect on me – he got up and stormed – I said exactly what you told me to and he replied that he knew thats what I wanted and he wasnt going to give it to me – it would make things far too easy for both of you (meaning you and me) … We're both liars he says and you are making me worse and he's going to put a stop to all or any correspondence coming for me at 168.*

Anticipating this, on 9 June (the day Freddy had sailed) she had sent a telegram to the *Morea* at Tilbury Docks – 'Send everything Fisher care GPO.' Her letter continued:

> *On Saturday he told me … I have always had too much of my own way and he was a model husband … He also told me he was going to be master and I was to be his mistress and not half a dozen mens (his words) … Avis … said that he said at 231 'I thought he was keen on you – Avis – but now I can see it was a blind to cover his infatuation for Edie.' Darlint its not an infatuation is it? Tell me it isn't.*

It was now a year since the Shanklin holiday, since their first kiss, since Freddy lodged with the Thompsons in Kensington Gardens, since the row and his departure, and since the declaration and consummation of their love. She now remembered and referred to these highlights in her life with fondness and yearning, and looked forward to his birthday, when he would be twenty. She wrote to him on 14 June 1922:

> *On our birthday [27 June] you will be left Aden on your way to Bombay – you'll be thinking of a girl whose best pal you are in England wont you … Time hangs so dreadfully … We are not busy this week and are leaving at five … Darlint, how can you get ptomaine poisoning from a tin of salmon? One of our boys Mother has died with it … Darlint this month and next are full of remembrances – aren't they … ? I was taken faint in the train this morning … On Saturday I'm going to see a Doctor.*

Six days later she wrote:

> *When you are not near darlint I wish we had taken the easiest way … The days pass – no they don't pass, they just drag on and on and the end of all this misery and unhappiness is no nearer in sight … There are 2 halves in this world who want nothing on earth but to be joined*

*together ... I went to see a doctor on Saturday he asked me lots of questions – could he examine
me etc – I said no ... Eventually he came to the conclusion I have 'chronic anaemia.'*

The doctor asked her if she had had an accident and lost a lot of blood. 'I said "No" –
because it wasn't really an accident and I didnt want to tell him everything – he might
have wanted to see my husband ... I lost an awful lot of blood.' Despite what appears to
have been a second abortion and a general depression, she was soon (if briefly) enjoying
herself. Her next letter was dated 23 June:

*Darlint, your own pal is getting quite a sport. On Saturday I was first in the Egg & Spoon
race & first in the 100 yards Flat race ... Then I was MC for the Lancers ... We had a
very good day indeed – until we got to Lpool St coming home & then he started to make
a fuss – says I take too much notice of Dunsford and he does of me. He gets jealous &
sulks if I speak to any man now ... It was rather fun on Thursday at the Garden Party –
They had swings & roundabouts & Flip Flaps cocoa-nut shies Aunt Sallies – Hoopla &
all that sort of thing I went in for them all & on them all & I shocked a lot of people I
think. I didnt care tho. It was rather fun.*

On 4 July she wrote:

*Last Wednesday I met your mother and she cut me ... things get worse and worse ... Why
arent you sending me something – I wanted you to – you never do what I ask you darlint
– you still have your own way always – If I don't mind the risk why should you?*

Absence and distance had not made Freddy's heart grow any fonder – rather the reverse.
It seems he had a good time on shore leave in Australia, in Fremantle, Melbourne and
Sydney. He missed the boat at Sydney and rejoined the ship at Melbourne.

In England, the Thompsons went on holiday for a fortnight to Bournemouth, an
event much dreaded by Mrs Thompson – 'No swimming lessons or tennis or anything
that Id [sic] really enjoy. However I must make the best of it & dance – Im so tired of it
all tho – this dancing and pretending.' She was also concerned about the paucity of his
letters and an attempt to distance himself. In her letter of 14 July she observed:

*You do say silly things to me – 'try a little bit every day not to think about me' ... When
you've got something that you've never had before and something that you're so happy to
have found – you're always afraid of it flying away – that's how I feel about your love ...
I never want to lose it and live.*

Bournemouth, she thought, was 'a very stiff and starchy place', not a bit like the fondly
remembered Isle of Wight. On her return to Kensington Gardens, where Mrs Lester was

'horrid' to her, she found herself becoming an insomniac like her husband. In her letter dated 15 August, she wrote:

> *Ever since Ive been back in Ilford Ive had most awful nights rest … I dream – sometimes theyre not very nice dreams. They are nearly always about you … One night I dreamed 1 had been to a theatre with a man I knew – I had told you about him & you came home from sea unexpectedly & when you found me you just threw me over a very deep precipice & I was killed …*

That dream strangely foreshadows events that were less than eight weeks away. Yet any thoughts or plans about divorce or the disposing of Percy seem now to have been abandoned. She wrote on 28 August: 'I said I would wait 5 years – and I will darlint … its only 3 years and ten months now.'

Then her 'darlingest boy', now homeward bound, stopped writing. Later, he told the court: 'I said I would not see her when I came to England, as it would not be so hard for her to bear … I was doing that for her sake, as I wanted to help her.' This was something she was unable to accept or acknowledge. On 12 September she complained:

> *I don't hear from you much you don't talk to me by letter and help me and I don't even know if I am going to see you … I feel so hopeless – just drifting … Things here are going smoothly with me – I am giving all – and accepting everything and I think I am looked upon as 'The Dutiful Wife' … Darlingest, only lover of mine – try to cheer me up.*

And on 19 September she wrote:

> *Darlingest boy – I don't quite understand you about 'Pals'. You say 'Can we be Pals only, Peidi, it will make it easier.' Do you mean for always? because if you do, No, no, a thousand times … Have you lost heart and given up hope? … Yes, darlint you are jealous of him – but I want you to be – he has the right by law to all that you have the right to by nature and love – yes darlint be jealous, so much that you will do something desperate.*

In this letter she included a cutting from the *Daily Sketch* headed 'Rat Poison Consumed by Fowl Kills Woman'.

The *Morea* docked at Tilbury on Saturday, 23 September. Freddy Bywaters never put to sea again. He went straight home to Upper Norwood, avoiding any meeting with Mrs Thompson, and refrained from seeing her until the Monday. Even then it was only for an hour after work. They met at Fenchurch Street station – as they did on the following Tuesday, Wednesday and Thursday.

What was discussed? Bywaters later told the court that he had never thought of marrying Mrs Thompson, or even of taking her away, for 'financial reasons'. Yet she was earning £6 a week and he £200 a year. She herself valued her job with Carlton & Prior's very much, as much as Mr Carlton valued her – he said she was 'a very capable woman'. But if she became involved in some scandal she would forfeit that job. It seems likely that she deceived herself and Freddy about her real intentions, subconsciously loath to lose her home, her job, her respectable status, even her husband, by letting her dreams become reality. Perhaps Freddy subconsciously realised all this, and fired once again by her presence, frustrated by snatched embraces and by her curious reluctance to seek a separation or divorce through proper channels – she never pursued this common-sense approach – was goaded into making fact of all the fantasy, talk and emotional uncertainty of the past year, on which she seemed to thrive, and into ending all the deceit and lies, which, it seems, he genuinely disliked.

Certainly something happened that weekend, some passionate experience that lit the touch-paper of his emotions and shattered the triangle. In court he described the weekend as follows: 'On Friday the 29th I met Mrs Thompson about midday and took her to lunch, and then she went back to her business. I went to Fuller's tea shop between three and four ... Later on Mrs Thompson came in. I left her in Ilford that evening about quarter to seven, and then I went home to my mother's. On the Saturday morning, about nine o'clock, I took her for a walk in Wanstead Park' – with a break for her to do some shopping. He left her there in the park at one o'clock. She went home to cook her husband's dinner and Bywaters returned to Norwood, where he remained for the rest of that day and all of Sunday.

On the morning of Monday, 2 October, she telephoned him and they met for lunch and again later on in Fuller's, after which he saw her home, leaving her in Ilford at quarter to seven. He then went to the Graydons for a couple of hours before making the long journey back to Norwood.

On the Saturday, the Sunday or the Monday – she said it was the Monday, although she saw him twice that day – she wrote her last, undated letter.

Darlingest lover of mine, thank you, thank you, oh thank you a thousand times for Friday – it was lovely – its always lovely to go out with you. And then Saturday – yes I did feel happy ... Darlint, we've said we'll always be Pals haven't we, shall we say we'll always be lovers ... Or is it (this great big love) a thing we can't control ... Your love to me is new, it is something different, it is my life ... It seems like a great welling up of love – of feeling ... just as if I am wax in your hands ... its physical purely ... Darlingest when you are rough, I go dead – try not to be please.

She went on to talk about a book she was reading and continued:

I tried so hard to find a way out tonight darlingest but he was suspicious and still is – I suppose we must make a study of this deceit for some time longer. I hate it ... I'd love to be able to say 'I'm going to see my lover tonight.' If I did he would prevent me − there would be scenes and he would come to 168 and interfere and I couldn't bear that ... Darlint its funds that are our stumbling block − until we have those we can do nothing. Darlingest find me a job abroad. I'll go tomorrow ... Darlint − do something tomorrow night will you? Something to make you forget. I'll be hurt I know, but I want you to hurt me − I do really − the bargain now seems so one sided − so unfair − but how can I alter it?

If she gave him the letter on the Monday, 'tomorrow night' refers to Tuesday night, when she had arranged to go to the theatre with her husband and her uncle and aunt, the Laxtons. She told the court that what Freddy was to do was to take Avis out, which would hurt her − as *he* would be hurt when she was out with Percy. Freddy did in fact see Avis at the Graydons' home on Monday and Tuesday night, although he never took her out.   The letter ended:

'He's still well − he's going to gaze all day long at you in your temporary home − after Wednesday. Don't forget what we talked in the Tea Room, I'll still risk and try if you will − we have only 3? years left darlingest. Try & help. Peidi.'

Her explanation in court of these ambiguities was that 'he' was the brass monkey Freddy had given her and the 'temporary home' was a sketch of the *Morea* that she was having framed for her desk. What they talked about in Fuller's, she said, was him getting her a job abroad. The mention of '3? years' would hardly seem to indicate that she was plotting her husband's murder and was prepared to wait.

Two letters from him that were found later that week at Carlton & Prior's, 168 Aldersgate, portray his tempestuous feelings. Though undated, they were probably written on Friday night and on Sunday evening.

Darling Peidi Mia. Tonight was impulse − natural − I couldn't resist − I had to hold you ... I thought you were going to refuse to kiss me − darlint little girl − I love you so much and the only way I can control myself is by not seeing you and I'm not going to do that. I must have you − I love you darlint − logic and what others call reason do not enter into our lives ... Peidi you are my magnet ... I shall never be able to see you and remain impassive.

On Sunday, 1 October, he wrote:

Peidi Mia I love you more and more every day − it grows darlint and will keep on growing. Darlint in the park − our Park on Saturday, you were my 'little devil' − I was happy then Peidi − were you? ... I mustn't ever think of losing you ... My darlint darlint little girl I love you more than I will ever be able to show you. Darlint you are the centre.

Did they plan murder that weekend? Did she urge him once too often to do something before he sailed again? Or, quite without her knowledge, was *he* planning to kill?

On Tuesday, 3 October, Mrs Thompson phoned Freddy Bywaters at about 9 am and they met for lunch at the Queen Anne restaurant, Cheapside. After lunch, she went back to Carlton & Prior's in Aldersgate. In the afternoon, he went once more to Fuller's, where she turned up at about ten-past five, meeting him at the door. They conversed for about fifteen minutes and he walked with her back to Aldersgate Street station, leaving her there about half-past five.

They both said later that arrangements for the following day were discussed: they would meet again for lunch. That was all, in fact, that was possible that day, for at 5 pm on the Wednesday both the Thompsons had arranged to go to Paddington Station to meet an arrival from Cornwall – a maid, Ethel Vernon, hired by Percy to relieve his wife of some of her domestic duties. Naturally Mrs Thompson would have to stay at home that night, tutoring the maid, and any meeting between the lovers was out of the question.

Bywaters knew of the maid's coming. He also knew – and had known for some days – that the Thompsons and the Laxtons were going to the Criterion Theatre on Tuesday night to see Cyril Maude in *The Dipper*. When he left Peidi at Aldersgate Street station, she was met there by her husband. Perhaps Freddy watched them walk away together, on their way to the West End. It would have been the first time he had seen the despised possessor of Peidi for many months.

Freddy travelled east to Manor Park, to see the Graydons in Shakespeare Crescent; Avis was there, with her parents and a brother, Newenham. Freddy stayed with them for over four hours, until 11 pm.

In his overcoat pocket was a knife, which he said later he had bought the previous November; such knives were on sale in Aldersgate Street. He said he always carried it in his overcoat pocket. It was a sheath knife – but the leather sheath was never afterwards found.

Before leaving the Graydons, he asked Avis to come to the pictures the following evening. Then he walked to East Ham station. 'I thought,' he said later, 'I don't want to go home – I feel too miserable – I want to see Mrs Thompson … I walked in the direction of Ilford. I knew Mr and Mrs Thompson would be together, and I thought perhaps if I were to see them I might be able to make things a bit better … I went to see Thompson to come to an amicable understanding for a separation or divorce … It kind of came across me all of a sudden …'

He must have had to wait. For it was not until midnight that the Thompsons began to walk up Belgrave Road from Ilford station. They had left the theatre about 11 pm, said goodbye to the Laxtons at the Piccadilly Circus underground station, and had travelled on to Liverpool Street Station, where they got the 11.30 pm train to Ilford.

It was a long walk up dark and badly lit Belgrave Road, which was intersected by suburban avenues left and right. The Thompsons walked along the right-hand pavement.

Mrs Thompson was, she said later, trying to persuade her husband to take her to a dance in a fortnight's time.

They were near the Kensington Gardens intersection when a man in an overcoat and hat overtook them in a rush. He pushed Mrs Thompson out of the way and she fell, banging her head on something, the pavement or a wall. She was momentarily dazed.

Said Bywaters later:

> *I pushed Mrs Thompson with my right hand, like that. With my left I held Thompson and caught him by the back of his coat and pushed him along the street, swinging him round …* *I said to him: 'Why don't you get a divorce or apparition, you cad?' … He said: 'I know that's what you want. But I'm not going to give it to you. It would make it too pleasant for both of you.' I said: 'You take a delight in making Edie's life hell.' Then he said: 'I've got her – I'll keep her – and I'll shoot you' … going at the same time like that with his right hand – as if to draw a gun from his pocket. As he said that he pushed me in the chest with his left fist, and I said: 'Oh, will you?' and drew a knife and put it in his arm … I had the knife in my left hand.* [Bywaters was right-handed.] *All the time struggling, I thought he was going to kill me … and I tried to stop him.*

That was what he told the court. Two months before this, on 5 October he told the police: 'I said to him: "You've got to separate from your wife." He said: "No." I said: "You'll have to." We struggled. I took my knife from my pocket and we fought and he got the worst of it … I didn't intend to kill him. I only meant to injure him.'

Percy Thompson was slightly cut in four places on his left side below the ribs. There were also two superficial cuts on his chin, two deeper cuts on the right of his lower jaw, one on the inner right arm by the elbow, and two two-inch stab-wounds in the back of his neck, one of which severed the carotid artery. He died, drowning in his own blood, a few minutes later.

The damage done, Bywaters fled, running in and out of the pools of lamplight through Seymour Gardens, where he thrust the knife down a drain, and on through Wanstead and Leytonstone to Stratford. By taxi and on foot he passed south across London, getting home about 3 am. 'Is that you, Mick?' said his mother, hearing him some in. 'Yes, Mum,' he said.

Mrs Thompson, meanwhile, struggled to her feet. 'When I came to my senses,' she said, 'I looked round for my husband, and I saw him some distance down the road. He seemed to be scuffling with someone … I saw somebody running away, and I recognised the coat and hat.' She went to her husband. Blood was pouring from his mouth, But she had no idea, she said, that he had been stabbed. 'He fell up against me and said, "Oe-er" … I helped him along by the side of the wall, and I think he slid down the wall onto the pavement … I went to get a doctor.'

He collapsed in one of the large dark spaces between the street lights. She ran back down the road, meeting a couple, Dora Pittard and Percy Clevely, who were walking up Belgrave Road from the station. She was sobbing, hysterical and incoherent, and cried: 'Oh, my God! Will you help me? My husband is ill – he's bleeding!'

They took her to the house of a Dr Maudsley, who was eventually roused from his slumbers. Mrs Thompson ran back to her husband, where a local resident, John Webber, drawn there by a match being struck, found her kneeling by a man who was propped against a wall. Webber, on the point of going to bed, had heard 'a woman's voice saying "Oh, don't! Oh, don't!" in a most piteous manner'. He was certain the voice was that of Mrs Thompson. But it may have been her husband's. On the other hand, his house was by no means the nearest to the stabbing – he may have made the story up.

The doctor arrived, and was followed at about 1 am by Police Sergeant Mew. After the body was removed, the sergeant escorted Mrs Thompson the fifty or so yards around the corner to her home. 'Will he come back?' she asked. 'Yes,' said the sergeant, assuming she meant her husband. 'They'll blame me for this,' she said.

Frederick Bywaters was arrested at the Graydons' house in Manor Park on the night of 4 October 1922 and taken to Ilford police station. Edith Thompson was detained later the same night.

He made a lying statement, saying he went straight home after leaving the Graydons. She made a lying statement the following morning, after which she happened to see Bywaters in the room where he was being detained. She said: 'Oh, God! Oh, God! What can I do? Why did he do it? I didn't want him to do it! I must tell the truth.' She then made a second, brief statement naming Bywaters as her husband's assailant. That evening Freddy was told that he and Mrs Thompson would be charged with the wilful murder of Percy Thompson. 'Why her?' said Bywaters. 'Mrs Thompson was not aware of my movements.' He then made a second statement, outlining his actions on the night of 3 October. They were then both charged.

It was not until a week later that her letters were found in his sea chest (or 'ditty-box') in his cabin on the *Morea,* which was anchored at Tilbury.

The trial began at the Old Bailey on Wednesday, 6 December. There were five other indictments against Mrs Thompson, besides that of murder – of conspiring to murder, of attempting to murder and of inciting Bywaters to murder Percy Thompson. But the couple were only tried on the first count. The judge was Mr Justice Shearman. The Solicitor-General, Sir Thomas Inskip, KC, led for the prosecution – Travers Humphreys was his second. Cecil Whitely, KC, defended Bywaters, and Sir Henry Curtis Bennett, KC, acted for Mrs Thompson.

Against the advice of her counsel, Edith Thompson gave evidence, as did Freddy Bywaters. Curtis Bennett observed later: 'She was a vain woman and an obstinate one. She had an idea she would carry the jury. Also she realised the enormous public interest, and decided to play up to it by entering the witness box.'

Mrs Thompson was rigorously cross-examined. The letters and her adultery seemed damning. There seemed to be no doubt that in the letters she had incited Bywaters to kill her husband. 'I never considered them as such,' said Bywaters. Mrs Thompson's explanation of her talk of poison was: 'I wanted him to think I would do anything for him, to keep him to me.'

'She worked and preyed on the mind of this young man,' said the Solicitor-General, and the judge appeared to agree – his summing-up was prejudicial and remorseless. Bernard Spilsbury's evidence – about the total absence of any poison or glass in Mr Thompson's body – was ignored. It seemed as if the jury were being asked to view the case as a breach of the third commandment, not the second.

The judge stated: 'This charge really is – I am not saying whether it is proved – a common or ordinary charge of a wife and an adulterer murdering the husband … You are told this is a case of great love. Take one of the letters as a test – "He has the right by law to all that you have a right to by nature and by love." If that means anything, it means that the love of a husband for his wife is something improper … and that the love of a woman for her lover, illicit and clandestine, is something great and noble. I am certain that you, like any other right-minded person, will be filled with disgust at such a notion.'

On Monday, 11 December, both the accused were found guilty. Bywaters said: ' I say the verdict of the jury is wrong. Edith Thompson is not guilty. I am no murderer – I am not an assassin.' After sentence was passed Mrs Thompson cried out: 'I'm not guilty! Oh, God. I'm not guilty!' Separately removed from the dock, they never saw each other again.

Despite many protests, the verdict against her was upheld in the Court of Criminal Appeal, a decision that shocked many people, and on 9 January 1923, Edith Thompson, although sedated, was dragged from her cell in Holloway Prison, screaming and fainting, towards the scaffold. She was hanged by John Ellis, the chief executioner, and two assistants. At the same time Freddy Bywaters was hanged by William Willis in Pentonville Prison half a mile away.

John Ellis, a neurotic man who drank a lot, retired in 1923, several months after the execution of Mrs Thompson – some said because of it. In August 1924, in Rochdale – eighteen months after she was hanged – Ellis tried to commit suicide by shooting himself. His aim was poor and he only succeeded in fracturing his jaw and lodging a bullet in his neck. 'Bloody hell,' observed executioner Tom Pierrepoint to his nephew, Albert. 'He should have done it bloody years ago. It was impossible to work with him.' When Ellis recovered he was sent for trial for the offence before a magistrate, who remarked: 'If your aim had been as true as the drops you have given it would have been a bad job for you.' On promising to stop drinking and to behave himself, Ellis was discharged. But, seven years later, in 1931, he cut his throat and died.

Edith Thompson's body was exhumed from the cemetery in Holloway Prison in March 1971 and reburied in unconsecrated ground near Woking in Surrey.

PATRICK MAHON

THE MURDER OF EMILY KAYE, 1924

The ghastliest murder case dealt with by Scotland Yard between the wars made police history of another kind. It led to the introduction of the Murder Bag, a case of forensic, medical and other items that was taken thereafter to the scene of every murder visited by detectives of the Metropolitan Police. This murder also illustrates yet again the terrible lengths to which a murderer will go to dispose of a corpse, and the unique terrors he faces. Mahon's method of disposal was so sensational, albeit unsuccessful, that it actually started a trend.

Miss Ethel Primrose Duncan was thirty-two and unmarried. A tall and dark-haired, well-built woman, she lived with her sister in Worple Avenue, Isleworth. On Thursday, 10 April 1924, at about ten o'clock at night, she was on her way home in pouring rain. In the High Street near Richmond Station she met an attractive man in his thirties with merry eyes and a ready smile. He offered to escort her part of the way towards Isleworth. This meant crossing the River Thames by way of Richmond Bridge. As they walked along with the rain dripping off his trilby hat, he told her that his name was Pat, that he was married, lived in Richmond and worked in Sunbury. His marriage, he said, was 'a tragedy'. Before he left her, he asked her if she would dine with him soon, and when she replied in the affirmative he said he would get in touch. She gave him her address, and he wrote it down in his diary. 'You'll probably hear from me on Wednesday,' he said, with murder in mind – though not that of Miss Duncan.

The following Tuesday she received a telegram in the late afternoon which read – 'Charing Cross seven tomorrow. Sure. Pat.' As requested, on Wednesday 16 April she went to Charing Cross at 7 pm. But it was not until about 7.50 pm that Pat appeared. His wrist was bandaged, and he said he had sprained it saving a lady from falling from a bus. He also said he had travelled up from Eastbourne, where he had borrowed a bungalow from a friend, and he asked Miss Duncan over dinner at the Victoria Station restaurant whether she would like to spend the Easter holiday with him in the bungalow. She agreed, and it was arranged that in two days' time (on Good Friday) he would meet her at Eastbourne. They left the restaurant at about half-past ten, by which time he had missed the last train back to Eastbourne. So after booking himself in for the night at the Grosvenor Hotel beside Victoria Station, he courteously accompanied her to Waterloo

Station and saw her safely on to the 10.36 pm train for Isleworth. There had been nothing at all in Pat's cheerful manner and conversation to suggest to Miss Duncan that he had just murdered another woman.

The next day, Thursday, Ethel Duncan received a telegraphic order for £4 and a telegram that read – 'Meet train as arranged. Waller.' Up to that point she had had no idea what Pat's surname was.

On Good Friday, she travelled on the 11.15 am train from Victoria to Eastbourne, arriving at 1.57 pm. Pat met her at the station – he was wearing a fawn-coloured suit – and after leaving her luggage in the station cloakroom they had lunch at the Sussex Hotel. In the afternoon they went for a drive in a taxi cab and dined that evening in the Royal Hotel, Eastbourne, leaving there about 10 pm. A taxi took them both (after they had collected her luggage) along the coast for about 3 miles towards Pevensey Bay, to a village called Langney, and finally to a bungalow by the shingly beach and the sea.

Here Pat and Ethel spent three nights, sleeping in the bedroom that was first on the left in the hall. Ethel realised as soon as she entered the room that another woman had been there before her, for a tortoiseshell brush and some cosmetics lay on a chest of drawers. Then the following morning, in tidying up, she discovered a pair of ladies' buckled shoes. Pat said they belonged to his wife. She had been down the previous week, he said, and would return there after Easter. He told Ethel she need not bother about cleaning the bungalow as his wife would do that. Ethel never saw the shoes again on her visit – Pat had hidden them away. But he could not conceal the bruising she had noticed on the back of his right arm.

On Saturday morning they drove into Eastbourne, where Pat left Ethel to do some shopping while he took the taxi on to Plumpton Races, 20 miles to the west. Unknown to Ethel, Pat stopped off at Lewes and entered the general post office, from where he sent a telegram to 'Walter, Officer's House, Pevensey.' It read: 'Must see you Tuesday morning nine Cheapside. Lee.' Pat reached the race course about 1.30 pm and remained there until the last race had been run. He had retained the taxi driver who had brought him there and returned in the same taxi to Eastbourne. There he met up again with Ethel at the railway station about 6.30 pm. They dined that night at the Sussex Hotel. On the way there he called in at the Sussex Stores and made some purchases.

On Easter Sunday, Pat busied himself in trying to change the lock on the door of the bedroom next to theirs. There were four bedrooms in the bungalow, as well as a sitting room, dining room, bathroom, kitchen and scullery. There was also a telephone. Pat's explanation for his task was that a pal of his had some valuable books in the room and he was concerned about their safety. The chisel he was using slipped and cut his left hand. Ethel bound it up for him, and through the partly open door glimpsed a bed and a large brown trunk. Pat said that if he had known the trouble the lock was going to be, he wouldn't have started. Later that afternoon he solved the problem another way. He told Ethel: 'I've screwed the door up. I don't know why I didn't think of that before.'

That night they dined at the Clifton Hotel in Eastbourne, travelling there and back by taxi. Pat seemed to have a lot of money on him in cash.

Earlier that day, Pat had shown her a telegram that had apparently arrived the night before when they were out. He opened it, told her what was in it. It was from someone called Lee, and he told her: 'We'll have to go up to London tomorrow. I have to be in town at nine o'clock on Tuesday morning.'

So, at 3:30 pm on Easter Monday, the couple left the bungalow and returned by train to London, where they dined together before going to the Palladium Theatre. After the show Pat travelled with Ethel from Waterloo to Richmond Station, where at midnight he left her, no doubt promising to see her again. Ethel's romantic weekend was over.

She did not see him again for more than five weeks. But a fortnight after their parting she was horrified to read in the newspapers that in a bungalow on Pevensey Bay the headless, mutilated remains of a woman had been found in a trunk.

Pat's real name was Patrick Herbert Mahon. He was thirty-four. Thin-faced, nice-looking, tall (5 ft 11 in) and with an athletic build, his most noticeable features were his deep-set eyes and thick brown wavy hair, which was already streaked with grey. Born in 1889 and brought up in West Derby, Liverpool, by Irish parents, as a boy he was a regular church-goer, good at games, a good mixer, intelligent, smart and an avid pursuer of girls, his activities in this field being undiminished by his marriage on 6 April 1910 to Jessie, aged twenty-three, from Walton, Liverpool. He gave his occupation then as 'literary publisher's book-keeper'. (His father was a stock-keeper in a clothing warehouse.) A year after his marriage, Mahon spent a weekend on the Isle of Man with another girl, a visit paid for by some forged cheques. For this he was bound over, but he was soon sent to prison on another charge of embezzlement. He moved to Surrey, and his constant picking up of women got him into trouble with his employers and eventually with the police. In 1916, during a robbery, he struck a maidservant with a hammer, but was so overcome with guilt that he remained on the scene until she recovered consciousness, reassuringly kissing her and apologising for what he had done. He was sentenced for five years in jail for this attack.

When he was released, he joined his wife and she got him a job as a £12 a week salesman in Sunbury with Consol Automatic Aerators (1914) Ltd; they marketed soda fountains and she worked as a secretary with the firm. The Mahons lived with their surviving child in Richmond – another child, a boy, had died while his father was in prison.

In May 1922, the company went bankrupt and came under the receiver. A chartered accountant, Mr Hobbins, was appointed by a firm of CAs, Robertson, Hill and Co., to sort out the company's affairs, and in effecting this he retained the services of Mr and Mrs Mahon and a chemist. In fac, he appointed Patrick Mahon as sales manager, on a salary and commission that averaged £42 a month. Mahon's duties sometimes took him into the City of London, to the offices of Robertson, Hill and Co. in Copthall Avenue,

Moorgate, where Mr Hobbins worked. His secretary and shorthand typist was Miss Emily Beilby Kaye.

Aged thirty-eight (born in November 1885), she was a tall, athletic woman, with fair bobbed hair and a round face – 'a cheery, loveable girl' according to a cousin. Her parents had died in Manchester when she was seventeen, since when she had supported herself locally as a clerk for over twenty years while living with her married sister, before eventually coming to London in October 1922.

It was in January 1923 that she was engaged as a typist by Robertson, Hill and Co. at £17 6s 8d a month, and in May she went to live in the Green Cross Club, Guilford Street, off Russell Square, where for a time she shared a room with Miss Edith Warren. Miss Kaye was described by Edith as placid and not easily roused. But she was also 'strong physically and unusually strong mentally'. Edith thought that Emily, whom she called 'Peter', was 'capable of very deep feeling'. Peter called Edith 'Phiz'. Peter was also a prudent woman. Over the years she had accumulated some £600, which she had invested in stocks and shares.

In the course of office business she soon met Patrick Mahon. He said later: 'Miss Kaye was aware that I was married, knew my wife by sight, and had spoken to her on many occasions on the phone. Miss Kaye frequently rang me up, and towards the end of August or September … suggested a day on the river, which suggestion, as I was anxious to gain some impartial knowledge of the legal proceedings in connection with the litigation in which the company was concerned, I accepted.' The events of that day, he said, showed him that Emily Kaye was 'a woman of the world'. After that, according to him, she often wanted to see him. He claimed that 'She reproached me on several occasions as being cold, and told me plainly she wished my affection, and was determined to win it if possible.'

On 21 October, she was dismissed for some unknown reason from Robertson, Hill and Co, but was able to obtain employment elsewhere. Over the New Year she went to stay with her sister, Mrs Elizabeth Harrison, in Cheshire, and when she returned to London she got a new job working as a shorthand typist and book-keeper for a financier, Lewis Schaverien, in Old Bond Street. She was only there a month.

In February 1924, she began to sell shares and to cash her savings, putting the proceeds into an account with the Midland Bank in Coleman Street. On 16 February, she cashed a cheque for £404, receiving the money in four £100 notes and four £1 notes. In March, she was ill with influenza and went down to Bournemouth for a week to recuperate. At the end of this visit, she was joined by Patrick Mahon in Southampton, where he bought her a diamond-and-sapphire cluster ring at Cranbrook's, a jeweller's in the High Street. That night they shared a double room in the South Western Hotel, signing the register as Mr and Mrs PH Mahon, Richmond.

On Emily Kaye's return to the Green Cross Club, she showed the ring to Edith Warren and said she was engaged to Pat. Edith thought that Peter seemed to be 'very fond' of Pat but not 'passionately in love'. Later he asked Edith not to use his name in front of the other girls as they knew some of his business acquaintances. Edith was to refer to him as 'Derek Patterson'.

Emily also told the club secretary, Ada Smith, about her engagement – 'She came bounding into my room exclaiming: "It's fixed, my dear – the date!"' – and that she and her fiancé were going to emigrate to South Africa. She wrote in a similar vein to her sister on 5 April, on the very day that Mahon, calling himself Waller, travelled to Langney to inspect a bungalow that had been advertised to let in *Dalton's News*. He agreed to rent it at three-and-a-half guineas a week from 1 April to 6 June.

On Monday, 7 April Emily Kaye packed her bags, said her goodbyes and moved out of the Green Cross Club. She went to Eastbourne and took a room in the Kenilworth Court Hotel, Wilmington Square, where she stayed until Saturday the 12th; Mahon had met Miss Duncan in Richmond on the 10th. About 2 pm on the 12th, Emily Kaye received a telegram – 'Regret extremely cannot come three-fifteen. Coming four forty-nine. Meet train. Pat.' Before she left the hotel she asked the receptionist to forward any letters to 'Poste Restante, Paris.' The receptionist noticed that Miss Kaye was wearing a smart grey costume, grey suede shoes and a fur coat with a dark collar.

In London at about lunchtime that day, Mahon had paid a visit to Staine's Kitchen Equipment Company in Victoria Street, and had bought a ten-inch cook's knife and a small meat saw. That evening he met Emily Kaye in Eastbourne as arranged and they drove out in a taxi to the bungalow by a stretch of coast known locally as The Crumbles.

The bungalow was called the Officer's House and was one of a row of white-washed properties once occupied by the coastguard on Pevensey Bay. Nearly three years earlier, and within a short distance of the bungalow, a seventeen-year-old London typist name Irene Munro had been battered to death and robbed of her holiday money by two young men – Jack Field, aged nineteen, and Bill Gray, twenty-nine. Both were subsequently hanged.

The bungalow had been let furnished to Mahon by a Mr Muir of Ashley Gardens in London on behalf of a Mrs Hutchinson of Prince's Gate. It had been cleaned up and made ready by Mrs Hutchinson's cook-housekeeper on 11 April, the day that Mahon had travelled down from London to meet Mr Muir at the bungalow and to receive the keys. He had returned to London that afternoon without seeing Emily in Eastbourne.

Strangely, Muir happened to meet Mahon again the very next day, Saturday, in Victoria Street between 12 noon and 1 pm. Mahon was carrying a kitbag in which would soon repose the newly bought knife and saw. That night he travelled down to Eastbourne, collected Emily Kaye and took her to the Officer's House.

No one knows for certain when Emily Kaye died. But she survived their first night together in the bungalow, which was spent in the bedroom that would be occupied by Miss Duncan the following weekend. Emily was seen through a window on the Sunday morning, 13 April, by a butcher who called to deliver some meat. On the same day, Emily called at a neighbouring bungalow to borrow some milk. On Monday, 14 April, she apparently visited Eastbourne, for a letter she wrote to Edith Warren was marked 'Kenilworth Court Hotel, Eastbourne, Monday', although it need not have been written there. The letter was not in fact posted until 16 April, when it was dropped by Mahon into a letterbox in south-west London. It read:

> *Pat arrived intact, but with his arm in a sling, on Saturday, and we are having a very nice time of it; quiet, a nice change from town. He particularly wants to get to Paris for Easter, and would like you and Fred both to have dinner with us when we return to town. We shall have a few days, about a fortnight, before setting on our final journey ... All news when we meet. Lots of love to all the pals and yourself, old bean − Pete.*

Miss Warren tore the letter up and threw the pieces into a bin, where they remained until the police, pursuing their enquiries, retrieved them and stuck them together.

The letter ties in, although somewhat loosely, with the fact that the last time Emily Kaye was seen alive was at the Kenilworth Court Hotel on either Monday or Tuesday (the 14th or 15th), when she called and enquired whether any letters or a parcel had arrived. The receptionist was uncertain about the exact date.

Despite Mahon's later insistence that Miss Kaye died on the *Tuesday* night after a day-trip to London − where he pretended to go to the passport office while she went to her club − it seems likely that she died on Monday the 14th. In cross-examination at his trial, he said that Miss Kaye was with him in Hastings on the 15th, when at 3.40 pm he sent the telegram to Miss Duncan asking her to meet him the following day at Charing Cross. If Miss Kaye was with him in Hastings, they could have gone there from London. But no evidence was ever produced to show that either Mahon or Miss Kaye was in London on the 15th, or that she was ever in Hastings.

What is fairly certain, however, is that she wrote a second letter to Edith Warren, dated 14 April − although Mahon later claimed that she actually wrote it on Tuesday the 15th. This letter read:

> *Dear old Phiz ... I am sorry that I shall not after all be able to see you before my departure. As you can imagine, there has been a lot to do ... We shall be travelling overland through France and Italy en route to the Cape. On arrival there I will write regarding prospects and other matters in general. I wish to thank you for all the kindness and friendship you have shown me in the past. One cannot put into words just what one feels, but I am sure you will understand and appreciate just what is in my mind. Any letters addressed to me care of Standard Bank, Cape Town, will find me. As I have said earlier, I will write fully on my arrival. Believe me, yours, Emily Kaye.*

There is something oddly formal about this letter. One wonders whether it was for some reason written under duress. It is hardly the kind of farewell letter that a woman writes to her best friend.

Mahon's accounts of the death of Emily Kaye vary in detail (and date). What follows is the story he told the Old Bailey court when he gave evidence in his own defence. He said that after they returned to the bungalow on Tuesday evening, 15 April, he lit a fire. In doing so he carried the coal scuttle from the dining room into the sitting room. There were some large lumps of coal in the scuttle, which he broke up with a small wooden-handled axe, laying it afterwards on the sitting-room table. at which Miss Kaye was seated, writing letters. He said she wrote two letters that night, both to Edith Warren. When she finished writing, he said, she looked up and stated: 'Pat, I'm determined to settle this matter one way or the other tonight.' She tossed the two letters over to him and said: 'These letters and my actions mean that I have burned my boats.' By this he understood that she meant leaving her club. 'For me there is no turning back,' she continued. 'Can't you realise, Pat, how much I love you, and that you are everything to me, and that I can never share you with another?' He said: 'Why can't we be pals?' She replied: 'What's the use of palship to me, to one of my nature?' 'That's all I can offer you,' he replied. Then, according to him, she became very excited. He realised that a crisis was coming. She was, he said, 'distracted and overwrought'.

At this point the judge intervened. 'This is a descriptive sort of narrative,' he said. 'We want to know what happened.'

Mahon continued: 'I said to Miss Kaye: "I'm going to bed," and I moved away from the table to go to the bedroom. Miss Kaye said something, and as I turned by the bedroom door she threw the axe. I barely had time to avoid it striking me on the right shoulder. It hit over the door or framework of the door. I was astounded by the suddenness of the attack. She leapt across the room clutching at my face.'

Here Mahon's voice broke; he staggered; his shoulders heaved and he burst into tears. When he had composed himself, drying his eyes with a silk handkerchief, he went on with his narration:

I did my best to keep her off. We struggled backwards and forwards, and I realised in a minute that I was dealing with a woman almost mad with anger. I tried to keep her off, but I realised she was getting the better of me ... In an almost despairing throw I pushed Miss Kaye off and we both fell over the easy chair on the left of the fireplace. Miss Kaye's head hit the cauldron and I fell with her — she was underneath. She had gripped me by the throat and I had gripped her by the throat. We were locked together. I think I must have fainted with the fear and shock. When I did become conscious of what had happened, Miss Kaye was lying by the coal scuttle and blood had flowed from her head. I tried to rouse her, pinched her, and called her by name, but she never moved or answered. I think I must have fainted again, or lay in a sort of stupor. I remember dashing water into her face. I must have gone half-mad. I went into the garden crazy with fear. I remember coming back to the bungalow later. Miss Kaye was still lying there, dead. That would be hours later, towards daybreak or at daybreak. It suddenly struck me what a fool I had been not to call for assistance, and it dawned on me what a horrible thing it was that she was lying there, and dead. The fact that she was dead flooded my mind.

The judge interrupted: 'You are asked what you did – not all this imagination.'

Mahon then told the court how he had dragged Miss Kaye's body into the second bedroom and covered it with a fur coat. He went to Eastbourne about breakfast-time, he said, and then to London to keep his appointment at Charing Cross with Miss Duncan.

It was on this day that the first letter to Miss Warren was posted from somewhere in south-west London, and that was the night he spent in the Grosvenor Hotel, returning to Eastbourne the following day, Thursday. Before he did so, he sent a telegram at 9.55 am to his wife from Vauxhall Bridge Road near Victoria Station – 'Expressed you urgent letter. Sorry impossible today. Mahon'

It was not until the morning of Good Friday, 18 April, according to Mahon, that he began to dismember Miss Kaye's corpse. He cut off her legs and then her head in order to pack her body into a trunk in the second bedroom. Having done so, he said, he then went by taxi to Eastbourne to meet Miss Duncan at the station just before 2 pm. He later told the police: 'I should have gone stark raving mad if I had not had her with me. It was ghastly.'

He and Miss Duncan returned to London on Easter Monday, and very late that night Mahon went home to Pagoda Avenue. But on Tuesday he was away again. He returned to the bungalow on Pevensey Bay, where he burnt the corpse's head in the sitting-room grate, as well as the feet and legs. Apparently, he did this during a thunderstorm, and later he told his counsel that when he put the head on the blazing fire the eyes opened – just as there was a clap of thunder overhead. Lightning flashed, and he fled from the room in terror. Returning yet again to the bungalow on the Saturday, he disposed of further portions of the now putrefying corpse.

He explained what he did in his first statement to the police:

I had to cut up the trunk. I also cut off the arms. I burnt portions of them and then I had to think of some other method of disposing of the portions. I boiled some portions in a large pot in the bungalow. I cut the portions up small, packed them in a brown bag, and I threw them out of the train while I was travelling between Waterloo and Richmond ... I had intended to go home Sunday night, and as I could not dispose of all the portions between Waterloo and Richmond, I went on to Reading and stayed at the Station Hotel in the name of Rees.

This was on the night of 27 April. He arrived about 7 pm, and as he had some luggage with him no deposit was required. 'Next morning I came to London and left the bag in the cloakroom at Waterloo – on the Monday morning.'

One wonders at Mahon's dreadful persistence, at the enormity of his terrible task and the mess he made of it. One wonders how the soda-fountain salesman remained in his right mind, and what Mrs Jessie Mahon thought of his comings and goings and of the strain that must have shown itself in his eyes, face and behaviour. She must have been very concerned and suspicious. But of what? Was she distressed by the thought that he was in the throes of another torrid affair? Or did she suspect something else?

On the last day of April, she took her worries to a friend, a former railway policeman. She also gave him a cloakroom ticket that she had found in her husband's pockets, and asked the ex-detective to find out what it was that Pat had left at Waterloo Station. This he did, presenting the ticket at the cloakroom of the south station at Waterloo. He was given a locked Gladstone bag. Easing the sides apart, he was able to see what appeared to be bloodstained female underwear, and a knife. He returned the bag to the cloakroom and the ticket to Mrs Mahon, instructing her to put it back in her husband's suit.

On Thursday, 1 May, the ex-detective communicated what he had been told and seen for himself to the Chief Constable of the CID, Frederick Wensley. DCI Percy Savage was asked to investigate. He visited the south station cloakroom at Waterloo himself about 7.15 pm with DS Frew, and after undoing the straps of the bag he was able to peer into it from the side. From then on the bag was kept under direct observation by the police, who were ordered to detain and question whoever came to collect it. They did not have long to wait.

About 6.30 pm the following day – 2 May – Patrick Mahon paid 5d to retrieve the Gladstone bag from the cloakroom, and as he walked towards the station's York Road exit he was brought to a halt by DS Thompson. 'Is that your bag?' enquired Thompson. 'I believe so,' said Mahon. Thompson asked if he might have a look inside the bag. Mahon replied: 'I haven't got the key.' Thompson said: 'You'll have to come with me to Kennington police station.' 'Rubbish!' retorted Mahon. Thompson said it was not rubbish and that the other man would have to do as he was told. At the police station, Mahon was searched. Sets of keys, 1,805 francs and a post-office savings book were found on him. He was seen at about 8.30 pm by DCI Savage, who took both Mahon and the bag, still unopened, for examination to Scotland Yard, where they arrived about 9 pm. Mahon was offered a drink and some sandwiches but refused them. The interrogation began about forty-five minutes later in the Chief Inspector's room.

'Look at the bag carefully,' said Savage. 'Is it yours?' Mahon said: 'Yes.' Savage opened the bag and took from it a torn and bloodstained pair of bloomers, two pieces of bloody white silk, a bloody scarf, a cook's knife and a brown canvas racket bag initialled 'EBK'. Everything had been liberally sprinkled with a disinfectant – Sanitas. 'How do you account for the possession of these things?' asked Savage. 'I'm fond of dogs,' replied

Mahon – 'I suppose I have carried home meat for dogs in it.' 'That explanation won't do,' said Savage. 'I'll have to detain you while we make further enquiries.' Mahon said: 'You seem to know all about it.' To which Savage replied: 'I cannot tell you what I know. It is for you to tell me what *you* know, and how these things came into your possession.'

At this point Savage had absolutely no idea what crime, if any, had actually been committed. He waited. The two men sat in silence for fifteen minutes, Mahon with his head hidden in his hands.

Then Mahon said: 'I wonder if you can realise how terrible a thing it is for someone's body to be active and one's mind to fail to act.' Savage said nothing. Mahon remained silent for another half-hour before speaking again. He remarked: 'I'm considering my position.' Fifteen minutes later he said: 'I suppose you know everything. I'll tell you the truth.'

After being cautioned, he made the first of several detailed and voluntary statements to the police. His story was taken down by DI Hall, and took well over two hours to tell. About 1.30 am Mahon collapsed and had to be revived with some whisky before he could complete the statement, which he did by 2 am. Then he read through what Hall had written. He made some corrections to the statement, initialled each page and signed the last one.

In this first long statement he revealed how he had quarrelled with Emily Kaye on 16 April in the bungalow, and that during a struggle she had hit her head on the coal scuttle and died. It was on the 17th, he said, that he bought a knife and saw in Victoria Street, and on the 18th that he began to dismember the body. He said he returned to London on Easter Monday. He made no mention of Miss Duncan. It was about 3.30 am before Savage left the room.

The Chief Constable, Frederick Wensley was informed about Mahon's statement straight away, and in the early hours of Saturday, 3 May he and Savage drove down to Sussex. After liaising with the East Sussex Constabulary they went to the Officer's House, still with no sure idea of what they might find.

The bungalow's porch was overhung with rambling roses. Inside it stank. In a large locked trunk marked 'EBK' was the quartered limbless body of a woman. In a hatbox and a biscuit tin were the heart and other organs. In a saucepan were portions that had been boiled. There were charred remains in the dining-room and sitting-room grates, and a quantity of bone fragments on an ash-dump outside. There were bloodstains on the sitting-room floor and on the door frame. There was no mark, however, on or near the door to indicate that it had been struck with an axe. The axe-head itself was eventually discovered hidden under some coal in the coalhouse; its broken shaft was found in the scullery. A saw was found by a fireplace and the coal scuttle was in the dining room. Miss Kaye's personal possessions and clothes, some of which had been torn up and wrapped around pieces of her flesh, had been stored in the same bedroom as the trunk.

DCI Savage returned to London, where Mahon had in the meantime corrected and expanded on his first statement, now revealing details about Miss Duncan's involvement.

On Sunday morning, Sir Bernard Spilsbury, who had been knighted earlier that year, visited the bungalow, and out in the back garden began to piece together the remains of Emily Kaye on a table, protected from the eyes of the curious – hundreds of people had gathered at the scene – by a high wall. The police began digging up the garden, searching for the missing limbs and the head. These were never found, and it was thought that Mahon had, as he claimed, destroyed them in the sitting-room fire. Spilsbury was able to establish that Miss Kaye had been about two months pregnant.

On the afternoon of Monday, 5 May, Patrick Mahon, in a grey suit, was taken to Hailsham in Sussex and charged with the murder of Emily Kaye. He replied: 'I've already made a statement. It wasn't murder, as my statement clearly shows.' Police investigations later that month revealed that Emily Kaye had given him the four £100 notes, presumably to pay in part for their trip abroad and the setting up of a home in South Africa. He had cashed two of the notes at the Bank of England before her death, and one after. The fourth note was thought by the police to have been changed at Plumpton Races.

A motive for murder now appeared. Having misled Miss Kaye into thinking that he would marry her, he acquired and spent most of her savings. When she became anxious about the non-realisation of his promises – and also became pregnant – he decided to kill her, for she had become a threat to his marriage, his financial solvency and was bound to be troublesome. He persuaded her to tell her friends that she was engaged to a man called Patterson and that they were going to South Africa to start a new life. She would then conveniently disappear. In his statements he said that *she* was the motivating force in their association, demanding that he leave his wife, that they get married and go abroad. He said that *she* bought the 'engagement' ring and that he never knew she was pregnant. Probably, if it had not been for Mrs Mahon's discovery of the cloakroom ticket, Miss Kaye would in due course have vanished entirely from the bungalow on The Crumbles and nothing would have connected Mr Waller of Eastbourne with Mr Mahon.

The trial of Patrick Mahon began at the Sussex Assizes in Lewes on Tuesday, 15 July 1924. Mr Justice Avory presided. Sir Henry Curtis Bennett, KC, led for the Crown, and the prisoner was defended by Mr JD Cassels, KC, MP. Thousands of people mobbed the courthouse and 200 were actually allowed inside.

The correspondent from *The Times* wrote: 'The accused appeared to be in much better health than when he appeared at the police court, although showing signs of weariness and fatigue.' In fact, he was looking his best: his face bore an artificial tan created, it is said, by tobacco juice; his hair was immaculate, his hands manicured; and he wore a smart, blue, specially tailored seven-guinea suit. He carefully scrutinised the all-male jury as they were sworn in – three were challenged by Mr Cassels and asked to stand down.

The second day of the trial was interrupted by the separate illnesses of two jurors, who had to be replaced. Two new ones were sworn in and the proceedings were recapitulated for their benefit. A third juryman then fainted, and a fourth asked to be excused. So another two jurors were sworn in and the prosecution's case was outlined again before the trial continued.

On the third day, Thursday, Ethel Duncan sobbed hysterically as she took the oath, and when she was asked by the judge to identify the prisoner as the man she had met at Richmond she cried: 'Oh, don't! Please!' and sobbed. When he stood up in the dock for her inspection, she stared at him fixedly, then burst into tears. When giving evidence, her voice was almost inaudible. Sir Bernard Spilsbury followed her. He supported the prosecution's view that Miss Kaye could not have received any fatal injuries from falling on to the coal scuttle, as the scuttle – a cheap one with insubstantial, hollow legs – was undamaged. He did not think that her throat had been cut. But the absence of her head prevented anyone from proving the theory that she had been hit on the head with the axe, and possibly strangled.

Later that afternoon, Mahon himself gave evidence on his own behalf. In telling of his renting of the bungalow he said: 'I promised Miss Kaye that we would go through with this experiment – this love experiment, we called it. I thought if I took the bungalow for two months it would kill two birds with one stone. After Miss Kaye had finished –' The judge interrupted: 'After Miss Kaye had *finished*?' Mahon explained: 'After we had finished our experiment and Miss Kaye had returned, my wife and I could use the bungalow.'

Later on he was overcome with emotion when he related how she had attacked him; he wept. Outside, the weather was close and sultry. During Mahon's narration of the dismemberment of the body, lightning flashed and there was a clap of thunder. Mahon shuddered and blanched, reminded perhaps of the thunderstorm that had accompanied his burning of the head and limbs.

He was cross-examined for nearly three hours on the Friday morning. When asked by Sir Henry about Miss Kaye's alleged assault on him, Mahon again broke down in tears. Towards the end of Sir Henry's interrogation, Mahon's face ran with sweat; he wiped his eyes repeatedly; he shuddered and seemed about to faint. When he was given a chair he sat on it with his left hand tucked under his right arm; his right hand shook.

Mr Justice Avory's one-and-a-half-hour summing-up was delivered on the morning of Saturday, 19 July, For the entire duration, Mahon never raised his head. He was quite listless and seemed to be in despair. Found guilty by the jury, he suddenly became animated, making a passionate denouncement of 'the bitterness and unfairness' of the summing-up before he was sentenced to death.

Patrick Mahon was hanged by Tom Pierrepoint and William Willis at Wandsworth Prison on 3 September 1924. He weighed 141 lb and was given a drop of 7 ft 8 in. During his time in prison, unable to eat most of his meals, he had lost 9 lb.

On the day itself, he was quite composed, according to Tom Pierrepoint, unlike the day he had been taken to the condemned cell, when he had to be carried along before collapsing in the cell, crying and moaning. But as Pierrepoint pulled the lever, Mahon tried to avoid falling through the trap door by jumping upwards. As he fell, said Pierrepoint, his back struck the edge of the trap.

Later that morning, Sir Bernard Spilsbury performed the autopsy, noting that the neck had been broken in two places, as was usual.

When Spilsbury had arrived at the Officer's House on 4 May, he found DCI Savage using his bare hands to pick up pieces of decomposing flesh. 'Are there no rubber gloves?' he asked, concerned about the risk of infection. There was none. But the Yard, in consultation with Spilsbury and other forensic experts, subsequently devised and assembled the Murder Bag that was thenceforth taken to the scene of any such crime.

NORMAN THORNE

THE MURDER OF ELSIE CAMERON, 1924

Sheer stupidity seems to be a characteristic of most murders – not surprisingly, as murder is seldom the act of a sensible person. But having committed the fatal deed, some behave so stupidly that even if not technically insane they would certainly seem to be abnormal. They are careless, they lie, they make a mess of disposing of the body and the evidence, and they cannot resist assisting the police. It sometimes seems they want to be caught, or else cannot believe they ever will be, as if they thought they had put themselves beyond the reach of society and the law.

Elsie Emily Cameron was far from being a typical pretty flapper. A London typist, aged twenty-six, she was small, plain, bespectacled, nervous, even neurotic, and very obstinate. Nonetheless, she was engaged to John Norman Holmes Thorne, a chicken farmer two years younger than she, who lived in a hut on a muddy, rundown small holding at Crowborough in Sussex.

They had met in 1920 at Kensal Rise Wesleyan Church in north London, and although Norman may not have been the brightest boy around, she decided he was quite good-looking and better than nothing. For besides being nice and amenable, he was also a Sunday school teacher, attended Band of Hope meetings and concerts, helped to run the local Scout group and was involved in all kinds of chapel work. Perhaps more than anything else, he had a certain physical attraction. Elsie began walking out with him and eventually determined to marry him.

Norman was then an electrical engineer with Fiat motors at Wembley. He was born in Portsmouth in 1902. His mother died when he was seven; his father, who remarried, was an engineer, an overseer and inspector for the Admiralty. In March 1918, Norman joined the Royal Naval Air Service as a mechanic. Stunned by a bomb blast after he went to Belgium in October 1918, three weeks before the end of the war, he was demobbed in November the following year and on returning to England became a civilian mechanic.

With thousands of others, he was forced to go on the dole in the summer of 1921. Norman, however, was not prepared to put up with this – he was made of sterner stuff – and having bought a field with money from his father for £100, he established the Wesley Poultry Farm, Blackness, Crowborough, Sussex, on 22 August 1921. To begin with, he used to lodge locally while he built his chicken runs and huts. At weekends he bicycled back to London. Then, to simplify matters, he turned one of his brooding houses into a shack for himself, where he set up a sort of home. At this point Elsie began travelling down by train to see him at the weekend, staying with local people at night and with Norman during the day.

They became engaged at Christmas 1922. The following month, Elsie was sacked from her job after being with the same firm for nine years: she was said to be moody and forgetful. Four other jobs followed in fairly quick succession. But in June 1923, she had something else to occupy her mind. It was about then, as Norman later told the police, 'We became on intimate terms, that is feeling one another's person and from that it went that I put my person against hers, but in my opinion I did not put it into her. This practice continued on almost all the occasions when Miss Cameron came to the hut. We had previously made up our minds that she should not become pregnant.'

Having given herself to him in this way Elsie, both sexually aroused and frustrated, wrote a long letter to Norman on 28 June, full of passion and repeated endearments such as 'Oh my pet – lovey – beloved – dearie – treasure – sweetheart – darling'. She wrote:

> Our courtship is like a fairy-tale and it will end with 'They lived happily ever after' Oh my treasure, how I adore you, you mean everything to me, and oh, if only we could get married. Oh pet, let's try and do so this year and manage as I said, Lovey. We can manage in a little hut like yours; your Elsie is quite well now and there is no fear of any children for three or four years … Oh, my Darling, how I adore you, what you mean to me you cannot realise … For ever and always. Your own true little sweetheart Elsie. PS. Do not forget my weekend letter.

Elsie's brother and sister both married in 1923, but the anniversary of her engagement came and went (she spent Christmas with Norman's neighbours, Mr and Mrs Cosham) without Norman showing any inclination to name the day – understandably, as the chicken farm wasn't doing very well. It wasn't a success, and Norman was in debt. But Elsie was quite prepared for any sacrifice. Love in a hut was, after all, still love.

Unfortunately, Norman's interest was diverted in the spring of 1924 by a simpler, more immediate attraction. For at a local dance that Whitsun he met a jolly young dressmaker, Miss Elizabeth Coldicott (Bessie). He began to walk out with her, and she ventured as far as his shack in September, where she had tea with him. Norman found her to be warm and understanding, much more fun than Elsie and probably much more receptive to his 'person'. Casting about for some way of diminishing and distancing his fiancée's ardour, he took Elsie one day to the Wembley Exhibition, where they visited the stand of the Alliance of Honour. Norman, already a member, paid his subscription and persuaded Elsie to join the Women's Section for one shilling. The Alliance was of those who pledged to keep themselves pure in deed as well as words.

By this time, Elsie had been out of work for months. Her mental and physical condition, which had never been stable, began to deteriorate. She became hysterical and abusive, or deeply depressed and lethargic, where before she had been merely moodily listless. A doctor diagnosed neurasthenia and prescribed sedative remedies. At the end of October, Elsie stayed in Crowborough for a week. She lodged with the Coshams, and according to Norman they had no sex. Nonetheless, towards the end of November, becoming desperate, Elsie wrote to him informing him she was pregnant – he would have to marry her now.

To convince him, and herself, she met him at Groombridge, between Crowborough and Tunbridge Wells, and talked repeatedly of her pregnancy and their forthcoming marriage. She urged him to fix a date for their wedding and to get the banns called at Tunbridge Wells. Norman was somewhat sceptical of Elsie's pregnancy – in fact, it was imaginary – and by now he was quite enamoured of Bessie Coldicott, whom he was seeing every night between half-past eight and half-past ten, mainly at the shack.

He wrote to Elsie on Tuesday, 25 November, after the Groombridge visit: 'You seem to be taking everything for granted. I shall not be going to Tunbridge Wells this week … There are one or two things I haven't told you … it concerns someone else … I am afraid I am between two fires.' Elsie replied on 26 November:

My own darling Norman … Certainly I take everything for granted, and especially after what you said on Friday, and I shall expect you to go and arrange our marriage as soon as possible. I really do think you might comfort me in your letters … This worry is very bad for the baby … I feel sick every day and things will soon be noticeable to everybody, and I want to be married before Christmas … I really think an explanation is due to me over all this.

He replied to this letter the following day.

What I haven't told you is that on certain occasions a girl has been here late at night … When you gave in to your nerves again and refused to take interest in life I gave up hope in you and let myself go … She thinks I am going to marry her, of course, and I have a strong feeling for her or I shouldn't have done what I have.

His clumsy letter destroyed her. She wrote on 28 November:

You have absolutely broken my heart. I never thought you were capable of such deception. You have deceived me, and I gave you myself and all my love … You are engaged to me and I have first claim on you … Oh Norman, I wouldn't have believed it of you. It's a poor thing for a man to let himself go because his girl has her nerves bad … You don't seem to care how I feel. You don't write a single word of love to me, and I have stood by you through all your out of work and farm trouble … Well, Norman, I expect you to marry me, and finish with the other girl, and as soon as possible. My baby must have a name, and another

thing, I love you in spite of all ... I have been told in times gone by that 'You can't trust
no man,' but oh Norman, I thought you were different ... For ever and always, your own
loving Elsie.

On Sunday, 30 November, Elsie arrived unexpectedly at the chicken farm before eleven
in the morning. She was aggressive and demanding. Who was the other girl? Was she in
trouble? Why hadn't he gone to Tunbridge Wells? When were they going to be married?
To pacify her, Norman assured her they would get married soon. He managed to defer
the matter of the date by saying he had to sort that out with his father.

Mollified but still suspicious, Elsie left the farm at 7.50 pm, getting the 8.18 train from
Crowborough back to London. Having seen her off at the station, Norman hurried back
to the farm, where Bessie Coldicott duly arrived after half-past eight. He told her about
his plight. She consoled him and was agreeably sympathetic.

Three days later, on Wednesday, 3 December, Norman's father visited the hut in
response to a letter from his son. They discussed his financial problems and his fiancée.
Mr Thorne suggested that Norman, if he had doubts about the pregnancy, should wait
until after Christmas before committing himself to any marriage.

Norman wrote a note to Elsie saying his father had been to the farm. On receiving
it, Elsie made up her mind: she decided to force the issue. As far as she was concerned,
she was practically married to Norman already, so she might as well burn all her boats
and go and live with him.

On Friday, 5 December, she had her hair done in a new style. She was cheerful,
according to a female lodger living in her parents' home, and when she left the house,
86 Clifford Gardens, Kensal Rise, about 2.0 pm, she was wearing a green knitted dress,
a new jumper and new shoes. She set off for Victoria Station carrying an attaché case
containing no underwear but two pairs of shoes, toiletries, and a baby's frock.

All she had when she walked from Crowborough Station towards the farm was a
penny-halfpenny in her purse, and an iron resolve.

Early on 10 December, five days later, her father (a Scottish commercial traveller) sent
a telegram to the chicken farm: 'Elsie left Friday have heard no news has she arrived reply.'
Norman's answer came by return: 'Not here open letters cannot understand.' Mr Donald
Cameron waited for a day, then informed the police about his daughter's disappearance.

On 12 December, PC Beck visited the farm and was given a photo of Elsie by her
helpful fiancé. The following day, Norman called at Crowborough police station, eager
and anxious to help. He gave them the following account of his movements around the
time that Elsie disappeared. He said that on the actual day of her disappearance he cycled
to Tunbridge Wells about 1.30 pm, and bought some shoes and a chess set. Returning
home about 3.45 pm, he fed his fowls and got milk from the Coshams. He then had his
tea. He was in the shack, he said, from about 5 pm to 9.45 pm, when he went to
Crowborough Station to meet Bessie Coldicott and her mother. They had been to

Brighton for the day and he had arranged to meet them on their return and escort them home from the station. He did so and was back in his shack by about 11.30 pm. On Saturday, 6 December, he went to Groombridge station, expecting to meet Elsie. She had written to him, he said, asking him to meet her there. On finding no sign of Elsie at the station, he got the next train to Tunbridge Wells, where he did some shopping and then came home. As usual about tea time he collected some milk from the Coshams, and learning from them that a party at their house that night had been cancelled, he went instead to the cinema with Bessie Coldicott. The next day he wrote to Elsie Cameron – 'My own darling Elsie ... Well, where did you get to yesterday?'

The police were able to confirm much of this. But they also discovered that Elsie, carrying her attaché case, had been seen by two homeward-plodding flower growers, Bert and George. She had been walking purposefully along a road that passed the chicken-farm at about 5.15 pm on the 5th. Meanwhile, Norman – 'I want to help all I can' – was showing policemen and reporters around the farm, inviting them into his shack (11 ft 8 in by 7 ft 5 in) and guiding them about the chicken runs. He talked freely with the reporters, posing for photographs with his dog and among his chickens. 'What about here?' he asked. 'Feeding the chickens?' And he was snapped in the very chicken run under which what remained of the unfortunate Elsie was interred.

Questioned again by the police, Norman, though as helpful as ever, was definite: Elsie Cameron had never arrived at the farm – the horticulturists were mistaken. On New Year's Eve he wrote to Bessie:

> My darling Bessie. Looking back over the last few months I perceive many changes in my life ... I have been in love twice ... the second was with Elsie ... had a strange disposition and strange parents ... They tried to force her on me ... Honour bright, darling, I never felt for any girl as I do for you ... No one knows the struggle that has raged within, but dearest of pals, you have pulled me through. Love, Honour, Bessie – my watchwords for 25 ...

A month had passed since Elsie disappeared, but the local police were still doggedly pursuing their enquiries. At the beginning of January 1925, they made a routine call on one of Norman's neighbours, Mrs Annie Price, who when asked said she had actually seen Elsie walk through the chicken-farm gate on 5 December at about 5.15 pm.

Scotland Yard were called in by the Sussex police and before long Chief Inspector Gillan of the Yard decided he had no option but to arrest Norman Thorne on suspicion of having had something to do with Elsie's disappearance or death.

At 3.30 pm, on 14 January 1925, he was picked up at the farm by CI Gillan and detained at Crowborough police station. When the police arrived at the shack Norman was sitting at a table with a letter to Bessie in front of him, in which he suggested that they should not see each other for a while. While he was in the police station, the farm buildings were searched, and an Oxo-cube tin, discovered in a toolshed, was found to contain Elsie's wristwatch – damaged – some jewellery and a bracelet. Meanwhile, the police, armed with spades and shovels, had begun to dig.

They struck lucky the very next day. At 8.25 am on a cold, wet morning, Elsie's sodden attaché case was unearthed by PC Philpott. Among its scanty contents were her broken glasses.

At 9.30 am, at Crowborough police station, CI Gillan told Norman he might be charged with murder, if and when they found her body. The police assumed he had buried it somewhere on the 1-acre farm. All day long Norman sat in a cell thinking, while the police continued to dig. At 8 pm he announced: 'I wish to tell you the truth of what happened …' He then made a statement. He said he hadn't killed Elsie, but he knew where her body was buried.

He was, he stated, having tea when Elsie arrived, much to his surprise. She was belligerent, he said, but when she calmed down she joined him in a cup of tea and had some bread and butter. He said: 'I asked her why she had come down without having written and where she intended to sleep. She replied that she intended sleeping in the hut, Furthermore, she also stated she intended stopping until she was married.' At about 7.30 pm he went to the Coshams, to see whether they would put her up for the night. But they were out. On his return to the hut there was an argument about his association with Bessie Coldicott and about his unfaithfulness. He and Elsie, he said, then had some supper. About 9.30 pm, he said, he had told her he had to go to the station to meet the Coldicotts. 'She protested … and she suggested that we should go to bed. I again refused and told her to go to bed.' He departed at quarter to ten. 'She remained in the hut with the dog … When I returned about half-past eleven, the dog came down to meet me. When I opened the hut door I saw Miss Cameron hanging from a beam by a piece of cord as used for the washing-line. I cut the cord and laid her on the bed. She was dead. I then put out the lights. She had her frock off and her hair was down. I laid across the table for about an hour. I was about to go to Doctor Turle and knock up someone to go for the police and I realised the position I was in … I got my hacksaw … and sawed off her legs, and the head, by the glow of the fire.'

The head with its new hair-do he crammed into a biscuit tin, and the other pieces were wrapped in newspapers, all being buried in the chicken run in which he kept his Leghorns – 'the first pen from the gate'. It was there, at 10.46 pm, after Norman had completed his statement, that the police discovered the remains of Elsie Cameron.

Two days later, Sir Bernard Spilsbury examined the decomposing body, and on 26 January it was reburied in Willesden. But a month later the remains were exhumed on Norman's insistence. He was sure the mark of the rope, which Spilsbury had failed to find, must be visible on Elsie's neck. He had *seen* such a mark, he said. When her body was finally reburied, he sent a wreath saying: 'Till we meet again.'

Norman Thorne was charged with the murder of Elsie Cameron and sent for trial at Lewes Assizes on 4 March 1925. The judge was Mr Justice Finlay; Thorne was defended by Mr JD Cassels, KC; Sir Henry Curtis Bennett led for the Crown.

The medical experts disagreed about the cause of Elsie's death. She seemed to have died from shock. Spilsbury, for the prosecution, said there were several bruises and injuries on her head and body, all caused shortly before her death, and no evidence of hanging. He also said that a 'crushing blow' on her forehead could conceivably have been caused by one of the Indian clubs found outside the hut. The experts agreed, however, that she had died one-and-a-half to two hours after eating a light meal and was dismembered six to seven hours after her death.

The defence's chief medical expert, of the three who were called, was an extrovert Irishman, Dr Robert Brontë. He had examined the corpse a month after Spilsbury, and now said that creases on the neck might have been made by a rope. Spilsbury said the marks were naturally found on most female necks. The police said there were no traces of any rope-markings on the only wooden beams in the hut, across its centre. 'The upper beam was very dusty ... The lower beam was entirely free from dust.' There had been hats on the lower beam, and Norman told the court, while giving evidence and speaking of the cord that Elsie had used to hang herself – 'I believe it was tied around some of the paper I used to keep the dust off my hats.' He also said of her unexpected arrival – 'She seemed to be highly strung' – and of her death – 'I realised the awful end that neurasthenia had brought to her.'

Her glasses were on the table, he added, along with her brooch, bracelet and hairpins. He was unable to say how her watch and glasses were damaged and why he had burnt her dress and jumper. Mr Justice Finlay enquired: 'You never thought of getting a doctor, and you did not get one?' To which the answer was 'No.'

The accused also said, by way of explaining his actions, that he was 'trying to build up evidence that I knew nothing about Miss Cameron's death ... I had gone so far and I could not stop. One lie meant another ...'

On the night of Elsie's death, however it happened, he may have been fatally influenced by his apparent interest in and knowledge of the grisly murder that had occurred earlier that same year less than 20 miles away. In April another determined and possessive shorthand typist, Emily Kaye, had been murdered by her lover, Patrick Mahon. He had also been tried at Lewes Assizes, and was convicted largely through the forensic evidence of Sir Bernard Spilsbury. Patrick Mahon had been hanged on 9 September 1924, almost three months to the day before Elsie Cameron's death. Newspaper cuttings about the Mahon case were discovered in Thorne's hut. The idea of dismembering Elsie's body probably came from them, teaching him how to profit, as he thought, from Mahon's mistakes.

Norman Thorne was found guilty by the jury of Elsie Cameron's murder and was sentenced to death. The next day, 17 March, he wrote to his 'Dad and Mother' about the 'extraordinary verdict ... They say a man has to be *proved* guilty. In what way was it proved against me? ... What happened while I was out I do not know.' An appeal was rejected, although he had expected it to succeed. He was taken from the Appeal Court crying: 'It isn't fair! I didn't do it.'

He was hanged by Tom Pierrepoint, assisted by Robert Wilson, in Wandsworth Prison on 22 April 1925, on what would have been Elsie's twenty-seventh birthday.

The minister who attended the execution believed Norman Thorne to be innocent of murder. Most murderers, said the minister, would confess to him what they had done and try to seek forgiveness. But Norman had maintained his innocence to the end. A Sunday School teacher at the Kensal Rise Wesleyan Church, who had known both Norman and Elsie, also never believed – like his father – that Norman had actually and intentionally killed her. It's possible in this case that an innocent man was hanged.

The day before he died he wrote a last letter to his parents: 'The world seems bright and beautiful, but how much better must be the Kingdom of Heaven … A flash and all is finished, *no,* not finished, but just starting; and I shall wait for you, just as others are waiting for me. By Christ I am free from all sin; all forgiven, I go to Him. All's well. With all my love, your loving son, Norman.'

Perhaps he told the truth – that Elsie stage-managed her death, timing it to coincide with his return so that he might save her. This could account for the lack of marks of hanging – if she stepped off a chair or the bed as he opened the door. Perhaps she bungled it somehow and was shocked to death by the experience. Her injuries may have been caused by his clumsy manoeuvres when he cut her down. They certainly happened near the time of her death. Or they may have been caused by his fists or the Indian clubs during some row, in which he struck her several times and threw her out of the hut. Perhaps, thus rejected and despised, she died indeed of shock, of a broken heart.

In any event, Norman Thorne would probably never have been hanged if he had been wholly honest from the start about the manner of Elsie's death, however it happened – if he had not dismembered her body, if he had not concealed it in the ground, and if he had not continuously lied, so persistently and for so long.

24

JOHN ROBINSON

THE MURDER OF MINNIE BONATI, 1927

Dismemberment of a murdered person never inclines a judge or jury towards a tolerant view of the murderer. Not only is this a clear attempt to thwart justice by hiding the body and thus the evidence, but it also shows disrespect and is, as it were, double murder. Within three-and-a-half years of Mahon and Thorne dismembering their ladyloves, John Robinson was at it himself, believing no doubt that it was the only way to remove a body from his premises – which happened to be opposite a police station. Surely there have not been many times that murder has been committed so close to the eyes of the law.

On Friday, 6 May 1927, a man with a soldierly bearing deposited a large black trunk in the left-luggage office at Charing Cross railway station. It had a rounded top and was made of wickerwork, the whole encased in black American cloth and bound with a wide strap. He urged that the trunk be carefully handled, then departed in the taxi in which he and the trunk had arrived. The left-luggage attendant on duty the following Monday noticed an offensive smell coming from the trunk. A policeman was sent for and the trunk was opened.

Inside it, roughly parcelled in brown paper and tied with string, were five portions of a woman – her limbs had been severed at each shoulder and hip joint and the sections wrapped in items of female clothing, towels and a duster, the latter being wound around her head. A police surgeon was called to certify the woman was dead before the bits of her body were removed to a mortuary.

The Home Office pathologist, Sir Bernard Spilsbury, pieced the body together and concluded that several bruises on the woman's forehead, stomach, back and limbs had been caused before she died. The cause of her death, he decided, was asphyxia, resulting from pressure on her mouth and nostrils while she was unconscious. She had been dead, he deduced, for about a week, and when alive had been short and stout and about thirty-five years old. A pair of black shoes and a handbag were also found in the trunk. Some of the clothing was marked. Two items bore laundry marks (581 and 447) and a pair of knickers carried a tab marked 'P HOLT'.

Initials were painted on the trunk itself – FA – and a label read 'F AUSTIN to ST LENARDS.' The initials and the name were later found to be blameless and to have no connection with the case. But the police were now checking the other clues.

Within twenty-four hours, the knickers and the laundry marks were traced to a Mrs Holt, who lived in Chelsea and was very much alive. The woman who was likely to have purloined her clothing must have been in Mrs Holt's employment, and the police now set about checking the whereabouts of ten female servants employed by Mrs Holt in the past two years. All but one were accounted for, and to clinch the matter the genteel employer was asked to identify the head. She did so. The dead woman was a Mrs Rolls.

A *Mr* Rolls was soon found, but it transpired he was not her husband – she had merely lived with him for a time. Her real but estranged husband turned out to be an Italian waiter called Bonati, who was soon cleared of suspicion. The victim's real married name was Mrs Minnie Alice Bonati; her maiden name was Budd. She was thirty-six, on the game, it was said, and had last been seen alive in Sydney Street, Chelsea, between 3.45 pm and 4 pm on Wednesday, 4 May.

In the meantime, photographs of the trunk had appeared in the newspapers under lurid headlines – and with satisfying results. A Brixton Road dealer in second-hand luggage told the police he had sold the trunk for 12s 6d on or soon after 4 May to a dark man with a small moustache: a man of average height, well dressed, well spoken, a military sort of man, who looked as if he might have served in India.

A shoeblack produced the left-luggage receipt, which he had happened to pick up in the station forecourt after seeing it thrown out of a taxi window as the taxi left the station. The ticket was numbered, and by tracing the owner of the ticket issued immediately *before* it the police established that the black trunk had been deposited in the left-luggage office soon after 1.50 pm on Friday, 6 May. Then the taxi driver who had carried the trunk to Charing Cross Station came forward with information about his male passenger and the trunk.

He said that some time after 1 pm on the Friday he had taken two young men from the Royal Automobile Club in Pall Mall to the police station in Rochester Row, SW1, at the back of the Roman Catholic Westminster Cathedral. The charge sheet at the station revealed that the two men had been summonsed for motoring offences and arrived in the station at 1.35 pm. After dropping his passengers, the taxi driver was hailed by a gentleman standing in the doorway of an office block across the street, and assisted him in carrying a heavy trunk from the building, across the pavement and into the cab. When the cabbie commented on the trunk's weight, he was told that it was full of books. The passenger's destination was Charing Cross Station (although Victoria Station was much nearer) and there the trunk, which the taxi driver identified, was left after being taken to the left-luggage office by a station porter. The office block in Rochester Row was identified as Number 86, which was now viewed with considerable interest by the police from their premises diagonally opposite.

Most of 86 Rochester Row was occupied by a firm of solicitors. But one of the occupants of a seedy two-roomed, second-floor office overlooking the street was missing. He turned out to be a struggling estate agent, who had written on 9 May to his landlord to explain that he was moving out because, frankly, he was broke. His name was John Robinson and His office was named: *Edwards and Co., Business Transfer Agents.*

Born at Leigh in Lancashire, young Robinson had been taken from school at the age of twelve and sent to work. Over the years he had worked variously as an errand-boy for the Co-op, a clerk, a tram conductor, a bartender – and a butcher's assistant. He married in 1911 and his first wife bore him four children. His second wife was a girl from Tasmania.

Nothing incriminating was found in his office in Rochester Row and not a speck of blood was visible. However, a window pane was cracked and the fireplace fender was found to be broken and an iron bar detachable. Mr Robinson's clerk, Miss Moore, was traced. She said that on 4 May Mr Robinson had returned about 3 pm to the office, obviously drunk, with a man in military uniform. Alarmed by this, no doubt by something that was said or done, she left the office early at 3.30 pm and never returned.

The police visited John Robinson's lodgings in Kennington, but he had gone from there without leaving a forwarding address. However – and this was another stroke of luck for the police – a telegram addressed to 'Robinson, Greyhound Hotel, Hammersmith' had been returned to his lodgings, addressee unknown. This led them to the Greyhound Hotel, where they found, not Robinson, but *Mrs* Robinson, who worked there. The telegram had been returned to its sender by a new maid ignorant of Mrs Robinson's presence in the hotel. She in turn was ignorant, until informed by the police, of the sorry fact that she was not the only Mrs Robinson, for he had another wife – his first. She agreed to cooperate with the police, and when she went to meet Robinson at his telephoned request on Thursday, 19 May at a pub, the Elephant and Castle in Walworth, Chief Inspector George Cornish went with the aggrieved woman.

John Robinson, aged thirty-six, thus identified and then questioned by the police, was quite amenable to being interviewed at the Yard that evening and to take part in an identity parade. Here he was very lucky. For neither the taxi driver, the station porter nor the trunk dealer recognised him. As he naturally denied any knowledge of his crime, or of buying the trunk, or of Mrs Bonati, he was released.

There was a conference at Scotland Yard on 21 May, in which all the evidence was reviewed. Chief Inspector Cornish decided that the bloodstained and grimy duster should be washed. His hunch proved correct, for a thin tab on the hem was revealed bearing the word 'GREYHOUND'.

In the meantime, a fresh scouring of Robinson's office in Rochester Row produced a bloodstained match, which had been caught in the wickerwork of a waste-paper basket.

Robinson was picked up at his lodging on 23 May and brought back to the Yard. Now his luck deserted him. For fearing perhaps that the police knew more than they did – or possibly overwhelmed by feelings of guilt – he elected to make a statement. He said: 'I realise this is serious … I met her at Victoria and took her to my office. I want to tell you all about it. I done it and cut her up.'

His story was that on 4 May, about 4.15 pm in the afternoon, he was accosted by Mrs Bonati at Victoria Station. Back in his third-floor office she asked him for money but he refused to give her any, saying he had none. She became abusive and made as if to strike him. He shoved her away and she fell, hitting her head on a coal scuttle. Having thus silenced her – and perhaps it was the presence of the police station across the road that made him fearful of the noise she made – he left the office. He said he thought she was only dazed and would go when she recovered. But when he returned the following morning, he said, she still lay on the carpet, face down. How was he to get rid of her?

Perhaps he remembered Mahon and Thorne. It seems more than coincidence that led him to the very shop in Victoria Street where Mahon had bought a carving knife and a saw. Here, Robinson merely purchased a knife. Then, in that shabby office of his, under the eyes of the law, he set about dismembering Minnie Bonati.

Having parcelled up her remains in brown paper after wrapping them in her own clothes, in a duster and a towel, he went away, no doubt exhausted. Doggedly, he returned to the office the following morning. He brought a trunk with him and travelled by omnibus, and the bus conductor helped him carry the trunk up the stairs to the top deck of the bus. Having got off the bus in Vauxhall Bridge Road at about 10 am, he dragged the trunk along Rochester Row and up the stairs to his office. Here he loaded the trunk with the parcelled portions of Mrs Bonati, throwing her shoes and her handbag into the trunk as well, and then dragged it out on to the landing. Perhaps he also did some scrubbing and cleaning of the premises to ensure that no sign of Mrs Bonati's visit remained.

His labours came to an end at about noon, and in need of a drink he went out to a local pub, where he fell into conversation with a Mr Judd. They chatted about property. Robinson told Mr Judd about a flat that he had to let and the two men returned to the office, where Judd was furnished with the flat's particulars. He was then asked if he would mind giving Robinson a hand with the trunk and help him take it downstairs to the hall. Judd obliged. The trunk was very heavy. 'Are you travelling in lead?' he puffed. 'No, I'm taking some books to the country,' replied Robinson.

A few minutes later Robinson hailed the taxi that had just stopped under the blue lamp of the police station. It seems incredible that he could behave so matter-of-factly and yet be so stupid. For after having acted with such deliberation and care that morning and the day before, he now publicly associated himself with the trunk and left it where it was bound to be discovered before long. The knife, as he later showed the police, was buried under a hawthorn tree on Clapham Common.

The trial of John Robinson began at the Old Bailey on Monday, 11 July. The judge was Mr Justice Swift. Mr Percival Clarke led for the Crown, assisted by Mr Christmas Humphreys. Robinson was defended by Mr Lawrence Vine.

Robinson himself gave evidence, in which he admitted more or less everything, except an intention to kill. When asked why he did not go to the police, he said: 'Because I was in a blue funk and did not know what to do.'

Dr Brontë was called by the defence to combat Sir Bernard Spilsbury's evidence. Spilsbury had said, and was supported by the police surgeon who did the post mortem, that the bruises on Mrs Bonati had been caused by direct blows and pressure, probably from a knee. Congestion in the lungs, Spilsbury had maintained, showed that she had lain on her back for some time and that no coal-gas poisoning, heart disease or epilepsy was involved. He concluded that she had been asphyxiated after a violent assault. And a cushion found in the office seemed the most likely object to have been used to silence any cries she made.

Brontë, supporting Robinson's contention that on returning to the office he had found Mrs Bonati face down on the floor, suggested that she could have suffocated with her face in the folds of the carpet (which was threadbare), or in the crook of her elbow. He disputed Spilsbury's timing of the bruises, saying they could have been caused several hours before death, before she and Robinson met.

Another witness for the defence was the dead woman's former husband, Frederick Rolls, who said Minnie Bonati was much addicted to drink and was sometimes very violent – she had attacked him many times.

The jury were not convinced by Dr Brontë's vigorous assumptions, nor was the judge impressed. As in Thorne's case, the judge asked the accused why he did not summon help and inform the police when he found the woman dead in his room. Robinson replied: 'I did not look at it in that light.'

After being out for an hour, the jury returned a verdict of 'Guilty'. John Robinson was sentenced to death on Wednesday, 13 July and hanged at Pentonville Prison on 12 August 1927.

25

BROWNE AND
KENNEDY

Apart from soldiers, the uniformed men most likely to be killed are policemen. Unarmed, unless in special circumstances, for well over a hundred years they had little defence against the law-breakers they attempted to apprehend in the execution of their duties.

At dawn on Tuesday, 27 September 1927, a post-office worker called Bill Ward was driving north across Essex from Romford to Abridge, delivering mail. He stopped at Havering and Stapleford Abbotts. His next port of call was Stapleford Tawney. Just before six o'clock, as he approached Howe Green, he came to a right-hand bend in the road on a slight incline and on rounding the bend he saw a man propped up against the opposite bank with his legs sticking out into the road.

Mr Ward stopped his car and investigated. A thick trail of blood led across the road to where the body lay; it was that of a uniformed and caped policeman. His helmet lay near him, as did a pocket book. A pencil was still clutched in his right hand. Despite the fact that the policeman's head was a bloody mask, Mr Ward recognised the dead man as PC George Gutteridge.

Ward ran back up the road to Rose Cottage. His knocking awakened Alfred Perritt, an insurance agent, who dressed and went back to the body with Ward. Mr Perritt, picking up the feet, swung the body round so that it lay parallel to the hedge and was not in danger of being run over. Next on the scene was the driver of a country bus. Ward drove on to Stapleford Tawney, from where he telephoned Romford police station.

By about quarter to eight, Detective Inspector Crockford had arrived. He saw that PC Gutteridge had been shot in the face. The dead man seemed to have been taken completely by surprise by the attack, as he was clearly about to make a note in his pocket book: his truncheon was in its place at his side, his torch was in a pocket. His whistle hung loose, however, outside his tunic.

Dr Robert Woodhouse was called out from Romford by nine o'clock and surmised that the murdered policeman had been dead for four or five hours. The body was removed to a cart-shed at the Royal Oak public house and taken the following morning to Romford mortuary, where Dr Woodhouse made a post-mortem examination. He found that PC Gutteridge had been shot four times at close range, twice through the left cheek near the ear – and once in each eye.

PC Gutteridge had lived with his wife, Rose, at Stapleford Abbotts. He had been out on night patrols on the 26th and 27th, covering his beat on foot. It was his custom and duty to meet up with another policeman PC Taylor, for a conference about 3 am outside Grove House at Howe Green. Taylor was a little late in the early hours of the 27th and when he turned up at the rendezvous the two men stood chatting in the quiet autumnal night until 3.25 am. 'It was not an exceptionally dark night,' said PC Taylor. 'But it was fairly dark. There was a fog, or what I would describe as a summer mist, in certain of the lower places … but not on the high hill.' Taylor was home and in bed by half-past four. Gutteridge set off homewards along the Ongar-Romford road, passing Rose Cottage and walking downhill as the road turned left. As he approached this bend, a car came speeding towards him.

Less than an hour before this, 10 miles to the east, a blue four-seater Morris-Cowley car, TW 6120, had been stolen from the garage of Dr Edward Lovell's house in London Road, Billericay. He had parked it in the garage about 7.30 pm on Monday the 26th and had locked the garage door, leaving two cases of surgical instruments and dressings and a small case with some drugs inside the car. The following morning, after breakfast, he found the garage door had been forced and the car had gone. Later, neighbours remembered a car being started up about half-past two and passing with headlights ablaze down the Mountnessing Road. Dr Lovell reported the theft of his car to the police and was able to tell them that the mileometer must have read about 6640.9 when the car was stolen.

The Morris had already been spotted, 42 miles away in south London, in a narrow passage behind 21 Faxley Road, Brixton. Albert McDougall, a crippled clerk, who lived at that address, left home by the back door at about half-past seven on his way to work. 'It was a very cold morning,' he said, 'with a mist.' He edged around the car, and happening to touch it 'on account of my disability', noticed that the radiator was 'very warm'. When he returned home at about 5.50 pm, the car was still there. He noticed that the nearside mudguard had been torn off, and after some thought reported his find to a policeman he chanced to find in Brixton Road. PC Alfred Edmonds casually inspected the car – it was empty of any cases – and telephoned Brixton police station.

At about 6.45 pm, Sergeant Hearn arrived, and as it was now dark he drove the car to the police station yard, where he and DC Hawkyard examined it by the light of a torch. Having checked the registration number, they now knew that it was Dr Lovell's stolen car and had come from Essex. They discovered an empty cartridge case under the front nearside seat, marked RLIV on the cap, indicating it was a Mark IV made at the Royal Laboratory in Woolwich Arsenal – a type of flat-nosed bullet that had been issued to the British Expeditionary Force in 1914. It was later noticed to have been scarred by a fault in the breech-block of the gun that had fired it. The two policemen also discovered bloodstains on the running-board by the driver's door. The mileometer read 6684.3. The distance from Dr Lovell's house to Brixton police station, via Faxley Road, was later found to be about 42 miles.

There were no further developments for four months, although hundreds of policemen were employed in a determined hunt to find the killer of PC Gutteridge. The murder weapon had been a Webley revolver, according to the expert gunsmith Robert Churchill, and two Webleys were found in the mud of the Thames. But it was proved that neither had fired the cartridge found in the car, for neither left the same small mark on the cartridge cases of test bullets fired by Mr Churchill. Meanwhile, a watchful eye was kept on known car thieves and associated criminals in south London.

One of these suspects was Frederick Guy Browne, whose real name was probably Leo Brown. Aged forty-six, he was described as a 'tall (5 ft 7 in), well-built, dark-complexioned man with a heavy moustache' and grey eyes. A strong, powerful man, born in Catford in 1881, he was a very capable mechanic, was easily provoked to anger and as easily assuaged. He suffered from complex feelings of resentment against society and the law – not surprisingly, as he had been in and out of jail (four sentences of hard labour and four years' penal servitude) since the age of twenty-nine, when he had been living with his widowed mother in Eynsham, repairing bicycles by day and stealing them at night.

His first conviction was in 1910 for carrying firearms. In 1915, he married a cook-housekeeper called Caroline. They had a daughter and settled in Clapham. 'With all his faults,' said Mrs Browne later, 'my husband has been decent to me.' Indeed, he was not a typical ruffian, being a teetotaller, a non-smoker, and faithful to his wife. During the Great War, in March 1917, he joined the Royal Engineers, serving in the Railway Operating Department; he never went overseas. 'I was never a soldier,' he said. 'I was a worker in khaki.' Convicted for stealing a motorcycle in Petersfield, he was discharged from the army on 5 November 1918 – 'character, indifferent' – after which he worked in garages in Clapham and Essex, stealing and altering cars and fraudulently claiming the insurance on them. For this he was arrested with others on Christmas Eve 1923 and sentenced at the Old Bailey on 20 February 1924 to four years' penal servitude.

He became too violent for Parkhurst Prison and was eventually moved to Dartmoor. There he met and made friends with Fred Counter, who was serving three years for burglary, and was released in March 1927. In June, Browne rented what had been a milk yard next to the Globe cinema in Lavender Hill and turned it into a garage/repair-yard/paint-shop, also called the Globe, at 7a Northcote Road. 'I profess to be a motor-engineer,' said Browne in court. 'And my instruments, I say, are far different to the average garage man. That is to say, I do better-class work, finer things.' There were spaces for seven cars, a fitter's shop, and a primitive office at the back in which there was also a bed. Here slept a man employed to keep the books and do odd jobs, of whom Browne said: 'I got him from the Salvation Army to give him a start.' This was forty-two-year-old Pat Kennedy.

They had probably already met, in Dartmoor Prison. Kennedy, whose Christian names were either Patrick Michael or William Henry, was born in Ayrshire in 1895. His parents were Irish, though, and he retained an Irish accent all his life. Trained as a compositor, he worked mainly in Liverpool, where in 1911 his first conviction (for indecent exposure) earned him two months' hard labour. Before that, he was a teenage soldier in South Africa from 1902 to 1903, and for the next eight years served with a Lancashire regiment as William Herbert, ending up as a Lance-Corporal ('character, indifferent'). Other fines and convictions soon followed the first one: for theft, for being drunk and disorderly, for loitering, for house-breaking and larceny, and again for indecent exposure. For the larceny he was sentenced to three years' penal servitude. On his release in April 1916 he enlisted in the Hussars, deserted, enlisted in the King's Liverpool Regiment, deserted, rejoined the King's under a different name and was discharged with ignominy. His petty criminal career continued from 1920 to 1927. He was hardly ever out of prison, doing time as before for theft, indecent exposure and burglary.

In 1927, the Discharged Prisoners' Association got him a job on a farm in Cheshire. He was there when he received a letter from Fred Browne. Said Kennedy later:

> *He invited me to come down and act as manager. He said he would probably have a number of boys under him later, and that he would want me to look after them whilst he was away on repair jobs. He said he could not offer me much money at first, but it would cost me nothing for board and lodgings, as I could live at the garage. He sent me my fare, exact amount, and I borrowed ten shillings … My duties consisted of attending to correspondence, keeping the books, making and dealing with accounts. The man Fred Browne was also sleeping on the premises at the time.*

Mrs Browne was still in service then. A handyman, John Dyson, came to work at the garage in August for 25s a week, and Curly Billy, aged twelve, helped here and there.

Business prospered, and on Saturday, 24 September, Browne and his wife rented two rooms in 33a Sisters Avenue, Lavender Hill. Mrs Browne later told the court: 'Occasionally, if anyone was coming into the garage late, so as not to disturb me he slept in the garage.' But, she said, on the night of 26 September 'he returned from work between nine and ten that night … He was at home all night.'

Kennedy told the police a different story, in a very carefully considered and lengthy statement he made after his arrest. 'I well remember the day of 26th September,' he said. 'Browne suggested that I should accompany him to Billericay, to assist him in stealing a Riley car at the end of the High Street, away from the station.' They went there by train from Liverpool Street station, arriving about 8 pm. They hung about waiting until people went to bed. But Browne was unnerved and deflected from his purpose of taking the Riley from its garage by the barking of a dog. He told Kennedy: 'We'll try somewhere else.' They walked off down the road – both were wearing overcoats and trilby hats – and at the other end of the village they came to Dr Lovell's house, which had a garage. They waited in a field until well after midnight. Then Browne forced the doors of the garage. Inside was a Morris-Cowley with plenty of petrol in the tank. They pushed it down the gravelled drive on to the road and then for another hundred yards along the road before getting in, Browne in the driver's seat, Kennedy beside him. The car started noisily and they raced away, avoiding the main roads, having to check signposts as they drove westwards through country lanes, heading back to London. They were on a road leading to Ongar when a man by a bank ahead of them flashed a light as a signal for them to stop.

Kennedy continued:

We drove on, and then I heard a police whistle and told Browne to stop. He did so quite willingly, and when the person came up we saw it was a policeman ... He came up close to the car and stood near Browne and asked him where he was going and where he came from. Browne told him we came from Lea Bridge Road garage, and had been out to do some repairs. The policeman then asked him if he had a card. Browne said: 'No.' The policeman then again asked him where he came from and Browne stammered in his answer, and the policeman said: 'Is the car yours?' I then said: 'No – the car is mine.' The policeman flashed his light in both our faces, and was at this time standing close to the running-board on the offside. [PC Gutteridge could also see the occupants by the dim light from the dashboard. Being 6 ft tall, he had to stoop to talk to them.] *He then asked me if I knew the number of the car and Browne said: 'You'll see it on the front of the car.' The policeman said: 'I know the number, but do you?' I said: 'Yes, I can give you the number,' and said: 'TW 6120.' He said, 'Very well, I'll take particulars,' put his torch back in his pocket, pulled out his notebook, and was in the act of writing when I heard a report, quickly followed by another one. I saw the policeman stagger back and fall over by the bank at the hedge. I said to Browne: 'What have you done?' and then saw he had a large Webley revolver in his hand. He said: 'Get out quick.' I immediately got out and went round to the policeman, who was lying on his back, and Browne came over and said: 'I'll finish the bugger,' and I said: 'For God's sake don't shoot any more – the man's dying,' as he was groaning. The policeman's eyes were open, and Browne, addressing him, said: 'What are you looking at me like that for?' and, stooping down, shot him at close range through both eyes.*

They returned to the car, driving on into London. Browne told Kennedy to reload the gun, and in his excitement Kennedy dropped a spent cartridge. The other three he threw out of his window. Hitting a patch of fog, Browne smashed the car into a tree, sheering off the nearside mudguard. The car was abandoned about 5.30 am in Brixton, and laden with the doctor's cases, the pair returned by tram to the Globe garage, where 'business carried on as usual'.

As the days passed, Kennedy had moments of panic, wanting to flee when he read accounts of the murder in the papers. Browne told him: 'You'll stop here and face it out with me.' Kennedy said later that Browne also threatened him with a gun.

But after two months had passed Browne must have thought they were safe, and Kennedy, whose drinking habits had begun to distress the older man, was told to go. Said Browne: 'He was a persistent drunkard. I tried all I could – I kept him short of money. I watched him from half-past nine to ten at night, and I could not stop him from drink, and I gave him the sack.' On 17 December 1927, Browne drove Kennedy to Euston Station, where Kennedy got on a train for Liverpool. Kennedy remained in West Kirby until 13 January 1928 when he returned by train to London with a woman whom he had married on 18 January.

In the meantime, Browne had gone on a binge of burglary, theft and stealing cars, making eight such criminal forays that winter with other villains, starting in October. Robbing railway station offices became a speciality. One of the cars he stole, a Vauxhall that was taken in Tooting in November, was sold a few days later by Browne to a butcher in Sheffield, Benjamin Stow, who gave him £100 and a grey Angus-Sanderson car, registration CW 3291, in part exchange. Browne used the car to drive down to Devon in the New Year. 'I do a lot of driving,' said Browne. 'I do thousands of miles. I do more miles than the average man, because the average man will stop at night to put up and garage and I do not. I keep straight on.'

In Devon, he picked up Fred Counter, who had been released from Dartmoor on Friday, 20 January. Browne, who intended to employ Counter in the garage, had dressed himself up as a chauffeur in a blue coat and a peaked cap. He drove Counter the 200 miles back to London, dropping him off near New Scotland Yard, where Counter had to report to the Convict Registration Office. This done, Browne returned to his garage near Clapham Junction about 7.50 pm. The police, having traced the stolen Vauxhall car by now, were waiting for him in force.

The police version of what happened next, as related in court with the use of notebooks, was generally stilted and stiff. Browne was presented as a dangerous thug and the police as stern and silent. Browne's version, substantially the same, is far more lively – and more likely. 'I went into the garage,' he said, 'and saw a light in there, and found Mrs Browne there. She said: "I thought you would be back soon," and I said: "I've brought the man's luggage." And I went out to get the luggage – that was a big case and a small case – and I put it in the office. I started talking to my wife, and – well, in rushed a man who was – I will tell you it was a detective. And behind him rushed a lot more.' Said DS Miller: 'I entered the inner office belonging to the garage with Inspector Barker, and I was present when Inspector Barker arrested Browne and searched him.'

Inspector Barker: 'He seemed to be boiling inwardly, holding himself in … He went pale and gripped his hands tightly together, as though he was trying to master his feelings.' Browne said: 'I really do not know what happened, because I had my back to him, but anyhow he caught hold of me and said: "I am going to charge you with stealing a Vauxhall car." I said: "I know nothing about a Vauxhall car," and that is all I troubled.' Barker continued: 'He said: "What do I know about stealing a car?"' Browne: 'Then he went on to explain that I got a Vauxhall car and sold it, and then I knew the car he was referring to was a car I sold to a butcher at Sheffield. I then said to him: "Yes, I sold the car. But why say I stole it? I got the car and paid the price for it" – words very similar to that – "and I sold it."' Barker: 'He said: "Well, you can't prove I stole it."' Browne: 'There was some argument about it and I said: "Well, anyhow, I was going to make myself some cocoa, because I have had a long run and I have had nothing." He said: "Well, wait a minute, I'm going to search you." I had these cartridges in my pocket, and I did not want him to see them. I made an excuse I wanted to go to the lavatory, and I did not want to – I wanted to get rid of the cartridges. He got the cartridges, and I said: "That's done it now."' Barker: 'He said: "That's done it. Now you've found them, it's all up with me."' Browne: 'The atmosphere was changed … Presently this revolver was brought in.' Barker: 'Browne looked at it and said: "Ah, you've found that, have you? I am done for now."' Browne: 'I said: "It's all up now," because I knew they would have me for having firearms and ammunition and no licence.' He was escorted to the lavatory by four policemen. DS Miller: 'He said: "Why all this precaution? I have never seen so many officers in my life!"'

He was then taken in a car – by two men, according to the police, by five, according to Browne – to Tooting police station. Nothing had yet been said about the murder of PC Gutteridge.

'They were quite decent,' said Browne. 'They put me in a big room with a big table, and they were laughing about something about "You won't go for a 200-mile run …" There was a lot of chatter. In the midst of it in comes another detective with a little revolver. He put it down on this table and he passed some remark … Anyway they were laughing about it and I said: "Oh yes, you can laugh about it. You think it's a toy. But it wouldn't only tickle you …" I knew there was something in it.'

DS Miller: 'Browne said: "Oh, you've found that, have you? That's no good. It would only tickle you unless it hit you in a vital part."' Browne: 'They explained they wanted to get me while I was in the car, and one said: "No. Wait until he's in the garage!" I didn't hear this – this was explained to me. And one said to me: "What would you have done, Browne, if we had stopped you in the car?" And I said: "I do not know." He said: "Perhaps you would have stopped us." And I said: "I have not been put to the test" … Then it came to my knowledge that there were ten men who had come to arrest me – ten! And all those ten men were armed. And they said had I tried it or something … they would have blown me to pieces, if I had shown any resistance. That is what it amounted to. But they were good-tempered … laughing about it.' 'No laughing at all,' said DS Miller. Browne: 'It was to this effect – "There would have been little left of you, Browne, if you had used it …" I said: "Good heavens! Ten! Why – it would take a man with a machine-gun to cope with you!" Those were the words.' DS Miller: 'What he did say was: "I shall have to have a machine-gun for you bastards next time."'

The police searches discovered twelve .45 cartridges in the back hip-pocket of Browne's trousers; a stockinette mask in his jacket pocket; a forceps, and a Webley revolver, fully loaded with six cartridges, in a pocket inside the driver's door of the Angus-Sanderson; sixteen .45 cartridges wrapped in some paper in the inner office, as well as another forceps, several rolls of bandages, some gauze, lint and an ethylchloride spray. In the Brownes' rooms off Lavender Hill were found a roll of plaster, a convex lens, an ear speculum, twenty-three .22 cartridges, a small nickel-plated revolver, loaded, and a fully loaded Smith and Wesson. A further search of the Angus-Sanderson revealed another fully loaded Webley revolver in a secret recess behind the driver's seat. This was the gun that was later proved to have fired one at least of the fatal shots: its breech block had the peculiar fault that imprinted itself on every cartridge case fired by the gun.

Kennedy, ignorant of Browne's arrest, arrived at the garage a day later, at 2 pm on Saturday, 21 January. Since his return to London he had been there twice before. Of these visits Browne said: 'I was surprised to see him again, because I told him not to come near the place again on account of the drink ... On the first occasion he insinuated he would come back to the garage, and I would not have anything to do with him. On the second occasion he wanted to know if he could come to Devon ... and again I said: "I cannot have you for drink." And he finished.'

On the day that Browne drove to Devon – Wednesday, 18 January – Kennedy got married in Liverpool. On the Saturday, finding the garage doors locked and two men who he thought were detectives inside the garage, Kennedy hurried back to his wife at 2 Huguenot Place and urged her to pack. They returned to Liverpool on the midnight train from Euston. The Kennedys had three more nights of married bliss before the police closed in. It was on Wednesday the 25th that Kennedy was arrested. That night, at about 11.40 pm, he was hurrying away from his home along St Andrew's Street, hiding his face, when DS Bill Mattinson, who knew Kennedy of old, approached him from behind and said: 'Come on, Bill. Now then, come on, Bill.'

Kennedy's response was to swing around and pull a pistol out of his pocket. He recognised the policeman, said: 'Stand back, Bill – or I'll shoot you!' and fired. There was a click. Mattinson seized Kennedy's gun with his left hand, hit him with the other and wrenched the gun, a Savage, from the other man's grasp. Shouting to his distant colleagues, Mattinson propelled Kennedy back up St Andrew's Street into Copperas Hill, where three other policemen came to his assistance. 'It's all right!' cried Mattinson, raising the pistol. 'I've got it!' Realising now how close he had been to being shot, he collapsed and was sick. In fact, the safety catch was found to be in the safety position.

Kennedy was taken into custody. He had clearly left his digs in a hurry, for under his coat he wore no shirt, just a vest; his trousers were undone and his boots unlaced. Having heard some policemen arrive in a taxi in the street below – they gave the cabbie a clear instruction to drive around the corner – he had taken flight. 'I had a premonition something was going to happen to me today,' he said.

He came face to face with DS Mattinson again at Warren Street police station, where he was charged with being concerned with Browne in stealing a Vauxhall motor car. He said to Mattinson: 'I'm sorry. I've no grudge against the police. But you should be in heaven now. And there was one for me.' Mattinson looked at him and said: 'I did not expect that from you.'

The following evening, Chief Inspector Berrett visited Kennedy, now in custody in New Scotland Yard, and asked him if he had any information to give about the murder of PC Gutteridge. Kennedy asked to be allowed to think, and did so for several minutes, head in hand, elbows on a table. 'Can I see my wife?' he eventually asked. Mrs Kennedy, who had travelled with him from Liverpool, was fetched. She kissed him. Berrett made notes of what they said.

Kennedy said: 'Well, my dear … These officers are making enquiries about that policeman murdered in Essex.' She exclaimed: 'Why? You didn't murder him, did you?' 'No,' he replied. 'I didn't. But I was there, and know who did. If I'm charged with murder and found guilty, I shall be hanged, and you will be a widow … If I'm charged and found guilty of being an accessory I shall receive a long sentence … and be a long time away from you. Will you wait for me?' She said: 'Yes, love. I'll wait for you any time.' Kennedy asked: 'Well, what shall I do then?' 'Tell these gentlemen the truth of what took place,' she said. He replied: 'All right, I will.'

It took him over three hours to dictate his statement, which Browne derided later in court as 'one pack of wilful or imaginative lies, either wilfully told or misled by some kink of the brain … It is a horribly concocted statement that has taken hours to consider. That is my opinion.' However, what Kennedy said is probably largely true, although he naturally tried to minimise his involvement in the death of PC Gutteridge. It is quite possible that Browne and Kennedy were *both* armed – even that Kennedy fired the first or second pair of shots. Browne could make no counter-allegations, as his defence was that he was never in Essex that night; he had claimed that he was in bed with his wife.

On 6 February, Browne and Kennedy were both charged by CI Berrett with the murder of PC Gutteridge. 'It's absurd,' said Browne. 'I know nothing about it.' Kennedy was silent.

Their trial began at the Old Bailey on Monday, 23 April 1928, before Mr Justice Avory. The Solicitor General, Sir Boyd Merriman, led for the Crown; Mr Lever defended Browne and Mr Powell appeared for Kennedy. Browne's appearance in the witness box unleashed a torrent of verbosity. Generally impatient with the proceedings and indignant, one minute he muttered, the next he ranted. The barristers, including his own, intervened with difficulty. He even argued about taking the oath. 'How can I tell the whole truth,' he exclaimed, 'of something I do not know?'

Kennedy elected to make a statement from the dock. He said that he had loaded the Webley after Gutteridge had been shot because he was terrified and did not know what he was doing. Browne also gave him the Savage, he said. And he had only intended to frighten Sergeant Mattinson. He concluded: 'I can only now express my deep regret to Mrs Gutteridge that I should have been in the car on the night of the crime.'

The ballistics evidence, concerning the bullets, the cartridges, and the gun prints made by the breech-shield of the Webley, was damning – the first time such evidence had been used to such effect in a murder trial. Four firearms experts were called, including Robert Churchill, the Crown's chief expert in this and other trials involving guns.

Both Browne and Kennedy were found guilty. Both made a speech, Browne repeating that he had had nothing to do with the murder, but was 'quite content to leave it', as penal servitude was worse than death. Kennedy said the verdict was preordained – it was fate – and they all were accessories of that fate. He said he wasn't afraid to die, and asked if he could see his wife.

Their appeals were heard on 22 May and dismissed. On 31 May 1928, Browne was hanged at Wandsworth by Tom Pierrepoint and Kennedy by Robert Baxter at Pentonville. The year 1928 had begun well for Pierrepoint and Baxter financially – in January, they each carried out five executions – Tom performing five in four days, at Manchester, Lincoln, Durham, Leeds and Birmingham.

The night before his execution, Kennedy, who had been converted to Roman Catholicism while awaiting execution, wrote a long, eloquently passionate letter to his wife, urging her to join him soon in heaven – 'Our word is au revoir.'

He added two postscripts, written a few hours before he died. 'Perhaps the worst is to know the exact hour, and yet perhaps the best ... Darling, my last word. I again assert that I had no previous knowledge of what was going to happen that night. I go to my death knowing that, and that my statement is true, and that my own darling believes me. B x x x x.'

Interviewed by a reporter from the Yorkshire Observer *in February 1930, Tom Pierrepoint, who was now 59 and had been assistant or chief executioner since 1906, said: 'Why should a murderer be nursed for the rest of his life? I think it would be encouraging people to murder if the death penalty were abolished. But it would make no difference to me either way.'*

In 1930, executions reached another low, only five people being hanged – the same number as those executed in 1921. Convicted murderers tended now to be reprieved. And in the years before the Second World War some overdue reforms were made in the laws governing capital punishment. The Infanticide Act of 1922, which had abolished the execution of mothers who killed their newborn babies, was tardily followed in 1931 by the Sentence of Death (Expectant Mothers) Act, which decreed that pregnant women should not be hanged.

Then, in 1933, the Children and Young Persons Act raised the age of convicted persons who might be hanged. No one who was under the age of eighteen when murder was committed could henceforth be sentenced to death. They were to be detained during His Majesty's pleasure.

26

SAMUEL FURNACE

THE MURDER OF WALTER SPATCHETT, 1933

There seems little doubt that various forms of mayhem, from mugging to murder, attract some imitators when sensationally and lengthily described by the press. For instance, a mentally unbalanced youth called Ernest Rhodes was so obsessed with the murderers Patrick Mahon and Norman Thorne that when the latter was awaiting execution, Rhodes went out on 9 April 1925 and cut the throat of a girl he thought he loved. He was found guilty but insane. The much-publicised murder committed by Alfred Rouse in November 1930 may have had a similar effect a few years later. He faked his own death by strangling a complete stranger and burning the body in his car so that he might assume a new identity. Two years after Rouse was sentenced to death, a man called Furnace tried the same fiery trick.

On the evening of Tuesday, 3 January 1933, Mr Wynne, of 30 Hawley Crescent, north of Camden Town underground station, was startled to see that a shed in his back yard was on fire. It had been rented from him by a builder and decorator, Sam Furnace. After firemen had extinguished the blaze they discovered the charred body of a man slumped on a high stool before what had been an office desk.

Furnace's home was in Crogsland Road, Chalk Farm, about 500 yards to the north-west. A native of St Neot's, he was married with children, the eldest being a ten-year-old boy. Earlier in life he had been a ship's steward, and had served in the Rifle Brigade and with the Black and Tans. A tenant of his, Mr Abbot, was able to identify the body as that of his late landlord. A note was found that said: 'Goodbye all. No work. No money. Sam J Furnace.'

At the inquest, which began on 6 January in St Pancras coroner's court before Mr Bentley Purchase, a life insurance claim was declared to be void as the person insured had committed suicide. The sympathetic insurance company agreed, however, to provide the widow with a generous grant.

The coroner, Mr Purchase, more suspicious than sympathetic, took it upon himself to examine the charred remains personally. He concluded that he was dealing with neither *felo de se* nor Furnace. For there was what appeared to be a bullet wound in the corpse's back, and its teeth were those of a man much younger than forty-two-year-old Sam.

A full post mortem revealed that the burnt man had in fact been shot *twice*, and had probably been dead before he was set on fire. He was identified by a sodden post-office savings book found in an overcoat in the shed. Both coat and book belonged to Walter Spatchett, aged twenty-five, a rent collector for Messrs TB Westacott and Son of Camden Road, who lived with his parents in Dartmouth Park Road, Highgate. He was last seen on the evening of the Monday before the fire, when he had about £40 of rent on him. He and Furnace were known to have been acquainted.

A nationwide hunt for Furnace was instituted by the police. On 9 January, BBC Radio brashly announced that the missing man was wanted for murder. Furnace, said to have been sighted all over the country, was finally traced to Southend. There he made the not uncommon mistake of criminals on the run – he wrote a letter, in his case to his wife's brother, Charles Tuckfield, who received it on Saturday, 15 January. It read:

I am at Southend, quite near the station, making out I have been ill with the flue [sic] … I am far from well through want of sleep. I don't think I have slept one hour since the accident happened. Now what I want you to do is not for me but for May and the kiddies. My days are numbered. I want you to come down Sunday, on your own, please. Catch the 10.35 from Harringay Park, that gets you down in Southend at 12.8. Come out of the station, walk straight across the road and down the opposite road. Walk down on the left side. I will see you. I am not giving my address in case you are followed. Just walk slowly down. If you come, will you bring me 15 1/2 shirt and two collars, any colour will do. Also one pair of socks, dark ones, and one comb. I think that is all now. Best of luck. Mine is gone.

Tuckfield gave the letter to the police. Shadowed by them, he went as instructed to Southend and walked down Whitegate Road. A curtain twitched in Number 11, and Furnace looked out and beckoned. Tuckfield entered the house and conversed as easily as he could with his brother-in-law until the police, led by Superintendent Cornish, entered the house through a rear door. Furnace, who was thought to be armed, was rushed and overpowered. He was taken back to London.

In a statement made at Kentish Town police station that night, he claimed that the shooting of Spatchett was accidental. Furnace said that on the Monday evening they had both been in the shed, which also served as an office. He said: 'I showed him the revolver. He cocked it. I told him it was loaded … I was showing him through the door, with the gun in my left hand, and as he was going through the door the gun went off and shot him. He fell to the ground groaning. I realised my position and lost my head. I went out. When I got back there I found that he was dead … I took the gun away and did not tell anyone I had shot him … Next morning about 7.15 I dragged him into the office … The idea struck me to destroy the body by a fire at my shop, making out that the body was mine. The idea at first seemed too terrible, but no other way seemed possible.' The same afternoon he returned to the shed. He sat the body on a chair and poured spirits and oil over it. 'I screwed up a lot of paper on the floor and set a candle, which I lit, in the middle of it … I came outside and pulled the outer door to, locking it.'

One wonders whether his story, if it had been used as a defence, would have been believed in court. But no trial was ever held.

Having made the statement Furnace was locked overnight in a cell in Kentish Town police station. During the night he could be heard pacing restlessly about. As it was very cold, he asked for his overcoat to be returned. It happened to be the only article of clothing that had not been searched. Towards dawn on Monday there was silence. A PC peered through the spy-hole at 7 am, and saw Furnace raise something to his mouth. The PC hastily opened the cell door, to find the prisoner now writhing on the floor. He had swallowed some hydrochloric acid, the contents of a small bottle that had been sewn into the lining of his overcoat.

He died twenty-four hours later, on Tuesday, 18 January in St Pancras Hospital, in whose mortuary Spatchett's body already lay. A coroner's jury concluded that the death of Spatchett was not accidental and they found Furnace guilty of murder.

In April 1931, Albert Pierrepoint, a wholesale grocer's deliveryman, aged 27, living with his first wife, Mary, in Manchester, wrote to the Prison Commissioners at the Home Office in London, applying for as job as assistant executioner, mentioning the fact that Harry Pierrepoint had been his father and that Tom Pierrepoint was his uncle. He was interviewed at Strangeways Prison in Manchester, but it was not until September 1932 that he was employed as an assistant executioner, his first task being to assist his uncle, Tom, carry out an execution in Dublin that December.

PARKER AND PROBERT

The Murder of Joseph Bedford, 1933

Murders committed in the course of a robbery are almost as common as sexual or domestic murders, and the murderers are commonly a pair of thugs, usually young, whereas their victims are usually middle-aged or old. The following case history was brutally commonplace. It is unusual in that the executions that settled the law's and the victim's account were the last, it is believed, to have been witnessed by a reporter – in this case, the chief crime reporter of the Press Association, WG Finch.

Joseph Bedford, an eighty-year-old bachelor, maintained a dilapidated general store in Clarence Street, Portslade, a run-down suburb between Worthing and Hove. On a slate in one of the shop's windows was written – 'Bankrupt Stock'. Somewhat doddery and deaf, he was also something of a miserly recluse, keeping his money in two chocolate boxes. One or two motherly women in the neighbourhood kept an eye on him and cared for him in a small way.

Bedford's shop usually remained open until 8 pm, and it was about fifteen minutes before this on Monday, 13 November 1933 that Miss Kathleen Russell called on the old man to prepare a simple evening meal for him, as was her wont. When she left the shop about eight o'clock, she saw two young men, both strangers, outside – 'hanging about' as she put it. One of them said something to her, but she was later not allowed by the courts to reveal what that was.

The suspicions of another neighbour were aroused about two hours later when at 9.50 pm or so he observed that the light in Bedford's shop was still on. This neighbour, Edward Myers, the son of the publican whose hostelry was on a street corner opposite the shop, was puzzled by this irregularity. Not only that – some of the old man's stock was still outside on the pavement. Myers summoned a police constable.

PC Peters was also aware of Mr Bedford's habits and investigated. He tried the shop door – it was locked. Hearing sounds 'as if someone were stumbling against something', he flashed his torch into the dimly lit interior through the glass panel of the door, across which a ladder had been placed. He said: 'The light fell full across the face of Mr Bedford, and I could see that it was covered with blood. The next moment I saw him stagger backwards. He fell against some gardening shovels resting against a showcase. I then forced the door, and found Mr Bedford lying in a heap on the floor.'

Mr Bedford was taken to hospital, where the following morning he died of shock occasioned by multiple injuries to his head. On the same day, Tuesday, Scotland Yard were called in, and DCI Askew, after examining the premises, came across a bowler hat with a dent in the crown and an overcoat button that seemed to have been torn off. Both were on the shop floor among several copper coins that were scattered about: halfpennies, pennies and farthings. The old man had kept his coppers in one of the chocolate boxes and his silver coins – sixpences, shillings, florins and half-crowns – in the other.

Mr Bedford was buried in Portslade Cemetery a week after the attack on him. His two assailants had already been picked up in Worthing, on or about Thursday, 16 November, charged with loitering with intent to commit a felony. The actual circumstances of their arrest are not known, but a week later, on the morning of Thursday, 23 November, they appeared before the Worthing magistrates, who gave them a nominal sentence of one day's imprisonment. After being taken back to their cells the two men were re-arrested by Superintendent Fairs at 10.40 am on a charge of murder. Handcuffed, they were driven to Portslade police station, where they were officially charged. Fifteen minutes later, they appeared before a special sitting of the Hove County Bench and were remanded until 1 December. Both men were granted legal aid. The chairman of the Bench and the younger of the accused men had the same name: Frederick Parker. Frederick William Parker was a twenty-one-year-old labourer. His partner in crime was a fitter, Albert Probert, aged twenty-six.

While in custody in Worthing, Fred Parker had been asked by Inspector Lewis about the attack on Joseph Bedford. Parker, who had not been told that Bedford was dead, said: 'Why don't you ask my mate? I don't see why I should give someone else away.'

Later he confessed. 'I don't see that I shouldn't tell you,' he said. 'We knocked an old man out in a shop at Portslade on Monday night. It was a shop where they sold bankrupt stock, and we took the money from the till.' Lewis then asked Parker if he realised the seriousness of what he was saying. 'Yes,' replied Parker. 'I want to get it off my mind':

> We decided to hold up a chap in a shop in Portslade. It was an old dirty shop of bankrupt stock. We both walked to the shop window to see that all was clear. After investigating we walked into the shop and spoke to the old shopkeeper. I then turned and locked the door. No one was passing at the time, and I brought my revolver into play. The gun was not loaded, but I had no other choice of making the old shopkeeper put up his hands. I held him up and the other chap with me – I don't want to mention his name – went around the counter and just knocked him out. I went to the boxes, and we both took money out and put it in our pockets. Those farthings you found on me are some I took from the till.

Later that night, Parker asked Lewis how Bedford was. Lewis was presumably non-committal, for the young man went on to say, still ignorant of Bedford's death: 'I wish it had been a bigger job. It was not worth doing for £6. He was an old miser; I thought we should have found buckets of money.'

Fred Parker first knew that Bedford was dead when told so by DCI Askew. 'You don't mean to say the old chap is dead?' exclaimed Parker, who then made a statement elaborating what he had told Lewis and naming Bert Probert as his partner in the raid on Bedford's store.

He said he first met Probert 'by accident' in the Church Army Hostel at Brighton. The police later established that on 7 November the two were in lodgings in Portslade, from which they disappeared on the 10th. The next day, Saturday, Parker was temporarily employed selling tickets for a sweepstake draw. Sometime during this period, Parker gave the older man, Probert, his blue overcoat, as the other man wanted one to match his blue suit. To replace it, Parker stole another coat.

On Monday the 13th, said Fred Parker, 'Probert asked if I would "do" a jeweller's. I said that the shop was bound to have alarms all over, but Probert said he was desperate. I tried to get him to talk sense. We walked round Portslade and we came to the shop. I explained to Probert that it was a big risk and I would not take any part except holding the gun.' They entered the shop.

The gun, according to Parker, had been given to Probert by a man he knew. His statement continued: 'While Probert was talking to the old man I turned the key, already in the door, and coming back I told Probert that the old man was deaf and could not hear what we were saying, but if he did hear to hit him gently. I took the revolver from my pocket and asked the old man to put up his hands. He resisted at first and Probert struck him. Probert was leading him backwards and as he struck the old chap went down. Probert did not take any notice of what I said and kept on asking if I had got the money. I told him to put a scarf under the old man's head. He was knocking his head on the floor and I could hear that distinctly. I told Probert: "I have found the money," and he left the old chap and we left the shop together.'

The police discovered that later that night, between 9.30 and 10 pm, the pair had a meal in a tea room in Worthing. The following morning, they went to an outfitter's and bought new suits and shirts. While they were there, Probert had a new button sewn onto his blue overcoat to replace the one that was missing.

After their arrest and after Probert had been told about Parker's allegations, he denied any involvement in Bedford's death and having ever been in his shop. But he could not or would not say where he was on the night in question. When arrested, Parker was found to have twenty-seven farthings on him; Probert had twenty-nine.

During their various appearances before the magistrates at Hove in the first week of January 1934, Fred Parker fainted seven times in the dock and had to be revived. On 4 January, DCI Askew also collapsed. He was being cross-examined when he suddenly fell backwards down the steps of the witness box. After being given first aid, DCI Askew re-entered the box and almost immediately fell forward in a faint. He was taken into an adjoining room, where he was revived by the doctor who had been standing by to resuscitate Parker.

Fred Parker made a statement denying that he had struck the fatal blow:

> I held up the old man with a gun and told him we had come for money. He put his hands up eventually. I stepped back for Probert to tie him up … We had tied my scarf and Probert's together for that purpose. I thought we were going to carry out the whole thing by merely tying him up. I told him to stop hitting him … Finally, I hit Probert over the knuckles to separate him from the old man. I told him the old man had had enough … He told me to keep my mouth closed, and said that if I did not, he would do the same to me as he had done to Mr Bedford.

Parker and Probert appeared at Sussex Assizes in Lewes on Wednesday, 14 March 1934. Both gave evidence. Mr Justice Roche was the judge and Sir Henry Curtis Bennett, KC, was the Crown's chief prosecutor. Mr John Flowers defended Probert.

Mr JD Cassels, KC, defending Parker, claimed that the charge against his defendant should be at the most one of manslaughter, as Parker alleged it was Probert who used the excessive violence that resulted in the old man's death. The judge remarked: 'I am afraid I shall have to tell the jury that that proposition is not correct in law.' Mr Cassels then suggested – as did Mr Flowers for Probert – that Bedford, in falling backwards, possibly frightened by PC Peters's flashlight, had struck his head on something sharp, had fractured his skull, and so died by misadventure.

The Crown's view, supported by the judge, was that if two persons set out to commit a robbery and if one used violence, the other standing by was as guilty as the person striking the blow. Mr Justice Roche in his summing-up told the jury that if they accepted Parker's evidence that he contemplated robbery and the use of some degree of violence, it was not manslaughter but murder. If they thought Mr Bedford fell because of the injuries he had previously received and died from the effects of that fall, then the original injuries were the cause of death.

After retiring for thirty-five minutes, the jury found both men guilty of murder. They were sentenced to death. An appeal was dismissed on 18 April by the Lord Chief Justice, Mr Justice Avory and Mr Justice Humphreys, and Parker and Probert were hanged in Wandsworth Prison on Friday, 4 May 1934. Tom and Albert Pierrepoint carried out the double hanging, assisted by Thomas Phillips and Stanley Cross.

28
CHARLOTTE BRYANT

THE MURDER OF FREDERICK BRYANT, 1935

Poisoners, especially female poisoners, who, with very evident malice aforethought, deliberately plan the deaths of their victims, and would seem to take some pleasure from their suffering, have invariably been treated with a corresponding lack of pity by the law.

Charlotte McHugh was an illiterate Irish girl and something of a slut, whom Frederick John Bryant, a corporal in the military police, met when he was serving in Ireland. This was during 'The Troubles', the guerilla warfare and savage reprisals of 1920-21 that followed the First World War, resulting in the official division of Ireland into Eire and Ulster in 1921-22. Corporal Bryant was at that time serving in Londonderry. He brought young Charlotte back with him to England and they were married in Somerset in March 1922. She was just nineteen and he was twenty-five or twenty-six.

But life with the upright, amiable Fred soon deteriorated. Jobs were hard to find – the country no longer needed or wanted its soldiery, and the best employment Fred Bryant could find was as a farm labourer. In 1925, they moved into a tied cottage on a Dorset farm on the Somerset border, at Over Compton east of Yeovil. Here, Mrs Bryant soon acquired a reputation for harlotry and excess. She was known locally, mainly in the public bars of inns, as 'Compton Liz', 'Black Bess' and 'Killarney Kate'. It seems she had an insatiable desire for amorous adventure and sex.

Although her hair was lousy and she was virtually toothless, she had many affairs, which presumably consoled her mind and body and distracted her from the humdrum poverty of a labourer's life. Along the way she produced five children, whose paternity must have been in doubt, and let the family cottage slide along with her local fame into squalor and disorder. However, her extramarital activities were able to supplement the family income, and this was apparently of some importance to Fred. He was earning less than £2 a week. As he said to a neighbour: 'Four pound a week is better than thirty bob. I don't care a damn what she does.' Accordingly, he was not displeased when at Christmas 1933 a pedlar and horse-dealer of gypsy origin, Leonard Parsons, began lodging at the cottage as a paying guest, sleeping on a couch in the kitchen and sharing Fred's razor – and his wife.

Fred was forced out of his complacency when early in 1934 he was sacked by the farmer, largely on account of the scandal caused in the neighbourhood by Mrs Bryant's amours. All the Bryants did, however, was to move east to another cottage on another farm not far way, at Coombe, a mile north of Sherborne, and carry on much as before.

Parsons was not a regular lodger, since his roving nature and occupation took him periodically elsewhere, sometimes in the direction of his 'natural wife', Priscilla Loveridge, a gypsy woman who bore him four children and later bitterly described him as 'a woman's fancy man, the kind of man who would break up any man's home'. But his reappearances at the Bryants' cottage, unshaven and unkempt, apparently excited Mrs Bryant so much that like a drug, she wished to have more – could not have enough of him, in fact – and began to consider how she might rid herself entirely of her marital obligations, loose as they were.

She was fairly besotted with Parsons and more than once went off with him on his travels, staying with him as his wife in Dorchester and Weymouth. During these absences as well as during his visits, her duties as mother and housewife were further neglected and the cottage lapsed even further into squalor and filth.

Parsons was lodging with the Bryants in May 1935, when on 14 May Fred Bryant became suddenly ill, vomiting and suffering from acute pains in his stomach. The local medic, Dr MacCarthy, diagnosed gastro-enteritis, and his patient's strong constitution soon assisted him towards a full recovery. Another such attack on 6 August was similarly diagnosed and Fred Bryant was soon on his feet again and back at work.

By October, Parsons's feelings for Charlotte Bryant seem to have cooled, for towards the end of the month, deterred perhaps by her demands, he went away and never returned. Indeed, he told her he was not coming back. She became more distraught as time passed, and on 11 December a third poisonous assault on her husband's innards laid him very low. A week later, when he was still incapacitated, although believed to be recovering, she travelled north to a gypsy camp near Weston-super-Mare, seeking Parsons. She encountered instead Priscilla Loveridge and her pipe-smoking crone of a mother, Mrs Penfold. Mrs Bryant was heartily abused by both and sent away.

The next day, Friday, 20 December, Fred Bryant's condition suddenly worsened. On Saturday he was in agony, saying there was something inside him like a red-hot poker that was driving him mad. A neighbour, Mrs Stone, saw him that day, and when his employer's wife, Mrs Priddle, called, he was so ill he could not speak. On Sunday he was removed from the cottage in an ambulance to the Yeatman Hospital, Sherborne, and that afternoon he died. He was thirty-nine.

This time Dr MacCarthy was suspicious and refused to sign a death certificate. He communicated his concern to the police. There was an inquest. 'What is an inquest?' asked Mrs Bryant, and waxed indignant when she understood – not surprisingly, as on 28 December 4.09 grains of arsenic were discovered by the Home Office analyst, Dr

Roche Lynch, in the corpse of poor Fred. But even before this, Scotland Yard's assistance had been sought by the Dorset police.

Meanwhile, Mrs Bryant and her five children were lodged in the Poor Law institution at Sturminster Newton, a former workhouse, while the Bryants' cottage was minutely examined by the police in the shape of DCI Bell and DS Tapsell of Scotland Yard. The place was virtually taken apart, but not before Tapsell, equipped with three paint-brushes, had gone about carefully sweeping shelves and cupboards and acquiring in all about 146 samples of dust, dirt and refuse, of which thirty-two samples later revealed some traces of arsenic.

Parsons was questioned and was luckily able to convince the police that he had had nothing to do with Mr Bryant's demise. He said he had met Mrs Bryant towards the end of 1933, when he was lodging at Babylon Hill and going under the name Bill Moss. Soon afterwards they became intimate and remained so for two years. In the summer of 1935, he said, she remarked more than once that she 'would soon be a widow', after which they might marry. To this he had unkindly replied: 'I wouldn't marry any woman.'

An elderly widow, Mrs Lucy Ostler, who had lately lodged with the Bryants, related that Mrs Bryant had once said: 'I hate Fred.' When Mrs Ostler asked her why she didn't leave him, Mrs Bryant replied that she did not want to leave the children. The older woman revealed that on the night of 21 December – Bryant died the following day – his wife had coaxed him to take some liquid Oxo, a meat extract. On another occasion, Mrs Bryant, said Mrs Ostler, had disposed of a tin of weed-killer, saying: 'I must get rid of this.' On being told what an inquest implied, the young widow had said: 'If they can't find anything, they can't put a rope around your neck.'

The police discovered that an insurance agent, Mr Tuck, had been approached by Mrs Bryant in December 1934, when she said: 'I would like to insure my old man.' This was not followed up, but a year later, on 20 December 1935, Mr Tuck happened to call at the Bryants' cottage. Mr Bryant, he thought, looked a very sick man – gastritis, said his wife – and Mr Tuck concluded that the husband was not a fair risk. However, he effected some insurance for the children. On 22 December, Bryant died. Mr Tuck, unaware of this, returned to the cottage on Monday the 23rd. Finding only the children at home he drove off, but on the way met Mrs Bryant and Mrs Ostler returning to the cottage on foot. He gave them a lift. Mrs Bryant had a bundle with her and she told him that she had been to the hospital to pick up her dead husband's clothes. 'Well, he's gone,' she said. 'I've been a good wife to him – nobody can say I haven't. And nobody can say I poisoned him.' Mr Tuck, mystified by this remark, said: 'No. Why should they?' She replied: 'Well, you never know what will come of these things.' She did not seem to the insurance agent like a woman who had just been widowed.

The police also made an exhaustive search of the area about the cottage and an empty, battered tin was found in some rubbish, and in it traces of arsenic. The tin was identified by a firm who manufactured weed-killer.

On Monday, 10 February 1936, Superintendent Cherett of the Sherborne police visited Mrs Bryant in the Sturminster Newton institution. After being cautioned and formally charged with the murder of her husband, she said: 'I have never got any poison from anywhere, and that people do know. I don't see how they can say I poisoned my husband.' She was taken by car to Exeter Prison. Her five children, aged twelve, ten, six, four, and fifteen months, remained in the Institution, despite an offer from the NSPCC to find them a home.

On Wednesday, 27 May 1936 the trial of Charlotte Bryant began in Dorchester at the Dorset Assizes. The judge was Mr Justice Mackinnon; the Solicitor-General, Sir Terence O'Connor, KC, led for the Crown; and the accused was defended by Mr JD Casswell.

Neither the defendant nor the principal witnesses for the prosecution, Parsons and Loveridge, seemed to comprehend the gravity of the situation – Mrs Bryant munched caramels in the dock. In giving evidence, she said she knew nothing about poison and had never bought any weed-killer, and she denied nearly all the prosecution's allegations, including what Parsons and Mrs Ostler had told the court. She was, she said, on very good terms with her husband. 'Never a breath wrong with my husband in my life until Leonard Parsons come along.'

The jury didn't believe her, and on Saturday, 30 May 1936, she was found guilty of murder and duly sentenced to death.

An appeal was heard on 29 June and dismissed. Ten days later the Labour MP for Nelson and Colne, Mr Silverman, asked the Home Secretary, Sir John Simon, whether he was aware that the appeal judges had refused to admit certain additional evidence on the ground that it could have been produced at the original trial, where, said Mr Silverman, the defence had been conducted by junior counsel only, whereas 'such a heavy battery of leading counsel' appeared for the Crown that 'the minds of a rustic jury' might have been considerably affected. The Home Secretary replied that counsel for the Crown were not a battery directed against the accused, and that in his view the defence was most adequately conducted.

Meanwhile, in Exeter Prison, Mrs Bryant's hair turned white at the roots. She refused to see her children so as not to upset them any further. The day before her execution she sent a telegraph appealing for mercy to the new, uncrowned king, Edward VIII – to no effect. 'Mighty King,' she wrote. 'Have pity on your afflicted subject. Don't let them kill me on Wednesday.'

Charlotte Bryant was hanged by Tom Pierrepoint and Tom Phillips in Exeter Prison on Wednesday, 15 July 1936. She was thirty-three. It is said that she went to her death bravely. Said a priest: 'Her last moments were truly edifying.' Mrs van der Elst, a leading campaigner for the abolition of capital punishment, staged a small demonstration outside the prison and was fined £5 for obstructing an officer. She also handed in £5 for the police sports fund and said she was going to pay for the maintenance and education of Mrs Bryant's five children.

At the inquest on the body of Mrs Bryant the jurors asked the coroner if they might give their fees to her children. The coroner replied that it was a small amount and provision had already been made for the children. The jury then handed their fees to the prison governor to give to the Discharged Prisoners' Aid Society.

Three months before the execution of Charlotte Bryant, another woman was hanged for murder: Dorothea Waddingham. She was thirty-six, and also had five children. Nurse Waddingham, who ran a small nursing home in Nottingham, had been charged with the murder by poison (morphia) of two elderly women in her charge: Louisa Baguley, aged eighty-nine, and Ada Baguley, fifty, who weighed 16 stone and suffered from disseminated sclerosis. Found guilty of the murder of Ada Baguley, Nurse Waddingham was executed at Winson Green Prison, Birmingham, on 16 April 1936, the execution being carried out by the two Pierrepoints.

It was the last time that two women (both poisoners) were hanged in the same year – in which six other women who had been sentenced to death were reprieved. No woman would be executed in Britain for over twelve years, the next being a forty-two-year-old lesbian, Margaret Allen, hanged on 12 January 1949 for the murder with a hammer of an elderly eccentric, Mrs Chadwick.

LESLIE STONE

THE MURDER OF RUBY KEEN, 1937

Only one policeman has ever been tried for murder at the Old Bailey. This was PC William Teasdale, who strangled his wife in bed in their Clapham home during a row about his association with another woman. Teasdale was tried at the Old Bailey in April 1938, found guilty and sentenced to death. He was reprieved in May. The year before this, two policemen were among the main suspects in a murder case outside London to which the Metropolitan Police's CID were called.

Ruby Anne Keen was an attractive young woman, aged twenty-three, who lived with her widowed mother, elder sister and her lorry-driver brother in Leighton Buzzard, Bedfordshire. She worked in a factory in the nearby town of Dunstable, and when she was free liked to go out and have a good time, which several young men in the district were glad to provide. She enjoyed the attention, the affirmation and exercise of her attractions, and if invited out by one of her admirers was not loath to accept.

One of her regular boyfriends was a builder's labourer, Leslie George Stone, aged twenty-four, who lived in the hamlet of Heath and Reach, a mile north of Leighton Buzzard. He and Ruby had been friends since 1931, and it was thought by their families that one day they would get married. But Stone was a soldier, serving with the Royal Artillery, and in 1932 he was posted to Hong Kong. After a year or so, Ruby's letters became less frequent and then stopped altogether. Out of sight meant out of mind. Besides, her other admirers – in particular, two young policemen – were not slow to occupy her time and affections. Before long one of them was favoured above all other suitors, and in 1936 she became engaged to a PC with the Bedfordshire Constabulary. Not long after this, in December 1936, Stone was discharged from the RA on medical grounds and returned to Leighton Buzzard.

It was more than two months before he saw Ruby again, and when he did she was in the company of another man. Stone said later: 'I did not speak to her as I did not want to look a fool.' However, he spoke to her the following Sunday, 4 April. He bought her a drink in a pub, the Golden Bell, and she said they must have a night out together for old time's sake. She would not commit herself to an actual date.

But a week later, after going to evening service in a local church with a girlfriend, she dropped in again at the Golden Bell about seven o'clock; Stone was waiting. In expectation and in honour of the occasion, he had put on a new blue serge suit, one he had never worn before. He had three pints of mild and she had a glass of port. They moved on to the Cross Keys and ended up in the Stag Hotel. They sat in a corner of the saloon bar, their conversation being overheard in part by some of the locals drinking at the bar. Leslie Stone was trying to persuade Ruby Keen to give up her fiancé and marry *him*. After he had drunk two more pints and she two ports, they left just before closing time at ten o'clock.

Two of the more inquisitive locals followed the couple, who walked past Ruby's home in Plantation Road and entered a lover's lane, the Firs, on the outskirts of the town about 300 yards from her home. The locals gleefully hurried back to the Stag with this bit of gossip, leaving the couple alone.

Stone later told the police that he left Ruby about 10.15 pm outside the Stag; they went their separate ways, he reaching home about 10.45 pm.

Ruby's presence in the Firs was accidentally confirmed in a curious way by a married couple who chose to take a short cut home along the lane about 10.30 pm. In the shadows they saw Ruby in the arms, they said, of a policeman – an assumption easily made, for the man was dressed in what they swore was a dark blue uniform with silver buttons. And who but a policeman would be embracing Ruby?

Early next morning, about 7 am, her almost naked body, wet with dew, was found in the lane by a railwayman, Mr Cox, on his way to work. No attempt had been made to hide her. She had been strangled with her own black silk scarf. Although most of her clothing had been torn off her, she was still wearing her gloves, and there was no sign of sexual assault. But there was every evidence in the sandy ground of the desperate struggle she had made, presumably to avoid being raped. She had been struck on the chin before being strangled, and her assailant had knelt as he killed her. The assault must have been swift and silent, for dogs in a nearby cottage had not been disturbed sufficiently to bark.

On the afternoon of 12 April, Les Stone called at the house of PC McCarthy, who was out. Mrs McCarthy thought that Stone looked very worried and agitated. He said he had heard about Ruby's death and asked her to telephone Leighton Buzzard police station as he had been with Ruby the previous night and wanted to make a statement to clear his name. He did so. But the police were more concerned about the evidence of the couple in the lane and the involvement of two local policemen with the murdered girl.

The assistance of Scotland Yard, in the person of Chief Inspector Barker, was speedily sought. He had been closely involved in 1927 in the arrest of Frederick Browne. It fell to Barker to question the two young policemen who had been the friend and the fiancé of Ruby Keen, as well as the young workman who had been drinking with her on the night she died. The fiancé said he had last seen Ruby on the Sunday afternoon, before he went on duty at the village of Hockliffe, 3 miles east of Leighton Buzzard. It was an unbreakable alibi. But he and the other PC owed their ultimate elimination from the enquiry to Leslie Stone's new suit.

All footprints beside the body had been trampled and defaced in the frantic struggle between Ruby and her assailant. But his knee marks – shallow, rounded depressions in the ground – remained. Plaster of Paris casts were made of them, and when they were examined by Sir Bernard Spilsbury a clear imprint of the trouser crease and the material was revealed.

The dark-blue trousers of the main suspects were inspected. Despite the fact that the trousers of Stone's new suit, as well as the jacket, had been cleaned or brushed – so hard at the knees that the nap had worn away – Spilsbury's microscope picked out granules of sandy soil in the fibres of the suit, and similar specks in the turn-ups. They were identical with the trampled earth by the dead girl's body. The fact that the suit had been worn by Stone on 11 April for the first time meant he could not claim to have got earth on his suit on any other night. Just as incriminating was a single silk fibre found embedded in the lining of Stone's jacket. It matched the cream underslip Ruby had been wearing the night she died. Stone was charged with her murder on Wednesday, 24 April 1937.

His trial began at the Old Bailey on Monday, 28 June before the Lord Chief Justice, Lord Hewart. The chief prosecutor was Mr Richard O'Sullivan, KC, assisted by Mr Christmas Humphreys, son of Mr Justice Travers Humphreys. Christmas Humphreys had become a Treasury Counsel in 1934, when he was thirty-three. Mr Maurice Healy, KC, defended the accused.

The evidence was scant and circumstantial. But on the second day of the trial, Stone changed his story in the witness box, saying in his defence that he and Ruby had quarrelled – she had struck him and he had choked her. He explained, saying that in the old days Ruby had had a trick of poking her little fingers in his ears and tickling them. This annoyed him. He had once struck her when thus provoked, but had missed and hit a brick wall. On the night of the murder she referred to this, and asked him if he had any trouble with his hand. He told the court:

I told her she was lucky that I hit the wall instead of hitting her. She called me a dirty devil and hit me above the left ear. It was a full-arm swing. I was surprised and went up to her, and she struck again at me with her other hand. It made me jump at her. I caught hold of her scarf I think and pulled it. I think I knotted it again after that ... She started to fall down and I caught hold of the front of her clothes. I was in a kind of rage. Her clothes were torn off as she was falling.

Then, he said, he knelt. He decided that she was not dead, only stunned. He said he did not try to interfere with her and walked away, thinking she would revive. When he got home he brushed his clothes.

The jury were out for twenty-five minutes. They found him guilty and he was sentenced to death.

When he appealed against the verdict on the grounds that the jury had been misdirected, it was on the basis that the judge had replied: 'Yes, undoubtedly,' to a question from the jury, sent to him as they considered their verdict: 'If as the result of an intention to commit rape a girl is killed – although there was no intention of killing her – is a man guilty of murder?'

Stone's appeal was dismissed. He was hanged by Tom Pierrepoint, assisted by Alfred Allen, at Pentonville Prison on Friday, 13 August 1937.

In 1938, Tom Pierrepoint dealt with all eight of the executions carried out that year, the first time in over twenty years that the chief executioner had done so. His nephew, Albert, assisted him on three occasions. Fewer hangings were now being carried out. More than a dozen people were reprieved that year, three of them women.

30

EDWARD CHAPLIN

The Manslaughter of Percy Casserley, 1938

Mr and Mrs Casserley married in 1927 when he was forty-seven and she was twenty years younger. Nothing is known of their lives till then, except that in his youth he had been a long-distance runner of some distinction and had represented his country in France. His club was South London Harriers. In 1937, the Casserleys were living in suburban comfort in Wimbledon, at 35 Lindisfarne Road.

Percy Arthur Casserley was managing director of John Watney and Co., Ltd, a London brewers, earning £1,500 a year. Tall, spare and still with an athletic build, he was due to retire in February 1938, but certain circumstances caused him to stop work the previous September. He was an alcoholic. His wife later told the police that he drank a bottle and a half of whisky every day, that he began drinking after returning home from work and continued, hardly bothering to eat dinner with her, until well after midnight. Irascible rather than violent, he was abusive, unsociable and moody, and as a result the Casserleys had few friends locally and seldom went out together. They had no children. This was said to be Mr Casserley's wish and not his wife's.

There may have been other reasons, for in 1936 he had an unspecified operation that led to the total cessation of sexual relations between them. His consumption of whisky increased in 1937, and Mrs Casserley's frustrations, seeking some release, focused on Ted Chaplin.

Lindisfarne Road was a cul-de-sac south of Wimbledon Common. In the spring of 1937, work began on the building of a house next to the Casserleys' home. The builders' foreman, there every day, was a strapping, handsome man aged thirty-five: Edward Royal Chaplin. Married in 1928, he had been divorced in 1934. One day, Mrs Georgina May Casserley (Ena) asked him if he would like a cup of tea. From there grew an association that deepened into an affair.

By September, Percy Casserley stopped going to work and his state of health was such that he started having treatment for his alcoholism. He was in a home for inebriates between 16 January and 17 February 1938. In his absence, Chaplin more than once stayed overnight in 35 Lindisfarne Road. Mrs Casserley also visited him in his flat 2 miles away in Abbotsbury Road, Morden. On her husband's return, she had news for him: she was pregnant.

This was another painful humiliation for Mr Casserley – his pride was hurt as well as his manhood. On 23 February, he told his brother-in-law, James Barry: 'One way out would be for me to shoot myself.' He presumed that his wife's lover must be 'a tea-planter home on six months' leave from Ceylon'. Before long he was back in the nursing home, described in court as a 'home for nervous disorders', and was said to have suffered a nervous breakdown.

While he was away from 8 to 22 March, Ted and Ena indulged themselves, careless now of what people might think or say. The live-in maid, Lydia Scott, had already been cast as Mrs Casserley's confidante and messenger. As far as Ena Casserley was concerned, something had to be done about making her baby legitimate. There was no question of an abortion. Ena, at the age of thirty-eight, wanted the baby very badly, and she also wanted its father to be her husband. Ted Chaplin wanted both woman and baby to be his in name as well as in fact. So while Percy Casserley was still in the nursing home Ena wrote to him asking for a divorce. He replied: 'Do you think I am such a fool as to give you up for someone else?'

Mr Casserley came home on to Lindisfarne Road on 22 March, and the next night he was dead.

On the morning of Wednesday, 23 March, Lydia Scott, who had the evening off, asked Mrs Casserley if she would like to go with her to the pictures that night. Mrs Casserley agreed, but later on said her husband did not want her to go. He had threatened, she said, to shoot her, and had put her into a state of fear and great distress. As Lydia Scott left the house at 6.45 pm, Mrs Casserley said to her: 'If you happen to see Ted, tell him I shall only be able to see him for a minute or two. I won't be able to get out. If he comes to the back door I'll be able to see him … Do try and see him.'

Chaplin had, in fact, arranged to meet Mrs Casserley at 7.30 pm at Coombe Lane. Lydia Scott turned up there instead, and explained: 'Madam can't get out tonight. Will you go up to the house to see her, if only for a few minutes?' Chaplin walked up the road to the Casserleys' home and arrived, according to him, as Mrs Casserley came out of the front door, wearing hat and coat and in tears. They walked to Copse Hill, where at 7.45 pm she bought a bottle of whisky at an off-licence – presumably on his orders, or to account for her absence to her husband if required to do so. She told Ted of her husband's threat and that she was afraid to go home.

They returned to the house in Lindisfarne Road and conferred in the scullery. Chaplin, wearing a raincoat over his sports jacket and trousers, and still wearing his hat, said: 'You had better leave this to me.' He sent her upstairs to her bedroom, from where she heard men's voices raised in anger, the sounds of a scuffle, two gunshots, and then someone coming up the stairs. The door opened – it was Chaplin.

That was the story Mrs Casserley told the police. Chaplin's story, as told in court, was as follows.

Percy Casserley was in an armchair beside the fireplace when Chaplin entered the lounge intending to have a man-to-man talk. 'Good evening,' said Chaplin, and removed his gloves to shake hands as Casserley got to his feet; his spectacles had fallen on the carpet. Chaplin made a speech: 'I've called to see what the trouble is between you and Mrs Casserley. I've just left her and she's terribly upset. You know about her condition. I'm responsible for it. I want to suggest to you that either she comes away with me tonight or I'll phone and get her police protection, as I understand you've threatened Mrs Casserley.' Percy Casserley stared at the other man as if shocked or dazed – or drunk. He said: 'Oh, so it's you, you swine!'

Chaplin waited, pulling on his gloves again, as Casserley went and sat at a writing bureau with his head in his hands. Then he opened a drawer and took out a gun. Chaplin dived forward and seized the other man's right forearm with both his hands, twisting the arm so that Casserley was forced to drop the gun. Chaplin then released his grip as the older man 'looked ill'. Chaplin was half supporting him. Casserley then leaned over and picked up the gun with his *left* hand, which was grasped at once by Chaplin's right hand. With his left he seized the other man's right wrist and there was a stand-up, face-to-face struggle, during which Chaplin endeavoured to keep the gun pointing in the air and away from him. The gun went off.

The bullet penetrated the back of Casserley's neck, exiting at once – a superficial wound – whereupon Chaplin released his grip on Casserley's right wrist and put his left arm around the other man's waist, intending to throw him to the floor and disarm him. As he did so, Casserley's right hand (the left one still held the gun) gripped Chaplin's genitals – referred to in court as 'a portion of his body'. Enraged by this, and in some pain, Chaplin reached out for a torch lying on the bureau and, left-handed, struck Casserley on the head three times. Casserley's head – he was stooping – was by then on a level with Chaplin's stomach and his left arm and the gun were held high in Chaplin's right-handed grasp. After the second blow on Casserley's skull, the head of the torch came off. The third blow was struck with the base of the torch.

Casserley let go of the younger man's genitals as Chaplin made another determined effort to throw him to the ground. Casserley stumbled and fell backwards, pulling Chaplin down on top of him. Their faces touched, and in their fall Chaplin banged his head on a bookcase. All the time, fifty-eight-year-old Casserley struggled violently, trying to point the gun at Chaplin and using both his hands now. There were a couple of clicks from the gun. 'He was like a maddened bull,' said Chaplin. With both of his hands he seized the other man's left wrist and pulled his left arm down and across his neck. Casserley, overpowered and unable to move under Chaplin's weight, said: 'All right. I give in.'

Chaplin relaxed his hold and began to get up. As he did so he heard another click and saw that both of Casserley's hands were on the gun. He pounced and forced the other man's hands back to the side of his head. The gun went off.

Casserley went limp — shot in the head, just in front of his left ear.

Chaplin removed the gun from Casserley's left hand and stood up, wrapped the gun in a handkerchief and put it in his raincoat pocket. He closed the open drawer in the bureau after taking out a box of cartridges he saw there and putting that too into a coat pocket. Noticing his gloves were stained with blood, he wiped them on his raincoat. He then went into the hall and upstairs to Mrs Casserley. 'My God!' he said.

They both came down and went to the kitchen. Chaplin then returned to the lounge, where Casserley lay on his back, stretched out diagonally opposite the door and in front of the small bookcase, on top of which was a large framed photograph and a bowl of yellow tulips. His head was near the skirting board, resting in a pool of blood. He was still alive, groaning but unconscious. Chaplin knelt and touched the wounded man's head. He began to panic. He thought of getting medical help, then thought of staging a burglary 'to save the publicity and to keep Mrs Casserley's name out of it as far as possible'.

When the police arrived, at about 9.30 pm, they found the house in some disorder. They had been summoned after Mrs Casserley rushed to a neighbour's house at 9.10 pm, sobbing and crying out that something terrible had happened — an intruder had broken into the house and her husband had been injured. The neighbour, Mr Burchell, went next door with his son, turned on the lights in the sitting room and saw Mr Casserley lying on the floor with every sign of an interrupted burglary. He sent for the police.

Mrs Casserley told the police she had gone out for a walk earlier that evening, being absent for about forty minutes. On her return, she said, she found her husband dying in the lounge and the house much disordered. Indeed, in the hall a coat stand had been knocked over; the kitchen window was open; silverware was scattered about the dining-room floor and other pieces lay on the floor of the lounge. A broken and bloodstained torch also lay on the lounge carpet and there was a grey button by the door. On the settee reposed one of the dying man's slippers. An empty cartridge case lay against the skirting board by Casserley's head, and about a foot above it there was a bullet-hole in the wall, which was spattered here and there with blood, as was the furniture and the floor.

Percy Casserley died soon after the police arrived.

Meanwhile, Chaplin went to Raynes Park and thence to his flat in Morden. There he put the gun, handkerchief and box of cartridges in the drawer of a bedside cabinet. Also in the drawer was a life preserver (a cosh), which Chaplin said later he had bought for his ailing father in October the previous year. He washed the front of his raincoat, burned the handkerchief and later the box, and then washed the life preserver, as some blood from the gun or handkerchief had got on to it. The following morning he went very early to Epsom and hid the gun and the cartridges in the cavity wall of a half-completed villa. Then he went to work.

Soon after the police investigation started they began to suspect that burglary was not the background to Percy Casserley's death.

The autopsy, carried out by Sir Bernard Spilsbury, was on the 25th. On 29 March, the police visited Ted Chaplin, builders' foreman, on his current site in Northey Road, Epsom. 'Are you Mr Chaplin, known as Ted?' enquired Detective Inspector Henry. 'Yes, that's right,' responded Chaplin. DI Henry continued: 'I wish to speak to you concerning the death of Percy Arthur Casserley.' 'Yes,' said Chaplin. 'It's terrible. I read about it in the papers.' He was asked to accompany DI Henry to a police station to be interviewed. Chaplin fetched his raincoat from a shed and put it on; it was still damp and was missing a button.

At the police station, after initially making a statement denying that he had been to Lindisfarne Road the night before, he suddenly decided to confess, and having done so, he obligingly took the police to the villa where the gun was hidden. 'I'll show you where the gun is,' said Chaplin. 'You'll never find it on your own.'

He was charged at Wimbledon police station with the murder of Percy Casserley on the same day that the murdered man was buried at Gapp Road Cemetery, Wimbledon. His widow sent a wreath of red roses from 'Sorrowing Ena'.

Three days later, Mrs Casserley was arrested in a nursing home and charged with being an accessory after the fact. She was remanded in custody in the hospital in Holloway Prison, where she was forbidden to have a bath and made to scrub floors. Her lawyer protested about her treatment when he asked for bail, saying his client was a lady, whose social position, refinement and pregnancy did not justify such harsh and humiliating treatment. Bail was granted.

The trial of Edward Royal Chaplin began at the Old Bailey in Court No. 1 on Tuesday, 24 May 1938, before Mr Justice Humphreys. Mr Norman Birkett, KC, defended Chaplin, and Mr St John Hutchinson appeared for Mrs Casserley, whose trial for being an accessory was to follow Chaplin's. Mr GB McClure, KC, led for the Crown, assisted by Mr Christmas Humphreys.

Sir Bernard Spilsbury, appearing for the prosecution, said the blows on the dead man's head could have been caused by the life preserver, as could three marks or injuries on his back. Casserley's body was in fact bruised or injured in more than seventeen places. Not a single mark had been found on Chaplin when he was examined by a doctor soon after his arrest.

The judge told the jury in his summing-up: 'What you have to decide is – did Chaplin unlawfully cause the death of Mr Casserley, and if he did, did he do it with the intention of causing his death, or of causing him grievous injury?'

The prosecution's case was that Chaplin went to the house, and knowing that Casserley had a gun took the life preserver with him, which he then used to batter the older man before shooting him twice.

Having lodged in the house in Mr Casserley's absence, Chaplin might well have known where the gun was kept. It was also possible that Mrs Casserley could have told him. He might have intended that Mr Casserley's death should look like suicide. Perhaps the struggle in the lounge was not caused by Casserley's efforts to kill Chaplin but by his own efforts not to be killed himself. However, Spilsbury suggested that the blows on Casserley's head had been struck from *behind,* and that the bullet that sliced through the back of his neck must have been fired from a distance of *more* than 12 inches, as there were no powder marks on the neck. Neither man was left-handed. But Chaplin said he struck the other man with the torch in his left hand, and that the gun was in Casserley's left hand each time it was fired.

Another problem was that Casserley, who was fifty-eight and ill, was unlikely to have put up much of a fight against a fit thirty-six-year-old with large, strong hands (Chaplin was asked to hold them up in court), even if he was fighting for his life. The prosecution also pointed out that Chaplin was unmarked in the struggle and that he had made no attempt to get help for the injured man. There was, after all, a telephone in the house. When Mr McClure asked Chaplin: 'Why didn't you hit him in the face with that large hand of yours?' Chaplin answered: 'I had no intention of harming Mr Casserley.'

Mr McClure, in his closing speech, again drew attention to the blood that had been washed off the life preserver – how did it get there? There were other questions too. Why was a diamond ring worn by Casserley found hidden in a basket in Chaplin's flat? How could he have been in a panic if he troubled to remove the ring? Why did the accused never mention that Mr Casserley cocked the gun before the first shot was fired? Did this mean the gun in the bureau drawer had already been cocked? Why did Chaplin, with his superior strength, need a weapon with which to strike the older man? Would not Casserley, having been struck three times, be dazed at least and even less capable of resistance? Why, after disarming Casserley once when the gun was in his right hand, was it so difficult to disarm him when he held the gun in his left hand? Were the jury to believe that a man like Chaplin would take his eyes off the gun for a moment, and allow Casserley to get both hands on it? 'Chaplin was holding the hand that was holding the pistol,' said Mr McClure. 'Whose was the force that was pressing that pistol against the skin? The man was flat on his back.' His suggestion was that Chaplin's story was made up later to fit the facts.

One point in the accused's favour was that the little gun, a .25 Webley and Scott automatic, had a defective mechanism. The firearms expert Robert Churchill concluded that the weapon would be more effective in the hands of the man accustomed to handling it – its owner. When the gun misfired, therefore, Casserley would have been more knowledgeable and quicker at clearing the jammed cartridge. On the other hand, the pistol had not been oiled, which seemed to indicate that Casserley knew or cared little about the maintenance of such weapons.

The judge reminded the jury that if they decided that Mr Casserley had been shot 'in the heat of passion in the course of a quarrel so serious that the accused lost complete control of himself', they might convict the accused not of murder, but of manslaughter.

This they did, and on Friday, 27 May 1938, Ted Chaplin was found guilty of manslaughter and sentenced to twelve years' penal servitude.

Mrs Casserley – who was six months pregnant at the time – was waiting outside the courtroom and fainted when she heard the verdict. Twenty minutes later, supported by policewomen she was brought into the court to be dealt with as an accessory after the fact. She wept without pause.

Her counsel, Mr Hutchinson, began his plea by saying that for years she had been an excellent wife. The judge, Mr Justice Humphreys, interposed: 'You are not putting her forward as an excellent wife now?' Later, Mr Hutchinson said: 'Also, I would ask you to take into account her condition at the moment.' 'We know she is pregnant,' snapped the judge. 'As hundreds of other women are pregnant. But there's nothing the matter with her, no disease or anything like that?' 'No,' replied Mr Hutchinson. 'But the nervous strain …' 'She can pull herself together if she wants to,' remarked the judge.

As with Mrs Thompson and Mrs Rattenbury, the judge's censure of the dead man's widow was severe. He said: 'The less said about you and your part in this case the better. I am not going to treat you with lenience because I think there is nothing particular in your condition that calls for it. Your case has aroused the most ridiculous nonsense. A great many people have treated you as though you were a sort of heroine. You were a participator in a vulgar and sordid intrigue.' He ended: 'Now please go!' Mrs Casserley was given a nominal sentence of eleven days in prison and immediately released.

Ted Chaplin served eight years of his sentence. When he was freed from prison on the Isle of Wight after the Second World War had ended, Ena Casserley was waiting at the gates. He put on a new suit and they went to a register office. On 17 May 1946, they became man and wife.

WILLIAM BUTLER

THE MURDER OF ERNEST KEY, 1938

The body of Ernest Percival Key, a sixty-four-year-old jeweller, was found in his lock-up shop at 74 Victoria Road, Surbiton, just before noon on Saturday, 24 December 1938, by his son, Jack Key, and his daughter, Mrs Arthur Bell. Covered in blood and unconscious, the old man was still alive despite one of the most savage knife attacks on record. He had been stabbed about thirty-one times in his head, face and neck, and there were well over a dozen cuts on his arms, which had been made as he tried to defend himself. He died on the way to hospital.

Mr Key, a Yorkshireman from Hull, was well known locally, having been in business as a jeweller in Surbiton for over twenty years. He had been murdered during the course of a robbery – some jewellery was missing from the shop. A bowler hat, however, had been left behind by the assailant, and Dr Eric Gardner, the County Pathologist for Surrey, was able to use the size of the hat and hairs found within it to give the police investigating the murder some hints about its owner before Sir Bernard Spilsbury arrived on the scene.

The owner of the hat turned out to be an unemployed driver called William Thomas Butler, aged about twenty-nine. He was married with two children and lived in Laurel Road, Hampton Hill, Teddington, about 3 miles north-east from the jeweller's shop, beyond Hampton Court Palace and the park. He had previous convictions for housebreaking.

Less than an hour after the knife attack on Mr Key. Butler took a taxi from Kingston railway station to the Kingston county hospital. Blood was issuing from his gloves. He was seen by Dr Day, who also examined Ernest Key. Butler gave his name as Charles Jackson, of Norbiton, and said he had been accidentally injured by a wood-cutting machine. He later told the police that his hands had been cut when he was knocked down by a motorcycle combination and that he gave a false name and address at the hospital because he could not afford the fees. The cuts had in fact been caused by a dagger or knife without a guard, which he had used to stab Mr Key.

Butler was charged with the murder of Mr Key on 17 January 1939, and was put on trial at the Old Bailey a month later, on Wednesday, 15 February. The judge was Mr

Justice Singleton, and the prosecutor Mr GB McClure. Butler was defended by Mr David Maxwell Fyfe, KC, MP – later to become Solicitor-General, and in 1951 Home Secretary. He claimed that Butler had acted in self-defence, and that the charge should be reduced to manslaughter.

The trial ended on its second day. Butler was found guilty and sentenced to death. An appeal was lodged on 23 February and dismissed. He was hanged by Tom Pierrepoint and Tom Phillips at Wandsworth Prison on 29 March 1939.

UDHAM SINGH

THE MURDER OF SIR MICHAEL O'DWYER, 1940

On Wednesday, 13 March 1940, there was a joint meeting at Caxton Hall of the East India Association and the Royal Central Asian Society. Held in the Tudor Room, it was attended by about 160 people who had assembled to hear a lecture – 'Afghanistan: the Present Position' – given by Brigadier-General Sir Percy Sykes. The Secretary of State for India, Lord Zetland, was in the chair and several distinguished elderly gentlemen sat beside him on the platform, including Sir Michael Francis O'Dwyer, who had been Lieutenant-Governor of the Punjab in 1919 at the time that the Amritsar riots were brutally suppressed by General Dyer. Sir Michael, now seventy-five, had succeeded Sir Louis Dane, who was now nearly eighty-four. Also seated on the platform were Lord Lamington, aged seventy-nine, former Governor of Bombay and President of the East India Association, and Sir Frank Brown, the Association's honorary secretary.

After the lecture, which lasted for about forty-five minutes and concluded at about four o'clock, Sir Michael O'Dwyer made what *The Times* called 'A witty speech, which was warmly received. The substantial unanimity of the Moslem world in support of the Allied cause in the war was emphasised. After Mrs Malan (formerly Miss Audrey Harris) and Sir Louis Dane had spoken, a vote of thanks was moved by Lord Lamington.' It was now about half-past four.

When the applause had died away the officials on the platform stood up and moved to congratulate each other on the success of the meeting. As they did so, a burly Sikh walked down a gangway to the front of the hall and at very close range fired all six rounds of a .45 Smith and Wesson revolver into the group on the platform. Sir Michael O'Dwyer, who had been sitting at the end of the front row, was shot twice in the back, one bullet passing through his heart and right lung, the other through a kidney. A bullet broke Sir Louis Dane's arm. Lord Lamington's right wrist was injured. Lord Zetland had a miraculous escape: he was hit by two bullets in the chest, but their impact was minimised by the use of .44 cartridges, ammunition which was thirty years old and by his clothes. 'I felt a sharp pain in my ribs,' he said later. 'It rather knocked me out, and while I was lying down I heard some other shooting going on, but did not see what happened.'

The Sikh was overpowered by two members of the audience (one in RAF uniform) as he ran for the exit, shouting 'Make way!' and waving the gun. Found also to be carrying a knife, he was charged at Bow Street police station on 14 March with the murder of Sir Michael O'Dwyer, whose death was described by Mr Clement Attlee in the House of Commons as an 'abominable outrage'. In India it was also officially deplored and condemned and Mr Gandhi said it was 'an act of insanity'.

The assassin was Singh Azad, a thirty-seven-year-old engineer who lodged in Mornington Crescent. He was also known as Udham Singh. A note of Sir Michael's name was found twice in Singh's diaries for 1939 and 1940, once spelt 'O'Dyer'. It seems that Singh may have confused O'Dwyer with General Dyer.

In custody Singh, who was excitable and spoke English badly, made several disjointed statements: 'I did it because I had a grudge against him. He deserved it. I don't belong to any society or anything else. I don't care. I don't mind dying. What is the use of waiting until you get old? That is no good … Is Zetland dead? He ought to be. I put two into him. I bought the revolver from a soldier in a public house. My parents died when I was three or four … Only one dead, eh? I thought I could get more.'

In prison, awaiting trial, Singh went on a forty-two-day hunger strike.

His trial began at the Old Bailey on 4 June 1940. The judge at the trial was Mr Justice Atkinson. Mr GB McClure led for the Crown and Mr St John Hutchinson for the defence. Singh said in his defence that the shooting was an accident. He had intended, he said, to fire at the ceiling in protest at the difficulty of getting a passport and at the treatment of Indians by the British government in India.

Sir Bernard Spilsbury gave evidence. Looking far from well, having had a slight stroke a few weeks earlier, he spoke from the well of the court and was not cross-examined. On 5 June, the jury retired for ninety-five minutes before deciding Singh was guilty. He made a speech that the judge directed should not be reported in the press.

An appeal heard on 15 July was dismissed and on 31 July 1940 Udham Singh was hanged in Pentonville Prison. On this occasion, Stanley Cross was the chief executioner. Albert Pierrepoint was his assistant. It was Cross's first job as the chief executioner and he miscalculated the drop, which was corrected by Albert Pierrepoint. Cross carried out four more executions but was removed from the list of executioners after that.

Albert Pierrepoint, who was born in 1905 at Clayton in Yorkshire, had become an assistant executioner in December 1932. But he was not given his first job as the 'Number One' executioner until October 1941. He remarried in August 1943. He and his uncle, Tom, worked together on many executions, and although Uncle Tom was employed as a hangman for forty years, retiring in 1946 when he was seventy-five, having hanged 294 people, it was 'Our Albert' who was able to say on his retirement: 'I have carried out the execution of more judicial sentences of death (outside the field of politics) than any executioner in any British record or archive.'

To this end, on behalf of the Allies, he executed 200 people convicted of war crimes at

Zuchthaus, Hameln in Westphalia, Germany, sometimes thirteen or fifteen in one day. Spies, saboteurs, traitors, deserters, German prisoners-of-war and some American soldiers were also among those he hanged. These executions continued after the Second World War until December 1949. Altogether, Albert Pierrepoint hanged 435 men and women in his twenty-three years as a hangman.

HAROLD TREVOR

THE MURDER OF MRS GREENHILL, 1941

Few murderers have exhibited quite as many of the characteristics of an archetype as HD Trevor, whose self-interest, self-pity, self-deception, self-dramatisation, stupidity, conceit, mendacity, charm and indolence were unbounded and apparently unending. Nonetheless, of minor criminals he seemed the least likely to end up as a hanged man. In doing so, he provided the police with one of their swiftest solutions of a crime – one made at the scene of the crime itself.

Mrs Theodora Jessie Greenhill was the sixty-five-year-old widow of Major Greenhill and lived in a block of flats in Elsham Road, West Kensington. In the autumn of 1941, anxious to move out of bombed and blacked-out London, she decided to let her flat, furnished, and advertised this fact through a local estate agent.

On Tuesday, 14 October, she was visited by a tall, slim, elderly gentleman, wearing a monocle and with thinning grey hair, who expressed a keen interest in renting the flat. Indeed, he was so pleased by it that he agreed to take it then and there. The few pounds she had requested as a down payment were forthwith produced – an advance or first instalment of the rent. No doubt much gratified by this speedy and satisfactory development, Mrs Greenhill seated herself at her bureau in the drawing room and began writing out a receipt for the money in her large bold hand – 'Received from Dr HD Trevor the sum of s—'

The pen jerked in her hand, making a jagged line down the note paper, as the monocled gentleman struck her on the head with a beer bottle, using such force that it shattered. Pieces fell on to the floor and into a wastepaper basket. Mrs Greenhill collapsed unconscious on to the carpet, where the phoney doctor got down on his knees and strangled her with a ligature. This done, he ransacked the flat, rifling through the drawers of the bureau and emptying a cash box that he found in the bedroom; he prized it open with a nail file. Having retrieved the rent advance, he left the flat. But before doing so he laid a handkerchief decorously over the dead woman's face. Thus she was discovered by a daughter of her first marriage, Miss Tattersall, who, on receiving no reply from her ringing of the doorbell, let herself into her mother's flat.

DCS Fred Cherrill, called to the scene from Scotland Yard to assist the investigation begun by DCI Salisbury, examined the various fingerprints that had been found – four on fragments of the beer bottle, two on a small table near the body, and one on the cash box.

Something seemed familiar to Cherrill about the name on the incomplete receipt – 'Trevor'. Yet surely no one would be so stupid as to leave his actual *name* on the murdered woman's desk, in her own hand? The name must be fictitious. Nonetheless, Cherrill contacted the Criminal Record Office at the Yard and asked for all the files bearing that name to be brought to him. When they arrived he began, with the aid of a magnifying glass, to compare the records of fingerprints in the files with the suspect prints in the flat. Before long he was able to tell the astonished Salisbury that the murderer was Harold Dorian Trevor.

A warrant was issued for Trevor's arrest and he was traced to Birmingham, where he had pawned and sold a cabin trunk and other articles that he had removed from Mrs Greenhill's flat by taxi to King's Cross station. There he had pawned two of her rings.

He was picked up on Saturday, 18 October, as he stepped out of a telephone box in Rhyl, north Wales. After being cautioned by DCI Salisbury, Trevor said: 'It wasn't murder. There was never any intent to murder. I have never used violence to anyone in my life before. What came over me I do not know. After I hit her my mind went completely blank and is still like that now. Something seemed to crack in my head.'

It was not surprising that the name 'Trevor' was familiar to DCS Cherrill – the sixty-two-year-old Yorkshireman had spent nearly all of his previous forty years in jail. In that time he had in fact known only eleven months of freedom, and had just been released from prison when he called on Mrs Greenhill, with robbery, it seems, in mind. He had never before, however, been involved in any kind of violence, the crimes for which he was so often incarcerated being those of petty theft and fraud. Posing as Commander Crichton, Sir Charles Warren, or Lord Herbert, he would ease money from any susceptible source, preferably female. His apparent aim was to avoid work and to live in the style and comfort he affected in his impostures. His subconscious intention seems to have been to dramatise and magnify a vacuous existence by making himself the centre of attention in police investigations and in a court of law. He must also have unconsciously sought the organised security of life in prisons, where he was known and cared for.

The murder of Mrs Greenhill is so uncharacteristic and unnecessary, and his stupidity in virtually leaving his calling card, his name and fingerprints, so extraordinary, that he appears to have almost consciously sought the final satisfaction in his old age of being tried on a capital charge and making a spectacular and perfectly legal exit. Certainly he never lost the chance in all his court appearances to address the judge and jury, speaking the utmost humbug with dignity and courtesy, and with his honour apparently unsoiled.

Trevor was tried at the Old Bailey on 28 and 29 January 1942. Mr Justice Asquith was the judge; Mr LW Byrne appeared for the Crown and Mr John Flowers, KC, and Mr Derek Curtis Bennett for the defence, which tried to prove that the accused was insane.

Harold Trevor's greatest moment came when he was asked if he had anything to say before sentence of death was passed. He declared:

I would like once and for all, finally to say this ...that I, as a man who stands, so to speak, at death's door, would like to confirm all I have already said regarding this lady's death, that I have no knowledge of it. Even as I am speaking the moving finger is writing on the wall, and the words, once written, can never be recalled. I sincerely hope that each of you, gentlemen of the jury, and the judge too, in passing sentence, will remember these words — that when each of you, as you surely must some day, yourself stand before a higher tribunal, you will receive a greater measure of mercy than has been meted out to me in this world ... If I am called upon to take my stand in the cold grey dawn of the early morning, I pray that God in his mercy will gently turn my mother's face away as I pass into the shadows. No fear touches my heart. My heart is dead. It died when my mother left me.

There was much more. And if this were not enough, in the death cell he penned a long farewell in which he wrote: 'I have lived my life not as I would have liked to live it – but as it was forced upon me by fate. I was educated at a first-class school in Birmingham, and was the friend and playmate of men who are Bishops today. Some of them are sitting in the Episcopal Chairs, while I am waiting the short walk from the condemned cell to the scaffold.'

He was hanged on 11 March 1942 in Wandsworth Prison by Albert Pierrepoint and Herbert Morris. In the condemned cell he became much distressed and couldn't eat. He went to his death in a state of terror, shuffling along the short distance to the drop.

34

GORDON CUMMINS

The Murder of Evelyn Oatley, 1942

The fantasies of many murderers are seldom as fantastic as the stories about them perpetrated by some newspapers in the guise of news and truth. Facts are misrepresented, elaborated and dressed up in a feverish style that is supposed to attract the public and sell papers – or in the case of television to fill the space, as it sometimes seem, between the advertisements. Nothing unlocks the crime-writer's cupboard of clichés more than the sexual murder of a woman or a child, when the murderer is presented as a monster or beast and the victim as pretty, if not attractive, and as innocence personified. In many cases, the victims have been far from pretty and have often been much more sophisticated than the reports suggest. No man is a monster, however monstrous his acts, and it is an unfortunate fact that many sex murderers have been good-looking, good company and good fun.

Such a one was Gordon Frederick Cummins, aged twenty-eight, who went on a sudden, barbarous murder binge in wartime London in 1942. He killed four women in six days, horribly mutilating three of them. He picked up his victims in West End pubs and clubs, older women, some of them prostitutes, who were on the look-out for pleasant young servicemen to give them a good time.

Nice-looking, agreeable Gordon Cummins was a most unlikely Ripper. But so was the Yorkshire Ripper, lorry driver Peter Sutcliffe, who at the age of thirty-four was sentenced to life imprisonment on 22 May 1981 for the murder of thirteen women over a period of six years. Another pleasant and plausible lady-killer was Neville Heath, a twenty-nine-year-old ex-air-force officer, who was active four years after Cummins. The two are, in fact, quite similar in many ways. But because Cummins's atrocities were committed in wartime, they never received the press attention that made the other two men notorious. Nonetheless, the attacks on Cummins's four known victims are almost unparalleled in their perverted savagery. They are also the most inexplicable. Little has been written about him. The few known facts are these.

Gordon Cummins was a well-educated boy, of good family and of more than average height (5 ft 7 in), but unreliable, dishonest and unable to hold down a steady job. His father was the superintendent of an approved school. Cummins was born in New Earswick, to the north of York. He was educated at Llandoveris County School, and when his family moved to Northampton he attended the technical school there before going to work in London in a laboratory. He married a theatre producer's secretary in 1936; they had no children. Called up in 1941, two years after the outbreak of war, he joined the RAF, became an air cadet, trained for the air-crew, and was billeted in the New Year in north London. His air force colleagues remarked on his phoney Oxford accent and pretensions and called him 'The Duke'.

On Saturday, 8 February 1942, he left an RAF establishment in a requisitioned block of flats in St John's Wood, visited his wife, borrowed some money and then went into the West End for a night on the town. Early on Sunday, the body of forty-year-old chemist's assistant Miss Evelyn Margaret Hamilton was discovered by an electrician in a brick-built air-raid shelter in Montagu Place, W1, just north of Marble Arch. She had been in London on her way from Hornchurch in Essex, where she worked, to her home in Newcastle-upon-Tyne. Her clothes were disarranged and her scarf had been wound around her head. But Cummins's motive for murder, apart from an unexplained lust to kill, seems to have been theft: her handbag had vanished and with it £80. Although she had been strangled, there was no sign of sexual assault.

This was only a prelude.

That night, a thirty-five-year-old former actress and Windmill showgirl (now a prostitute), Mrs Evelyn Oatley, also known as Nita Ward, encountered Cummins and took him home to her Wardour Street flat. Here she was strangled. Her nearly naked and crudely mutilated body was found on her bed on Monday, 10 February. After she was strangled, her throat had been cut, and the lower part of her body cut open with a tin-opener or a knife. Nearby was a pair of curling tongs.

A few days later, on Thursday, 13 February, another prostitute, Mrs Margaret Florence Lowe, aged forty-three and known as Pearl, was murdered in her tiny flat in Gosfield Street, W1, parallel to Great Portland Street. She was strangled on her divan bed with a silk stocking and then cut and disfigured. By the body were the knife and razor used on her. There was also a candle. In the kitchen was a half-empty bottle of stout. While DCI Greeno, Sir Bernard Spilsbury and DI Higgins were still at the scene of the Lowe murder, they received news of yet a fourth.

This time the victim was Mrs Doris Jouannet, aged thirty-two. The wife of an elderly hotel manager, she was also known as Doris Robson. Strangled with a scarf, and with her naked body obscenely mutilated, she lay in the two-roomed ground-floor flat she shared with her husband in Sussex Gardens, north-west of Marble Arch. A fountain pen and a comb had been taken from the flat. As with Miss Hamilton, her home town was Newcastle-upon-Tyne. DCI Greeno, who with DCS Cherrill was investigating the murders, realised after the discovery of the bodies of Mrs Lowe and Mrs Jouannet that a new Ripper was at large. Even the case-hardened Bernard Spilsbury was moved to say, on viewing Mrs Lowe's injuries, that they were 'quite dreadful' and that their perpetrator was a savage sexual maniac.

On Friday, 14 February, Cummins, now insatiable but careless, chatted up Mrs Greta

Heywood in Piccadilly. They went for a drink and a sandwich in the Trocadero and then walked down Haymarket. She said later that he became unpleasantly forward, so she said goodbye and tried to leave him. 'You must let me kiss you goodnight,' he said, trying to do so. Having no wish to be his Valentine, she hurried away in the blackout. He chased after her, she claimed, catching up with her in St Alban's Street. In a dark doorway he seized her by the throat and began to choke her. She struggled in vain and passed out. But her life was saved by a delivery boy who happened to be taking some drink to a bottle-party in the nearby Captain's Cabin. He heard some scuffling, saw a flash of silk stocking as Mrs Heywood's legs gave way and went to investigate. Cummins ran off, leaving behind an RAF gas mask that bore his name, rank and number (525987).

A few hours later, still bent on a fifth kill, he acquired another companion, a young prostitute called Mrs Mulcahy, in Regent Street and returned with her in a taxi to her Paddington flat in Southwick Street. On the way there he gave her five £1 notes. It had been snowing and was very cold. Mrs Mulcahy lit the gas fire, and as her room was icy she kept her boots on while she removed her clothes. Cummins had hardly removed his great coat and belt when a 'strange expression', as she later described it, came over his face. He gripped her neck and squeezed. Mrs Mulcahy kicked him hard on the shins, making him cry out. As if recovering his senses he shook his head, put on his coat, and left, but not before giving her another £5 in notes. Perhaps he panicked, fearful of the noise he himself had made and of being caught in the act again. This time he stupidly left behind his belt.

This, along with the gas mask and the £1 notes, enabled DCI Greeno to trace Cummins to his St John's Wood billet, where Greeno at once came up against an apparently perfect alibi – Cummins's name in the billet pass book showed that he had reported back to the billet and been signed in before midnight all that week, and must accordingly have been in bed when Evelyn Oatley Mrs Lowe and Mrs Jouannet had been murdered. He, of course, when interviewed, denied having had anything to do with the killings. It was not until Greeno ascertained that the airmen in the billet often vouched for each other's return, and that on the nights in question Cummins, leaving the building by way of a fire escape, had gone out with another airman *after* being checked in, that the alibis were proved false.

There was enough other evidence to clinch the case against Cummins, though. A white metal cigarette case belonging to Mrs Lowe was found in a pocket of his tunic; items belonging to Miss Hamilton were found in a dustbin outside the billet. The fountain pen belonging to Mrs Jouannet, and marked 'DJ', was found in his number-one uniform, and a cigarette case belonging to Mrs Oatley was discovered in a refrigerator in the billet. In her flat a print from a left thumb on a mirror and a print of a left little finger on the tin opener were identified as his. In Mrs Lowe's flat, fingerprints from a left hand were detected on the bottle of stout and a candlestick. Cummins was left-handed. He was arrested on Sunday, 16 February.

Above left: Gordon Cummins, who went on a barbaric murder binge in wartime London.

Above right: How the *Daily Express* covered the Cummins murders.

Below: The gun used by Jack Tratsart, who killed his brother and sister in a Lyons Corner House in London. He then tried to take his own life, but failed.

The Evening News

WORLD'S LARGEST EVENING NET SALE

NO. 20,923   LONDON, THURSDAY, MARCH 3, 1949   ONE PENNY

LATE EXTRA

STORY OF THE VAMPIRE KILLER

Lured Victims One by One, Then Sold Up Their Property, Believe Yard

Outside No. 79 Gloucester-road a big crowd waited as the search went on in the basement.

Then thre saw men emerge with picks and shovels, and then came police officers carrying paper parcels and canisters.

In the picture below Div. Det.-Inspector Jennings is seen leading the way

THE DUCHESS BUYS A TOY

The Duchess of Kent remembered her own children when she visited the "Daily Mail" Ideal Home Exhibition at Olympia to-day.

In the Children's section she bought a set of "The Walkie Wonders"—a quaint set of three animals with springy legs—and asked for it to be sent to her home.

Earlier she had seen the gardens, admired fine Irish linen in the Pavilion of Beautiful Things and made friends with toddlers in the playland.

Court Told of Whisky, Fur Coat, Radio and Refrigerator

B.O.T. Man Is Accused of Accepting Gifts

'CARS FROM U.S.' CHARGE

"Evening News" Reporter

A BOARD of Trade official appeared at Bow-street this afternoon to answer four summonses which alleged that he accepted rewards in relation to his principal's affairs. He is Edmund Hadfield, of The Chalet, Salcombe-road, Ashford, Middlesex.

The prosecution said that the alleged gifts were a radio set from Sir Geoffrey Duveen, a refrigerator from Sidney Winton, two bottles of whisky, two bottles of sherry and 20 yards of carpet from Philip Hyams and a fur coat from John Shackman.

It was stated that the four charges were under Section 1 of the Prevention of Corruption Act 1906.

The first case was concerned almost entirely with the importation of motor-cars from the U.S.

Mr. R. E. Seaton, prosecuting, said the importation of cars from the U.S. was at one time prohibited unless the car was a free, unsolicited gift and was granted a licence by the Board of Trade.

The Board's Licensing Department was in Greek-street, Soho, and Hadfield was a Higher Clerical Officer there.

His Duty

It was part of his duty to deal with the issue of licences for importing cars.

Sometimes he interviewed people, examined documents and the application form, and then passed them up to a senior officer.

Generally speaking, in a great many cases he acted entirely on his own in granting licences, said Mr. Seaton.

Letters purporting to come from friends or other strangers, wanting U.S. permits to import cars.

MORE FINDS IN LONDON CELLAR

Canisters Taken Away: Police Dig 3 Hours

By SAM JACKETT

SCOTLAND YARD detectives investigating the disappearance of five London people today gathered fresh evidence to support their view that each was the victim of a modern Dracula-like murderer.

They believe that the murderer of Mr. and Mrs. W. D. McSwan and their son and Dr. and Mrs. Archibald Henderson either shot them or bludgeoned them to death. He appears to be the most sadistic criminal in the history of the Yard.

Inquiries are by no means complete in these "Vampire" murders, but day by day the Yard men are unfolding a story of cold-blooded murders.

The Yard are convinced that all the murders were committed for money, and that the murderer gained probably between £12,000 and £10,000 from the McSwans and Hendersons.

This is their story as the Yard have it to date:

The McSwans were an elderly couple and they lived quietly with their son in various parts of London, their last known address being

... man, of some means and that the wife owned some thousands of pounds' worth of jewellery, the "Vampire" decided to murder them.

Again he laid his plans with precision and the fact that he was doing so the doctor sold his property in Notting Hill and moved to another property in Dawes-road, Fulham, which he bought, did not delay him.

This time he drove up the plan

CROWDS SEE POLICE AT No. 79

NEIGHBOURS TELL OF McSWANS' LIFE THERE

"Evening News" Reporters

RENEWING their search of the basement of 79, Gloucester-road, Kensington, today, police dug and sifted for 3 hours 20 minutes. All the time, Dr. Holden, the director of the Yard's forensic laboratories, was with them, carrying out on-the-spot chemical tests of the fragments the men dug up.

Then the detectives left, carrying picks, shovels and a wire sieve. They were wearing hobnail boots, and their trousers, tied around the tops of the boots were covered in dust and dirt.

Next, out came Div. Det. Insp. Jennings and another Yard officer, each carrying two canisters. They left at once for the science laboratory.

Among articles taken away by police for examination were, it is believed, small pieces of bone dug from a hole in the back room of the basement. The police also made a thorough inspection of the drainage system.

Crowd Rush

As the group crossed the pavement other policemen had to exert themselves to prevent a rush of spectators across the pavement. When the doors of the police car were closed, traffic was held up, and the crowd dispersed as the car sped away.

More than 200 people, later swelled to a considerable number, had waited from the time they saw ... in broad daylight.

ALEXANDER ON WESTERN DEFENCE

HE CALLS FOR POLICY OF COLLECTIVE SECURITY

MR. A. V. ALEXANDER, Defence Minister, moving a resolution approving the Government's statement on defence, as with regard to our own defence services the main development have been the measures of equipment involving new problems put in hand since September.

"It is abundantly clear that we have to go on the basis of collective security under the U.N Charter.

"It has always been our belief that we have to act collectively because it is quite impossible to show in our world as it is now that you can plan to secure defence of our country alone by their own resources."

He reported considerable progress in the West First Defence, ...

Above: A news story about John Haigh, who murdered widow Olive Durand-Deacon, amongst others.
© John Frost Collection

Below: Neville Heath, who was hanged for murder in 1946.   *© Getty Images*

FROM ALL GOOD OUTFITTERS

SUNSPEL
shirts — pyjamas

39,950

Evening Standard

TUESDAY, NOVEMBER 22, 1949 ● ONE PENNY

MRS. GOODMAN'S BROTHER-IN-LAW KNEW NOTHING OF £2518 SAFE

Raven is charged with murder of father-in-law

'Anonymous note' told Savoy about drinks sales

Evening Standard Reporter

An anonymous letter to the Savoy Hotel caused Mr. Arthur Collard, the assistant general manager to ask the security department to keep a closer watch on the sale of spirits, it was said in the High Court this afternoon.

He also said that after complaints he gave instructions that short measures were not to be served.

Other witnesses were questioned about allegations of "short measure" drinks and charges in the hotel bars.

They were giving evidence in the case brought by Mr Matthew Dent Bertram, 44, of St. James Road, Surbiton, Surrey, ex-policeman in London and a former head barman at the hotel. Claiming damages from Mr Collard, Mr. Stanley, a detective at the hotel and the hotel proprietors, he alleges slander, assault and battery, false

LATEST CENTRAL
(See also Back Page)

5000 ON STRIKE

ATHENS, Tuesday — Five thousand workers started a 24-hour strike to-day, but public services in the Greek capital were not interrupted. The strikes were extending to the Greek provinces.

imprisonment and wrongful dismissal.

The defendants deny the allegations, plead privilege and maintain that any dismissal was justified.

Suspicions

Mr. Roy Wilson, counsel for all defendants, asked Mr. Collard: "In December the hotel received an anonymous letter which made certain accusations. Did you think it right, bearing in mind your suspicions, to pay some regard to it?"

"I immediately conducted the security department to keep an even stronger watch if possible," Mr Collard replied.

Mr. Wilson said that the anonymous letter was addressed from the Council Houses, Twickenham on December 18, 1949. It said that it was written about one of the employees trying to sell spirits at £3 10s. and £4.

The writer said that he had been to the same "local" as he usually did when going home from Teddington. There he saw the same man who obtained the gin.

The letter was signed "I.P." Mr Wilson suggested that the Twickenham address was in

♦ Back Page, Col. Six

'CHARRED SUIT IS VITAL'

Evening Standard Reporter

Daniel Raven, 23, of Edgwarebury Lane, Edgware, pleaded not guilty to-day to murdering his 49-year-old father-in-law, Leopold Goodman, at Ashcombe Gardens, Edgware, on October 10.

A large crowd waited outside the Old Bailey hoping to catch a glimpse of 22-year-old Mrs Marie Raven.

But they were disappointed. She did not appear.

Those in the public gallery craned forward when the court usher called "Daniel Raven."

He stepped into the dock, accompanied by three police officers, wearing a brown overcoat tightly buttoned over a smart dark grey suit, his wavy auburn hair neatly brushed.

As each juror, all men, took the oath, he regarded them fixedly, his face pale with circles under his eyes.

He raised no objection to any

The chief points

Mr. Anthony Hawke, K.C., for the prosecution, told what took place at the home of Mr. and Mrs. Goodman on October 10 while Mrs Raven lay in a nursing home at Muswell Hill with her four-day-old son.

It was on this night, soon after 10 o'clock, that her parents were discovered in the dining-room of their home, only an hour after they, with her husband, had been to visit her.

Mr Anthony Hawke said that the chief points of the story revolved around the rare blood group A.B. to which both Leopold Goodman and his 47-year-old wife belonged, and to the prompt action of Detective-inspector J. Diller who, in the words of Mr. Hawke, "saved one of the most vital pieces of evidence."

This piece of evidence was the suit which, it is alleged, Daniel Raven wore when he paid his last visit to see his four-day-old son.

Detective - inspector Diller found it half destroyed in the boiler of Raven's house in the Edgwarebury Lane, about 500 yards from his parents-in-law's home.

Mr. Hawke told how Mr. Frederick Fraiman, 35, a brother-in-law of Mrs. Goodman and a partner in business with Mr. Goodman, arrived at Ashcombe Gardens with his 17-year-old daughter, June, at about 10 o'clock in the evening of October 10 to ask after Marie and the baby.

He got no answer

He described how Mr Fraiman, receiving no answer, climbed through a window of the house and discovered first the body of Mrs. Goodman in the dining-room door, and, in the dining-room itself, the body of her husband.

Mr. Fraiman at once telephoned doctor and police," Mr Hawke said.

"First to arrive was P-c Hill closely followed by the doctor and an ambulance.

"The doctor found Mrs. Goodman was already dead, but there was a flicker of life in Mr. Goodman. He gave an injection but Mr. Goodman died almost at once."

Mr. Hawke said that Dr

● Back Page, Col. Four

DANIEL RAVEN. A new picture, with his wife.

MR. GOODMAN
The dead man.

FIRE ENGINE WRECKS SHOP

Five hurt—and call was a hoax

Evening Standard Reporter

Five people were injured when a fire engine skidded into two shops in Rye Lane, Peckham, S.E., to-day.

The engine, a big one with a ladder on top, was on its way to a "fire" which turned out to be a hoax.

It crashed between two shops, a grocer's and a wool shop. The engine smashed the street window of the grocer's. The ladder went right through the top windows of the wool shop.

Breakdown lorry sent

The driver of the fire engine was among those hurt. The others were people in the street. A breakdown lorry had to be sent for to get the engine away.

J. H. Thomas £15,032

Evening Standard Reporter

Mr. "Jimmy" Thomas, once an engine-driver and a former Cabinet Minister, left £15,032 when he died last January.

The residue he left on trust to pay £500 for the benefit of his wife "in such manner as she shall direct."

MAHARAJAH IS RECALLED

'Return to India'

NEW DELHI, Tuesday. — The Maharajah of Baroda, who is at present staying in England with his second wife, Sita Devi, has been summoned to return to India.

The announcement of the summons was made to-day by the Ministry of States of the Government of India.—Exchange.

U.S.—LONDON— 8hrs. 55 mins.

Two records in two days

The stratocruiser Flying Cloud arrived at London Airport to-day having flown non-stop from New York in eight hours 55 minutes—a new record.

Average speed was 420 mph Only yesterday another Pan-American stratocruiser knocked 13 minutes off the previous record.

U.S. asks our help

'Plead with Communists'

America has asked the British Foreign Office and 29 other nations—including Russia—to intervene with the Chinese Communists on behalf of Mr. Angus Ward, U.S. Consul-General in Mukden, who is being held by them. The Foreign Office said to-day they are "studying" the request.

The Communists say Mr Ward and his staff were arrested for beating a Chinese employee, but these charges have been described in Washington as "trumped up."

Sid Field ill?

'Exaggeration,' he says

Sid Field, who was taken ill on Sunday on board the liner Durban Castle until the following day from Port Elizabeth last night to a friend in London "Gross exaggeration. Nothing to worry about. Inform Press. Love, Sid."

Children's airliner is found—'Some alive'

OSLO, Tuesday. The Dutch airliner with 28 Jewish children aboard was found wrecked this afternoon on the bank of a fjord 30 miles from here.

Nine people were inside. Some of them were thought to be alive. Rescue teams are on the way. The airplane had cut a 40-yards-wide path among trees as it fell, and was badly damaged but had apparently not caught fire.

Some report said several bodies were lying near it. About 1500 people have been

JET AIRPLANE HITS TANK: PILOT KILLED

The pilot of a twin-engined Meteor jet fighter was killed instantly when his aircraft crashed during an attack on a column of tanks in a large-scale army exercise in the Stanford Battle Area, near East Wretham (Norfolk) to-day.

According to troops, the airplane touched the ground as it flew in low to the attack, struck the rear tank of the column and burst into flames.

The airplane crashed close to the column of tanks and gun which were moving forward in a mock attack.

One engine was thrown over the column, and across a road. The tank was only slightly damaged and no one in it was injured. The aircraft came from Horsham St. Faith (Norfolk).

Night theft at canteen

Cash and cigarettes were stolen during the night from the staff canteen at Fenchurch Buildings, City of Messrs. Bowring and Co. of Leadenhall Street.

City police surrounded the premises but no one was found

'My 5 girl friends,' perfect secretary share man's will

A legacy of £50 to each of "my five girl friends," has been left by Mr. Leonard Newman, of High Street, Tring, Herts, in his £16,000 will, published to-day.

The five girls are: Elsie H Cope, of Folly Farm, Tring; Edith A. Littlefield, of Valley Farm, Radway, Warwick; Annie Welch, of Chiltern Villas, Tring; Mabel J. Pitkin, of West Leith Farm, Tring; and Adelaide M Gibson, of Cottage Farm, Northchurch, Berkhamsted.

He left them the money "as a recognition of my affection for them, and as a reciprocation of their many kindnesses to me."

Mr. Newman also left a further £1000 each, after his wife's death, to Mabel Pitkin and Adelaide Gibson.

To Miss Doris I Richards, of Ferndale Road, Clapham, S.W. he gave £100 "as a recognition of her great help to me whilst acting as my secretary—the most efficient anyone could possibly have."

Most of Mr. Newman's money goes to his wife and daughter.

Main Picture: The *Evening Standard* reported on Daniel Raven, who battered his parents-in-law to death.

© *John Frost Collection*

Inset: Daniel and Marie Raven on their wedding day.   © *Topfoto*

Above left: The kitchen at Rillington Place, where three bodies were found.

© The Metropolitan Police

Above right: John Reginald Christie, hanged in 1953.

© Mirrorpix

Below left: Ethel Christie, Reg Christie's wife and one of his victims.

©Mirrorpix

Below right: A *Daily Mirror* front page from the day Christie was charged with murder.

© Mirrorpix

Above left: Derek Bentley hanged for the murder of PC Miles in 1953. In 1998, his conviction was quashed by the Home Office.

© *PA Photos*

Above right: Guenther Podola's arrest in 1959 – he was said to be unfit to plead because he had lost his memory.

Below: The scene outside Wandsworth Prison on the day of Podola's execution.

© *The Metropolitan Police*

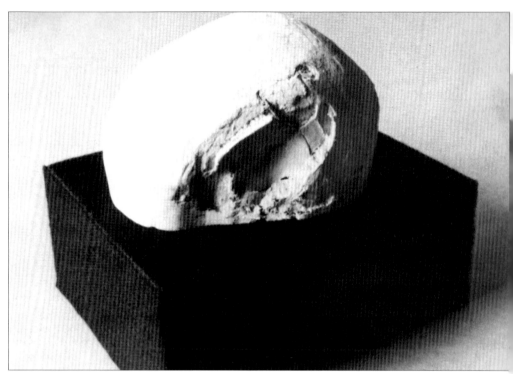

Above: The plaster cast of Colin Saunders' head. Saunders was killed by Stanley Wrenn, who made no attempt to conceal the crime or to evade capture.

© *The Metropolitan Police*

Below and right: Harry Roberts and the scene of the murders of the three policemen.

© *The Metropolitan Police*

Above: Reggie and Ronnie Kray, who ruled East London with an iron fist. © *Mirrorpix*

Below left: The Blind Beggar, where George Cornell was shot. © *Topfoto*

Below right: Jack 'The Hat' McVitie.

© *Getty Images*

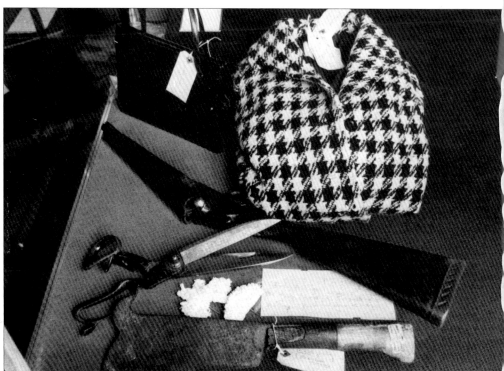

Above left: Arthur Hosein, who kidnapped Mrs McKay and demanded a £1 million ransom.

© Mirrorpix

Above right: Mrs Muriel McKay, the victim of the first-ever kidnap and ransom crime in Britain.

© The Metropolitan Police

Below: Evidence from the McKay murder, including a letter written during her imprisonment, her coat and her handbag; the paper flowers, sawn off shotgun and billhook found in the Hoseins' car.

© The Metropolitan Police

Two other murders, then unsolved, were later attributed to him: that of nineteen-year-old Miss Maple Church, whose body had been found the previous October in a bombed house in Hampstead Road, near Euston station, and that of a Mrs Humphries, whose body was discovered in Gloucester Crescent, north-east of Regent's Park.

Gordon Cummins was charged on 17 February 1942 with the murders of Mrs Oatley, Mrs Lowe, and Mrs Jouannet, and on 20 February with assaulting Mrs Heywood and Mrs Mulcahy. Finally, on 27 March, the murder of Miss Hamilton was added to the list.

While on remand in Brixton Prison, Cummins was escorted to and from prison by DI Robert Higgins, who with a detective sergeant from Tottenham Court Road police station had discovered the body of Mrs Lowe after forcing open the door of her flat with a jemmy. Higgins was also with Cummins in court, and in his memoirs had this to say of his charge:

> He chatted to me on everyday subjects as though he had not a care in the world. He seemed to be completely unaware of the seriousness of the charges against him … He had an irritating habit of wanting to shake hands each time we met … Observed at close quarters, he was not an obviously unpleasant person … He was inclined to be slow and steady in his speech. From the physical point of view he appeared quite normal, being well built and proportioned, and would not have attracted special notice if put among a group of ordinary people. I did, however, take particular note of his unusually large, strong hands, which had been well kept. He was deceptively gentle in manner and quite good-looking – a man not unattractive to women.

The trial of Gordon Cummins began at the Old Bailey on Monday, 27 April 1942 before Mr Justice Asquith, and he was indicted, as was usual, on just one count: the murder of Evelyn Oatley. The prosecutor was Mr GB McClure, KC. Cummins was defended by Mr John Flowers, KC. The evidence was conclusive and the trial was brief, ending the following day on 28 April. The jury took thirty-five minutes to find him guilty and he was sentenced to death.

Gordon Cummins was hanged by Albert Pierrepoint and Harry Kirk in Wandsworth Prison on 25 June, during an air-raid. His wife, who had stood by him throughout, visited him until the day of his execution, believing, it seems, that he was totally innocent, as he himself continued to claim. The post mortem on his body, as with many other executed murderers, was carried out by the pathologist who had examined the murderer's victims – in this case, Sir Bernard Spilsbury.

JONES AND HULTEN

The Murder of George Heath, 1944

No full-length study has been made of the relationship between murder and wartime, when official military murder is rife. Some connections undoubtedly exist, as is shown by the increase and the casual nature of wartime murders, when life seems cheap. Living is difficult, passions are raised and people are on the move. Many post-war murders also had their roots in wartime, when the imagination of boys fired by experiences of death and glory, by the guns their fathers wore and used, sought some equivalent peace-time realisation. Then there were also the demobilised servicemen, their reason and feelings marred and bent by slaughter. In fact, while the majority of all murderers have previous criminal records, another large proportion, related to the first, are servicemen or ex-servicemen.

In the autumn of 1944, the Allies were following up the D-day invasion on all fronts in Europe and in the Pacific. The liberation of Paris on 23 August had preceded the recapture of Antwerp and Brussels as well as the Allied advance through Belgium, Holland and France to the borders of Germany, forestalled for a time by the Arnhem disaster and the German counter-offensive in the Ardennes. British forces invaded Greece on 5 October. Meanwhile, V2 rockets had begun falling on the south-east of England and on London, as well as doodlebugs – the flying bombs.

In the late afternoon of Tuesday, 3 October 1944, an American GI met a striptease artiste in wartime London. He was Private Karl Gustav Hulten, aged twenty-two, dark-haired and Swedish in origin, and absent without leave for six weeks from his paratroop regiment. He was now passing himself off as a lieutenant and called himself Ricky (Richard Allen). She was Elizabeth Maud Jones, aged eighteen, fair-haired and blue-eyed. Her stage-name had been Georgina Grayson, and it was as 'Georgina' that Betty Jones was introduced to 'Ricky' in a little café in Queen Caroline Street, Hammersmith Broadway, by Len Bexley, a coach trimmer who happened to know them both.

Said Hulten: 'I saw Len Bexley sitting there with a young lady. I took another seat, but he asked me to come over and join them, which I did.' She said: 'I thought he was a gentleman.' 'We were there a while in the cafeteria,' said Hulten, 'and afterwards we all got up together and left together. Mrs Jones and I walked down towards the Broadway. I asked her if she would care to come out later on … She agreed and then she left us. I told Bexley: "I don't believe she will turn up."'

Hulten went off to see a girlfriend, Joyce Cook, whom he had only known for three days. They had met the previous Sunday by chance at the local Gaumont cinema. Betty Jones returned to her rented room in 311 King Street, Hammersmith.

Born in South Wales on 5 July 1926, she had married at the age of sixteen. Her husband was a Welsh soldier and ten years older. On their wedding day he struck her and she left him there and then. Two months later in January 1943 she came to London, obtaining employment as a barmaid, usherette, waitress and ultimately striptease dancer at the Panama and Blue Lagoon clubs. But from the spring of 1944 she was out of work, living on the separation allowance of £11 5s 6d a week provided by her husband, who was then serving abroad. He went missing in September, and the letter confirming that fact was delivered to her on 13 October – the day she was formally charged with murder.

On the night of Tuesday, 3 October, she turned up at the Broadway cinema at 11.30 pm as arranged, but Hulten failed to make an appearance. She was walking back to her room in King Street when a 2 1/2 ton ten-wheeled US army truck pulled up in front of her, driven by Hulten, now in a leather jerkin and khaki slacks. He hailed her and she climbed into the huge truck beside him. 'I told her I was a paratrooper,' he said, 'and she said that was a dangerous profession to be in. I told her it was … She said she would like to do something exciting, like becoming a "gun moll", like they do back in the States. At first I thought she was kidding … I then explained to her that we had a stolen truck. We drove on towards Reading.' He also told her that he had broken into a pub and had run around with a mob in Chicago. He showed her a stolen pistol.

At about 1 am, just outside Reading, they passed a girl on a bicycle. Hulten turned the truck around, drove past the girl again and stopped the truck. He got out, and as the girl cycled by he shoved her over. She scrambled away, and he seized her purse, which was hanging from the bicycle's handlebars. After throwing the purse up to Betty Jones, he got into the cab (it had a left-hand drive) and they drove back to London. Their haul was a few shillings and some clothing coupons, which he later sold for £1. 'During the night,' she said, 'he taught me to drive.' At about 5 am, he dropped her off in King Street, parked the truck in a car park and slept there.

He saw her again on the Wednesday night, but they didn't make another foray in the truck. Instead, they went to bed in her rented room. Hulten discovered she had a rash on her stomach. 'That put me cavy,' he said, and accordingly, although they slept together, they went only as far as 'the next thing to sexual intercourse'.

On Thursday, 5 October, he called on her about 5 pm. They went out for a meal and then to the Gaumont cinema in Hammersmith. On leaving the cinema at about 8.45 pm, they entered a café. 'Just as we got to the door,' she said, 'the sirens sounded.' After the air raid they went to the car park, got in the truck and drove towards Reading again, to a pub near Sonning which Hulten intended to rob. But either his nerve failed or something disturbed him, for he drove the truck back to London, to Marble Arch.

'When we got there,' Hulten recalled, 'she suggested that we rob a cab. She pointed one out to me and I followed it ... out to Cricklewood.' Having used the truck to force the taxi to stop, Hulten pulled a gun on the taxi driver and said: 'Let me have all your money.' However, the presence of a passenger in the back seat alarmed him and he fled. He and Mrs Jones drove slowly back through deserted, blacked-out London to Marble Arch. In Edgware Road, at Jones's suggestion, he offered a young girl pedestrian a lift to Paddington, where she hoped to catch a train to Bristol. Hulten offered to take her as far as Reading. He put her suitcase, which was tied with rope, into the back, and she sat in the cab between Jones and Hulten, thankful for the lift.

Said Hulten: 'When we were almost through Runnymede Park going towards Windsor, I stopped the truck off the road. I told the girls we had a flat tyre. We all got out ... I told Georgina to get the girl's back to me. She said: "All right." Georgina gave the girl a cigarette and lit one for herself ... I hit the girl over the head with an iron bar.' As she did not fall, he put an arm-lock around her neck, forced her to the ground and knelt on her back as Jones went through the helpless girl's pockets. She found about five shillings. 'By this time the girl had ceased struggling. I picked up her shoulders and Georgina picked up her feet. We carried her over and dumped her about three feet from the edge of a stream.' The girl survived.

The robbers returned to Georgina's bed in King Street and stayed there till 3 pm on Friday afternoon. When Hulten left King Street an hour or so later he went to see his other girlfriend, Joyce. They went out to the pictures, returned to her house in Fulham Palace Road, and he left about 11 pm.

Betty Jones had been expecting her American friend since six o'clock. She now had a very bad cold. Despite this and his broken promise she went out with him apparently without complaint or reservation when he whistled for her down in the windy street. They decided to rob a taxi. They were sheltering from the wind in a doorway opposite Cadby Hall in Hammersmith Road when a grey Ford V8 saloon slowly approached them as if seeking their custom. Betty Jones called out – 'Taxi!' – and the car stopped.

It was a private-hire car, driven by thirty-four-year-old George Heath. Earlier that night he had twice called for work at a Godfrey Davis garage in Eccleston Street, the last time at about 11.05 pm. But no work was forthcoming and he set off on his own to find some passing trade. His charge for taking his two young customers to the Chiswick roundabout marking the end of the Great West Road was an exorbitant ten shillings. Between them Jones and Hulten then had less than £2; she had 10s 3d. They expected to have more money soon.

The Ford set off with its two passengers sitting in the back, Hulten behind the driver. It was now about 2 am. Once past the Chiswick roundabout, Hulten, the loaded gun in his lap, told the driver: 'We'll get out here.' Heath brought the car to a halt at the kerb and leaned to his left over the back of the front seat to open the near-side door for the female passenger. Hulten fired – accidentally, he said later, claiming his jacket sleeve caught on something on the door and jerked his arm as he started to get up. Later, Betty Jones recalled:

> As Heath was leaning over I saw a flash and heard a bang. I was surprised there was not a loud bang because Ricky had told me it would make a big noise when it went off ... Heath moaned slightly and turned a little towards his front. Ricky said to him: 'Move over or I'll give you another dose of the same.' I saw that he still had the automatic in his hand. Heath seemed to understand what Ricky said, because he moved further over to the left-hand side of the front seat ... I heard him breathing very heavily and his head slumped on his chest.

Heath had been shot through the middle of his body. Hulten now occupied the driver's seat and drove speedily towards Staines. Said Jones: 'Ricky then told me to go through Heath's pockets. I leaned over and I heard his breath coming in short gasps. Ricky told me to look for his wallet in the breast pocket of his jacket. I felt in that pocket but did not find the wallet. I found it instead in the left-hand outside pocket of his overcoat.' She emptied the dying man's pockets, including his trouser pockets. She removed his wrist-watch. That and the pound notes, pennies, fountain pen, silver pencil and cigarette case she found were given to Hulten. Everything else was thrown out of a window: his cheque book, identity card, licence, petrol coupons, photos and letters. Paralysed by a bullet deflecting off his spine, Heath died of haemorrhage within fifteen minutes, drowning in his own blood.

His body was dumped in a ditch on the edge of Knowle Green near Staines. Jones found the bullet that had killed Heath – it had ricocheted off the front nearside door, striking the dashboard and dropping to the floor. It too was thrown from a window.

The couple drove back to London, parking the Ford in the old Gaumont cinema car park behind Hammersmith Broadway at about 4 am. They wiped it clean of fingerprints, ate in the Black and White café and then asked some cab drivers there to take them home. None of them would, so they walked. In Jones's room they examined all their trophies before going to bed about 5 am on Saturday, 7 October.

Three hours later, at about eight o'clock, an electrician's apprentice, John Jones, was walking along the Great Southwest Road that leads to Staines when he came across the wallet, identity card, driving licence and cheque book that had belonged to George Heath. The body was discovered soon after 9 am by an auxiliary fireman attached to the National Fire Service, Robert Balding. He had just finished a night duty at the Ship Garage, London Road, and was taking a short cut across Knowle Green on his way home.

Tyre marks on the grass verge helped to identify the car. Police enquiries about the murdered man traced his movements the previous night and a description of his car, registration RD 8955, was circulated to all police stations.

Meanwhile, Jones and Hulten got up at ten to eleven. He went out to a barber's shop at 16 Queen Caroline Street and sold Heath's wristwatch to a hairdresser, Morris Levene, for £5. The fountain pen and silver pencil were sold to Len Bexley for eight shillings. 'He said he was broke and wanted some money,' said Bexley, who then went to a pub with Hulten before returning with him to 311 King Street. On the way there, Hulten bought a small bunch of flowers for Georgina.

The three then took a taxi to the White City Stadium where they bet on the greyhound races. Jones looked very tired, according to Bexley, but the couple, he said, seemed very fond of each other. She won some money, and when she and Hulten returned to King Street she asked her landlady, Mrs Evans, to mind some money for her, £7 in all. 'I said to her,' said Mrs Evans later, 'if she had any money at any time, as the buzz-bombs are about, I put anything of mine in the oven, and let me put it in the oven for her ... and she did.' Later, Mrs Evans, like Bexley and Levene, said Hulten was 'a very decent chap'. The couple went out for a meal and then saw a film, *Christmas Holiday*, starring Deanna Durbin.

On Sunday, 8 October, Ricky Hulten spent the afternoon with Joyce and most of the night with Georgina, during which they drove about in the Ford V8, using it as a hired car, having further unknown adventures and returning to King Street – the car was parked behind an air-raid shelter – about 7.30 am. They slept until about 1.45 pm. When Hulten left King Street, he picked up the car, saw Joyce at the bakery where she worked, drove to his camp near Newbury in Berkshire, and called on Joyce about 6 pm, when he had promised to visit Betty Jones. He parked the car in Lurgan Avenue.

At about ten-past eight on the night of Monday, 9 October, PC William Walters observed the Ford and its number, RD 8955, when he was out on his beat. After telephoning Hammersmith police station from a police box, he was soon joined by Inspector Read and a sergeant, who arrived at the scene in a police car. All three waited, PC Walters at the rear of the Ford.

At about nine o'clock, Hulten emerged from Joyce's house and entered the stolen Ford. Walters dashed up, seized his hand, and said: 'Is this your car, sir?' Hulten was silent. Walters shouted – the police car put its lights on and the other policemen ran up. Hulten was dragged out and searched. In his left-hand hip pocket there was a Remington automatic, the safety catch cocked; ammunition was found in a trouser pocket. He was taken to Hammersmith police station, where he said he was 2nd Lt Richard Allen, 501 Parachute Infantry Regiment, US Army.

The police communicated with the American authorities, as an act passed that year had laid down that no American serviceman could be tried in a British court. At 3 am on Tuesday, 10 September, Lt Robert Earl de Mott, aged twenty-seven – an American CID officer who had once been a lawyer in Denver, Colorado – interviewed the suspect and established his real name and that he was a deserter. Hulten said he had found the car abandoned near Newbury. He was removed to the American CID HQ in Piccadilly and questioned further. This time he said he had spent Friday night with Georgina Grayson.

On Wednesday morning, he offered to show de Mott where Georgina lived. He did so, and two British inspectors entered the house at noon, found Jones in bed and took her to Hammersmith police station, where she made a statement and was allowed to go home, not as yet being thought to have been involved in the shooting of Heath.

That afternoon, at about half-past four, she happened to go into a cleaners' in Hammersmith where she met a War Reserve constable, Henry Kimberley, whom she had not seen for two years – not since she had been a very young waitress. He had gone to the cleaners' to pick up a suit. She said: 'Hello.' Struck by her haggard appearance, he remarked how tired she looked. 'I should think so,' she said. 'I've been over at the police station for hours about this murder.' She pointed to a newspaper she held, which reported the murder of George Heath. The papers called it the 'Cleft Chin Murder' and the 'Inky Fingers Murder', both descriptions applying to Heath. Kimberley asked her why that should worry her if she had nothing to do with the murder. She said she knew the man they had got inside – adding that he couldn't have done it as he was with her all Friday night. Before she left, he commented once again on her worn-out appearance. She said to Kimberley : 'If you had seen someone do what I have seen done, you wouldn't be able to sleep at night.'

A few hours later, Inspector Tansill and Constable Kimberley called at 311 King Street. Betty Jones arrived at the same time. Alone for a moment with Kimberley, she asked him why he had brought the inspector. 'I think you should tell him the truth,' said Kimberley. 'All right, I will,' she said.

She made a full confession, implying that Hulten had led her astray and that she was only obeying his orders. She denied helping him carry the body out of the car. A fortnight later she elaborated this idea, writing to the police and saying she had acted throughout in fear of Hulten's threats and violence. This was to be the mainspring of her defence. Hearing of her confession, Hulten made a statement of his own, blaming her for egging him on 'to do something exciting' and participating far more than she had admitted. 'If it hadn't been for her, I wouldn't have shot Heath,' he told the police.

The American government waived its rights on the Visiting Forces Act and allowed Hulten to be tried in a British court.

Hulten and Betty Jones appeared before Mr Justice Charles at the Old Bailey, on Tuesday, 16 January 1945. Mr LA Byrne led for the prosecution, Mr John Maud and Mr JD Casswell for Hulten and Jones respectively. Mrs Lloyd Lane also appeared for Jones, the first woman barrister to defend a prisoner accused of murder. And for the first time in legal history, a female accused in a murder trial was allowed to appear hatless and with no covering on her head.

After a six-day trial, both the accused were found guilty and were sentenced to death. Eighteen-year-old Betty Jones was taken shrieking and sobbing down to the cells. Appeals pleading manslaughter were heard – and dismissed – in February.

Elizabeth Jones was reprieved, just two days before the date set for her execution.

There was no reprieve for Karl Hulten, though. He was hanged by Tom Pierrepoint and Harry Critchell at Pentonville Prison five days after his twenty-third birthday, on 8 March 1945. The war in Europe ended two months later.

Betty Jones was released from jail on licence in January 1954. She was twenty-seven.

36

JACK TRATSART

THE MURDERS OF JOHN AND CLAIRE TRATSART, 1945

Lyons Corner Houses — tea rooms and restaurants of some distinction — were celebrated features of the London scene for more than fifty years. In their heyday before the Second World War, there were 250 of them, employing hordes of swift-footed, aproned waitresses known as 'nippies'. The first Corner House was opened in Piccadilly in 1894, and the last bearing that name closed in 1969. They were phased out in the 1960s, being converted into self-service restaurants under the name of Jolyon. The Corner Houses were large, bright, cheerful establishments, providing cheap but agreeable teas and meals. They were popular places of rendezvous and formed the familiar setting of many tête-à-têtes and scenes of domestic affection, argument, parting and celebration. The Oxford Street Corner House, near Tottenham Court Road, was once the setting for a very unusual double murder.

At about 5 pm on 20 April 1945, the ground-floor restaurant was crowded, buzzing with conversation and busy nippies. The end of the war was in sight – the surrender of Germany was only a fortnight away. Few people glanced at the family of six gathered around one of the tables, although one or two of those sitting nearby noticed that a young man wearing glasses was fooling, so it seemed, with a pistol. A water pistol or an air-pistol, they assumed, naturally enough as the other members of the family continued to laugh and joke as if nothing at all was amiss.

Then, six shots cut across the tea-time chatter.

Customers screamed and some ducked below tables, as three members of the family fell from their chairs, their heads and bodies spurting blood. The young man wearing glasses stood over them, a smoking gun in his right hand.

Two soldiers, quicker to react than most, seized him, and the police and a doctor were sent for. The initial panic soon subsided. After five years of war, the Blitz and flying bombs, Londoners were accustomed to violent sights and sounds. The Corner House staff soon calmed their customers and persuaded them to stay put, coolly screening off the scene of the crime. No more teas were served that day. Meanwhile, the first police constable to arrive on the scene – he had hurried in from Oxford Street – informed the local police station in Tottenham Court Road.

By the time DI Robert Higgins arrived, the bodies were being removed. One man was dead; a woman was dying; and a young man was seriously injured, shot through the jaw. The bespectacled gunman, still guarded by the two soldiers, sat calmly in a chair. Higgins asked where the gun was. No one could tell – no one knew. He approached the gunman, assuming that he had concealed the murder weapon somewhere on his person, and after introducing himself Higgins asked the young man for the gun. Speaking clearly and firmly the killer informed the police officer that as *he* was a detective it was up to him to find it.

A search of the gunman and of the floor-space round him produced no gun, although nineteen bullets were found in a pocket. Higgins was becoming anxious when something odd in one of the light fittings on a pillar caught his eye. Through the bowl-like glass of the lights he saw the silhouette of a gun. It had been thrown there after the shooting, but to Higgins's amazement no one in the restaurant had noticed the gunman doing this. No one, it also appeared, had actually seen the shooting – presumably because, on hearing the bangs, everyone automatically dived for cover under the nearest table or chair.

The short-sighted young man was removed to Tottenham Court Road police station for questioning. To this he was not at all averse and spoke freely, his words being carefully written down in longhand as he sipped at a cup of tea.

His name was Jack Adrian Tratsart. He was twenty-seven, unmarried, and a toolmaker by trade. His father, John Tratsart, was a Belgian, who had come to Britain before the First World War and had settled in Norbury, south London. He designed shoes for a living. He and his wife had six children. When she died in 1937 he married his housekeeper. After the start of the Second World War, the Tratsarts left London for Northampton, except for the eldest son, Jack, who remained 'for business reasons' in Norbury.

As the war came to an end, the family in Northampton began to think about returning to Norbury. A meeting to discuss the move was arranged by Jack, who had plans of his own. It was decided that Mr Tratsart (aged fifty-seven), his son Hugh, and two of his daughters (Claire, twenty-eight, and Anne, thirteen) should meet Jack and Mr Tratsart's first wife's middle-aged sister, Miss Coemans, at the Lyons Corner House in Oxford Street.

Claire had been an epileptic for seven years. Young Hugh suffered from a kind of palsy. Jack himself was an insomniac and a manic depressive. He had been to see a specialist about his depressions, but having no faith in doctors he soon terminated his visits. The casualties and suffering caused by the war used to excite his concern. He was particularly outraged, according to his aunt, by the Italians' treatment of the Abyssinians. As it was, life seemed to him to be full of almost intolerable pain, delusions and difficulty, and when disabilities were added, as in the case of his sister Claire and brother Hugh, the sufferers might as well be dead. For that matter, so might his father, whom he hated and despised.

Thus reasoning, he resolved to kill the three of them and then commit suicide himself, and he decided that the family gathering in the Lyons Corner House would provide the best occasion for the deed. He already had a revolver, bought two years previously 'from a sailor' for £5. 'They say that opportunity only comes once,' remarked Jack Tratsart.

In the long statement he made to the police he declared:

I have considered killing my brother Hugh and my sister Claire for some time, four or five years really, ever since I came back from Belgium when I was nineteen. My sister Claire is an epileptic and my brother Hugh has never been able to use his hands – a sort of semi-paralysis. They've never stood a chance and my father didn't help them in their deficiencies. He is miserably, terribly bigoted, and the worst person to have as a father. You know what an epileptic is? She can't get married, and her life isn't worth living whatsoever. My sister Claire is a staunch Roman Catholic, and all she thinks about is going to heaven. She's got every possible disadvantage and couldn't keep her job. I have been contemplating killing myself for a number of years. I tried once, but failed. That was in Belgium. I was the only one of the family who could help Claire and Hugh. My father only thought of making money. I had decided to commit suicide, so I thought I would do a good job while I was about it.

So on the afternoon of 20 April, Jack Tratsart travelled up to London with his aunt to meet the other members of his family at the Oxford Street Corner House. In a pocket was his gun and twenty-five bullets, six of which had been loaded in the breech. The family took their seats and gave their orders to the waitress. The three women – Anne, Claire and the aunt – sat opposite the three men, Mr Tratsart, Hugh and Jack. Said the latter:

I sat in the right position so that nobody could interfere with me shooting them and myself. We all sat talking normal gossip. I got the gun out and the funniest thing happened. I tried three times to fire it and couldn't. I didn't know you have to pull the top back. I decided to shoot Claire first then my father, then Hugh, then myself. I pointed the gun across the table at Claire and pulled the trigger. But nothing happened and only Hugh saw me and grinned. Ten minutes later I repeated the performance and pulled hard at the trigger, with the gun only about two feet from Claire. But again nothing happened. They did not seem to realise that I was going to kill, and when my aunt asked, jokingly, what I had there, I said: 'Only a water pistol.' They joked about it and I put it under the table. Then I carried my plan through. I fired two bullets at Claire, but did not see what happened. I then fired two at my father and two at Hugh, coming round in a line. I was then standing up and pointed the gun at my head and pulled the trigger once or twice. But nothing happened.

Mr Tratsart died almost at once. His daughter died on the way to hospital. Hugh, shot through the chin, survived.

Jack Tratsart was charged with double murder and attempted murder. After a preliminary hearing at Marlborough Street court he was sent for trial at the Old Bailey. But he never appeared there. Doctors and psychologists who examined him in prison decided he was unfit to plead. He was declared insane and sent to Broadmoor, where two years later he died.

Before he died he learnt how to play tennis and to play the piano. He became quite good at both. He also began writing a book, which opened: 'This is a world of youth, all men over forty scram.'

NEVILLE HEATH

THE MURDER OF MARGERY GARDNER, 1946

It is difficult to comprehend why some men who kill women should go on to grossly mutilate their bodies. Such obscene acts may have some origins, probably sexual, in things that happened when the murderer was child. But, as with Jack the Ripper, mutilation with a knife or other instrument would seem to be the ultimate thrill in the murderer's mind, not the actual murder.

Such a one was Mrs Margery Gardner, a thirty-two-year-old film extra. She had rather masochistic tendencies, her bent being flagellation and bondage. With this, it seems, in mind, in May 1946 she went with a good-looking, well-built and gentlemanly younger man to the Pembridge Court Hotel in Notting Hill Gate, where she was saved from a fate worse than flogging by the intrusion of a hotel detective.

Some weeks before this another woman, naked and bound as Margery Gardner had been, was saved in a hotel in the Strand by a similar intervention prompted by her screams. This woman later refused to prefer charges, presumably to avoid appearing in court and to escape the ensuing publicity.

On the other hand, Yvonne Symonds, who had no predilection for bondage or anything of the sort – or indeed even any knowledge of such things – was saved a few weeks later when she spent a night in a hotel room with the same man by what one can only suppose was her own innocence and trust.

Yvonne Symonds was nineteen. She was staying at the Overseas Club, and on Saturday, 15 June 1946, she went to a WRNS dance in Chelsea. There she chanced to meet a charming army officer in civvies who called himself Lt Col Heath. He was ten years older than she, quite young to be a colonel, but it was possible for him to have achieved such a rank in the war. He took her to the Panama Club in South Kensington and then back to the Overseas Club. Much enamoured of him, she spent most of Sunday in his company and agreed, after he made a proposal of marriage, to spend the night with him at the Pembridge Court Hotel, 34 Pembridge Gardens, Notting Hill Gate. He booked them in as 'Lt Col and Mrs NGC Heath'. Nothing untoward happened to her in Room 4, despite Heath's recent and frustrating experiences with the lady in the Strand hotel and with Mrs Gardner.

None the worse, the next day she returned to her parents' home in Worthing, leaving

Heath alone in the hotel. He telephoned her in Worthing several times and amused himself in unknown ways on Monday, Tuesday and Wednesday. He also telephoned Margery Gardner, and as fate would have it she agreed to see him on Thursday, 20 June.

That night they visited the Panama Club in Cromwell Place and left just after midnight, getting a taxi back to Pembridge Gardens. Both were the worse for drink. Heath took a minute or so to count out the fare – 1s 9d, to which he added 5d – and then walked off towards the Pembridge Court Hotel with his arm round his companion's waist. The taxi driver, Harold Harter, later recalled that Heath wore a grey, pin-striped suit and that Mrs Gardner had a tight-fitting hat and a three-quarter tweed coat. To the man on the door at the Panama Club she had seemed 'rather dowdy'.

Mrs Margery Aimée Brownell Gardner, three years older than Heath, led what was then known as a bohemian life. Married before the war, she had recently separated from her husband and was occasionally employed as a film extra. Heath, who had stayed twice before at the hotel under the name of Lt Col Armstrong, let himself into the nineteen-bedroom hotel with a front door key – there was no night porter – and took Mrs Gardner up to Room 4 on the first floor: it had two single beds. The occupants of three other adjacent bedrooms slept on, undisturbed by any sound.

The following afternoon, a chambermaid, receiving no answer to her knocking, went into the unlocked room. The curtains were drawn; both beds were disordered; and a body under the bedclothes of one so alarmed her that the assistant manageress was fetched. Mrs Alice Wyatt entered the room and drew back the curtains.

When she recovered from her shock and horror at seeing the state of the body in the bed nearest the door, the police were called. Sergeant Fred Averill walked over from Notting Hill police station, arriving at the hotel at about 2.35 pm.

The naked body of Margery Gardner lay on her back under the bedclothes, her right arm underneath her. Her ankles were tied tightly together with a handkerchief, and her hands had also been tied behind her back. This was later deduced from the marks on her wrists, although the ligature was missing – as was the material with which she seemed to have been gagged and which would have stifled her screams. Her face and chin were bruised, as if she had been hit by a fist and as if a hand had gripped her jaw to prevent her opening her mouth or moving her head. She had been scourged seventeen times by something that had left a criss-cross diamond-like pattern on her face (twice) and on her front and back. Her breasts had been bitten and the nipples nearly bitten off. In addition, some rough instrument had been thrust up her vagina and fiercely rotated, causing much bleeding. All these injuries had been inflicted before her death, which had been caused by suffocation – either by the gag, a pillow, or the bed clothes, or by having her head, face down, pressed into a pillow.

There were many bloodstains in the bedroom, especially on the sheets of the other disordered bed by the window. This suggested that the main injuries had been inflicted there, and that the woman's body had been moved.

Her face had been washed, but there was still some dried blood caught in her nostrils and in the lashes of her left eye. There was no evidence that any intercourse had taken place. The handkerchief that bound her ankles was embroidered with a 'K' and marked 'L Kearns'. But this clue was later found to be misleading and the handkerchief's owner had nothing to do with Mrs Gardner's death.

That morning, Friday, 21 June, Neville Heath telephoned his unofficial fiancée in Worthing and travelled down by train to see her. He and Yvonne had lunch together and he booked himself a room at the Ocean Hotel. Miss Symonds met him again the following morning, when he mentioned a murder in London that was featured in the morning papers. He said he would tell her something about it later. She introduced him to her parents and they all went to the local golf club. That night, he took Yvonne out for dinner at the Blue Peter Club in Angmering. During the meal she said: 'Look here, you told me you were going to tell me more about that murder.' He obliged.

'He told me,' she said later, 'that it happened in the room he booked at the Pembridge Court Hotel.' The amazed Miss Symonds heard that he had actually seen the body – 'a very gruesome sight', he said – and that he had met the victim earlier in the evening and lent her his keys; she had had a man with her and they had nowhere else to go. He had slept elsewhere. He told her Inspector Barratt had telephoned him at this other place, had picked him up and had taken him to the hotel where he was shown the body. She continued: 'He said Mr Barratt had said he thought she had been suffocated … that a poker had been used on her … had been stuck up her … had probably killed her.' Heath seemed concerned about the victim. He said that the sort of person who could do a thing like that must be 'a sexual maniac'. After dinner, he escorted Yvonne back to her home.

The Sunday morning papers were full of the murder, and Miss Symonds's parents were most distressed to read that Scotland Yard wished to interview a six-foot man named 'Neville George Clevely Heath', aged twenty-nine. Their daughter anxiously telephoned her fiancé at the Ocean Hotel. She told him her parents were rather worried by what they had read. 'Yes, I thought they would be,' he replied. He reassured her, saying he was going back to London to talk to the police and would telephone her that evening. He never did, and fortunately for Miss Symonds she never heard from him or saw him again until she gave evidence at the West London magistrates' court and then at the Old Bailey.

Neville Heath left Worthing that Sunday afternoon and took a train to Bournemouth. Before he left he posted a letter that he had begun, or written, the day before. It was addressed to Chief Inspector Barratt of New Scotland Yard, and arrived at the Yard on Monday, 24 June. The letter, signed 'NGC Heath', embellished what he had told Miss Symonds, excluding any reference to Barratt himself. Heath said that he had lent his hotel keys to Mrs Gardner, who had met an acquaintance 'with whom she was obliged to sleep' for financial reasons. Mrs Gardner, he said, intimated to him that if he returned after 2 am he might spend the remainder of the night with her. He did so, he said, and on his return 'found her in the condition of which you are aware. I realised that I was in an invidious position, and rather than notify the police, I packed my belongings and left.' He then described Mrs Gardner's acquaintance, called Jack, and ended: 'I have the instrument with which Mrs Gardner was beaten and am forwarding this to you today.'

This he neglected to do, and the police neglected to provide the newspapers with any photo of him – with the result that he was able to stay at the Tollard Royal Hotel in Bournemouth for thirteen days without attracting much attention, other than that he was over-familiar with the head porter and seemed to have nothing other than a light-brown sports jacket, flannel trousers and some shirts to wear.

He arrived at the hotel on the evening of Sunday, 23 June, calling himself Group Captain Rupert Brooke. The hotel was on the West Cliff, overlooking the sea. He was given Room 71, and was moved on 27 June to Room 81 on the second floor as he wanted a room with a gas fire; he complained of being cold. Room 4 at the Pembridge Court Hotel had also had a gas fire but, according to the manageress there, a poker had not been part of the furnishings. Otherwise, according to the Tollard Royal's head porter, Heath was just like any other male guest, reading, drinking beer and going out at night to shows and dances. There was also dancing at the hotel twice a week.

Ten days passed without apparent incident, except that Heath met a girl called Peggy at a dance at the Pavilion. On the morning of Wednesday, 3 July, he was sitting on the promenade under the West Cliff when he saw her again, walking along the front with another girl. He joined them, and when Peggy left in about half an hour he asked the other girl, Doreen Marshall, who was staying at the Norfolk Hotel, to have tea with him that afternoon. She was twenty-one. Heath later told the police something of what happened that afternoon and that night:

> I met her along the promenade about 2.45 pm in the afternoon, and after a short stroll we went to the Tollard Royal for tea at about 3.45. The conversation was fairly general and covered the fact that she had served in the WRNS. She mentioned the fact that she had been ill, with influenza, and was down in Bournemouth to recuperate. She left the hotel at about 5.45 after accepting my invitation to dinner in the evening. At approximately 7.15 I was standing outside the hotel when I saw Miss Marshall approaching the hotel on foot down West Hill Road. [She had, in fact, left the Norfolk Hotel in a taxi.] I entered the hotel, went to my room to get some tobacco and came downstairs again just as she was entering the lounge. We dined at about 8.15 pm and sat talking in the lounge after dinner, moving into the writing room at about 10 pm. [His timings were vague as he had no wristwatch.]

He continued:

The conversation was again general but she told me she was considering cutting short her holiday in Bournemouth and returning home (to Pinner) on Friday instead of Monday. She mentioned an American staying in the hotel (her hotel) and told me that he had taken her for car rides into the country and to Poole. She also mentioned an invitation to go with him to Exeter, but I gathered, although she did not actually say so, that she did not intend to go. Another American was mentioned – I believe his name was Pat – to whom I believe she was unofficially engaged some while ago ... Conversation continued general until approximately 11.30 pm. At 11 pm (approx) Miss Marshall suggested going away, but I persuaded her to stay a little longer. At about 11.30 pm the weather was clear and we left the hotel and sat on a seat near the hotel overlooking the sea.

The night porter, who had served them with drinks, thought that Miss Marshall seemed tired and pale and a little distressed. It seems she asked another hotel guest to order a taxi for her and that Heath countermanded this, saying he would walk her home. When they left just after midnight, he told the porter he would be back in half an hour. 'No, in quarter of an hour,' said Miss Marshall. Hatless, she was wearing a black frock and a yellow camel-hair coat and carried a handbag. Around her neck was a single string of twenty-eight pearls. She was 5 ft 3 in tall.

According to Heath, they walked down towards the Pavilion and he left her at the pier, from where she headed back to the Norfolk Hotel in Richmond Hill through the public gardens. He said he returned to his hotel on foot via Durley Chine, west of the hotel – a very circuitous route. 'It rained heavily before I reached the hotel,' he said. He continued: 'I guessed that the night porter would be waiting for me to come in, and as a ladder had that day been placed up against my window, I decided to practise a small deception on him, and entered my hotel bedroom via the ladder.'

So he did, and there he was, asleep in bed, when the night porter, wondering whether the playful group captain was in or not, peeped into Room 81 at 4.30 am. He noticed that Mr Brooke's shoes outside the door were caked with sand.

The following morning, Heath joked about his little deception with the staff. He continued to stay at the hotel, his manner and appearance unchanged apart from the fact that he had a couple of scratch marks on his neck, took to wearing a scarf, and for once paid for his drinks in cash.

On Friday, 5 July the manager of the Norfolk Hotel notified the police that Miss Marshall had been missing for two days. He also telephoned the Tollard Royal manager, Mr Relf, as he believed she had dined there the previous Wednesday.

On Saturday morning, about 10.15 am, Mr Relf asked Group Captain Brooke whether his dinner guest on Wednesday had been a Miss Marshall from Pinner. Heath laughed this off, saying: 'Oh, no. I've known that lady for a long while, and she certainly doesn't come from Pinner!' The manager suggested nonetheless that Mr Brooke should get in touch with the police.

He did so, telephoning Bournemouth police station within half an hour. The officer in charge of the case was out, so Heath said he would phone again. He did so at half-past three and spoke to DC Souter, who asked him if he would come and look at a photograph of the missing Miss Marshall. Heath agreed, and arranged to visit the police station at 5.30 pm.

There he happened to meet Doreen's father and sister, who had travelled to Bournemouth from London. He consoled them, looked at Miss Marshall's photo, and was able to say that the girl with whom he had dined was indeed the missing girl. As he gave an account of his dealings with her, DC Souter was struck by the group captain's resemblance to the photo of a man wanted for murder that had been circulated by Scotland Yard. He told his superiors about his suspicions and suggested to Rupert Brooke that his real name was Neville Heath. Although the group captain denied this, he was detained in the police station by delaying tactics until DI George Gates saw him at about 6.30 pm. Heath was searched. £4 10s was found on him in notes and cash. It was later established that he had pawned Doreen Marshall's ring for £5 on Friday and her watch for £3 on Saturday morning.

When Heath was told he was being officially detained for further questions, he complained of feeling chilly and asked if he could get his jacket from the Tollard Royal: he was wearing a buttoned-up tieless flannel shirt and flannel trousers. He said he would come back. DI Gates fetched the jacket himself.

It was searched at the police station in front of Heath. In a pocket was found a cloakroom ticket issued at Bournemouth West railway station on 23 June, as well as a single artificial pearl and the return half of a first-class railway ticket from Bournemouth to London, which had belonged to Doreen Marshall. Heath said he found it on a seat in the lounge of the Tollard Royal. Gates then went to the railway station to claim the luggage Heath had left there. It turned out to be a suitcase.

Inside was some clothing: a mackintosh, a hat, and other articles marked with the name 'Heath'. There was also a blue neckerchief and a dark blue woollen scarf, both bloodstained, the latter with several hairs stuck to it that had come from Margery Gardner's head. Finally, there was a leather-bound riding switch, with a striking criss-cross weave. Where the end had worn away, a bunch of wire filaments was exposed. The switch had been washed or wiped, but some blood still remained on it.

At about 9.45 pm, DI Gates told Heath he knew who he was and that he would be further detained until officers of the Metropolitan Police arrived to interview him in connection with the murder of Mrs Gardner. 'Oh, all right,' said Heath.

He began writing out a carefully worded statement at about half-past eleven, finishing it at 2.45 am on 7 July. That same day, Detective Inspector Reg Spooner arrived in Bournemouth and followed up the investigations already made by the Bournemouth police. He eventually saw Heath in the early hours of Monday, 8 July, at about 5.20 am. Heath said: 'I will make a statement after I've had some sleep.' He was taken by car to

London a few hours later. That evening he was charged with the murder of Margery Gardner but declared: 'I have nothing to say at the moment.'

About the time that he was charged, the body of Doreen Marshall was found. Earlier the same day a young woman, Miss Evans, out exercising her black spaniel dog in Branksome Chine after returning home from work, noticed a swarm of flies in some rhododendron bushes. Later, after reading a newspaper account of the missing girl, she discussed her suspicions with her father over their evening meal. Mr Evans was intrigued. At about eight o'clock, he and his daughter visited the chine and found the body. By half-past eight, the find had been reported to the police.

Branksome Dene Chine is a deep wooded valley running inland from the sea, about a mile west of what used to be the Tollard Royal Hotel, in the opposite direction from the pier and the Norfolk Hotel. It can be reached by a long walk past three other chines, along the seafront under the cliffs. The body was found some distance away from the beach, to the right of a path in a subsidiary chine, dumped in some thick rhododendron bushes and covered first with the victim's clothes, the black dress and the yellow coat, and then with a fir-tree bough. The body, naked except for a left shoe, had apparently been moved a short distance: bloodstains and a broken string of pearls were found some twenty feet away, and nearby was a torn stocking. Another stocking was found high up in some bushes, and a blue powder compact 70 yards south of where Doreen Marshall's body lay.

She had been struck several times on the back of her head. There were also abrasions on her back, a bruise on her right shoulder and an area of redness around the left collar-bone, as if someone had knelt on her. The left side of her chest was bruised and a rib had fractured, piercing the left lung. Her left arm was bruised, as were both wrists, which appeared to have been tightly tied. They also bore fingernail imprints of her assailant. The fingers of both her hands were badly cut on the inside, as if she had seized a knife in self-defence. All these injuries had been inflicted before she died, her death itself having been caused by two deep knife cuts across her throat.

After death, a nipple had been bitten off and her body had been mutilated. A jagged series of slashes reached from her vagina vertically up to her chest, where they were joined by a deep diagonal cut from each nipple to the centre of her body, forming a Y. A rough instrument, possibly a branch, had also penetrated and torn her vagina as well as her anus.

No knife was ever found, nor was any blood on any of Heath's clothing. It is thought he stripped naked before the attack, and afterwards washed himself in the sea, into which he also threw the knife.

Heath's trial at the Old Bailey began on Tuesday, 24 September, concluding on the Thursday of that week at 5.45 pm. He pleaded not guilty. The judge was Mr Justice Morris; Mr EA Hawke led for the Crown and Mr JD Casswell for the accused.

The question was not whether Heath was guilty, but whether he was insane. He gave no evidence in his own defence, as his counsel felt that his calm detachment and agreeable manner would never support the defence's contention that he was mad. Mr Casswell, in his cross-examination of DI Spooner, tried to establish Heath's instability and criminal nature by a detailed account of his career.

Neville George Clevely Heath was born on 6 June 1917 at Ilford, Essex. His father was a barber, and his mother is said to have been a large, dominant woman. He was educated to begin with at a local Catholic school, where he seems to have been a bully and a tormentor of animals. He was good at athletics and rugby, but failed his exams. An office boy at £1 a week for a time, he joined the Artists' Rifles when he was seventeen, and finding a service life to his liking he enlisted in the RAF on a short-service commission in February 1936. Court-martialled the following year for being absent without leave, for escaping while under arrest and for stealing a car, he was dismissed from the RAF in September 1937. In November, he was charged with fraud and false pretences, eight other offences being taken into consideration, including two of posing as Lord Dudley. He was put on probation. In July 1938, after working for a fortnight as a sales assistant in an Oxford Street store, he was sent to a borstal in Suffolk for three years for robbing a friend's house of jewellery worth £51. Ten other offences were taken into consideration. Years later, he revisited the borstal at Hollesley Bay, giving the inmates a talk on how he had made good. Released from the borstal on the outbreak of war, he joined the RASC as a private, being commissioned in March 1940 when he was sent to the Middle East. This time he got into trouble with a brigadier, mainly over dishonoured cheques. He went absent without leave, was again court-martialled and then cashiered in August 1941. Sent back to Britain on the troopship *Mooltan,* he absconded at Durban and went to Johannesburg, where he masqueraded as Captain Selway MC for a time, until he enlisted in the South African Air Force, calling himself Armstrong. His past record came to light eventually, but because of his good work he was allowed to remain, although he was never put on operational duties. Obtaining the rank of captain, he was seconded to the RAF in May 1944, to 180 (Bomber) Squadron, and flew a few sorties over Holland. In October his Mitchell bomber – he was the pilot – was hit by anti-aircraft fire and he and his crew bailed out.

Early in 1945, he returned to South Africa, and in October his wife – he had married in February 1942 – divorced him for desertion, taking custody of their son. She was a wealthy woman and he tried to blackmail her family over the divorce. In December, he was court-martialled for the third time, being convicted of undisciplined conduct and of wearing unauthorised decorations. Dismissed from the service, he returned to England, to Wimbledon, where his parents lived in Merton Hall Road. Before long he was fined £10 at Wimbledon magistrate's court in April for wearing medals and a uniform to which he was not entitled. He studied for a 'B' commercial flying licence, but failed to turn up for the necessary exams.

The assault on the woman in the Strand hotel occurred in March, and the first assault on Mrs Gardner in May. He killed her in the early hours of 21 June 1946.

Mr Casswell's defence was that Heath's mind was 'not behind his hand,' that he was not responsible for his actions and was 'morally defective' or 'morally insane'. Was there any anticipation or premeditation? Were his actions in London, Worthing and Bournemouth the actions of a sane man – not hiding, discussing the murder with Miss Symonds, writing to the police, reporting to the police, behaving in an apparently normal manner after the most savage of crimes? He may have known what he was doing, said Mr Casswell, but he did not know that what he was doing was wrong. Besides, the man must have been mad to have done what he did. Therefore, his deeds came within the scope of the McNaghten Rules on insanity and Heath must be found guilty but insane.

Dr WH de Bargue Hubert, produced by the defence as an expert psychiatrist who could vouch for this line of reasoning, was carved up in cross-examination. (Within a year Dr Hubert, who was a drug addict, committed suicide.) Two prison doctors testifying for the Crown announced that Heath was a most abnormal person, a sadist, a sexual pervert and a psychopath, but that although he had behaved in an extraordinary way he was not insane.

Heath seemed indifferent to what was being said. Wearing a light-grey suit with a wide chalk stripe, he presented a clean, almost heroic appearance with his fresh complexion, blue eyes, and fair wavy hair, carefully brushed and pomaded.

The question of why his petty criminality took such a sadistic, murderous bent in 1946 was hardly raised and never answered. Nothing was said of his early sexual experiences – Heath himself was reluctant to talk about them to the doctors who examined him – but as a schoolboy he had assaulted a girl, and then a woman much later in South Africa.

The jury, who included one woman, were out for an hour. They found him guilty of murder. Asked if he had anything to say, Heath replied: 'Nothing.' There was no appeal. He never showed any remorse or made a confession. He wrote to his parents: 'My only regret at leaving the world is that I have been damned unworthy of you both.'

He was hanged at Pentonville Prison by Albert Pierrepoint and Harry Kirk on 26 October 1946. According to Pierrepoint, Heath was the most handsome man he had ever hanged.

Some two weeks earlier in Germany, Pierrepoint had hanged sixteen war criminals at Hameln – in one day (8 October) – and on 11 October he had a hand in the deaths of another twelve. Following these executions, he had been entertained in the evening by some RAF officers, who had been in Heath's old squadron and were aware that their former comrade was about to be hanged in London. It seems they talked about him rather fondly. One recalled Heath's answer to an admiring comment that he must have had hundreds of affairs. After some careful thought, as if calculating numbers, Neville Heath replied: 'Not hundreds, old boy, but thousands. And the funny thing is I've never been the slightest bit in love with any of them.'

Heath was smoking a pipe when Pierrepoint and Kirk entered the condemned cell. To the warders he said: 'Come on, boys. Let's be going.' Earlier that morning he had asked for a whisky as a final request, adding: 'In the circumstances, you might make that a double.'

38

JENKINS, GERAGHTY AND ROLT

THE MURDER OF ALEC DE ANTIQUIS, 1947

Chance plays as large a part in murder as in life, and it was pure chance that motor mechanic Alec de Antiquis happened to be riding on a motorcycle along Charlotte Street in central London one sunny April afternoon just after two o'clock. Aged thirty-four and married with six children, he had a garage and repair business at Collier's Wood in south London, and was on his way back there after picking up some spare parts for his workshop. It was not chance that he acted the way he did, but it was chance that the man whose path he blocked had a gun and had no hesitation in using it. The inadvisability of having a go was seldom better demonstrated than in this case, which is also notable for the emergence of one of Scotland Yard's celebrated investigators, Superintendent Robert Fabian, and for the last appearances of Sir Bernard Spilsbury and Robert Churchill at an Old Bailey murder trial.

Just before 2 pm on Monday, 28 April 1947, three masked gunmen burst into Jay's, a jeweller's shop at 73-75 Charlotte Street, W1, on the corner of Tottenham Street and not far from the Scala Theatre. Two of the gunmen went in by the front door, the third by a side entrance. This man ordered the two assistants in the back to keep quiet. The two other bandits in the front of the shop grabbed at the jewellery on the shelves. What happened next has been confusedly reported. It seems that during the raid a gun was thrown at the firm's director, Ernest Stock, as he slammed shut the door of a safe. One of the raiders clubbed him to the ground with another gun. The assistant manager, Bertram Keates, aged seventy, managed to set off a burglar alarm, and when he was asked for the safe's keys he threw a stool at the gunmen, whereupon a shot was fired. It missed him, passed through a glass door leading to the inner room and struck the panelled wall beyond. No doubt alarmed by the noise, resistance, and their own violence, the gunmen fled outside, empty-handed apart from the guns that two of them held. They piled into a getaway car, found their exit was blocked by a lorry and scrambled out. They then ran, it seems, across Charlotte Street towards the section of Tottenham Street that leads into Tottenham Court Road. Women screamed; pedestrians scattered; some dropped to the ground. Alec de Antiquis drove his motorcycle across their path in an attempt to obstruct their escape.

One of the raiders shot him in the head. He fell dying into the gutter while the three robbers disappeared among the crowds and traffic. He is alleged to have said to someone before he died: 'I'm all right ... Stop them ... I did my best.'

Another bold and public-spirited passer-by, a surveyor from Kenton in Middlesex named Charles Grimshaw, also had a go. He described how he saw the three gunmen come out of Jay's and then run towards him:

> At that moment a motorcyclist drew up in front of me. He more or less stood up from his machine on one leg, as though to dismount, and I heard a shot and saw him fall. I saw two men come round the front of the machine, which had fallen over, still running towards me across Charlotte Street. They were side by side and the taller of the two was removing a white scarf from his face. There seemed to be a third person on the other side of the fallen motorcyclist. I stepped off the kerb behind a stationary car and, as they drew near to me, trip-kicked the shorter man. He fell full length on the pavement and dropped the gun he was carrying. I jumped on top of him, but his companion, who had run on a few paces, turned back and kicked me on the head. That made me release the man, as I was dazed, and he pushed me over and stood up. He picked up the gun, pointed it at me and said: 'Keep off!' I stayed where I was.

Albert Pierrepoint, the chief executioner, who had left a pub in Soho shortly before the shooting, happened to walk along Charlotte Street soon afterwards and saw a lot of people gathered around a body in the road. But he walked on, late for an appointment. He was in London on an official visit to the War Office concerning the carrying out of further executions in Germany.

One of Pierrepoint's police friends, Acting Superintendent Robert Fabian, was put in charge of the case, assisted by DCI Higgins and DI Hodge. The many eye-witness accounts of the robbers varied considerably, and it was thought they escaped in a car, which was incorrect.

Two days after the shootings a taxi driver walked into Tottenham Court Road police station and said he had seen two men in a hurry enter Brook House, an office block at 191 Tottenham Court Road. They had had knotted handkerchiefs around their necks. When the building was searched, a raincoat was found in an empty top-floor office, where one of the gunmen at least had sought temporary shelter. Stuffed into the coat's pockets were a cap, a pair of gloves and a piece of white cloth, triangularly folded and knotted. The maker's name had been torn from the coat and cap, but a dissection of the coat revealed, in the lining, a manufacturer's stock label bearing trade numbers and marks. The expert help of a man in the clothing business enabled the police to trace the raincoat to a multiple tailors' in Leeds. They in turn informed the police that the coat was part of a consignment delivered to three of their branches in London. The coat found in Brook House was traced to a tailor's shop in Deptford High Street.

At that time, to prevent the acceptance of forged clothing coupons, a customer's name and address were noted as a precaution, and as a result a record of the coat's sale, on 30 December 1946, led the police to a man in Bermondsey who revealed, after some prevarication, that his wife had lent the coat a few weeks before the shooting to her brother, Harry Jenkins.

Charles Henry Jenkins, aged twenty-three, was soon picked up. A handsome braggart and ex-borstal boy, he was a minor criminal with a record for assault, including two convictions for assaulting policemen – he broke the jaw of one of them. But twenty-seven witnesses failed to pick him out at an hour-long identity parade.

In the meantime, an eight-year-old schoolboy discovered a gun lying just above the low-tide mark of the River Thames at Wapping. It was a .32, loaded with five rounds (three of which had misfired) and an empty case, which proved to have been that of the bullet that killed Alec de Antiquis. Then another gun was recovered from the foreshore of the Thames, a rusty old .455 Bulldog revolver loaded with six rounds, one of which had been fired. This bullet was extracted from the woodwork in the jewellers' shop. The rounds in the Bulldog were over fifty years old. Both guns were found a quarter of a mile from the block of flats in Bermondsey where lived the parents of Jenkins's wife.

Two years before this, Harry Jenkins's older brother, Thomas, had been convicted of manslaughter for a very similar crime. In another raid on a jewellers', this time in the City (on 8 December 1944) a retired naval captain, Ralph Binney, a passer-by, tried to stop two thieves from getting away by stepping into the road and stretching out his arms before the getaway car. The driver, Ronald Hedley, knocked him down with the car and ran over him twice. The captain's clothing caught on the body work of the car and he was dragged for over a mile, across London Bridge, before his broken and battered body was flung clear. He died soon afterwards. Hedley was later hanged. Thomas Jenkins, who was with him in the car, was sentenced to eight years' penal servitude. Both he and Hedley belonged to a south London gang called the Elephant Boys.

Harry Jenkins was not so fortunate as his brother. Two of his friends were also picked up by the police and interrogated: Christopher James Geraghty, aged twenty, and Terence John Peter Rolt, who was seventeen. Geraghty had been with Jenkins in borstal and had twice escaped. Both he and Rolt eventually made incriminating statements and all three were charged on 19 May 1947 with the murder of Alec de Antiquis.

Rolt's story was that on Saturday, 26 April, two days before the shooting, the three of them had broken into a gunsmith's shop, F Dyke and Co., in Union Street, between Waterloo and London Bridge stations. Here they spent the night, playing with the guns on display and eventually choosing the three that were used in the Charlotte Street raid. On the morning of Monday the 28th they met up again at Whitechapel underground station and travelled by tube to Goodge Street. Walking here and there, all armed, they tried to evaluate the possible pickings in jewellers' shops in the vicinity of Tottenham Court Road. This took some time as they edgily nerved themselves for the robbery. Jay's at last was chosen, but by this time it was the lunch hour and the streets were thronged. The raiders retreated to a café for lunch.

They now encouraged each other by sneaking across the street to make further assessments of what was in the window of Jay's – first Rolt, then Geraghty, who derided Rolt's timorous estimates by saying the contents of the window were worth £5,000. Procrastinating yet further, they decided to acquire a getaway car, although it was never used as such. But after a black Vauxhall 14 saloon had been stolen from Whitfield Street by Jenkins and Rolt, there was nothing now to stop them staging the raid. Rolt drove the car up Charlotte Street with Geraghty beside him. Jenkins walked ahead. The plan was that all three, having parked the car near the shop, would first assemble on the pavement and then, when the coast was clear, would enter the shop. Rolt parked the car and Geraghty joined Jenkins. Then Rolt, in a high state of tension and nervous excitement, mistook a signal from Jenkins and scrambled out of the car. He burst into the shop, brandishing a gun. Jenkins and Geraghty, hastily pulling up their scarves as masks, had no option but to follow him.

In the confusion the two elderly salesmen in Jay's were assaulted and a shot was fired from the Bulldog. The gun that was thrown at Mr Stock had faulty ammunition, which rendered it incapable of being fired. When the robbers fled outside they found that a lorry had pulled up in front of their getaway car and obstructed its departure. In a panic, they ran down the street. It was Chris Geraghty who shot the motorcyclist who got in his way. All three were found guilty at the Old Bailey of the murder of Alec de Antiquis.

Their trial began on Monday, 21 July before Mr Justice Hallett and ended a week later. The chief prosecutor was Mr Anthony Hawke. Jenkins was defended by Mr Vick, KC; Rolt by Mr O'Sullivan, KC, and Geraghty by Mr Wrightson. The jury were out for fifty minutes. Rolt, because of his youth – he was not yet eighteen – was ordered to be detained at His Majesty's pleasure for at least five years. Although Harry Jenkins killed no one, he was deemed to have been an accessory engaged in a joint enterprise of armed robbery. He was sentenced to death with Chris Geraghty. Despite pleas for a reprieve on account of their youth, he and Geraghty were hanged at Pentonville Prison by Albert Pierrepoint, assisted by Harry Allen and Harry Critchell, on 19 September 1947.

Their executions caused an outcry, reinforcing the demands for the abolition of the death penalty. But very little was said or done about Mrs de Antiquis and her six children – except that the police gave her a medal commemorating her husband's bravery.

Terence Rolt was released from prison on licence in June 1956.

Sir Bernard Spilsbury committed suicide two months after Jenkins and Geraghty were hanged; he was seventy. He had never fully recovered from the wartime deaths of his wife and two of his sons. His mental and physical health had deteriorated: he had become absent-minded and unobservant, and had suffered from several strokes and arthritis in his hands. On 17 December, after leaving the Hampstead hotel where he lived, he performed a post mortem, gave his staff Christmas boxes, destroyed notebooks and papers in his laboratory in University College, Gower Street, and wrote out his last post-mortem report. After an early dinner at his club he returned to his laboratory and turned on the gas. A post mortem said he died of coronary thrombosis and carbon monoxide poisoning. He was cremated at Golders Green.

39

DONALD THOMAS

THE MURDER OF PC EDGAR, 1948

Another petty criminal shot a policeman to avoid arrest in 1948. This case was different in that the gunman had a north London and middle-class background – and, because of a temporary suspension of capital punishment, he was never hanged.

Shortly after 8 pm on 13 February 1948, a woman was walking along a suburban road, Broadfields Avenue in north London, with her brother. They heard three shots coming from the direction of another road, Wades Hill, and then a man ran past them, in and out of the street lights. The couple found a badly wounded policeman lying in the drive of 112 Wades Hill. They summoned help.

The policeman, PC Nathaniel Edgar, aged thirty-three, married with two children, had been patrolling in plain clothes an area called Winchmore Hill on the look-out for any break-ins. There had been a spate of burglaries in the Southgate district. Seeing a young man acting suspiciously, he had stopped to question him, going as far as writing the man's name and address in his notebook, when the suspect suddenly pulled out a gun, fired three times and fled. PC Edgar, shot in the back – in the base of the spine, the buttocks and right thigh – was able to tell his colleagues what happened – 'I got his identity card and name … The pocket book's in my inside pocket' – before he died an hour later in hospital. The notebook referred to 'Thomas Donald 247 Cambridge Road, Enfield. BEAH 257/2'.

Donald George Thomas turned out to have a record. He was twenty-three and had been born and brought up in Edmonton, a suburb adjacent to both Enfield and Southgate. A member of the Boys' Brigade, he had been educated at a good school where he had become the cricket captain and had done well academically. However, he had been put on probation several times, and once, when he was sixteen, was sent to an approved school. Called up for military service in January 1945, the last year of the Second World War, when he was nineteen, he had soon deserted. After nearly two years on the run he gave himself up and was sentenced to 160 days in detention. On being returned to his unit, however, he absconded again. This was in October 1947, since when the army had been on the look-out for him.

The police now joined the hunt, but failed to find him at his Enfield address. They appealed for help on the radio as well as in the papers, saying that they wished to interview Donald George Thomas as he 'might be able to help them in their enquiries'. It was apparently the first time that this familiar formula was used in a press release.

As a result, a Mr Winkless, living in Camberwell, south London, got in touch with the police. He had known Thomas for about three months, and within that time Mrs Winkless had fallen passionately in love with the debonair younger man and had absconded with him, leaving her home, her husband and her three children.

Her photograph, supplied by Mr Winkless, was published in the papers on 17 February. It was seen that morning by a Mrs Smeed, the landlady of a house converted into bed-sits in Clapham. She immediately telephoned the police, saying that the woman in the picture was, she thought, in the top flat with a young man.

Four policemen arrived a few minutes later and it was agreed that Mrs Smeed should, as usual, take a breakfast tray up to her lodgers. This she did, closely attended by the police. She put the tray down outside the door of the top-floor room, knocked and said that breakfast was outside. There was a pause before a key turned in the lock. The door opened an inch or so.

Simultaneously the police and Thomas, in his underpants, glimpsed each other. The police rushed forward, preventing him from shutting the door. He sprang for the bed, in which was the shrieking Mrs Winkless and a Luger pistol under the pillow, but was overpowered and disarmed before he could use the gun. He said: 'You were lucky. I might just as well be hanged for a sheep as a lamb.'

Bullets from the Luger matched those extracted from PC Edgar. Mrs Winkless made a statement saying that Thomas had told her about his involvement in the shooting. Seventeen rounds of ammunition were found in the bedroom as well as a jemmy and a rubber cosh.

Donald Thomas was tried at the Old Bailey in April 1948, before Mr Justice Hilbery, and was found guilty and sentenced to death. But the Home Secretary had announced that no executions would be carried out while the House of Commons debated an experimental five-year suspension of the death penalty. So Donald Thomas did not hang.

Nor did James Camb, a ship's steward who had been sentenced to death in March, also by Mr Justice Hilbery, for the murder of twenty-six-year-old Eileen Gibson, known as 'Gay', a first-class passenger on the *Durban Castle* en route from Cape Town to Southampton. She was believed to have been strangled and her body, which was never found, pushed through the porthole of Cabin 126.

The sentences on Donald Thomas and Camb were commuted to life imprisonment. Soon afterwards the 'no hanging' clause, passed in the Commons by twenty-three votes, was deleted from the Criminal Justice Bill in June in the House of Lords by 181 votes to 28. Lord Goddard, making his maiden speech, spoke against the amendment. The death penalty was restored. Nonetheless, a Royal Commission was set up in May 1949 to consider whether capital punishment should be modified or limited.

James Camb was released from prison in 1959. Donald Thomas was released on licence in April 1962.

Between 1909 and 1949, life imprisonment lasted on average for eleven years. No one was detained for more than twenty years during this period and only a few served as many as fifteen years. Most lifers now serve ten years or less. However, in a few cases, life can still mean life.

40

HARRY LEWIS

THE MURDER OF HARRY MICHAELSON, 1948

In the early hours of Sunday, 26 December 1948, Boxing Day, the night porter at Furzecroft, a large block of flats in George Street, Marylebone, was startled out of his night-time reverie by a cry for help. It came from the basement. The porter trotted down the interior stairs and saw, standing outside the entrance door of No. 75, one of the basement flats, Mr Harry Saul Michaelson, a well-known commercial artist and cartoonist. Mr Michaelson was dazedly using a towel to dab the blood that spilled from a deep wound on his forehead. Although seriously injured and in pain, he was quite coherent. But he had absolutely no idea how the injury had been sustained. His wife, who lived with him in the basement flat, happened to be away on holiday.

Mr Michaelson was taken to St Mary's Hospital, Paddington, where his condition swiftly worsened: his ribs had been fractured as well as his skull. An operation on his brain was performed, but he died on the 27 December without regaining consciousness. The head wound and his other injuries had clearly not been self-inflicted or caused by accident. But who had struck him, with what, and why?

The police soon answered the first two questions. The assailant had left bloody finger- and palm prints on a tubular metal chair, which proved to be the unwieldy and unusual weapon used to batter Mr Michaelson. The prints matched a set in the Criminal Record Office at Scotland Yard. They belonged to a young known thief, Harry Lewis, aged twenty-one. He was arrested on 18 January 1949 and charged with murder.

His story was of a chance break-in. Penniless at the time, he happened to be on the prowl in George Street when the sight of an open basement window invited his inspection. He clambered over the railings edging the basement area and cautiously climbed through the window. He found himself in a bedroom: a man lay asleep in a bed. In the darkness Lewis fumbled his way about the room, finding a pile of clothes, some loose change and a wallet, which he pocketed. Exploring further, he opened the bedroom door and crept into the hallway of the flat. As he did so a fuddled voice behind him called out from the bedroom – 'Who's there?'

Lewis panicked. He told the court: 'I went back into the bedroom. The chap was getting out of bed. I picked up the metal chair. It was the first thing I could put my hand on … I admit I gave him two bashes.'

Having temporarily incapacitated the occupant of the flat, Harry Lewis fled via the basement window. Out in the street he hailed a passing taxi and was driven away from the scene of the crime.

He was tried at the Old Bailey on 7 March 1949. The judge was the Lord Chief Justice, Lord Goddard; the prosecutor was Mr Anthony Hawke. Lewis's counsel tried to attribute Mr Michaelson's death to the hospital operation, claiming that it was not Lewis who killed the cartoonist but the surgeon. Pathologist Dr Donald Teare, appearing for the Crown, said the patient would have died in any case, the operation not having contributed substantially to his death.

The defence hoped for a verdict of manslaughter. But Lord Goddard told the jury that the accused man should be found guilty if they thought that the deceased had been killed by a burglar seeking to evade apprehension. Persuaded by this and by the facts of the case, the jury found Lewis guilty of murder, although they added a recommendation for mercy.

The recommendation was ignored. Harry Lewis was duly sentenced to death. An appeal was likewise ignored by the Home Secretary, and at the age of twenty-one, on 21 April 1949, Lewis was hanged at Pentonville Prison by Albert Pierrepoint and Harry Allen, who invariably wore a bow-tie when assisting at executions.

41
JOHN HAIGH

THE MURDER OF MRS DURAND-DEACON, 1949

Gross insensitivity and vanity characterise most murderers, as does a limited imagination. In some cases the daring, almost divine aspect of depriving a human being of life seems to infect the murderer with a belief in his own invulnerability. Or perhaps some death wish is at work. For whatever reason, many murderers, like Haigh and Norman Thorne, feel compelled to assist the police with their enquiries, convinced, it seems, that they can get away with murder. Or is it that they feel they should not be allowed to get away with murder, and wish subconsciously to be caught?

Mrs Olive Henrietta Helen Olivia Robarts Durand-Deacon, aged sixty-nine, was a stout, intelligent widow whose husband had left her well provided for. For over six years she had lived in South Kensington at the Onslow Court Hotel, Queen's Gate.

She was in the habit of exchanging pleasantries with another long-term resident, a neat, smiling little man with twinkling eyes and nice manners, who sat in the dining room on his own at a table next to hers and had done so for over four years. He was somewhat younger than the other residents, being only thirty-nine, and when he first appeared in the hotel about six months before the end of the war she was probably curious about his single status and the source of his income, but was too well bred to ask personal questions. However, a nodding acquaintance developed in time into a certain friendship, and whatever he told her about his antecedents and irregular absences – she was a lady of regular habits herself – must have sounded very plausible. Although he was clearly not a gentleman born and bred – he had a slight accent and was rather flash – she learned he was a Yorkshireman, an engineer, a company director, and that he patented inventions. She often chatted to him as they sat at their separate tables. She had no idea, and would never have believed, that nice and gentlemanly Mr Haigh had already murdered five people for monetary gain.

On St Valentine's Day, 1949, Mrs Gwendoline Birin, assistant secretary of the Francis Bacon Society, lunched, as she usually did on a Monday, with Mrs Durand-Deacon, and during the meal her hostess, after excusing herself, produced a box of plastic fingernails, which she showed to their neighbour, Mr Haigh, and discussed briefly with him. She told him about an idea she had had for a new type of artificial fingernail. Later, she showed him some she had made of paper and glued to her own nails. Could he make something of her idea, she wanted to know. Would it be possible to manufacture and market such fingernails? He said he would think about it – it seemed like a good idea. But the idea she had actually given him was quite a different one.

John George Haigh was in debt. His gambling losses, on horses and dogs, had of late been rather heavy, and he had no regular income. His bank account was overdrawn by £83; his cheques were beginning to bounce; and he had not paid his hotel bill (£5 15s 6d a week, plus 10% for services) since the beginning of January. He now owed the Onslow Court Hotel nearly £50, as the manageress discreetly but firmly continued to remind him. To avoid further embarrassment he had to acquire some instant cash.

He looked at Mrs Durand-Deacon and saw money in what she wore.

The next day, Tuesday, he set about depriving her of her jewellery and of her life. He drove south to Sussex, to Crawley, then little more than a large village. He drove to Leopold Road, where he had acquired the use of a small workshop in Giles Yard. The ramshackle, weedy yard also contained some lock-ups for cars. The workshop itself belonged to Hurstlea Products Ltd, for whom Haigh had once worked, and when they had discarded it, he borrowed it off them.

He called on a business acquaintance, a welding engineer called Mr Davies, and instructed him to collect a carboy of acid from London. Mr Davies had performed a similar task for Haigh a year before. He also called on the manager of Hurstlea, Mr Jones, and asked him for a £50 cash loan. This he was given on condition the money was repaid that week.

On the Wednesday he paid his hotel bill in full, using the money he had borrowed, and was left with 4s 11d in change.

In Crawley, Mr Davies went to Haigh's workshop in Giles Yard and emptied one of three carboys of sulphuric acid that were there by filling up the other two. He took the empty one away, and on Thursday exchanged it for a full one at White's, Dallington Street, EC1 – one carboy contained about 10 gallons of acid. Haigh had previously telephoned White's and ordered the carboy in his own name. Davies brought the carboy back to Haigh's workshop and dumped it there.

That afternoon Haigh himself went to Barking, and at Victor Blagden's wharf obtained a 45-gallon black drum, which he then exchanged for a green drum, specially prepared to resist corrosive acids. He had in the meantime told Mrs Durand-Deacon that he thought he could do something with her idea for false fingernails and suggested that she should come down to his factory at Crawley. He asked her whether Friday would be convenient for her.

In the hotel dining room at breakfast on Friday, 18 February, he told Mrs Durand-Deacon that everything was arranged for later, but he would confirm the appointment at lunchtime. He drove down to Crawley, helped Mr Jones to move some steel sheeting from Giles Yard to the Hurstlea premises in West Street, and was back at the hotel in time for lunch.

Mrs Durand-Deacon had already eaten, and he met her in the Tudor Lounge of the hotel and asked her if she was still free to come with him to Crawley. She was. He drove her there in his Alvis. They left about half-past two. On the back seat was a square leather hat box, in which was a .38 Enfield revolver and eight rounds of ammunition.

The last time Mrs Durand-Deacon was seen by anyone else was when she and Haigh called at an ancient coaching inn, the George Hotel in Crawley, and visited the cloakrooms. It was about 4.15 pm.

What happened next was later described by Haigh himself in his third statement to the police:

She was inveigled into going to Crawley by me in view of her interest in artificial fingernails. Having taken her into the storeroom at Leopold Road, I shot her in the back of the head while she was examining some paper for use as fingernails. Then I went out to the car and fetched in a drinking-glass and made an incision, I think with a penknife, in the side of the throat. I collected a glass of blood, which I then drank. Following that, I removed the coat she was wearing, a Persian lamb, and the jewellery, rings, necklace, earrings and cruciform, and put her in a 45-gallon tank. Before I put the handbag in the tank I took from it the cash, about thirty shillings, and her fountain pen and kept these, and tipped the rest into the tank with the bag. I then filled the tank up with sulphuric acid, by means of a stirrup pump, from a carboy. I then left it to react. I should have said that in between having her in the tank and pumping in the acid I went round to the Ancient Prior's for a cup of tea.

He also had a poached egg on toast with his tea and chatted cheerily to the proprietor. (For several years, the owner of the restaurants and bars that would later occupy the historic timbered building was the former middleweight boxing champion, Alan Minter.)

Haigh's account of his activities in Giles Yard omits the fact that soon after shooting Mrs Durand-Deacon, at about 4.45 pm, he called on Mr Jones in West Street. Haigh said the person he had intended bringing down to Crawley to discuss artificial fingernails had not turned up. Mr Jones was in something of a state, though – he had just sacked some of his employees – and Haigh left a few minutes later.

He was next seen about ten-past six by a van driver who left his vehicle in Giles Yard, where there were also several lock-up garages. By the light of the headlights the van driver saw a man in a fawn overcoat going to and fro between a car and the workshop, the bottom half of whose windows were blacked out.

It was not, in fact, until about 6.45 pm that Haigh went to Ye Olde Ancient Prior's restaurant in The Square for some refreshment. Having consumed his poached egg and drunk his tea, he left the restaurant just after seven o'clock, returning to the workshop to fill the drum with acid. Soon after 9 pm, with his tasks completed, he was back in the George Hotel, where he treated himself to a full-blown three-course dinner. He then drove back to London and was safely ensconced in the Onslow Court Hotel before 11 pm.

The following morning at breakfast, the waitress, Mary, asked Haigh if anything was wrong with Mrs Durand-Deacon as she had not been down to dinner the previous night. Mrs Constance Lane, who had lived at the hotel for nine years and was 'a great friend' of Mrs Durand-Deacon, was then approached by Mr Haigh, 'a nodding acquaintance only'. After an exchange of polite 'Good morning' he asked her: 'Do you know anything about Mrs Durand-Deacon? Is she ill? Do you know where she is?' 'No,' said Mrs Lane, who had noticed that her friend's table had been unoccupied the night before. She added: 'I haven't seen her ... Don't you know where she is? I understood from her you wanted to take her to your factory in Horsham?' 'Yes,' said Haigh. 'But I wasn't ready. I had not had lunch, and she said she wanted to go to the Army and Navy Stores and she asked me to pick her up there.' He said he had waited an hour for her there but she never arrived. Mrs Lane was worried. 'Well,' she said, 'I must do something about it.'

She went upstairs to Room 115, Mrs Durand-Deacon's room, and spoke to a chambermaid. But the room had clearly not been used overnight, and Mrs Lane, becoming increasingly anxious, sought some explanations from the staff and other guests for her friend's disappearance.

Meanwhile, Haigh was elsewhere employed that Saturday, as he later told the police. 'I eventually went back to Crawley, via Putney, where I sold her watch, en route, at a jewellers' shop in the High Street for £10.' It was a ruby and diamond wristwatch and he signed the receipt with a false name and address. 'At Crawley, I called in to see how the reaction in the tank had gone on. It was not satisfactorily completed, so I went on to Horsham, having picked up the coat and put it in the back of the car. I called at Bull's the jeweller's for a valuation of the jewellery, but Mr Bull was not in. I returned to town, and on the way dropped in the coat at the "Cottage Cleaners" at Reigate.' The second-hand value of Mrs Durand-Deacon's black Persian lamb coat was about £50.

On Sunday morning, Haigh again approached Mrs Lane's table in the dining-room and solicitously asked her if she had any news. 'No,' said Mrs Lane. 'I haven't had any news.' She added that she intended going to Chelsea police station after lunch to ask them to take the matter up. Haigh went away, but before long came back to Mrs Lane in the Tudor Lounge where she was reading a morning paper. Haigh said: 'I think we had better go together to Chelsea police station.' 'I think so too,' said Mrs Lane.

He drove her there about 2.15 pm. Unhappily for Haigh, he and Mrs Lane were interviewed by a policewoman, Sergeant Lambourne, whose instincts – based on experience – led her to mistrust the male informant. She visited the hotel and what she learned about Mr Haigh from the manageress gave colour to her suspicions. On Monday, a call was put through to the Record Office at Scotland Yard and very soon Chelsea police station was supplied with the information that Mr Haigh had thrice been imprisoned for crimes connected with the fraudulent obtaining of money.

Meanwhile, on Monday morning, Haigh drove south again:

> *I returned to Crawley to find the reaction almost complete, but a piece of fat and bone was still floating on the sludge. I emptied off the sludge with a bucket and tipped it on the ground opposite the shed, and pumped a further quantity of acid into the tank to decompose the remaining fat and bone. I then left that to work until the following day. From there I went to Horsham again and had the jewellery valued, ostensibly for probate. It was valued at just over £130. I called back at the West Street factory and eventually returned to town.*

At the Onslow Court Hotel, two police officers were waiting to see him, Detective Inspector Symes and DI Webb. The former said to Haigh: 'I am a police officer and I am making enquiries with respect to a lady named Mrs Olive Durand-Deacon who is missing from the hotel.' Haigh replied: 'Yes, I thought you would see me as I went with her friend, Mrs Lane, to the police station to report her missing. I will tell you all I know about it.'

He made a statement, written down by DI Webb, about his appointment with Mrs Durand-Deacon at the Army and Navy Stores, her failure to arrive, his trip to Crawley (without her) and his subsequent conversations with Mrs Lane.

Apparently undisturbed by the police visit, and with money uppermost in his mind, Haigh returned to Horsham on Tuesday, 22 February, and sold the jewellery to Bull's the jeweller's for £100, of which he was given £60, the remaining £40 being handed over the following day. He gave the jeweller's a false name and address. Money in hand, he drove to Crawley and gave Mr Jones £36 of the £50 debt.

At the workshop, Haigh decided the acid had done its work and emptied the drum of its sludgy contents in the yard. Mrs Durand-Deacon's plastic handbag had not been much affected by the acid's action, although its handle and base had come apart, and Haigh stuffed the handbag behind some bricks beside a fence. But her disappearance was not as complete as he thought: the minor contents of the handbag and bits of Mrs Durand-Deacon remained, hidden in the sludge.

On Wednesday, Haigh was back in Horsham, collecting the £40 that was owed him by the jeweller's. He put £5 into his bank account in Crawley. He then called on Mr Jones just before lunch to settle his debts. But Mr Jones had other matters on his mind, for the police had interviewed him the night before. He said he hoped Haigh was not in any trouble. Haigh shrugged, said 'No,' and laughed. 'If there is any trouble,' said Jones, 'I prefer you not to come to the works. I prefer you to stay away.' Haigh left, and Jones never received the £14 Haigh owed him.

The next afternoon, the police returned to the Onslow Court Hotel and interviewed Haigh again. He helpfully provided them with a second statement, very similar to the first, but with more details. He must have realised that Jones would lead the police to the workshop, but nothing daunted he stayed on at the hotel, full of foolish confidence that nothing incriminating would be found.

Nothing happened on Friday, except that the police continued to pursue their enquiries and had a conference. It was on Saturday, 26 February that Mr Jones took DS Pat Heslin of the West Sussex Police to Giles Yard.

The workshop door was padlocked and had to be forced, as Haigh had the keys. Inside, Heslin noted the presence of three carboys, a stirrup pump, a rubber apron, rubber gloves, a mackintosh, a gas mask, an attaché case and a locked leather hat box. A key from the attaché case opened the hat box, in which were found a revolver, ammunition and a receipt from a Reigate cleaner's for a black Persian lamb coat.

On Sunday and Monday, DI Shelley Symes visited Crawley, Horsham and Reigate and picked up various items.

At 4.15 pm on Monday, 28 February, DI Albert Webb was waiting at the hotel when Haigh drove up in his Alvis. 'I want you to come to the Chelsea police station at once,' said DI Webb, 'and see Superintendent Barratt and Detective Inspector Symes.' 'Certainly,' said Haigh. 'I'll do anything to help you, as you know.'

At the police station, Barratt and Symes were busy, and it was not until about 7.30 pm that Symes appeared and said: 'I have continued my enquiries into the disappearance of Mrs Durand-Deacon and I want you to answer some more questions.' Haigh nodded. 'I'm quite willing to answer anything I can,' he said. 'And to help you all I can.' Symes then questioned him about the Persian lamb coat and Haigh's visits to Horsham. How many times had Haigh been there? 'I used to go to Horsham a lot,' said Haigh. 'But lately I've only been there once in the evening, to the pictures.' 'You've been there in the morning recently on no less than four occasions,' said Symes. 'Ah,' said Haigh. 'I can see you know what you're talking about. I admit the coat belonged to Mrs Durand-Deacon and that I sold her jewellery, as you know, to Bull's in Horsham.' Symes then produced the cleaner's ticket. Haigh said: 'Yes, I wondered if you'd got it when you started.' 'How did you come by this property?' demanded Symes. 'And where is Mrs Durand-Deacon?' He then cautioned Haigh about anything he might say. There was a pause before Haigh replied. 'It's a long story,' he said. 'It's one of blackmail, and I shall have to implicate many others. How do I stand about that?' Symes retorted: 'What you have to say is entirely a matter for you.'

At this point some other business summoned Symes and Barratt from the room for about ten minutes. Haigh was left alone with DI Webb.

Haigh looked at him and said: 'Tell me, frankly, what are the chances of anyone being released from Broadmoor?' Said Webb: 'I can't discuss that sort of thing with you.' 'Well,' said Haigh. 'If I told you the truth, you wouldn't believe me. It sounds too fantastic for belief.' Webb cautioned him. Haigh interrupted: 'I understand all that – I'll tell you all about it. Mrs Durand-Deacon no longer exists. She's disappeared completely. And no trace of her can ever be found again.' Webb was non-committal. 'What's happened to her?' he asked. 'I've destroyed her with acid,' Haigh replied. 'You'll find the sludge that remains at Leopold Road. Every trace has gone. How can you prove murder if there's no body?'

Webb fetched Symes and Barratt. In Haigh's presence, Webb remarked: 'He's just told me that Mrs Durand-Deacon doesn't exist, and that he's destroyed her by acid.' 'It's perfectly true,' said Haigh. 'But it's a very long story and it'll take hours to tell.' 'I'm prepared to listen,' said Symes.

What the police officers thought as Haigh told his story about the death of Mrs Durand-Deacon is not on record. If they were not amazed by the end of it, they certainly were when Haigh mentioned McSwann and Henderson – 'the subject of another story.' Invited to tell them about it, Haigh merely remarked that he had disposed of Mr WD McSwann and his mother and father, as well as Dr and Mrs Henderson, 'in a similar manner to the above'.

Pressed for details, he said that in the summer of 1944 he chanced to meet William Donald McSwann, a man in his thirties whom Haigh had first met in 1936. The acquaintance was revived. Haigh was popular with McSwann's parents and often visited them. One night, on 9 September 1944, the two men had a drink at The Goat in Kensington High Street, and then went to 79 Gloucester Road, where Haigh had a basement workshop, in which he was repairing a pin-table for McSwann. He hit McSwann on the head with a cosh, drank his blood (he said), removed any valuables and put the body in a purloined water butt, which he had filled with acid, later disposing of the sludge down a manhole in the basement. He visited Mr and Mrs McSwann and told them their son had gone underground to avoid being called up. The deception was maintained by Haigh, who forged letters from McSwann to his parents, somehow contriving to post them from Glasgow and Edinburgh. In July the following year, Haigh dealt separately with Mr and Mrs McSwann in the Gloucester Road basement, disposing of them as he had their son.

Posing as the son, he then obtained legal control of all his victims' assets, including the freehold in four properties, their furniture and belongings, which he sold, and the gilt-edged securities they owned. He made over £4,000 out of the extermination of all the McSwanns.

Haigh then told the astounded police how he had cultivated and disposed of another couple, Dr and Mrs Henderson, whom he met in 1947 over a property deal. In February 1948 he took them one by one from the Metropole Hotel, Brighton, where all three were staying, to his new workshop in Crawley. Here, both Hendersons were shot and dumped in two drums of acid, but not before he had drunk their blood and removed any money and valuables they had on them. Their hotel bill in Brighton was paid by Haigh and he took charge of their red setter dog until it contracted night blindness, when he sent it to a kennels. Again he kept the relatives quiet by forging occasional letters to Mrs Henderson's brother, who lived in Manchester.

Six victims were more than enough for the Chelsea police officers. After his confession, Haigh was detained in custody. The next day, Tuesday, 1 March, Symes searched Haigh's room at the Onslow Court Hotel, Room 404, and removed certain items and papers. He, DCI Mahon and the Home Office pathologist, Dr Keith Simpson, drove down to Crawley to examine the scene of Mrs Durand-Deacon's alleged disappearance.

Specks of blood were found on the whitewashed wall above the workshop bench, a hat pin was found in the bottom of the green drum, and a gall stone was spotted by the observant Dr Simpson in the sludge outside in the yard. The sludge itself was ladled into five wooden boxes and carted to the police laboratory in New Scotland Yard. Carefully sifted and analysed, it produced 28 lb of animal fat, two more gall stones, part of a foot, eighteen corroded bone fragments, a lipstick container, the handle of a handbag, and a full set of dentures, which were later identified by Mrs Durand-Deacon's lady dentist.

Left in acid or even in the sludge, these exhibits would all have dissolved within a month, apart from the gall stones, thus preventing the identification of the remains and proving Haigh's claim that Mrs Durand-Deacon had indeed vanished without any trace.

He was charged with her murder at Horsham police station on 2 March, and taken to Lewes Prison in Sussex.

Two days later, he asked to see DI Webb and made yet another statement, in which he said he had murdered three other people, strangers whom he met accidentally. He had coshed them and disposed of their bodies in acid. One was a woman in her thirties whom he had met in Hammersmith and killed in February 1945. The second was a man in his thirties called Max whom he encountered in The Goat in Kensington and killed about September 1945. The third was a Welsh girl called Mary, whom he met in Eastbourne in the summer of 1948. The first two, he said, were disposed of in the Gloucester Road basement, the third in Crawley. Haigh said he robbed all three of what they had, which was very little, and drank their blood.

No evidence was ever unearthed by the police to substantiate these claims. Most probably Haigh fabricated these murders to enforce the idea of insanity, which was to be his defence. He may have thought, like Christie, that the more the merrier, and decided to invent victims who were slaughtered just for their blood and not for their money, as the other six obviously were.

There is no evidence, of course, to prove whether or not he drank anybody's blood, except that a penknife with faint traces of blood on it *was* found in his Alvis. Blood if drunk would, however, tend to act as an emetic.

The blood-supping and his alleged dreams of blood and crucifixion were elaborated by the defence at the trial, as was Haigh's claim that he had habitually drunk his own urine since he was a boy. At the trial he was reported to have done just that in the presence of a prison doctor.

His life had, in fact, been rather unusual. He was born on 24 July 1909 at Stamford in Lincolnshire, and brought up in a Yorkshire village, Outwood, situated between

Wakefield and Leeds. The only child of a colliery foreman, his solitariness was enforced by the fact that his parents belonged to a religious sect, the Plymouth Brethren, who frowned on sport, light entertainment, social amusements of any frivolous or unedifying sort, and daily prayed together and read the Bible, isolating themselves from the sins, pleasures and evils of the world and refusing to have even a wireless or a newspaper in the house. But Haigh was not unhappy and was fond of his mother and father. He was always neat and smart. Educated at Wakefield Grammar School until he was seventeen, he was a good mixer, eager to please, and mischievous, and although no scholar or athlete, he wrote well and won a Divinity prize with an essay on St Peter. At the same time, to avoid trouble or offence, he became an accomplished liar. He was also an accomplished pianist, music being his greatest indulgence and passion. Between the ages of ten and sixteen he sang with the Wakefield Cathedral Choir, and occasionally played the organ at minor services. Much was also made at his trial of the presumed disturbing dichotomy between the lavish High Church cathedral rituals and the austere religion of his parents, but it is doubtful whether his sensitivity or intellect were sufficiently deep to be disturbed by anything much.

Apprenticed for a time to a motor engineer, he began at the age of twenty-one to experiment with various speculative business ventures concerned with insurance and brokerage. Then, on 6 July 1934, he married, left home and stopped attending meetings of the Brethren. Looking around for some means of making money, he devised a method of swindling a hire-purchase company dealing in cars by forging documents for non-existent cars hired by non-existent owners. Within a few months he was found out and was sentenced at Leeds Assizes in November 1934 to fifteen months for conspiring to defraud.

He wrote later: 'When I first discovered there were easier ways to make a living than to work long hours in an office, I did not ask myself whether I was doing right or wrong. That seemed to me to be irrelevant.'

While he was in prison his wife left him and he was rejected by the Brethren. His next venture, a successful dry-cleaning business, collapsed when his partner was killed in a car crash. The firm went into liquidation. Haigh came to London in 1936.

He was employed as the chauffeur and secretary of the manager of an amusement arcade called McSwann, whom – as we have seen – he later murdered. He became quite friendly with the McSwanns, but soon he embarked on another swindle. Posing as a small-town solicitor winding up the estate of a client who wished to dispose of some non-existent shares at a good price, he offered them for sale to anyone who paid a 25% deposit. For a time he was successful, collecting the cheques and moving on from town to town. In all, he made over £3,000. But eventually the law latched on to him and in November 1937 he was charged at Surrey Assizes in Kingston with obtaining money by false pretences. He pleaded guilty and was sentenced to four years' penal servitude.

He was released in August 1940, and during the Blitz was employed as a firewatcher in Pimlico. Within a year he was back in prison, sentenced to twenty-one months for stealing household goods.

This third experience of prison, together with his experiences as a firewatcher, seems to have hardened and darkened his mind. He wrote later: 'The ghastly sights after two land-mines had wiped out a block of buildings are fixed indelibly in my memory.' He began to doubt the existence of God. He is thought to have studied the effects of acid on mice, seeing how long their bodies took to dissolve if immersed in a mug of sulphuric acid. He resolved not to get caught again and to abandon the generally unrewarding petty crimes of the cheap crook.

On his release, he became a salesman for an engineering business at Crawley, where he lived for about two years, often being seen in the lounge of the George Hotel having tea. In March 1944, he was involved in a motor accident in which his head was cut. Some months later, now living in London, he chanced to meet young McSwann.

The brief trial of John George Haigh began at Lewes Assizes court in Sussex on Monday, 18 July 1949. It finished the following afternoon. The judge was Mr Justice Humphreys; the Attorney-General, Sir Hartley Shawcross, KC, MP, led for the Crown, and Sir David Maxwell Fyfe, KC, MP, for the defence.

The prosecution produced thirty-three witnesses, of whom just four were cross-examined, and then but briefly, by the defence. Haigh gave no evidence and only one witness was called for the defence, Dr Henry Yellowlees, a leading psychiatrist, with little or no court experience at that time. Dr Yellowlees was an early exponent of forensic psychiatry and later on appeared for the defence in other trials, successfully supporting verdicts of guilty but insane. Of the nine doctors who had examined Haigh in prison, he was the only one prepared to speak on the prisoner's behalf, after talking with him on three occasions for a total of twenty-four hours and ten minutes.

Dr Yellowlees maintained that Haigh had a paranoid constitution that could produce paranoid insanity. Early influences in his life had contributed, the doctor said, to this condition. But when cross-examined, Dr Yellowlees was forced to admit that Haigh knew he had done something which was 'punishable by law', and therefore 'wrong by the law of the country'.

In his book, *To Define True Madness*, published in 1953, Yellowlees wrote about the 'sadly overrated Haigh case', and said that the only point of real interest was that Haigh was 'medically mad' but not 'McNaghten mad'. Yellowlees said that he had been prepared in court to admit that Haigh 'did not satisfy the McNaghten criteria'. But so 'unfriendly and hostile' was the atmosphere in the court that when his evidence was attacked *in toto*, he felt 'improperly treated'.

No medical evidence was called by the Crown in rebuttal, the Attorney-General submitting there was nothing to rebut. The judge, commenting in his summing-up on Dr Yellowlees' statement that there was no sex element in the case, said that this was 'really rather a comfort in a way. One gets rather tired in these courts of sex complexes.'

The jury were out for seventeen minutes, returning at 4.40 pm. They found Haigh guilty of murdering Mrs Durand-Deacon. Asked if he had anything to say, Haigh replied: 'Nothing at all.'

Before his execution he wrote a remarkable account of his life, which appeared in the *News of the World*. He was hanged by Albert Pierrepoint and Harry Kirk at Wandsworth Prison on 6 August 1949, thirteen days after his fortieth birthday.

Pierrepoint used a special strap of pale calf leather to bind Haigh's wrists, as he had done with Heath. He used this special strap on only about a dozen occasions, on those occasions when he made a red-ink entry in his diary on the day of an execution – to indicate, as he said, 'more than a formal interest in this particular execution'.

42
DANIEL RAVEN

Among the murderers who kill without apparent motive are a number of sons who for some reason or other cannot exist without extinguishing members of their families – frequently a mother or father, or both. Such inimical offspring tend to plead guilty or to be found insane, and so no explanation or motive is ever officially put forward for their fatal deeds.

In this case, the deadly son was actually a son-in-law. No motive for his extraordinary actions was ever aired before or during his trial. But on Monday, 10 October 1949, after visiting his young wife, Marie, in a maternity home in Muswell Hill – where on 6 October she had given birth to their first child – the father, a dapper twenty-three-year-old Jewish advertising agent called Daniel Myer Raven, drove to the home of his parents-in-law and savagely battered them both to death.

The fact that Mr Leopold Goodman, aged forty-nine, and Mrs Esther Goodman, aged forty-seven, were Russian Jews and possessively proud of their daughter and of their new grandson, is probably not as relevant as the fact that they were also at the maternity home that evening, sitting beside their daughter and watched by their son-in-law. Something surely must have been said, some opinion, prejudice or attitude expressed by the middle-aged couple that provoked their son-in-law to exterminate them.

The Goodmans left the nursing home at about 9.05 pm, followed soon after by their son-in-law. He drove to the Goodman home in Ashcombe Gardens, Edgware, where at about 9.30 pm he attacked them, battering Mrs Goodman seven times on the head and Mr Goodman at least fourteen times. In both cases the weapon was the base of a television aerial.

The presence of a television set in the house gives some indication of the Goodmans' affluence. For television was then in its infancy and sets showing the few black-and-white TV programmes the BBC broadcast on one channel were expensive. The BBC's transmissions from Alexandra Palace, begun in November 1936, had been discontinued during the war, only being resumed on 7 June 1946. Daniel Raven, earning about £20 a week, was not monied enough to own a TV set.

After the attack, Raven drove around the corner to Edgwarebury Lane, where he lived with his wife in a house bought for them by Mr Goodman. Here he tried to remove the bloodstains on his dark blue suit, and having failed to do so satisfactorily, he stuffed the suit into a coke-boiler in the kitchen, hastening the burning process by leaving a lit gas-poker in the boiler.

At about 10.30 pm, he received a telephone call from the police, possibly while he was still trying to clean his suit. The police requested him to come round to his in-laws' house straight away – they had some rather bad news for him. If the telephone call interrupted him in his efforts to clean the suit, he must have set about burning it in some haste before dressing himself in a new shirt and tie and suit.

Unfortunately for Raven, about twenty minutes after he left Ashcombe Gardens Mrs Goodman's brother-in-law, Mr Frederick Fraiman, had called at the house with his wife and eldest daughter to enquire about Marie Raven and the baby. (Mr Fraiman was a business partner of the Goodmans in L Goodman Radio Ltd.) When the three Fraimans received no response to their knocking and ringing at the front, side and back doors, Mr Fraiman climbed into the house through an open window and came across the savaged bodies of the Goodmans in their blood-soaked dining room. He dialled 999 at 10.02 pm. The police and a doctor were soon at the scene, the police investigations being led by DI Diller. The aluminium aerial that had been the murder weapon was found in a sink in the scullery.

Robbery as an associated motive for the murders was discounted when bundles of pound notes were found untouched in the house, including one cache of notes under a mattress. There was also over £2,500 in a safe.

When Daniel Raven arrived he was overcome with emotion and sat sobbing on the stairs, crying: 'Why did they tell me to go? Why didn't they let me stop?' He had wanted to stay, he said, as his in-laws were apprehensive about being burgled. But they had insisted, he said, that he left. 'I don't get on with Mr Goodman too badly,' he confessed. 'Although we do quarrel at times. But Mrs Goodman and me didn't get on at all well.'

DI Diller was doubtful about the young man's explanations and sorrow, and was given further cause to be so when one of his policemen, who had questioned other relatives of the Goodmans, passed on the information that the young man had been wearing a dark-blue suit earlier that evening – not the light-grey suit he now wore. Diller also noted that Raven's shirt seemed very crisp and fresh.

The lamenting son-in-law was asked to accompany the police to Edgware police station for further questioning. But before this happened Diller asked Raven for the keys to his house. he handed them over reluctantly, adding: 'But you won't find anything there – I only had a bath.'

It was not until 11.45 pm that Diller entered the Raven's nest. As soon as he did so, he noticed a smell of burning. It came from the kitchen. He saw the gas-poker projecting from the blazing boiler, removed it, closed the vent and flue, and was able to retrieve part of a suit. Later it was found to be stained with blood (from the Goodmans' rare blood group AB), as were a pair of shoes that had been washed and hidden in the garage. The driver's seat in Raven's car had also been scrubbed.

When asked to account for the burning, bloody suit in the boiler – he had admitted the suit was his – Raven replied: 'How the blood got on it I don't know.' He had left it, he said, in the bathroom, where the police found no evidence of a bath having been recently taken.

Daniel Raven was charged by DCI Albert Tansill at Edgware police station on the night of Tuesday, 11 October with the murder of Mr Leopold Goodman. In proclaiming his innocence, Raven said that his father-in-law had made several enemies as a result of crooked business deals.

This was elaborated in court by counsel for the defence, who suggested that Mr Goodman had been a police informer, assisting the police with information about persons suspected of currency offences, and that the elderly couple had been murdered in revenge by a person or persons unknown. Raven's story by now had also been elaborated. When he gave evidence he said that after leaving the Goodmans alive and well he had called on his cousins nearby, who were out, and then decided to return to Ashcombe Gardens as he knew the Fraimans would probably call that night. Receiving no reply, he said, to his knocking at the door, he entered the house through a window and found Mrs Goodman in the dining room, her skull cracked open. He felt sick at the sight, he said, and in the witness box he swayed and appeared on the point of collapse. He continued by saying that blood got on his clothes and shoes when he knelt by her body. Overwhelmed by fear, he said, he fled from the house and drove to his own home, where he burned his suit and washed his shoes.

No defence involving the accused's mental instability or possible insanity was ever broached.

He appeared at the Old Bailey on Tuesday, 22 November 1949 before Mr Justice Cassells, with Mr Anthony Hawke appearing for the Crown and Mr John Maude, KC, for the defence. Found guilty on 24 November, Daniel Raven was sentenced to death.

In support of an appeal, a solicitor, Mr Rutter, then produced evidence that Raven was insane, that on account of his 'severe anxiety neurosis' he had been discharged from the RAF after a plane crash that he alone survived. He had joined the RAF when he was sixteen. A doctor who had treated Raven in the past stated that he used to suffer from 'black-outs and brain-storms'. Another said he had a kind of epilepsy. The appeal was heard on 20 December 1949 and dismissed.

All other appeals for clemency as well as a petition failed. Daniel Raven was duly hanged in Pentonville Prison on Friday, 6 January 1950, the executioners being Albert Pierrepoint and Harry Kirk.

CRAIG AND BENTLEY

THE MURDER OF PC MILES, 1952

Few murder trials exemplify the instinctive 'Them and Us' attitudes of those who uphold the law as starkly as Regina v Bentley and Craig in 1952. It was Regina (nor Rex) versus the accused as although Elizabeth II would not be crowned until June 1953, she had become Queen in February 1952, when her father, King George VI died. Seldom has an execution raised so many agonising problems. Questions were later asked in the House of Commons. Mr RT Paget said: 'A three-quarter witted boy is to be hung for a murder he did not commit, which was committed fifteen minutes after he was arrested. Can we be made to keep silent when a thing as horrible and as shocking as this is to happen?' But the law was determined to make an example of Craig and Bentley in order to deter young criminals in post-war Britain, and in doing so succeeded in making a disturbing example of itself. Bentley was hanged; he was nineteen. But crimes of violence committed by boys and youths continued to increase.

Christopher Craig was born on 19 May 1936, three years after Derek William Bentley. Both lived in south London, in Norbury, and both went to Norbury Secondary Modern School and left when they were fifteen. Craig suffered from word blindness, dyslexia, a disability that was hardly recognised then and rarely treated. As a result, he was scarcely able to read or write, only comics being within his comprehension. Other boys, he said, 'used to take the mickey out of me'. To improve his status he cultivated athletic skills – he was a good swimmer – and carried weapons, guns and knives. The guns he took to school, displaying them and swapping some with other boys. Between the ages of eleven and sixteen he possessed in all about forty guns: his ambition was to be a gunsmith. This interest arose from the fact that his father, a chief cashier in a bank, had been an army captain with the London Scottish during the First World War and was himself the possessor of two wartime revolvers. He also took his sons target-shooting, using air guns. Christopher, the youngest of nine children, was included. He proved, however, not to be a good shot, unlike his oldest brother, Niven.

Christopher's fantasies involving firearms were fed by the films he saw – he went to the pictures three or four times a week – and gangster films were his favourites. Niven, who was ten years older, had turned those fantasies into fact. Convicted of shop-breaking when he was fourteen, he was found guilty as a juvenile of two other offences and sent to an approved school. He was convicted twelve times in the army, being eventually court-martialled for armed robbery and given a five-year sentence. In March 1952, Niven was involved with four other men, one of whom died later in prison, in an armed robbery at Waltham Abbey. The haul was a cigarette lighter and £4. Niven Craig, aged twenty-six, a motor mechanic, denied any involvement in the robbery: he said he was elsewhere at the time. Nonetheless, he was convicted of the offence and of possessing a pistol at the time of his arrest. He denied making a grab at it when the police burst into his bedroom.

On Thursday, 30 October 1952, he was sentenced at the Old Bailey to twelve years in prison. Some of his family were in court, including his youngest brother, Christopher. They heard the judge, Mr Justice Hilbery, say to the prisoner: 'You are not only cold-blooded, but … I believe that you would shoot down, if you had the opportunity to do so, any police officer who was attempting to arrest you.'

Three days later, on Sunday, 2 November 1952, Christopher Craig, then aged sixteen, went to the pictures with a girlfriend. They saw a film in which the hero was hanged after a gunfight during which a policeman was shot. The film was called *My Death is a Mockery*. Between 8 and 9 pm, after going home for a meal, Craig called at the home of Derek Bentley.

Bentley, born on 30 June 1933, was then nineteen; his father owned an electrical business. He is said to have fallen off a lorry in 1938, landing on his head, an accident that allegedly cause him to suffer from epilepsy all his short life, and when he was bombed out twice during the Blitz, when bricks and rubble fell on him, injuring his head, this was claimed to have resulted in the fact that he was of below-average intelligence and illiterate. He was later adjudged by a prison doctor to be 'feeble-minded' and a psychiatrist at the trial adjudged his mental state to be bordering on being retarded. Perhaps to compensate for his intellectual failings, he took up body-building. He was proud of his physique, and was a tall, nice-looking boy. On leaving school, he worked occasionally as a dustman or removal man. Convicted of shop-breaking, he was sent to an approved school in March 1948, being released in July 1950. About the time of Niven Craig's arrest in 1952, he began an infrequent association with young Christopher Craig whom he rather admired, an association that his parents did their best to stop after some trouble in May that year. Worth a mention here is the fact that Bentley once refused to go on a raid with Craig when he found out that Craig carried a loaded gun.

On 2 November 1952, when Craig called at the Bentley home about 8.30 pm, Mrs Bentley said Derek was out. Derek was, in fact, watching television. He said later: 'A little later Norman Parsley and Frank Fazey called … My mother told me that they had called and I then ran out after them. I walked up the road with them to the paper shop, where I saw Craig standing. We all talked together and then the other two left. Chris Craig and I then caught a bus to Croydon, a 109 bus.'

'What for?' demanded the judge at the trial. Said Bentley: 'Just for the ride, sir. An ordinary ride.'

He and Craig had already met that morning. According to Craig, who gave Bentley a knuckle-duster on the short bus ride into Croydon, Bentley had dared him to break into a butcher's shop. This Bentley later denied. But both now had weapons. Craig had a revolver with a sawn-off barrel, some ammunition, and a sheath knife, which he wore on his belt. Bentley had a smaller knife and the knuckle-duster, which Craig said he had made. He also said in court: 'I did not know what Bentley had got, sir, and he did not know what I had got.' According to him, their common intent that night was burglary.

They got off the bus at West Croydon station and went down Tamworth Road. Said Bentley: 'We walked down to Reeves' Corner and crossed over, and then we came back up … We looked into the window of the sweet-stuff shop … I was still looking in it and Craig had got over this iron fence.' It was in fact a 6-ft-high iron gate.

It so happened that at that time − about 9.15 pm − a woman named Mrs Ware chanced to be putting her little girl to bed in a house opposite the wholesale confectioner's, which was called Barlow and Parker. The child drew her mother's attention to the two men near the side entrance of the confectioner's. 'They were just standing there,' said Mrs Ware, 'talking for a few minutes, and pulling their hats over their eyes.' 'I was always messing around with my hat, sir,' said Bentley later. Mrs Ware: 'All of a sudden the shorter one jumped right over the fence at the side on the left.' The taller man, she said, 'waited for a few more minutes, and then a motor came round the corner and he waited for that to go by, and when there was no one in sight he jumped over'. Her husband telephoned the police.

Bentley stated: 'Chris then climbed up the drainpipe to the roof and I followed. Up to then Chris had not said anything. We both got out onto the flat roof at the top … Someone shone a light in the garden, and so we got behind a stack or lift-shaft . .. Someone called out down in the garden. Chris said: "It's a copper. Hide behind here …" We were there waiting for about ten minutes.' They hid themselves in the shadows of the lift house at the far end of the roof. It was a dry night, but dark − 'there was not much moon' according to a police witness.

At about 9.25 pm, a police van arrived outside the confectioner's, moments before a police car. In the van were DC Frederick Fairfax in plain clothes, PC Norman Harrison, PC Bugden and PC Pain. In the car were PC Sidney Miles and PC James McDonald. All six were from Z Division. What happened in the next thirty minutes or so was to be variously interpreted by the accused and the police.

In 1991, PC Pain, by then aged 83 and long retired, stated: 'I was the first officer called that night. The scene on the roof was pandemonium. It was very chaotic. There were police sirens, an ambulance and a fire engine, people shouting. It was impossible to hear Bentley say anything. But if he had said, "Let him have it, Chris!" I would have heard it. And I didn't.' PC Pain was never called to give evidence at the trial.

Fairfax's story, and that of his colleagues, was as follows. He said his attention was caught by a footprint on a window sill of the warehouse and that he then climbed up a drainpipe onto the flat roof. Somehow aware of the presence of the burglars behind the lift house at one end of the roof, he approached them, walking carefully between four roof lights. 'I'm a police officer!' he shouted. 'Come out from behind that stack!' Craig retorted: 'If you want us, fucking well come and get us!' 'All right,' said Fairfax, and showing great courage and determination, he rushed towards the lift house and grabbed the nearest figure he saw, who happened to be Bentley. Fairfax dragged him out into the open. Still holding Bentley he tried to close in on Craig. But Bentley broke free, allegedly shouting: 'Let him have it, Chris!'

Craig fired, said Fairfax, 6 ft away from him, and a bullet grazed his right shoulder. He fell, got up and chased after Bentley. Fairfax floored Bentley with his fist and Craig fired again.

With Bentley as a shield, Fairfax ducked down behind a roof light and frisked his captive, finding a knuckle-duster and a knife. 'That's all I've got, guvnor,' said Bentley. 'I haven't got a gun.' Firmly holding onto Bentley, Fairfax edged around the roof lights, finally finding shelter behind the staircase head to one side of the roof. Craig retreated back to the area of the lift house and was now about 40 feet away from them.

PC McDonald, whose weight had made climbing the drainpipe difficult, was assisted onto the roof by Fairfax, who let go of Bentley in the process. Then Fairfax called to Craig: 'Drop your gun.' 'Come and get it!' came the answer, accompanied by another shot. According to McDonald, Fairfax said to him: 'He got me in the shoulder,' and Bentley said: 'I told the silly bugger not to use it.'

Meanwhile, PC Harrison had climbed onto an adjacent roof to the right of the lift-shaft (from Fairfax's point of view) and to the left of Craig, who fired two shots in Harrison's direction when the policeman edged out onto a connecting roof of asbestos and glass tiles. Harrison retreated behind a chimneystack, which he said was struck by a bullet – although no corroborative evidence of this was ever produced.

McDonald then asked Fairfax: 'What sort of a gun has he got, Fairy?' Bentley intervened, saying: 'He's got a .45 Colt and plenty of bloody ammunition too.' From then on, Bentley was allegedly silent.

Several minutes later, police reinforcements arrived below. Some were armed. At least six guns are believed to have been issued to the police, some of whom surrounded the warehouse.

PC Syd Miles, who had arrived at the scene with PC McDonald, had gone in search of the confectioner's manager. From him, Miles obtained the keys to the warehouse. On his return, Miles was one of the policemen who entered the building and came up the interior staircase to the roof. PC Harrison was with him. PC Miles kicked the roof door of the stair-head open and stepped out. As he did so, a shot was fired and he fell down dead, a bullet having entered his head above the left eyebrow. It made a horizontal exit wound at the back.

A second shot was fired as Fairfax and McDonald dragged Miles' body behind the stair-head, leaving Bentley again unattended.

Moments later, PC Robert Jaggs climbed on to the roof from the drainpipe and joined his colleagues. Whenever he poked his head around the stair-head he heard shots. Craig shouted: 'Come on, you brave coppers! Think of your wives!' Bentley allegedly said to Jaggs: 'You want to look out. He'll blow your head off.' PC Harrison, after hurling his truncheon, a milk-bottle and a piece of wood in Craig's direction – during which Craig cried: 'I'm Craig! You've just given my brother twelve years! Come on, you coppers! I'm only sixteen!' – dashed out of the stairhead door and joined his other three colleagues.

Meanwhile, PC Lowe Stewart, who had arrived about 9.45 pm, had climbed a drainpipe to the roof, seen that Miles was dead, climbed down again and positioned himself in a small yard west of the building and below Craig's vantage point. There was a dilapidated greenhouse in the yard. He heard Craig say: 'It's a Colt .45! Are you hiding behind a shield? Is it bullet proof? Are we going to have a shooting match? It's just what I like … Have they hurt you, Derek?'

Fairfax, McDonald and Jaggs now pushed and pulled Bentley around the open stair-head door and inside the entrance. Bentley is said to have shouted: 'Look out, Chris! They're taking me down!' The three policemen, and Harrison, went down the stairs with their captive, Bentley.

Before long Fairfax returned, armed with a .32 automatic. 'Drop your gun – I also have a gun!' he shouted. Craig replied: 'Come on, copper – let's have it out!'

Fairfax darted out of the stair-head. A shot was fired, and he fired two shots in return as he rushed around the roof lights, crouching behind them and moving towards Craig, whose own gun, misfiring, clicked more than once – four times, according to PC Lowe Stewart, who then heard a shot and Craig say: 'See – it's empty!' Craig said later there were just two clicks.

Craig swung his body over the railings that edged the roof, stood for a moment and said: 'Well, here we go. Give my love to Pam!' He jumped.

The drop was 25 feet. But on the way down, according to Stewart, Craig hit the edge of the greenhouse. Stewart ran over to Craig. Later, Stewart said: 'I jumped on him and he said: "I wish I was fucking dead! I hope I've killed the fucking lot."' Craig's spine was fractured, as was his breastbone and his forearm. However, it seems highly unlikely that his leap took him as far as the greenhouse, which was 15 feet away from the warehouse wall. His injuries may have been caused when he hit a shed in falling: it was immediately below him on his right.

It was now about 10.45 pm. Craig was put in the same ambulance as DC Fairfax and taken to Croydon General Hospital, where he and Fairfax lay overnight in adjacent cubicles.

Although Craig was in considerable pain, he was only given two codeine tablets (at 2 am on Monday the 3rd) in the twelve hours between his admission and the operation to set his wrist, at 11 am on the Monday morning. At 9.45 pm on the Monday night he was given a pain-killing injection of pethedine, another dose of the same at 4 pm on Tuesday, and more codeine at 10 pm on Wednesday the 3rd. On Wednesday morning he had another operation on his wrist.

Craig said later in court that he dived head first off the roof, intending to kill himself. He said he landed on his head and knocked himself out. He remembered nothing thereafter, he said, until the early morning of the 3rd. He said in court: 'I was in hospital and I woke up when someone hit me in the mouth and called me a murdering bastard, sir.' He claimed later, and this must refer to the operation on his wrist on Monday morning: 'They were pushing me down a corridor on a trolley and they were running me into the walls and all over the bumps so they could hurt me.' He added, explaining his difficulty in remembering what the police claimed he said: 'I was injected every twelve hours, sir … I was hardly conscious half the time, sir.' 'Hardly conscious!' exclaimed the Lord Chief Justice. 'Don't talk such nonsense!' Said Craig: 'I was only half conscious. I was crying for my mother.'

Six policemen from Z Division gave evidence at the trial about Craig's callous and boastful remarks as he lay in a hospital bed under police surveillance. He said: 'Is the copper dead? How about the others? We ought to have shot them all! – Did I really kill a policeman? – I shot him in the head and he went down like a ton of bricks – All you bastards should be dead – Is the policeman I shot in the shoulder still in hospital? I know that the one I shot in the head is dead – That night I was out to kill because I had so much hate inside me for what they did to my brother.' Much of this was later denied by Craig.

DS Shepherd said in court that he went to Croydon General Hospital at 11 pm on 2 November and saw Craig – who later denied seeing Shepherd until 11 November.

DCI John Smith – who had already visited the scene of the crime, had seen the dead policeman's body and spoken with DC Fairfax – said he charged the young gunman at about 11.30 pm on 2 November with the murder of PC Miles.

This is contradicted by Fairfax himself, who some years later told author David Yallop: 'Craig did not talk to anyone either voluntarily or any other way until the following day. He was *out* and stayed that way.'

At 1.15 am, Smith and Shepherd went to Craig's home, where they found a .45 bullet in his bed and 137 rounds of ammunition in a tin box in the attic. At 4 am, they saw Bentley in Croydon police station. Bentley said to Smith: 'Are you in charge of this, guvnor? … I didn't kill him, guv. Chris did it.' He was then cautioned and made a statement, written down by DS Shepherd. It was read back to the illiterate Bentley, who scrawled a signature on each page. He was then charged. He said: 'Craig shot him. I hadn't got a gun. He was with me on the roof and shot him then between the eyes.' In his statement he said: 'I did not have a gun and I did not know Chris had one until he shot.'

This contradicts a remark Bentley is said to have made in the police car taking him from Tamworth Road to the police station. After being taken down the warehouse stairs, Bentley had been handed over by Inspector Bodley to PS Edward Roberts, who cautioned him. Bentley said to him: 'I didn't have a gun. Chris shot him.' Sitting between PS Roberts and PC Alderson in the rear of a police car driven by PC Stephens, Stephens and Roberts heard Bentley say: 'I knew he had a gun, but I didn't think he'd use it. He's done one of your blokes in.' According to Roberts, nothing else was said by anyone in the car. However, the driver, Stephens, added that Roberts also said: 'I shouldn't make any other statement now. You'll be given a chance to make a statement at the station.'

Apart from the fact that both Craig and Bentley later denied most of what police witnesses alleged they had said – on the roof, in the police car and in hospital – including the phrase 'Let him have it, Chris!' which was said to have been heard by Fairfax, McDonald and Harrison, these officers and others sometimes disagreed about the alleged shouts and remarks made by Bentley and Craig, who both also denied that Fairfax apprehended Bentley in the manner he described.

Their version was that Fairfax, having seized Bentley, took him back across the roof, while McDonald was still struggling up the drainpipe. It was then, said Craig, that he fired 'to frighten him away', when Fairfax was about 30 ft from him. He said he fired at the ground, 6 ft in front of himself, and his defence suggested that the bullet flew up and grazed Fairfax's shoulder. Said Bentley: 'Fairfax leaned on me and fell over like *that*. He did not touch the floor, though … He got up – well, leaned up – and put me behind that staircase … I gave him the knuckle-duster. I took it out of my pocket myself.'

Oddly, the alternative interpretation of the phrase 'Let him have it, Chris!'– i.e., 'Hand him the gun' – was never mentioned in court, not even by the defence.

Craig's defence was that although guilty of manslaughter, he was innocent of murder: he never intended to injure or kill. He fired at the policemen, he said, obliquely, not directly, and what he shouted was 'Bluff, sir, so that they would not come at me.' His version of PC Miles's death was this. 'The door flew open and I thought someone was rushing at me, sir, saw someone was coming out, and I fired another one to frighten them away … over the roof" i.e., to his right. The fatal bullet, he said, 'might have ricocheted off". Of Fairfax's final armed charge at him, he said: 'Someone fired two shots at me from somewhere I could not see.'

Bentley's defence was that the 'joint enterprise' had ended fifteen minutes *before* Miles died, that at the time of Miles's death he was already under arrest, had made no move to rejoin Craig or escape when he might have done so, that he did not know Craig had a gun and did not urge him to use it.

The prosecution had to prove that Bentley and Craig had a common purpose. The law was that an accomplice, although he did nothing, was as guilty as the person who struck a blow or shot a gun. It had to be proved that Bentley knew Craig had a gun before the shooting began and that he was prepared to use it, as Bentley urged him so to do, according to the prosecution. Bentley himself had two weapons in his possession, a knife and a knuckle-duster. But it was the latter that excited the interest and disapprobation of the judge in the trial – the Lord Chief Justice, Lord Goddard. Slipping it on his hand, he asked the jury: 'Have you ever seen a more horrible sort of weapon? … Did you ever see a more shocking thing that that?'

As regards Craig, the judge told the jury that in the special law concerning policemen, if a person 'does a wilful act which causes the death of the officer, he is guilty of murder, whether or not he intended to kill or to do grievous bodily harm'. The defence, said the judge, had to show the *act* was accidental in order to reduce the charge to manslaughter.

The trial of Bentley and Craig, who was now on crutches, began at the Old Bailey, on Thursday, 9 December 1952 – less than six weeks after the shooting. It ended on the morning of Saturday, 11 December. The chief prosecutor was Mr Christmas Humphreys. Craig's counsel was a barrister from Leeds, Mr John Parris, and Bentley's was Mr FH Cassels, son of Mr Justice Cassels. Mr Parris, busily employed in a trial in Leeds, was given the brief concerning Craig three days before the Old Bailey trial was due to start, originally on Monday, 6 December. When he complained, the start of the trial was postponed for three days.

Twenty-four witnesses were called by the prosecution – sixteen of whom were police officers of Z Division – and only two by the defence, the accused themselves. The police witnesses failed to agree on how many shots were fired and some of their evidence was inconsistent. But, as the judge told the jury, speaking of Fairfax, McDonald and Harrison: 'Those three officers in particular showed the highest gallantry and resolution. They were conspicuously brave. Are you going to say that they are conspicuous *liars*? Because if their evidence is untrue – that Bentley called out "Let him have it, Chris" – those officers are doing their best to swear away the life of that boy. If it is true, it is, of course, the most deadly piece of evidence against him.'

Craig himself said he reloaded his gun once and fired it eleven times, two shots being misfires. The prosecution produced Mr Lewis Nicholls, MSc, Director of the Metropolitan Police Laboratory, as their ballistics expert. He revealed that the gun was not strictly speaking a Colt .45 but a First World War standard issue .455 Eley Service revolver with a sawn-off barrel. He pointed out that 'This weapon … was quite an inaccurate weapon.' He agreed that it would be inaccurate to a degree of 6 ft at a range of 39 ft, although 'if one aimed at the centre of a human being, one would more or less guarantee to hit him at 6 ft.' This seemed to suggest that Craig was far more likely to have hit Miles, some 39 ft away, if he had *not* been aiming at him – a point that the defence failed to follow up.

Nicholls said that of the twelve bullets and cartridge cases given to him on 15

November, nearly a fortnight after the shooting, one was a .32 and three were under-sized and would make a shot completely inaccurate. These three had been fired, one being found later caught up in Fairfax's braces. The rest were 45 Tommy-gun rounds, two of which were duds. The police had found only two spent bullets on the roof, and apparently none (apart from that in Fairfax's clothing) elsewhere. One .45 bullet (Exhibit 8) was inside the doorway of the staircase head, and the other was in a far corner of the roof. Mr Nicholls agreed that Exhibit 8 was 'badly distorted' and had been fired by a revolver similar to Exhibit 6, Craig's gun. However, he added: 'I could find no evidence of blood on it whatsoever. Therefore, in all probability, it is not the fatal bullet.'

Some years later, Dr David Haler – who had carried out the post mortem on PC Miles – told the author David Yallop that the bullet that killed Miles was a large-calibre bullet of a size ranging between .32 and .38. The standard Metropolitan Police pistol at that time was a .32 Webley automatic.

What happened to the bullet that killed PC Miles? It was never produced as such in court. Nor was any forensic expert, or indeed any other ballistics expert, asked by the defence to examine and comment on all the bullets, the ammunition and the gun.

It has been alleged that one of the policemen involved in the later stages of the confrontation at the warehouse, situated on an adjacent roof, could have shot PC Miles by accident or mistake. Craig himself always seemed to believe that *he* had shot Miles. However, Yallop quotes him as saying years later: 'What I've never been able to understand is how I shot him between the eyes when he was facing away from me and was going the wrong way.'

During the brief trial, Lord Goddard made over 250 interjections, most of them harmful by implication to the accused. As the jury retired, the foreman asked the judge if they could examine Fairfax's jacket and waistcoat. Lord Goddard retorted: 'You will remember you are not considering the wounding of Sergeant Fairfax. You are considering the murder of a policeman!' He was still wearing the knuckle-duster, which he had put on his hand again towards the end of his summing-up. He now strongly smote the bench with it.

The all-male jury were out for seventy-five minutes, between 11.15 and 12.30 am. While they were out, Lord Goddard dealt with another case in which Craig and a sixteen-year-old grammar school boy, Norman Parsley, both masked, had robbed an elderly Croydon couple at gunpoint. Parsley was sentenced to four years in jail.

Craig and Bentley were both found guilty of the murder of PC Syd Miles, but in Bentley's case the jury added a recommendation for mercy. Neither prisoner said anything when invited to speak before sentence was passed. Lord Goddard donned his black cap and formally sentenced Derek Bentley to death.

Christopher Craig was too young to hang – though he was, said the judge: 'One of the most dangerous young criminals who has ever stood in that dock.' He was sentenced to be detained at Her Majesty's pleasure. 'You are the more guilty of the two,' said Lord

Goddard. 'Your heart was filled with hate, and you murdered a policeman without thought of his wife, his family or himself. And never once have you expressed a word of sorrow for what you have done.'

The Lord Chief Justice then asked DS Fairfax (recently promoted to detective sergeant), PCs McDonald and Harrison, as well as the Chief Inspector of Z Division, to step forward. He told them that their conduct was worthy of the highest commendation and that the thanks of all law-abiding citizens was their due.

Three weeks later, on 6 January 1953, *before* Bentley's appeal was heard, it was announced that DS Fairfax had been awarded the George Cross, PC Harrison and PC McDonald George Medals, and PC Jaggs a BEM.

Bentley's appeal was heard on 13 January and dismissed. Although the press were largely in favour of his execution – four policemen had been killed by villains in 1951 – there were widespread protests, petitions and expressions of outrage by some MPs and many others. But the Home Secretary, Sir David Maxwell-Fyfe, remained inflexible and did nothing.

Derek Bentley, aged nineteen, was hanged by Albert Pierrepoint and Harry Allen in Wandsworth Prison at 9 am on Wednesday, 28 January 1953, just over three months after the shooting of PC Miles.

Some 5,000 people demonstrated outside the prison, crying 'Murder!' and singing 'Abide With Me' when the hour struck. The notice of Bentley's execution, hung on the prison gates, was torn down and smashed.

It was rumoured that Bentley wept as he was taken to be hanged. Pierrepoint would later categorically deny this, saying in his autobiography: 'I did not shake hands with the prisoner on the afternoon before his death. I did not make any notes about him. The Governor of Wandsworth did not have to urge me to get on with my job. Bentley did not cry on the way to the scaffold.'

Steve Fielding, in his book *Pierrepoint: A Family of Executioners*, had more to say about the event:

> *Rising early, Albert tested the equipment and with everything in readiness* [he and Harry Allen] *returned to their room, where Albert was served his favourite prison breakfast of fried plaice and potatoes. At a few seconds to nine the hangmen approached the condemned cell and took their places next to the governor. 'Good morning, Pierrepoint,' the governor whispered. 'I see that this has got to be done.' 'That's all right, sir,' Albert replied. Moments later the signal was given and they entered through the green cell door. Bentley got to his feet and as Harry took hold of his right arm, Albert fastened the wrist-strap. Bentley looked around confusedly as the door was thrown open leading to the drop.*

At the Bentley home in Norbury, the clocks in the house had all been silenced. Mrs Bentley lay upstairs in bed, heavily sedated. In the living room sat Mr Bentley, his daughter Iris, and his youngest surviving son, Dennis, aged nine. Mr Bentley wore a wristwatch and he could not help glancing at it from time to time as the hour of his eldest son's execution approached. At nine o'clock he suddenly rose from his chair and grabbed Dennis. 'No one's ever going to take my son away from me,' he said and wept.

Christopher Craig spent ten-and-a-half years in prison and was released on licence in May 1963. He settled in Buckinghamshire, became an engineer and married in 1965 when he was twenty-eight. Lord Goddard died in May 1971, at the age of ninety-three.

Interviewed for a Thames TV programme called *Thames Reports,* Craig said in September 1991: 'It was a conspiracy. Everybody knew at the time that if a policeman dies, somebody has to pay for it ... The guns and things gave me a sort of security. I suppose it's like a child with a dummy.' He also said: 'Fairfax's evidence that, er, Bentley struggled and I shot at him from 6 ft is totally untrue ... I fired at him from 39 ft at least, not 6 ft ... I tried to shoot myself earlier in the incident, and I had the gun to my head, not my mouth, as people portrayed, but to my temple. And I just couldn't do it ... I had run out of ammunition. I threw the gun to my right and dived off the roof.'

Asked whether Bentley had ever said 'Let him have it, Chris!' Craig replied: 'He didn't say a word. I didn't hear Bentley speak the whole time, even when Fairfax grabbed him by the shoulder, behind the lift ... He was just taken away, meek and mildly ... He didn't say [those words] ... If he had said it, I would have heard it ... Everyone else seemed to hear it ... All the police ... It never was said.'

Craig volunteered to have a polygraph test, which the company's managing director, Jeremy Barratt, conducted. Craig answered questions about salient points concerning what happened on the warehouse roof with a 'Yes' or a 'No'. At the end of the test Mr Barrett said: 'The machine doesn't lie and neither do you.'

Bentley's family tried for years to get the verdict on their son repealed, but to no avail. Mr Bentley died in July 1974 and his wife two years later. Iris Bentley struggled on alone. Dennis, who grew up to be a bitter, sullen young man, himself fell foul of the law more than once. In 1980, when he was thirty-eight, he was sentenced to a term of imprisonment for various driving offences. For forty years, Iris Bentley campaigned to get her brother's conviction quashed. Wearing the bracelet he had given her on the eve of his execution, she wrote over 150,000 letters. Along the way she had sixteen operations for cancer. In 1993 she said: 'I have undergone a lot of stress in my fight. There have been so many setbacks, so many disappointments, so much stress. But I am not the sort of person who gives in.' She died of cancer in 1997. Four years earlier, in July 1993, Derek Bentley had been granted a royal pardon.

Before Derek Bentley died, he told his parents: 'I didn't kill anyone. So why are they killing me?' In his last letter to them, someone wrote at his dictation: 'I tell you what, Mum, the truth of this thing has got to come out one day.'

In July 1998, almost forty-six years after the trial, the Court of Appeal overturned the conviction of Derek Bentley. The Lord Chief Justice, Lord Bingham, said that Lord Goddard had been 'blatantly prejudiced', had misdirected the jury, had never mentioned Bentley's mental problems, had lavishly praised the police, and that his summing-up had pressurised the jury into convicting Bentley, who had been denied, he said, 'that fair trial that is the birth-right of every British citizen'.

JOHN REGINALD CHRISTIE

THE MURDER OF MRS CHRISTIE, 1953

More has probably been written about the murders at 70 Rillington Place than about any other case investigated by the Metropolitan Police since the Whitechapel murders. At least six women were killed at Number 70. But what has caused the greatest argument is whether or not two murderers were at work at the same time in the same house. The undisputed fact is that a man who had already strangled two women was the chief witness for the prosecution at the trial of another man who lived in the same house and was alleged to have strangled his wife and child.

John Reginald Halliday Christie was a thin, bald, weak, neurotic, unlikeable person, a hypochondriac, a liar and one-time thief. One of seven children, five of whom were girls, he was born on 8 April 1898 in Yorkshire and brought up in Chester Street, Boothtown, on the edge of Halifax. His father was a carpet designer. As a child, Christie was often ill, often beaten by his father and known as a sissy at Halifax Secondary School, where he proved to be quite bright and sang in the school choir; he was also a boy scout and liked to do some gardening.

After leaving school when he was fifteen, he got a job with the Halifax police. He was sacked for petty pilfering, however, and then sacked for petty theft by the carpet factory that gave him his next job. He became a cinema operator at the Gem and then at the Victoria Hall cinema in Halifax, from where he was called up in April 1917 just after his nineteenth birthday. He served as a signalman with the Duke of Wellington's Regiment and with the Notts and Derby Regiment in Flanders and France. Injured by an exploding mustard-gas shell, he was gassed twice, blinded for some months, and lost his voice, as he claimed, for over three years. Thereafter, he always spoke in low, uncertain tones. He was also short-sighted and wore glasses. His sex drive was apparently as feeble as his constitution – he had pneumonia when he was seventeen – and a girl who led him down a lover's lane in Halifax dubbed him 'Reggie-no-dick' and 'Can't-do-it-Christie'.

He married Ethel Simpson Waddington in May 1920; they had no children. He moved from job to job, working as a cinema operator, a clerk and a postman, and in April 1921 he was sentenced to three months' imprisonment for stealing postal orders. Two years later, he was bound over for obtaining money by false pretences and put on twelve months' probation for violence. Presumably disgruntled with the attentions of the law and the imperfections of his all but sexless marriage, he came to London in 1923, leaving his wife in Sheffield where she worked as a shorthand typist. The pattern of shiftlessness continued. He moved from place to place and job to job. In September 1924, he was given nine months' hard labour at an Uxbridge court for theft.

Two months after this, Timothy John Evans was born in south Wales.

Christie then held down a clerical job for five years until, in May 1929, he was sentenced to six months' hard labour for striking a woman with whom he was temporarily living with her son's cricket-bat. His last sentence, in 1933, was three months for stealing a car. His wife visited him in prison and on his release came to live with him in London, ten years after their separation. Her presence gave him some stability, for it was twenty years before he was again charged with an offence – her murder. Their sex life, although it apparently revived for a time, was sporadic and eventually ceased.

In 1938, they rented three small rooms, the ground floor flat in 10 Rillington Place – at the time a seedy cul-de-sac near Ladbroke Grove underground station. Since demolished and rebuilt as a terrace of modern houses, the street, off St Mark's Road, is now known as Ruston Mews.

Christie lived in Rillington Place for fifteen years, during which time seven women were murdered in the house. The first was Ruth Fuerst, a tall Austrian girl, aged twenty-one at the time of her death, who came to England in 1939 as a student nurse and was then employed in a wartime munitions factory in Davies Street, Mayfair. In 1939, Christie had begun to wear the dark-blue uniform and peaked cap of a special constable in the War Reserve Police. Based at Harrow Road police station, he patrolled the streets making sure black-out regulations were observed and law and order maintained. This he apparently did with a thoroughness that verged on the officious. Off duty one day, but still making enquiries about a man wanted for theft, he met Ruth Fuerst in a snack bar. As his wife was away in Sheffield, where she fled when the bombing became unbearable, he asked Miss Fuerst back to Rillington Place on two or three occasions. It was August 1943 and Christie was forty-five. He later declared:

She was very tall. Almost as tall as me, and I was 5 ft 9 in … One day … she undressed and wanted me to have intercourse with her. I got a telegram while she was there, saying that my wife was on her way home. The girl wanted us to team up together and go right away somewhere together. I would not do that. I got on to the bed and had intercourse with her. While I was having intercourse with her, I strangled her with a piece of rope. I remember urine and excreta coming away from her. She was completely naked … She had a leopard skin coat and I wrapped this around her. I took her from the bedroom into the front room and put her under the floorboards. I had to do that because of my wife coming back. I put the remainder of her clothing under the floorboards too. My wife came home in the evening; my brother-in-law, Mr Waddington, came with her. Mr Waddington went back home the next day and during the afternoon my wife went out. I think she was working at Osram's.

While she was out I picked the body up from under the floorboards and took it into the outhouse. Later in the day I dug a hole in the garden, and in the evening, when it was dark, about ten o'clock I should say, I put the body down the hole and covered it up quickly with earth. It was the right-hand side of the garden, about halfway along towards the rockery. My wife never knew. I told her I was going to the lavatory. The only lavatory is in the yard.

The outhouse served as a wash-house and lavatory and was situated outside the back door leading into the yard or garden.

That statement was made nearly ten years after the event it describes, and – like most of what Christie so cautiously said – has to be viewed with equal caution. The facts are that Ruth Fuerst was last seen on 24 August 1943 in her Notting Hill digs and that her skeleton was recovered in the area indicated by Christie in March 1953. There was no evidence to show how, in fact, she met her death.

Four months after the Austrian girl's disappearance, Christie ceased to be a War Reserve constable because of his association with a married woman employed at Harrow Road police station. Her soldier husband, returning home on leave, assaulted Christie and cited him as co-respondent in the ensuing divorce case. Meanwhile Christie – whom everyone knew as 'Reg' – got a clerical job with Ultra Radio in Acton. There he met a small, stout woman, Muriel Eady, aged thirty-two, who worked in the canteen. She had a boyfriend, and the two of them used to visit the Christies in Rillington Place. Said Christie later:

On one occasion she came alone. I believe she complained of catarrh, and I said I thought I could help her. She came by appointment when my wife was out. I believe my wife was on holiday. I think I mixed some stuff up, some inhalants, Friar's Balsam was one. She was in the kitchen, and at the time she was inhaling with a square scarf over her head. I remember now, it was in the bedroom. The liquid was in a square glass jar with a metal screw-top lid. I had made two holes in the lid and through one of the holes I put a rubber tube from the gas into the liquid. Through the other hole I put another rubber tube, about two feet long. This tube didn't touch the liquid ... She inhaled the stuff from the tube. I did it to make her dopey. She became sort of unconscious and I have a vague recollection of getting a stocking and tying it round her neck. I am not too clear about this ... It may have been the Austrian girl that I used the gas on. I don't think it was both. I believe I had intercourse with her at the time I strangled her. I think I put her in the wash-house. That night I buried her in the garden on the right-hand side nearest the yard.

Last seen alive on 7 October 1944 at her Putney home, Muriel Eady's skeleton was unearthed in the garden in March 1953. The cause of her death could not be established, but that same month the police discovered a square glass jar (but no lid) in the kitchen of Christie's flat. They also found that a gas-pipe on the kitchen wall by the window had been stopped up with putty, and that one of the burners on the gas-stove, minus its top, was merely a nozzle.

Christie probably devised a method of gassing women visitors so that he could indulge his sexual whims with their immobile, unconscious bodies. This may have involved some form of masturbation rather than intercourse. For as the women were apparently willing, with the possible exception of Miss Eady, there was no need to gas them before a normal act of intercourse. None of his later victims died of carbon monoxide poisoning: the gas was used, it seems, only to incapacitate them.

Miss Fuerst and Miss Eady may not have been the only women so treated, but in their case strangling may have resulted when they panicked and resisted, or when they suddenly revived. Strangulation in the case of his last three victims may by then have become part of some masturbatory rite in which necrophilia was also involved. Christie's statements probably 'improved' on what he did, making it more manly. Few men with unusual sexual tastes – and Christie was otherwise quite a prim and proper person who neither smoked nor drank – are willing to admit in detail the special tricks and techniques and practices by which they obtain ejaculation.

What is especially odd, among so much that is strange about this case, is that after killing two women (in 1943 and 1944) he killed no more – if one excepts Beryl Evans – for nine years. And then he killed four women in four months.

Why did he stop after Muriel Eady? Possibly because his wife was more or less permanently in the house. Or perhaps he found some partner who suited his peculiar sexual requirements. Perhaps his health, which was always poor, became his main preoccupation. He had been visiting Dr Odess since 1934 with a string of minor complaints, fibrositis being the most consistent and severe. Dr Odess said at Christie's trial that he was 'a nervous type … He had fits of crying, sobbing. He complained of insomnia, and headaches, and giddiness.' He also suffered from diarrhoea, flatulence and amnesia.

After the war, Reg Christie became a clerk in a post-office savings bank, a job that lasted four years, until his previous convictions came to light. His next and final job was a clerical post with British Road Services.

Meanwhile, on 20 September 1947, Timothy Evans (who was now twenty-three) married Beryl Thorley, a pretty but dull eighteen-year-old telephonist working at Grosvenor House in Mayfair. Evans was a van driver, a thin and wiry Welshman (5 ft 5 1/2 in) with an uncertain temper, whose constitutional, tubercular weakness kept him in sanatoria when he was a boy and kept him out of National Service, from which he was rejected on medical grounds. Poorly educated and hardly able to read or write, he was nonetheless not illiterate. For he read comics, signed his own name, and must have had some understanding of the writing on the packages, receipts etc., which he handled in his job. He was not, as had been claimed, a pathetic 'near mental defective'.

Beryl Thorley, who came from a respectable family and worked in upper-class surroundings, is unlikely to have married an idiot. The Tim Evans whom she met on a blind date must have been an attractive, sparky young Welshman – not too bright perhaps, but not a dim-witted lout either. He was also a bit of a braggart, a heavy drinker and a fantastic liar. A senior police officer thought him 'quite worldly'.

For a while the young couple lived with Evans's mother, Mrs Probert (she had remarried), in St Mark's Road, and when Beryl learned she was pregnant the couple decided to move into a place of their own. This they did in March 1948, renting the two rooms on the top floor of 10 Rillington Place. The middle flat was occupied by a solitary, elderly man called Kitchener. The Christies lived on the ground floor.

Geraldine Evans was born on 10 October 1948.

A year passed without apparent incident, except that Mr and Mrs Evans often had rows, mainly about money but also about a blonde girl, Lucy, who came to stay for a few weeks in August. She was seventeen and a friend of Beryl. It is said that the two girls shared the marital bed while Evans slept on the kitchen floor. Before long Mrs Probert and a probation officer were involved: once Evans threatened to throw his wife out of a window. Eventually he walked out with Lucy, staying away for two nights before he returned to Beryl.

Then, in October 1949, Beryl told him she was expecting another baby.

It seems she decided to have an abortion, apparently reluctant to lose her figure and possibly her husband, as well as the extra money she earned through part-time work. Both the Christies knew of her intentions and advised her against the abortion. Evans himself was also opposed to the idea, as he explained in his first statement to the police:

> She told me she was about three months gone. I said: 'If you're having a baby, well, you've had one. Another won't make any difference.' She then told me she was going to try and get rid of it. I turned round and told her not to be silly, that she'd make herself ill. Then she bought herself a syringe and started syringing herself. Then she said that didn't work, and I said: 'I'm glad it won't work.' Then she said she was going to buy some tablets. I don't know what tablets she bought because she was always hiding them from me. She started to look very ill, and I told her to go and see a doctor, and she said she'd go when I was in work. But when I'd come home and ask her if she'd been, she'd always say she hadn't. On the Sunday morning, that would be the sixth of November, she told me that if she couldn't get rid of the baby she'd kill herself and our other baby, Geraldine. I told her she was talking silly. She never said no more about it then, but when I got up Monday morning to go to work she said she was going to see some woman to see if she could help her.

In his *second* statement Evans told a different story:

> About a week before my wife died, Reg Christie ... approached me and said: 'I'd like to have a chat with you about your wife taking these tablets ... If you and your wife had come to me in the first place I could have done it for you without any risk.' I turned round and

*said: 'Well, I didn't think you knew anything about medical stuff.' So he told me that he
was training for a doctor before the war. Then he started showing me books and things on
medical … He told me the stuff that he used one out of every ten would die with it. I told
him I wasn't interested. So I said goodnight to him and I went upstairs. When I got in, my
wife started talking to me about it. She said that she had been speaking to Mr Christie and
asked me if he had spoken to me … I told her she wasn't to have anything to do with it.
She turned round and told me to mind my own business and that she intended to get rid of
it and she trusted Mr Christie … On the Monday evening [7 November] … my wife said
that Mr Christie had made arrangements for the first thing Tuesday morning. I didn't argue
with her. I just washed and changed and went to the KPH [a pub] until ten o'clock. I came
home and had supper and went to bed. She wanted to start an argument, but I just took no
notice. Just after six I got up the following morning to go to work … I had a cup of tea and
a smoke and she told me: 'On your way down tell Mr Christie that everything is all right.
If you don't tell him, I'll go down and tell him myself.' So as I went down the stairs he came
out to meet me and I said: 'Everything is all right.' Then I went to work.*

In his first statement Evans had said that on the Monday he met a man at a transport
café who gave him some 'stuff' in a bottle that would fix the matter of his wife's
pregnancy. He said that on the Tuesday when he returned from work at about 6.30 pm
the lights were out and he found his wife, who had apparently taken the liquid 'stuff',
dead on the bed. That night, he said, he put her body down a manhole or drain outside
the house and got someone to look after the baby the next day. This statement was made
on the afternoon of Wednesday, 30 November, to the Merthyr police in Wales. When
they told him later that night that there was no body in the drain and that three men
had been needed to lift the manhole cover, Evans then said: 'I said that to protect a man
named Christie. It's not true about the man in the café either.'

He then made his second statement, the longest of the four he made, accusing
Christie of causing his wife's death in an attempt to carry out an abortion. Evans said:
'When I came home in the evening [Tuesday] he was waiting for me at the bottom of
the staircase. He said: 'It's bad news. It didn't work.' Christie allegedly refused to tell Evans
what had happened except that Beryl had died about three o'clock and that her stomach
was 'septic poisoned'. Evans found his wife lying on the bed – 'I could see that she was
dead and that she had been bleeding from the mouth and nose and that she had been
bleeding from the bottom part. She had a black skirt on and a check blouse and a kind
of light blue jacket on.'

This story was repeated by Evans at his trial. He also said that about seven o'clock he
helped Christie, who was 'puffing and blowing', to carry Beryl's body down the stairs
and into Mr Kitchener's kitchen, as the old man was away in hospital. According to
Evans, Christie said he would dispose of the body 'down one of the drains' and would
see about getting someone to look after the baby. This was done in Evans's absence at

work on the Thursday, when a 'young couple from East Acton' – so Christie informed him – took the baby away.

What actually happened on the Thursday (and from now on Christie's and Evans's versions of events roughly tally) was that Evans was sacked from his job, although he told everyone he had left of his own accord. 'He seemed extremely angry,' said Christie at Evans's trial. 'Really wild.' That evening, Evans told his mother that Beryl and the baby had gone to her father in Brighton.

On Friday the 11th, Evans visited a second-hand furniture dealer in Portobello Road, and went out drinking as well as to the pictures over the weekend. The Christies fed him on Sunday, and on Monday afternoon the furniture dealer bought and took away most of the Evans's hire-purchase possessions, including the lino on the floor. Evans received £40. He then left Rillington Place, going again to the pictures and to various pubs before he caught the 12.55 am milk train from Paddington Station to Wales.

Early on Tuesday, 15 November, he arrived at the home of his aunt, Mrs Lynch, in Merthyr Vale. He told her and her husband that Beryl and Geraldine had gone to Brighton and would spend Christmas there. Apparently no further questions were asked and Evans idled about Merthyr for almost a week until, on Monday, 21 November, the day after his twenty-fifth birthday, when he returned to London.

His whereabouts on Monday and Tuesday are unknown, but he appeared at the door of 10 Rillington Place on Wednesday the 23rd and had a discussion on the doorstep with Christie, allegedly about the baby's well-being. That night, Evans was back in Merthyr in South Wales.

By now his mother and her married daughters in St Mark's Road were becoming anxious: they had heard neither from Beryl nor from Evans for over a fortnight. The Christies, when asked for information, said they knew nothing of Beryl, except that she had gone away with the baby. A telegram was sent on 29 November to Beryl's father in Brighton and resulted in the disclosure that she was not there either.

On that same day Mrs Probert wrote to Mrs Lynch in reply to a recent letter from her sister-in-law saying that Tim had been in Merthyr for two weeks on his own and was jobless. Mrs Probert wrote:

> I don't know what lies Tim have told you down there I know nothing about him and I have not seen him for 3 weeks ... There is some mystery about him you can tell him from me he don't want to come to me I never want to see him again ... He have put years on my life since last August [when Lucy lodged with the Evanses] ... He is like his father no good to himself or anybody else ... His name stinks up here everywhere I go people asking for him for money he owes them. I am ashamed to say he is my son.

At breakfast on the 30th, Mrs Lynch read this letter to Tim Evans, who was dismissive and made little comment. But after some thought, that afternoon at 3.10 pm he walked into

Merthyr Vale police station and told an astonished DC Evans: 'I want to give myself up. I have disposed of my wife.' 'What do you mean?' enquired DC Evans. 'I put her down the drain,' said his namesake. 'You realise what you're saying?' queried DC Evans. 'Yes,' Tim Evans replied. 'I know what I'm saying. I can't sleep, and want to get it off my chest.'

Evans then made his first statement – about his wife's abortion attempts and the man in the café – in which neither himself nor Christie were implicated in Beryl's death. The Welsh police telephoned London, and the manhole cover outside 10 Rillington Place was raised with great difficulty by three policemen and no body was found 'down the drain'. When informed of this, Evans made his second statement, naming Christie as the abortionist and killer.

At Evans's trial, Christie denied knowing about or assisting in any abortion, and no evidence was produced to refute this. He told the court that on Tuesday, 8 November: 'I was in bed a lot of the time with the illness I had, which is enteritis and fibrositis in my back. I was in a great deal of pain and I rested as much as possible under doctor's orders with a fire in the room day and night, and on Tuesday evening at about twenty-past five I went up to the doctor.' Doctor Odess lived in nearby Colville Square. On the way back, Christie collected his wife at the local public library, where she had gone while he was seeing the doctor. The Christies went home and he went to bed 'feeling pretty bad' and his wife prepared some milk food for him. 'As a matter of fact she slipped and fell and the milk food went over the bed, and I didn't have it.' About midnight, he said, they were both in bed when they were startled awake by a very loud thud. 'We listened for a few seconds and didn't hear anything, and I gradually knelt up in bed and looked through the window which overlooks the yard. It was very dark and I couldn't see anything there, and so I went back and we laid down, and shortly after that I heard some movement which appeared to be upstairs … as though something heavy was being moved.' Mrs Christie said in court it was 'as if furniture was being moved about'.

There was no sign of Beryl or the baby on Wednesday, according to both the Christies, and when Evans returned that night at about half-past ten he told Mrs Christie, in answer to her question about the whereabouts of Beryl and the baby, 'Oh, she's gone away to Bristol.' 'Gone away to Bristol?' queried Mrs Christie. 'She never told me she was going.' 'She said she would write,' Evans replied, adding: 'She didn't tell my mother either.' None of this was ever contradicted or refuted by either of the Christies, by Dr Odess, or by any other witness at Evans's trial, apart from Evans himself.

At Christie's trial, Dr Odess said that his patient had had a severe attack of fibrositis that had lasted from 1 November to 27 December 1949, and he doubted whether Christie could lift a human being down two flights of stairs. He said: 'At the time I was seeing him, he could hardly get off the chair sometimes. I had to help him up.' He said later that Christie visited him on Tuesday the 8th complaining of enteritis, or diarrhoea, and again on the 12th when his fibrositis was so bad his back had to be strapped.

On 1 December 1949, the day after Evans made his first two statements, the police in Merthyr Tydfil and London pursued their enquiries by interviewing Mrs Lynch, Mrs Probert and Mr and Mrs Christie, who were questioned at some length and independently. The two rooms of Evans's former flat were found to be empty, apart from a stolen briefcase and some newspaper cuttings about the 'Torso Murder' of Stanley Setty. The yard and garden, which were also examined, showed no signs of digging or disturbance.

In Merthyr Vale, Evans added some details to his second statement, saying he helped Christie to carry his wife's body down the stairs and that he visited Christie on Tuesday the 15th.

Investigations in Brighton and Bristol concerning the whereabouts of Beryl and the baby drew a blank. She might have gone elsewhere, but Evans's statements seemed to indicate that her body, *if* there was a body, was somewhere in or around the house at the end of the cul-de-sac. On the morning of Friday, 2 December a thorough search was made of 10 Rillington Place by Chief Inspector Jennings, accompanied by DCS Barratt. The door of the wash-house was found to be locked. Mrs Christie said the wash-house was not used as such, adding that the tap inside was used to swill out the slop-pail. The lock, she said, was faulty, and the door locked itself, though it could be opened with a piece of metal that pushed back the catch. She proceeded to do so. Christie was also present, with his hands pressing into the base of his back, suffering from an attack of fibrositis.

Under the sink, hidden by bits of wood, was a bundle wrapped in a green tablecloth and tied up with sash cord. Mrs Christie was invited by the police officers to explain its presence, even to touch the bundle. She did so and was mystified. The bundle was dragged out into the yard, the cord was untied, and Beryl's naked feet flopped out. Baby Geraldine, with a striped tie knotted tightly around her neck, was found concealed by some kindling behind the door.

Dr Donald Teare, the Home Office pathologist who carried out the autopsies, established that both mother and daughter had been strangled – Geraldine by the tie and Beryl by what appeared from the abrasions on her neck to have been a rope. Clothed but without any knickers, she was more than three months pregnant, and the only evidence of interference was a slight bruise in her vagina and an old scar. She had evidently been struck in the face about twenty minutes before she died – her right eye and upper lip were marked and swollen – and there were two bruises on the inner, upper part of her left leg.

Timothy Evans, ignorant of these discoveries, was brought to London that night and taken to Notting Hill police station. He was shown two piles of clothes, Beryl's and Geraldine's, as well as the tablecloth, a blanket in which Beryl had been wrapped, and the striped tie. He was told by CI Jennings that the bodies of both mother and daughter had been discovered in the wash-house that morning 'and this clothing was found on them'. Both had been strangled, said Jennings. (It was disputed at Evans's trial whether

Jennings had also revealed the exact positions of the bodies and that they had been obscured by pieces of wood.)

As Jennings talked, Evans picked up some of the garments. He picked up the tie. Tears came to his eyes. If his first two statements were true, this was when he discovered that his baby was dead, and the manner of her death. It was also when he found out how Beryl had died and where her body had been put. Said Jennings: 'I have reason to believe you were responsible for their deaths.' 'Yes,' replied Timothy Evans.

He made a brief statement, his third. 'She was incurring one debt after another,' he said. 'I couldn't stand it any longer, so I strangled her with a piece of rope and took her down to the flat below the same night … I waited till the Christies had gone to bed, then I took her to the wash-house after midnight. This was on Tuesday, 8 November. On Thursday evening after I came home from work I strangled my baby in our bedroom with my tie, and later that night I took her down into the wash-house after the Christies had gone to bed.'

According to Jennings he then said: 'It's a great relief to get it off my chest. I feel better already. I can tell you the cause that led up to it.' He then went on to make a long statement, his fourth. As in the third there was no attempt to incriminate Christie and no mention of any abortion attempt.

Beryl, he said, was always moaning about the long hours he worked and about how little he was paid. She was in debt, and he had to work overtime to pay off her debts. He also had to borrow money. Then he discovered she was behind with their HP payments and with the rent. There was a row. 'I told her if she didn't pull herself together I would leave her, so she said: "You can leave anytime you like."' There was another row on the morning of Sunday, 6 November, after which he went out to the pictures. She nagged him on his return and until he went to bed. The following morning, he said, 'She gets up and starts an argument straight away. I took no notice of her … My wife told me that she was going to pack up and go down to her father in Brighton … She was going to take the baby with her … So I said it would be a good job and a load of worry off my mind.' When he returned from work that night he put the kettle on, sat down, and his wife walked in. 'I thought you was going to Brighton,' he remarked. She replied: 'What, for you to have a good time?' He went downstairs to fetch the push-chair. 'I came upstairs and she started an argument again. I told her if she didn't pack it up I'd slap her face. With that she picked up a milk bottle to throw at me. I grabbed the bottle out of her hand. I pushed her, she fell in a chair in the kitchen, so I washed and changed and went out.' When he got home later, they argued again.

On Tuesday morning he went to work as usual. 'I came home at night about 6.30 pm, my wife started to argue again, so I hit her across the face with my flat hand. She then hit me back with her hand. In a fit of temper, I grabbed a piece of rope from a chair, which I had brought home off my van, and strangled her with it. I then took her into the bedroom and laid her on the bed with the rope still tied round her neck. Before

10 pm that night I carried my wife's body downstairs to the kitchen of Mr Kitchener's flat …' He fed and sat up with the baby and then put her to bed. Later, 'when everything was quiet', he wrapped his wife's body in a blanket and a green tablecloth from the kitchen table and tied the bundle up 'with a piece of cord from out of the kitchen cupboard.' He took the bundle – Mrs Evans was quite small – down to the wash-house, put it under the sink and 'blocked the front of the sink up with pieces of wood so that the body wouldn't be seen'.

For two days, on Wednesday and Thursday, he fed, washed and changed the baby and went to work, sitting by the fire in the evenings. After he was sacked on Thursday, he came home, he said, 'picked up my baby from her cot in the bedroom, picked up my tie and strangled her with it'. That night he hid the baby's body in the wash-house 'behind some wood'.

Why would Evans kill the baby? One explanation was put forward, but never used in the court, by PS Trevallian, who guarded Evans in his cell at Notting Hill Gate. Trevallian said later that as they conversed he remarked that he was unable to understand how or why anyone would kill a baby. Evans replied, according to Trevallian, that it was the continual crying of the baby that got on his nerves and that he strangled it to silence its noise.

There are other questions. Why did he remove the rope from his wife's neck and not the tie from Geraldine's? The tie, if it was his – and this was never clearly established – would obviously incriminate him. How was it that the baby was silent, according to the Christies, for two days, though left unattended for twelve hours at a stretch for two days? If alive, she must have cried and must have been heard by the Christies. It was on Wednesday evening that Mrs Christie asked Evans: 'Where's Beryl and the baby?' To which he replied that they had gone away to Bristol. Why did he say he strangled the baby on the *Thursday* night? Was there some reason for this in his story in the second statement about the baby being given by Christie on Thursday to a couple from East Acton? Was he again trying to protect Christie? Or indeed someone else, some *woman* to whom he had given the baby on the *Tuesday* night?

It seems unlikely that Evans should wish to protect Christie. There is no reason to suppose that either man had any respect or liking for the other, or that Evans was dominated by the older man. Evans – a heavy-drinking, excitable, brawling wiry Welshman – must have been despised by his tall, quiet, nervous, teetotal neighbour. The Christies tended to keep themselves to themselves. The wives might have become familiar, but next to nothing is known about this.

Although Mrs Christie's role in the events of that week is far from clear, the police apparently never doubted her innocence or her mystified reaction to the bundle under the wash-house sink. She was believed when she said in court that the last time she saw Beryl and the baby was on the Monday of that week: she had looked after the baby when Beryl was out. There is also no reason to suppose that the police terrorised Evans into making a false confession. No complaint or allegation about this was ever made by Evans, by his lawyers, or by his relatives.

On 3 December 1949, Timothy Evans was charged with the murder of his wife, to which he replied: 'Yes, that's right.' When charged with the murder of Geraldine, he made no reply. On his way to the magistrate's court in a police car, he told Inspector Black: 'After I killed my wife I took her ring off her finger and sold it for six shillings in Merthyr.' The ring was, in fact, found in a Merthyr jewellers' shop. But when his mother, Mrs Probert, saw him after the magistrate's hearing, he told her: 'I never done it, Mum. Christie done it. Tell Christie I want to see him. He's the only one who can help me now.' She tried to talk to Christie, but he refused to see her and sent for the police.

When Evans was examined by the prison doctor in Brixton, he voluntarily repeated his account of Beryl's death as contained in his fourth statement, and made no accusations against Christie. He was cheerful in prison, playing dominoes and cards, and never professed to be innocent – at least, not until he saw his solicitor on 15 December, when once again Evans accused Christie.

Timothy Evans was tried at the Old Bailey on Wednesday, 11 January 1950, before Mr Justice Lewis, a sick man who died a few weeks later. Mr Christmas Humphreys, then Britain's leading Buddhist, led for the Crown: it was his first case as Senior Treasury Counsel. Evans, defended by Mr Malcolm Morris, was charged with the murder of Geraldine, as it was assumed by the prosecution that there would or could be no excuse of provocation – which might have been put forward as a defence in the case of Mrs Evans.

Christie was a good but cautious prosecution witness and Evans himself was the only witness, a poor and muddled one, for the defence. He was patently a liar. His counsel's assault on Christie, revealing his previous convictions, was viewed with disfavour by the court, as were counsel's allegations that Christie was an abortionist, a murderer and a liar. All this was firmly denied by Christie.

Evans's explanation of his last two statements, a 'load of lies', was that they were made because he was 'upset' after hearing about Geraldine's death, because he thought the police would 'knock him about' if he said otherwise, and because he wanted to protect Christie.

When asked by Mr Humphreys to suggest why Christie had strangled Mrs Evans, the accused replied: 'Well, he was home all day.' 'Can you suggest why he should have strangled your wife?' demanded Mr Humphreys. 'No, I can't,' said Evans. 'No,' he said again, when the question was applied to his daughter.

Mr Humphreys' closing speech was probably the shortest ever made in a murder trial. It lasted less than half an hour. The defence's allegations and attack on Christie were dismissed as 'Bosh!'

On Friday, 13 January, the jury took forty minutes to find Evans guilty of the murder of Geraldine Evans. Christie, who was in court, burst into tears. Evans said nothing and was sentenced to death.

Taken to Pentonville Prison, he was as cheerful as he had been in Brixton. He showed no sorrow for his dead family, nor displayed any outrage at his sentence or even when his appeal was dismissed, although he still maintained that 'Christie done it.' He was well behaved, good tempered and calm. Before he was hanged by Albert Pierrepoint and Syd Dernley on 9 March 1950, Evans, a Roman Catholic, received the sacrament and made his last confession to a priest. There were no petitions, demonstrations or outcry before or after the execution of Timothy Evans.

Later that year, in August 1950, 10 Rillington Place was bought by a Jamaican hotel commissionaire, Charles Brown. The upstairs rooms – Kitchener had left by now – were occupied by several Jamaicans and others, much to the annoyance and distress of both the Christies. They complained several times to the Poor Man's Lawyer Centre about noise, intrusion and assault, which they said were affecting their health. Christie was still suffering from fibrositis, enteritis, insomnia and amnesia. His wife suffered from nerves and depression and was regularly taking sleeping pills and pheno-barbitone as a sedative.

In the spring of 1952, Christie was advised to go to Springfield Mental Hospital for treatment for an anxiety neurosis, but he was reluctant to leave his wife. Deteriorating mentally and physically, he stopped seeing Dr Odess in September and gave up his £8-a-week job with British Road Services on 6 December. He was fifty-four. Three years had now passed since the death of Beryl Evans.

On 10 December 1952, Mrs Christie wrote a letter to her sister. Christie kept it and altered the date to the 15th, when he posted it. By then Ethel Christie was dead. She was last seen at a laundry on Friday, 12 December.

Christie later told the police: 'She was becoming very frightened from these blacks … and she got very depressed. On 14 December [Sunday] I was awaked at about 8.15 am. I think it was by my wife moving about in bed. I sat up and saw that she appeared to be convulsive, her face was blue and she was choking … I couldn't bear to see her, so I got a stocking and tied it round her neck to put her to sleep … I left her in bed for two or three days and didn't know what to do.'

He alleged she had taken an overdose of pheno-barbitone, but no traces of it were found later in her body. He eventually buried her under the floorboards of the front room after wrapping her body (which was naked apart from unsecured stockings) in two dresses and a blanket, with a pillow case around her head and a vest between her legs.

Why did Christie kill his wife, with whom he had lived closely and amicably for nineteen years? Despite the alteration of the date on the letter, which could have been lying about, accidentally not posted, and then put to use as an afterthought, there is little to suggest premeditation. Nor is there any reason, beyond being wise after the event, to suggest that he wanted to rid himself of her so that suddenly, and after a nine-year gap, he could revert to his murderous wartime habits. There is also no reason to suppose that three years after the murder of Beryl Evans Mrs Christie had to be killed because what she knew had made her so fearful and guilt-ridden that Christie had to silence her in case she talked. Fictional murderers may be infinitely cunning, but Christie was sunk in apathetic despair. The murders that followed were made more possible because of Mrs Christie's absence and because of his isolation. They probably happened *because* of her death, and not the other way around.

There is an interesting coincidence of events between the actions of Christie and Timothy Evans after the deaths of their respective wives: Mrs Christie's body was wrapped up and hidden under wood; her wedding ring was sold on the 17th for £1 17s; the neighbours were told she had gone away; Christie sold nearly all his furniture (for £13) to the same dealer Evans had chosen; and eventually he left the house.

The furniture was sold on 6 January 1953, but Christie kept a mattress, some blankets, a table, two chairs, some crockery and cutlery. For ten freezing weeks he squatted in the back room with his mongrel bitch, Judy, and a cat. One of the chairs was a deckchair, with knotted webs of string in place of canvas. Once a week he received £2 14s from the unemployment exchange. Daily he disinfected the hallway, the drains, the front and back of the house with Jeyes Fluid, as he had begun to do towards the end of December.

During this period he murdered three prostitutes and put their bodies in a coal-cupboard in the kitchen.

On Friday, 13 March, a week after the last murder, he sublet his three rooms to a Mr and Mrs Reilly for £7 13s, getting three months' rent in advance. He had decided to go away. After taking his dog to a vet to be destroyed, he walked out of 10 Rillington Place on 20 March with all he owned in a battered suitcase. That night he turned up at a Rowton House hostel for down-and-outs in King's Cross.

Despite an unpleasant smell in the kitchen, the Reillys moved into Christie's rooms and unknowingly spent one night with the corpses of four women before they were visited by the landlord, Charles Brown, and thrown out. Three days later, Mr Beresford Brown, a Jamaican who lodged upstairs, was clearing up the mess in the downstairs flat before it was reoccupied, and was inspecting the fabric as he did so. He knocked on a kitchen wall and heard a hollow sound. He tore off a loose piece of patchy wallpaper, covering what had been the coal-cupboard door, and by the light of a torch he saw a naked back through a gap in the boards.

It was not until DCI Griffin, senior police officers and the Home Office pathologist, Dr Camps, had gathered at the house at about 7.30 pm that the cupboard was opened up. Inside were three bodies. They were photographed, and removed in the reverse order of their concealment.

First out was Hectorina MacLennan (Ena), aged twenty-six, from the Hebrides. She was naked apart from her brassiere, and was squatting, head bowed, on a heap of rubble and ash. Next was Kathleen Maloney, also twenty-six. She was partly clothed and wrapped in a blanket, as was Rita Nelson, aged twenty-five, from Belfast; the latter was six months pregnant. The last two had probably been killed towards the end of January, and Ena MacLennan about 6 March. All three prostitutes had had VD and had been strangled with some ligature, not manually. All three had also been gassed – there was carbon monoxide in their blood – but not fatally. All three had a vest or some material between their legs, like a diaper, and intercourse had taken place about the time of their various deaths.

Later that night, the decomposing body of Mrs Christie was discovered under the floorboards of the front room. Although she also wore a kind of diaper there were no signs of intercourse. She had been strangled by some ligature and had not been gassed, injured or bruised.

The morning papers, reporting the finding of the three bodies in the cupboard, must have been read by Christie. He left Rowton House on 25 March, leaving his few belongings in a locker. He wandered about London for six days, sleeping rough, while 10 Rillington Place was stripped and searched and the garden dug up, a disruption that so crazed Christie's cat that it had to be destroyed. In the garden an assortment of bones was unearthed, which when pieced together formed two skeletons – those of Ruth Fuerst and Muriel Eady. In the yard, a tobacco tin was found that contained four sets of pubic hairs.

Despite the photographs in every newspaper and an intensive police hunt, the thin, bald, middle-aged man with glasses went unobserved until Tuesday, 31 March. At about ten-past nine on a cold grey morning, PC Tom Ledger was walking along the embankment south of the river by Putney Bridge. He saw a shabby, unshaven, hungry-looking down-and-out leaning on the embankment wall, looking at the river.

PC Ledger went up to the man and asked him: 'What are you doing? Looking for work?' The man replied: 'Yes, but my employment cards haven't come through.' Ledger asked the man for his name and address and was told it was 'John Waddington, 35 Westbourne Grove.' Said Ledger: 'Have you anything on you to prove your identity?' 'Nothing at all,' the man replied. Some instinct or suspicion prompted the PC to ask the man to remove his hat. He did so, revealing a bald dome, and PC Ledger recognised John Christie.

The wanted man was taken to Putney police station. Coins amounting to 2s 3 1/2d were found on him, as well as a wallet containing identity cards, ration books (his own and his wife's), his marriage certificate, a union card, a St John's Ambulance badge, three pawn tickets, a rent book and a newspaper cutting outlining the evidence Christie had given at the trial of Timothy Evans.

When told by DCI Griffin that his wife's body had been found under the floorboards of his flat, Christie began to cry. He said: 'She woke me up. She was choking. I couldn't stand it any longer. I couldn't bear to see her suffer.' He then made a long statement describing the murders of his wife and the three prostitutes. He was diffuse and vague, often saying he 'thought' or 'believed' or 'must have done' something and failing to remember details. Not once did he actually admit to strangling any of them, or gassing the last three, or having sex with them. According to him, all four unaccountably seemed to have died after some sort of struggle.

Christie was charged at Notting Hill police station with the murder of his wife and taken to Brixton Prison after a preliminary hearing at the West London magistrates' court, to which he was accompanied by a very young PC called Bill Waddell, who also sat with him in a cell. That PC would one day become Curator of the Black Museum.

On 15 April, Christie was also charged with the murders of the three women in the cupboard, by which time his lawyers had told him his defence had to be one of insanity. To this end he was interviewed more than ten times by Dr Hobson, a psychologist. At the first interview Christie indignantly denied killing Mrs Evans. But after 22 April, when he first heard that the skeletons in the garden had been dug up and identified, he told Dr Hobson he had also murdered these women, by gas or strangulation or by both.

It was five days later that he said he had killed Beryl Evans – but not the baby, Geraldine. 'The more the merrier,' as he remarked to the prison chaplain. On 18 May, Mrs Evans and the baby were exhumed and their bodies examined.

It was not until 5 June, however, that Christie made a statement to the police in the presence of his solicitors, saying he was responsible for the deaths of Miss Fuerst and Miss Eady. For the first time he mentioned strangling and gassing, though confusedly, and admitted for the first time that he had had intercourse with his victims. In his last statement, made on 8 June, he described how he had killed Beryl Evans.

He said that in November 1949 he disturbed her in a suicide attempt – she was lying on a quilt on the kitchen floor with the gas on. The next day he happened to go upstairs at lunchtime, he said, and she asked him to help her commit suicide:

> She begged of me to help her to go through with it … She said she would do anything if I would help her. I think she was referring to letting me be intimate with her … She lay on the quilt … I got on my knees but found I was not physically able of having intercourse with her owing to the fact that I had fibrositis in my back and enteritis. We were both fully dressed. I turned the gas tap on … held it close to her face. When she became unconscious I turned the tap off. I was going to try again to have intercourse with her but it was impossible … I think that's when I strangled her. I think it was with a stocking …

When Evans returned that evening, Christie told him his wife had gassed herself. Evans carried her body into the other room and put it on the bed:

> I told Evans that no doubt he would be suspected of having done it because of the rows and fights he had had with his wife. He seemed to think the same. He said he would bring the van down … and take her away and leave her somewhere … He did not know his wife had been strangled … I never mentioned it to him. I never had intercourse with Mrs Evans at any time. We were just friendly acquaintances, nothing more. I went up that first afternoon to have a cup of tea … I had some shoring timber and old floorboards from my front room which had been left behind by the work people and I asked Evans to take it to the yard for

me, as I could not carry it owing to my fibrositis … I suggested he put it in the wash-house
out of the way. I saw it in the wash-house afterwards and some of it was stacked in front of
the sink … I feel certain I strangled Mrs Evans and I think it was with a stocking. I did it
because she appealed to me to help her to commit suicide … I don't know anything about
what happened to the Evans's baby.

He then went on to say that he had gassed the three prostitutes as they sat in the deckchair by the kitchen window. He attached a piece of rubber piping to the plugged gas-pipe at the window – 'I put a kink in the tube with a bulldog clip to stop the gas escaping' – and, letting it dangle behind the chair, he then removed the clip.

Some substantiation of this was provided by the fact that a bulldog clip and a piece of half-inch rubber tubing were discovered in the flat – although how did he avoid being gassed himself? However, his version of Beryl Evans's death, about the assisted suicide and the invitation to intercourse, seems most unlikely. Few activities, let alone these, are likely to be contemplated or carried out by a sick man suffering from backache and diarrhoea. The autopsies on Beryl Evans showed that she had not been gassed, that she had been punched more than once, and strangled not with a stocking but with a rope. However, he may well have tried, when unexpectedly provided with an inert female body, to have intercourse with her, after her death.

Whatever the truth, it seems that Christie's self-love was such that he could admit to nothing nasty or perverted about himself. Reluctantly and cautiously he confessed, not to 'murder', but to having killed. And he tried to dignify and obscure his motives and his actions as much as he could. In no circumstances would he ever admit, to himself above all, to such vile and vicious behaviour as baby-killing, sadism, onanism, abortion and necrophilia.

Was there, nonetheless, some truth in Evans's story about the fatal abortion attempt? One fact contradicts this, and poses many more questions – a fact that was mentioned at both trials but never attested to. In the week that Beryl Evans died, there were workmen in the house as well as in the yard. Two were actually at work on the wash-house, repairing the roof, pointing and plastering. It was not a big job, but they worked slowly, storing their tools and equipment in the wash-house overnight. They finished working on the roof on Tuesday, 8 November (the day Beryl Evans is said to have died), but did not finish their plastering until the Friday, when they removed their tools and left the wash-house bright and *empty*.

In addition to these two workmen there was a carpenter at work inside the house, repairing the floorboards in the front room and in the hall. He worked from Thursday the 10th until noon on Monday the 14th, when at Christie's request he gave Christie the broken bits of floorboard for firewood.

The presence of workmen in and about one's house is disruptive at the best of times. They make requests and require cups of tea. It is most unlikely in these circumstances, with workmen *and* Mrs Christie in the house, that Christie planned an abortion, which could have waited until the following week, or have carried out a murder. After all, it was only when he was alone in the house that he felt safe enough to set about killing the first two and the last three of his victims.

It is, however, conceivable that at night, in the heat of a row, Evans might well have struck and strangled his wife. But if so, how could he or Christie or both of them have put her body in the unfinished wash-house? There can be little error about the workmen's dates – their employer kept time-sheets, and they all made statements in 1949 to the police. These statements were never, it seems, supplied to Evans's counsel and never used by the prosecution, probably because they made nonsense of Timothy Evans's confession of murder (on which the prosecution based their case) in respect of his alleged date of the disposal of the bodies.

Were the bodies hidden in Kitchener's flat until Monday evening, by which time all the workmen had gone and Evans had sold his furniture? And if Beryl's body was put in the wash-house on Monday night, was that why Evans caught such a late train, at 12.55 am, to South Wales?

Perhaps Christie, investigating the bumps and movement of the Tuesday night, came across Beryl's body in Kitchener's flat the following day. What would he do? He would hardly welcome the attentions of the police. But her body might have invited the attempt at intercourse that he later described. Later that night, avowedly anxious to help Evans, might he not have advised Evans to leave everything to him, to sell up and go? And might not the concealment of the bodies in the wash-house have been a *temporary* measure, as it had been with Fuerst and Eady? Might not Christie have intended *burying* the bodies, but have been prevented from doing so because of his fibrositis? All might have been well, as far as he was concerned, if Evans had kept quiet. This he failed to do. But what, unless it were a feeling of guilt, led Evans to make that first odd confession to the Merthyr police?

The trial of John Reginald Halliday Christie for the murder of his wife began in the Number 1 Court at the Old Bailey before Mr Justice Finnemore on Monday, 22 June 1953. The Attorney-General, Sir Lionel Heald, was the prosecutor and Mr Curtis-Bennett, QC, appeared for the defence, which aimed to show that Christie was guilty but insane.

It was Curtis-Bennett who brought the attention of the court to the murders of all seven women, including that of Mrs Evans, which the accused said he had also committed. His memory of events, however, was poor and vague. Christie spoke slowly, with long pauses, and in such a low voice that a microphone was set up so that he could be heard.

The only other witness for the defence was Dr Hobson, who said the accused suffered from gross hysteria which affected his reason, and that it was highly probable that at the time of the crime he did not know that what he was doing was wrong. Hobson also noted:

He has this abnormal memory. I am prepared to believe that the abnormality of his memory is in some way purposeful, but that he himself is not aware of the fact that it is motivated … He often makes statements one after the other which to the listener seem self-contradictory, but Christie is unable to see the contradiction. I found … that those things about which he has been most certain, and most sure, and most indignant when the opposite was suggested, were things we ultimately found him most mistaken about or deceiving himself about.

He was most indignant, said Dr Hobson, when it was suggested that his wife had died in other ways and for other reasons than those described by Christie, and that he had picked up Kathleen Maloney in a pub. Dr Hobson said: 'I have never … felt able to place any reliance on any of his statements without confirming the facts externally … I think he has tried to be as cooperative as possible. I believe that these tricks of memory, or avoidance of getting down to disturbing topics, is to preserve his own self-respect … rather than to avoid incriminating himself.'

Dr Matheson, prison doctor at Brixton, appearing for the prosecution in rebuttal, described Christie thus:

He is a man of weak character. He is immature. Certainly in his sex life he is immature. He is a man who in difficult times and in the face of problems tends to exaggerate in an hysterical fashion … I would call him not a man suffering from hysteria, but a man with an hysterical personality … He spoke quite freely, but when it came to what might be incriminating facts … he became vague, and started saying: 'Well, it must have been so' – 'I think it must be that' – 'I can't be certain' – 'I can't remember.'

Dr Curran, a psychiatrist, who also interviewed Christie on behalf of the prosecution, said he was 'an inadequate personality with hysterical features, and a very extraordinary and abnormal man'.

Summarising the ward reports, Dr Curran stated:

Christie was somewhat emotional, tremulous and fearful on admission but soon settled down. He has been meticulously clean and tidy in his person and habits. He has always kept himself well occupied. He has mixed freely with the other patients. He has been noticeably egocentric and conceited. He keeps a photograph of himself in his cell. He has been a great talker and has seemed to enjoy discussing his case, bringing the conversation round to it. He has been cheerful and boastful. He has compared himself to Haigh. He has admitted in conversation that he 'did some of them in'. He appeared to be above average intelligence He has always been polite and well behaved … He has slept well, his appetite has been good and he has gained 11 pounds in weight.

Dr Curran added: 'I do not believe Christie's alleged loss of memory is genuine. It is in my opinion too inconsistent, variable, patchy and selective to be genuine ... His lies seem to be purposive if not convincing ... [He has] like many other criminals and murderers, a remarkable capacity for dismissing the unpleasant from his mind ... He is a man with a remarkable capacity for self-deception.'

The trial ended on 25 June 1953. The jury were out for eighty-five minutes, and found Christie guilty of the murder of his wife. He was sentenced to death.

Much unease was felt before and after the trial about the case of Timothy Evans. Had an innocent man been hanged? As a result, a private enquiry initiated by the Home Secretary, Mr David Maxwell-Fyfe, QC, MP, was carried out by a senior QC, Mr John Scott Henderson. After reading all the relevant depositions, documents, transcripts and briefs, including the statements of the workmen, and after interviewing the police and lawyers concerned as well as Christie himself – who was more guarded and ambiguous than ever – Scott Henderson concluded that Evans *had* killed both his wife and child. His report was published on 13 July and presented to parliament.

On 15 July Christie, was hanged in Pentonville Prison by Albert Pierrepoint, who had also hanged Evans. Pierrepoint was assisted this time by Harry Smith. Christie's height was noted the previous afternoon as being 5 ft 8 1/2 in, his weight being 149 lb.

A large, raucous crowd had gathered overnight in the Caledonian Road. In the morning, when Pierrepoint and Smith entered the condemned cell less than a minute before 9 am, they observed that Christie was regarding the chaplain and his final ministrations with a sneer. They swiftly secured Christie's thin wrists before Pierrepoint removed Christie's spectacles. As the door leading to the drop was opened, Pierrepoint noticed the look on Christie's face. He recalled later: 'It was more than terror ... At that moment I knew Christie would have given anything in his power to postpone his own death.' He stumbled towards it, and seemed as if he would faint.

Some Labour MPs believed that the Scott Henderson report was a piece of official white-washing aimed at protecting the police, and so the matter was strongly debated in the House of Commons two weeks later, on 29 July. The Home Secretary refused to order a public enquiry. The report was again debated in November, and the Evans case continued to be discussed whenever the issue of the abolition of the death penalty was raised.

On 10 February 1955, the Rt Hon James Chuter Ede, who had been Home Secretary at the time of Evans's trial and execution, told the Commons: 'I think Evans's case shows ... that a mistake was possible, and that, in the form in which the verdict was actually given ... a mistake was made.'

Later the death penalty was abolished for most crimes in a free vote in the Commons. But the pressure to re-investigate the murder of Beryl Evans and her daughter continued.

In the winter of 1965-6, the case was reheard in public by Mr Justice Brabin. The main hearings of the enquiry covered thirty-two days. In a definitive report, published by HMSO in 1966, the judge concluded that it was 'more probable than not' that

Evans had killed his wife, but that he did not kill his daughter. As Evans had been convicted and hanged for the murder of Geraldine, and not of his wife, he was given a free and posthumous pardon. His remains were exhumed and reburied outside Pentonville Prison.

Among all the uncertainties of his statements, Christie had said 'I feel certain' twice – that he strangled Mrs Evans – and that the pubic hairs in the two-ounce tobacco tin found in the yard came from the three women in the cupboard and from his wife.

It is highly likely that his very certainty indicated a lie. He later amended this second certainty, telling his solicitor that one of the sets of hair in the tin *might* have come from Beryl Evans. Forensic experts established that the type of one of the four teased-out tufts was the same as Beryl's, but was also common to millions of women and could not in fact have been cut from her at the time of her death. One of the souvenirs was of a type that could have come from Mrs Christie. But none could have come from the three prostitutes, although two of the trophies might have come from Muriel Eady and Ruth Fuerst. It was impossible to be sure.

On the other hand, *all four* could have come from four separate and completely unknown women.

It was Christie who claimed ownership of the tobacco tin. But was it his? It could have belonged to Timothy Evans – he was a heavy smoker and Christie never smoked at all. Or did the tin have nothing to do with either, having been thrown into the yard by Mr Kitchener or some other occupant of 10 Rillington Place?

On 13 July 1955, the last woman to be hanged in Britain, Ruth Ellis, was executed in Holloway Prison for the murder of her lover. The executioner was Albert Pierrepoint. He resigned the following year on 23 February 1956 and was succeeded by Harry Allen and Jock Stewart, who between them carried out thirty-five executions over the next eight years.

The real reason for Pierrepoint's resignation was not known at the time. What had happened was that in January 1956 he was employed to carry out an execution in Manchester. The night before the execution, after Pierrepoint had got everything ready, the condemned man, called Bancroft, was reprieved. The snowy weather was so bad that night that Pierrepoint stayed overnight in a Manchester hotel, driving back home to his wife in the Rose and Crown at Hoole, near Preston in Lancashire, the following morning. Because of the reprieve, the £25 he would have received for a hanging wasn't paid. In due course he received £1 for his expenses. He was so offended he returned the pound 'with his compliments'. The sum of £4 then arrived in the post. He sent it back and resigned. In March his memoirs began to be serialised in the Empire News *for a very large sum of money. The Home Office intervened, and after a third instalment the articles came to an end.*

Albert Pierrepoint died in a nursing home at Southport on 10 July 1992; he was 87. During his 23 years as a hangman he had been involved in the executions of 435 people. In his autobiography he wrote, in 1974: 'Capital punishment, in my view, achieved nothing except revenge.'

Mr Sidney Silverman's Death Penalty (Abolition) Bill, given a second reading in 1956 in the Commons by 286 votes to 262, was rejected by the House of Lords. However, in March 1957 the Homicide Act was passed. The death penalty was now only to be exacted for five kinds of murder (a) committed in the course or furtherance of theft, (b) caused by shooting or by an explosion, (c) in the course or for the purpose of resisting or avoiding or preventing a lawful arrest, (d) of a police officer acting in the execution of his duty or a person so assisting him, (e) of a prison officer or murder done by a prisoner. A previously convicted murderer who killed again could also be sentenced to death.

45
JOHN DONALD MERRETT

Unlike lightning, murderers sometimes strike twice. More than one convicted murderer has within a year or two of his release from jail or Broadmoor killed again. In fact, about one per cent of the dangerous criminals released from Broadmoor commit crimes similar to those for which they were incarcerated. Donald Merrett's murders are doubly unusual, however, in that they occurred twenty-seven years apart.

Vera Chesney, aged forty-two, was surprised to see her forty-five-year-old husband, Ronald Chesney, on the night of 10 February 1954. Not only had she seen little of him in recent years, but the last time he called on her in the old people's home she ran with her mother in Montpelier Road north of Ealing Broadway, he had looked quite different. He had then been his usual self, hugely extrovert, if unusually amiable, and with his bulk, his beard, his big nose and one gold earring, he looked as piratical as ever. They had had a fine night out, going to the cinema and downing quantities of gin, Vera's favourite tipple. Now, exactly a week later, he was back again and quite altered – without a beard or the earring, with his hair brushed back and wearing horn-rimmed glasses.

He had flown over from Germany, as he had done the last time, specially to see her. She did not know he was travelling with a false passport, using the name of Leslie Chown, a real photographer whom he resembled in this disguise. She probably never realised the purpose of his second visit, as she was fortunately in a drunken stupor when he overpowered her, dragged her into the bathroom, and held her face down in the bath in six inches or so of water.

It was all part of a plan to provide Ronald Chesney with some money – money that he must have felt was rightly his. For after he and Vera had married in 1928, by eloping to Scotland when he was twenty and she was seventeen, he had at the age of twenty-one inherited a fortune of £50,000 from a grandfather, of which he settled £8,400 on his teenage bride. The interest on this sum was to be hers as long as she lived. When she died, the capital would revert to her husband.

For a time this did not mean much to him, as he spent the rest of the inheritance in the ten years before the Second World War, acquiring in the process a taste for adding to his diminishing income by criminal means: theft, smuggling, blackmail and fraud. Any thoughts of acquiring his wife's nest egg were further diverted by the war and by various illegal wartime enterprises. During the war he served in the RNVR and was captured by the Italians at Benghazi. After the war his criminal career branched out into black-market activities, mainly in the ruins of post-war Germany. But by 1954 he was short of funds and devised a new scheme to enrich himself. He was not sentimental. After twenty-five years of marriage, much interlarded with mistresses, he decided to reclaim the £8,400 that had been part of his inheritance by killing his wife.

It was not the first time he had killed a woman. His first victim had been his none other than his mother.

Chesney's real name was John Donald Merrett – Donnie to his friends. Born in New Zealand on 17 August 1908 at Levin in the North Island, he was the only son of an electrical engineer who deserted his wife, Bertha, in 1924. Bertha returned to England with sixteen-year-old Donnie, who was sent to school at Malvern College. He was an intelligent, enthusiastic boy, good at languages. He was also very tall for his age and well developed, and his enthusiasm for the pursuit and conquest of girls soon resulted in his being removed from the school and in Mrs Merrett's move in January 1926 to Edinburgh, where Donnie was sent to the university to study art.

On 10 March, mother and son moved into a first floor flat at 31 Buckingham Terrace. In the meantime, Donnie had been enjoying himself, spending much of his time in the Palais de Danse studying the art of the foxtrot and the female form, his studies being financed by his unsuspecting mother. For by now he had discovered another talent – that of forging her signature on cheques. By this means, he withdrew £458 from her two accounts by means of twenty-nine cheques, although he was prevented from making it an even thirty by a worried letter that reached Mrs Merrett from a bank manager querying the size of her overdraft. This filled her with a certain unease, which was nonetheless nothing compared to the uneasiness felt by Donnie, who in order to avoid any future financial embarrassment – and to avail himself of her annual income of £700 – decided to kill her.

Her death was carefully planned, but the plan misfired. It was supposed to look like suicide. On Wednesday 17 March 1926 at 9.40 am, Mrs Merrett's maid, Mrs Sutherland, was disturbed in the kitchen by the large seventeen-year-old youth, who rushed in crying: 'Rita, my mother has shot herself!' And indeed, Mrs Merrett lay on the sitting-room floor by her bureau with a gunshot wound in her right ear and a gun in her hand. However she was still alive, though unconscious.

She was removed to the Royal Infirmary – the grieving Donnie being driven there by the police. As an attempted suicide – a criminal act – she was isolated and was asked no questions when she recovered consciousness. However, she was able eventually to tell Dr Roy Holcombe: 'I was sitting down writing letters and my son Donald was standing beside me. I said: "Go away, Donald, and don't annoy me!" and the next thing I heard was a kind of explosion, and I don't remember anything more.'

She died on 1 April. Her death might still have been classed as suicide had not the Edinburgh police discovered one of her cheque books in Donnie's bedroom.

Further slow but diligent enquiries revealed that the signatures on some of Mrs Merrett's cheques were forgeries, and almost reluctantly, it seems – so unbelievable was the charge – Donald Merrett was eventually arrested on 29 November 1926 for the murder of his mother. He was at that time staying with family friends at Hughenden Vicarage in Buckinghamshire, 'preparing for an academic career'.

His trial began at the High Court of Justiciary, Parliament Square, Edinburgh, on 1 February 1927 and lasted until 8 February. The Lord Justice-Clerk, the Rt Hon Lord Alness, was the judge and the Lord Advocate, the Rt Hon William Watson, KC, led for the prosecution. Mr Craigie M Aitchison, KC, defended the tall, pleasant-looking teenager, now eighteen, his defence being that Mrs Merrett had shot herself and had not been shot by her son. The suicide theory was disputed by the absence of any powder marks on or near Mrs Merrett's ear, no blackening or 'tattooing'. Sir Bernard Spilsbury, appearing for once for the defence, said that this fact could be consistent with either suicide or accident.

The jury were bemused by the whole matter and returned a verdict possible in Scottish courts – 'Not Proven'. Donald Merrett was, however, found guilty of 'uttering as genuine' twenty-nine forged cheques. For this he was sent to jail for a year, though after serving eight months of his sentence he was released. While in jail he was visited by a friend of his mother, Mrs Mary Bonnar, and on his release he went to stay with her in Hastings. A few months later he eloped with and married her daughter Isobel, who was known as Vera.

Mrs Bonnar apparently never believed that Donnie *did* shoot his mother. But Vera, in later years when her husband insisted they call themselves Chesney, sometimes borrowed a book from the local lending library – a book in the Notable British Trials series – and read about the trial in 1927 of young John Donald Merrett. What did *she* believe? Whatever it was, she could never have believed that twenty-seven years after shooting his mother, Donnie/Ronnie would drown his wife. But in 1954 Vera Chesney died, drowned in her own bath.

Unfortunately for Chesney/Merrett, the perfect murder plan once again went wrong. Mrs Bonnar, now calling herself Lady Menzies, encountered him accidentally him in the suite of rooms in Montpelier Road that she shared with her daughter. She recognised him, despite his disguise, and accordingly had to be silenced. Small and elderly though she was, she fought for her life until she was eventually overpowered, battered and strangled by her hulking son-in-law.

He left the house and flew back to Germany. But someone had noticed a heavily built stranger in the neighbourhood that night, of the same build as Mr Chesney, and the police knew from their files that Mr Chesney had once been Mr Merrett. Was it possible after all this time that he had now killed not only his wife but also his mother-in-law?

The police in France and Germany were alerted and asked to find Chesney/Merrett. But less than a week after the murders of Vera and her mother, on 16 February 1954, his body was found in a wood near Cologne. He had shot himself.

Pink fibres from Lady Menzies's scarf were found on his clothes, as were hairs from her dog and traces of blood. Dark hairs similar to his were found on her cardigan, and under her fingernails were slivers of skin. They came from his arms, scratched and bruised by the frail old woman as she struggled for her life.

The British police asked the Germans if this evidence could be checked, and with Germanic thoroughness his arms were cut off and dispatched to London to assist the police with their murder investigations there. These arms, which were later displayed as evidence at a coroner's inquest in London, are now the most strikingly grisly exhibit in the Crime Museum – two arms, severed above the elbows and crossed, erect, in a tank of formaldehyde.

46

GINTER WIORA

THE MURDER OF SHIRLEY ALLEN, 1957

Ginter Wiora was a Polish art student aged thirty-four, who lived with his twenty-four-year-old girlfriend, Shirley Marguerite Allen, in a basement flat in 21 Leinster Square, Bayswater. They had moved into the flat in November 1956, she posing as his wife and calling herself Mrs Wiora. He was known as Peter. A jealous man, he suspected her of having posed for pornographic pictures and was angered by her carefree attitude to and association with other men, whether real or imagined.

On Saturday, 4 May 1957 – it was Cup Final Day (Aston Villa beat Manchester United 2-1) – the landlady, fifty-five-year-old Mrs Doreen Dally, was awakened at 8 am by a loud banging noise. She lived in a basement flat opposite that occupied by Wiora and Shirley Allen. Mrs Dally then heard a woman cry out: 'No, Peter! No! Oh, Peter, please.' This was followed by a terrible scream of agony and fear.

The landlady, in her night-dress, apprehensively went to the door of her flat, opened it and looked out into the passage. She saw Shirley Allen, wearing a red dressing-gown, emerge from the door of Wiora's flat, with blood streaming down her neck from a head wound. But something or someone seemed to be holding her back and Miss Allen, seeing Mrs Dally, said softly: 'Oh, Mrs Dally. Help me, please. Peter's gone mad.' Mrs Dally seized the other woman's right arm and was able to pull her away. The door was only slightly ajar and she saw nothing of Wiora.

She guided Shirley Allen into her own flat and told her to lock the door. She then hastened towards the basement stairs, intending to reach a telephone on the floor above, but had only mounted two or three steps when she heard a sound behind her. She turned and saw Wiora standing in the passage, gazing at the door of her flat. His hands, crossed high on his chest in an oriental pose, held what the police said later was a Japanese samurai sword. In fact, it was a long, thin-bladed, slightly curved sword with a long hilt called a *dha*, which was used in Burma and other adjacent countries in South-east Asia.

Wiora turned and looked at her. Suddenly swirling the sword in the air, he pointed the sword at her and lunged. The point pierced her left breast and entered her chest. He withdrew it and then returned the sword to its previous position, his arms ceremonially crossed over his chest.

Mrs Dally fled up the stairs, blood staining her nightdress. She aroused the occupant of a ground-floor flat and telephoned for the police. Meanwhile, screams could be heard coming from her flat below.

When the police arrived they found Mrs Dally sitting in an armchair in the ground-floor flat, waiting to be taken to hospital. She told them what had happened. Cautiously, PC Tennyson descended the stairs into the basement.

The door of Mrs Dally's flat was open, and Shirley Allen lay dead on her back behind the door, her head against the wall. A sword with a bent blade lay on the floor by her right leg. Nearby was a broken standard lamp with which she had been battered on the head. She had died of a haemorrhage caused by a deep stab wound in her chest.

With PC Tennyson was DC Patrick Drown. He discovered that the door to Wiora's flat had been locked. He listened, and could hear the sound of a radio and some moaning. There was also a smell of gas. The door was kicked open and the police burst in, hastening to turn off an unlit and hissing gas fire and a kitchen stove. On a bed in a corner lay Wiora, writhing and moaning. He had tried to commit suicide by stabbing himself with another sword and by cutting his wrists with a bread knife. He and Mrs Dally were taken to St Mary's Hospital, Paddington.

Ginter Wiora was tried at the Old Bailey on 25 July 1957. His defence was that of diminished responsibility. The jury found him guilty of manslaughter and he was sentenced to twelve years in prison.

He tried to commit suicide in prison and was transferred to Broadmoor on 31 October 1958. A special restriction on his discharge expired in July 1969. But he remained in Broadmoor until 1987, when he was transferred into the care of a local psychiatric hospital.

47

MICHAEL DOWDALL

THE MURDER OF VERONICA MURRAY, 1958

The body of Veronica Murray, a thirty-one year-old prostitute, was found in her room in a boarding house at 58 Charteris Road, Kilburn, on Christmas Eve 1958. She had been dead for five or six days. Sprawled on her bed, she was naked except for a pullover drawn up over her head, which had been battered six times by a blunt instrument, apparently a bloodstained 6 lb dumbbell that was lying on the floor by the bed. The fatal injuries she sustained, which had fractured her skull and caused her death, were evident on her forehead above her left eye. There were slight lacerations and abrasions on her body, including a series of small circular marks that had been inflicted after death.

Fingerprints of her possible assailant were found on a cup, but police investigations into the murder produced no result for nearly a year.

Then, on 10 October 1959, a certain Mrs Hill, celebrating her birthday in the West End, met a youth whom she invited back to her flat in Ismailia Road, Fulham. When she refused to have sex with him he hit her, tore her clothes off and strangled her with a silk stocking until she became unconscious. She survived the attack, however, and from her evidence and the young man's fingerprints the police were able to connect the assault with another on a sixty-five-year-old woman who had been battered with a poker as she slept in her home near Sloane Square. She had been robbed, as had Mrs Hill, of money and a bottle of whisky.

The assailant's fingerprints also connected him with a series of break-ins and burglaries over the previous year, including three in Chelsea, one in a Fulham pub and another in the Westbury Hotel, Mayfair. Apart from possessing the burglar's fingerprints, the police now knew he was young, drank heavily, chain-smoked and was called Mick.

DI Peter Vibart of Chelsea police station, investigating the Fulham attack, was struck by a curious feature of the assault on Mrs Hill. There were odd circular marks on her body, indicative of some sexual perversion. Vibart recalled that such marks had been found on another woman's body some time previously. He checked the files, studied the unsolved murder of Veronica Murray, and saw that the fingerprints in the Murray file matched those of the youth called Mick who had attacked Mrs Hill. The police were now convinced that they were dealing with not just a dangerous criminal but a psychopathic, perverted killer who might murder again.

Previous burglaries and assaults on women in the London area were double-checked and a further detail emerged: Mick had a cigarette-lighter bearing the unusual name 'Texas Gulf Sulphur Co.' A picture of a similar lighter was published in the newspapers one month after the attack on Mrs Hill. It produced a response, from a young guardsman stationed at Pirbright in Surrey, the depot of the 1st Battalion Welsh Guards. He informed his CO that another guardsman, called Mick, had just such a lighter. His full name was Michael Douglas Dowdall.

The police were informed. Dowdall's army record was checked against the police file on Veronica Murray, the attacks on Mrs Hill and other women, and the weekend burglaries. At the time of Miss Murray's murder, Guardsman Dowdall, then barely eighteen, had been absent without leave. He frequently spent his weekends off duty in London and he drank and smoked a great deal. He had in fact been AWOL four times, and once, when in military detention, had tried to hang himself. His CO, Lt Col Mansell Miller, later described Dowdall as 'a bit odd' and thought that the boy had delusions of grandeur despite (or perhaps arousing from) the fact that he was in reality 'small, weak and insignificant'.

Mick Dowdall had joined the Welsh Guards as a drummer boy. He was born on 12 December 1940 and his father, an army captain, was killed during the Second World War in 1943. Described as 'quite uncontrollable' at school, he had been a problem child from the start, being referred to a child-care officer with the London County Council when he was six-and-a-half. He was also said to be 'destructive'. He had a tendency to become hysterical, and once, according to his brother, he tried to set fire to the Dowdall home. His mother died in 1948, after which he was brought up by an aunt in Wales. He was an unruly child and a violent, vicious youth. After joining the Welsh Guards he would brag about his prowess with women and burst into tears when he was disbelieved. To prove himself he drank heavily, stealing money to buy both drink and women.

On his eighteenth birthday he went with Sgt Clotworthy, Cpl Hopkins and other guardsmen, all older than he, to a hotel in Guildford, where he drank four or five half-pints of gin. At Dowdall's trial the judge asked Sgt Clotworthy: 'You did not feel it incumbent upon you to stop him? Did you have no responsibility for him?' Replied Clotworthy: 'Not while he was out of barracks.' Cpl Hopkins, who said that the rest of the group drank beer, told the judge that after two hours, and two pints of gin, Dowdall had to be carried out of the hotel and taken back to camp in a taxi. He was unable to go on parade the following morning and was taken for a walk by Hopkins.

On 24 November 1959, Dowdall was interviewed by the police at Pirbright. His fingerprints were taken and were found to match matched those in the Murray file. Dowdall was brought to London, to Chelsea police station, where he was questioned by DCI Acott. Dowdall said: 'Everybody has been against me. It's when I get drink in I do these things. I'm all right when I'm sober. It's been worrying me for a long time, and I wanted to go to a doctor. I'm glad it's over. I'll tell you all I can remember.' He went on:

Just before Christmas 1958, I had been drinking in the West End and I got very drunk. I picked up with a prostitute in Trafalgar Square. She called a taxi and I remember she gave an address somewhere in Kilburn. We got to her house and climbed the stairs to her room. I had sex with her and went to sleep. When she woke me up we had a row over something and she called me a filthy little Welsh bastard. I threw a vase at her. I believe it smashed. She came at me and hit me with something on the back of the neck and head and scratched my nose and eyes. I rushed at her, and I knocked her down and hit her head or face. I think she was half getting up. I pulled her onto the bed and I remember chucking some clothes over her. I took a bottle of whisky and then I left the place. I went back to the Union Jack Club and went to sleep. When I woke up, I found blood on my hands, and my shirt and suit were covered in blood. I chucked the shirt away in the dustbin at the camp. I tried to wash it, but I could not get rid of the blood. I sent the suit to the cleaners. A day or two afterwards, I read in the newspapers that a prostitute had been found murdered at Kilburn, and I knew then I had killed the woman.

He went on to confess to a series of house-breakings and burglaries and to the assault on Mrs Hill. 'There are a lot of other jobs I've done in the last year,' he admitted. 'But I can't remember where all of them were exactly.' Trying to explain his criminal activities, he said: 'My army mates think I'm queer. I've tried to show them they're wrong … My mates make me feel a nobody. So I have a drink, and then I feel better and more important. Once I started the heavy drinking bouts, I liked it and kept it up. When I was drunk, very drunk, I would try anything. I wasn't fussy about what I did or what woman I went with. I'm glad I've been caught. I feel much better now already.'

He was charged with the murder of Veronica Murray on 3 December 1959, nine days before his nineteenth birthday.

Dowdall's two-day trial began at the Old Bailey on 20 January 1960. The judge was Mr Justice Donovan; the prosecutor was Mr Alastair Morton, and Mr Desmond Trenner defended the accused, who pleaded not guilty to murder. His defence was that of diminished responsibility, which if accepted would reduce the charge to one of manslaughter.

The pathologist, Dr Donald Teare, gave evidence for the Crown. The defence produced a child-care officer, as well as Dowdall's brother, various guardsmen and officers, and the principal MO at Brixton Prison, Dr Brisby. The latter described the accused as 'a psychopath', a 'social misfit' and 'an untruthful type' who believed people mocked and maligned him.

Dr Leigh, a psychiatrist at Bethlehem Hospital, said Dowdall was a psychopath and sexual pervert. The characteristics of a psychopath, he said, were aggressiveness, impulsiveness, lying, sexual perversion and often alcoholism, with no remorse or sense of guilt. The judge, in his summing-up, told the jury that if they accepted that the accused was suffering from an abnormality of mind that substantially impaired his responsibility for the killing, they should find him guilty of manslaughter.

The jury were out for three hours, before returning to seek advice on the degree of impaired responsibility necessary to mean 'substantially impaired mental responsibility'. After another eight-minute retirement, the jury found Dowdall guilty of manslaughter on the grounds of diminished responsibility.

On 21 January 1960, the judge sentenced him to life imprisonment, to be detained until, as he said, the authorities 'are satisfied that you can safely mingle with your fellow creatures once again'. An appeal was dismissed.

Mick Dowdall was released on licence from prison in July 1975, suffering from a serious illness from which he died in November 1976. He was thirty-six.

48
GUENTHER PODOLA

THE MURDER OF DS PURDY, 1959

Between 1900 and 1975, thirty-three men serving with the Metropolitan Police were murdered on duty, mainly by criminals evading arrest. The trial of one such murderer made legal history on the opening day. The accused was said to be unfit to plead, because he had lost his memory.

Guenther Fritz Erwin Podola, the only child of a banker, was born on 8 February 1929 in Berlin. He was a studious, piano-playing boy, the nature and direction of whose life was altered irrevocably by the Second World War. His early teens were spent in the lawless atmosphere of the bombed and ruined city. He became a member of the Hitler Youth. He was fourteen when his father was killed at Stalingrad and sixteen when the Russians invaded Berlin and Hitler died in his bunker. The men in the block of flats where Podola lived were machine-gunned by the Russians and some of the women, including his mother, were raped.

He somehow survived the deprivations and hardships of post-war Germany, and in 1952, when West Germany became an independent nation, he escaped from East Berlin to the West, leaving behind him a woman, Ruth Quant, with whom he had lived and who had borne him a son, Micky. Podola emigrated to Canada and stayed there for six years. But in July 1958, he was deported after being jailed for a year for theft and burglary. For a time he worked in Dusseldorf. Then, in May 1959, when he was thirty, he came to London, affecting a gangster pose in Soho night clubs and calling himself Mike Colato. During the day he was involved in various legitimate, though shady, activities. At night, he added to his wages by house-breaking and burglary.

One of the flats he burgled, on 3 July 1959, was occupied by Mrs Verne Schiffman, a thirty-year-old English-born American model, on holiday in London. The flat was in Roland Gardens, South Kensington, and she lost some furs and jewellery. A few days later she received a letter from a man called Levine, who claimed to be an American private detective and said he possessed some compromising photos and tapes of her. These would be returned to her, he wrote, on the payment of $500.

Five days later on Sunday, 12 July Mrs Schiffman was telephoned by Podola, posing as a Mr Fisher. He said he was acting on behalf of Mr Levine and wanted to know her response to the letter. Unimpressed by the letter and the threat of blackmail, she had already complained to the police investigating the burglary. On their advice her telephone was tapped, and when the blackmailer rang again at about half-past three on Monday, 13 July, she kept him talking for fifteen minutes while the call was traced to a telephone box in South Kensington underground station – KNI 2355.

At 3.50 pm she heard the man say: 'Hey! What do you want?' There was the sound of a scuffle and she heard another man say: 'Okay, lad, we're police officers.' The same man then spoke to her: 'Mrs Schiffman,' he said. 'This is Detective Sergeant Purdy. Remember my name.'

DS Raymond William Purdy, aged forty, was a married man with three children. He had driven over from Chelsea police station with DS John Sandford to apprehend the caller. They hauled Podola out of the call box. But as they went up the stairs that led from the underground station led to the street, he broke loose and ran down Sydney Place into a block of flats in 105 Onslow Square, about a hundred yards from the tube. He hid behind a pillar in the hall but was soon spotted and seized by the two detectives, both of whom were in plain clothes and unarmed. DS Purdy took charge of Podola, ordering him into a corner of the hall to the right of the entrance, where there was a window.

Here Podola was briefly questioned, but not searched. Purdy removed the blue sunglasses Podola was wearing – the summer of 1959 was the hottest and driest for fifty years – and stuffed them in the suspect's breast pocket. He told Podola to behave himself and sit on the window sill. Podola did so, hoisting himself on to the marble ledge as DS John Sandford crossed the hall to ring a bell summoning the caretaker, his intention being to enlist some assistance before he himself returned to the police car and communicated with the police station.

There was no response to his ringing of the caretaker's bell and Sandford so informed Purdy, calling out to him across the hall. Purdy, momentarily distracted, turned his head towards the other detective – at which point Podola pulled out a gun, a 9mm FB Radom V15, shot Purdy through the heart and fled out into the sunny street. Sandford rushed over to his fallen colleague. When he ran outside there was no sign of the gunman.

DS Ray Purdy was not Sandford's usual partner, who that afternoon had been elsewhere engaged. Although Purdy had been about to go off duty when Sandford was detailed to go to the call box, he volunteered to partner the other sergeant. Before he did so, he telephoned his wife to say he would be late coming home that evening.

Sandford later described Podola as: 'A man about thirty, height about 5 ft 10 in, slim build, brown hair, speaking with an American accent, last seen wearing dark glasses, a light sports coat, light grey trousers and suede shoes.'

Podola was identified by fingerprints left on the marble ledge in the hall of 105 Onslow Square. Two days after the shooting, Purdy's widow said that the address book that had been returned to her with his personal possessions was not his. It belonged to Podola. It was thought that Purdy, seeing it in the call box when Podola was picked up, put it in his pocket. Although Podola's name was not in the address book, the names, addresses and telephone numbers of many other people were. They were all contacted, and variously confirmed Sandford's description of the gunman. Some thought Podola was German, others Canadian.

Then a hotel manager told the police that one of his guests, Paul Camay, was acting 'very strangely'. He seemed to be in hiding in the hotel. On the same day, the Royal Canadian Mounted Police sent particulars and a photograph of an immigrant German, Podola, who had been deported in 1958. The hotel manager thought that Camay and Podola were probably one and the same.

The police went in force to the Claremont House Hotel, 95 Queen's Gate, Kensington, where Mr Camay had hidden himself in Room 15.

Here he had cowered for two days since the shooting, in great fear of the law, it seems, and of being caught – not eating, nervously smoking and listening to the news on the radio about the police hunt for him. He had hidden his gun and its ammunition in the attic of the hotel, wrapping the weapon in a copy of *The Times* dated 13 July. It was later found there by the police.

At 3.45 pm on the afternoon of Thursday, 16 July, there was a banging on the bedroom door. 'Police! Open the door!' said a voice.

After a brief hesitation Podola, wearing a vest and trousers, went to the door. Perhaps he removed the key to peer through the keyhole, for the police outside said later that they thought they heard a click like the cocking of a gun.

DS Albert Chambers, who weighed 16 stone, charged the door. It burst open, the handle striking Podola in the face as Chambers crashed down on him. Podola was overpowered and put on the bed by DCI Acott and DI Vibart. He then apparently became unconscious or fainted. When he had somewhat recovered he was taken from the hotel at about 4.15 pm, minus his shirt and shoes and with his jacket thrown over his head.

Some newspapers later exaggerated the doubtful aspects of Podola's arrest, including the actions of a police dog, which was also present with its handler. It was rumoured that Podola had been beaten up by the police and bitten by the dog. But Podola himself never made any complaints, nor did his lawyers. What was seldom mentioned was that the police officers concerned had showed some courage in tackling an armed (as far as they knew) gunman, and that DS Chambers had received a George Medal four years earlier in October 1955, awarded for his courageous actions in overpowering and arresting an armed gunman in Mayfair.

A police surgeon, Dr John Shanahan, was summoned to examine Podola within half an hour of Podola's arrival in Chelsea police station, and found him to be 'dazed, frightened and exhausted' and suffering from muscular tremors, as if he were shivering, with a 'withdrawal reaction to his arrest'. Minor injuries included a cut over the left eye, some bruises and some scratches on his face. The worst bruise was under his left eye. It still showed at his trial two months later. Dr Shanahan examined Podola again at midnight and found no change.

Podola was taken to St Stephen's Hospital on the following day, 17 July, where he was handcuffed by one wrist to a bed in a public ward and guarded by two policemen. Here he was seen by Dr Harvey, the consultant physician. Podola seemed to be severely shocked, in a stupor and only partially aware of his surroundings, although tests revealed no fractures or internal bleeding.

Over the next few days, he began to recover, although he remembered hardly anything of his life before 17 July. Interestingly, although he wanted to know where he was and why, he apparently never asked why he was chained to the bed.

On 20 July, Dr Harvey allowed him to be seen by the police and a solicitor. That afternoon Podola was removed from the hospital and taken to West London magistrates' court where, in a state bordering on collapse, he was charged with the murder of DS Purdy. He was then driven to Brixton Prison, where a posse of doctors examined him over the ensuing weeks to determine whether or not his loss of memory was real.

His trial began at the Old Bailey on 10 September before Mr Justice Edmund Davies; Mr Maxwell Turner led for the Crown. Podola was represented by Mr Frederick Lawton, QC. Although the Homicide Act of 1957 had limited the death sentence to seven kinds of murder – with a gun, with explosives, in the furtherance of robbery, of a police officer, of a prison warder, while assisting arrest or escaping, and committing two separate murders – Podola's crime was such that he could, if found guilty, be hanged. But certain legal issues had first to be resolved. Were the prosecution or the defence to open the debate? On which of them was the burden of proof, and what indeed was the nature of that proof?

The judge ruled that it was up to the defence in the first place to prove that the loss of memory was genuine. If they succeeded, they would have to submit that Podola could not therefore be tried as charged. This legal discussion took nine days.

Mr Lawton said at the start of his opening address to the jury: 'I stand here today, my learned friend by my side, Podola's solicitor in front of me, and the three of us have no idea what his defence is at all.' He said that Podola's loss of memory meant that he was unable to defend himself, and suggested that it had been caused by concussion and severe fright occasioned by the circumstances of his arrest at the Claremont House Hotel. Podola's injuries, acquired then, were not severe, said Mr Lawton – 'A good deal of blood was shed, however. Two pillow cases were deeply stained with blood; a coverlet was stained … There was blood spattered on his trousers.' All this was unlikely to have come from a cut above Podola's eye. It was more likely to have come from a nose bleed. Not that there was so far any complaint against the arresting policemen, said Mr Lawton: 'Podola does not know whether he has any complaint at all. It may have been an accident. It may have been that he struggled violently … It may be, of course, that more force was used than was necessary.'

Mr Lawton detailed the findings of Dr Shanahan and Dr Harvey, and then those of Dr Edwards, Dr Ashby and Dr Larkin, who all concluded that Podola's amnesia was more than likely to be genuine.

All these doctors gave evidence at the medical trial before the murder trial. The last four, who had studied Podola, agreed that although it was possible for him to be feigning amnesia, it was most unlikely. He could not have the psychiatric knowledge or superior intelligence, they said, to sustain such a deception. And the fact that he had not lost certain acquired skills – he remembered how to play chess, pontoon, and could speak English, German and French – was quite consistent with his claim. Nonetheless, two doctors found it surprising that his virtually total loss of memory had persisted for two months.

Podola himself gave evidence. He said he remembered two names, Micky and Ruth, whom he thought were his son and a girlfriend. He also remembered a time when he was lying under a train, and another time when a policeman whispered: 'I am your friend. Say it was an accident.' He remembered nothing else of his life before 17 July, although he said he knew how to speak English and German, to play cards and chess, and certain bits of general knowledge, such as the names of national rulers.

The prosecution produced a letter he had written from Brixton Prison to a man called Ron Starkey, who was also produced and said he had met the accused three times and that the accused once stayed with him. Podola said he had no memory of this man, and had only replied to the man's postcard in order to acquire a visitor and some cigarettes.

Starkey's postcard read: 'Dear Mike. Is there anything I can get you in the way of tobacco and eats? If so, drop me a visiting card and I will come and see you. Best of luck, Ron.' Podola replied:

> Dear Ron. Thank you for your card. I was very pleasantly surprised to hear from you. How are you keeping yourself these days, old boy? I reckon you have heard all about the mess I am in ... I think it is very nice of you to write and now you want to come all the way to London to see me. You don't need a special visiting-card, you can see me any day Monday through Saturday from 10 to 11.30 and 1.30 to 3.30. Naturally I would appreciate anything in the line of smokes and eats but it really isn't necessary ... However, Ron, if you should be able to pick up a bunch of old magazines or reading matter I will be sure glad and grateful ... There is not much doing around here. The food isn't bad but lacks variety ... It was sure nice to hear from you, Ron. Cordially yours, Mike.

Two doctors were called by the prosecution: Dr Brisby, the prison doctor at Brixton, and Dr Leigh, who saw Podola on ten occasions. They concluded that Podola was malingering, faking his amnesia. They said there had never been a case of hysterical amnesia involving such total memory loss that did not have some clinical or medical symptoms. In rebuttal, the defence summoned another psychiatrist, Dr Stafford-Clark, who said that he had dealt with twenty cases of complete hysterical amnesia and that such persons might lose all personal knowledge but retain certain skills and general knowledge. These medical discussions covered four days.

On 23 September, the ninth day of the trial, the judge asked the jury to go away and consider whether the defendant was or was not suffering from a genuine loss of memory 'covering at least all the events with which he was concerned between 1 July 1959 and the time of his arrest on 16 July 1959' and whether he was fit to stand trial. The jury returned after three-and-a-half hours. Podola, they thought, was not suffering from a genuine loss of memory. This had not, they felt, been established.

Podola's trial for murder, with a new jury but the same judge and lawyers, began on 24 September. It lasted two days.

The main prosecution witness was DS John Sandford, who told how Podola had shot DS Purdy. In his defence Podola made a statement from the dock: 'I understand the various accusations that have been made, and now the time has come for me to defend myself against these accusations. I cannot put forward any defence ... I cannot remember the crime. I do not remember the circumstances leading up to the events or to this shooting. I do not know if I did it or whether it was an accident or an act of self-defence ... For these reasons I am unable to admit or deny the charge against me ... Thank you, my lord.'

The jury took half an hour to find Podola guilty and the judge sentenced him to death for a 'foul and terrible deed'.

Guenther Podola, the last man to be hanged for killing a policeman, was executed at Wandsworth Prison by Jock Stewart and Harry Allen on 5 November 1959 after an appeal to the House of Lords was turned down by the Attorney-General. The appeal judge said: 'Even if the loss of memory had been a genuine loss of memory, that did not of itself render the appellant insane.'

DS Purdy's widow received a pension of £546 a year.

The last two men to be sentenced to death for murder and hanged were executed on the same day at the same time, at 8 am on 13 August 1964. They were Peter Anthony Allen, aged twenty-one, and Gwynne Owen Evans, aged twenty-four, both dairymen, who had been convicted of the murder in the furtherance of theft of John Alan West, aged fifty-two, in Seaton, Cumberland. A laundry-van driver, West was brutally beaten to death with a cosh in his home and stabbed. This happened on 6 April 1964. Allen and Evans were tried in June and their appeal was dismissed on 21 July by the Lord Chief Justice, Lord Parker, by Mr Justice Widgery and Mr Justice Winn. Allen and Evans were hanged three weeks later, the former at Walton Prison, Liverpool by Jock Stewart, and the latter by Harry Allen at Strangeways Prison, Manchester.

Four months after the executions, Mr Sidney Silverman's Murder (Abolition of Death Penalty) Bill, which suspended capital punishment for murder for an experimental period of five years, was given a second reading by the House of Commons by a majority of 185 votes. However, the bill did not become law until 9 November 1965.

ROBERTS, WITNEY AND DUDDY

THE MURDERS OF DS HEAD, DC WOMBWELL AND PC FOX, 1966

The murders of policemen invariably result in letters to the newspapers demanding the restoration of capital punishment – something the police themselves would generally support. After the triple murders of DS Head, DC Wombwell and PC Fox there was such a public outcry, such widespread demonstrations of outrage, that it seemed the death penalty might be restored for some sorts of murder.

The last time three policemen had been shot dead in one incident was at midnight on 16 December 1910 in Houndsditch, when seven anarchists were surprised digging their way through the rear wall of a jeweller's shop. These deaths resulted in the fiasco of the Siege of Sidney Street, when two of the gang were trapped in a three-storey tenement at 100 Sidney Street, Whitechapel, on 3 January 1911. In the ensuing gun-battle, in which thirty-six guardsmen and many policemen were involved, the building burnt down, two anarchists were killed, and a fireman died when part of the building collapsed. Four other firemen were badly injured, and five policemen, four civilians and a soldier were wounded. Of the nine persons arrested by the police in connection with the shooting of the three policemen, not one was convicted, because of lack of evidence. The deaths of the policemen were later dignified by a memorial service in St Paul's Cathedral.

In between these two cases, twenty-four policemen had been murdered on duty, eleven after 1956. There had also been a general rise in crimes of violence, of gang warfare and robbery in London, and many people believed that because hanging had been abolished the growing number of criminals armed with guns would not hesitater to use them.

It was warm and sunny on Friday, 12 August 1966, when the three-man crew of Q car Foxtrot Eleven took over their car, a Triumph 2000, at Shepherd's Bush police station in Uxbridge Road. The three men, who were on duty from 9 am to 5 pm that day, had been working together for just a few weeks. The area they patrolled, F Division, centred on Hammersmith and took in Shepherd's Bush and Fulham. A major murder enquiry in F Division, concerning the strangling of six prostitutes whose naked bodies had been dumped around the division, mainly by the river, had recently been closed after the suicide of the chief suspect, a security guard.

The driver of Foxtrot Eleven was forty-one-year-old PC Geoffrey Roger Fox. Married with three children, he lived in a council flat north of Northolt and had been a PC at 'the Bush' for the sixteen years he had been in the police force. (His wife, Marjorie, said later: 'I always knew my Geoff would get killed some day.') PC Fox was the regular driver of the Q car and, like the other two, he was in civilian clothes.

DS Christopher Tippett Head, aged thirty and unmarried, was in charge of the team. Born in Dartmouth on 24 December 1935, one of four children, he was five when his mother was widowed. She brought the children up on her own and Christopher went to the local grammar school. He became a police cadet when he was seventeen and did his National Service with the RAF police in Scotland. After he was demobbed, he worked in an aircraft factory in Newton Abbot until June 1958 when he was accepted by the Metropolitan Police in London and posted to Fulham after his training. He joined the CID in 1964 and was promoted to sergeant just before his move to Shepherd's Bush.

DC David Stanley Bertram Wombwell, aged twenty-seven, was also a newcomer to the Bush and had only just become a temporary detective constable three years after joining the force. The only child of divorced parents, he had been brought up by his father and grandmother. After studying motor engineering at a polytechnic, he became a car salesman. When he was twenty-three, he married a seventeen-year-old hairdresser, Gillian Hague, in St Albans in 1962. They had two children and lived in East Acton.

On the morning of Friday the 12th, the crew of Foxtrot Eleven took DI Coote to Marylebone magistrate's court, where he gave evidence against five men who had escaped from Wormwood Scrubs Prison in June. Coote had with him several court exhibits such as the ropes that had been used in the escape. Foxtrot Eleven went back on patrol, and the three policemen had lunch in the Beaumont Arms in Uxbridge Road before setting off again, driving up Wood Lane, past the BBC TV Centre and the White City stadium, where they turned left into Western Avenue.

At about 3 pm Foxtrot Eleven was in the East Acton area. So was a battered blue Standard Vanguard estate car, containing three other men. All three were petty criminals with previous convictions. They were on the look-out for a car to replace the one they were in. The stolen car was then to be fitted with a pair of false number plates, which lay in the back of the Vanguard, and would be used in the robbery of a rent collector that the three planned to carry out the following week. The Vanguard was untaxed and uninsured. It had failed an MOT test, and the insurance covering the car had expired at noon that very same day.

Its owner was John Edward Witney, aged thirty-six and unemployed, who lived in a basement flat with his wife, Lilian, in Fernhead Road, Paddington. Previously a lorry driver, he had ten convictions for petty theft. His longest prison sentence had been eighteen months. Earlier that year, he had met another lorry driver and petty criminal, Harry Roberts, and the two teamed up, stealing metal and lead until they were joined by a third man, John Duddy, aged thirty-seven, when they began raiding betting shops and robbing rent collectors. Duddy later said that Witney was 'the brains of this outfit'.

Duddy was a Scot, born in Glasgow's Gorbals district on 27 December 1929. He was

37, 5 ft 5 in tall, slightly corpulent, brown haired, fresh complexioned, and his right forearm was tattooed with a skull, a heart and the motto 'True to death'. Four of his convictions were for theft: the offences had all been committed before he was twenty and none had involved violence. He was sent to borstal once and imprisoned twice for three months. But after 1948, no further convictions had been added to his record. He married and came to London, working from there as a long-distance lorry driver, and for seventeen years kept out of trouble. Then in 1966 he began drinking heavily and frequenting dubious West London clubs, in one of which he met Roberts and Witney.

Apart from the fact that they all had previous convictions, had all been lorry drivers, wanted easy money and lived within a mile of each other in London W9, they had little in common – except that Duddy's father had been a policeman and that Roberts as a boy had wanted to be one. Oddly, in 1966, Roberts was living with an ex-policeman's wife.

Harry Maurice Roberts was three weeks past his thirtieth birthday at the time of the shooting, having been born on 21 July 1936 at Wanstead in Essex, where his parents managed a pub, the George. An only child, he was cared for by a nanny who called him 'Robin'. On the outbreak of war his father, who had a savage temper and sometimes assaulted his wife, joined the RAF. 'I thought he was mental,' she said much later of Roberts Senior. 'He was always taking money off me and putting it on the dogs or drinking it.' When her son was seven or eight she sent him to a Roman Catholic boarding school in Norwood, for which she had to pay, being determined that he would have a good education; she was convent-educated herself. Hard times followed. Mr Roberts walked out, and Mrs Roberts was left to bring up young Harry in post-war London. She slaved to pay for his education, sometimes working twenty-two hours a day, and lived on a council estate near Euston. She became manageress of a local restaurant. When Harry was thirteen he became, at his own insistence, a day boy at St Joseph's, and as his mother was out working nearly all the time, he began to play truant. He started taking money from her handbag and pilfered the restaurant till. Later, his mother reflected:

Every time my boy got into trouble and I tried to thrash things out of him, I got nowhere. I just couldn't seem to get through to him somehow ... I know now where the turning-point was. It was when he was sixteen or seventeen, and I hauled him out of a fellow's flat. He hadn't been working; but he would go out all dressed up, obviously up to something ... The man was no good. A criminal type. I went up one afternoon and banged on the door till they let me in. In front of my son, and this man's wife, I told him I knew he was no fit company for a young lad, and he was never to see my son again. I made Robin come home with me. He said nothing until he got into my flat, then he turned on me like a savage and punched me in the face, splitting my lip open. I couldn't believe he would do such a thing to his mother ... I didn't go to the police. I couldn't bring myself to turn my own boy in ... All his life he has liked the company of rotten people.

Her care and devotion, and his education, were wasted. Already, by the time he was fifteen, he had been put on probation for receiving stolen goods, and when he left school, early, he was variously a porter, an electrician's mate, a street trader and a lorry driver, filling in time until National Service claimed him.

He then joined the Rifle Brigade, became a marksman and a lance corporal and served in Malaya during the emergency. Jungle training and guerilla warfare taught him much and hardened him. After he was demobbed, according to his wife Margaret: 'He seemed bitter, and talked about killing and the fear of battle and the danger … He seemed to have become slightly ruthless and much more tough.' He had met his future wife – a small, attractive barmaid and former vaudeville dancer, Margaret Rose – at a party while he was on leave. She called him 'Robbie'. She said later that he was very clean and tidy and made no demands on her sexually. They were married on 3 March 1958, at which time he was employed as a motor mechanic/driver earning £7 14s 1d a week – slightly less than his wife, who worked for £8 a week as a barmaid.

For a time the couple lived with his mother, and there were rows. Then, in January 1959, he was convicted at Chelmsford in Essex for attempted store-breaking and larceny and sentenced to a total of twenty-one months in prison. While he was inside, his wife became worried by the knowledge that during another foray the previous November he had robbed and beaten up a seventy-eight-year-old man – for before her marriage, she had lodged with the same old man. The latter was now dangerously ill in hospital, and it was said a ring had been cut off his finger. Roberts admitted the assault when she questioned him. But – 'I didn't know what to do,' she admitted. 'I was his wife, after all.'

When Roberts was released from prison, he seemed different to her. 'All his quiet manners had gone,' she said. 'Only his tidy habits and neat dressing remained. He did not seem to care how he got money from somewhere.' They had a serious row when he suggested she could make some money for them both if she picked up men. A few nights later they were both in a Soho night club, drunk, when he repeated the suggestion. She was furiously indignant. He knocked her off the bar stool, punched and kicked her. Enraged, she staggered out to a call box, phoned the police, and told them about the assault on the old man in November.

Harry Roberts, aged twenty-two, was sentenced in March 1959 to seven years for robbery with violence. 'You are a brutal man,' said the judge. The maximum sentence was life, and Roberts could have been hanged if the old man had died. Instead he was in jail for four years and eight months. When he was sentenced he swore he would be revenged on his wife, who was seven months pregnant at the time. She collapsed in court and soon afterwards miscarried. She later became a stripper, calling herself Mitzi, and was billed as the Pocket Venus. She never saw Harry Roberts again.

In prison, despite an erratic, explosive temper that erupted over card games, Roberts was quite popular, although he had no interest in betting and football. He took courses in brick-laying and plumbing and did well in both.

In January 1963, he was transferred from Wormwood Scrubs to Horfield Prison in Bristol. A 'trusty', he was allowed to live in a prison hostel and do a normal job – brick-laying – provided he returned to the hostel by 10.45 pm. At weekends he went drinking with other inmates, some of whom, tempted by so much freedom, absconded.

It was in a pub that Roberts met Mrs Lilian Margaret Perry. She was auburn-haired, about thirteen years older than he, and was in the process of getting a divorce from her ex-policeman husband. She and Roberts became friendly.

When he was released in November 1963 he lodged with her in Horfield, continuing to work as a brick-layer for Wimpey's in Weston-super-Mare. He worked hard for several years, earned good money, and bought a second-hand Daimler for £650, his only personal extravagance.

But by March 1966, he had had enough. Leaving a large overdraft and several sizeable debts behind him, he returned to London. Mrs Perry went with him. They stayed in Maida Vale with a married couple, the Howards, who had witnessed his wedding to Margaret and had three young children. By now Roberts was twenty-nine.

A police description of him issued later that year read: 'Height 5 ft 10 in, slimmish built, slightly sunken cheeks, quiff of hair in centre of forehead that falls down frequently, George Robey eyebrows, left side of mouth twists up slightly, a big eater, drinks little and then brown or light ale or Coca Cola, has a passion for suede shoes, occasionally takes purple hearts, smokes tipped cigarettes fairly heavily, spends freely … Has long fingers and bites his nails … Needs to shave only occasionally.'

Mrs Perry later revealed:

We never had a cross word the whole time we were together … He said he had often rowed with his mother and would walk out of the room to avoid one. He was a very quiet man who kept himself to himself. He hated pubs and clubs and just liked to sit at home and watch television or read … I think he had never had a real home life before. He loved getting home at night, seeing a big fire and finding a steak grilling for him. He used to say that was the life, and we'd sit there so peaceful and happy. Wrestling was his favourite programme and he read all the James Bond books. He was a deeply lonely man and wanted me to go everywhere with him … If the Labour Government hadn't put the squeeze on and killed the building trade, Robbie wouldn't be inside now. It was only when the building trade flopped that he took to doing jobs … Robbie had to have money. He always had money as a boy. His mother gave him plenty because she was working and could not spend much time with him … He reckoned it salved her conscience … He could always buy friends with money but he could never rid himself of this horrible loneliness. That's why he was happy with me … There was no sex between us. I'm sexless, and Robbie didn't like it either.

He vowed, she said, that he would do anything to avoid going inside again – that he would shoot it out rather than go back to prison.

Mrs Perry and their landlady, Mrs Howard, knew of Roberts's association with Witney and Duddy – he was very fond of Witney, she said – and Mrs Howard often warned him about the loaded guns they had. 'You'll get fifteen years if you're caught with them!' she would say. 'If only they hadn't had the guns,' said Mrs Perry. 'Robbie always swore they were for frighteners.' Said Mrs Howard: 'If they were only for frighteners, they wouldn't have been loaded, would they?'

At 3.10 pm on Friday, 12 August, Witney's ramshackle, noisy blue Vanguard left East Acton underground station car park with Witney at the wheel, Roberts beside him and Duddy in the back with the false number-plates, a stocking mask and some overalls. A small canvas bag containing three guns occupied the space between the two front seats.

Apart from a break for lunch in Eastcote, they had spent the day driving around the Harrow and Wembley areas looking, mainly in station car parks, for a car to steal. No suitable car or opportunity had presented itself, and on leaving East Acton the three decided to abandon their search, take a break, and discuss their next move. Witney was also reluctant to go home as his wife thought he was at work. They headed for nearby Wormwood Scrubs common, intending to lie in the sun on the grass not far from the prison walls.

At 3.10 pm, Foxtrot Eleven received a radio message from DI Coote in Marylebone magistrate's court: the five men who had escaped from the prison had just been committed for trial, and Coote asked the Q car to pick him up with his exhibits. DS Head told Coote they would be at the court in twenty minutes. They were then in Acton.

Exactly where they were and how they chanced to spot and follow the blue Vanguard is unknown. But something about its appearance or movements must have attracted the policemen's attention. DS Head probably decided to check the other car before they headed east to Marylebone Road.

All six men, three in one car, three in the other, were totally unprepared for what happened in the next five minutes.

The Vanguard entered Braybrook Street, whose southern end ran along the thirty-foot-high perimeter wall of the prison. The rest of the street was bordered on the north by the wide stretch of the common. The residents of the council houses lining the opposite side of the road were used to drivers parking in the quiet street for a nap or a snack. That sunny afternoon, women idled about their household duties and children on holiday played on the pavement and out on the common.

The police car overtook the Vanguard and DS Head flagged it down. Both cars came to a halt, the police car some yards in front of the other, which was much closer to the kerb. Head and Wombwell got out of the Q car and approached the Vanguard, both coming to the driver's window. Fox remained in the Q car, the engine running.

DS Head asked Witney if he was the owner of the car. Witney replied: 'Yes.' Then he was asked for his road fund licence. He replied that he didn't have one. Head enquired why. Witney said he couldn't get the car taxed until it had been given an MOT certificate. Head asked to see his driving licence. Having examined it, he asked for the car's insurance certificate. After studying it he remarked: 'It's three hours out of date.'

DC Wombwell produced a notebook to write down the car's and the driver's particulars. So far Roberts and Duddy had said nothing. Head moved away to inspect the rear of the car. 'Can't you give me a break?' cried Witney. 'I've just been nicked for this a fortnight ago.'

As DC Wombwell inclined his head to talk to Witney through the open window Roberts shot him in the left eye. Wombwell staggered back and fell.

Roberts told Duddy to grab a gun and leapt out of the car, closely followed by Duddy, as Head ran for his life towards Foxtrot Eleven. 'Get the driver!' Duddy was told. Roberts fired at Head and missed. 'No, no, no!' cried Head, trying to hide behind the bonnet of Foxtrot Eleven. Roberts shot him in the back, and Head fell dying in front of the car.

Shocked senseless, Fox was slow to respond. But in any case, with Head in front of the police car he could not advance, and if he reversed he would approach the gunmen. Duddy fired at him three times, once through the rear near-side window, shattering the glass. This and another shot missed Fox. The third shot, which Duddy fired through the open passenger window, entered Fox's left temple and exited the other side.

As it did so his foot stamped on the accelerator. The car lurched forward over DS Head, who was still alive. He was caught underneath the car. Smoke poured from the engine as the rear wheels, lodged against Head's body, repeatedly banged against him, unable to advance. Fox lay dead at the wheel.

Witney had stepped out of the car to see what was happening. Roberts and Duddy ran back towards him and piled into the Vanguard.

'Drive!' cried Roberts. 'You must be fucking potty!' yelled Witney. 'Drive, you cunt!' Roberts retorted. 'Unless you want some of the same!'

Unable to stomach passing the fallen policemen, Witney reversed, and the blue Vanguard careered backwards with its loose exhaust, tied with string, sparking on the road. The brakes screeched as the car stopped, was swung left and sped down Erconwald Street and away from what would come to be known by the press as the Massacre of Braybrook Street.

A young couple, Bryan and Patricia Deacon, driving up Braybrook Street on their way to see his parents, were alarmed by the Vanguard reversing towards them. Bryan Deacon, a thirty-year-old security officer, who had been on duty the previous night, swore at the men in the blue car, and thinking that they might be mixed up in some prison-break shouted at his wife, who was seven months pregnant: 'Get the number!' He drove on, cursing, intending to telephone the police about the incident.

'Then I came across the first body,' he said later. 'I now know it was David Wombwell. He was lying with his feet towards the common. There was blood everywhere. Pat said:

"He's dead!" There was a green police car in the middle of the road, with smoke pouring from it. A lorry driver ran down the street, shouting: "Get the police! Get the police!"" It was the lorry driver who reached across PC Fox and switched off the ignition. The engine died and there was silence in the street.

At round about that time, a blackbird flew in the kitchen window of Mrs Roberts's flat in Euston. She was unable to get rid of it for some time and felt it was some kind of omen.

Bryan Deacon drove on past the police car and found a telephone in a nearby butcher's shop. He dialled 999. Although his wife was sobbing and hysterical, he returned to Braybrook Street on foot and gave the Vanguard's number, which he had written down on the butcher's wrapping-paper, to the driver of one of the many police vehicles that were soon on the scene. The number was PGT 726.

There were other witnesses – women and children. But there were discrepancies in their statements, and their descriptions of the three men involved in the shooting proved to be very inaccurate.

It took some time to trace the owner of PGT 726, as the records of car owners were in those days kept in county council offices and at 5 pm they had closed for the day.

DCS Richard Chitty was put in charge of the murder enquiry, and by 9 pm DI Steventon and a sergeant were knocking at the door of Witney's basement flat in Paddington. 'We are making enquiries concerning the owner of a blue Vanguard shooting-brake, PGT 726, which we understand is yours.' 'Oh, no! Not that!' said Witney, and explained: 'We've just seen on the telly about the coppers being shot.' He told Steventon that he had sold the car that day to a stranger for £15. 'You told me you'd been to work,' said Mrs Witney. 'You didn't tell me you'd sold the car. What's going on?' 'I haven't been to work for five weeks,' Witney replied. 'I had to get some money for you.' He was trembling and sweating: he mopped his face with a towel. Steventon, after further questions, asked Witney to come to the police station. Mrs Witney, much upset by now, said: 'Please, darling, tell them the truth.'

Witney was questioned at Shepherd's Bush police station. He made a statement, elaborating what he had told DI Steventon, and was detained. A search of his flat revealed no weapons or anything incriminating.

Meanwhile, the car's number and descriptions of the wanted men had been issued to the press and broadcast on radio and television. Masses of information, most of it useless, began to pour in, and at a press conference on Saturday evening the police appealed for other witnesses and information. Witney's detention was not mentioned.

The previous evening, Harry Roberts had returned to Wymering Mansions in Maida Vale at seven o'clock. 'I knew at once something was wrong,' said Mrs Perry. 'He looked as if he had been running. He was all breathless and very flushed. I told him I had some nice rock salmon and chips for his tea. He looked disgusted. "I can't eat anything," he said, complaining of a headache.' Soon after this Mrs Howard left the shared flat and

Lilian Perry mentioned the shootings to Robbie – she had heard about them on the radio. 'Did you hear about the three policemen?' she said. 'Shut up!' said Roberts, and added: 'It was us.'

He told her what had happened. Repeatedly he said: 'If only that fool hadn't asked to look inside the car. I knew if the coppers turned the car over they'd find the guns and put us all away. I thought it was better to shoot it out than go down for fifteen years.' If the police had found the guns, he said, they would have done time for nothing. He neither ate nor drank and sat staring at the television set all evening, seeming to Mrs Perry to be very far away. She didn't know what to say or do.

On Saturday morning, they went shopping. On their return, John Duddy was in the flat: he had the guns. Roberts hid them under a bed. In the afternoon, Roberts, Duddy and Mrs Perry went for a walk in Paddington Recreation Ground, taking a pram and two of Mrs Howard's children with them, Barry, aged four, and Samantha, two, whom Roberts carried in his arms to hide his face. They returned to the flat in time to watch the wrestling on ITV.

Roberts wanted Duddy to go with him and get rid of the Vanguard, which Witney had left in a lock-up garage in Tinworth Street, Vauxhall, near the River Thames. But Duddy refused to go anywhere near the car. Eventually, at about 8 pm, Mrs Perry agreed to accompany Roberts to Vauxhall, leaving Duddy behind in the flat to babysit, as the Howards had gone out. Duddy poured himself a drink.

The lock-up garage was under the arches of the main railway line to Waterloo. Mrs Perry and Roberts peered through the slats of the garage door at the car within. The door was locked and they did not have the garage key or car key. Roberts said he wished Duddy would help him do something to get rid of the car, burn it or something. But he did nothing himself. Returning to the flat with Mrs Perry, he kept on at Duddy to do something, to help him. But the other man repeatedly said: 'No.'

Later that night, a man telephoned the police to say that he had seen a blue Vanguard being driven into the Tinworth Street garage on Friday. Within minutes the police visited the scene, and some time after midnight they discovered that the lock-up was rented by Witney. Three .38 cartridges were found in the car from the .38 Colt that Duddy had fired. The next day – Sunday – the Commissioner, Sir Joseph Simpson, and the Home Secretary, Roy Jenkins, called at Shepherd's Bush police station, outside which a crowd was shouting: 'Bring back the rope!'

That evening, John Witney was charged by DCS Chitty with the murders of all three policemen 'with others' and taken back to his cell. Soon afterwards he decided to make another statement. 'I'm not scared for myself,' he said. 'I know I'm going away for a long time, but I'm frightened for my family. As God is my judge I had absolutely nothing to do with the shooting of the three policemen.' He told the police his version of what had happened in Braybrook Street, naming Roberts and Duddy as the gunmen. Unable to remember their exact addresses, he was taken in a police taxi late at night to point out where Roberts and Duddy lived. Both buildings were discreetly surrounded by armed policemen.

They were raided at 5 am on Monday, 15 August, to the shock and alarm of the occupants. Duddy's two teenage daughters were on their own. They had not seen their father since Saturday, and their mother had walked out weeks ago. The Howards and their children were alone in their flat. Mrs Perry and Roberts were absent. Mrs Roberts's flat in Euston was also visited by the police and searched, and was kept under observation from then on. Harry Roberts's one-time wife was put under police protection. But of Roberts himself, there was no sign.

On the Sunday morning, Roberts and Duddy had gone to Hampstead Heath to bury the guns. On their return, Duddy opted to go to Scotland and Roberts decided to go to ground. He told Mrs Perry to pack a suitcase for him, and that afternoon they went to the Russell Hotel. He booked them in as Mr and Mrs Crosby. After a meal in a local restaurant – he couldn't eat, as food still made him feel sick – they went up to their twin-bedded room. They lay on top of the single beds, talking. Roberts smoked a cigarette.

It was a very warm night, for London was having a heatwave. He said: 'What a mess I've made of things. What a bloody mess. If only that fool hadn't wanted to inspect the car … I've got to get away, pet. If I can keep hidden, lie low for a while, the whole thing may blow over.'

It seems he intended to go to Scotland, for on Monday morning he and Mrs Perry walked from the hotel to Euston Station. There, however, Roberts changed both is mind and the direction of his flight. He put his case in a left-luggage office, and then tore up the ticket he had bought.

They then went to a second-hand army surplus store near King's Cross Station, where he bought some camping equipment, including some clothes, a haversack, a primus stove and a sleeping bag. He also bought some tins of food from a grocer. From King's Cross, they journeyed by bus to Camden Town, where they got on a Green Line bus for Epping. Roberts hardly spoke. They left the bus beyond the Wake Arms and walked back to the crossroads opposite the pub.

He looked at Mrs Perry and said: 'This is as far as you go, love … I'm on my own now. I'll have to make my own way from here.' She asked him where he was going. 'I don't know,' he said, 'I haven't really made up my mind.' He began to cry. So did she. 'You better go,' he said, 'before I get any worse.' Taking £6 out of a pocket he gave her 6s 6d, and told her how to get back to Maida Vale from there. 'That should be enough for your fare,' he said. 'I reckon I'm going to need the rest more than you.' Although she wanted to stay with him, he told her to go and saw her on to a coach. On her return to Wymering Mansions, she was interviewed by the police. She told them what she knew about Roberts and his whereabouts.

On Tuesday, 16 August – another hot, sunny day – a photograph of Harry Roberts was issued with a description of the khaki combat jacket, khaki trousers, shirt, socks and boots he might be wearing. The public were warned he might be armed.

That same morning, acting on a tip-off, the police arrested John Duddy in Glasgow, catching him in bed in a Calton tenement. He did not resist arrest. That night he was brought back to London on a scheduled flight from Glasgow airport.

Handcuffed, he sat between two Yard detectives – DCI John 'Ginger' Hensley and DI Slipper. The latter took a statement from him on the plane, which Duddy later denied having made. It said: 'I must tell you what happened … It was Roberts who started the shooting. He shot two who got out of the car and shouted to me to shoot. I just grabbed a gun and ran to the police car and shot the driver through the window. I must have been mad.' At Shepherd's Bush police station, Duddy made another statement. It ended: 'I didn't mean to kill him. I wanted quick money the easy way. I'm a fool.'

At dawn on Thursday, over 500 policemen, many of them armed, began searching the 6,000 acres of Epping Forest, backed up by police dogs and tear-gas guns, with a helicopter overhead observing and directing. On Saturday the search was called off – Harry Roberts had gone to ground elsewhere.

The man-hunt intensified, spreading all over Britain and into the continent, where Interpol were alerted. Roberts was seen everywhere. Sightings were as many as the theories about where and how he was living – was he disguised? – and every piece of information had to be followed up. There were further raids, chases and searches. A £1,000 reward was offered and advertised on 16,000 posters. It was the biggest police operation since the Great Train Robbery in August 1963.

In London, the police had two rest days, on 31 August and on 6 September. On the first day, the three murdered policemen were buried after a funeral service in the church opposite Shepherd's Bush police station. Over 600 policemen lined the route of the funeral procession. At Scotland Yard, in the wind and rain, a lone piper played a lament in the courtyard. On 6 September, a memorial service was held in Westminster Abbey, attended by 2,000 policemen from all over Britain, as well as by the Prime Minister, Harold Wilson, by Mr Heath, by the Home Secretary and other leading politicians. In Whitehall, signatures were collected for a petition demanding the restoration of the death penalty.

More sightings than ever before were reported – over 6,000 in all. Roberts was seen in Ireland, Wales, the Isle of Man, on planes, trains and boats. A hundred and sixty reported sightings came from Liverpool, 106 from Bournemouth. And over 50,000 people sent money and gifts to the Bush for the dead men's families.

September ended. Press and public interest waned and was then diverted by another sensation – the escape, on 22 October, of the spy George Blake from Wormwood Scrubs Prison, where, six years previously, Roberts had met him. Blake had been sentenced in 1961 to forty-two years in prison, the longest sentence ever passed by a British court.

The weeks passed. October ended. The trial of Witney and Duddy was set for

Monday, 14 November. By then, the real Harry Roberts had been seen by several people, who thought they recognised him but did nothing about it.

It must have been in October that three teenage boys, hunting rabbits in Thorley Wood near Bishop's Stortford in Hertfordshire, 3 miles up the A11 from Epping Forest, found a camouflaged tent, hidden in undergrowth and surrounded by a low stockade of twigs and branches. A man was inside and a radio was on. Without disturbing him they went away. One of the boys told his mother about the man in the woods. He said: 'I wonder if it's Harry Roberts.' 'That's not possible,' replied his mother with a laugh.

Since the beginning of October a dishevelled man in a combat jacket had regularly visited a grocery shop 2 miles away from Thorlwy Wood. He went there once a week and bought bread, eggs and tins of food, for which he paid in silver and other coins. 'My gosh, that chap looks like Harry Roberts!' said the manageress to her assistant, who laughed. They continued to see him. Said the manageress later: 'I meant to telephone the police. But I was afraid of feeling a little foolish. Now I feel an even bigger fool.'

Then, in November, four days before the trial of Witney and Duddy began, a gypsy farm labourer – twenty-one-year-old John Cunningham – was prowling at night in Thorley Wood armed with a catapult and looking for small game. His eye was caught by a light from a tent buried in the undergrowth and fallen autumn leaves. A tin can rattled; the occupant was having a meal. Cunningham returned to the family caravan and mentioned his discovery to his father, who was incurious and dismissive. But on Saturday, a policeman making enquiries about thefts in the area chanced to visit the Cunningham caravan and heard about the stranger in the wood. He determined to investigate. With another policeman, he set out for the wood that afternoon.

After some difficulty they found the hide-away. There was no one inside. But it was admirably situated and constructed, its carefully built framework of boughs and branches being covered with tarpaulin and plastic sheeting painted green and brown. Branches screened it all around; a hand-made chimney poked out of the roof, connected within to an iron stove; kindling cut to size was stacked in a box; a camp bed, sleeping bags, blankets, a primus stove, a cache of food tins, two transistor radios, a fishing rod, and all the necessary equipment for cooking and washing completed the homely scene; two suits and some shirts were neatly folded away.

The policemen watched and waited all day and night, but the tent's occupant failed to appear.

Fingerprints in the hide-away were taken by the Hertfordshire police and identified the occupant as Harry Roberts, and Scotland Yard was at once informed.

DCS Chitty received the news in the Old Bailey on the first day of the Witney–Duddy trial. That night, Thorley Wood was silently surrounded by well over a hundred policemen. At dawn on Tuesday, they moved in.

Harry Roberts was found just before noon on the edge of neighbouring Nathan's Wood. PS Smith and PS Thorne were poking around bales of straw piled up in a disused hangar. Smith noticed a jar of methylated spirits. Pulling apart the bales behind the jar, he unearthed a primus stove and a torch. Heaving aside another bale he saw a sleeping bag. He prodded it with a rifle. At one end, Roberts's bearded face emerged: he had been asleep. He said: 'Don't shoot. You won't get any trouble from me. I've had enough. I'm glad you caught me.' A loaded Luger lay inside the sleeping bag, the one used to kill Head and Wombwell. But this time he let it lie.

News of his capture reached DCS Chitty, the police and the press in the Old Bailey as they listened to Mrs Perry's evidence. Some left the court at once. But nothing was said officially before the court adjourned for lunch and for the day.

Chitty saw Roberts that afternoon in Bishop's Stortford police station. Roberts denied killing PC Fox but made a statement admitting everything else. A large crowd had gathered outside Shepherd's Bush police station when he was taken there that night. His mother saw him for ten minutes. At first she failed to recognise him, with his ginger beard and long hair. He looked thin and tired, she thought. She wept and he hugged her. She asked him if the police had harmed him, and he said: 'No, they've been the essence of kindness.'

On Wednesday, 16 November, Harry Roberts made brief appearances at West London magistrate's court and at the Old Bailey, where it was decided that he should be tried with Witney and Duddy. A new date was set for that trial.

It began at the Old Bailey on Tuesday, 6 December 1966. Witney and Duddy, represented respectively by Mr WM Hudson and Mr James Comyn, QC, pleaded not guilty to all the indictments against them. Roberts, defended by Mr James Burge, QC, pleaded guilty to the murders of DS Head and DC Wombwell and not guilty to the murder of PC Fox. He admitted the other charges – of being an accessory to the murder of PC Fox, and to possessing firearms. The Crown was led by the Solicitor-General, Sir Dingle Foot, QC. The judge was Mr Justice Glyn Jones.

All three accused were found guilty of murder and of possessing firearms. The judge said: 'You have been justly convicted of what is perhaps the most heinous crime to have been committed in this country for a generation or more ... Lest any Home Secretary in the future should be minded to consider your release on licence I have to make a recommendation. My recommendation is that you should not be released on licence, any of the three of you, for a period of thirty years, to begin from today's date.'

Roberts and Witney appealed, but their applications were dismissed.

John Cunningham, the gypsy, was given £300, part of the £1,000 reward offered for information leading to Roberts's capture. Mrs Wombwell, Mrs Fox and the mother of DS Head each received £26,250, three-eighths of the £210,000 that was raised for and given to the dead policemen's families. The rest of the money was put into a trust fund for the children.

Mrs Dorothy Roberts, Harry Roberts's mother, went to work in a hotel. She later revealed: 'When I come home from work I shut myself away and keep myself to myself.

Everybody round here knows who I am. It's not pleasant … I've got to go on living for my son's sake. When everybody else has forgotten him, I'll still be visiting him. But there doesn't seem much point in living now, and most nights I cry myself to sleep.'

David Wombwell was, like Harry Roberts, an only child. His grieving mother declared:

> *I saw Roberts at the trial. I had to go … He was so cocky, so arrogant. I couldn't understand why he should be there, alive and swaggering, when my boy who was so good was dead. Yet I couldn't hate him, because it all seemed so unreal … It was all so pointless, so wicked … Everybody wants something for nothing these days it seems. That's the attitude that breeds the Harry Roberts of this world, and then it's the honest, hard-working boys like my son who have to die … What was it all for? What's it all about? Why did it have to happen to him? … Sometimes I feel I shall break, or go out of my mind.*

John Duddy died in the hospital of Parkhurst Prison on the Isle of Wight in February 1981, having served half of the recommended thirty years of his life sentence, to which the automatic one-third remission did not apply. He was fifty-two.

John Witney was released on licence in 1991 and died in 1999.

No one in the twentieth century had ever served a full thirty-year prison sentence. But Harry Roberts, forty-two years after the Massacre of Braybrook Street, has now (in 2008) been in prison since December 1966.

Over the years he made several attempts to escape. However, in 2001 he was moved to an open prison. Parole was denied, as he had allegedly been involved in drug-dealing in prison. In 2005, he appealed against parole being refused, and in September 2006 he applied for a judicial review over the apparent delays by the Parole Board in granting him parole. In December 2006, parole was again refused. But on 29 June 2007 he was given leave to seek a High Court review over his failed parole bids. In July 2008, Harry Roberts was 72.

50
REGGIE AND
RONNIE KRAY

THE MURDERS OF GEORGE CORNELL AND JACK MCVITIE, 1966-7

The trial of the Kray brothers and eight other men at the Old Bailey in 1969 was at that time the longest and most expensive criminal trial in British history. It was also unique in that the main defendants, both charged with murder, were thirty-five-year-old identical twins, although by then their varying lifestyles and their divergent mental and emotional problems had subtly altered their appearance. If ever two men were fated to follow a violent life of crime it was these two, doomed by their nature and their circumstances, and bound by the very fact of being identical twins to imitate and protect each other and finally to share in each other's ruin.

They were born on 24 October 1933 in Hoxton, in the East End of London. Their father was Charles Kray, aged twenty-six, an itinerant dealer in old clothes, silver and gold. Their mother, Violet, aged twenty-one, called the first child Reginald and the second, who arrived an hour later, Ronald. The Krays already had another son, six-year-old Charles, a placid, pleasant child. The twins were different. Said their mother: 'They was so lovely when they was born, so small and dark, just like two little black-haired dolls.'

Their Romany ancestry showed more than the Jewish and Irish blood in them. Ronnie nearly died when they both got measles and diphtheria. After that he was moody and slower than Reggie, who was more of an easy-going charmer.

In 1939, the family moved to 178 Vallance Road in Bethnal Green, then an East End ghetto and a hot-bed of boxers, gamblers, hard drinkers and assorted villains. Half of it was destroyed in the Second World War, but the Kray twins survived, constantly fighting each other and other boys. They were little demons and were known as the Terrible Twins – though they were polite and considerate to their elders; although inseparable, they never stopped vying with each other all the time. 'Even as a kid,' said Reggie, 'if I was challenged to a fight and I backed down, Ronnie would know. He'd be a sort of conscience, and I'd find it hard to face him afterwards.'

Other boys thought them weird. They had no interest in girls and fought with a cold fury, piling into enemy gangs with coshes, bicycle chains and broken bottles. And Ronnie used a sheath knife. 'You're a born devil, Ronnie,' said his Aunt Rose, adding that his eyebrows, meeting in the middle, meant he was born to hang. This, of course, also applied to Reggie.

In 1950, a sixteen-year-old Hackney boy called Harvey was found badly beaten up by fists, boots and bicycle chains. There were witnesses, but when the twins were put on trial at the Old Bailey – their first appearance there – the case was dismissed for lack of evidence.

They bought their first revolver when they were sixteen. In 1951, aged seventeen, they became professional boxers – lightweights. Reggie was the better boxer, Ronnie the slogger. They always won. On 11 December 1951, Reggie, Ronnie and Charlie all appeared in a boxing contest at the Albert Hall. Charlie lost; Ronnie was disqualified; Reggie won.

Sometimes they hit their father, especially when he had drunk too much. He began to avoid them. They loved their mother and she them. 'I used to worry about the twins … I wasn't their mother for nothing,' she later declared. 'But if they was involved in any trouble I didn't want to know. It only upset me … Both of them was good boys at heart.'

Called up for National Service, they reported to the Waterloo Building in the Tower of London on 2 March 1952, and having decided they didn't care for the Royal Fusiliers or the army, they walked right out, after dotting a corporal on the jaw. 'We're off home to see our mum,' remarked Ronnie. The next day, they were picked up by the police.

For the next two years they were either on the run, in jail, in guard-room cells or military prisons. On the run and in jail, they learned many lessons from minor criminals. From the army, they learned about weapons, discipline and power – the power of propaganda and of fear. United they could get away with nearly anything, behave as badly as they liked and make nonsense of society's conventions. Once they assaulted a policeman sent to arrest them. It was Christmas and they were reluctant to spend it in a barracks. 'Kray Brothers Beat Up PC' read a headline in a local paper, accompanied by a photo of them. They spent a month in Wormwood Scrubs Prison. All this merely added to their status and their self-esteem.

On one occasion, while awaiting court-martial in a Canterbury guard room, they went crazy, screaming abuse, refusing to eat, setting fire to their bedding and their uniforms, wrecking what they could and escaping again. The army could have thrown the book at them, but at their trial on 11 June 1953 they were charged only with striking an NCO, going AWOL, and with conduct prejudicial to good order and discipline. They pleaded guilty and were sentenced to nine months in custody.

These were spent in Shepton Mallet military prison, where they made contact with incipient and actual criminals and prepared for a life of crime to achieve their vision of the good life: wealth, property, cars, power and fame. Ronnie's heroes were TE Lawrence, General Wingate and Al Capone. He wanted to be famous as well as feared.

The twins acquired a billiard hall in Mile End, which became their HQ and centre for the advising and aid of petty criminals. They started a protection business and waged war on other gangs. Within six months of being dismissed from the army, Ronnie was known as the Colonel. The twins' organisation became known as the Firm, and their mother's home Fort Vallance.

By 1956, aged twenty-two, their control over thieves, clubs, pubs and businesses had spread over Hackney, Stepney, Bow and Shoreditch. They ruled through fear and thrived on danger. But they still lived with their mother, Violet, in Vallance Road, which now contained an armoury of assorted guns and knives. Ronnie dressed like a gangster and had his own barber. But at night he slept with the light on and a gun under his pillow.

One day, he shot a young docker in the leg. The docker was a member of a rival gang and had threatened a car-site owner favoured by the Krays. Money changed hands, threats or promises were made, and the docker, in hospital, found he couldn't quite remember how or where the accident happened. Although he picked out Ronnie in an identity parade, the police had no option but to let him go when Ronnie said: 'I'm not *Ronnie* Kray. I'm *Reggie* Kray. I wasn't nowhere near where this bloke was shot.' Reggie was, however, furious with Ronnie. 'You must be raving mad!' he shouted. 'You shoot a man, and leave me to clear it up!' Retorted Ronnie: 'All you're fit for is clearing up! You couldn't shoot a man if you tried.'

In the summer of 1956, two business friends of the Krays, club owners, were beaten up by the Watney Street gang. A punitive raid was made by the Firm on a pub where the gang was thought to be. As the Firm's large cars arrived at the entrance the gang escaped out the back. But a boy who happened to remain behind was seized, slashed and stabbed with a bayonet. He was also kicked unconscious. This time the victim couldn't be fixed, and at the Old Bailey, on 5 November 1956, Ronnie Kray, now aged twenty-three, was sentenced to three years for causing grievous bodily harm to Terence Martin of Stepney. Nothing was proved against Reggie, however.

With his dangerous brother in Wandsworth Prison, Reggie now took the lead and much improved the Firm's business operations. He opened a club in Bow Road, the Double R. A club owned by Terence Martin's family in Poplar was destroyed by fire. The Double R prospered, being a success both with villains and celebrities. The twins' older and married brother, Charlie, became involved. The Krays bought a car site, another club in Stratford, and set up an illegal gambling club beside Bow police station.

Meanwhile, in Wandsworth, Ronnie made friends with a mild-mannered but psychopathic giant called Frank Mitchell, known as the 'Mad Axeman'. While in Wandsworth, Ronnie read books, and didn't cause any trouble. But then he was moved to Camp Hill Prison on the Isle of Wight. Isolated from his contacts and his family he lost touch with reality, becoming obsessed with Reggie's successes and his own apparent failure. He became silent and refused to eat, as he had done in the army, certain that everyone was his enemy and out to get him. For a time the only thing that reassured him was his reflection in a mirror. Then one night he went berserk and was transferred to Winchester prison.

The MO there said Ronnie had prison psychosis. Heavily sedated, he appeared to recover. Then, one day, Reggie wrote saying that their Aunt Rose had died. The following day Ronnie Kray was certified as insane. He was twenty-four.

On 20 February 1958, he was transferred to an asylum in Surrey, Long Grove Hospital, suffering from paranoid schizophrenia. He soon responded to the drugs he was given and was about to be sent back to prison – the doctors had concluded that he was now 'quiet, cooperative, and mentally sub-normal' – when Reggie arranged his escape. He swapped places with his twin during Sunday visiting hours.

Ronnie was hidden away in a four-berth caravan in Suffolk to begin with, making secret and sensational appearances at old haunts in London. But his mental imbalance remained, and despite all the family's attempts to cure him, with the help of psychiatrists, Ronnie's condition worsened. One night he tried to kill himself. His family were forced to accept the unimaginable – they informed Scotland Yard of his whereabouts.

He was picked up and taken back to Long Grove, before being returned to Wandsworth Prison. Still prone to violence and delusions, he was nonetheless released in the spring of 1958, a changed man indeed. No longer the image of Reggie, his face and figure had thickened; he looked brutish. The picture, it was said, of a homicidal psychopath.

The twins still lived in Vallance Road with their mother. They had fearful rows. Reggie guiltily modified his pursuits and ambitions to fall more in line with Ronnie's, whose aggression now began to imperil the Firm's business. 'He's ruining us,' said Reggie. 'I know we ought to drop him. But how can I? He's my brother and he's mad!'

East End violence increased; gang fights became bigger and more bloody. In February 1960, Reggie was accidentally caught backing up a demand for protection money and sentenced to eighteen months in Wandsworth Prison. Now Ronnie was on his own.

The Double R began to lose money. Then Ronnie met Peter Rachman. Rachman's empire had been threatened by the frequent beating up of his rent collectors, and so he arranged to pay off the Krays by giving them a fashionable night club in Knightsbridge, Esmeralda's Barn, which later became a discothèque. Freed from East End opinion, Ronnie now openly paraded his homosexuality with a fast turnover of teenage boys. His contacts with like-minded persons – politicians, businessmen, actors, academics, DJs and clerics – proliferated. 'I'm not a poof,' he said once reprovingly, adding proudly, 'I'm homosexual.' He despised pansies as much as he despised women. He liked his men, and boys, to be manly.

Reggie came out of prison when he was twenty-seven, and somewhat surprisingly fell in love with a sixteen-year-old schoolgirl, Frances Shea, the sister – and, significantly, a look-alike – of Frankie, a Hoxton boy whom Ronnie had admired and had perhaps desired, if not more. Reggie put Frances on a pedestal. Ronnie vilified them both. There was a row and Ronnie walked out of Esmeralda's Barn and the West End, back to the East End, to a flat in Cedra Court, Walthamstow, where parties at which he and his boys were the centre of attraction were very well attended.

Meanwhile, he planned to set up an English branch of Murder Incorporated, a private army of East End villains. He read *Mein Kampf.* He came to believe he was the reincarnation of Attila the Hun.

Reggie now began to expand the protection business and rackets involving fraudulent companies. Between them, the Krays dominated London's criminal world.

In March 1962, after the gala première of *Sparrers Can't Sing* in Bow Road, the cast and their friends celebrated at the twins' new club, the Kentucky. Their fame and power spread. They moved in on other clubs in Birmingham and Leicester. In 1962, three attempts to kill them were thwarted by their excellent network of informers. By now, they were making about £500,000 a year. They bought their mother a race horse and themselves a restaurant in Kingston – the Cambridge – where Ronnie, insulted one night by an old friend, a boxer called Joe, knifed him in the washroom. Joe's face needed seventy stitches. Another old friend, Jonathan, also offended Ronnie, and his face was branded. Ronnie's depressions, drinking, paranoia and sadism increased along with his wealth, notoriety and power. Red-hot pokers were used to brand the Krays' victims, and claw hammers to smash their hands.

A sensational revelation in the *Sunday Mirror* on 12 July 1964 of the alleged homosexual relationship between a peer and a well-known gangster resulted in a detailed denial of the allegations by Lord Boothby in *The Times,* an apology by the *Sunday Mirror,* the payment of £40,000 in compensation, and the total embarrassment of the press and the police.

This was compounded when, in 1965, the twins – together with Teddy Smith – were arrested and charged with demanding money with menaces from Hew McCowan, owner of the Hideaway club in Soho. Bail was refused. The Firm got to work; the jury failed to agree about their verdict. In the re-trial, McCowan was successfully discredited as a witness and the trial was stopped. (Partly because of the McCowan case, the law was changed so that verdicts in future could be accepted from a majority of the jury.)

The Krays were freed and celebrated by buying the Hideaway, renaming it El Morocco. They celebrated there with the biggest party they had ever given, to which the police and press were also invited. Among the celebrities they claimed as friends were Diana Dors, Barbara Windsor, George Raft, Judy Garland and Frank Sinatra. Ronnie wrote in his autobiography that the 1960s were 'the best years of our lives'. He wrote: 'They called them the Swinging Sixties. The Beatles and the Rolling Stones were rulers of pop music, Carnaby Street ruled the fashion world … And me and my brother ruled London. We were fucking untouchable.'

The West End party of the year was followed by the East End wedding of the year. On 20 April 1965, Reggie, now aged 31, married Frances Shea. They moved in below Ronnie in Cedra Court. Two months later, Frances left her husband, going back home to her parents. Six months after her marriage, she was visiting the same Harley Street psychiatrist who had seen Ronnie.

Ronnie himself was now dreaming of becoming an international racketeer, dealing in drugs, guns, forgery and crooked deals. The twins became involved with the Mafia, disposing of some securities stolen in Canada. They acquired a stuttering Jewish banker called Alan Cooper to handle their affairs. He needed their protection, having been threatened by the Richardson gang; the Krays needed him. The middle-class Richardsons had made Ronnie feel threatened: they were getting too big, encroaching on the West End, where the Krays hoped to enter into business in the gambling world with the American Mafia, then attempting to infiltrate and flourish in London.

During Christmas 1965 there was a confrontation between the Richardsons and the Krays at the Astor Club. A Richardson henchman, George Cornell, referred to Ronnie as a 'fat poof'. An all-out gang war was declared and two attempts were made on the lives of the twins.

Then, early on 8 March 1966, there was a shoot-out at Mr Smith's club in Catford between the Richardsons and a local gang. The Krays were not involved, but one of their associates, Richard Hart, was killed. One of the Firm later stated: 'One of ours had gone, so it was up to Ronnie to do one of theirs.' But of the leading members of the Richardson gang only George Cornell, who had been absent from the Catford shoot-out, was not behind bars. This suited Ronnie, who had a personal insult to avenge.

He asked Jack Dickson, a Scot, to drive him to the Blind Beggar pub in Whitechapel Road. With him was another Scot, Ian Barrie. Both had guns, Ronnie a 9mm Mauser automatic. There were few people in the pub apart from the barmaid. Cornell, sitting on a bar stool, was drinking a light ale with two friends when Ronnie and Ian Barrie entered. The juke box was playing 'The Sun Ain't Gonna Shine Anymore'. Barrie fired two shots into the ceiling. Everyone froze. Then, Ronnie drew his gun from a shoulder holster and shot Cornell between the eyes.

No one talked. Ronnie Kray was included at a police identity parade at Commercial Street, but the barmaid failed to recognise the killer in the line-up. She had a poor memory for faces, she explained. Freddie Foreman said in a television interview in 2000 that he had been employed to intimidate witnesses who had seen Ronnie shoot George Cornell.

The Firm's business suffered as a result of the killing. The twins were now very bad news. They themselves became nervous. They absconded for a time to Morocco, from where they were soon ejected. Reggie now drank more than ever. His wife, Frances, attempted suicide.

In an effort to improve their underworld status, the twins helped Frank Mitchell, the 'Mad Axeman', to escape from Dartmoor Prison on 12 December. Just before this, Ronnie went into hiding in a Finchley flat to avoid giving evidence in a forthcoming police corruption trial.

Frank Mitchell, cooped up and out of sight in a flat in Barking Road, became impatient and dangerous, threatening to shoot any policeman he encountered, and the Krays, although he had been provided with a blonde night-club hostess called Lisa to pass the time. Before long he fell in love with her. (Later she would declare: 'His virility was greater than that of any man I have ever known.')

On Christmas Eve, Mitchell disappeared. One of his keepers later said that Mitchell was shot in a Thames van occupied by three men and that his body was dismembered and disposed of. The murder has never been solved, and for many years Mitchell was still officially on the run from Dartmoor.

Freddie Foreman claimed in 2000 that he helped to dispose of the body of Frank Mitchell, dumping it in the North Sea – as he did with the body of Tommy 'Ginger' Marks, a used-car dealer, whose body disappeared after he was shot in Stepney in 1965. Foreman also said he disposed of the body of Jack "The Hat' McVitie in 1967.

There were other disappearances. One was Ronnie's driver, Frost; another was Teddy Smith. There was also a death in the family. Frances Kray, aged twenty-three, took an overdose on 7 June 1967, the day after Reggie bought them both tickets for a second honeymoon on Ibiza. Her funeral at Chingford was a lavish one. She was buried in her wedding dress. A prison associate of Reggie would one day be told by Reggie (according to him) that Ronnie had somehow contrived the death of Frances, and then a few days later told Reggie what he had done.

. Reggie went to pieces, drank more than ever, and was full of hate. He began to seek revenge on those who had betrayed him. Drunk on gin, he shot at a man whom he thought had maligned his dead wife. All the shots missed, except for one that struck the victim's leg. 'Drunken slag!' said Ronnie later. 'Risking our necks like that! You risk everything shooting one of our friends, you drunken pig … You couldn't kill a man if you tried. You're too soft. When I did my one, I made a job of it.' To prove he was as tough as Ronnie, Reggie shot another man who owed the Firm money, again through the leg. He knifed a third in the face.

The Firm's business had now expanded into fruit machines, drugs and pornography. Assassination plots now occupied Ronnie's mind: those of President Kaunda, the President of Zambia, formerly Northern Rhodesia, and of Colin Jordan, leader of the far-right Nationalist Socialists. He also had a death-list of the Firm's enemies. He got the idea that murder would unite the Firm's members, test their loyalties and make them more of a brotherhood.

He decided to try out his idea on a drunken, loud-mouthed suspect associate called Jack 'The Hat' McVitie, who habitually wore a hat to hide his baldness. Ronnie had given him a gun and £100 to rub out a former associate, Leslie Payne, for which McVitie would get £400. But Payne was on his guard and remained alive. Ronnie failed to get his money back, so Reggie went to collect it. But McVitie told him a sob story and Reggie gave him £50 instead. Ronnie went wild, abusing Reggie and demanding payment. McVitie, feeling aggrieved and frightened by the twins' blowing hot and cold, got drunk, and armed with a sawn-off shotgun went looking for them in the Regency club, saying he was going to get them.

Such defiance was unendurable. A few nights later, in November 1967, Reggie, drunk himself, entered the Regency looking for McVitie, intending at last to emulate Ronnie's murder of Cornell. McVitie wasn't there. Meanwhile, Ronnie was making other arrangements. He took over a basement flat in Stoke Newington, belonging to a woman called Carol, and, when Reggie arrived, he sent their cousin, a former merchant seaman called Ronnie Hart, and two half-Greek brothers called Lambrianou, who had yet to be blooded, to find McVitie and invite him to a party at Carol's place. Two boys were with Ronnie. They danced together as Ronnie and Reggie waited, along with a man called Ronnie Bender.

Just before midnight, the drunkenly bold McVitie barged in, looking for a party. 'Where's all the birds and booze?' he cried. Reggie, behind the door, pointed a gun at McVitie's head and fired. The gun jammed.

There was a furious struggle. Ronnie's boys fled. McVitie got half out of a window – in doing so, his hat fell off. He was hauled back by the legs. Ronnie seized him from behind, pinioning his arms. Reggie now had a carving knife. 'Kill him, Reg!' screamed Ronnie. 'Do him! Don't stop now!' 'Why are you doing this, Reg?' cried McVitie.

He was stabbed in the face, the stomach and chest, and finally impaled through the throat on the floor – by Reggie, according to Ronnie Hart, who was later counter-accused of this crime by Reggie. But the twins' honour had been satisfied.

McVitie's body was never found. Rumour said it had been buried in concrete, consumed by pigs, cremated in a furnace, or concealed in a coffin by a fearful undertaker and cremated. The twins went off on a week's holiday at an expensive hotel in Suffolk.

Years later, in June 1991, Tony Lambrianou told *The News of the World*:

Jack is buried in Gravesend. In a grave under the coffin of a person buried shortly after ... It was a bad night when he was killed. I'll never forget the way his guts and liver hung out of his stomach.' Tony Lambrianou said that Reggie told him to invite Jack to a party, to which he was driven by Tony, his brother, Chris, and two other brothers called Mills. 'Jack loved a party ... He was a cocky villain, who often took pot-shots at people he didn't like, and he certainly knifed his fair share of enemies ... I was the first one through the door, with Jack following me. All of a sudden two gay boys, friends of Ronnie, started whacking The Hat. A bloke called Ronnie Hart, a second cousin of the Krays, then passed Reggie his gun. The Hat was pushed into an arm-lock and Reggie put the gun to the back of his head. The Hat said: 'What's the matter? What have I done?' I saw Reggie pull the trigger, but the gun jammed. Reggie clicked the trigger a few more times. The Hat made a dash for the window and punched it, breaking the pane of glass ... Reggie thrust a twelve-inch long carving-knife into his belly. Twice more he stabbed him, twisting the blade in and out of his body. Reggie then plunged the knife into his neck ... leaving a great gaping wound. It was over in seconds. Reggie turned to me and said: 'Get rid of it!'

Ronnie Bender assisted Tony Lambrianou, and they wrapped McVitie's body in a bedspread. 'We took Jack's hat too,' said Bender. McVitie's body was placed on the back seat of his own Zodiac. 'The smell was disgusting,' said Lambrianou. 'I wanted to be sick.' They drove off southwards, until the petrol gauge showed zero, when they dumped the car on the other side of the Thames, at Rotherhithe, near a church; here, McVitie's body was picked up by Chris Lambrianou and Ronnie Bender, who'd followed in another car. The knife and gun were thrown into the river, as were the keys to McVitie's car. His body is said to have been dismembered and burnt before being buried in a sack.

A month earlier, Scotland Yard had set up a special team led by Detective Superintendent Leonard (Nipper) Read to investigate the Krays and find some charges against them that would stick. Leslie Payne, McVitie's intended victim, was routinely questioned about his former business associates and decided to talk. He was secretly interrogated for three weeks and his final statement ran to over 200 pages. Other statements were acquired, but many people would not speak until the Krays were safely inside. There was still no corroborative proof against them. Meanwhile, the twins were planning their retirement. They knew about Read's investigation, and considered killing him. Ronnie's mind was still on murder.

To test the Firm's Jewish banker, Alan Cooper, Ronnie suggested he should kill a minor villain whose death would score off one gang while putting another in his debt. Cooper agreed, even though it meant killing the man when he was appearing as a witness at the Old Bailey. Cooper produced an unusual murder weapon – an attaché case that would jab a cyanide-filled hypodermic needle into the man's leg – and arranged for a tall, bespectacled young man called Paul Elvey to do the job. He failed to do so, because, he said, the victim never appeared at the Old Bailey. Another weapon was provided by Cooper: a cross-bow. Again Elvey's mission failed.

Meanwhile, Ronnie flew to New York with Cooper, but for some reason failed to make contact with the Mafia. Perhaps his reputation put them off. On his return, to impress the Mafia that he was the king of criminal London, he took on a contract to eliminate a Las Vegas gambler staying at the London Hilton, who proved, however, to be very wary and elusive. An easier target then presented itself: a Maltese night-club owner, George Caruana, whom Ronnie planned to blow up in his car, a red Mini. He asked for Cooper's assistance, and Cooper again brought in Paul Elvey, sending him by plane to Glasgow to fetch four sticks of dynamite. As he boarded the plane on his way back to London, however, Elvey was arrested. The attaché case and cross-bow were found in his house. Elvey confessed, implicating Cooper.

Cooper's story was almost incredible. He told Nipper Read that he was an undercover agent, working largely on his own and that he had been working for the Yard and the American Treasury Department for two years, trying to compromise the Krays. The weapons he supplied them, he said, were faulty (for instance, the gun that had jammed when used against McVitie), and Elvey could be relied on to bungle everything. It had been a most dangerous game, and was very hard to believe.

But now Nipper Read had three attempted murders, arranged by Cooper, to pin on the Krays, as well as Payne's statement. At dawn on 9 May 1968, the police raided Violet Kray's new council flat in Braithwaite House, Shoreditch. Reggie was in bed with a girl from Walthamstow; Ronnie with a fair-haired boy. They had spent the night until 4.0 am at the Old Horn pub in Bethnal Green and at the Astor Club, Berkeley Square.

With the Krays behind bars, people were now persuaded by the police to talk, including the barmaid from the Blind Beggar. Twenty-eight criminals were promised freedom from prosecution if they cooperated with the police. Ronnie Hart and Jack Dickson were among those who turned Queen's evidence.

The Krays were charged with the Cornell and McVitie murders. Others of the Firm, like Charlie Kray and Bender and the Lambrianou brothers, were charged with being accessories.

The trial, before Mr Justice Melford Stevenson, lasted thirty-nine days, beginning in January 1969 and ending on 8 March. Ronnie Kray gave evidence, arrogantly denying everything, claiming it was all a police plot. He shouted at the prosecutor: 'You're a fat slob!' He told the judge: 'You're biased too!'

Reggie Kray's defence could have been that he was dominated by his brother Ronnie. But the twins, pleading not guilty, were tried and sentenced together to life imprisonment, the judge recommending that this should not be less than thirty years. They were thirty-five years old.

The Lambrianou brothers were also given life sentences, with a recommended incarceration of fifteen years. Ronnie Bender was sentenced to twenty years.

The Krays were later found not guilty of the murder of Frank Mitchell. Other charges remained on police files.

For a time, the twins were reunited, in 1972, in Parkhurst Prison on the Isle of Wight. But in 1979 Ronnie Kray was once again declared to be a paranoid schizophrenic and moved to Broadmoor Hospital in Crowthorne. He was also a heavy smoker and a diabetic. In 1981, Reggie Kray was transferred to Long Lartin Prison in Leicestershire. For 'humanitarian reasons' he was occasionally allowed to visit his twin in Broadmoor. They lunched together, exchanged news and views and talked about old times.

In March 1995, Ronnie Kray died in Broadmoor of a massive heart attack; he was sixty-one. The twins' older brother, Charlie, who had been imprisoned for twelve years for smuggling cocaine into the country, died of a stroke in prison in April 2000; he was seventy-three. Reggie was released from prison to attend Charlie's funeral service in Chingford. As with Ronnie's funeral, huge crowds, cherishing the Krays' legend, lined the streets and mobbed the church. The *Daily Mail* described Reggie as 'a wizened little old man, with grey hair and a shaky demeanour'. He had become a born-again Christian and was now terminally ill with cancer of the bladder and secondary tumours.

Because of his illness, he was freed on compassionate grounds from Wayland Prison in Norfolk by the Home Secretary, Jack Straw, on 26 August 2000. Reggie Kray died in a Norwich hotel on 1 October, three weeks short of his sixty–seventh birthday. His second wife, Roberta, whom he had married in prison, was with him, as were some of his surviving henchmen.

In November 1969 the five-year experimental period during which the death penalty for murder was suspended came to an end, and on 16 December 1969 the House of Commons confirmed the abolition of capital punishment by a majority of 158 votes. The decision was reaffirmed by the House of Lords two days later, by a majority of 46.

However, the scaffold at Wandsworth Prison was not dismantled, as the death penalty could still be exacted for treason and piracy with violence, and it still remained in force on the Isle of Man, which came within the jurisdiction of the Manx courts. In December 1982, a nineteen-year-old labourer, Stephen Moore, convicted of the murder of his girlfriend's baby son in Douglas, Isle of Man, was sentenced to death by the island's senior judge, Deemster Jack Corrin. In an outmoded ritual, outlawed on the mainland, he formally donned a black cap and declared: 'You will be taken from this place to the Isle of Man Prison and thence to a place of lawful execution, where you will be hanged by the neck until you are dead.' The sentence was never carried out.

STANLEY WRENN

The Murder of Colin Saunders, 1969

Violent offences against homosexuals increased after the passing of the Sexual Offences Act of 27 July 1967, which legislated that 'a homosexual act committed in private shall not be an offence, provided that the partners consent thereto and have attained the age of twenty-one years.' The increase in violence was probably due to the fact that so-called gays tended, since the Act was passed, to pursue their sexual activities more openly and so make themselves more obvious targets for those whom they antagonised. Murders of homosexuals are not often solved, because of the random nature of the pick-up that may be involved. The following case is unusual in several respects: in the deliberate but casual way the murderer chose and killed his victim; in the choice of one of the weapons; in the absence of any attempt to conceal the crime or to evade capture; and in the acknowledgement of guilt.

Stanley Wrenn was born in Liverpool on 20 January 1950. When he was sixteen, he joined the army as a junior private in the RAMC, but was discharged later the same year. After that, he drifted, finding employment as a car-sprayer, shop assistant, labourer and barman. In October 1969, he was in London, and one night during the first half of the month was in the concourse of Piccadilly Circus underground station when an older man came up to him and said: 'How are you getting on? Haven't I met you before?'

Wrenn was nineteen. The other man was thirty-five-year-old Colin George Saunders, who was born in Bedford on 12 June 1934 and was now a chauffeur with Warley Car Hire Services in Bromley, Kent. Saunders, who had previous convictions for importuning and gross indecency, continued: 'Where are you living?' 'Nowhere,' replied Wrenn. Saunders took him for something to eat in a café and asked him if he would like to come back to his place. 'Yeah,' said Wrenn.

They went to 13 College Road in Bromley, a Victorian type of terraced house that was divided into various flats and single rooms. Saunders occupied a ground-floor room at the front. That night they slept in a double bed, but Saunders soon acquired two single beds. According to Wrenn, the older man had sex with him – 'I did nothing' – every night.

This went on for five or six weeks. In the third week of November 1969, Wrenn discovered that Saunders had infected him with gonorrhoea. The relationship became very strained. On Monday, 24 November, 'out of spite', Wrenn made up his mind to kill Saunders.

He went shopping for a knife, and having passed over one that cost 12s 6d – it was too dear – he bought a fisherman's knife for 4s 6d. He also dismantled and removed a gas ring from another room in 13 College Road and concealed both it and the knife in a cubby-hole by the television set in their shared bed-sitting-room. The following night, Wrenn hid both weapons under his bed, going to bed himself at 10.45 pm.

He later told the police that he stayed awake until 5 am on the morning of Wednesday, 26 November, listening to Saunders snore. Then he got out of bed – he was wearing a T-shirt – took the gas ring and knife from their place of concealment, and with the gas-ring struck Saunders, who was asleep on his side, on the head.

'The second time I hit him,' said Wrenn later, 'he looked up. He was facing the wall. I then stuck the knife in his throat.' Wrenn then went berserk, stabbing Saunders many times about the head. After drying his hands on his T-shirt, Wrenn pulled a sheet up over the corpse's head and covered it with a dressing gown. He then found time to wash and shave.

He remained in the room for some time, going through the dead man's possessions. Eventually, Stanley Wrenn took what he wanted – money, clothes, car keys and some other articles – and packed the larger items into a suitcase. Carrying the suitcase, he left the flat.

Saunders's employer's car, a Humber, was outside the house and Wrenn got in. He was not, however, familiar with cars or with automatic gears. The Humber reversed at speed and struck a Ford Consul being driven along Hammelton Road. The driver remonstrated with Wrenn, saying: 'That's a nice thing to do!'

There was an argument that concluded with the driver of the Ford suggesting that they should telephone the police. Wrenn volunteered to do so and returned to 13 College Road, where he made no phone call but instead put Saunders's chauffeur's cap on the dead man's bed. He returned to the impatient driver of the Ford and pretended he had telephoned for the police. Once more he returned to the house, this time leaving the car keys on Saunders's bed before leaving the house once agin, this time avoiding the driver of the Ford. He walked to Bromley North railway station, where he got on a train to London.

Wrenn spent that night in the West End. In the morning, he bought a newspaper and saw that he had been named in connection with the death of Colin Saunders. Police investigating the car accident had gone the previous day to Saunders's address and discovered his body. Wrenn, seeing his name in the papers, decided to give himself up.

He approached a police constable in Piccadilly Circus and said who he was. The PC took him to West Central police station, where he was charged on Thursday, 27 November.

Put on trial at the Old Bailey on 24 March 1970 before Justice Sir Ralph Cusack, Stanley Wrenn pleaded guilty and was sentenced to life imprisonment. He served ten years of his sentence, being released from prison in June 1980, when he was thirty.

52

MUSTAPHA BASSAINE

THE MURDER OF JULIAN SESSÉ, 1970

Sixty would seem to be a dangerous age for homosexual men, for those who invite, solicit or pay for the attentions of younger men. Such men, who grew up in the first part of the twentieth century, when their sexual inclinations and activities were of necessity closeted or repressed, once formed the majority of the gay minority who became murder victims. This was also true in 1970, despite the Sexual Offences Act of 1967. But then, as now, although some homosexual men still become victims of 'gay-bashing', of violence committed by deeply prejudiced and apparent straights, most of the more violent homosexual homicides are committed by and among homosexual men, resulting in an overkill of multiple stabbings and gross and brutal injury.

Julian Louis Georges Sessé was the butler of Lord Bernstein, chairman of Granada TV. A Belgian, though born in Scotland, Sessé was sixty-five at the time of his murder and was living in a basement flat in his employer's grand London residence at 32 Wilton Crescent, off Belgrave Square. When Lord Bernstein went on holiday to Bermuda on Friday, 18 December 1970, Sessé was left in sole charge of the house. He was last seen alive by a milk roundsman on the Saturday morning.

At 9 am on Monday, 21 December, a van driver from Granada TV called at the house to make a delivery but received no reply to his knocking and ringing at the big front door. However, he noticed newspapers lying outside the basement flat below. He went down the steps into the basement area and banged on the door of the flat. There was no response. Apparently, when he found that the door was unlocked, he went inside, stood in the hallway, called out and after getting no reply he left.

A part-time cleaner, fifty-five-year-old Mrs Malmon, was the next person to arrive. She also tried to attract the attention of someone within the house, and after waiting for a while, uncertain what to do, she telephoned Bernstein's private secretary, Jean Hazelwood, from a phone box. The cleaner waited for some time outside the house until Miss Hazelwood turned up with a key. She unlocked the front door and they went inside. Calling out Mr Sessé's name, they made a search of some of the rooms. Eventually Miss Hazelwood, who was twenty-four, went down the inner stairs to Sessé's flat. She found the living room spattered with blood: there was blood on the settee, on the walls and in the kitchen. There were also bloodstains on the floor outside the bathroom. But its door was locked. Alarmed, she ran upstairs and dialled 999.

An ambulance and two local policemen, from Chelsea police station in Lucan Place, arrived soon after 11 am. At 11.15 the policemen forced open the bathroom door, which had been locked on the outside. Inside the bathroom Julian Sessé, wearing a crewneck sweater and trousers, lay on the floor in a pool of blood, partly covered by a large and bloody bath towel. His throat had been cut. There were stab wounds in his head and lower chest, and his stomach had been hacked open by another instrument – a meat cleaver.

The Home Office pathologist, Professor Keith Simpson, who carried out the post-mortem, established that Sessé had died of haemorrhage, shock and loss of blood, and that he had been killed late on Saturday night or early on Sunday. Anal intercourse had occurred before his death.

DCS John 'Ginger' Hensley, aged fifty, was put in charge of the case. He was assisted by DS Bernie Davis, aged thirty-three, who had just joined the Murder Squad. Arriving at the house about 12.30, they examined the basement flat and found a pair of bloodstained trousers in a washing machine, and a small meat cleaver and a knife in the lavatory bowl; its seat was down. Both implements had evidently come from the kitchen, where the killer had apparently picked up the knife and attacked the butler. The assault seemed to have continued in the living room. Sessé had apparently resisted and tried to escape. But after his throat was cut he had been dragged into the bathroom, where the killer, it seemed, had hoped to conceal the body and the weapons. The killer had also exchanged his trousers for a clean pair taken from Sessé's wardrobe.

Correspondence found in the flat and other inquiries revealed that Sessé, a kind and generous man and highly regarded by his employer, was homosexual and in the habit of picking up young men, entertaining them and paying some of them for sex. There were names, addresses and phone numbers in Sessé's correspondence, but the police were far from certain that any of this information would lead them to the killer, who could have been a total stranger, picked up that Saturday night.

Two days later, however, they had an unexpected breakthrough. On Wednesday, 23 December, Hensley and Davis received a message that a girl living in Tufnell Park, London N7, appeared to know something about the murder. She had dialled 999 in an agitated state and then talked to two policemen in a Q car who had called at her address.

Jean Fitzgerald was a twenty-two-year-old Irish girl, who worked as a waitress in a café. She had met Julian Sessé through her boyfriend, a Moroccan male nurse called Mustapha Bassaine, whom she had known for over a year. Born in May 1944 in Rabat, Bassaine was twenty-six, unemployed, and had been living in a bed-sit with Jean Fitzgerald for several months. She told Hensley and Davis that on Saturday, 19 December, she had gone drinking in the West End with Bassaine and that after a while he telephoned Sessé's flat. He then told her that he was going to call on Sessé to get some money off him. He left her around the pub's closing time, about 11 pm.

She next heard from him at about 9 pm on the Sunday night, when he telephoned her at the Tufnell Park bed-sit and told her that he wanted her to come to the Bernstein mansion in Wilton Crescent. He was apparently phoning from there. It seems that he remained in the house overnight on Saturday and most of Sunday. In hindsight, perhaps he wanted her to assist him in the disposal of Sessé's body.

Something in his voice or words made Fitzgerald fearful and she declined to do as he wished. He then threatened to kill her if she failed to obey him. She still refused. He concluded the conversation by telling her to get his clothes together and pack them as he was going away.

Later that night, Bassaine turned up at the bed-sit, letting himself in with his key. He had been drinking. There was blood on his shoes and there were scratches on his neck. He said he had cut himself on some glass. She noticed that he was wearing a new pair of trousers that were too big for him. Too frightened to go to sleep, she sat up with him all night, as he sobbed and drank gin, smitten with uncertainty, self-pity and remorse.

On the morning of Monday, 21 December, he went out and bought a newspaper. Later, he told her that he was going back to Morocco as his mother was ill. Later still, she went with him to Regent Street. There, at an airline ticket agency, he paid £44 in cash for a single ticket to Casablanca and also exchanged $50 American dollars for English pounds. The money had presumably been stolen from Sessé or from the Bernsteins. The two of them then journeyed out to Heathrow Airport, where Bassaine departed on a flight to Casablanca that left at 3.10 pm.

Before leaving, he gave Jean Fitzgerald an address in Morocco and instructed her to send cuttings of any newspaper story that mentioned his name. Two days later, having read in the papers about Sessé's murder, she dialled 999.

The police found Bassaine's bloodstained shoes and Sessé's trousers in a dustbin in Tufnell Park. The blood on the shoes would later prove to match that of Sessé. But there was little that Hensley and Davis could do about an arrest, as there was no extradition treaty between the UK and Morocco. So Sessé's killer was safe as long as he remained in North Africa.

Nonetheless, an application for his extradition was made and a warrant issued on 23 December 1970 for his arrest. A description of the murdered man was also issued to the press, who were told that the police wanted to interview a young man who had been seen near Lord Bernstein's house. For a time, Jean Fitzgerald's lodging was put under police guard. But nothing more was seen or heard of Bassaine for nearly two years.

Meanwhile, Hensley and Davis attended Julian Sessé's funeral. Few others did. None of his family chose to be there. Lord Bernstein acquired another butler.

Then, in October 1972, news reached New Scotland Yard that Mustapha Bassaine had been arrested for some alien's offence at Rotterdam in the Netherlands. The Dutch police, via Interpol, had learned that he was wanted for murder in the UK. Extradition arrangements were made.

DS Bernie Davis flew to Rotterdam to collect Bassaine, who turned out to be a man of good family, of average height and build, with a heavily pock-marked face. On the flight back to England they sat, handcuffed together, at the front of the plane. A stewardess suggested that the handcuffs should be removed, in case there was an emergency during the flight. Davis refused to oblige, saying: 'If the plane crashes, we're all in trouble, love.'

Mustapha Bassaine, now twenty-eight, was tried at the Central Criminal Court in London in February 1973 before Mr Justice Forbes. The trial began on Thursday, 8 February, and ended the following Monday. John Buzzard, QC, was the chief prosecutor, and the defence was led by Mr Howard, QC.

Bassaine pleaded not guilty to the murder of Julian Sessé and not guilty to stealing £80 from Lady Bernstein's bedroom. He gave evidence on his own behalf and said that although he had spent the Saturday night with Sessé, he did not kill the Bernsteins' butler. His story was that Jean Fitzgerald, when told of his association with Sessé, had threatened 'to harm the old man'. Bassaine said that on the Sunday she left their digs and didn't return until late that night. When she did, she was trembling, he said, and told him she was sick.

The jury decided there was no truth in these allegations. Bassaine was found guilty of murder and sentenced to life imprisonment.

Privately, the police surmised that Bassaine had tried to blackmail Sessé, that Sessé had refused to be intimidated, and that angry words were exchanged. In a rage, Bassaine had then picked up the knife.

DCS Ginger Hensley retired from the police in 1975. He died of cancer two years later. Bernie Davis remained with the Murder Squad for another five years and was promoted to DCS. He retired in 1989.

Mustapha Bassaine was released from prison in July 1984 and duly deported from the UK.

In the five-year period from 1986 to 1991 inclusive, there were sixty-six known non-domestic murders of homosexual men nationwide, of which twenty-nine remained unsolved. Most of these murders involved older men, in their fifties and sixties, who were killed by young men, usually in their twenties. Young homosexual men are in fact less likely to be killed by their contemporaries, as they are capable of defending themselves and do not arouse deep feelings of loathing and disgust. Young gay men are more likely to be beaten and roughed up. The law courts have generally taken a lenient view of those who murder gays. Invariably the charge is not murder but manslaughter, and the resulting sentence three to five years, sometimes ten. There is even a recognised mitigating defence of 'homosexual panic', when it is felt that a heterosexual man's killing of a homosexual man may in part be excused because of his shock, revulsion and consequent loss of self-control at being the object of homosexual advances and desire.

ARTHUR AND
NIZAMODEEN HOSEIN

THE MURDER OF MRS MCKAY, 1970

Kidnap victims must be among the most pathetic and wretched victims of crime, living in acute discomfort, isolation and terror until, as sometimes happens, they are done to death. Kidnappers must be among the most cowardly and callous of killers. One of the many extraordinary features of the McKay case was that it was the first kidnap-and-ransom crime ever perpetrated in Britain. It was also one of the worst examples of cooperation between the police, the press and the victim's family, and the ensuing investigation suffered as a result. It was also only the third case in fifty years in which a murder conviction was obtained without the body ever being found. The questions still remain. Whatever happened to Mrs McKay? When, and where, and how did she die? The prime irony in the case is that she was kidnapped by mistake.

Muriel Freda McKay, née Searcy, aged fifty-five, was the epitome of a wealthy middle-class woman, with a large comfortable house in Wimbledon, many social and charitable interests, three fond married children, and a successful, loving husband, Alexander Benson McKay, who was known as Alick. They were both Australians.

Born in Adelaide on 4 February 1914, Muriel Searcy met and fell in love with Alick McKay at a Sunday school when she was thirteen and he was eighteen. They married in June 1935. It was through her brother that Alick became involved in the newspaper business, in the management of Sir Keith Murdoch's News Ltd. Eventually, in 1957, he came to London as the advertisement director of Daily Mirror Newspapers. The family settled in a red-brick, mock-Georgian mansion, St Mary House, 20 Arthur Road, Wimbledon.

Alick McKay continued to prosper, becoming advertisement director of the newly formed IPC in 1963 and acquiring many powerful friends in politics and the newspaper world. Two years later, he was awarded the CBE. He was all set to retire in August 1969 after two heart attacks – he was now sixty – when Rupert Murdoch, son of Alick's first newspaper employer, offered him a job.

Murdoch's company, News Ltd, had gained control in January 1969 of the world's best-selling Sunday paper, the *News of the World* (circulation: six million). Its success was based on the public's appetite for sensational stories about sex, crime, scandal and murder. In June, Murdoch became the paper's chairman, and then bought an ailing daily paper, *The Sun*, from IPC, relaunching it in November. The previous month Alick McKay had retired from the IPC with a golden handshake said to amount to £40,000. Instead of returning to Australia as his wife had hoped and his colleagues expected, he accepted Murdoch's offer of a job as deputy chairman of the *News of the World,* becoming temporary chairman when Murdoch decided to return to Australia with his attractive young wife for a six-week holiday. Alick McKay was left in charge on 19 December and given the use of the company car, a dark-blue Rolls-Royce.

The car had already caught the eyes of two Indian Muslim brothers from Trinidad who wanted to know where Rupert Murdoch lived. They had scanned the London telephone directory, tried directory enquiries, consulted a library copy of Kelly's Street Directory – all without success. They then drove to the *News of the World* offices in Bouverie Street, where some chance sighting or snippet of information led them to identify the blue Rolls-Royce as the chairman's car. Who else but he would have such a car at his disposal?

They noted its number, and on Friday, 19 December, the very day that Rupert Murdoch flew with his wife to Australia, the younger Trinidadian brother, Nizamodeen Hosein, called at the offices of the GLC at County Hall and, using a false name, said he was anxious to trace the owner of ULO 18F with which, he said, he had been involved in a slight accident. A girl in the vehicle registration department could only tell him that the Rolls was owned by the *News of the World*. This merely seemed to confirm what the brothers already suspected.

They now surmised that the simplest way of finding out where the chairman lived was to follow the car from Fleet Street to its destination. This they did just before Christmas, oblivious of the fact that the identity of its passenger had changed a few days before. They followed the Rolls across London. It led them to 20 Arthur Road, Wimbledon, to the kind of up-market house a wealthy executive was likely to inhabit. They went home to plan the kidnapping (as they thought) of Mrs Anna Murdoch, for whom they intended to ask a ransom of £1 million.

Home for the Hosein brothers of Railway Road, Dow Village, Trinidad, was now a run-down seventeenth-century farmhouse set in 11 acres of Hertfordshire, 40 miles north of London. Rooks Farm, by the hamlet of Stocking Pelham, had been bought by the older brother, Arthur Hosein, on a mortgage in 1967.

Arthur Hosein was a vain and natty little man – 'like an advert for Babycham', said a publican – about 5 ft 4 in, moustached, ever-talking, volatile, jokey, ambitious, boastful, and determined to make good in England, to make money – lots of it – to make and be worth a million. He had emigrated to England in September 1955, hoping to become a student. He became a ledger-clerk instead, earning £7 a week. He was then called up for National Service. Army life had little appeal for him and he often absconded, finally being court-martialled for desertion in 1960. 'Immeasurably the worst soldier it has been my misfortune to have under me,' said one officer, and Private

Hosein of the Royal Pioneer Corps was sentenced to six months in Aldershot military prison and discharged.

However, while a British soldier stationed at Colchester, he met Else Fischer, a married woman ten years his senior. She and Arthur married after she got a divorce from her soldier husband. She had a ladies hairdresser's in Mare Street, Hackney, and it was there that Arthur began a tailoring business that won him a solid reputation as a very good trouser-maker and craftsman. He was also a keen gambler and owned two greyhounds, which he raced at various tracks around London. The East Enders called him 'nutty Arthur', and he might have stayed among them and prospered – he was now earning up to £150 a week, of which £65 a month was sent to his parents in Trinidad – but for his ambition to become a country gentleman and realise some of his fantasies. This led him to abandon his 'business in town' and acquire an 'estate in the country': Rooks Farm.

He moved there in May 1968 and relied mainly on hire-purchase to furnish the house to his taste: there was a gilt cocktail bar in the lounge. One of the outhouses became a tailor's workshop, where he cut his famous trousers, taking them into the East End to be finished. He had two cars, a dark-blue Volvo saloon and a Morris Minor. At night he liked cutting a dash in local pubs, buying lavish rounds of drinks for village worthies – whisky was his favourite tipple – and talking grandly of the money he had made and planned to make, of influential friends and contacts. He also liked making up calypsos mocking the Labour government; Arthur was a Liberal. He saw himself as an English squire – some villagers called him 'King Hosein' – and when an altercation with Captain Barclay, Master of the Puckeridge Hounds (they had cut across Arthur's land), involved the police and legal correspondence and the actual social acquaintance of a real country gentleman, Arthur must have felt he had made his mark. He applied to Captain Barclay to become a member of the Puckeridge Hunt.

None of this appealed to Nizam, who was an awkward youth, introverted and emotional. He came to England, lured by Arthur's fantasies, in May 1969, a year after he had wounded his father in a fight. He was twenty-one and worked as a labourer on the farm in return for pocket -money and his keep. But little pleased him and he was disparaging about Arthur's illusions and exaggerations. Where was the wealth, the affluent and socially successful life that Arthur had bragged about in Trinidad, and which he had promised his parents should they come to visit England? The discrepancy between Arthur's heady aspirations and cold reality had to be faced. The solution was obvious – get rich quick. But how? How could Arthur, now thirty-four, realise the ultimate fantasy of making a million, which would in turn make fact of all his dreams?

The answer was provided by a television show. On 30 October, the brothers were watching David Frost interviewing Rupert Murdoch about the ethics of reprinting Christine Keeler's memoirs. But what was of greater interest to the brothers was the huge amount of money mentioned in connection with the take-over of the *News of the*

World. Clearly, Mr Murdoch was a millionaire many times over. They heard he also had a young, attractive wife. Obviously, he would part with one of his millions to ransom her if she were kidnapped …

The brothers probably made some preliminary enquiries in November, but did not go into action until after 13 December, when Arthur's German wife, their two children and his thirteen-year-old sister left England on a Christmas visit to Else's parents in Germany. They would return on 3 January, soon after which Nizam's visitor's permit was due to expire. The brothers had three weeks in which to make a million.

It took them a week to find out where – as they thought – Mrs Murdoch lived. Then there was the Christmas break, a long one as Christmas Day fell on a Thursday. Nobody would be back at work until Monday, 29 December.

The McKays spent a pleasant family Christmas at Lingfield in Sussex with their daughter, Diane, who was married to David Dyer, a business executive with the Wilkinson razor-blade company. The Hosein brothers were on their own in Rooks Farm, although they were joined on Boxing Day by a Trinidadian nurse called Liley, who was Nizam's girlfriend. She was twenty-nine and had left her husband and three children. Her presence excited Arthur, who thought all women found him irresistible, and there was a punch-up between the brothers in which Nizam was worsted and was so distraught that he reported Arthur to the police. But when Liley departed on the following day, fraternal harmony was restored.

On the morning of Sunday, 28 December 1969, two policemen visited Rooks Farm, making enquiries about an assault on an old farmer the previous Sunday. Both Hoseins denied being involved in this case of grievous bodily harm and the detectives withdrew. That night, about 9.30 pm, the brothers appeared in a pub, the Plough, at Great Munden. Arthur was full of beans. He said he had been invited to a dinner party at Mr Rupert Murdoch's house, but had had to refuse. The following Monday morning, about 11 am, PC Felton called at the farm in connection with Nizam's complaint against his brother. Nizam said he didn't wish to prefer any charges. Of Arthur and the Volvo there was no sign.

Later that day, at 8 pm and again at 10.30 pm, Liley telephoned the farm to talk to Nizam. No one answered the first call. The second was answered by Arthur, who said Nizam was out.

That Monday morning Alick McKay had set off for work at half-past nine in the dark-blue Rolls-Royce, driven by his chauffeur Bill. Mrs McKay waved goodbye at the door of St Mary House. It was very cold: the ground was still white with frost, but some Christmas roses flourished.

Not long afterwards, Mrs McKay got into her Ford Capri and drove to Haydon's Road to collect the household help, Mrs Nightingale. Back at the house, after dealing with various tasks including the preparation of two steaks for the evening meal, Mrs McKay went shopping on foot, visiting a cobbler's, a bank, and a smart dress-shop where she bought a silk dress and matching coat for £60. She lunched in the kitchen with Mrs Nightingale and then visited her dentist in Wimpole Street for a routine check-up, returning home about 5 pm, when she drove Mrs Nightingale home, stopping to buy the evening papers. She must have been back in St Mary House about 5.40 pm, when she made herself a cup of tea and settled down to read the papers in the snug at the rear of the lounge, with a log fire blazing in the grate and her dachshund, Carl, at her feet.

She turned on the television to watch the news but, as was her wont, kept the volume down until news-time arrived. The front door was locked, with a chain across it. Mrs McKay had become wary of strangers ever since the house had been burgled three months before: silver, jewellery, a television set and a record player being taken.

At about ten to six, the doorbell rang.

At six o'clock a neighbour, Mrs Lydiatt, walked by the house and noticed a dark car parked in the drive. She also saw that the light above the front door was on.

Alick McKay returned from work at 7.45 pm. After dismissing the chauffeur-driven Rolls, he rang the doorbell in a pre-arranged code (three shorts and a long) to let his wife know who it was. There was no response. He tried the door – it was neither locked nor chained. He went into the house.

The scene in the hall, as DS Birch described it later, was 'as if it had been set up for an amateur production of an Agatha Christie thriller'. The telephone lay on the floor, its lead ripped from the wall, as well as Mrs McKay's reading glasses. The contents of her handbag were scattered on the stairs, and littering various pieces of furniture were a tin of Elastoplast, a ball of string and a wooden-handled billhook. Everything else was in order, and Carl the dachshund lay dozing in front of the fire in the snug.

At 8 pm, Alick McKay telephoned the police from a neighbour's house. Within five hours, the house was besieged by the press and garrisoned by CID and uniformed policemen. Mrs McKay's two married daughters moved in with their husbands, and several influential newspaper friends arrived, including the editor of *The Sun* and the chairman of IPC.

The disappearance of Mrs McKay was potentially just the kind of story that would be blasted across the front page of *The Sun* and the *News of the World* – as, in fact, it was – and the police, headed by DCS Bill Smith and DI John Minors from Wimbledon, were at first suspicious about everyone's motives and about everything to do with the case. Initially, they thought that Mrs McKay's disappearance might be part of some publicity stunt – the *News of the World* had a regular item dealing with missing persons, as it happened – that Alick McKay, who seemed strangely calm, might be in some way involved; that Mrs McKay had run off on her own accord, possibly with another man; that there had been a family row; or that she had had some kind of breakdown. In any event, they felt that 'the whole thing smelt' and that her disappearance had been stage-managed.

They rather doubted she had been abducted at all, it seemed. There was, after all, no ransom note, and middle-aged women who went missing were a regular occurrence in London, numbering about fifty a week. Earlier that year, another Wimbledon housewife, thirty-seven-year-old Mrs Dawn Jones, had vanished in similar circumstances, her body being eventually found in a hut in Morayshire, Scotland. What aggravated the police most was the involvement and the presence of the press. A *Sun* reporter and photographer were the first journalists at the scene, and a statement was sent by *The Sun's* editor to the Press Association in time to catch the morning papers.

That night, at 1 am, Mrs McKay's disappearance was announced in very vague terms by BBC radio. Fifteen minutes later, the McKays' telephone, which had been busy all night after being reconnected, rang.

David Dyer, the McKays' more aggressive son-in-law, answered it. The operator said he was putting a call through from a call box at Bell Common, Epping. A voice said: 'Tell Mr McKay it is M3, the Mafia.' The house fell silent as the family and the policemen who were there looked at Mr McKay.

He took the receiver from Dyer. DS White picked up an extension in the kitchen. The voice, evidently disguised and later described by the operator as 'an American or coloured voice' continued: 'We are from America – Mafia. M3. We have your wife … You will need a million pounds by Wednesday …' 'This is ridiculous!' cried Mr McKay. 'I haven't got a million!' 'You had better get it,' said the voice. 'You have friends. Get it from them. We tried to get Rupert Murdoch's wife. We couldn't get her – so we took yours instead … You have a million by Wednesday night. Or we will kill her.' 'What do I have to do?' demanded Mr McKay. The voice said: 'All you have to do is wait for the contact … Have the money or you won't have a wife.'

The family were both relieved and horrified: Mrs McKay was apparently alive but in the hands of a lunatic gangster. The police found it hard to believe that any kidnapper would make a ransom demand from a public call box – and 'Mafia M3'! It was most unlikely and surely must be a hoax.

The Sun's front-page headline on the morning of Tuesday, 30 December was 'MYSTERY OF PRESS CHIEF'S MISSING WIFE'. Mr McKay felt that the maximum publicity could only help in his wife's return. But the police were far from sure about this, as were some members of his own family.

From the police point of view, Mr McKay was still the most obvious suspect. The house, the attic and the garden of 20 Arthur Road were carefully searched. Frictions developed between the family and the police, who they thought should be pursuing their enquiries elsewhere. This was indeed being done, and a press conference revealing details of the £1 million ransom demand was held that morning.

At the same time, a description of Mrs McKay – '5 ft 9 in, medium build, dark complexion, dark brown hair, straight nose, green eyes, oval face' – was circulated, and a crime index was set up at Wimbledon police station. The index was a filing system, heavily cross-referenced, dealing with all the sightings, statements and other information that began to come in as the police made enquiries about cars and people seen in the area. They questioned friends and neighbours of the McKays and investigated the activities of local cranks and crooks. A tape-recorder was provided by a detective working on the case – it would have taken over two months to obtain one through official channels – and was fixed to the telephone in the snug, which had been taken over by the police. The McKays' number was soon jammed by hoaxers and reporters, but there was not a word from M3. This tended to confirm police suspicions that the Mafia call was probably a hoax.

But at 4.56 pm, M3 finally got through. Again, he was ringing from a callbox; David Dyer, who took the call, heard the pips. The voice said: 'Your wife has just posted a letter to you. Do cooperate ... for heaven's sake. For her sake, don't call the police ... You have been followed. Did you get the message? ... Did you get the money?'

Again, no instructions were given as to where or how the money was to be delivered. The family's fears increased, and that night Diane Dyer appeared on the 8.50 BBC TV News – much to the vexation of the police and with a corresponding increase in nuisance calls.

On Wednesday morning a letter, postmarked '6.45 pm. Tottenham. N17', arrived. On lined blue paper was a feeble, unaligned scrawl from Mrs McKay: 'Please do something to get me home. I am blindfolded and cold. Only blankets. Please cooperate for I cannot keep going ... I think of you constantly ... What have I done to deserve this treatment? ... Love Muriel.'

The police decided to keep the letter's contents secret and it was not mentioned at the midday press conference. Nonetheless, it was leaked to *The Sun* and the Press Association, and most morning papers carried the text in full. The police in charge of the case were furious, and DCS Smith felt he now had no option but to enlist the family's full cooperation and explain his every move, against all police principles.

That night, New Year's Eve, both Mrs McKay's daughters and David Dyer, who had become the McKays' spokesman, appeared at the evening press conference, and Diane Dyer made another emotional appeal on television, this time on ITN's news.

Early that same morning, the Hoseins had had a visitor. He was a business friend and a master tailor and arrived by appointment at Rooks Farm about 7.30 am to collect some trousers. This he did, seeing nothing of Arthur nor anything suspicious. Later that morning, both brothers picked up Liley in London by car and brought her back to the farm, where she stayed until 2 January, during which time she noticed nothing odd. She said Arthur spent most of the time watching television.

The telephone in 20 Arthur Road continued to ring. One call came from a nurse who recommended that a medium be consulted. The McKay family, determined to explore any avenue to obtain Mrs McKay's release, contacted a spiritualist who said she was too busy to see them just then but had already received a message from the spirit world about the abduction. Three people were involved, she said, as was Seven Sisters

Road – which ended just south of Tottenham, N17. The motive was spite or malice, she said, and Mrs McKay was being held in a 'very scruffy place'. This impressed the family and they resolved to go further – without telling the police.

They next consulted a famous clairvoyant, Gerard Croiset, who lived in Utrecht in Belgium. A family friend took a photo of Mrs McKay to Croiset, who said: 'The impression I get is of a white farm ... Around it are trees and a green barn.' It was approached by a road going north-north-east out of London. In the vicinity, said Croiset, were another farm, a disused airfield, a concrete building, and a pond in which was an old motorcycle. He added: 'If she is not found within fourteen days, she will be dead.'

Somewhat reluctantly, the police followed up the information, finally identifying a deserted building on the Essex-Hertfordshire border. Rooks Farm happened to be only a few miles away.

When the newspapers published their accounts of the McKays' dealings with Croiset the police were doubly aggrieved – firstly by the implication that the supernatural might be more reliable than police detection and secondly by the influx of related information that now swamped them. 'Because of Croiset's intervention,' said Commander Guiver of the CID, 'we wasted thousands of man hours. Not through following up his ideas, but because of all the imitators.' In addition, the McKays' telephone was again jammed by useless, cranky calls.

But on the evening of Thursday, 1 January, at 7.40 pm, M3 got through again.

Diane Dyer answered the untraceable STD phone call. But M3 was unwilling to talk to her. 'I'll contact you later,' he said. 'Why don't we talk now?' asked Diane. 'You've gone too far,' said M3. 'It has gone too far now.' 'What's gone too far?' persisted Diane. But M3 rang off. A few minutes later, he was back. He said: 'You tell them they've gone too far ... They've gone to the police ... They've got to get a million, a million pounds. I'll contact them tomorrow, and they've got to get it in fivers and tenners.' 'Where do you get a million pounds from?' demanded Diane. 'That's not my business,' said M3 and rang off.

Nothing more would be heard from the kidnappers for nine days.

On 3 January, Mrs Hosein and the children returned to Rooks Farm. Nine days later, when she found that Liley had stayed at the farm in her absence, there was a row – Arthur hit Else and she walked out with the children, going to live with a friend for a few days. By now the police, the press and the family all tended to believe that Mrs McKay had indeed been kidnapped. But by whom? The ransom demand was so excessive as to appear absurd, and it was felt that the kidnapping could be an act of malicious revenge directed against the *News of the World* by someone who had been exposed in its pages or who disapproved of the paper's lurid and explicit stories. In the meantime, Ian McKay (the McKays' son), and his wife Lesley, had arrived in England from Australia. Displeased with the way things were going, he would nonetheless soon be instrumental in getting his family to treat the police approach with more respect.

The telephone in 20 Arthur Road rang constantly. There were always two policemen in the house as well as two or more outside, where the press and television crews still stuck to their posts, their numbers swelled by sightseers.

On Friday, 2 January a man had telephoned offering to return Mrs McKay for £500. The hand-over was to be effected on Platform 5 at Wimbledon railway station. DI Minors, in Mr McKay's hat and coat and carrying a suitcase containing £150 and some paper money, kept the appointment. As a result, a nineteen-year-old waiter was arrested and later fined £100 for attempting to obtain money by deception.

On Saturday evening, at a press conference, the police were harassed by questions they were unable to answer. By then, although most senior officers were inclined (like the McKays and the press) to believe that Mrs McKay *had* been kidnapped, some were still suspicious of Alick McKay. So the house, the garden and the garage were searched again.

Alick McKay was now allowed to read a statement and was photographed in his dressing gown and pyjamas; this was arranged to give the impression that he was ill. The statement implied that Mrs McKay was also ill and needed certain drugs to maintain her health. It said: 'I ask whoever is holding Muriel to get in touch with me immediately and let me know exactly what they want. If it is money, then I must know how and where it can be exchanged for my wife. In order to be certain I am dealing with the person who is holding Muriel I must have positive proof that she is safe.' Six days later, he appeared on television and once more appealed for proof that his wife was still alive.

During that week, the police effort was largely dissipated in the necessary but useless investigation of phone calls and sightings all over Britain. There were also yet more hoax ransom demands. In following up one of them, DS Chalky Whyte, disguised as Diane Dyer in a wig and mini-skirt and carrying £5,000 in a suitcase, travelled on a 47 bus across London to a hand-over point at Stamford Hill, as instructed by an anonymous caller. Two other detectives, dressed as workmen and sitting separately, accompanied Whyte all the way, and the bus was shadowed by two Q cars – so closely that the bus-driver reported their suspect presence to the Stamford Hill police. In another hoax, the telephone caller was caught outside a public toilet in an east London underground station and jailed for three years.

Increasingly, the police were accused both of doing too much – because of the status and connections of the McKays – and also of not doing enough. One line of enquiry they followed led them to Hertfordshire, to Bishop's Stortford, 8 miles from Stocking Pelham. The billhook found in the hall was said by a Sheffield manufacturer to have been one of many sold and used in Hertfordshire. But that trail was apparently followed no further.

When twelve days had passed since Mrs McKay's disappearance, and nine days since the last communication from M3, the accumulated fears and frustrations of all those most closely concerned with the case were relieved for a while the morning after Mr McKay's television appearance. A letter received by the editor of the *News of the World* on Saturday, 10 January complained that the writer had telephoned Arthur Road several times but the line had always been engaged. The million-pound ransom was now to be delivered in halves, at two collection points. Instructions would follow.

But again there was silence, this time for four days. Then, on Wednesday, 14 January, M3 rang both the *News of the World* and Arthur Road, the latter call being taken by Alick McKay.

Both calls were brief, and neither contained any new information. 'You cooperate,' M3 told Mr McKay, 'and you'll get your madam back.' The tape recording of this conversation, as of the others, was sent to an acoustics laboratory – the first time this had happened in a murder case. Voice-printing, then as now, was an uncertain but improving method of identification. As a result, M3's voice was deduced to be West Indian with American overtones.

The next and longest call to date, lasting thirty-five minutes, was answered on the afternoon of Monday, 19 January, again by Alick McKay, who was in an emotional state after the police had openly admitted their fears that Mrs McKay was dead – a fear already expressed by some of the family.

M3 asked for a first payment of half a million pounds and said, as before, that instructions would follow. Mr McKay demanded that some proof be sent that his wife was still alive. 'Bring a gun here and shoot me,' he cried, 'rather than make impossible demands! ... Nobody's got a million pounds ... and it's ridiculous to talk about it ... I can't give you what I haven't got!' 'If you don't cooperate,' said M3, 'you will be responsible for not seeing your wife again.' 'What have I done to deserve this?' 'I don't know,' said M3. 'But I'm very sorry we had to do this because your wife is such a nice person.' When Mr McKay offered to pay £20,000, M3 replied: 'That's not enough ... It must be half a million, first delivery.' 'Take me instead!' said Mr McKay. M3 rang off.

By this time, press interest in the story had waned, as had the interfering telephone calls. After Mr McKay's outburst the police persuaded the family that Ian McKay should reply to all calls and try to establish some rapport with the kidnappers. He answered the next call, which came two days later on Wednesday, the gist of which was that the family should have no dealings with the police and that two letters from Mrs McKay were on their way to Arthur Road.

These, and a ransom demand with detailed instructions, arrived on Thursday the 22nd inside an envelope postmarked Wood Green, a northern suburb parallel to Tottenham. The letters referred to Diane's television appeals (on 31 December and 2 January), one of which Mrs McKay had apparently *heard*. Her faltering hand wrote: 'I am deteriorating in health and spirit ... Excuse handwriting, I'm blindfolded and cold ... Please keep the Police out of this and co-operate with the Gang ... The earlier you get the money the quicker I may come home ... Please keep Police out of it if you want to see me alive ... The gang is too large to fool.'

The ransom demand told Mr McKay to put half a million pounds, in five and ten pound notes, into a black suitcase and to bring it, using his wife's Capri, to a telephone box on the corner of Church Street and Cambridge Road (the A10) in Edmonton at 10 pm on 1 February. There he would receive further instructions.

The following day, Friday, Ian McKay answered three calls from M3, who was anxious to confirm that the letters and the demand had been received and to repeat his threats. Ian's belligerent attitude and counter-demands for proof of his mother's well-being produced an excited volubility from the caller and two more letters from Mrs McKay, plus another ransom demand and three bits of material cut from the clothes she had worn on 29 December. They arrived in one envelope on Monday, 26 January.

The letters were hard to decipher. They were despairing, and, it seems, the last that she ever wrote – probably some weeks earlier. 'If I could only be home ... I can't believe this thing happened to me ... It seems hopeless ... You betrayed me by going to Police and not co-operating with the M3 Gang ... Love Muriel.'

The ransom note ended:

Looking forward in settling our business on the 1st February at 10 pm as stated on last letter in a very discreet and honest way, and you and your children will be very happy to join Muriel McKay, and our organisation also will be happy to continue our job elsewhere in Australia ... You see we don't like to make our customer happy, we like to keep them in suspense, in that way it is a gamble ... We give the order and you must obey. M3.

The police made their plans. The ransom was made up of £300 in real £5 notes, provided by Mr McKay, and of convincing forgeries in bundles with real notes at either end. An electronic homing device was attached to the suitcase.

It was decided that DI Minors would dress as a chauffeur while DS Roger Street posed as Ian McKay, with his arm in a sling in which a two-way radio would be concealed. 'I'll have to come in the Rolls,' the real Ian told M3 on 30 January, after several other conversations between the two. 'I don't know the north of London very well, and I've also injured my hand a bit and I want to bring the chauffeur.' 'Oh, I see,' said M3 doubtfully. But he raised no objections.

On Sunday, 1 February the Hoseins left Rooks Farm at about 6.30 pm in the Volvo, after entertaining some friends to lunch. At 9 pm the Rolls set off from 20 Arthur Road. Lying in wait about the A10 were over 150 policemen and over fifty unmarked police cars.

DS Roger Street entered the Church Street call box soon after 10 pm. The phone rang. 'Who's that?' said a voice. Street replied: 'Ian McKay. Who's that?' 'This is M3. These are your instructions ...' Street was directed to another call box farther up the A10, on the corner of Southbury Road. The Rolls set off again. In the second call box, M3 told Street that further instructions were written in a cigarette pack on the floor, a pack of Piccadilly cigarettes, which was empty apart from directions to High Cross, where the suitcase was to be left. M3 said that if Street then returned to the first call box at Church Street, he would receive a call saying where Mrs McKay could be found.

The Rolls drove on north, past a petrol station in High Cross, until it came to a left turning leading to Dane End. Here, two paper flowers stuck in a bank marked the spot where the suitcase was to be abandoned. This was done – it was midnight. The Rolls headed back to London.

But the trap failed. So many policemen, variously disguised, some as Hell's Angels, drove up and down the road and lurked in ditches and hedges, that the fantasy of catching the kidnappers turned into a farce. In the two-and-a-half hours that followed the drop, almost five times as many police vehicles were noted by the CID men concealed across the road from the drop as civilian cars, of which only ten were logged in that time.

One was a Volvo 144. In it, unknown to the police, were the Hoseins, who drove slowly past the suitcase to a transport café, where they parked and debated their next move. Two policemen in plain clothes happened to pull in after them, giving themselves and the game away by their loud comments on the operation. The Hoseins fled back to Stocking Pelham, 8 miles to the east. At Rooks Farm Else gave them a meal and they went to bed.

Early that morning, Ian McKay was primed at 20 Arthur Road by DI Minors and DS Street on where they had gone and what they had done, in case M3 rang again. It seemed a hopeless prospect. Everyone in St Mary House was sadly depressed.

But a day later, on 3 February, an indignant M3 telephoned, accusing Ian McKay of setting a trap. Police cars, he said, had been seen around the pick-up spot. Ian tried to convince M3 that he knew nothing of this. The conversation, as was now usual, was a lengthy one. M3 said he would only talk in future to Alick McKay. He was now off, he said, to a meeting of the gang to discuss Mrs McKay's fate. 'I am going to plead for your mum,' said M3. 'I'm fond of her – your mum – you know … She reminds me of my mum.'

The day before this, and not until then, the Hertfordshire police were officially involved in the enquiry. At the same time, some Flying Squad detectives making routine investigations around the scene of the drop asked a sergeant in the local police station if any West Indians lived in the neighbourhood. The sergeant replied in the negative, but added that he believed two Pakistanis were living in Stocking Pelham.

The detectives went there and made further enquiries, establishing that the 'Pakistanis' were called Hosein and were not too popular. The sergeant, questioned again, said he knew about the Hoseins because of some motoring offences; they had two cars, a Morris Minor and a Volvo. On the detectives' return to London, the information was filed away in the crime index.

The Hoseins, undeterred by the evident odds against them and blindly confident about the outcome of the game they were playing – and probably excited by the sight of the suitcase – telephoned Arthur Road twice on Thursday, 5 February, the day after Mrs McKay's birthday. This time, M3 spoke at length to Mr McKay. The £500,000, he said, was to be put in two suitcases and taken by Mr McKay and his daughter Diane in the Rolls to the Church Street call box at 4 pm the following day.

Preparations were swiftly made, and more wisely after the overkill of the previous Sunday. In Wimbledon, DI Minors shaved off his moustache in order to impersonate Mr McKay and donned a fur hat and a camel-haired coat. DC Joyce Armitage dressed herself in Diane's clothes. This time, the Rolls had an unseen passenger. DS John Bland was hidden in the unlocked boot with an oxygen mask and two cylinders.

They set off at 3 pm on Friday, 6 February, half an hour after M3 made his final call. It came from the East End, where Arthur Hosein was delivering trousers. Ian McKay answered the call. 'They're on their way,' said Ian. 'This is the last and final chance,' said M3. It was, for all concerned.

DI Minors was kept waiting at the Church Street call box for forty-five minutes. When M3 rang, he was told to go to the East End of London to a call box in Bethnal Green Road, 6 miles away.

Commander Guiver, supervising police manoeuvres from an ops room in Scotland Yard, moved some of his forces south. The Hoseins, who were in the area already, parked not far from the second call box and at about 6 pm observed the Rolls arrive. They then moved on to make the call that Minors now awaited. He and Joyce Armitage were told to leave the Rolls at Bethnal Green underground station and to take the Central Line tube to Epping, where they would receive another call on a booking-hall telephone. Unwilling to risk any trouble on a train crammed with commuters, the police took another risk.

After consulting the ops room, Minors drove the Rolls, not to Bethnal Green, but to Theydon Bois – the stop *before* Epping – with the intention of boarding a train there, with Joyce Armitage. He drove slowly thither so that the police forces could again be repositioned. When he and Joyce Armitage reached Theydon Bois underground station, DS Bland, who had been in the boot for over four hours, got out. With Minors carrying the suitcases, all three boarded a train bound for Epping, as did assorted policemen in various civilian disguises. Nothing happened on the short journey. All the policemen left the train and disappeared, except for Minors and Armitage, who waited beside the suitcases in the hall.

Meanwhile, at about 7.15 pm, Arthur Hosein turned up on his own in a pub, the Raven, in Berden, Essex, a few miles from Rooks Farm.

It was 7.34 pm when the next and final telephone call was answered by the police waiting at Epping station. The call is believed to have been made by Nizamodeen Hosein from a pay phone in a house converted into flats in Bishop's Stortford.

Minors and Armitage were told to go by taxi to Bishop's Stortford, 13 miles to the north on the A11 and 8 miles east of Stocking Pelham. They were to leave the two suitcases beside a mini-van – registration UMH 587F – parked in the forecourt of Gates Garage. 'We deal with high-powered telescopic rifles,' said M3. 'Anyone trying to interfere with the cases, we will let them have it.'

A mini-cab driver, Robert Kelly, was sent by his office to pick up a 'Mr McKay' at Epping station after that gentleman had telephoned for a cab. Kelly found that 'Mr McKay' was accompanied by a young woman and that they had two white suitcases with them. He put the cases in the boot. They set off, and had hardly gone two hundred yards when 'Mr McKay' told him to stop the car, whereupon a man (DS Bland) dashed out of the darkness, plunged into the back of the car and curled up on the floor at the female passenger's feet. Kelly, enquiring about this strange behaviour, was told: 'We're playing a joke on a friend.' He was also advised to ask no more questions and drive on.

At Bishop's Stortford, Kelly was told to drive past Gates Garage, do a U-turn and stop beside a hedge. Here the woman got out and the man in the back crawled out and disappeared into the hedge. The suitcases were then removed from the boot and deposited by a beige mini-van outside the garage. Minors and Armitage then returned in the mini-cab to Epping station, where they waited for a call that never came. Kelly also waited, as curious as he was apprehensive, and eventually drove the couple back to Theydon Bois, to the Rolls. He was paid £5 for his five-hour mystery tour. He revealed later: 'There were times when I thought of leaving the car and running for it … I didn't sleep properly for about three days puzzling over it, and I don't mind admitting I was frightened.'

Meanwhile, DS Bland, concealed by the hedge across the road from the garage, observed the slow approach of a dirty dark-blue Volvo, registration XG0 994G. Its driver seemed to take an interest in the cases. Other cars passed. Thirty minutes later, the Volvo returned, went past the garage, did a U-turn, passed the cases again, and then – the driver having apparently been alarmed by people pouring out of a bingo hall – drove on back into Bishop's Stortford.

Arthur, meanwhile, had been enjoying himself in the Raven, remaining there until 10 pm, chatting with an actor – Griffith Davies – who lived locally, and two girls. He boasted about the fact that he would soon be a millionaire. He was joined at the Raven by Nizam and after an earnest private conversation they both left.

The Volvo reappeared again outside the garage at 10.47 pm. This time there were two men inside. Again, it slowed noticeably as it passed the cases. DS Bland and other policemen hidden about the garage cocked their guns. They were waiting for the kidnappers to pick up the cases and take them back to their hide-out, where Mrs McKay might be or might have been. But the Volvo once more moved away.

Then, at 11 pm, the trap was sprung. By the wrong mice.

A public-spirited couple, the Abbots, seeing the cases lying unattended in the garage forecourt, became concerned. Mrs Abbott kept watch on the cases while her husband reported their find to the local police, who in due course visited the garage and removed the cases, taking them to the local police station where the duty officer was astounded to see what was in them – half a million pounds.

The operation was abandoned at 11.40 pm.

Back in Wimbledon, Minors and Armitage, sitting with the McKays in case M3 telephoned, were as depressed as the family. They had failed again. But about 3 am, DCS Smith came to the house – and he was smiling. Bland's sightings of the Volvo had tallied with other entries in the crime index. 'We think we may be on to them,' said Smith.

At 8 am on Saturday morning the police visited Rooks Farm in force. They saw that a dark-blue Volvo was parked outside.

Else Hosein answered the door. DCS Smith said he was investigating the disappearance of some jewellery (Mrs McKay's). Arthur Hosein appeared and cheerfully invited the police inside, despite the flooded kitchen and living room – the washing machine had just burst. With Arthur's consent, the house was searched. 'You can look where you like,' he said. 'I know nothing. I earn over £150 a week. I do not deal in stolen property.'

The police found some paper flowers made by Liley for the Hoseins' children. They found an exercise book whose pages had been used for Mrs McKay's letters, as well as a billhook, a sawn-off shotgun, a tin of Elastoplast and a packet of Piccadilly cigarettes. There was a paper flower on the floor of the Volvo. DS Bland identified Nizam as the man who had driven the Volvo the previous night.

The brothers were taken to London for further questioning. Arthur Hosein's fingerprints turned out to be the same as those that had been found on the ransom demands, the envelopes and the cigarette packet.

He and Nizam were charged on Tuesday, 10 February. Handwriting experts agreed that Arthur had probably written two ransom notes, and voice experts concluded that Nizam had made most of the phone calls. But neither brother said anything incriminating. Arthur seemed to exult in all the attention and hardly ever stopped talking. Nizam, on the other hand, tried to kill himself twice, and seemed constantly afraid and on the point of tears. He hardly spoke at all. There was little doubt that he was, and always had been, dominated by his older brother. 'Arthur always gets me into trouble!' he wailed at one point.

They were remanded in custody – appearing seventeen times in Wimbledon magistrate's court – for seven months. For weeks, hundreds of policemen scoured Rooks Farm and the neighbourhood. But no pathologist was ever consulted, and not a trace of Mrs McKay was found.

The trial of Arthur and Nizamodeen Hosein, charged with murder, kidnapping and blackmail, among other indictments, began at the Old Bailey on Monday, 14 September 1970. The judge was Mr Justice Sebag Shaw; the Attorney-General, Sir Peter Rawlinson, led for the Crown; Arthur was defended by Barry Hudson, QC, and Nizam by Douglas Draycott, QC. The trial ended on 6 October.

On the last day, all the McKays were present, as was Else Hosein and the brothers' father from Trinidad. Arthur wore a natty dark-blue suit, made specially for the occasion. Both Hoseins were found guilty, the jury adding a recommendation for leniency in Nizam's case. Asked if he had anything to say, Arthur shouted: 'Injustice has not only been done, it has also been seen and heard by the gallery to have been done! They have seen the provocation of your lordship and they have seen your immense partiality!'

Both brothers were sentenced to life imprisonment on the murder charge. Arthur was also given twenty-five years on the other charges and Nizam fifteen years. Their appeals were dismissed.

St Mary House and Rooks Farm were both sold, the house for £30,000 and the farm for £18,500. Mrs Hosein obtained a divorce. *The Sun's* circulation rapidly increased, passing the two million mark in February 1971. A special tie was made for those policemen who had worked on the case: dark blue, its crest was a black red-eyed rook and two crossed billhooks.

Alick McKay remarried in 1973, his second wife being Beverley Hylton, the widow of the impresario, Jack Hylton. In 1976, he became managing director of News International, the company owning *The Sun*, the *News of the World, The Times* and *The Sunday Times*. He was knighted in 1977 and died of a heart attack, aged seventy-three, in January 1983.

What happened to Mrs McKay? The police believe she was murdered and disposed of at Rooks Farm. Some believe her dismembered body was fed to the pigs at the farm – seven Wessex Saddlebacks. When the police eventually raided the farm, the boar and four of the sows had been sold and slaughtered, although this did not happen until 19 January. Two sows and their litters remained. But not one of the animals, sold by Mrs Hosein on 26 February, was killed or examined for any traces of the drug cortisone, which Mrs McKay had been taking.

It would have been difficult to conceal her at the farm after Else Hosein, the children and Miss Hosein returned to Rooks Farm from Germany on 3 January. The police theory is that Mrs McKay was drugged, shot and dismembered before the other Hoseins arrived.

There are two other possibilities: that Mrs McKay died of natural causes, of shock perhaps or hypothermia; and that she was never at Rooks Farm, being held captive and killed somewhere else. A few of the police officers who worked on the case were of the opinion that a third man was involved, someone who was the brains behind the kidnapping and then dropped out when Mrs McKay died.

Nonetheless, the obvious suppositions remain the most likely explanations of what happened. There were reports of a gun being fired at the farm on or about New Year's Day and of a burning smell coming from the farm after 6 January, also of unidentified men and cars being seen near the farm. But only the Hoseins know what really happened to Mrs McKay.

Nizamodeen Hosein was released and deported to Trinidad in 1990. Arthur Hosein was not granted a release from prison by the Parole Board until 2003 and has subsequently died.

APPENDIX A

Extract from *My Experiences as an Executioner*, by James Berry, concerning his first execution, which was in Edinburgh.

On Thursday, March 27th, 1884 ... I arrived at Waverley Station 4-20pm, and I hired a cab to drive me to the gaol. On arrival at the prison I was met at the doors by a good-looking warder, dressed in ordinary prison garb, and very courteous; and on entering the large portal gate, was asked my name, and after entering it down in the prison book, time, etc ... he pulled a string, which rang the Governor's bell, and in a few moments I was confronted with the Governor, a very nice gentleman, of military appearance, and very good-looking. After passing the usual conversation of the day, and the weather, and what kind of journey I had up from Bradford, he said after such a long journey I should require a good, substantial tea: and as soon as I had washed, and combed my hair, the tea was there, everything that could be desired. I sat down, and quite enjoyed my first Scotch meal in Bonnie Scotland ...

I spent the Thursday night smoking and reading. At 10.0 o'clock pm I was escorted to my bedroom, a round house at the back part of the gaol, a snug little place, and was informed that the last man who slept inside that room was William Marwood, five years previous to my visit ... The chief warder, whom I spoke to, seemed to touch upon the subject with great reluctance, and said that he felt quite upset concerning the two culprits (Robert Vickers and William Innes), and that he hoped they would get a reprieve. I sat me down on my bed after he had gone, locked my door, and could hear the trains depart from the station under the prison wall ... I then knelt down and asked the Almighty to help me in my most painful task, which I had undertaken to carry out ...

At 8.0 am on the morning of the 28th, Friday, my breakfast was brought into my room, consisting of toast, ham and eggs, and coffee ... At 10.0 am I was introduced to the Magistrates and those responsible to see the execution carried out. I exposed my ropes and straps for their inspection, and, after a long and careful investigation of all points, they retired, quite satisfied with their visit. After that we paid another visit to the scaffold; the builders, not having finished the contract, were making a final touch to the new-erected shed to keep the execution private, and so that nobody outside could see. After testing it with bags of cement, same weight as the prisoners, and calculating the length of drop and its consequences, and other details, the committee departed. After, I filled my time walking about the prison grounds, and thinking of the poor men who were nearing their end, full of life, and knowing the fatal hour, which made me quite ill to think about. My meals did not seem to do me good, my appetite began to fall off … and I felt as I wished I had never undertaken such an awful calling. I regretted for a while, and then I thought the public would only think I had not the pluck, and I would not allow my feelings to overthrow me, so I never gave way to such thoughts again.

At 1.0 pm my dinner had arrived. I went up to my room, and sat down to pudding, beef, and vegetables, Scotch broth, and Cochrane & Cantrell's ginger ale. At that time I was a total abstainer; and I think it is the safest side, since what I have seen brought on by its sad consequences of taking too much alcoholic liquor … After tea, I had a chat with the warders coming off duty for the day.

Saturday morning, 29th … After breakfast, had another interview with the Magistrates, and made the final arrangements. I tested the scaffold in their presence, with the ropes I was going to use on the Monday morning, with bags of cement, each bag being placed in the same places as was marked for the criminals … I tested the ropes by letting off the traps, and down went the bags, and I got my calculations from that point … The rope was of Italian silk hemp, made specially for the work, 5/8 inch in thickness, and very pliable, running through a brass thimble, which causes dislocation and a painless death if rightly adjusted … After dining, I had the honour of having a drive in an open carriage, provided by the Governor, for a couple of hours … I retired to bed as usual at 10.0 pm, after reciting my prayers, and thinking only another night and I shall be back with my wife and children. Saturday night I was very restless, and I did not feel so much refreshed for my night's sleep, as I was thinking of the poor creatures who was slumbering their hours away, in the prison cell, just beyond where I was laid. Two men, in full bloom, had to come to such an untimely end, leaving wives and large families. One poor woman, I was informed, her mind was so affected that she was removed to the asylum, she took it so to heart.

(Sunday) I retired to my day-room at the front entrance, where I only partook very sparingly of the nice and tempting ham and poached eggs put before me. I spent most of the forenoon looking round inside the prison, while the prisoners was at chapel, until dinner time. My dinner did not arrive until 4 o'clock, which is called late dinner, consisting of rice pudding, black currants, chicken, vegetables, potatoes, bread, and the usual teetotal beverages. I tried to make the best of it, but all that I could do was to look at it, as my appetite was gone; but I managed to eat a little before going to roost for the last night … I retired at 10.0 pm on Sunday, but only had cat naps all night, one eye shut and the other open, thinking and fancying things that never will be.

(Monday, 31 March 1884) I was dressed and up at 5.0 am; and felt more dead than alive as I had such a responsible part to play in the programme for the day. I fancied the ropes breaking; I fancied I was trembling, and could not do it. I was nearly frantic in my *mind, but I never let them know. 6.0 am arrived. I heard the sound of the keys, clattering of doors, sliding of bolts. Breakfast had to be served earlier than usual. No prisoner allowed out of his cell until all was over. The public had begun to assemble on Calton Hill in groups. 7.0 am arrived. I made my way to the scaffold, made my arrangements secure, and cleared the scaffold shed ...*

At 7.45 the living group wended their way to the prison, and into the doctor's room, ready for the last scene of the drama. The prisoners were brought face to face for the first time since their conviction. They kissed each other; and the scene was a very painful one, to see mates going to meet their end on the gallows.

They were conducted to the room adjoining the doctor's room, and were in prayer with the two ministers in attendance after 8.05. I was called to do my duty. I was handed the warrant, which was made out by the judge who condemned them to die. I then proceeded to pinion the prisoners, previously shaking hands, bidding good-bye to this world. Both men seemed to feel the position very much.

The procession was formed, headed by the High Bailiff, the Chaplain reading the litany for the dead. Both the prisoners walked without assistance to the place of execution; they was at once placed under the beam on the drop, where everything was done as quick as lightning, and both culprits paid the highest penalty of the law.

Elsewhere in his book, Berry adds:

Vickers was buoyed up with hope throughout and continually asked if 'the reprieve' had come. Hope rendered him almost cheerful. Even when we were on the scaffold he was convinced that he was not to die ... It was not until the noose touched his neck that he realised that his execution was to be an actual solemn fact, and when the dread reality burst upon him, he fainted. His companion in crime and death stood unmoved upon the scaffold, resigned and calm, without either hope or fear. The white cap was over his face when Vickers fainted, and no sound gave him any hint that Vickers was overcome. The fainting man was supported for a moment, then a touch on the lever, and it was necessary to support him no longer.

APPENDIX B

Two accounts of the execution of Abel Atherton, aged thirty, are given here. He was a miner condemned to death for the murder by shooting of his former landlady, Mrs Patrick, at Chopwell near Durham. He claimed it was an accident. The accounts were written by Harry Pierrepoint, the chief executioner, and a local newspaper reporter, his account being one of the last of its kind. Pierrepoint's assistant was William Wallis. Atherton was hanged in Durham Jail on Wednesday, 8 December 1909.

Pierrepoint: *It was a cold wintry day when I arrived at Durham on the afternoon before the execution. I called in at an hotel opposite the prison from where the landlord used to send our meals across to the prison. While I was talking to the landlord at the counter, who should come in but Atherton's father and sister-in-law in deep mourning dress. Atherton's father was talking about his son and saying he was innocent. He pulled out some last letters they had just received from him while paying their last visit. I took a seat until they had gone, and pretended to interest myself in some curios that hung on the wall. It was now time for us to go to the prison, and as I was walking across the road I saw Atherton's father and sister-in-law standing watching to see if I went into the prison. I knew they had guessed from my speech who I was when they came into the hotel.*

I made my usual arrangements after my arrival. Then I went to Atherton's cell. I found him fairly cheerful, but a sad downcast look upon him. He was only of short stature, 5 feet 1? inches high, but of strong build.

Reporter: *After the visit from his father Atherton seemed reconciled, and retired to rest at about ten o' clock on Tuesday night. He slept pretty well, and at half-past five was aroused, washed, and dressed in his own clothing. The Chaplain arrived at the Gaol before seven o'clock, and administered the Communion to Atherton in the condemned cell. Atherton partook of a light breakfast, after which the Chaplain again joined him, and remained with the condemned man until a few minutes to eight, then he left to robe to take part in the final act. Wednesday morning broke clear and frosty. At ten minutes to eight Mr AA Wilson, Acting Under Sheriff, entered the Prison, and was followed by the three Press representatives.*

D Gilbert was the last of the officials to enter. Principal Warder Hunt took charge of the Press men, and at about four minutes to eight conducted them to a position immediately in front of the execution shed. Warders were already in position, at a signal from Engineer Stanton, to throw back the doors of the execution shed, and officers were stationed to signal to Warder Elliott, who had ascended to the prison bell, ready to toll the passing knell. Although all was perfectly quiet within the walls, imagination readily supplied the grim details which were being enacted within the Prison.

Pierrepoint: *When all the officers arrived to witness the last dread act, I entered the condemned cell. Atherton was looking a little terrified. I pinioned his arms and prepared his neck. Then I gently tapped him on the shoulder, and said, 'Keep your pluck up, my lad.' This put life in him. I said I would get it over as quickly as possible. I brought him into the corridor. The procession started.*

Reporter: *The colliery buzzers had commenced to sound, and the first stroke of eight on the clock over the Assize Courts had sounded, when the voice of the Chaplain was heard reciting the opening sentence of the burial service: 'I am the resurrection and the life, saith the Lord.' A second later the procession came in view, in the following order: Chief Warder Barlow; the Chaplain, the Rev D Jacob; the pinioned culprit, with Assistant Warder Hutton and Assistant Warder Duke on either side; the executioner and his assistant; Principal Warder Lenthrall, and Schoolmaster-Warder Dawson; the Acting Under Sheriff; Captain Temple, the Governor; the medical officer; Assistant Warder Jones bringing up the rear.*

The culprit, who seemed remarkably calm and composed, and walked with a firm step, fixed the Press representatives with a look which betokened that he had something to communicate. However, the procession hurried on, and Atherton saw the preparations which had been made for the carrying out of the dread sentence. From the beam there was the rope reaching well nigh to the floor. On the drop there was the ankle strap lying ready for use, and across the drop there were two stout boards with foot-pieces, ready for the attendant warders to render Atherton assistance if required.

At the door the Chaplain stepped aside, and the remainder of the procession passed inside. The moment the threshold had been passed, Atherton's cap had been removed from his head, and the executioners urged him forward to the mark in the drop. The assistant instantly dropped on to his knees and fastened the ankle strap, and while Pierrepoint was adjusting the noose, Atherton in a husky voice cried out, 'Yer hanging an innocent man.'

Pierrepoint: *Whether or not, I could not flinch … I pulled the lever, which gave Atherton a drop of 7 feet 3 inches, and launched him into the hereafter.*

Reporter: *Atherton shot from view before – incredible as it may seem – the clock had ceased striking … As the Press representatives stepped forward and looked into the pit the body was hanging perfectly still. The execution house was then closed till nine o'clock, when the executioners withdrew the body from the pit, released it from the rope, and removed the other paraphernalia of their dread office. In the meantime the official notices were posted at the Prison gates, certifying that judgment of death had been duly executed on Atherton.*

The inquest was held at nine-thirty in the Governor's office at the Prison, by Mr Coroner J Graham, assisted by a jury. Prior to the enquiry the jury viewed the body of the law's victim which was lying on the floor of the execution house enclosed in a plain black deal coffin. Atherton's lips were very blue, and there was a swelling of the neck. Otherwise his features were placid, and gave no appearance of a violent death.

APPENDIX C

Albert Pierrepoint's own account of his first execution as chief executioner follows. It took place at Pentonville Prison in 1941, the victim being a club manager, Antonio Mancini, aged thirty-nine, sentenced to death for the killing of Harry Distleman, who was stabbed at the Palm Beach Bottle Party club in London's Soho. Pierrepoint's assistant was Steve Wade.

At five minutes to nine we were given the signal that the Sheriff had gone to the Governor's office. Wade and I walked across the prison yard with an officer who led us up to the corridor outside the condemned cell. I think the next minutes of waiting were the worst, not only then but on every occasion. It is impossible not to feel apprehension and even fear at the prospect of the responsibility of the moment, but with me the frailty passed as soon as there was action. At half a minute to nine a small group came down the corridor. There was the Sheriff, the Governor, the doctor and some senior prison officers. I suddenly had a strange realisation. I was the youngest man there, and the eyes of everyone were on me. The party paused at the next door to that of the condemned cell, the door of the execution chamber. A finger was raised and they passed in. The chief opened the door of the cell and I went forward with a strap in my hand.

The prisoner was standing, facing me, smiling. In his civilian clothes he looked as smart as I had already registered him. In my civilian clothes, amid all those uniforms, we might have been meeting for a chat in a club in Leicester Square. But who would have foreseen a robed priest in the room? I quickly strapped his wrists and said 'Follow me.'

The door in the side wall of the cell had been opened as I came in, and I walked through it into the execution chamber. He followed me, walking seven paces with the noose straight ahead of him, and the escorting officers mounting the cross-planks gently stopped him as he stood on the T. I had turned in time to face him. Eye to eye, that last look. Wade was stooping behind him, swiftly fastening the ankle strap. I pulled from my breast pocket the white cap, folded as carefully as a parachute, and drew it down over his head. 'Cheerio,' he said. I reached for the noose, pulled it down over the cap, tightened it to my right, pulled a rubber washer along the rope to hold it, and darted to my left, crouching towards the cotter pin at the base of the lever. I was in the position of a sprinter at the start of a race as I went over the cross-plank, pulled the pin with one hand, and pushed the lever with the other, instinctively looking back as I did so. There was a snap as the falling doors were bitten and held by the rubber clips, and the rope stood straight and still. The broken twine spooned down in a falling leaf, passed through a little eddy of dust, and floated into the pit.

I went to the side of the scaffold and walked down into the pit. I undid the prisoner's shirt for the stethoscope, and the doctor followed me. I came up again, and waited. The doctor came back to the scaffold. 'Everything is all right,' he said. It was a curious way for a doctor to pronounce death. I suppose his intention was to reassure the Governor and possibly me …

At ten o'clock Wade and I returned to the execution chamber. He went down into the pit and, kneeling on the scaffold floor, I complied with a strange requirement. By regulation, I had to measure from the heels of the hanging man to the level of the scaffold from which he had dropped. This measurement was longer than the drop I had given him. The extra length was made up by the stretch of the man's body after death … He had been hanging for an hour, and the stretch was considerable …

I put the tape measure away, and went below. I stared at the flesh I had stilled. I had further duties to perform, but no longer as executioner. I had been nearest to this man in death, and I prepared him for burial. As he hung, I stripped him. Piece by piece I removed his clothes. It was not callous, but the best rough dignity I could give him, as he swung to the touch, still hooded in the noose. He yielded his garments without the resistance of limbs. If it had been in a prison outside London, I should have left him his shirt for a shroud, and put him in his coffin. In London there was always a post-mortem, and he had to be stripped entirely and placed on a mortuary stretcher. But in common courtesy I tied his empty shirt around his hips.

Wade had fixed the tackle above. I passed a rope under the armpits of my charge, and the body was hauled up a few feet. Standing on the scaffold, with the body now drooping, I removed the noose and the cap, and took his head between my hands, inclining it from side to side to assure myself that the break had been clean. Then I went below, and Wade lowered the rope. A dead man, being taken down from execution, is a uniquely broken body whether he is a criminal or Christ, and I received this flesh, leaning helplessly into my arms, with the linen round the loins, gently with the reverence I thought due to the shell of any man who has sinned and suffered.

APPENDIX D

The Home Office memorandum given to the Royal Commission set up in 1949 to consider whether capital punishment should be limited or modified detailed the routine of the last days of a man condemned to death.

Immediately a prisoner sentenced to death returns from court, he is placed in a cell for condemned prisoners and is watched night and day by two officers. Amenities such as cards, chess, dominoes, etc, are provided in the cell and the officers are encouraged to – and invariably do – join the prisoner in these games.

Newspapers and books are also provided. Food is supplied from the main prison kitchen, the prisoner being placed on hospital diet, with such additions as the medical officer considers advisable. A pint of beer or stout is supplied daily on request and ten cigarettes or half an ounce of pipe tobacco are allowed unless there are medical reasons to the contrary. The prisoner may smoke in his cell as well as exercise.

It is the practice for the Governor, medical officer and chief officer to visit a prisoner under sentence of death twice daily, and the chaplain or minister of any other denomination has free access to him.

He may be visited by such of his relations, friends and legal advisers as he desires to see and as are authorised to visit him by the Visiting Committee and the commissioners, and he is given special facilities to write and receive letters.

The executioner and his assistant arrive at the prison by 4.0 pm on the day preceding the execution, and are not permitted to leave the prison until the execution has been carried out.

They see the prisoner at exercise and test the execution apparatus with a bag of sand approximately of his weight. The bag is left hanging overnight to stretch the rope … It is common practice for the Governor to visit a prisoner before he retires for the night to talk to him and give him an opportunity to say anything he may wish. Some like to take advantage of this opportunity, others do not, but no one is forced to say anything.

On the morning of the execution it is usual for the chaplain to spend the last hour with the prisoner and remain with him until the execution is over.

Some twenty minutes before the time fixed for the execution the High Sheriff, or more usually the Under Sheriff, arrives at the prison, and a few minutes before it is due, proceeds with the Governor and medical officer to the place of execution.

The executioner and his assistant wait outside the condemned cell, with the chief officer and officer detailed to conduct the prisoner to the execution chamber. On a signal given by the Sheriff they enter and the executioner pinions the prisoner's arms behind his back. He is escorted to the drop with one officer on either side. The Sheriff, the Governor and the medical officer enter the execution chamber directly by another door.

The prisoner is placed on the drop on a marked spot so that his feet are directly across the division of the trap doors. The executioner places a white cap over the prisoner's head and places the noose round his neck, while the assistant pinions his legs. When the executioner sees that all is ready he pulls the lever.

The medical officer at once proceeds to the pit and examines the prisoner to see that life is extinct. The shed is then locked and the body hangs for one hour. The inquest is held the same morning.

Burial of the body takes place in the prison graveyard during the dinner hour. The chaplain reads the burial service.

Burial within the prison precincts, where suitable space is strictly limited, gives rise to increasing difficulties. In some prisons bodies are already buried three deep.

The duty thrown on prison staffs and others concerned is a distasteful one not only in carrying out the execution itself, but in the long-drawn preliminary stages. Indeed the actual execution may come as a relief from the mounting tension of the previous days.

Anything tending to increase this atmosphere of tension in the prison generally has been, as far as possible, eliminated. The hoisting of a flag and the tolling of a bell were discontinued many years ago, and today the prisoners are no longer locked in the cells during an execution. The time fixed is after the normal routine of the prison is under way, and all prisoners are out at work or about their normal business.

AFTERWORD

I operated on behalf of the state, what I am convinced was the most humane and the most dignified method of meting out death to a delinquent – however justified or unjustified the allotment of death may be – and on behalf of humanity I trained other nations to adopt the British system of execution …

I do not now believe that any one of the hundreds of executions I carried out has in any way acted as a deterrent against future murder. Capital punishment, in my view, achieved nothing except revenge.

Albert Pierrepoint, 1974

SELECT BIBLIOGRAPHY

BEATTIE, John, *The Yorkshire Ripper Story,* Quartet Books, 1981

BERRY, James, *My Experiences as an Executioner,* reprinted by David & Charles, 1972

BLOM-COOPER, Louis, *see* MORRIS, Terence

BRABIN, Hon. Mr Justice, *The Case of Timothy John Evans,* HMSO, 1966

BROWNE, Douglas G, and TULLETT, EV, *Bernard Spilsbury,* George G Harrap, 1951

COBB, Belton, *Murdered on Duty,* WH Allen, 1961

DEARDON, Harold, *Some Cases of Bernard Spilsbury and Others,* Hutchinson, 1934

DEELEY, Peter, and WALKER, Christopher, *Murder in the Fourth Estate,* Victor Gollancz, 1971

DEW, Walter, *I Caught Crippen,* Blackie & Son, 1938

DOWNIE, R Angus, *Murder in London,* Arthur Barker, 1973

Famous Trials, Geoffrey Bles (Norman Thorne)

FARSON, Daniel, *Jack the Ripper,* Michael Joseph, 1972

FIELDING, Steve, *Pierrepoint: A Family of Executioners,* John Blake, 2006

FURNEAUX, Rupert, *Famous Criminal Cases, Vol* 1, 6, 7, Oldham Press, 1954–62

HASTINGS, Macdonald, *The Other Mr Churchill,* George G Harrap, 1963

HIGGINS, Robert, *In the Name of the Law,* John Long, 1958

HUGGETT, Renee, *Daughters of Cain,* Allen & Unwin, 1956

HUMPHREYS, Travers, *A Book of Trials,* Heinemann, 1953

KNIGHT, Stephen, *Jack the Ripper: The Final Solution,* George G Harrap, 1976

LA BERN, Arthur, *The Life and Death of a Ladykiller,* Leslie Frewin, 1967

LESSON, B, *Lost London,* Stanley Paul, 1934

LINKLATER, Eric, *The Corpse on Clapham Common,* Macmillan, 1971

LUSTGARTEN, Edgar, *The Woman in the Case,* André Deutsch, 1955

MORRIS, Terence and BLOM-COOPER, Louis, *A Calendar of Murder,* Michael Joseph, 1964

NICHOLSON, Michael, *The Yorkshire Ripper,* WH Allen, 1979

Notable British Trials, William Hodge (Peace, Maybrick, Dougal, Crippen, Morrison, the Seddons, Smith, Armstrong, True, Bywaters and Thompson, Browne and Kennedy, Craig and Bentley, Christie and Evans)

O'DELL, Robin, *Exhumation of a Murder,* George G Harrap, 1975

O'FLAHERTY, Michael, *Have You Seen This Woman?,* Corgi, 1971

Old Bailey Trials, Jarrolds, 1945 (Jones & Hulten)

PEARSON, John, *The Profession of Violence,* Weidenfeld & Nicolson, 1972 (The Krays)

PIERREPOINT, Albert, *Executioner Pierrepoint,* George G Harrap, 1974

PITMAN, Pat, *see* WILSON, Colin

ROWLAND, John, *The Fingerprint Man,* Lutterworth Press, 1959

RUMBELOW, Donald, *The Complete Jack the Ripper,* WH Allen, 1975

SAMUEL, Raphael, *East End Underworld: Chapters in the Life of Arthur Harding,* Routledge & Kegan Paul, 1981

SIMPSON, Keith, *Forty Years of Murder,* George G Harrap, 1978

SPENCER-SHAW, E, *A Companion to Murder* (1900-1950) Cassells, 1960. *A Second Companion to Murder,* Cassells, 1961

TULLETT, EV, *see* BROWNE, Douglas G

TULLETT, Tom, *No Answer from Foxtrot Eleven,* Michael Joseph, 1967. *Murder Squad,* Triad/Granada, 1981 (First published as *Strictly Murder,* Bodley Head, 1979)

WALBROOK, HM, *Murders and Murder Trials,* 1812-1912, Constable, 1932 (Peace, Cream, Prince, Crippen, the Seddons)

WALKER, Christopher, *see* DEELEY, Peter

WHITTINGTON-EGAN, Richard, *A Casebook on Jack the Ripper,* Wildy, 1975

WILD, Roland, *Crimes and Cases of* 1933-34, Rich and Cowan

WILSON, Colin, and PITMAN, Pat, *Encyclopedia of Murder,* Arthur Barker, 1961

WILSON, Patrick, *Murderess,* Michael Joseph, 1971

Websites on the Internet can be of great help in any kind of research. Wikipedia was particularly helpful with the biographies of individuals.